STUDY GUIDE

for Stiglitz and Driffill's

Economics

STUDY GUIDE

for Stiglitz and Driffill's
ECONOMICS

CHRISTINE OUGHTON
Birkbeck, University of London

LAWRENCE W. MARTIN
Michigan State University

W · W · NORTON & COMPANY · NEW YORK · LONDON

Copyright © 2000, 1997, 1993 by W. W. Norton & Company, Inc.

Printed in Great Britain by Redwood Books, Trowbridge

ISBN 0-393-97585-1 (pbk.)

W. W. Norton & Company, Inc., 500 Fifth Avenue, New York, N.Y. 10110
www.wwnorton.com

W. W. Norton & Company, Ltd., 10 Coptic Street, London WC1A 1PU

1 2 3 4 5 6 7 8 9 0

CONTENTS

Part Seven: Dynamics and Macro Policy

Part Eight: Issues in Macroeconomic Policy

PREFACE

This *Study Guide* is designed to aid in your understanding, assimilation, and use of the material in Joseph Stiglitz and John Driffill's *Economics*. The chapters in this volume correspond to those in the main text, and each one is divided into three parts. The first part contains a Chapter Review, an Essential Concepts section, and a Behind the Essential Concepts section. The Chapter Review begins with a brief paragraph explaining how the chapter fits into the overall structure of the text. The Essential Concepts section is a summary of the chapter, bringing out the main points covered. Behind the Essential Concepts offers suggestions about how to avoid common mistakes and provides some intuitive explanations for difficult concepts. This section also brings out the similarities among related ideas and the common structure of many economic theories and concepts.

The second part of each chapter includes a Self-Test with true-or-false, multiple-choice, and completion questions.

After reading the chapter in the text and going over the first part of the *Study Guide* chapter, you should take the self-test. It will help you determine those areas which need further study.

The final part of each chapter is called Tools and Practice Problems. This part is designed to teach you the basic skills of economics. The only way to do this is to sharpen your pencil and try some exercises. If you're willing (or your teacher has assigned this material), you'll find the problems useful. For each type of problem, there is a Tool Kit box that gives step-by-step instructions about how to use the appropriate tool, a worked problem with a step-by-step solution that follows the procedure outlined in the Tool Kit box, and several practice problems for you to do. Answers are provided at the end of each chapter.

Best of success with your course!

Part One

INTRODUCTION

Chapter 1

THE MOTOR INDUSTRY AND ECONOMICS

Chapter Review

The story of the automobile is a rich one, introducing as it does the principal ideas of economics. The dominant idea is that economics is about the choices made by the three major groups of participants: individuals or households, firms, and the government. These choices control the allocation of resources, another central concern of economics. The automobile story also highlights the three markets on which this book focuses: product, labor, and capital. The chapter closes with a discussion of how economists use models and theories to describe the economy and why they sometimes disagree. This chapter sets the stage for the introduction of the basic economic model in Chapter 2.

ESSENTIAL CONCEPTS

1   The brief history of the automobile given here illustrates the broad and varied subject matter of economics and many of the important themes of this book. We see the importance of investors and entrepreneurs and the risks they face, and the central roles of research, technological advance, and patents. The problem of incentives appears both in the conflicting interests of Henry Ford and his investors and in the effect of high wages on his workers.

The upheavals in the British car industry caused by oil price increases in the 1970s and the influx of competition from foreign producers show us how the British economy functions in the world economy. Finally, government has enacted environmental and safety regulations, supplied money to bail out major producers, nationalized and privatised the British Leyland car company and provided protection against foreign competition.

2   Economics studies how **choices** are made by individuals, firms, governments, and other organizations and how those choices determine the allocation of resources. **Scarcity,** the fact that there are not enough resources to satisfy all wants, requires that choices must be made by individuals and by the economy as a whole. The fundamental questions that an economy must answer are the following:

What is produced, and in what quantities?
How are these goods produced?
For whom are these goods produced?
Who makes economic decisions, and by what process?

3   Most Western economies are mixed economies that rely primarily on private decisions to answer the basic economic questions. **Markets,** which exist wherever and whenever exchanges occur, influence the choices of individuals and firms, but government also plays a promi-

nent role. For starters, the government sets the legal structure within which market forces operate. It also regulates private activity, collects taxes, produces some goods and services, and provides support for the elderly, poor, and others.

4   Trade takes place between individuals and firms in three major markets: the **product market,** the **labour market,** and the **capital market.** Figure 1.1 sketches the interactions. Notice that in general, individuals buy goods and services from firms; they also supply labour and funds for investment to firms.

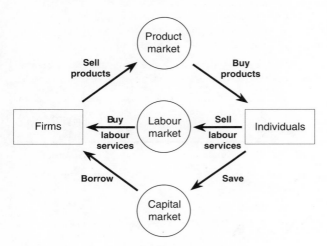

Figure 1.1

5   There are two broad branches in economics. **Microeconomics** studies the product, labour, and capital markets, focusing on the behaviour of individuals, households, firms, and other organizations that make up the economy. **Macroeconomics** looks at the performance of the economy as a whole and at such aggregate measures as unemployment, inflation, growth, and the balance of trade.

6   Economics uses models and theories, which are sets of assumptions and conclusions, to understand and predict the behaviour of the economy. Economists want to discover and interpret relationships among economic variables and especially to distinguish where there is causation and where there is only correlation.

7   Economists are frequently asked to give advice regarding public policy, and often they disagree, for two major reasons: they disagree about what is the appropriate theoretical model of the economy and about the effects a policy will have.

BEHIND THE ESSENTIAL CONCEPTS

1   In this book you will learn many economic theories and models. Models and theories are simplified representations of the vast and complex economic world. The way that a model is made simple and workable is through assumptions. We assume that only certain factors are relevant to the problem at hand. Then we derive conclusions

from the assumptions and test the model by comparing its predictions with what we know of the world.

You need to do two different things with the models that you will come across in your study of economics. First, you must understand how the model works—specifically, what is assumed and how the conclusions follow. The second task is to evaluate how well the model explains what it is supposed to explain. As you read the many arguments and pieces of evidence, keep in mind how they fit with the model's basic assumptions and conclusions.

2   Economic **variables** are measurable, and they change. The price of potatoes is an economic variable; so is the rate of unemployment. We look for two types of relationships among these variables. First, we are interested in whether certain economic variables move together. For example, during the 1970s, imports of foreign cars into Britain rose and production of cars in Britain fell. Foreign imports of cars and British production are negatively **correlated.** But we are also interested in whether a change in one variable **causes** a change in another variable. Specifically, did the rise in foreign imports cause British production to fall? Before economists make conclusions, they require a sound model that shows how a change in an economic variable was caused and also some evidence that the model's assumptions are appropriate and that its predictions have actually occurred.

3   **Positive economics** focuses on questions about how the economy works. What does it do, and why does it do it? For example, how were foreign car imports into Britain and car production in Britain related? **Normative economics,** on the other hand, typically asks what should be done. Should we increase the competitiveness of the British car industry? Keep in mind, however, that normative economics cannot prescribe which value to hold; it describes the appropriate policy given the value.

4   Microeconomics and macroeconomics are two ways of looking at the economy. Microeconomics looks from the bottom up; it starts with the behaviour of individuals and firms and builds up to an understanding of markets and the economy as a whole. Macroeconomics, on the other hand, is a top-down look, beginning with a description of the performance of aggregate economic variables and then constructing explanations. Micro- and macroeconomics must fit together. The models that explain how individuals, firms, and markets work must be consistent with the models that we use to describe the economy as a whole. An important theme of this book is that the microeconomics in Parts One, Two, and Three provides a firm foundation for the macroeconomics to follow in Parts Four, Five, and Six.

SELF-TEST

True or False

1   Henry Ford patented the internal combustion engine.

2   The history of the car industry illustrates that in some cases, higher wages can lead to higher productivity,

through greater loyalty, harder work, and less absenteeism.

3 By and large, government has kept out of the car industry.

4 Patents give exclusive rights to market an innovation for a limited period of time.

5 The British government imposed a tariff on car imports in 1915.

6 Economics studies how individuals, firms, governments, and other organizations make choices and how those choices determine the allocation of the economy's resources.

7 The four basic questions concerning how economies function are what is produced and in what quantities, how are the goods produced, for whom are they produced, and who makes the decisions?

8 In most Western economies, resource allocation decisions are made primarily by governments.

9 In centrally planned economies, most decisions are made by the government.

10 The three major markets are the product, labour, and insurance markets.

11 Microeconomics focuses on the behavior of the economy as a whole.

12 Macroeconomics studies the behavior of firms, households, and individuals.

13 Two economic variables are correlated if there is a systematic relationship between them.

14 When two variables are correlated, it is because changes in one cause changes in the other.

15 Normative economics deals with questions concerning how the economy actually works.

Multiple Choice

1 Henry Ford paid his workers more than the going rate chiefly because

  a he feared that the government would set minimum wages if he paid low wages.
  b he could thereby obtain a hard-working, productive labour force.
  c he did not care about profits, only the well-being of his workers.
  d his highly paid workers would buy more of his cars.
  e his highly paid workers would pay more taxes.

2 Patents

  a give inventors exclusive rights to produce and market their inventions for a limited time.
  b allow inventors to charge high prices without fear of competition.
  c provide incentives to encourage new inventions.
  d are awarded for innovations, not ideas.
  e all of the above.

3 In 1915 the British government imposed a tariff of 33.3 percent on the import of cars. As a result,

  a the British car industry faced more foreign competition.
  b imports of cars declined.
  c foreign firms set up production in Britain.
  d car prices declined.
  e *b* and *c*.

4 Because resources are scarce,

  a questions must be answered.
  b choices must be made.
  c all except the rich must make choices.
  d governments must allocate resources.
  e some individuals must be poor.

5 Which of the following is *not* a fundamental question concerning how economies funtion?

  a What is produced, and in what quantities?
  b How are the goods produced?
  c For whom are they produced?
  d Who makes the decisions?
  e All of the above are fundamental questions.

6 In market economies, the four basic questions are answered

  a by elected representatives.
  b in such a way as to ensure that everyone has enough to live well.
  c by private individuals and firms, interacting in markets.
  d according to the traditional way of doing things.
  e by popular vote.

7 In market economies, goods are consumed by those who

  a are most deserving.
  b work the hardest.
  c are politically well connected.
  d are willing and able to pay the most.
  e produce them.

8 Which of the following is not one of the three major markets?

  a The goods market
  b The labour market
  c The capital market
  d The Common Market
  e All of the above

9 The detailed study of firms, households, individuals, and the markets where they transact is called

  a macroeconomics.
  b microeconomics.
  c normative economics.
  d positive economics.
  e aggregate economics.

10 The study of the behaviour of the economy as a whole, especially such factors as unemployment and inflation, is called

  a macroeconomics.
  b microeconomics.

c   normative economics.
d   positive economics.
e   market economics.

11   An economic theory or model is a

a   mathematical equation.
b   prediction about the future of the economy.
c   recommended reform in government policy that pays attention to the laws of economics.
d   set of assumptions and conclusions derived from those assumptions.
e   small-scale economic community set up to test the effectiveness of a proposed government program.

12   Which of the following statements provides an example of causation?

a   Imports are too high.
b   The reduction in British car production in the 1970s was a direct result of the lack of competitiveness in the British car industry.
c   During the 1970s British car production fell and foreign imports increased.
d   In mixed economies there is a role for government and a role for markets.
e   British car production fell during the 1970s.

13   Which of the following is an example of correlation?

a   The reduction in British car production in the 1970s was caused by the lack of competitiveness in the British car industry.
b   Production is too low.
c   During the 1970s British car production fell and foreign imports of cars into Britian increased.
d   In mixed economies there is a role for government and a role for markets.
e   Economics studies choices and how choices determine the allocation of resources.

14   Which of the following is an example of normative economics?

a   The reduction in British car production in the 1970s was caused by the lack of competitiveness in the British car industry.
b   During the 1970s British car production fell and foreign imports of cars into Britian increased.
c   Increasing the competitiveness in the British car industry would increase the volume of cars produced in Britain.
d   The competitiveness in the British car industry should be increased.
e   Increasing investment will increase competitiveness.

15   Which of the following is an example of positive economics?

a   Imports are too high.
b   British car production is too low.
c   Increasing the competitiveness in the British car industry would increase the volume of cars produced in Britain.
d   The competitiveness in the British car industry should be increased.
e   Car production in Britain should be increased.

16   In most Western economies, the question of what is produced and in what quantities is answered

a   primarily by private decisions influenced by prices.
b   by producing what was produced the previous year.
c   primarily by government planning.
d   randomly.
e   according to majority vote.

17   In which of the following does the government determine what is produced, how, and for whom?

a   Market economies
b   Mixed economies
c   Centrally planned economies
d   Tradition-bound economies
e   All of the above

18   Choices must be made because

a   resources are scarce.
b   human beings are choice-making animals.
c   government regulations require choices to be made.
d   economic variables are correlated.
e   without choices, there would be no economics as we know it.

19   Anything that can be measured and that changes is

a   a correlation.
b   a causation.
c   a variable.
d   a value.
e   an experiment.

20   In the labour market,

a   households purchase products from firms.
b   firms purchase the labour services of individuals.
c   firms raise money to finance new investment.
d   households purchase labour services from firms.
e   borrowing and lending are coordinated.

Completion

1   Exchanges take place in _____.

2   In a _____ economy, some decisions are made chiefly by government and others by markets.

3   All the institutions involved in borrowing and lending money make up the _____ market.

4   The behaviour of the economy as a whole, and especially of certain aggregate measures such as unemployment and inflation, is called _____.

5   The branch of economics that focuses on firms, households, and individuals and studies product, labour, and capital markets is called _____.

6   The statement that crime rates are higher in low-income areas is an example of _____.

7   The statement that poverty leads to crime is an example of _____.

8   Economists use _____, which are sets of assumptions, conclusions, and data, to study the economy and evaluate the consequences of various policies.

9 _____ economics rests on value judgments; _____ economics describes how the economy behaves.

10 The four basic questions that economists ask about the economy are (1) what is produced and in what quantities, (2) _____, (3) for whom are they produced, and (4) who makes the decisions?

Answers to Self-Test

True or False

1	F	6	T	11	F
2	T	7	T	12	F
3	F	8	F	13	T
4	T	9	T	14	F
5	T	10	F	15	F

Multiple Choice

1	b	6	c	11	d	16	a
2	e	7	d	12	b	17	c
3	e	8	d	13	c	18	a
4	b	9	b	14	d	19	c
5	e	10	a	15	c	20	b

Completion

1 markets
2 mixed
3 capital
4 macroeconomics
5 microeconomics
6 correlation
7 causation
8 theories or models
9 Normative, positive
10 how are these goods produced

Chapter 2

BASIC PRINCIPLES

Chapter Review

The concept of scarcity discussed in Chapter 1 implies that choices must be made. This chapter begins to explain how economists think about choice and how choices are influenced and coordinated by markets. A basic economic assumption is that of rational choice, which simply says that people select the alternative they prefer most from among all those which are available. The alternatives available to any particular firm or individual, of course, depend upon the choices made by other firms and individuals. All of these rational choices must somehow fit together, and markets serve the function of coordinating them. How they do so is the subject of Chapters 3 through 5.

ESSENTIAL CONCEPTS

1   The **basic economic model** includes three elements: individuals, firms, and markets. Economic decisions such as what and how much of each type of good to produce, how to produce them, what kind of career to pursue, and how to spend one's earnings are made by **rational, self-interested individuals** and **rational,** profit-maximising firms. **Markets** serve the economic role of coordinating these decisions.

2   The basic economic model assumes that markets are **perfectly competitive.** In perfectly competitive markets, there are many consumers and firms, and each is small relative to the size of the overall market. One key feature of perfect competition is that any firm charging more than the going price will lose all its customers. Without any ability to influence the market price, the firm is a **price taker.** (Later in this book, we will encounter monopolists and others known as **price makers,** who have the power to charge higher prices without losing all their customers.)

3   Private **property rights** play an important role in the basic model. They include the right to use resources in certain ways and the right to sell them in markets. These two aspects of property rights provide incentives to use resources efficiently and to transfer resources to their most valuable use. Inefficiencies can arise when property rights are ill defined or restricted.

4   When compensation is tied to performance, people have strong incentives to work hard and be productive, but those who are more fortunate and successful also will earn higher incomes. On the other hand, distribut-

ing the output more equally undermines incentives. This **incentive-equality trade-off** is one of the basic questions facing societies: how should the tax, social security, and welfare systems be constructed to balance the competing ends of providing strong incentives and promoting equality?

5   **Scarcity** implies that not everyone who desires a good or resource can have it: there is an allocation problem. In market economies, goods are allocated to the highest bidder. Another solution to the allocation problem is to **ration**. Rationing schemes include queues; first-come, first-served; lotteries; and coupons. Unless supplemented by markets, rationing schemes are likely to lead to inefficiencies.

6   The basic economic model assumes that decisions are made rationally, which simply means that individuals and firms balance the benefits and costs of their decisions. Economists see rational decision making as a two-step process. First, find what alternatives are available. This step is the construction of the **opportunity set**. Next, select the best alternative from those within the opportunity set.

7   The chapter presents three types of opportunity sets. The **budget constraint** shows which combinations of goods can be consumed with a limtied amount of money. The **time constraint** indicates to which uses limited time can be put. Finally, the **production possibilities curve** depicts the combinations of goods that a firm or an entire economy can produce given its limited resources and the quality of the available technology.

8   The best alternatives in an opportunity set will lie along the outer edge. This is because people prefer more goods to less. Operating on the outer edge also implies that there will be a **trade-off**: more of one option means less of another. For example, on the budget constraint, consuming more of one good means that less money is available to spend on another good. On the time constraint, if an individual devotes more time to one activity, there is less time available for other endeavors. A society that chooses to produce more of one good must settle for less production of other goods.

9   The **opportunity cost** of a good or activity is the option forgone. The opportunity cost of consuming more of one good is consuming less of some alternative good. The opportunity cost of an activity is the other endeavor that would have been but now cannot be undertaken. The opportunity cost of producing one good is the necessarily lower production of another.

10   The opportunity cost, not the price, is the proper measure of the economic cost of any choice. For example, in addition to the ultimate purchase price, the opportunity cost of buying a car includes the time and expense devoted to investigating alternatives, searching for the best deal, and negotiating the terms.

11   Opportunity costs are measured in toto and at the margin. When a firm is deciding where to locate its plant, it compares the **total costs** at each location. When a firm is considering how large a plant to build, it looks at the costs of increasing or decreasing the size. These are the **marginal costs**, the costs of a little bit more or a little bit less.

BEHIND THE ESSENTIAL CONCEPTS

1   The basic competitive model introduced in this chapter is critical to your understanding of economics. It will be expanded and applied in all the chapters that follow, but you should master the concepts given in this chapter: rational individuals choose the best combinations of goods along their budget constraints, firms maximise profits, and trading takes place in competitive markets, where each individual and firm is a price taker.

2   The opportunity set itself shows all of the alternatives that are available. Because more is generally preferred to less, however, economists focus on the outer boundary of the opportunity set. For example, Figure 2.1 shows an opportunity set for a firm that must divide its resources between the production of canned and frozen vegetables. The entire shaded area shows all of the combinations that are possible. The economist's attention is drawn to the outer edge, the production possibilities curve, because to choose a combination inside (such as point A) would be inefficient.

3   The terms *opportunity set, budget constraint, trade-off,* and *opportunity cost* are related, but they are distinct and you should take care to understand each one. Figure 2.2 shows the opportunity set for a student who consumes hamburgers and pizzas. The **opportunity set** shows all of the combinations of hamburgers and pizzas that are affordable. Points A and B are affordable; they lie within the opportunity set but have the critical characteristic of lying along its outer edge, which is the budget constraint. The trade-off is that more hamburgers mean fewer pizzas. If Joe chooses B rather than A, he eats another pizza and exactly two fewer hamburgers. The trade-off between any

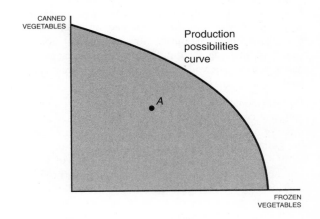

Figure 2.1

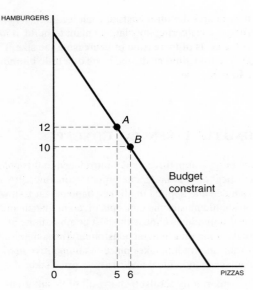

Figure 2.2

two points measures the opportunity cost. In this case, the opportunity cost of this extra pizza is the two forgone burgers. When the outer edge of the opportunity set is a straight line, the trade-offs will be the same all along the line; when it is a curve, the trade-offs will change.

4   Opportunity costs are forgone alternatives—not money, not time, and not resources. For example, if you spend one hour in class tomorrow, the opportunity cost of attending that class is not the hour itself. That hour will pass whether you go to the class or not. The opportunity cost is what you could have done with that hour. It is the activity you give up. Strictly speaking, the opportunity cost of buying a book for £20 is not the money, but what would have been purchased with the £20 if it had not been spent on the book.

5   **Sunk costs,** outlays that cannot be recovered, are not opportunity costs. Because these expenditures are not affected by the choice of any alternative, they do not represent the opportunity cost of any alternative. For example, suppose that you sign a one-year lease on a house and are forbidden to sublet it. When you consider whether to stay at home for the summer or travel abroad, the rent owed your landlord is irrelevant. You cannot do anything about it. Regardless of which alternative you choose, you must pay the rent. The rent is a sunk cost, not an opportunity cost.

6   Be clear about the difference between total costs and marginal costs. Marginal costs are the costs of a little more or a little less of some activity. Before considering going into business, you evaluate the total opportunity costs of the enterprise—all of the costs of setting up the plant, designing and producing the product, and locating the market. When you are considering whether to produce another unit of output, however, it is the marginal opportunity cost that is important. The marginal cost of producing a little bit more is

just the added cost incurred when producing more with the plant already set up, the product designed, and the market found. These latter costs are not marginal.

7   **Diminishing returns** can be confusing at first. What the term means is that as more inputs are used in a production process, output increases at a diminishing rate. For example, suppose more workers are hired to pick apples. Each additional worker results in more apples being picked in toto, but the marginal contribution of the newest worker, how many extra apples are picked when he is hired, is not as great as that of the previously hired new workers. We can also say that the opportunity cost of increasing output—the marginal cost—is higher as output increases.

8   Another way to approach diminishing returns is to think about why the output of the marginal input is declining. The extra inputs are just as good at producing; however, as more are used, the production process becomes crowded. For example, when more workers are hired to pick apples, there are fewer apple trees per worker, and it is more difficult to pick apples.

SELF-TEST

True or False

1   The basic model of economics seeks to explain why people want what they want.

2   According to the basic competitive model, firms maximise profits (or stock market value).

3   Generally, inequality will be greater when society is organised to provide stronger incentives to perform efficiently.

4   A firm selling in a perfectly competitive market is a price taker because it cannot raise its price without losing all of its customers.

5   Both the right to use a resource in certain ways and the right to transfer that resource are important aspects of private property rights.

6   Commonly owned property is the reason for diminishing returns.

7   A legal entitlement—that is, the right to use a resource in certain ways but not to sell or trade it—probably prevents the resource from going to its highest-valued use.

8   Lotteries are an inefficient means of allocating resources because they do not allocate goods to the highest bidder.

9   Rationing by queues wastes the time spent queuing.

10 The opportunity set includes only the best available alternative.

11 The production possibilities curve shows the boundary of the opportunity set.

12 The principle of diminishing returns says that as more units of any input are added to a production process, total output eventually falls.

13 If an economy is not using its resources in the most productive way, economists say that there is inefficiency.

14 Sunk expenditures do not represent opportunity costs.

15 If one pizza sells for £8 but two pizzas can be purchased for £12, the marginal cost of the second pizza is £6.

Multiple Choice

1 Which of the following is *not* a building block of the basic economic model?

   a Assumptions about how firms behave
   b Assumptions about how consumers behave
   c Assumptions about markets
   d Assumptions about the behavior of government
   e All of the above are building blocks of the basic economic model.

2 Individuals and firms in the economy must make choices because of

   a diminishing returns.
   b rationality.
   c scarcity.
   d all of the above.
   e none of the above.

3 The concept of rationality refers to the

   a fact of scarcity.
   b principle of diminishing returns.
   c assumption that individuals have sensible goals.
   d assumption that individuals and firms weigh the costs and benefits of their choices.
   e assumption that individuals and firms are certain of the consequences of their choices.

4 A firm that cannot influence the price it sells its product for is called a

   a price maker.
   b price taker.
   c rational decision maker.
   d all of the above.
   e none of the above.

5 In a pure market economy, incentives to work hard and produce efficiently are provided by

   a the profit motive.
   b government regulations.
   c private property rights.
   d both the profit motive and private property rights.
   e all of the above.

6 When property is commonly owned, users

   a do not maximise profits.
   b violate the principle of rationality.
   c ignore the principle of diminishing returns.
   d have little incentive to maintain and preserve the value of the property.
   e none of the above.

7 If owners are not allowed to sell their resources, then

   a the resources will not go to the highest value users.
   b the owners will not act rationally.
   c their choices will not be limited to their opportunity sets.
   d the market will be perfectly competitive.
   e none of the above.

8 Allocating goods by lotteries, queues, and coupons are examples of

   a rationing.
   b not selling to the highest bidder.
   c efficient ways of allocating resources.
   d the profit motive.
   e *a* and *b*.

9 Rationing by queues

   a leads to an efficient allocation of resources.
   b allocates goods to those willing to pay the most money.
   c wastes the time spent queuing.
   d is an efficient way of allocating scarce goods.
   e *a* and *c*.

10 When goods are rationed by coupons and the coupons are not tradable,

   a the goods do not go to the individuals who value them most.
   b a black market may be established.
   c individuals will not act rationally.
   d *a* and *b*.
   e none of the above.

11 Choices of individuals and firms are limited by

   a time constraints.
   b production possibilities.
   c budget constraints.
   d all of the above.
   e none of the above.

12 Fred has £10 to spend on football cards and hamburgers. The price of football cards is 50 pence per pack. Hamburgers sell at a price of £1 each. Which of the following possibilities is *not* in Fred's opportunity set?

   a 10 hamburgers and zero packs of football cards
   b 5 hamburgers and 10 packs of football cards
   c 2 hamburgers and 16 packs of football cards
   d 1 hamburger and 18 packs of football cards
   e None of the above

13 The production possibilities curve

   a shows the amounts of goods a firm or society might produce.
   b is not a straight line because of the principle of diminishing returns.
   c illustrates the trade-offs between goods.
   d all of the above.
   e none of the above.

14 Henry spends an hour shopping and buys one shirt for £30. The opportunity cost of the shirt is

a one hour.
b £30.
c one hour plus £30.
d the next-best alternative uses of the hour and the £30.
e none of the above.

15 Renting a house, Jorge signs a lease promising to pay £400 each month for one year. He always keeps his word, and therefore he will pay the £400 each month whether he lives in the house or not. The £400 each month represents

a an opportunity cost.
b a sunk cost.
c a trade-off.
d a budget constraint.
e diminishing returns.

16 One box of Nature's Crunch Cereal sells for £1.55. Each box comes with a coupon worth 50 pence off the purchase price of another box of Nature's Crunch Cereal. The marginal cost of the second box of this product is

a £1.55.
b £2.05.
c £1.05.
d 55 pence.
e none of the above.

17 Making a rational choice involves

a identifying the opportunity set.
b defining the trade-off.
c calculating the opportunity costs.
d all of the above.
e none of the above.

18 Fred is considering renting a flat. A one-bedroom flat rents for £400, and a nice two-bedroom flat can be had for £500. The £100 difference is

a the opportunity cost of the two-bedroom flat.
b the marginal cost of the second bedroom.
c a sunk cost.
d the marginal cost of a flat.
e none of the above.

19 If a firm changes from paying commissions on total sales to paying each member of its sales force a fixed salary, it will likely

a experience lower total sales.
b have greater equality in earnings of its sales representatives.
c see no difference because compensation is a sunk cost.
d *a* and *b*.
e none of the above.

20 Reducing taxes

a makes no difference because incentives do not matter.
b will likely increase inequality because those who

work harder can keep more of their higher earnings.
c will likely increase inequality because those who are luckier can keep more of their higher earnings.
d *b* and *c*.
e none of the above.

Completion

1 Economists assume that people make choices _____, taking into consideration the costs and benefits of their alternatives.

2 A market with large numbers of buyers and sellers, each of whom cannot influence the price, is an example of _____.

3 The right of an owner of a resource to use it in certain ways and to sell it is called a _____.

4 Allocating goods and services by some means other than selling to the highest bidder is called _____.

5 The collection of all available opportunities is called the _____.

6 _____ limit choices.

7 The amount of goods that a business firm is able to produce is called its _____.

8 The idea that as more inputs are used in a production process, each successive input eventually adds less to output is an example of the principle of _____.

9 The fact that more time spent studying means less time available for other activities illustrates a _____.

10 An expenditure that cannot be recovered is a _____ cost.

Answers to Self-Test

True or False

1	F	4	T	7	T	10	F	13	T
2	T	5	T	8	T	11	T	14	T
3	T	6	F	9	T	12	F	15	F

Multiple Choice

1	*d*	6	*d*	11	*d*	16	*c*
2	*c*	7	*a*	12	*e*	17	*d*
3	*d*	8	*e*	13	*d*	18	*b*
4	*b*	9	*c*	14	*d*	19	*d*
5	*d*	10	*d*	15	*b*	20	*d*

Completion

1 rationally
2 perfect competition
3 property right
4 rationing
5 opportunity set
6 Constraints
7 production possibilities
8 diminishing returns
9 trade-off
10 sunk

Tools and Practice Problems

For the problem sets in this section, we reach into the economist's tool box for five important techniques, each of which will reappear throughout the remainder of the book. Three relate to the opportunity set: budget and time constraints, for which the outer edge of the opportunity set is a straight line; multiple constraints, which involve limits on both time and money; and production possibilities curves, which can be straight lines but more often exhibit diminishing returns and are curved. The remaining two techniques relate to costs: the distinction between sunk and opportunity costs, and the use of marginal analysis to balance costs and benefits.

STRAIGHT-LINE OPPORTUNITY SETS

The simplest type of opportunity set has an outer boundary that is a straight line. Examples include budget constraints, time constraints, and production possibilities when there are constant returns. The budget constraint indicates which combinations of goods can be purchased with a limited amount of money. The time constraint indicates which combinations of time-consuming activities can be undertaken with a limited amount of time. The production possibilities curve (in this case it is a straight line) indicates which combinations of goods can be produced. Tool Kit 2.1 shows how to construct these opportunity sets.

Tool Kit 2.1 Plotting the Straight-Line Opportunity Set

Budget constraints, time constraints, and production possibilities are examples of straight-line opportunity sets. To draw the budget constraint, you must know the size of the budget and the prices of the goods. The time constraint can be drawn given the total time available and the time requirements for each activity. To plot the production possibilities curve, you need to know the resources and the technology. Follow this procedure to plot these straight-line opportunity sets.

Step one: Draw a set of coordinate axes. Label the horizontal axis as the quantity of one good or activity and the vertical axis as the quantity of the other good or activity.

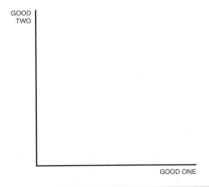

Step two: Calculate the maximum quantity of the good or activity measured on the horizontal axis. Plot this quantity along the horizontal axis.

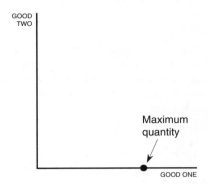

Step three: Calculate the maximum quantity of the good or activity measured on the vertical axis. Plot this quantity along the vertical axis.

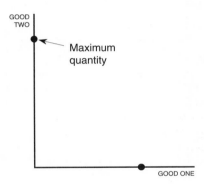

Step four: Draw a line segment connecting the two points. This line segment is the relevant part of the opportunity set.

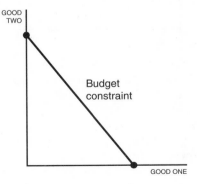

Step five: The slope is the opportunity cost of the good or activity measured on the horizontal axis. In the case of the budget constraint, it is called the relative price, the ratio of the price of the good measured on the horizontal axis divided by the price of the good measured on the vertical axis.

1   (Worked problem: budget constraint) Diana has an entertainment budget of £200 each month. She enjoys lunches with friends and going to the cinema. The price of a typical lunch is £10. Cinema tickets are £5 each. Construct her opportunity set.

Step-by-step solution

Step one: Draw coordinate axes and label the horizontal one "Lunches" and the vertical one "Cinema tickets." (There is no rule as to which good goes where. It would be fine if lunches were measured on the vertical axis and cinema tickets on the horizontal.)

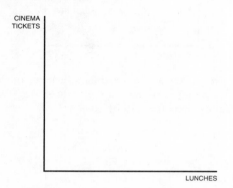

Step two: Calculate the maximum quantity of lunches. This number is £200/£10 = 20 lunches. Plot this quantity along the horizontal axis.

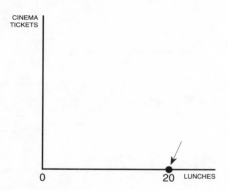

Step three: Calculate the maximum quantity of cinema tickets. This number is £200/£5 = 40 cinema tickets. Plot this quantity along the vertical axis.

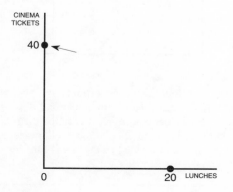

Step four: Draw a line segment connecting these two points. This line segment is the budget constraint.

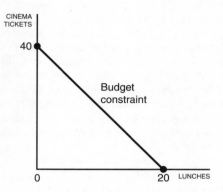

Step five: The slope of the budget constraint is 40/20 = 2. The price ratio is £10/£5 = 2. (Strictly speaking, these slopes are negative, but we follow the practice of dropping the negative sign as long as there is no confusion.)

2   (Practice problem: budget constraint) Velma Thomas must pay for both prescription medicine and nursing care for her elderly father. Each bottle of pills costs her £40, and the price of nursing care is £100 per day. She has been able to scrape together £1,000 each month for these expenses. Construct her opportunity set, going through all five steps.

3   (Practice problem: budget constraint) Construct the following opportunity sets.

   a   Clothing budget per year = £900; price of suits = £300; price of shoes = £90.
   b   Food budget = £200 per week; price of restaurant meals = £20; price of in-home meals = £5.
   c   School expense budget = £1,200 per semester; price of books = £50; price of courses = £200.
   d   Annual state transportation department budget = £100,000; cost of fixing potholes = £200; cost of replacing road signs = £500.

4   (Worked problem: time constraint) Ahmed likes to visit his invalid father across town. Each visit, including transportation and time with Dad, takes 3 hours. Another of Ahmed's favorite activities is his tango lessons. These are given at home and take only an hour each. With work and night school, Ahmed has only 15 hours each week to divide between visiting his father and tango lessons. Construct his opportunity set.

Step-by-step solution

Step one: The time constraint works very much like the budget constraint. Plot coordinate axes and label the horizontal one "Visits" and the vertical one "Lessons."

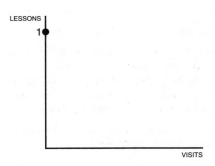

Step two: Calculate the maximum number of visits to his father. This number is 15/3 = 5 visits. Plot this quantity along the horizontal axis.

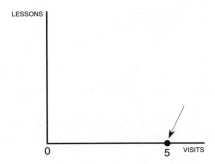

Step three: Calculate the maximum number of tango lessons. This number is 15/1 = 15 lessons. Plot this quantity along the vertical axis.

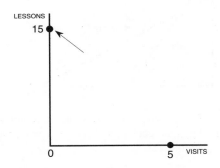

Step four: Draw a line segment connecting these two points. This line segment is the time constraint.

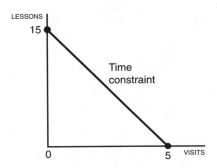

Step five: The slope of the time constraint is 15/5 = 3. The time-requirement ratio is 3/1 = 3.

5   (Practice problem: time constraint) Michael Terranova has 2 hours to make his house as clean as possible. The place needs vacuuming and dusting. He can dust one piece of furniture in 10 minutes. Each room takes 20 minutes to vacuum. Plot his time constraint.

6   (Practice problem: time constraint) Construct the following opportunity sets.

a   Total time available = 6 hours; time required to iron each shirt = 15 minutes; time required to iron each dress = 30 minutes.

b   Total time available = 20 days; time required to study each chapter = 1/2 day; time required to write book reports = 2 days.

c   Total time available = 40 hours; time required to counsel each disturbed teenager = 2 hours; time required to attend each meeting = 1 hour.

d   Total time available = 8 hours; time required to visit each client = 4 hours; time required to telephone each client = 10 minutes.

7   (Worked problem: production possibilities curve) First, assume that there is one resource, which can be used in the production of either of two goods, and that there are no diminishing returns. In this case, the production possibilities curve is a straight line, and we treat it just as we did the budget and time constraints.

There are 25 farm workers employed at Green Fields vegetable farm. Each worker can pick 4 bushels of cucumbers an hour. Alternatively, each worker can pick 1 bushel of peppers each hour. Each worker can work 8 hours a day. Plot the daily production possibilities curve.

Step-by-step solution

Step one: Plot coordinate axes and label the horizontal one "Cucumbers" (measured in bushels) and the vertical one "Peppers."

Step two: Calculate the maximum number of cucumbers that can be picked each day. This number is 25 (workers) × 8 (hours) × 4 (bushels an hour) = 800 bushels of cucumbers. Plot this number along the horizontal axis.

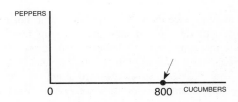

Step three: Calculate the maximum number of peppers that can be picked each day. This number is 25 (workers) × 8 (hours) × 1 (bushel an hour) = 200 bushels of peppers. Plot this number along the vertical axis.

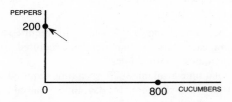

Step four: Draw a line segment connecting these two points. This line segment is the production possibilities curve.

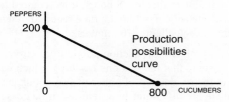

Step five: The slope is 200/800 = 1/4, which means that the opportunity cost of 1 bushel of cucumbers is 1/4 bushel of peppers.

8 (Practice problem: production possibilities curve) Football coach Alex has four assistant coaches. They make recruiting visits and also run clinics for local youth. Each can make 32 recruiting visits a week. Alternatively, each can run 8 clinics in a week. Plot the production possibilities curve.

9 (Practice problem: production possibilities curve) Construct the following opportunity sets.

  a Total amount of land available = 10 acres of land; output of corn per acre = 2,000 bushels; output of wheat per acre = 1,000 bushels.
  b Total amount of labour available = 40 hours; output of donuts per hour = 150; output of scones per hour = 50.
  c Total amount of floor space available = 1,000 square metres; sales of women's sportswear per square metre = £500; sales of home furnishings per square metre = £200.
  d Total amount of fuel available = 5,000 litres; kilometres per litre for tank travel = 3; kilometres per litre for armored personnel carriers = 9.

MULTIPLE CONSTRAINTS

Individuals often face more than one constraint. For example, many activities cost money and take up time. This means that the opporunity set includes only those alternatives which do not exceed both the budget and time constraints. Tool Kit 2.2 shows how to combine multiple constraints into a single opportunity set. Notice how the resulting opportunity set is convex.

Tool Kit 2.2 Plotting Multiple Constraints

When activities take both time and money, opportunities will be limited by two constraints. This is one example of the problem of multiple constraints. To plot the opportunity set when more than one constraint applies, follow this three-step procedure.

Step one: Plot the first constraint. (For example, this might be the budget constraint.)

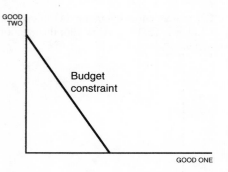

Step two: Plot the second constraint. (For example, this might be the time constraint.)

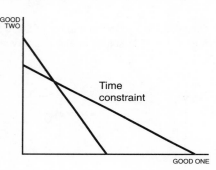

Step three: Darken the section of each constraint that lies under the other constraint. This is the outer edge of the opportunity set.

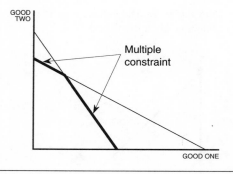

10 (Worked problem: multiple constraints) Out of work for six months, Donna feels that it is time to start looking for a job. Her father (gently) suggests that she apply in person to several of the shops in the city centre. Each application would require £5 in out-of-pocket expenses for transport and dry cleaning. (She realizes

that only those who wear clean clothes stand any chance of receiving an offer.) Each trip would require 5 hours.

Donna's mother (not so gently) says that she should send letters of application to a wide variety of potential employers. Each letter of application would require only £1 in postage and copying costs and 1/2 hour of time.

Donna can devote 30 hours and £50 each week to her job search campaign. Plot her opportunity set.

Step-by-step solution

Step one: Follow the procedure for plotting her budget constraint. Label the horizontal axis "Personal applications" and the vertical one "Postal applications." Your answer should look like this.

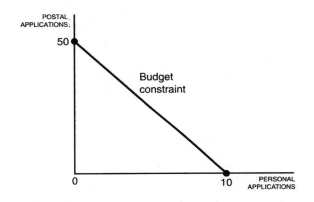

Step two: Follow the procedure for plotting her time constraint. Your answer should look like this.

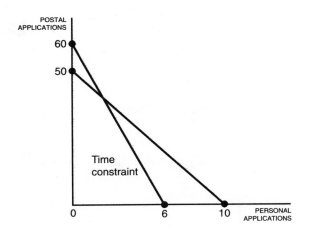

Step three: Darken the section of each constraint that lies under the other constraint. Notice that between points *A* and *B* on the diagram, it is the budget constraint that is binding, but between *B* and *C,* the time constraint is the limiting one.

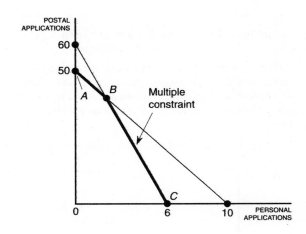

11   (Practice problem: multiple constraints) Harold's leaf-raking business is taking off. He has so many jobs to do that he is thinking of renting a leaf blower. This would cost him £20 per day. With a leaf blower, he could clean 10 lawns each day. He can only do 4 each day with his trusty rake, which costs nothing. Harold works 7 days each week, but has only £100 to spend. Plot his opportunity set for the week. (Hint: The axes should be labeled "Lawns cleaned with a leaf blower" and "Lawns raked by hand.")

12   (Practice problem: multiple constraints) The maintenance department at Alberti Van and Storage has 8 mechanic-hours to tune engines and replace mufflers. It takes 1 hour to tune an engine and 1/2 hour to replace a muffler. In addition, the parts budget is only £100, the parts required to tune an engine cost £10, and each muffler costs £20. Construct the department's opportunity set.

13   (Practice problem: multiple constraints) Lamont tests swimming pools and cleans changing rooms for local country clubs. He has 20 hours available, and it takes him 1 hour to test each pool and 1/2 hour to clean each changing room. He has a budget of £50 to spend. It costs him £10 to test each pool and £1 to clean each changing room. Construct his opportunity set.

PRODUCTION POSSIBILITIES WITH DIMINISHING RETURNS

Usually, production is subject to diminishing returns. This means that as more of a resource is used in production, the extra (or marginal) output is less. In other words, although output increases, it does so at a diminishing rate. With diminishing returns the production possibilities curve acquires a convex shape. Tool Kit 2.3 shows how to plot the production possibilities curves when there are diminishing returns.

Tool Kit 2.3 Plotting the Production Possibilities
Curve with Diminishing Returns

Diminishing returns mean that as more of some resource is used in production, the extra (or marginal)
output declines. Follow this five-step procedure to plot
the production possibilities curve with diminishing returns.

Step one: Draw and label a set of coordinate axes.

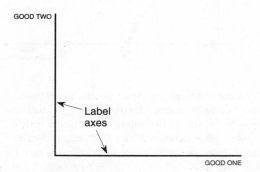

Step two: Calculate the total amount of the good measured on the horizontal axis that can be produced if all
the resource is used. Plot this quantity along the horizontal axis.

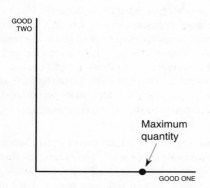

Step three: Calculate the total amount of the good
measured on the vertical axis that can be produced if
all the resource is used. Plot this quantity along the
vertical axis.

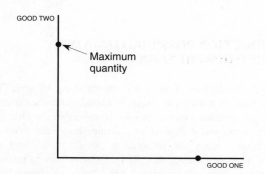

Step four: Calculate and plot several other feasible
combinations.

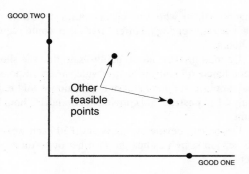

Step five: Draw a smooth curve connecting these
points. This curve is the production possibilities curve.

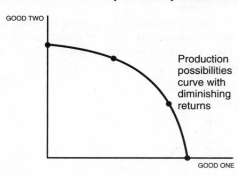

Step six: Verify that the slope is increasing along the
curve. Since the slope is the marginal opportunity
cost of the horizontal axis good, this reflects diminishing returns.

14   (Worked problem: production possibilities curve with
diminishing returns) Iatrogenesis, a medical laboratory, employs 4 lab technicians. Each is equally adept at
analysing throat cultures and distilling vaccines. The
table below shows output per day for various numbers
of lab technicians.

Technicians doing cultures	Throat cultures	Technicians doing vaccines	Vaccines
1	50	1	20
2	90	2	35
3	120	3	45
4	140	4	50

Plot the production possibilities curve for Iatrogenesis.

Step-by-step solution

Step one: Draw coordinate axes. Label the horizontal one
"Throat cultures" and the vertical one "Vaccines."

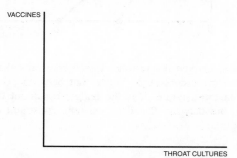

Step two: Calculate the maximum number of throat cultures. If all 4 technicians do throat cultures, the number is 140. Plot this number.

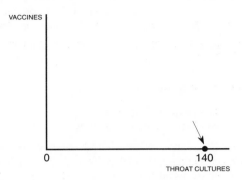

Step three: Calculate the maximum number of vaccines. If all 4 technicians do vaccines, the number is 50. Plot this number.

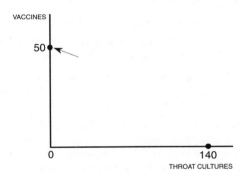

Step four: Calculate several other feasible points. For example, if 1 technician does throat cultures, then 3 can do vaccines. Reading off the table, we see that the combination produced is 50 throat cultures and 45 vaccines. Similarly, if 2 do throat cultures and 2 do vaccines, the outputs are 90 throat cultures and 35 vaccines. Another feasible combination is 120 cultures and 20 vaccines. Plot these points.

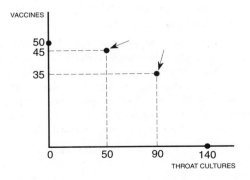

Step five: Draw the production possibilities curve through the points that have been plotted.

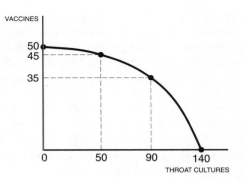

Step six: Observe that, as expected, the slope gets steeper as the number of throat cultures is increased. This indicates diminishing returns.

15 (Practice problem: production possibilities curve with diminishing returns) Large Town University has a crime problem. Members of the criminal element have stolen many bicycles and a great deal of stereo equipment. To address this crime wave, the campus police has hired 5 new officers. The following table gives the expected number of thefts for various assignments for these new officers.

New police officers assigned to bicycle duty	Reduction in bicycle thefts	New police officers assigned to dorm patrol	Reduction in thefts of stereo equipment
1	25	1	10
2	45	2	18
3	60	3	25
4	70	4	31
5	75	5	36

Plot the production possibilities curve.

16 (Practice problem: production possibilities curve with diminishing returns) Movaway Company has employed 4 maintenance inspectors for their fleet of trucks and forklifts. The following table shows how assigning inspectors leads to fewer breakdowns.

Inspectors assigned to check trucks	Reduced number of truck breakdowns	Inspectors assigned to check forklifts	Reduced number of forklift breakdowns
1	5	1	3
2	9	2	5
3	12	3	6
4	14	4	6

Plot Movaway's production possibilities curve, and verify that it shows diminishing returns.

17 (Practice problem: production possibilities curve with diminishing returns) The Stewart vegetable farm has 800 tons of fertilizer. The following table shows how output of endive and round lettuce is expected to respond to different amounts of fertilizer.

Fertilizer used on endive crop (tonnes)	Output of endive (bushels)	Fertilizer used on round lettuce crop (tonnes)	Output of round lettuce (bushels)
0	1,400	0	2,000
200	2,400	200	3,400
400	3,200	400	4,200
600	3,600	600	4,700
800	4,000	800	5,000

Plot the farm's production possibilities curve, and verify that it exhibits diminishing returns.

SUNK COSTS

Rational individuals make choices by carefully weighing the benefits and costs of their alternatives. Doing this requires a clear understanding of exactly what an opportunity cost is. Expenditures that cannot be recovered are not true opportunity costs. They are sunk costs and should be ignored when making decisions. Opportunity costs are forgone alternatives, and they are the only costs to consider. Tool Kit 2.4 shows how to distinguish true opportunity costs from sunk costs.

Tool Kit 2.4 Distinguishing Opportunity Costs and Sunk Costs

When an expenditure must be made regardless of which action is chosen, that expenditure is not an opportunity cost, it is a sunk cost. To find the opportunity cost of an action, it is necessary to see what is changed by undertaking that action rather than its alternative. Follow this four-step procedure.

Step one: To find the opportunity cost of an action, first specify the next-best alternative. This is what could be done if the action in question were not chosen.

Step two: Calculate the total cost for the action and its alternative.

Step three: Calculate the opportunity cost. Subtract the cost for the alternative from the cost for the action. This difference is the opportunity cost of the action.

Step four: Calculate the sunk costs. Any costs that are the same for both the chosen action and its alternative are sunk costs.

---

18   (Worked problem: opportunity cost and sunk costs) Northern Airlines is studying the question of when to cancel flights for its Glasgow to London route. Flying nearly empty planes seems like bad business. The company wants to know the opportunity cost of going ahead with a scheduled round-trip flight. There are two scheduled flights each day. Here are some relevant cost data.

Salaries of crew	£1,000 per day
Fuel	£ 400 per round trip
Loan repayments on plane	£ 100 per day
Landing fees	£ 50 in Glasgow
	£ 100 in London
Other in-flight costs	£ 100 per round trip

Calculate the opportunity cost of each round trip.

Step-by-step solution

Step one: The next-best alternative to going ahead with the scheduled round-trip flight is not flying.

Step two: Calculate the total cost for going ahead with the flight and canceling it. If the flight is made, the expenditures are all of those listed above. If the flight is canceled, the company saves on fuel, landing fees, and other in-flight costs. The salaries of the crew and the loan repayments must be paid whether the flight happens or not.

Expenditures if flight is not cancelled

$= £1,000 + £400 + £100 + £150 + £100 = £1,750.$

Expenditures if flight is canceled $= £1,000 + £100 = £1,100.$

Step three: Calculate the opportunity cost: $£1,750 - £1,100 = £650.$ This is the opportunity cost of the flight.

Step four: Calculate the sunk costs. The remaining £1,100 for salaries and loan repayments are sunk costs. Whether or not the flight is canceled, these cannot be recovered.

19   (Practice problem: opportunity cost and sunk costs) Often during the summer term, courses are scheduled but canceled at Large Town University's education building. In order to see whether this is a good policy, the administration needs to know the opportunity cost of going ahead with a scheduled course offering. Here are some cost data.

Compensation for instructor	£4,000
Air conditioning and lighting	£1,000
Custodial services	£2,000
Property rates	£2,500

Each course requires one room. Any rooms not used for summer courses can be rented to local groups for £1,200 for the summer term.

a   Find the opportunity cost of offering a course.
b   How much are sunk costs?

20   (Practice problem: opportunity cost and sunk costs) The Department of Trade and Industry is downsizing under Prime Minister Scissorhands. It is considering offering early retirement to 8 civil servants in its competitiveness division. Each is 2 years from normal retirement age. (For simplicity, you may ignore discounting the second year's pounds in this problem.)

Salaries	£50,000 each (per year)
Fringe benefits	£20,000 each (per year)
Office space for all 8	£10,000 annually (lease signed for 1 more year)
Pension benefit	£20,000 each if retired (per year)

a If the 8 do receive early retirement, what is the opportunity cost?

b How much are sunk costs?

MARGINAL BENEFITS AND MARGINAL COSTS

The rational individual always considers the benefits and costs of any action. Once you decide to do something, however, there is the question of how much of it to do. Answering this question involves looking at the benefits and costs of a little more or a little less, the marginal benefits and marginal costs. Tool Kit 2.5 shows how to calculate and balance the marginal benefits and marginal costs of economic decisions.

Tool Kit 2.5 Using Marginal Benefits and Marginal Costs

The marginal benefit of an activity is the extra gain brought about by increasing that activity a little. The marginal cost is the corresponding cost. Rational individuals make efficient decisions by carefully balancing benefits and costs "at the margin." Follow this four-step procedure.

Step one: Identify the objective of the activity and the benefits and costs of various levels of the activity.

Step two: Calculate marginal benefits. These are the extra gains from a little bit more of the activity.

Step three: Calculate the marginal costs. These are the extra costs from a little bit more of the activity.

Step four: Choose the level of the activity for which the marginal benefits equal the marginal costs.

---

21 (Worked problem: marginal costs and marginal benefits) A new inoculation against Honduran flu has just been discovered. Presently, 55 people die from the disease each year. The new inoculation will save lives, but unfortunately, it is not completely safe. Some of the recipients of the injections will die from adverse reactions. The projected effects of the inoculation are given in Table 2.1.

Table 2.1

Percent of population inoculated	Deaths due to the disease	Deaths due to the inoculations
0	55	0
10	45	0
20	36	1
30	28	2
40	21	3
50	15	5
60	10	8
70	6	12
80	3	17
90	1	23
100	0	30

How much of the population should be inoculated?

Step-by-step solution

Step one: Identify the objective, benefits, and costs. The objective is to minimise total deaths from the disease and the inoculations, and the problem is to choose the percentage of the population to inoculate. The benefits are reduced deaths caused by the disease, and the costs are the deaths caused by the shots.

Step two: Calculate the marginal benefits. The first 10 percent of the population inoculated reduces deaths caused by the disease from 55 to 45. The marginal benefit of the first 10 percent is 10. From the second 10 percent (increasing the percentage from 10 to 20), the marginal benefit is 45 − 36 = 9. The schedule of the marginal benefit is given in Table 2.2.

Table 2.2

Percent of population	Marginal benefits
10	10
20	9
30	8
40	7
50	6
60	5
70	4
80	3
90	2
100	1

Step three: Calculate the marginal costs. Inoculating the first 10 percent causes no deaths. The second 10 percent (increasing the percent of the population getting the shots from 10 to 20 percent) causes 1 death. The schedule for the marginal costs is shown in Table 2.3.

Table 2.3

Percent of population	Marginal costs
0	0
10	1
20	1
30	1
40	1
50	2
60	3
70	4
80	5
90	6
100	7

Step four: Choose the level of inoculation percentage for which marginal benefits equal marginal costs. The percentage of the population to inoculate is 70. To see why this is correct, notice that inoculating 10 percent of the population saves 10 lives (marginal benefits = 10) and causes no deaths (marginal costs = 0). The net savings in lives is 10. Increasing the percentage to 20 percent saves 9 lives at a cost of 1 death. The net savings is 9 lives. Continuing as long as deaths do not rise gives 70 percent. Notice that increasing the percentage to 80 percent saves fewer people (marginal benefits = 2) than it kills (marginal costs = 4). This is a bad idea. We should stop at 70 percent.

22   (Practice problem: marginal costs and marginal benefits) The transport department has 10 workers fixing potholes. It is considering allocating some of these workers to reprogram traffic lights. Each activity saves travel time for commuters, and this is the objective of the transport department. Table 2.4 gives time savings of each activity as the number of workers assigned to it varies. Remember that if a worker is assigned to reprogram lights, he cannot fix potholes.

Table 2.4

Workers assigned to reprogramming	Total time saved (minutes)	Workers assigned to fix potholes	Total time saved (minutes)
1	100	1	125
2	190	2	225
3	270	3	305
4	340	4	365
5	400	5	415
6	450	6	455
7	490	7	485
8	520	8	510
9	540	9	530
10	550	10	540

How should the workers be assigned? (Hint: Let the number of workers assigned to reprogramming be the activity. What are the costs of assigning these workers?)

23   (Practice problem: marginal costs and marginal benefits) Insectout pesticide kills insects that eat lettuce leaves. Currently 11 leaves per head are eaten by the insects. In the right concentrations, Insectout can be effective. On the other hand, there are side effects. When the concentration is too great, leaves fall off the lettuce head. Table 2.5 shows the relationship between concentrations of Insectout, leaves eaten, and leaves fallen. What concentration should the manufacturer recommend?

Table 2.5

Concentration (parts per million)	Leaves eaten per head	Leaves fallen per head
1	7	0
2	4	1
3	2	3
4	1	6
5	0	10
6	0	15

Answers to Problems

2

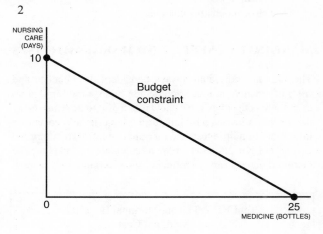

3   *a*

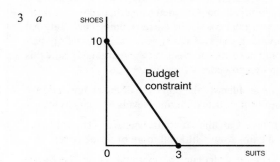

b

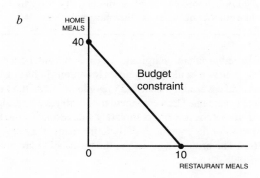

c

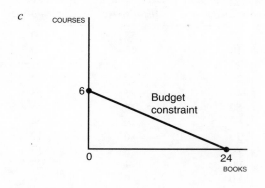

d
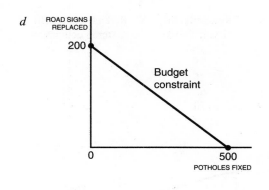

d
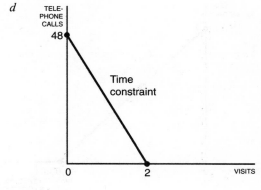

5
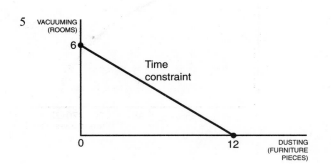

8
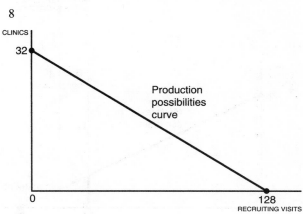

6 *a*
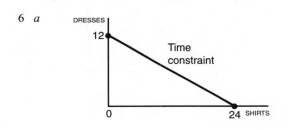

9 *a*
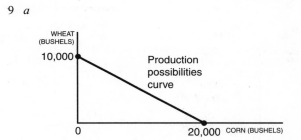

b
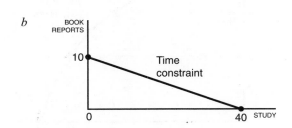

b
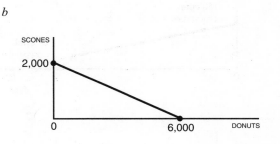

c
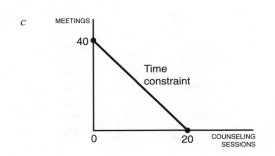

c
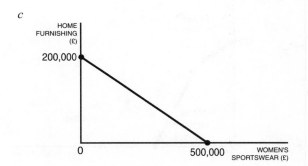

d

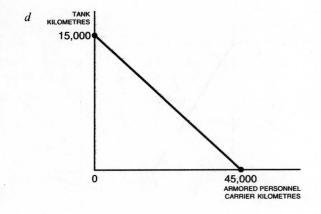

11

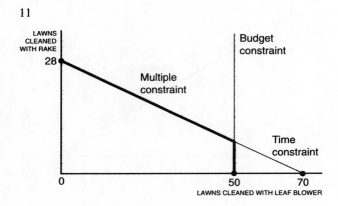

12

13

15

Reduction in bicycle thefts	Reduction in thefts of stereo equipment
0	36
25	31
45	25
60	18
70	10
75	0

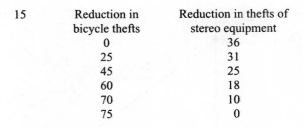

16

Reduced number of truck breakdowns	Reduced number of forklift breakdowns
0	6
5	6
9	5
12	3
14	0

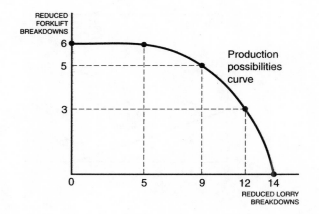

17

Endive (bushels)	Lettuce (bushels)
1,400	5,000
2,400	4,700
3,200	4,200
3,600	3,400
4,000	2,000

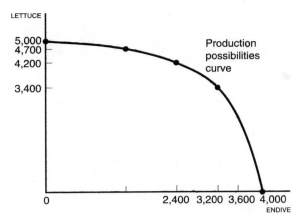

a Opportunity cost = £1,140,000 – £330,000 = £810,000.

b Sunk costs = £330,000.

22 The marginal benefit of assigning a worker to reprogram the lights is the time saved; the marginal cost is the time lost because the worker was not assigned to fix potholes.

Workers assigned to reprogramming	Marginal benefits	Marginal costs
1	100	10
2	90	20
3	80	25
4	70	30
5	60	40
6	50	50
7	40	60
8	30	80
9	20	100
10	10	125

Assign 6 to reprogramming and 4 to fixing potholes.

23 The benefit of recommending higher concentrations of pesticides are the fewer leaves eaten; the costs are the leaves that fall off.

Concentration of pesticide	Marginal benefits	Marginal costs
1	4	0
2	3	1
3	2	2
4	1	3
5	1	4
6	0	5

The manufacturer should recommend a concentration of 3 ppm.

19

	Costs of holding class	Costs of canceling class
Compensation for instructor	£4,000	0
Air conditioning and lighting	£1,000	£1,000
Custodial services	£2,000	£2,000
Property rates	£2,500	£2,500
Rent	0	– £1,200
Total	**£9,500**	**£4,300**

a Opportunity cost = £9,500 – £4,300 = £5,200.

b Sunk costs = £4,300.

20

	Cost of early retirements	Cost of retaining bureaucrats
Salaries	0	£50,000 × 8 × 2
Fringe benefits	0	£20,000 × 8 × 2
Office space for all 8	£ 10,000	£20,000
Pension benefit	£ 20,000 × 8 × 2	0
Total	**£330,000**	**£1,140,000**

TRADE

Chapter Review

Chapter 3 takes up the key feature of markets: exchange. The fundamental aspect of market-based economies is voluntary trade. By definition, voluntary trade is mutually beneficial; it creates a surplus for both buyer and seller. If this were not true, the trade would not take place! An important insight of trade theory is the principle of comparative advantage, which shows how individuals and countries can specialize in production and thereby increase the gains they receive from trade. Economists emphasise the benefits of these gains from trade. The next two chapters will show how markets help realise some of the potential gains from trade.

ESSENTIAL CONCEPTS

1   Voluntary trade between rational individuals is **mutually beneficial;** it is good for both buyer and seller. Naturally, the buyer would like a lower price, and the seller would prefer a higher price. Both might also benefit from better information. Nevertheless, the fact that the exchange takes place implies that given the information each has at the time of the transaction, both judge that they are better off trading than not trading.

2   Trade between individuals within a country and trade between individuals in different countries take place in markets. The three broad classes of markets are the product, labour, and capital markets. These three markets are all integrated internationally; this has led to a high degree of economic interdependence among countries.

3   Trade is many sided, or multilateral. A typical person sells labor to an employer and uses the wages she earns both to purchase goods and services from many other firms and to save for future consumption. Similarly, a country may import more from some trading partners and export very little to those countries. With other trading partners, the country may export more than it imports. A country may also buy more goods and services than it sells abroad and make up the difference by borrowing in capital markets or sending its workers to foreign labour markets.

4   The principle of **comparative advantage** says that individuals and countries will specialise in those goods that they are relatively more efficient in producing. To be relatively efficient means to have a lower opportunity

cost. Countries will have a comparative advantage in different goods. Each can import certain goods from abroad for a lower opportunity cost than it would incur producing them at home. Similarly, each can export to foreign countries those goods for which it has a comparative advantage.

5   Comparative advantage leads to **specialization** in trade, but specialization itself increases productivity and further lowers opportunity costs. First, individuals and countries grow more efficient at their specialties through practice. Second, producing for others allows a larger scale of operations, more **division of labour** into separate tasks, and more specialization. Finally, specialization creates conditions in which invention and innovation flourish.

6   Different countries and individuals have comparative advantages in different activities. Reasons for a comparative advantage can include natural endowments such as climate (for a country) or manual dexterity (for a tailor), human or physical capital, knowledge, and experience. These factors may be gifts of nature, or they may be the result of investment, experience, education, training, or other past actions.

7   **Protectionism** is the idea that the economy needs safeguarding against the perceived harmful effects of trade. Proponents of protectionism use many arguments; chief among them are the loss of domestic jobs, the vulnerability to foreign influences, the unfair trade practices of foreign governments, trade imbalances, and the potential damage to weak economies. To many economists, none of these arguments is convincing.

BEHIND THE ESSENTIAL CONCEPTS

1   An exchange creates and divides a surplus. The surplus is the difference between the value to the seller of what is traded and its value to the buyer. If there is no surplus, the exchange does not take place; the seller simply refuses to trade if he thinks the good is worth more than the buyer is willing to pay. The division of the surplus is another matter. Both the buyer and seller will receive some of the surplus. This is what economists mean when they say that trade is mutually beneficial: each party receives some of the surplus. The buyer pays somewhat less than the maximum she is willing to pay, and the seller receives somewhat more than the minimum he is willing to accept. Of course, whatever the division of the surplus, each would prefer to receive more.

2   When individuals trade, both buyer and seller gain. Each is better off with the trade than he or she would be if the trade did not take place. Likewise, countries also gain from trade. Trade allows specialization on the basis of comparative advantage, and countries benefit from more goods and services. But although each country as a whole gains from trade, not every individual in each country is better off. Some businesses lose out to foreign competition, and some workers lose jobs. Other

businesses gain new markets, and new jobs are created. Thus, international trade creates both gains and losses, but overall, the gains outweigh the losses.

3   The problem with protectionism is that it looks only at the losers from international trade. Tariffs, quotas, and other protectionist policies can, at least temporarily, protect the losers, but only by limiting the trade. Limiting the trade means limiting the gains as well as the losses. Because the gains from trade exceed the losses, protectionism can only make matters worse for the economy as a whole.

4   To better understand comparative advantage, it helps to distinguish it from **absolute advantage.** A country has an absolute advantage in the production of a good or service if it requires fewer inputs to produce the good than another country. Comparative advantage, on the other hand, pertains to opportunity costs. As we have seen, the opportunity cost is not the inputs used in production; rather, it is the alternative use of those inputs. Thus, a country (or individual) has the comparative advantage in the production of a good or service if it has the lower opportunity cost.

For instance, assume that only labour is required to produce tomatoes or bookcases. Workers in country A can produce a carload of tomatoes in 40 hours, while workers in country B require 80 hours. Country A has an absolute advantage in producing tomatoes. To determine comparative advantage, however, we must look at how productive those workers are elsewhere in the economy. If the 40 hours of labour in country A produce 2 bookcases, but 80 hours in country B produce only 1, then country B has a comparative advantage in tomatoes. Why? Because a carload of tomatoes has an opportunity cost of 1 fewer bookcase in country B.

SELF-TEST

True or False

1   Unless the gain from trade is divided equally between buyer and seller, an exchange cannot be mutually beneficial.

2   While imports to the United Kingdom as a percentage of gross domestic product (GDP) have grown over the past three decades, the percentage of GDP devoted to exports has fallen.

3   Because of problems of information, problems of estimating risks, and difficulties in forming expectations about the future, many exchanges are not mutually beneficial.

4   With multilateral trade, imports from a particular country may not equal exports to that country.

5   The country that can produce a good with the least amount of labour is said to have a comparative advantage in the production of that good.

6   Trade on the basis of comparative advantage leads to complete specialization.

7   The extent of the division of labour is limited by the size of the market.

8   Comparative advantage is determined by the endowment of natural resources, human and physical capital, knowledge, and the experience that comes from specialization.

9   The marginal rate of transformation measures the trade-off between two commodities, indicating how much more of one commodity can be produced at the sacrifice of a given amount of another commodity.

10 Opposition to trade between nations is called protectionism.

11 A country that exports more than it imports will run a trade deficit.

12 Although trade benefits the country as a whole, many individuals may lose from trade in a particular product.

13 A country that runs a trade deficit must borrow from abroad.

14 The United Kingdom has a comparative advantage in some high-technology manufactured products, such as jet engines and small aircraft, but must import whisky.

15 Free trade is in principle capable of bringing benefits to the entire economy, but the gains may not be evenly spread.

Multiple Choice

1   Voluntary trade between two rational individuals benefits

   a   the buyer only.
   b   the seller only.
   c   the buyer or the seller but not both.
   d   both the buyer and the seller.
   e   none of the above.

2   The gain from trade, that is, the difference between the value of a good to the buyer and its value to the seller,

   a   accrues entirely to the seller.
   b   accrues entirely to the buyer.
   c   is always divided equally.
   d   accrues to the government.
   e   none of the above.

3   When economists argue that both parties benefit from voluntary trade, they are assuming that

   a   both parties are well-informed.
   b   both parties place the same value on the traded good.
   c   both parties desire the same price.
   d   the surplus is divided evenly between buyer and seller.
   e   none of the above.

4   Goods produced in the United Kingdom and sold in foreign countries are called

   a   imports.
   b   exports.

   c   either imports or exports.
   d   capital flows.
   e   none of the above.

5   For decades, Japan has imported raw materials from Australia, while Australia has purchased heavy equipment from the United States. Furthermore, Japan has exported consumer goods to the United States. This is an example of

   a   multilateral trade.
   b   bilateral trade.
   c   absolute advantage.
   d   protectionism.
   e   trade deficit.

6   If the United Kingdom has a comparative advantage in the production of a good, then

   a   fewer resources are required to produce the good in the United Kingdom.
   b   the United Kingdom also has an absolute advantage in the production of the good.
   c   the relative cost of producing the good is lower in the United Kingdom.
   d   the United Kingdom will import the good.
   e   all of the above.

7   If the United Kingdom has absolute advantage in the production of a good,

   a   production of the good in the United Kingdom is more efficient and requires fewer resources.
   b   the United Kingdom also has comparative advantage in the production of the good.
   c   the relative cost of producing the good is lower in the United Kingdom.
   d   the United Kingdom will import the good.
   e   the United Kingdom will export the good.

8   The trade-off between two commodities is called

   a   comparative advantage.
   b   specialization.
   c   absolute advantage.
   d   the marginal rate of transformation.
   e   none of the above.

9   Suppose that in the United States increasing wheat output by 1,000 tons would require a reduction in steel output of 500 tons, but in Europe increasing wheat output by 1,000 tons would require reducing steel output by 1,000 tons. Then we can infer that

   a   Europe has an absolute advantage in wheat.
   b   the United States has an absolute advantage in wheat.
   c   the United States will export steel.
   d   the United States has a comparative advantage in steel.
   e   the United States has a comparative advantage in wheat.

10 The slope of the production possibilities curve is called

   a   the marginal rate of transformation.
   b   comparative advantage.

c   the trade deficit.
d   marginal benefit.
e   the marginal rate of production.

11   The principle of comparative advantage

a   applies only to international trade.
b   always leads to complete specialization.
c   forms the basis for the division of labour.
d   is relevant only in the absence of protection.
e   all of the above.

12   Which of the following is *not* a reason why specialization increases productivity?

a   Workers and countries grow more efficient by repeating the same tasks.
b   Specialization saves time needed to switch from one task to another.
c   Specialization allows larger-scale production with greater efficiency.
d   Specialization allows the assignment of tasks to those who have a comparative advantage.
e   None of the above.

13   Important sources of comparative advantage include

a   natural endowments.
b   human and physical capital.
c   superior knowledge.
d   experience.
e   all of the above.

14   If two countries have identical relative opportunity costs,

a   there will never be any basis for trade.
b   they might specialize in the production of certain goods and acquire a comparative advantage in those goods over time.
c   each will gain from protectionist policies.
d   the country with an absolute advantage will reap all of the gains from trade.
e   none of the above.

15   When two countries trade,

a   each individual and firm in both countries benefits.
b   any individual benefits from the trades that she engages in.
c   particular groups in each country may be hurt by trade in some goods.
d   b and c.
e   none of the above.

16   Increased immigration of unskilled workers into the United Kingdom will likely

a   lower consumer goods prices.
b   make British firms more competitive in international markets.
c   lower wages of unskilled workers already in the United Kingdom.
d   all of the above.
e   a and b.

17   If a country runs a trade deficit for several years, it

a   is importing more goods and services than it exports.

b   is exporting more goods and services than it imports.
c   must borrow from abroad.
d   b and c.
e   a and c.

18   Which of the following is *not* a basis of comparative advantage?

a   Natural endowments
b   Acquired endowments
c   Superior knowledge
d   Protectionism
e   Specialization

19   With voluntary trade between countries,

a   all individuals are made better off.
b   all individuals in the larger country are made better off.
c   some individuals are made worse off, but the gainers could more than compensate the losers.
d   businesses gain but consumers lose.
e   workers lose but consumers gain.

20   The repeal of the British Corn Laws in 1846 led to

a   a fall in the price of corn in Britain.
b   the impoverishment of British farmers.
c   greater wealth for British industrialists.
d   more rapid industrialization and growth in Britain.
e   all of the above.

Completion

1   The difference between what a person is willing to pay for an item and what she has to pay is a gain from trade, or _____.

2   If a country is relatively more efficient at producing a good than its trading partners, then that country is said to have the _____ in the production of that good.

3   _____ refers to having superior production skills or lower resource costs.

4   Because of trade possibilities, individuals and countries can produce more of what each has a comparative advantage in. This specialization or division of labor is limited by the _____ of the market.

5   _____, such as location, natural resources, and climate, are bases of comparative advantage.

6   Acquired endowments, such as physical and human _____, represent other sources of comparative advantage.

7   The doctrine that the economy of a country is injured by trade is called _____.

8   The marginal rate of transformation is the _____ of the production possibilities frontier.

9   The trade-off in producing two commodities is called the _____.

10   The _____ had the effect of raising farm incomes and the price of bread.

Answers to Self-Test

True or False

1	F	4	T	7	T	10	T	13	T
2	F	5	F	8	T	11	F	14	F
3	F	6	F	9	T	12	T	15	T

Multiple Choice

1	*d*	6	*c*	11	*c*	16	*d*
2	*e*	7	*a*	12	*e*	17	*e*
3	*e*	8	*d*	13	*e*	18	*d*
4	*b*	9	*e*	14	*b*	19	*c*
5	*a*	10	*a*	15	*d*	20	*e*

Completion

1   surplus
2   comparative advantage
3   Absolute advantage
4   size
5   Natural endowments
6   capital
7   protectionism
8   slope
9   marginal rate of transformation
10 British Corn Laws

Tools and Practice Problems

This chapter introduces comparative advantage, a very important concept. The principle of comparative advantage illustrates how individuals, firms, and countries can benefit by specialising in performing tasks or producing goods and trading with each other. This problem set will help you to identify comparative advantage and to see why comparative advantage determines the division of labour and the pattern of trade. You will also study the gains from trade when they proceed according to comparative advantage. Finally, you will use the idea of comparative advantage to construct the production possibilities curve for the case in which resources differ.

COMPARATIVE ADVANTAGE

The most important concept in exchange and production is comparative advantage. Countries have comparative advantage when their opportunity cost is lower. They will export the goods in which they have comparative advantage. Tool Kit 3.1 shows how to use production possibilities curve to identify comparative advantage and determine the pattern or production and trade.

Tool Kit 3.1 Identifying Comparative Advantage

When a country or individual has a comparative advantage in performing some task or producing some good, that country or individual is relatively more efficient; this means that the country or individual has a lower opportunity cost. The following procedure shows how to identify comparative advantage and predict the pattern of trade. It is written for the case of two-country trade.

Step one: Plot the production possibilities curves for each country. Be sure to be consistent and measure units of the same good along the horizontal axis in each case.

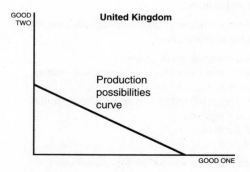

Step two: The slope of the production possibilities curve is the opportunity cost of the good on the horizontal axis, and it indicates the trade-off. The flatter slope implies comparative advantage for producing the good on the horizontal axis.

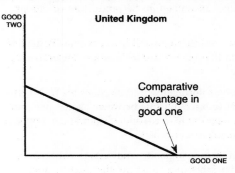

Step three: The steeper slope indicates comparative advantage for the good on the vertical axis.

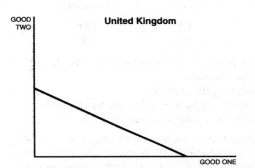

Step four: In a system of free trade, each country will produce more of the good in which it has a comparative advantage, and the relative price will lie somewhere between the opportunity costs of the two countries.

1   (Worked problem: comparative advantage) Workers in the United Kingdom and Portugal can produce shoes and computers. The annual productivity of a worker in each country is given in the table below.

Country	Computers	Shoes
United Kingdom	5,000	10,000
Portugal	200	5,000

a   Which country has a comparative advantage in computers? In shoes?
b   Predict the pattern of trade.
c   Indicate the range of possible relative prices that would bring about this pattern of trade.

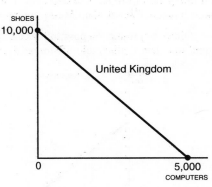

Step-by-step solution

Step one (a): Plot the production possibilities curves. In this problem, the production possibilities curve for one worker in each country will suffice. Measure computers on the horizontal axis.

Step two: The production possibilities curve for the United Kingdom has the flatter slope; therefore, the U.K. worker has a comparative advantage in the production of computers.

Step three: The production possibilities curve for Portugal is steeper, and the Portuguese worker has a comparative advantage in shoes.

Step four (b and c): Portugal will trade shoes for U.K. computers. The relative price must lie between 2 shoes per computer (the U.K. opportunity cost) and 25 shoes per computer (the Portuguese opportunity cost).

2   (Practice problem: comparative advantage) Workers in Nigeria and neighboring Niger produce textiles and sorghum. The productivities of each are given in the table below.

Country	Textiles (bales)	Sorghum (bushels)
Nigeria	100	500
Niger	50	400

a   Which country has a comparative advantage in textiles? In sorghum?
b   Predict the pattern of trade.
c   Indicate the range of possible relative prices that would bring about this pattern of trade.

3   (Practice problem: comparative advantage) For each of the following, determine which country has a comparative advantage in each good, predict the pattern of trade, and indicate the range of possible relative prices consistent with this pattern of trade.

a

Country	Fish	Wheat (bushels)
Greece	60	80
Poland	35	70

b

Country	Heart bypass operations	Car parts (containers)
United States	5,000	10,000
Canada	3,000	9,000

c

Country	Scrap steel (tonnes)	Finished steel (tonnes)
Thailand	20	20
Laos	10	2

d

Country	Wine (barrels)	Wool (bales)
Portugal	2	2
United Kingdom	4	8

GAINS FROM TRADE

When countries trade there is mutual gain, in the sense that their opportunity sets expand beyond their production possibilities curves. To exploit the potential of trade, production

---

Tool Kit 3.2 Showing the Gains from Trade

When the pattern of trade is based upon comparative advantage, both countries can gain. Specifically, they each can consume a bundle of goods that lies beyond their own production possibilities curve. Follow these five steps.

Step one: Draw the production possibilities curve for each country, identify the country with a comparative advantage in each good, and identify the trade-offs for each country.

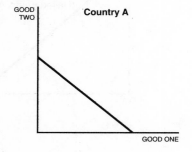

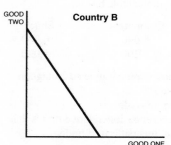

Step two: Choose a relative price between the trade-offs.

Step three: For the country with the comparative advantage in the horizontal-axis good, label the horizontal intercept *A* and draw a line segment from *A* with a slope equal to (–) the relative price. This line segment shows the bundles of goods that the country can consume by trading at the given relative price.

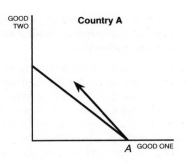

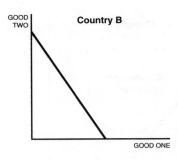

Step four: For the country with the comparative advantage in the vertical-axis good, label the vertical intercept *A* and draw a line segment from *A* with a slope equal to (–) the relative price. This line segment shows the bundles of goods that the country can consume by trading at the given relative price.

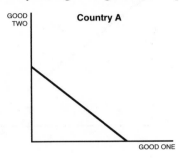

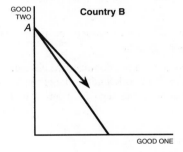

Step five: Pick a pair of consistent points, where A's exports equal B's imports, one on each line segment, and show how each country can benefit from trade.

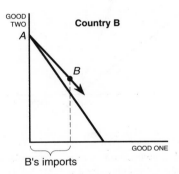

and trade must be organized according to comparative advantage. Tool Kit 3.2 shows how both trading partners can gain from trade.

4   (Worked problem: gains from trade) This problem builds upon problem 1. Show that a worker in Portugal and a worker in the United Kingdom can benefit by trading on the basis of comparative advantage.

Step-by-step solution

Step one: Identify the country with a comparative advantage in each good and the trade-offs for each country. The U.K. worker has the comparative advantage in computers, and the trade-off is 2 shoes per computer. The Portuguese worker

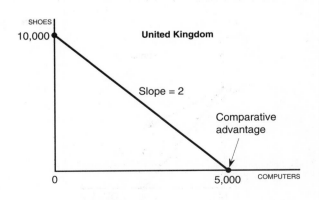

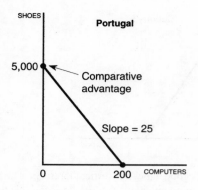

has the comparative advantage in shoes, and the trade-off is 25 shoes per computer.

Step two: Choose a relative price between the trade-offs. Let's choose 20 shoes per computer.

Step three: For the country with the comparative advantage in computers, which is the United Kingdom, label the horizontal intercept A and draw a line segment from A with a

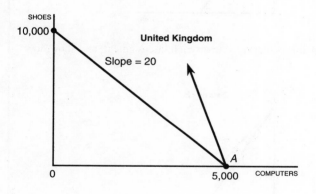

slope equal to –20. This line segment shows the bundles of goods that the United Kingdom can consume by trading at the given relative price.

Step four: For the country with the comparative advantage in shoes, label the vertical intercept A and draw a line segment

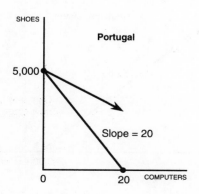

from A with a slope equal to –20. This line segment shows the bundles of goods that Portugal can consume by trading at the given relative price.

Step five: Pick a pair of consistent points, one on each line segment, and show how each country can benefit from trade. Let the U.K. worker produce 4,800 computers for domestic consumption. This leaves 200 for trade. At a relative price of 20 shoes, the 200 computers trade for 4,000 shoes. Plot the point (4,000, 4,800) and label it B. The Portuguese worker must then produce 4,000 shoes for trade. This leaves 1,000 shoes for domestic consumption. The

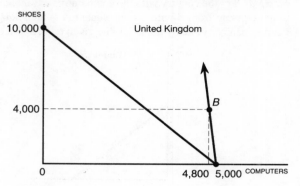

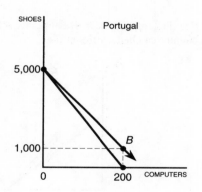

4,000 shoes for trade 200 computers. Plot the point (200, 1,000) and label it B. At this point, the United Kingdom exports 200 computers and imports 4,000 shoes, while Brazil imports 200 computers and exports 4,000 shoes. Trade is balanced, and each country consumes beyond its production possibilities curve.

5   (Practice problem: gains from trade) This problem builds upon problem 2. Show that workers in Nigeria and Niger can benefit by trading according to comparative advantage.

Production Possibilities with Different Resources

Free trade assigns to each country the task of producing those goods in which it has a comparative advantage. The same is true for trade between individuals. To see why this is efficient, we consider the joint production possibilities curve in the case where there are two or more different types

Tool Kit 3.3 Plotting the Production Possibilities Curve When Resources Are Different

When resources differ in their productivity, plotting the production possibilities curve requires that they be assigned to produce goods according to the principle of comparative advantage. Follow these six steps.

Step one: Draw a set of coordinate axes. Label the horizontal axis as the quantity of one good and the vertical axis as the quantity of the other good.

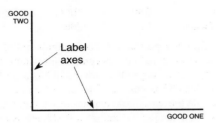

Step two: Calculate the maximum quantities of each good that can be produced. Plot the quantity of one good along the vertical axis and label the point *B*. Plot the quantity of the other good along the horizontal axis and label this point *A*.

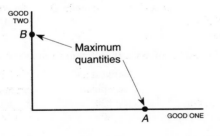

Step three: Identify the resource with the comparative advantage for each good.

Step four: Choose the resource with the comparative advantage in the horizontal-axis good and assign it to produce this good, while keeping the other resource producing the vertical-axis good. Calculate the total quantities produced, and plot this point. Label it *C*.

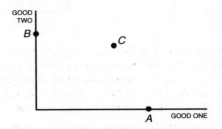

Step five: Connect the points *BCA* with line segments. This is the production possibilities curve.

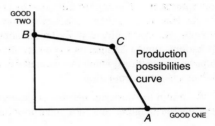

Step six: Verify that the slope is increasing. Because the slope measures the opportunity cost of the horizontal-axis good, this means that the opportunity cost is increasing, which is an implication of the principle of diminishing returns.

of resources that can be used in the production of two goods. To do this efficiently, it is necessary to assign resources to produce the good in which they have a comparative advantage. Tool Kit 3.3 shows how. Compare its shape with Chapter 2's opportunity sets for multiple constraints and diminishing returns.

6 (Worked problem: production possibilities curve) Harrigan and her daughter have formed a two-person firm to handle business incorporations and property transactions. The hours required for each type of task are given below. Each works 48 hours every week.

Lawyer	Hours required to perform each incorporation	Hours required to complete each transaction
Harrigan	4	8
Daughter	8	24

Plot their weekly production possibilities curve.

Step-by-step solution

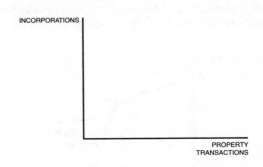

Step one: Draw and label a set of coordinate axes. Put property transactions on the horizontal axis and incorporations on the vertical.

Step two: Calculate the maximum number of incorporations they can do in a week. For Harrigan, this number is 48/4 =

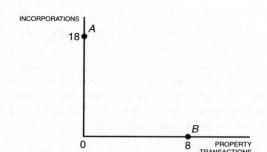

12; for her daughter, it is 48/8 = 6. The pair can complete 18 incorporations. Plot this point along the vertical axis, and label it *A*. Concerning property transactions, Harrigan can do 48/8 = 6; her daughter, 48/24 = 2. The pair can do 8. Plot this point along the horizontal axis, and label it *B*.

Step three: Identify the resource with the comparative advantage for each good. Since it takes Harrigan 8 hours to complete each property transaction but only 4 to do an incorporation, each property transaction requires enough time to do 2 incorporations. The opportunity cost of a property transaction for Harrigan is, then, 2 incorporations. By the same argument, the opportunity cost for her daughter is 24/8 = 3 incorporations; thus, Harrigan has a comparative advantage in property transactions, while her daughter has a comparative advantage in incorporations.

Step four: We assign to Harrigan the task of property transactions, leaving her daughter to do the incorporations. With

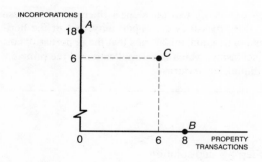

this assignment, they can do 6 incorporations and 6 property transactions (see step two). Plot this point, and label it *C*.

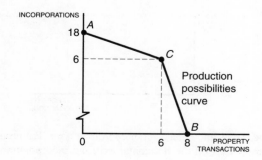

Step five: Draw line segments connecting the points. This is the production possibilities curve.

Step six: Note that between *A* and *C* the slope is 2, but between *C* and *B* the slope increases to 3. The shape of the production possibilities curve thus indicates diminishing returns.

7   (Practice problem: production possibilities curve) A farmer has 3 acres of land. Owing to various characteristics of the land, his ability to produce his two cash crops (corn and soya beans) differs on each acre. The technology of production is given in the table below.

Maximum outputs of each crop per acre (bushels)

	Acre 1	Acre 2	Acre 3
Corn	200	200	100
Soya beans	400	200	50

These figures represent the maximum output of each crop, assuming that only one crop is grown on the acre. That is, acre 1 can produce either 200 bushels of corn or 400 bushels of soya beans. Of course, the farmer can also divide the acre into one part corn and one part soya beans. For example, he can grow 100 bushels of corn and 200 bushels of soya beans on acre 1. Plot the production possibilities curve.

8   (Practice problem: production possibilities curve) Plot the following production possibilities curves.

  a   Maximum harvest of each type of fish per trawler (tonnes)

	Trawler 1	Trawler 2	Trawler 3
Salmon	2	3	4
Tuna	2	6	6

  b   Maximum amounts of pollutants removed (tonnes)

	Smokestack scrubbers	Coal treatment
Sulphur	100	50
Particulates	500	100

Answers to Problems

2   *a*   Nigeria has a comparative advantage in textiles. Niger has a comparative advantage in sorghum.
    b   Nigeria will trade its textiles for sorghum from Niger.
    c   The relative price will lie between 8 bushels of sorghum per bale of textiles and 5 bushels of sorghum per bale of textiles.

3   *a*   Greece has a comparative advantage in fish. Poland has a comparative advantage in wheat. Greece will trade its fish for Polish wheat. The relative price will lie between 4/3 bushels of wheat per fish and 2 bushels of wheat per fish.
    b   The United States has a comparative advantage in heart bypass operations, and Canada in car parts. The United States will trade heart bypass operations for Canadian car parts. The relative price will lie between 2 containers of car parts per operation and 3 containers of car parts per operation.
    c   Thailand has a comparative advantage in finished steel, Laos in scrap steel. Thailand will trade its finished steel for Laotian scrap steel. The relative price

will lie between 5 tonnes of scrap steel per ton of finished steel and 1 tonne of scrap steel per tonne of finished steel.

  d Portugal has a comparative advantage in wine, the United Kingdom in wool. British wool will be traded for Portuguese wine. The relative price will lie between 1 and 2 bales per barrel of wine.

5 Choose, for example, 6 bushels of sorghum per bale of textiles as the relative price. Nigeria can produce 100 bales of textiles and trade 20 to Niger for 120 bushels of sorghum. The point (80, 120) lies outside its production possibilities curve. Niger can produce 400 bushels of sorghum and trade 120 bushels to Nigeria for 20 bales of textiles. The point (20, 280) lies outside its production possibilities curve.

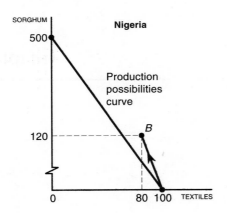

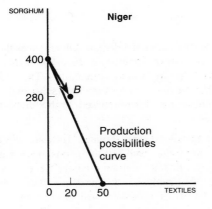

7

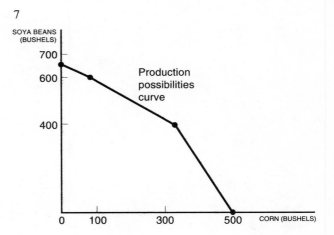

8*a*

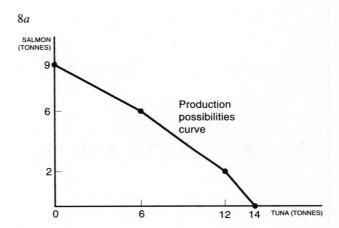

b

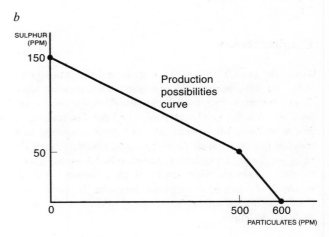

DEMAND, SUPPLY, AND PRICE

Chapter Review

Trade, the markets in which it occurs, and the gains it provides for both buyers and sellers are all important ideas from Chapter 3. Chapter 4 builds the basic model of markets, which is the supply and demand model. The focus is on prices and quantities—how they are determined and how they change when other factors change. Chapter 5 then applies the supply and demand model to major areas of concern to economists: what happens to the quantity demanded or supplied when prices change, and what happens when prices do not adjust, as when the government sets price floors or ceilings.

ESSENTIAL CONCEPTS

1   Consumers **demand** goods and services. They are willing and able to pay, and given a price, they will buy a certain quantity. Several factors influence demand, but the most important is **price.** As the price falls, people buy more of the good or service; as the price rises, they purchase less. The entire relationship between the price and the quantity that a person buys is called the individual **demand curve.**

2   Adding all the individual demand curves gives the **market demand curve.** For every price, ask how much each individual will buy. Add these quantities. The result is the market demand curve, which shows the total amount of the good that will be purchased by all individuals at each price.

3   Firms **supply** goods and services. They are willing and able to produce and sell the good, and at a given price, they will sell a certain quantity. Several factors influence the supply, but the most important is price. As the price rises, producers will supply more; as the price falls, producers will supply less. The entire relationship between the price and the quantity that the producer will sell is called the individual **supply curve.**

4   Adding up all of the individual supply curves gives the **market supply curve.** For every price, ask how much each producer will sell. Add these quantities. The result is the market supply curve, which shows how much of the good will be sold by all producers at each price.

5   The price at which consumers want to buy exactly the quantity that firms want to sell is the **equilibrium price.** This quantity, which is the same for demand and

supply, is the **equilibrium quantity.** It is an equilibrium because there are no forces that would cause it to change.

6   If the price were higher than the equilibrium price, firms would want to sell more than consumers would buy. Unable to sell all of their goods, many firms would compete, by lowering prices, to attract the relatively few consumers. Because this higher price would change, it is not an equilibrium. Similarly, if the price were lower than the equilibrium price, consumers would want to buy more than firms would sell. Seeing the glut of consumers, firms would raise their prices. In sum, if the price is above equilibrium, it falls; if it is below equilibrium, it rises. When price equals the equilibrium price, it does not change.

7   Many factors affect the demand and supply. For demand, these factors include changes in income, prices of substitutes and complements, the composition of the population, and people's tastes. This is only a partial list. When one of these factors—or anything else that affects the willingness to pay for the good—changes, the entire demand curve **shifts,** and a new equilibrium must be found.

Supply is affected by changes in technology and input price—more generally, anything that causes costs to change. Again, changes in these factors **shift** the supply curve and lead to a new equilibrium.

BEHIND THE ESSENTIAL CONCEPTS

1   The demand curve is the entire range, or schedule, that indicates how many goods will be purchased at each price. At a given price, this number is called the quantity demanded. In diagrams of demand curves, the quantity demanded is measured along the horizontal axis. To find the quantity demanded, simply read it off the demand curve at the current price. Economists, students, and sometimes professors are sloppy and say "change in demand" without being clear whether they mean a shift in the demand curve or a change in the quantity demanded. The latter is brought about by a change in price, and it involves only a movement along the same demand curve. To guard against confusion in stressful situations (like exams!), say "demand curve" when you refer to the entire schedule of prices and quantities and "quantity demanded" when you want to indicate the number of goods purchased.

2   It is very important to understand why the market demand curve is drawn as it is. When the price rises, the market quantity demanded falls for two reasons. First, each individual buys less. The principle of substitution says that other available goods and services can serve as alternatives, and at higher prices, people switch to consume these substitutes. Second, some individuals find the price to be too high altogether, and they leave the market completely. When the price falls, the oppo-site happens. People substitute away from other goods and buy more of the one with the lower price. Furthermore, the lower price attracts new consumers to the market.

3   The market supply curve slopes upwards. This means that as the price rises, more is offered for sale. Again, there are two reasons. First, firms are willing to sell more at higher prices. Second, higher prices attract new producers to the market.

4   Other factors that shift the demand curve include consumer income, tastes, prices of substitutes and complements, and the composition of the population. The supply curve shifts with changes in technology or input prices. While these factors are the most common causes of shifts, they do not make up a complete list. Anything that affects the willingness and ability to pay for goods shifts the demand curve, and anything that affects costs shifts the supply curve. For example, if it rains in April, the supply of crops may increase and the demand for umbrellas may also increase.

5   Successful supply and demand analysis proceeds in four steps:

   a   Start with an equilibrium.
   b   Figure out which curve shifts.
   c   Shift the curve and find the new equilibrium.
   d   Compare the price and quantity at the original and new equilibria.

Be careful to avoid a common pitfall. Suppose you are asked to show the effect of a change in tastes that shifts demand to the right. The failing student's analysis goes like this: "Demand shifts to the right; this increases quantity and price, but the increase in price leads producers to want to supply more, so supply also shifts to the right." What is wrong with this answer? Stop before the *but.* True, the demand shift does raise price and quantity, but that is the end of the story. The increase in price does lead producers to want to supply more. As they supply more, there is a movement along the supply curve but not a shift. Changes in the price of a good *never shift* the demand curve for that good or the supply curve for that good; rather, changes in the price of a good cause a *movement* along the demand curve or supply curve. There is more discussion on this point and lots of practice problems in the Tools and Practice Problems section of this chapter.

SELF-TEST

True or False

1   Prices provide incentives to help the economy use resources efficiently.

2   As the price falls, the quantity demanded decreases.

3   The market demand curve is the sum of the quantities and prices of each individual demand.

4   The individual demand curve is an example of an equilibrium relationship.

5   One reason why the supply curve slopes upwards is that at higher prices, more producers enter the market.

6   In equilibrium, there is neither excess demand nor excess supply.

7   If the price is above the equilibrium price, consumers can buy as much as they are willing.

8   If the price is below the equilibrium price, sellers cannot sell as much as they are willing.

9   The law of supply and demand says that the equilibrium price will be that price at which the quantity demanded equals the quantity supplied.

10   The individual supply curve is an example of an identity.

11   The price of diamonds is higher than the price of water because diamonds have a higher value in use.

12   A change in a consumer's income will shift her demand curve.

13   A change in the price of a good will shift its market demand curve to the right.

14   An increase in the price of a substitute will shift the demand curve for the good in question to the right.

15   A decrease in the price of a complement will shift the demand curve for the good in question to the left.

Multiple Choice

1   Market prices

   a   measure scarcity.
   b   communicate information.
   c   provide incentives.
   d   all of the above.
   e   a and b.

2   The individual demand curve for a good or service

   a   gives the quantity of the good or service the individual would purchase at each price.
   b   gives the equilibrium price in the market.
   c   shows which other goods or services will be substituted according to the principle of substitution.
   d   all of the above.
   e   a and c.

3   The idea that there are other goods or services that can serve as reasonably good alternatives to a particular good or service is called the

   a   law of demand.
   b   principle of substitution.
   c   market demand curve.
   d   principle of scarcity.
   e   none of the above.

4   If you knew the individual demand curves of each consumer, you could find the market demand curve by

   a   taking the average quantity demanded at each price.
   b   adding all of the prices.
   c   adding, at each price, the quantities purchased by each individual.
   d   taking the average of all prices.
   e   none of the above.

5   As the price rises, the quantity demanded decreases along an individual demand curve because

   a   individuals substitute other goods and services.
   b   some individuals exit the market.
   c   some individuals enter the market.
   d   the quantity supplied increases.
   e   a and b.

6   As the price rises, the quantity demanded decreases along the market demand curve because

   a   individuals substitute other goods and services.
   b   some individuals exit the market.
   c   some individuals enter the market.
   d   the quantity supplied increases.
   e   a and b.

7   As the price rises, the quantity supplied increases along an individual supply curve because

   a   higher prices give firms incentives to sell more.
   b   the principle of substitution leads firms to substitute other goods and services.
   c   the market supply curve is the sum of all the quantities produced by individual firms at each price.
   d   b and c.
   e   none of the above.

8   As the price rises, the quantity supplied increases along the market supply curve because

   a   at higher prices, more firms are willing to produce the good.
   b   each firm in the market is willing to produce more.
   c   the market supply curve is the sum of all the quantities produced by individual firms at each price.
   d   at higher prices, more firms substitute other goods and services.
   e   a and b.

9   If the market price is below equilibrium, then

   a   there is excess demand.
   b   there is excess supply.
   c   consumers will want to raise the price.
   d   firms will want to lower the price.
   e   all of the above.

10   If the market price is at equilibrium, then

   a   the quantity that consumers are willing to buy equals the quantity that producers are willing to sell.
   b   there is excess demand.
   c   there is excess supply.

d there are no forces that will change the price.

e *a* and *d*.

11 If the market price is above equilibrium, then

a there is excess supply.

b there is excess demand.

c firms will not be able to sell all that they would like.

d consumers will not be able to buy all that they would like.

e *a* and *c*.

12 The law of supply and demand is an example of

a an identity.

b an equilibrium relationship.

c a behavioral relationship.

d all of the above.

e none of the above.

13 The statement that market supply is equal to the sum of individual firms' supplies is an example of

a an identity.

b an equilibrium relationship.

c a behavioral relationship.

d all of the above.

e none of the above.

14 A diamond sells for a higher price than a litre of water because

a luxuries always have higher prices than necessities.

b only a few people demand diamonds but everyone needs water.

c the total use value of diamonds exceeds the total value of water.

d the total cost of diamond production exceeds the total cost of water production.

e none of the above.

15 Stationary exercise bicycles and stair-stepper machines are substitutes, according to the aerobically correct. An increase in the price of exercise bicycles will

a shift the demand for stair-stepper machines to the right.

b increase the price of stair-stepper machines.

c increase the quantity of stair-stepper machine sales.

d all of the above.

e none of the above.

16 As people have grown more concerned about saturated fat in their diets, the demand for beef has shifted to the left. The quantity of beef sold has also fallen. This change is a

a movement along the demand curve for beef.

b shift in the supply curve for beef.

c movement along the supply curve for beef.

d *a* and *b*.

e none of the above.

17 Which of the following is *not* a source of shifts in market demand?

a An increase in consumer income

b A change in tastes

c An increase in the population

d A technological advance

e None of the above

18 If the price of an input falls,

a supply shifts to the left.

b demand shifts to the right.

c demand shifts to the left.

d supply shifts to the right.

e none of the above.

19 If ski-lift tickets and skiing lessons are complements, then an increase in the price of lift tickets

a shifts demand for skiing lessons to the left.

b shifts demand for skiing lessons to the right.

c shifts supply of skiing lessons to the left.

d shifts supply of skiing lessons to the right.

e *a* and *d*.

20 A recent regulation requires tuna fishing companies to use nets that allow dolphins to escape. These nets also allow some tuna to escape. This regulation causes

a the supply of tuna to shift to the left.

b the demand for tuna to shift to the right.

c the demand for tuna to shift to the left.

d the supply of tuna to shift to the right.

e none of the above.

Completion

1 _____ is defined as what is given in exchange for a good or service.

2 If the price of a good or service falls, the quantity demanded _____.

3 The quantity of the good or service purchased at each price is given by the _____.

4 The quantity of the good or service offered for sale at each price is given by the _____.

5 In an economic equilibrium, there are no forces for _____.

6 The law of supply and demand says that at the equilibrium price, the _____ equals the _____.

7 The statement that market supply equals market demand is an example of an _____.

8 The statement that market supply is the total of all individual supplies is an example of an _____.

9 An increase in the price of a good leads to a _____ its demand curve.

10 A change in technology leads to a _____ the supply curve.

Answers to Self-Test

True or False

1	T	4	F	7	T	10	F	13	F
2	F	5	T	8	F	11	F	14	T
3	F	6	T	9	T	12	T	15	F

Multiple Choice

1	d	6	e	11	e	16	c
2	a	7	a	12	b	17	d
3	b	8	e	13	a	18	d
4	c	9	a	14	e	19	a
5	a	10	e	15	d	20	a

Completion

1 Price
2 increases
3 demand curve
4 supply curve
5 change
6 quantity demanded, quantity supplied
7 equilibrium relationship
8 identity
9 movement along
10 shift in

Tools and Practice Problems

Three techniques receive attention in this section. The first technique shows how to add individual demand and individual supply curves to get market demand and market supply curves. The next technique involves finding the equilibrium price and quantity, where the market clears. Finally, some general instructions about supply and demand analysis are given and developed in several problems. Each of these techniques is fundamental and will appear repeatedly throughout this book.

MARKET DEMAND AND MARKET SUPPLY

When the price falls, individual demanders want to buy more, and individual suppliers want to sell less. These individual demand and supply curves are behavioural relationships. The market demand and market supply curves are found by adding all of these individual demands and supplies. Tool Kit 4.1 shows how to do this.

Tool Kit 4.1 Calculating Market Demand and Supply

The market demand is the sum of the individual demands. The market supply is the sum of the individual supplies. This tool kit shows how to add the individual demands and supplies.

Step one: Make two columns. Label the left-hand column "Price" and the right-hand column "Quantity."

Price   Quantity

Step two: Choose the highest price at which goods are demanded. Enter it in the first row of the price column.

Price   Quantity
p_1

Step three: Find how many goods each individual will purchase. Add these quantities. Enter the total in the first row of the quantity column.

Price   Quantity
p_1 $Q_1 = Q_a + Q_b + Q_c + \cdots$

Step four: Choose the second highest price, and continue the process.

---

1 (Worked problem: market demand) The individual demands of Jason and Kyle for economics tutoring are given in Table 4.1. Calculate the market demand. (Jason and Kyle are the only two individuals in this market.)

Table 4.1

Jason		Kyle	
Price	Quantity	Price	Quantity
£10	6	£10	4
£ 8	8	£ 8	5
£ 6	10	£ 6	6
£ 4	12	£ 4	7

Step-by-step solution

Step one: Make and label two columns.

Price   Quantity

Step two: Choose the highest price. This is £10. Enter this in the first row under price.

Price   Quantity
£10

Step three: Find the market quantity. Jason would buy 6; Kyle would buy 4. The total is 6 + 4 = 10. Enter 10 in the corresponding quantity column.

Price   Quantity
£10   10

Step four: Repeat the process. The next lower price is £8. Jason would buy 8; Kyle would buy 5. The total is 8 + 5 = 13. Enter £8 and 13 in the appropriate columns.

Price   Quantity
£10   10
£ 8   13

Continue. The entire market demand is given below.

Price   Quantity
£10   10
£ 8   13
£ 6   16
£ 4   19

2 (Practice problem: market demand) Gorman's tomatoes are purchased by pizza sauce makers, by sandwich shops, and by vegetable canners. The demands for each are given in Table 4.2. Find the market demand.

Table 4.2

Pizza sauce		Sandwich shops		Vegetable canners	
Price	Quantity (bushels)	Price	Quantity (bushels)	Price	Quantity (bushels)
£5	25	£5	5	£5	55
£4	35	£4	6	£4	75
£3	40	£3	7	£3	100
£2	50	£2	7	£2	150
£1	80	£1	7	£1	250

3   (Practice problem: market supply) The technique for finding the market supply curve is the same as for the market demand. Simply sum the quantities supplied at each price. There are three law firms that will draw up partnership contracts in the town of Pullman. Their individual supply curves are given in Table 4.3. Find the market supply curve.

Table 4.3

Jones & Co.		Smith & Co.		Riley & Co.	
Price	Quantity	Price	Quantity	Price	Quantity
£200	0	£200	6	£200	4
£220	0	£220	8	£220	8
£240	0	£240	12	£240	10
£260	8	£260	24	£260	11

EQUILIBRIUM

In equilibrium, markets clear. The market price will settle where the quantity that demanders want to purchase exactly equals the quantity that suppliers choose to sell. Tool Kit 4.2 shows how to find the equilibrium.

Tool Kit 4.2 Finding the Equilibrium
Price and Quantity

The equilibrium price in the demand and supply model is the price at which the buyers want to buy exactly the quantity that sellers want to sell. In other words, the quantity demanded equals the quantity supplied. The equilibrium quantity in the market is just this quantity. Here is how to find the equilibrium in a market.

Step one: Choose a price. Find the quantity demanded at that price and the quantity supplied.

Step two: If the quantity demanded equals the quantity supplied, the price is the equilibrium. Stop.

Step three: If the quantity demanded exceeds the quantity supplied, there is a shortage. Choose a higher price and repeat step one. If the quantity demanded is less than the quantity supplied, there is a surplus. Choose a lower price and repeat step one.

Step four: Continue until the equilibrium price is found.

---

4   (Worked problem: equilibrium price and quantity) The supply curve and demand curve for cinder blocks are given in Table 4.4. The quantity column indicates the number of blocks sold in one year.

Table 4.4

Demand		Supply	
Price	Quantity	Price	Quantity
£2.00	50,000	£2.00	200,000
£1.50	70,000	£1.50	160,000
£1.00	100,000	£1.00	100,000
£ .75	150,000	£ .75	50,000
£ .50	250,000	£ .50	0

a   Find the equilibrium price and quantity.
b   If the price is £1.50, is the market in equilibrium? Will there be a surplus or a shortage? If so, what is the size of the surplus or shortage? What will happen to the price? Why?
c   If the price is 75 pence, is the market in equilibrium? Will there be a surplus or a shortage? If so, what is the size of the surplus or shortage? What will happen to the price? Why?

Step-by-step solution

Step one (a): Choose a price. At a price of, say, £2, the quantity demanded is 50,000 and the quantity supplied is 200,000.

Step two: The quantities are not equal.

Step three: There is a surplus. The equilibrium price will be lower.

Step four: Continue. Try other prices until the quantity supplied equals the quantity demanded. The equilibrium price is £1, where the quantity equals 100,000. We can now see the answers to parts b and c.

Step five (b): If the price is £1.50, the quantity demanded is 70,000, and it is less than the quantity supplied, which is 160,000. There is a surplus of 90,000 (160,000 − 70,000). The price will fall because producers will be unable to sell all that they want.

Step six (c): If the price is 75 pence, the quantity demanded is 150,000, and it is greater than the quantity supplied, which is 50,000. There is a shortage of 100,000 (150,000 − 50,000). The price will rise because producers will see that buyers are unable to buy all that they want.

5   (Practice problem: equilibrium price and quantity) The demand curve and supply curve in the market for billboard space space along busy roads are given in Table 4.5. The price is the monthly rental price. The quantity column shows numbers of billboards.

Table 4.5

Demand		Supply	
Price	Quantity	Price	Quantity
£100	5	£100	25
£ 80	8	£ 80	21
£ 60	11	£ 60	16
£ 40	14	£ 40	14
£ 20	22	£ 20	3

a   Find the equilibrium price and quantity.

b   If the price is £20, is the market in equilibrium? Will there be a surplus or a shortage? If so, what is the size of the surplus or shortage? What will happen to the price? Why?

c   If the price is £80, is the market in equilibrium? Will there be a surplus or a shortage? If so, what is the size of the surplus or shortage? What will happen to the price? Why?

6   (Practice problem: equilibrium price and quantity) Find the equilibrium price and quantity in each of the following markets.

a   The supply and demand curves for new soles (shoe repair) are given in Table 4.6.

Table 4.6

Demand		Supply	
Price	Quantity	Price	Quantity
£35	17	£35	53
£30	21	£30	37
£25	25	£25	25
£20	30	£20	15
£15	35	£15	0

b   The supply and demand curves for seat cushions are given in Table 4.7.

Table 4.7

Demand		Supply	
Price	Quantity	Price	Quantity
£8	4	£8	32
£7	8	£7	28
£6	12	£6	22
£5	16	£5	19
£4	17	£4	17

SUPPLY AND DEMAND

Supply and demand is probably the most useful technique in microeconomics. Economists use it to study how markets are affected by changes in such factors as tastes, technology, government programs, and many others. Supply and demand offers a wealth of insights into the workings of the economy. It is very important to master the procedure spelled out in Tool Kit 4.3.

Tool Kit 4.3 Using Supply and Demand

Supply and demand analysis provides excellent answers to questions of the following form: "What is the effect of a change in _____ on the market for _____?" You are well on your way to success as a student of economics if you stick closely to this procedure in answering such questions.

Step one: Begin with an equilibrium in the relevant market. Label the horizontal axis as the quantity of the good or service and the vertical axis as the price. Draw a demand and a supply curve and label them D and S, respectively.

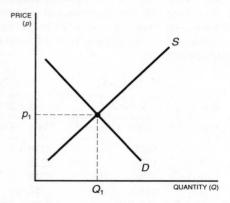

Step two: Figure out whether the change shifts the supply curve, the demand curve, or neither.

Step three: Shift the appropriate curve.

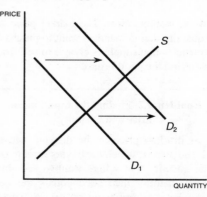

Step four: Find the new equilibrium, and compare it with the original one.

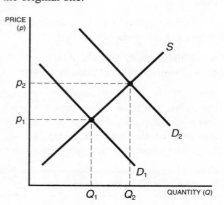

7   (Worked problem: using supply and demand) In response to concern about the fumes emitted by dry cleaning establishments, the government has issued regulations requiring expensive filtering systems. How will this regulation affect the dry cleaning market?

Step-by-step solution

Step one: Start with an equilibrium.

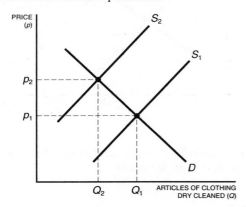

Step two: Figure out which curve shifts. The mandated filtering systems increase the dry cleaning firm's costs, shifting supply to the left.

Step three: Shift the curve.

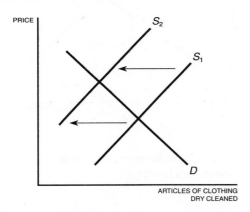

Step four: Find the new equilibrium and compare. The effect of the regulation is to raise the price and lower the quantity of clothes dry cleaned.

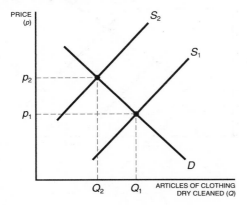

8   (Practice problem: using supply and demand) The Brazilian coffee harvest is hit by a climatic disaster that reduces the supply of coffee and increases its price. Explain the effect of the rise in the price of coffee on the market for tea.

9   (Practice problem: using supply and demand) For each of the following, show the effects on price and quantity. Draw the diagrams and follow the procedure.

   a   An increase in income in the market for a normal good
   b   A decrease in income in the market for a normal good
   c   An increase in the price of a substitute
   d   A decrease in the price of a substitute
   e   An increase in the price of a complement
   f   A decrease in the price of an complement
   g   An increase in the price of an input
   h   A decrease in the price of an input
   i   An improvement in technology

Answers to Problems

2 | Price | Quantity (bushels) |
    |-------|--------------------|
    | £5 | 85 |
    | £4 | 116 |
    | £3 | 147 |
    | £2 | 207 |
    | £1 | 337 |

3 | Price | Quantity |
    |-------|----------|
    | £200 | 10 |
    | £220 | 16 |
    | £240 | 22 |
    | £260 | 43 |

5   *a*   Equilibrium price = £40; quantity = 14.
    b   If the price is £20, there is a shortage of 22 – 3 = 19. The price will be driven up.
    c   If the price is £80, there is a surplus of 21 – 8 = 13. The price will be driven down.

6   *a*   Price = £25; quantity = 25.
    b   Price = £4; quantity = 17.

8   Coffee and tea are substitutes, and therefore the demand curve shifts to the right, the price increases, and the quantity increases.

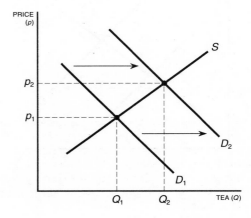

9   *a*   Demand shifts to the right, driving the price up and increasing the quantity.

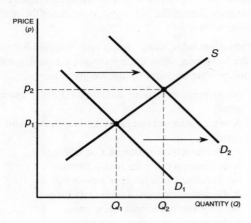

b   Demand shifts to the left, driving the price down and decreasing the quantity.

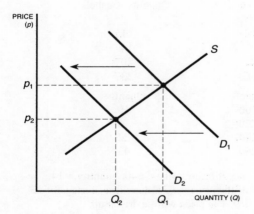

c   Demand shifts to the right, driving the price up and increasing the quantity.

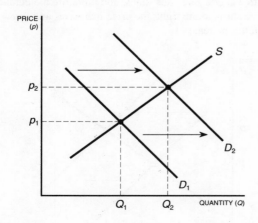

d   Demand shifts to the left, driving the price down and decreasing the quantity.

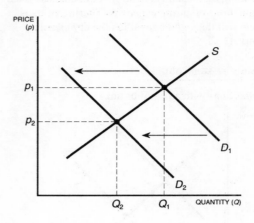

e   Demand shifts to the left, driving the price down and decreasing the quantity.

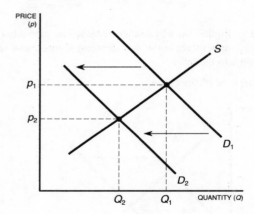

f   Demand shifts to the right, driving the price up and increasing the quantity.

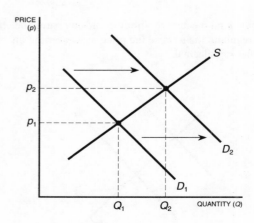

g Supply shifts up (vertically), increasing the price but decreasing the quantity.

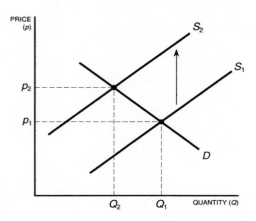

i Supply shifts down (vertically), decreasing the price but increasing the quantity.

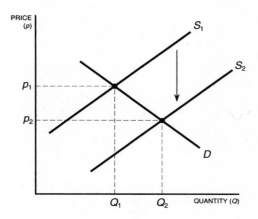

h Supply shifts down (vertically), decreasing the price but increasing the quantity.

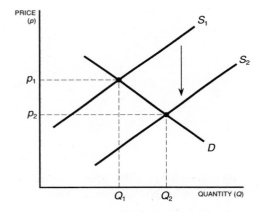

Chapter 5

USING DEMAND AND SUPPLY

Chapter Review

The model of demand and supply introduced in Chapter 4 is one of the most useful in all of the social sciences. The ideas of demand and supply form the basis of all economic study and will be used throughout this text. This chapter develops the model in more detail and introduces the concept of elasticity. Elasticity is best thought of as sensitivity. The price elasticity of demand, for instance, measures how sensitive the quantity demanded is to a change in price. The chapter then applies the model to the study of the effects of taxes and price controls. Chapter 6 extends the supply and demand framework to markets in which future goods and risk are exchanged.

ESSENTIAL CONCEPTS

1   When price falls, quantity demanded increases. If the demand curve is steep, the increase in quantity is smaller than it would be if the curve were flat. Although it might seem natural to measure how the quantity responds to price changes by the slope of the demand curve, economists employ the concept of **elasticity.** They do so because elasticity will produce the same measure no matter which units are used. The **price elasticity of demand**

is the percentage change in the quantity demanded brought about by a 1 percent change in price.

2   The **price elasticity of supply** is the percentage change in the quantity supplied brought about by a 1 percent change in price. It is the basic measure of how sensitive the quantity supplied is to changes in price.

3   The price elasticity of demand is greater when there are good, close substitutes available. Usually it is greater when the price is higher, because at higher prices, only those who consider the good essential remain in the market. Both the price elasticity of demand and the price elasticity of supply are greater in the long run because individuals and firms have more time to find substitutes and make adjustments.

4   When demand shifts, both the equilibrium price and quantity change. The price elasticity of supply determines which change is larger. If supply is more elastic, quantity changes by a greater percentage than price; if supply is less elastic, price changes more. Similarly, it is the price elasticity of demand that determines the relative changes in price and quantity when supply shifts. The more elastic the demand, the more quantity changes and the smaller is the change in price.

5   The economic effects of a tax are seen by focusing on the market affected by the tax. For example, a tax on the

sale of petrol shifts the supply curve up (vertically) by the amount of the tax, raises consumer prices, and reduces the quantity of petrol sold. Except in a case where supply or demand is perfectly inelastic or perfectly elastic, the increase in consumer price is less than the amount of the tax. This means that producers are able to pass on only part of the tax to their customers and must bear some of the burden themselves.

6   **Price ceilings,** when set below the market-clearing price, lead to shortages; in that case, the quantity demanded is more than the quantity supplied. **Price floors,** when set above the market-clearing price, result in surpluses; in this case, the quantity demanded is less than the quantity supplied. In each case, the quantity exchanged is less than it is at the market-clearing price.

BEHIND THE ESSENTIAL CONCEPTS

1   The concept of elasticity appears many times throughout the text and is worth mastering. Suppose that price falls by 1 percent. We know that quantity will increase as consumers substitute towards the lower price, but by how much? The price elasticity provides the answer. It is the percentage change in quantity brought on by a 1 percent change in price.

2   The relationship between elasticity and total revenue is very important. Total revenue is just price multiplied by quantity. If the price of a bicycle is £200 and there are 20 sold, then total revenue is £200 × 20 = £4,000. When price falls, total revenue is pushed down because each unit sells for less money; however, total revenue is pushed up because more units are sold. Whether on balance total revenue rises or falls depends on the elasticity. Table 5.1 helps to keep the relationship between elasticity and total revenue straight.

Table 5.1

If price rises,
   Total revenue *falls* if the price elasticity of demand is greater than 1 (elastic).
   Total revenue *rises* if the price elasticity of demand is less than 1 (inelastic).
   Total revenue *does not change* if the price elasticity of demand equals 1 (unitary elasticity).

If price falls,
   Total revenue *rises* if the price elasticity of demand is greater than 1 (elastic).
   Total revenue *falls* if the price elasticity of demand is less than 1 (inelastic).
   Total revenue *does not change* if the price elasticity of demand equals 1 (unitary elasticity).

---

3   What makes the demand for some goods (like motorboats) elastic, while the demand for others (like milk) is inelastic? The most important factor is the availability of substitutes. The **principle of substitution** says that consumers will look for substitutes when the price rises. If there are good, close substitutes available, then finding substitutes will be easy and consumers will switch. If good, close substitutes are not available, the consumers are more likely to swallow the price increase and continue purchasing the good.

4   Suppose that the government levies a tax on the supply of hotel rooms. Who pays the tax? While it is natural to think that the hotel pays the tax because it writes the cheque to the government, when you look at the issue through the lens of supply and demand, you see the value of economics. The tax increases the hotel's costs, and therefore it shifts the supply curve up and raises the price. Because they must pay higher prices for hotel rooms, consumers pay some of the tax.

5   The key to tax analysis is to find the market or markets in which the burden of the tax falls. Sometimes this is easy. A hotel room tax falls on the market for hotel rooms. In other cases, its not so clear. For example, an income tax affects the labour market, because workers must give up some of the earnings. It also affects the capital market because some of the interest earnings must be paid to the government. Once you find the relevant market, simply apply the basic method of supply and demand: start with an equilibrium, figure out which curve shifts (which side of the market is taxed), shift the curve, find the new equilibrium, and compare.

6   Price ceilings only make a difference if they are set below the market-clearing price (where the supply and demand curves intersect). A price ceiling set above the market-clearing price has no effect. Similarly, a price floor set below the market-clearing price does not do anything.

7   Price floors and ceilings also affect the quantity traded in the market. If there is a price ceiling, then the quantity demanded exceeds the quantity supplied. The supply is the short side of the market, and although consumers would like to buy more of the good, the quantity traded is what producers are willing to sell. This is shown in Figure 5.1A. With price floors, the opposite is true. The demand is the short side of the market, and the quantity traded equals the amount that consumers are willing to buy, as shown in panel B. In each case, we say that the short side of the market determines the actual quantity traded, and the actual quantity trade is less than the market-clearing quantity.

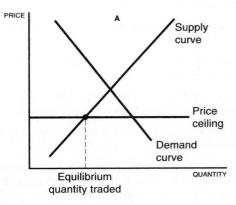

Figure 5.1

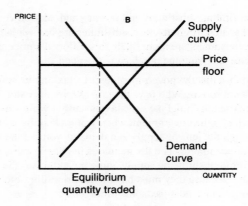

Figure 5.1

SELF-TEST

True or False

1   The price elasticity of demand is greater for goods and services that have better close substitutes.

2   The price elasticity of demand is always constant along the demand curve.

3   Total revenue increases as price falls when the demand is elastic.

4   A horizontal demand curve is perfectly elastic.

5   A vertical supply curve is perfectly inelastic.

6   If the supply curve is unitary elastic, then total revenue is constant as price changes.

7   If the supply curve is upward sloping, a rightward shift in the demand curve increases the equilibrium price and the equilibrium quantity.

8   If the demand curve is downward sloping, a rightward shift in the supply curve increases the equilibrium price and the equilibrium quantity.

9   When the demand curve is very elastic, relatively more of a tax on the production of some good or service will be borne by producers.

10 A tax on the sale of beer shifts the supply curve vertically by the amount of the tax.

11 When prices are sticky, shortages and surpluses can result in the short run.

12 A price ceiling set above the equilibrium price will have no effect on the market.

13 A price ceiling set below the equilibrium price will have no effect on the market.

14 A price floor set above the equilibrium price in the milk market will lead to a surplus of milk.

15 When demand and supply are more elastic, minimum wages set above the equilibrium wage lead to relatively more unemployment.

Multiple Choice

1   The quantity demanded is more sensitive to price changes when

   a   supply is relatively inelastic.
   b   close substitutes are available.
   c   consumers are rational.
   d   consumers are relatively more informed about quality for some goods.
   e   all of the above.

2   Suppose that price falls by 10 percent and the quantity demanded rises by 20 percent. The price elasticity of demand is

   a   2.
   b   1.
   c   0.
   d   1/2.
   e   none of the above.

3   Suppose that the price elasticity of demand is 1/3. If price rises by 30 percent, how does the quantity demanded change?

   a   Quantity demanded rises by 10 percent.
   b   Quantity demanded falls by 10 percent.
   c   Quantity demanded rises by 90 percent.
   d   Quantity demanded falls by 90 percent.
   e   Quantity demanded does not change.

4   Suppose that the price elasticity of demand is 1.5. If price falls, total revenue will

   a   remain the same.
   b   fall.
   c   rise.
   d   double.
   e   c and d.

5   Suppose that the price elasticity of demand is 0.7. The demand for this good is

   a   perfectly inelastic.
   b   inelastic.
   c   unitary elastic.
   d   elastic.
   e   perfectly elastic.

6   Which of the following are true statements concerning the price elasticity of demand?

   a   The price elasticity is constant for any demand curve.
   b   Demand is more price elastic in the short run than in the long run.
   c   If total revenue falls as price increases, the demand is relatively inelastic.
   d   a and c.
   e   None of the above.

7   If the supply curve is vertical, then the price elasticity of supply is

   a   0.
   b   inelastic.
   c   1.

d   elastic.

e   infinite.

8   The long-run elasticity of supply is greater than the short-run elasticity of supply because

a   in the long run, the stock of machines and buildings can adjust.

b   in the long run, new firms can enter and existing firms can exit the industry.

c   in the long run, customers can discover substitutes.

d   all of the above.

e   *a* and *b*.

9   Suppose that supply is perfectly elastic. If the demand curve shifts to the right, then

a   price and quantity will increase.

b   quantity will increase but price will remain constant.

c   price will increase but quantity will remain constant.

d   neither price nor quantity will increase.

e   price will increase but quantity will decrease.

10   Suppose that demand is perfectly inelastic and the supply curve shifts to the left. Then

a   price and quantity will increase.

b   quantity will increase, but price will remain constant.

c   price will increase but quantity will remain constant.

d   neither price nor quantity will increase.

e   price will increase but quantity will decrease.

11   The price elasticity of demand for tyres is 1.3, and the supply curve is upward sloping. If a £1-per-tyre tax is placed on the production of tyres, then the equilibrium price will

a   not change because the tax is on production and not on consumption.

b   increase by £1.

c   increase by less than £1.

d   fall by less than £1.

e   fall by £1.

12   In general, consumers bear more of a tax when the demand is

a   relatively inelastic.

b   unitary elastic.

c   relatively elastic.

d   such that consumers always bear the entire burden.

e   none of the above.

13   Suppose that the supply of a good is perfectly inelastic. A tax of £1 on that good will raise the price by

a   less than £1.

b   £1.

c   more than £1.

d   50 pence.

e   none of the above.

14   A price ceiling set below the equilibrium price will

a   create a shortage.

b   increase the price.

c   create a surplus.

d   *a* and *b*.

e   have no effect.

15   A price ceiling set above the equilibrium price will

a   create a shortage.

b   increase the price.

c   create a surplus.

d   *a* and *b*.

e   have no effect.

16   A price ceiling set below the equilibrium price will

a   increase the quantity demanded.

b   increase the quantity supplied.

c   decrease the quantity supplied.

d   *a* and *c*.

e   have no effect.

17   Rent control

a   creates a shortage of rental housing.

b   leads to a larger shortage in the long run.

c   lowers rents for renters who have apartments.

d   all of the above.

e   none of the above.

18   A price ceiling on insurance rates will shift

a   demand to the left.

b   demand to the right.

c   supply to the left.

d   supply to the right.

e   none of the above.

19   Which of the following is *not* a cause of surpluses or shortages?

a   Price ceilings

b   Price floors

c   Taxes

d   Sticky prices

e   None of the above

20   In the early 1990s the market for houses in Britain experienced a sharp downturn in demand, and as a consequence,

a   the price of houses fell.

b   the supply of houses to rent increased.

c   some people could not sell their houses because prices were sticky.

d   all of the above.

e   none of the above.

Completion

1   The percentage change in the quantity demanded as a result of a 1 percent price change is called the _____.

2   Price changes have no effect on revenue if the price elasticity of demand is _____.

3   If the price elasticity of demand lies between 0 and 1, then we say that demand is relatively _____.

4   A horizontal demand curve indicates that demand is _____.

5   If the supply curve is vertical, then the price elasticity of supply equals _____.

6   A 50-pence-per-litre tax on the production of petrol can be expected to shift the supply curve _____ by _____.

7   If demand is relatively inelastic, most of the tax is borne by _____.

8   A price ceiling set below the equilibrium price will create a _____.

9   A price floor set above the equilibrium price will create a _____.

10 The minimum wage is an example of a _____.

Answers to Self-Test

True or False

1	T	4	T	7	T	10	T	13	F
2	F	5	T	8	F	11	T	14	T
3	T	6	F	9	T	12	T	15	T

Multiple Choice

1	b	6	e	11	c	16	d
2	a	7	a	12	a	17	d
3	b	8	e	13	b	18	e
4	c	9	b	14	a	19	c
5	b	10	c	15	e	20	d

Completion

1   price elasticity of demand
2   1
3   inelastic
4   perfectly elastic
5   zero
6   vertically, 50 pence
7   consumers
8   shortage
9   surplus
10 price floor

Tools and Practice Problems

Three techniques receive attention in this section. You'll first learn how to calculate elasticity, then how to measure the effects of taxes, and finally how to analyze the effects of price controls.

ELASTICITY

When price changes, how much does quantity change? Economists answer this question with the concept of elasticity. The price elasticity of demand measures how responsive quantity demand is to changes in price. Similarly, the elasticity of supply measures the responsiveness of quantity supplied to price changes. Tool Kit 5.1 shows how to calculate elasticity. The problems focus on elasticity of demand and illustrate the relationship between elasticity and total revenue.

Tool Kit 5.1 Calculating Elasticity

Elasticity measures how sensitive the quantity is to changes in price. Follow these steps to calculate elasticity.

Step one: To find the elasticity between two points on the demand or supply curve, let p_1 and Q_1 be the price and quantity at the first point and p_2 and Q_2 be the price and quantity at the second point.

Step two: Substitute the prices and quantities into the formula

$$\text{Elasticity} = \frac{(Q_1 - Q_2)(p_1 + p_2)}{(Q_1 + Q_2)(p_1 - p_2)}.$$

---

1   (Worked problem: calculating elasticity) The demand curve for notice boards is given below.

Price	Quantity
£35	800
£30	1,000
£25	1,200
£20	1,300

a   Calculate total revenue for each price.
b   Calculate the price elasticity of demand between £35 and £30, between £30 and £25, and between £25 and £20. Does elasticity change along this demand?
c   Verify the relationship between elasticity and total revenue.

Step-by-step solution

Step one (a): Total revenue at £35 is 800 × £35 = £28,000. Total revenue at £30 is 1,000 × £30 = £30,000. Continue, and enter the numbers in the table.

Price	Quantity	Total revenue
£35	800	£28,000
£30	1,000	£30,000
£25	1,200	£30,000
£20	1,300	£26,000

Step two (b): Let £35 = p_1, 800 = Q_1, £30 = p_2, and 1,000 = Q_2. Substituting into the formula gives

$$\text{Elasticity} = \frac{(35 + 30)(1,000 - 800)}{(800 + 1,000)(35 - 30)} = 1.44,$$

which is elastic.

Step three: Between £30 and £25,

$$\text{Elasticity} = \frac{(30 + 25)(1,200 - 1,000)}{(1,000 + 1,200)(30 - 25)} = 1,$$

which is unitary elastic.

Step four: Between £25 and £$20,

$$\text{Elasticity} = \frac{(25 + 20)(1,300 - 1,200)}{(1,200 + 1,300)(25 - 20)} = 0.36,$$

which is inelastic.

Clearly, the elasticity is not constant. The demand curve is less elastic at lower prices.

Step five (c): Between £35 and £30, where the demand is elastic, total revenue rises from £28,000 to £30,000 as price falls. Between £30 and £25, where the demand is unitary elastic, total revenue is constant at £30,000 as the price falls. Between £25 and £20, where the demand is inelastic, total revenue falls from £30,000 to £26,000 as the price falls. Check Table 5.1 to verify that these numbers are consistent with the general relationship between price elasticity of demand and total revenue.

2 (Practice problem: calculating elasticity) The demand curve for bookends is given below.

Price	Quantity
£10	70
£ 8	90
£ 6	120
£ 4	130

a Calculate total revenue for each price.
b Calculate the price elasticity of demand between each of the adjacent prices. Does elasticity change along this demand?
c Verify the relationship between elasticity and total revenue.

3 (Practice problem: calculating elasticity) For each of the following, calculate the total revenue for each price and the price elasticity for each price change, and verify the relationship between elasticity and total revenue.

a

Price	Quantity
£12	6
£10	8
£ 8	10
£ 6	12

b

Price	Quantity
£100	80
£ 80	85
£ 60	90
£ 40	95

c

Price	Quantity
£9	10
£8	8
£7	6
£6	4

TAX INCIDENCE

The economic effects of taxes can be analysed using the method of supply and demand introduced in Chapter 4. The key idea is that the burden of a tax—its incidence—does not necessarily fall on the person or firm that must deliver the money to the government. Taxes affect exchanges, and their impact must be analysed by looking at the markets where the affected exchanges occur. The basic conclusions of this analysis are that, except when demand or supply is perfectly elastic or perfectly inelastic, consumers and producers share the burden of the tax, taxes reduce the level of economic activity, and, perhaps surprisingly, the effects of the tax are the same whether the supplier or the demander pays. Tool Kit 5.2 shows how to use supply and demand to calculate tax incidence.

Tool Kit 5.2 Using Supply and Demand to Calculate Tax Incidence

Supply and demand analysis shows how markets are affected by taxes and how the burden of taxes is allocated between suppliers and demanders. Follow this five-step procedure.

Step one: Start with an equilibrium in the relevant market.

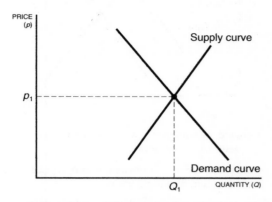

Step two: Identify whether the demander or supplier must pay the tax.

Step three: If the supplier must pay the tax, shift the supply curve up (vertically) by exactly the amount of the tax. If the demander must pay the tax, shift the demand curve down by exactly the amount of the tax.

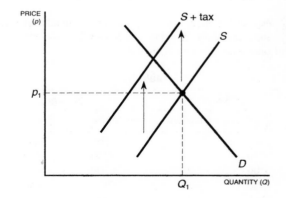

Step four: Find the new equilibrium.

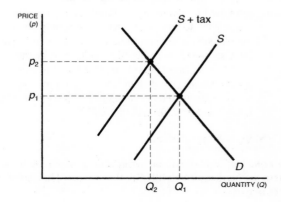

Step five: Determine the economic incidence of the tax. If the supplier must pay the tax, then use the following formulas to calculate economic incidence.

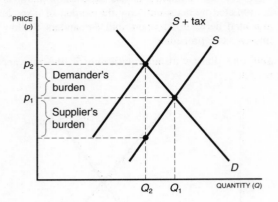

Demander's burden = new equilibrium price – original equilibrium price.

Supplier's burden = original equilibrium price – new equilibrium price + tax.

If the demander must pay the tax, use the following formulas to calculate tax incidence.

Demander's burden = new equilibrium price + tax – original equilibrium price.

Supplier's burden = original equilibrium price – new equilibrium price.

4   (Worked problem: tax incidence) The demand curve and supply curve for rented two-bedroom flats in central London are given in Table 5.2.

Table 5.2

Demand		Supply	
Price	Quantity	Price	Quantity
£800	100	£800	500
£750	200	£750	500
£700	300	£700	450
£650	400	£650	400
£600	500	£600	300

a   Find the equilibrium price and quantity.
b   Suppose that landlords are required to pay £100 per flat in a tax to the government. Use supply and demand analysis to determine the incidence of the tax.
c   Now suppose that rather than being paid by the landlords of flats (the sellers), the tax must be paid by the tenants (the demanders). Use supply and demand analysis to determine the incidence of the tax.
d   Does it matter who pays the tax?

Step-by-step solution

Step one (a): Find the no-tax equilibrium. When the price is £650, the market clears with 400 flats rented. This is the answer to part *a*.

Step two (b): Identify whether the demander or supplier must pay the tax. For part *b*, the supplier pays the tax.

Step three: Because the tax is paid by sellers, the supply curve shifts up by £100, the amount of the tax. The new supply curve is found by adding £100 to the price column, as in Table 5.3.

Table 5.3

Supply	
Price	Quantity
£900	500
£850	500
£800	450
£750	400
£700	300

Step four: Find the new equilibrium. The market clears at a price of £700 and a quantity of 300.

Step five: Determine the economic incidence of the tax.

Demander's burden = new equilibrium price – original equilibrium price = £700 – £650 = £50.

Supplier's burden = original equilibrium price – new equilibrium price + tax = £650 – £700 + £100 = £50.

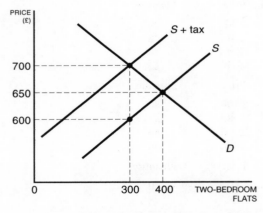

Step six (c): To answer part *c*, we repeat the procedure for the case where the demander must pay the tax.

Step seven (one): The original no-tax equilibrium is the same with the price equal to £650 and 400 flats rented.

Step eight (two): In this case, the demanders pay the tax.

Step nine (three): We shift the demand curve down by £100. The new demand curve is given in Table 5.4.

Table 5.4

Demand	
Price	Quantity
£700	100
£650	200
£600	300
£550	400
£500	500

Step ten (four): The market clears at a price of £600 and a quantity of 300.

Step eleven (five): We determine the incidence as follows.

Demander's burden = new equilibrium price + tax
 − original equilibrium price.
 = £600 + £100 − £650 = £50.

Supplier's burden = original equilibrium price
 − new equilibrium price
 = £650 − £600 = £50.

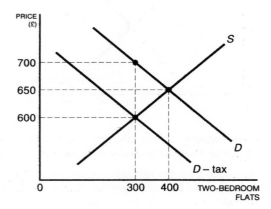

Step twelve (d): It does not matter who pays the tax! In either situation, the total amount that demanders pay is £700, the net amount that sellers receive is £600, and the equilibrium quantity is 300. The diagrams illustrate the solution.

5   (Practice problem: tax incidence) The demand curve and supply curve for unskilled labour are given in Table 5.5.

Table 5.5

Demand		Supply	
Wage	*Quantity*	*Wage*	*Quantity*
£6.50	1,000	£6.50	1,900
£6.00	1,200	£6.00	1,800
£5.50	1,400	£5.50	1,700
£5.00	1,600	£5.00	1,600
£4.50	1,800	£4.50	1,500
£4.00	2,000	£4.00	1,400

a   Find the equilibrium wage and quantity hired.
b   Consider the effect of National Insurance. Suppose that it equals £1.50 per hour and is paid by the employers (they are the demanders in this market). Use supply and demand analysis to determine the incidence of this tax.
c   Now suppose that rather than being paid by the employers, the tax must be paid by the workers. Use supply and demand analysis to determine the incidence of this tax.
d   Does it matter who pays the tax?

PRICE CONTROLS

When the government interferes with the law of supply and demand and sets price controls, the effects can be analysed with the basic method of supply and demand. To see the effects, start with an equilibrium.

The price control (if it is effective) will change the price without changing either the demand curve or the supply curve. The new equilibrium occurs at the price set by the government, but the quantity demanded is read off the demand curve and the quantity supplied is read off the supply curve. The actual quantity transacted is always the short side of the market (the smaller of the quantity demanded and the quantity supplied).

The basic results of this analysis are that price ceilings, when set below the market-clearing price, lower the price, cause shortages, and reduce the quantity transacted. Price floors, when set above the market-clearing price, raise the price, cause surpluses, and reduce the quantity transacted. Tool Kit 5.3 shows how to use supply and demand to analyse price controls.

Tool Kit 5.3 Using Supply and Demand
for Price Controls

The impact of price controls is made clear through the use of supply and demand. This four-step procedure shows how to analyse price controls.

Step one: Start with a market-clearing equilibrium.

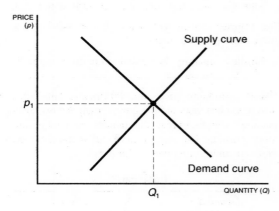

Step two: Identify the controlled price, and decide whether it is a floor or a ceiling.

Step three: Find the new equilibrium price. If it is a price floor set below the market-clearing price or a price ceiling set above the market-clearing price, then the equilibrium is the market-clearing one found in step one. If it is a price floor set above the market-clearing price or a price ceiling set below the market-clearing price, then the controlled price is the equilibrium price.

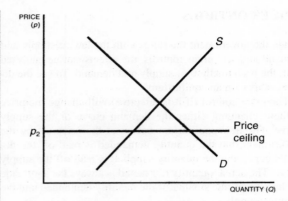

Step four: Determine the shortage or surplus. For a price floor set above the market-clearing price, there is a surplus:

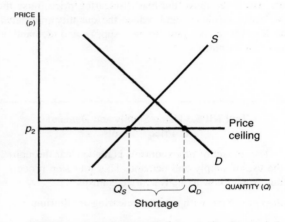

Shortage = quantity supplied – quantity demanded.

For a price ceiling set below the market-clearing price, there is a shortage:

Surplus = quantity demanded – quantity supplied.

6   (Worked problem: price controls) Private dental charges rose again last year and the government is considering placing a ceiling on fees that dentists can charge for tooth cleaning. The supply curve and demand curve for tooth cleanings are given in Table 5.6.

Table 5.6

Demand		Supply	
Price	*Quantity*	*Price*	*Quantity*
£65	100	£65	190
£60	120	£60	180
£55	140	£55	170
£50	160	£50	160
£45	180	£45	150
£40	200	£40	140

a   Find the equilibrium price and quantity for tooth cleanings.
b   The government introduces a price ceiling of £40 per cleaning. Use supply and demand analysis to determine the effects of the price control.

Step-by-step solution

Step one (a): Find the equilibrium price and quantity. The market clears at a price of £50 and quantity equal to 160.

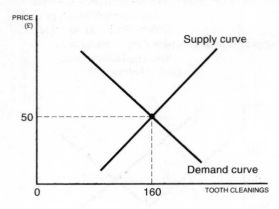

Step two (b): Identify the controlled price and whether it is a floor or a ceiling. The price control is a price ceiling set at £40.

Step three: Determine the new equilibrium price. The ceiling is below the market-clearing price; therefore, the new price is equal to the ceiling price of £40.

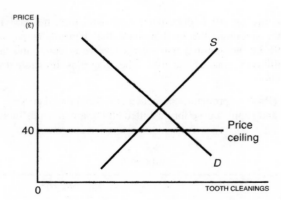

Step four: Determine the shortage or surplus. When the price is £40, the quantity demanded is 200 and the quantity supplied is 140. Although consumers would like more, there are only 140 cleanings actually performed. This results in a shortage of 200 – 140 = 60 tooth cleanings. The diagram illustrates the solution.

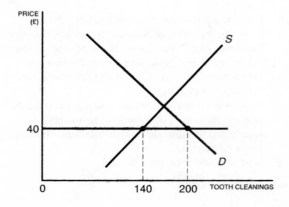

7   (Practice problem: price controls) The government is considering introducing price ceilings on car insurance premiums. The supply curve and demand curve for car insurance policies are given in Table 5.7.

Table 5.7

Demand		Supply	
Price	Quantity	Price	Quantity
£600	1,000	£600	1,800
£500	1,100	£500	1,500
£400	1,200	£400	1,200
£300	1,400	£300	900
£200	1,600	£200	600

a   Find the equilibrium price and quantity.
b   Suppose that a price ceiling of £300 is imposed. Use supply and demand analysis to determine the effects of the price control.

8   (Practice problem: price controls) Fearful of a restless urban population, Corporal Thug, the new supreme ruler of Guano, attempts to mollify the masses with a wage increase. He mandates that employers must pay at least £8 per day. The supply and demand curves for urban labour are given in Table 5.8.

Table 5.8

Demand		Supply	
Wage	Quantity	Wage	Quantity
£8.50	400	£8.50	4,000
£8.00	600	£8.00	3,200
£7.50	700	£7.50	2,600
£7.00	800	£7.00	2,200
£6.50	900	£6.50	1,800
£6.00	1,000	£6.00	1,000

a   Find the quantity demanded, the quantity supplied, and the size of the surplus or shortage if any.
b   Corporal Thug is overthrown and the minimum wage repealed. Use supply and demand analysis to determine the effects of the price control.

Answers to Problems

2   a
Price	Quantity	Revenue
£10	70	£700
£ 8	90	£720
£ 6	120	£720
£ 4	130	£520

b   Between £10 and £8,

$$\text{Elasticity} = \frac{(10+8)(90-70)}{(10-8)(90+70)} = 1.125.$$

Between £8 and £6,

$$\text{Elasticity} = \frac{(8+6)(120-90)}{(8-6)(120+90)} = 1.$$

Between £6 and £4,

$$\text{Elasticity} = \frac{(6+4)(130-120)}{(6-4)(130+120)} = 0.2.$$

c   When elasticity is 1.125, the demand curve is elastic, and total revenue rises from £700 to £720 as price falls. When elasticity is 1, the demand curve is unitary elastic, and total revenue remains constant at £720 as price falls. Finally, when elasticity is 0.2, the demand curve is inelastic, and total revenue falls from £720 to £520 as price falls.

3   In the following tables, the number in the elasticity column corresponding to each price refers to the elasticity over the interval between that price and the next highest price.

a
Price	Quantity	Total revenue	Elasticity
£12	6	£72	
£10	8	£80	1.57
£ 8	10	£80	1.00
£ 6	12	£72	0.64

b
Price	Quantity	Total revenue	Elasticity
£100	80	£8,000	
£ 80	85	£6,800	0.26
£ 60	90	£5,400	0.20
£ 40	95	£3,800	0.14

c
Price	Quantity	Total revenue	Elasticity
£9	10	£ 90	
£8	14	£112	2.430
£7	18	£126	1.875
£6	22	£132	1.300

5   a   Wage = £5.00; quantity = 1,600.
b   The new supply is given in Table 5.9.

Table 5.9

Supply	
Wage	Quantity
£8.00	1,900
£7.50	1,800
£7.00	1,700
£6.50	1,600
£6.00	1,500
£5.50	1,400

The new equilibrium wage = £5.50; quantity = 1,400. Demander's burden = £5.50 − £5.00 = 50 pence; supplier's burden = £5.00 + £1.50 − £5.50 = £1.00.

c   The new demand curve is given in Table 5.10.

Table 5.10

Demand	
Wage	*Quantity*
£5.00	1,000
£4.50	1,200
£4.00	1,400
£3.50	1,600
£3.00	1,800
£2.50	2,000

The new equilibrium wage = £4.00; quantity = 1,400. Demander's burden = £4.00 + £1.50 – £5.00 = 50 pence; supplier's burden = £5.00 – £4.00 = £1.00.

d   No. The demander's burden, supplier's burden, and equilibrium quantity are the same in each case.

7   a   Price = £400; quantity = 1,200.

b   Price = £300; quantity demanded = 1,400; quantity supplied = 900; shortage = 1,400 – 900 = 500.

8   a   Wage = £8.00; quantity demanded = 600; quantity supplied = 3,200; surplus = 3,200 – 600 = 2,600.

b   Price = £600; quantity = 1,000.

Chapter 6

TIME AND RISK

Chapter Review

When trades involve the future, as they do when individuals save, borrow money, or buy a house, people must be concerned with the time value of money and with the risk that the trade will not proceed as stipulated. Time and risk therefore affect today's demand and supply curves. This chapter explores markets for risk and insurance along with the broad class of capital markets (stock markets, foreign exchange markets, and so on) where firms raise funds to finance investment and where people transfer risks. Chapter 7 closes the introductory part of the book, with a look at the public sector and the large role government plays in the economy.

ESSENTIAL CONCEPTS

1   The value of a pound today is greater than the value of a pound to be received in the future. In other words, money has a time value. Any decision that involves present and future pounds must account for the time value of money. Economists calculate the present discounted value; they convert future pounds to their present equivalent. The formula for the present discounted value of £1 next year is £1/(1 + interest rate).

2   The market for loanable funds brings together all those who want to borrow and all those who want to save. The price in this market is the **interest rate.** Figure 6.1 shows the demand curve for loanable funds sloping downwards, which indicates that at lower interest rates, more borrowers would like to borrow more funds. The supply curve slopes upwards because at higher interest rates, individuals will save more. The interest rate adjusts to clear the market, and the equilibrium quantity of savings equals the equilibrium quantity of borrowing.

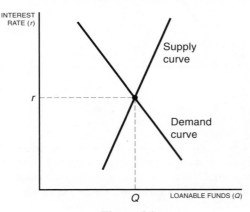

Figure 6.1

3   **Assets,** such as land, housing, stocks, and bonds, last a long time and can be bought today and sold in the future. The prices of assets are determined by supply and demand; however, supply and demand are affected by both today's conditions and what people expect future prices to be. Buyers and sellers of assets must form their **expectations** and make forecasts with care; nevertheless, they are likely to make mistakes, disagree, and revise their expectations. Changing expectations explain large changes in asset prices and make asset markets volatile and risky.

4   Most people are **risk averse** and would prefer to reduce the uncertainty about future economic conditions. The **market for risk** is a whole set of institutions and arrangements by which risk is transferred. People can manage risk by avoiding certain risk endeavors altogether, taking steps to keep options open, diversifying, and transferring risks through the **insurance market,** where individuals purchase policies that protect against the risk of specific events, such as disability or accidents.

5   There are important risks, however, for which insurance markets do not offer such protection. One reason is **adverse selection,** which means that the riskiest customers are the most likely to buy insurance. Another problem, **moral hazard,** arises because people who have bought insurance have less incentive to protect themselves against loss.

6   One of the most fundamental **trade-offs** in the economy involves **risks and incentives.** In markets for both risk and capital, when risks are reduced, so are incentives. Figure 6.2 shows the trade-off. At point *A,* there are small risks and limited incentives. Both risks and incentives increase by moving from *A* to *B.*

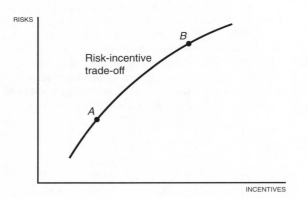

Figure 6.2

7   Entrepreneurs introduce new products, develop new ways of producing goods, and create new businesses. These activities are very risky, but they are not insurable. An important function for entrepreneurs is bearing the risks of these necessary endeavors.

BEHIND THE ESSENTIAL CONCEPTS

1   The distinction between real and nominal interest rates is very important, especially in macroeconomics. When you deposit money in your bank account, the bank pays you the nominal interest rate. Say it is 5 percent. Your money grows at 5 percent each year, but your purchasing power may not, because each year prices may also be changing. Suppose that the inflation rate (the rate of increase in the general price level) is 4 percent. This means that each year goods become 4 percent more expensive, and you can buy only 5 – 4 percent = 1 percent more goods. The 1 percent is the real interest rate, and also the rate of increase in your purchasing power.

2   Many economic activities, from purchasing an asset to making an investment, are oriented towards the future. Households and firms must form expectations about the future. Economists distinguish three ways of forming expectations. If you think that tomorrow will be like today, then your expectations are **myopic.** You have **adaptive expectations** if you think that current trends will continue. Finally, you have **rational expectations** (and are well on your way to becoming an economist) if you use all available information, including what you learn in economics.

3   Because people are risk averse, they are willing to pay something to reduce risk. The extra payment is called the **risk premium.** Here is how it works. Suppose that you have a £5,000 car, and its chance of being stolen is 1 percent. Your expected payment (if uninsured) is 1 percent of £5,000, or £50. If you buy a theft insurance policy for £55, then the risk premium is £55 – £50 = £5. In other words, it is the amount (beyond the expected payment) received by the insurance company to bear the risk of theft.

4   **Adverse selection** and **moral hazard** are important problems, and you should be clear about the difference. Adverse selection occurs when the mix of customers is affected by the insurance contract. For example, an insurance company may find that its policyholders have more accidents than the population at large. The company reasons that high-risk people buy more insurance. **Moral hazard,** on the other hand, involves the behavior of the insured. People who have insurance may not take the same precautions as those without insurance. They may fail to use seat belts or may even drive recklessly.

5   Adverse selection, moral hazard, and the risk-incentive trade-off are not limited to the insurance industry. They are pervasive in the economy. If you are a banker and charge higher interest rates, then you may find that only risky borrowers apply for loans. We say that the pool of applicants for your loans is adversely selected. It may be wise for you to move along the risk-incentive trade-off. You can do this by requiring collateral. This increases the borrower's risk—the collateral will be forfeited if she defaults—but it gives better incentives to repay the loan.

Here is another example. Suppose that you own a business and you pay your sales force a fixed salary. You may find that your workers do not work as hard as you would like and sales decline. Because it is the behaviour of your sales force that changes, it is called **moral hazard.** Again, you can move along the risk-incentive trade-off by replacing the fixed salary with commission payments based on how much each employee sells. This policy exposes your sales force to more risk, but gives the workers incentive to work hard.

SELF-TEST

True or False

1   The present discounted value of a future pound is what one would pay today for that future pound.

2   The interest rate is the price in the market for loanable funds.

3   The nominal interest rate is the real interest rate minus the inflation rate.

4   Current prices of assets are based upon expectations about their future prices.

5   Someone who always expects that what is true today will be true tomorrow has myopic expectations.

6   Someone who expects current trends to continue has adaptive expectations.

7   People with rational expectations do not make mistakes.

8   Keeping options open only exacerbates risk.

9   The risk premium equals the expected payment.

10 Individuals demand insurance because they are risk averse.

11 The adverse selection problem arises because insurance companies are not sure about the riskiness of their customers.

12 The moral hazard problem arises because insured individuals have less incentive to protect against loss.

13 When risks are higher, so are incentives to protect against losses.

14 The individuals who are responsible for creating new businesses, new products, and new production processes are called entrepreneurs.

15 Most of the risks faced by entrepreneurs, such as the risk that the business will not succeed, cannot be insured against.

Multiple Choice

1   If you deposit £1,100 in the bank today and the interest rate on your deposit is 10 percent, how much money will be in your account at the end of one year?

a   £1,200
b   £1,210
c   £121
d   £1,000
e   None of the above

2   If you are to receive £1,100 from a client one year from today, and the interest rate is 10 percent, what is the present discounted value of that future receipt?

a   £1,100
b   £1,000
c   £1,200
d   £979
e   None of the above

3   If the interest rate increases, the present discounted value of the future returns from investment projects

a   increases.
b   remains unchanged.
c   decreases.
d   *a* or *b*.
e   none of the above.

4   If you borrow £4,000 for a used car purchase at 11 percent interest, the 11 percent is the

a   real rate of interest.
b   rate of inflation.
c   nominal rate of interest.
d   real rate of interest – the nominal rate of interest.
e   nominal rate of interest – the rate of inflation.

5   Suppose that the interest rate offered by banks and building societies is 8 percent. The inflation rate is expected to be 5 percent. What is the real rate of interest?

a   8 percent
b   5 percent
c   13 percent
d   3 percent
e   None of the above

6   When market prices for assets change dramatically, it is usually because of

a   changes in the supply of assets.
b   government price floors.
c   changes in expectations about future prices.
d   changes in tastes.
e   changes in income.

7   People who use all available information to form expectations about the future are said to have

a   myopic expectations.
b   adaptive expectations.
c   rational expectations.
d   insider expectations.
e   random walk expectations.

8   Most people are risk averse. This means they

a   try to avoid or minimise serious risks.
b   have myopic expectations.

c   never take risks.

d   focus on the nominal rate of interest.

e   *a* and *b*.

9   An important market for risk is the insurance market. Which of the following is true about insurance markets?

a   Buyers are risk averse.

b   Insurance companies spread risks among its many owners.

c   Insurance companies can forecast accurately the annual amount of claims.

d   All of the above.

e   *a* and *b*.

10   For insurance companies, the selection problem refers to selecting

a   the best employees to hire.

b   the right premium to charge.

c   the best risks to insure.

d   the best corporate logo.

e   none of the above.

11   Adverse selection

a   is a consequence of the fact that the insurance company has limited information about the riskiness of individual customers.

b   implies that those more likely to buy insurance tend to be the higher risks.

c   causes those customers with lower risk to avoid insurance at high rates.

d   makes the fraction of customers who will have an accident larger when premiums are higher.

e   all of the above.

12   Moral hazard means that

a   insurance buyers are risk averse.

b   insurance companies predict losses accurately.

c   higher-risk individuals demand more insurance at higher prices.

d   insured individuals have less incentive to avoid accidents.

e   the premium must include an allowance for false claims.

13   An individual who sometimes drives under the influence of alcohol has a high demand for automobile insurance. This is an example of

a   adverse selection.

b   moral hazard.

c   risk aversion.

d   adaptive expectations.

e   none of the above.

14   After buying more professional negligence insurance, a solicitor spends less time on each case. This is an example of

a   adverse selection.

b   moral hazard.

c   risk aversion.

d   adaptive expectations.

e   none of the above.

15   Individuals respond to risk by

a   avoiding or mitigating risks.

b   keeping options open.

c   diversifying.

d   transferring risk to others.

e   all of the above.

16   Investing in a wide variety of stocks or in mutual funds, rather than owning a single asset, is an example of

a   avoiding or mitigating risks.

b   keeping options open.

c   diversifying.

d   transferring risk to others.

e   none of the above.

17   Suppose that a certain business is losing money on a certain product line. If it delays abandoning production for a while in the hope that demand will pick up, it is

a   avoiding or mitigating risks.

b   keeping options open.

c   diversifying.

d   transferring risk to others.

e   none of the above.

18   The risk-incentive trade-off shows that

a   insurance buyers have adaptive expectations.

b   bonds are riskier than shares.

c   fully insured individuals have less incentive to protect against risk.

d   as risk is decreased, the moral hazard problem becomes less severe.

e   *c* and *d*.

19   For the most part, the risk of business failure is borne by

a   insurance companies.

b   corporate lawyers.

c   accounting firms.

d   entrepreneurs.

e   the loanable funds market.

20   Those who provide new businesses with capital earn higher rates of returns. This extra return is

a   a risk premium.

b   adverse selection.

c   a moral hazard.

d   diversification.

e   insurance.

Completion

1   The return received for giving up current consumption in exchange for increased future consumption is called the _____.

2   The _____ of a pound to be received in the future shows how much that future pound is worth today.

3   The formula used to calculate the present value of £1 next year is _____.

4   When the interest rate rises, the present discounted value of future income _____.

5   The interest rate is the price in the market for
_____.

6   A savings account that pays 10 percent compounded
daily will return _____ to the saver than another
savings account that pays 10 percent compounded
monthly.

7   The interest rate that indicates how much consumption
tomorrow must be forgone for extra consumption
today is the _____ interest rate.

8   The real interest rate is the nominal interest rate minus
the _____.

9   Current prices of assets, such as land, depend upon
_____ about their future prices.

10 The fact that insured individuals have less incentive
to take precautions against accidents is called
_____.

Answers to Self-Test

True or False

1	T	6	T	11	T
2	T	7	F	12	T
3	F	8	F	13	T
4	T	9	F	14	T
5	T	10	T	15	T

Multiple Choice

1	b	8	a	15	e
2	b	9	d	16	c
3	c	10	c	17	b
4	c	11	e	18	c
5	d	12	d	19	d
6	c	13	a	20	a
7	c	14	b		

Completion

1   interest rate
2   present value
3   $1/(1 + \text{interest rate})$
4   falls
5   loanable funds
6   more
7   real
8   inflation rate
9   expectations
10 moral hazard

Tools and Practice Problems

Payments to be received in the future are not worth as much
as payments received today. This statement reflects the time
value of money. Decisions involving present and future
costs and returns require a consistent standard for comparison. This standard is present discounted value, and it is illustrated in Tool Kit 6.1.

Tool Kit 6.1 Calculating the Present
Discounted Value

To compare the worth of present and future payments, it is necessary to compute the present discounted value, which is the current pound equivalent of an
amount to be rendered in the future. Follow the steps.

Step one: Make a table with four columns, and label
them as shown.

Year	Amount	Discount factor	Present discounted value

Step two: For every payment or receipt, enter the year
and the amount. Let Y_1 be the amount in the first
year, Y_2 the amount the second year, and so on.

Year	Amount	Discount factor	Present discounted value
1	Y_1		
2	Y_2		

Step three: Calculate the discount factor for each
year. The formula is $1/(1 + r)^n$, where r is the interest
rate and n is the number of years until the payment or
receipt. Enter these discount factors in the table.

Year	Amount	Discount factor	Present discounted value
1	Y_1	$1/(1 + r)$	
2	Y_2	$1/(1 + r)^2$	

Step four: Multiply the number in the amount column
by the corresponding discount factor. Enter the product in the present discounted value column.

Year	Amount	Discount factor	Present discounted value
1	Y_1	$1/(1 + r)$	$Y_1 \times 1/(1 + r)$
2	Y_2	$1/(1 + r)^2$	$Y_2 \times 1/(1 + r)^2$

Step five: Add the numbers in the right-hand column.
The sum is the present discounted value.

Year	Amount	Discount factor	Present discounted value
1	Y_1	$1/(1 + r)$	$Y_1 \times 1/(1 + r)$
2	Y_2	$1/(1 + r)^2$	$Y_2 \times 1/(1 + r)^2$

$$\text{Present discounted value} = \frac{Y_1 \times 1}{(1 + r)} + \frac{Y_2 \times 1}{(1 + r)^2}.$$

---

1   (Worked problem: present discounted value) Ethel has
two years before retirement from a career of teaching
unruly high school children. Her salary is £40,000, paid
at the end of each year. The school board has offered
her £70,000 now to retire early. The relevant interest
rate is 7 percent. In monetary terms alone, is working
worth more than retiring?

Step-by-step solution

First, calculate the present discounted value of continuing to
work.

Step one: Make a table with four columns, and label them as shown.

Year	Amount	Discount factor	Present discounted value

Step two: For every payment or receipt, enter the year and the amount. Ethel receives £40,000 each year for two years.

Year	Amount	Discount factor	Present discounted value
1	£40,000		
2	£40,000		

Step three: Calculate the discount factor for each year. For the first year, the discount factor is $1/(1 + .07) = 0.93$, and for the second year it is $1/(1 + .07)^2 = 0.86$. Enter these discount factors in the table.

Year	Amount	Discount factor	Present discounted value
1	£40,000	0.93	
2	£40,000	0.86	

Step four: Multiply the number in the amount column by the corresponding discount factor. Enter the product in the present discounted value column.

Year	Amount	Discount factor	Present discounted value
1	£40,000	0.93	£37,380
2	£40,000	0.86	£34,400

Step five: Add the numbers in the right-hand column. The sum is the present discounted value.

Year	Amount	Discount factor	Present discounted value
1	£40,000	0.93	£37,380
2	£40,000	0.86	£34,400

Present discounted value = £71,780.

Next, compare the lump-sum payment with the present discounted value of continuing to work. Ethel can postpone retirement and increase the present discounted value of her earnings by only £1,780. The reason that the gain is so little is that earnings come in the future and must be discounted, while the retirement bonus is paid now.

2   (Practice problem: present discounted value) The Department of Transport is considering the bids of two paving companies for repaving South Street. The Do-It-Right firm will do the job for £200,000, and it will guarantee that its new process will make the road free of potholes for 3 years. The Let-It-Go company only charges £100,000, but estimated pothole repair costs are £40,000 each year. The interest rate is 8 percent.

   a   Calculate the present discounted value of the entire cost with the Let-It-Go firm.
   b   Which is the less expensive bid?

3   (Practice problem: present discounted value) Calculate the present discounted value of each of the following.

   a   Interest rate equals 10 percent.

Year	Amount	Discount factor	Present discounted value
1	£10,000		
2	£15,000		

   b   Interest rate equals 5 percent.

Year	Amount	Discount factor	Present discounted value
1	£ 0		
2	£20,000		

   c   Interest rate equals 15 percent.

Year	Amount	Discount factor	Present discounted value
1	£5,000		
2	£5,000		
3	£5,000		

   d   Interest rate equals 5 percent.

Year	Amount	Discount factor	Present discounted value
1	£ 5,000		
2	£ 0		
3	£25,000		

EXPECTED VALUE AND THE RISK PREMIUM

Markets provide incentives to take or accept risks. These incentives include the risk premium, which is the extra payment offered to one who accepts a certain risk. The ultimate consequence of the risky alternative is unknown, of course, so it is measured using the concept of expected value. Risk premiums appear in many settings, including insurance, investment, and risky employment. Tool Kit 6.2 shows how to calculate the risk premium.

Tool Kit 6.2 Calculating Expected Value and the Risk Premium

The risk premium is the extra payment that markets offer for accepting risk. It is calculated using expected value. Follow these three steps.

Step one: Identify the safe and risky alternative and also the amounts and probabilities of gain or loss.

Step two: Calculate the expected value of the risky alternative. Use the formula for expected value.

Expected value = (probability of bad event)
(payments if bad event occurs)
+ (probability of good event)
(payments if good event occurs).

Step three: Subtract the value of the safe alternative from the expected value of the risky alternative (calculated in step two). The difference is the risk premium.

Expected value of the risky alternative
– value of the safe alternative
= risk premium.

---

4   (Worked problem: risk premium) City Money Managers is a small firm that provides short-term money management to companies and depends upon the knowledge and personal reputation of its founder. Should he die or be forced to retire for health reasons, the value of the business would fall by £200,000. The probability of this happening is .01. An insurance policy is available for £2,500. This policy would compensate the business in the event of the loss of the founder.

a   Point out the safe and risky alternatives.
b   What is the expected loss?
c   How much is the risk premium?

Step-by-step solution

Step one: Identify the safe and risky alternatives. Buying the insurance is the safe alternative. Bearing the risk of the loss of the founder is the risky one.

Step two: Calculate the expected value (*EV*) of the risky alternative.

$$EV = .01(-£200,000) + .99(0) = -£2,000.$$

Step three: Subtract the value of the safe from the expected value of the risky alternative. The insurance policy costs £2,500.

$$\text{Risk premium} = -£2,000 - (-£2,500) = £500.$$

5   (Practice problem: risk premium) Barbara is considering leaving her safe job in government to strike out on her own as a consultant. She currently earns £40,000 and estimates that the consultant business will pay £75,000 if she wins an important contract but nothing otherwise. Her best guess is that the probability of her winning the contract is 2/3.

a   Point out the safe and risky alternatives.
b   What is the expected value of the consulting business?
c   How much is the risk premium?

6   (Practice problem: risk premium) If Kim keeps her retirement savings in safe assets she expects to have £250,000 at retirement. Her brother-in-law advises that she move into derivatives. Her financial adviser points out that following the advice of her brother-in-law might result in £600,000 at retirement. Losing it all is another possibility. The probability of each is 1/2.

a   Point out the safe and risky alternatives.
b   What is the expected loss?
c   How much is the risk premium?

Answers to Problems

2   *a*

Firm	Cost
Do-It-Right	£200,000
Let-It-Go	£100,000 $+ \dfrac{£40,000}{1.08}$

$$+ \frac{£40,000}{(1.08)^2} + \frac{£40,000}{(1.08)^3}$$

$$= £203,083.$$

b   The Do-It-Right bid

3   *a*   £21,488.   *b*   £18,141.
c   £12,447.   *d*   £26,358.

5   *a*   Safe alternative = government; risky alternative = consultant.
b   £75,000 × 2/3 + £0 × 1/3 = £50,000.
c   £50,000 – £40,000 = £10,000.

6   *a*   Safe alternative = safe assets; risky alternative = derivatives.
b   £600,000 × 1/2 + £0 × 1/2 = £300,000.
c   £300,000 – £250,000 = £50,000.

Chapter 7

THE PUBLIC SECTOR

Chapter Review

The text's focus so far has been on private markets. This is overly simple, as the history of the motor industry given in Chapter 1 illustrates. While the motor industry now consists of private firms, government has played a large role throughout the industry's history, by issuing patents and regulating safety and environmental standards, nationalising and privatising British Leyland, occasionally protecting domestic manufacturers from foreign competition, and providing benefits to unemployed workers. This blend of the public and private sectors is called a mixed economy.

This chapter considers the economic role of the public sector and how it operates differently from the private sector. Important roles for the public sector include improving the market's allocation of resources, stabilising the overall performance of the economy, and redistributing income. The chapter also discusses government policies and emphasises that government action may not always succeed in correcting market failures.

ESSENTIAL CONCEPTS

1   For the most part, the economic system relies on private markets to allocate resources, but government has al-
ways played a major role. The balance between the public and private sectors has changed over the years as government has privatised public corporations and taken on new regulatory responsibilities to improve perceived failures in the private economy. Government differs from private institutions in that its decisions are made by elected representatives or their appointed officers, and government has the power to force compliance with some of its orders.

2   Economists see roles for government in redistributing income and correcting market failures. These include stabilising the economy's fluctuations, enhancing competition, and improving the performance of the economy where there are externalities, public goods, missing markets, or information problems. Government also intervenes to discourage or prohibit certain actions, overriding the principle of consumer sovereignty.

3   The **public sector** has a variety of instruments with which to accomplish its goals. It can take direct action, either producing the good or service itself or purchasing it from private firms. It can legislate to enforce private sector action, regulate private activity, or ban certain behaviour altogether. Finally, with a somewhat lighter hand, the government can provide incentives to increase

or decrease certain types of actions through the use of its tax and subsidy powers.

4   While market failures imply that there is potential for improvement, government programs carry with them additional problems. Imperfect information, poor incentives for government administrators, waste, and the failure to foresee all of the consequences of government actions can cause public failures.

BEHIND THE ESSENTIAL CONCEPTS

1   **Externalities** exist whenever individuals or firms do not face the full costs and benefits of their decisions, and left alone, externalities create incentive problems. Negative externalities are costs borne by others, such as pollution, congestion, and noise. Positive externalities are benefits received by others, such as contributions for medical and other research, innovation, public parks, and endangered species preservation. Because decision makers can ignore the costs that spill over onto others, private firms overproduce negative externalities. Similarly, because they are not compensated, producers of positive externalities do not create enough. Governments can improve the allocation of resources by inducing individuals to produce fewer negative and more positive externalities.

2   **Public goods** have two important characteristics. Once they are provided, the marginal cost of another consumer's enjoying the good is zero. For example, a second, third, or fourth person can view a public statue without affecting the first person's enjoyment. The second characteristic is that it is costly to exclude individuals from enjoying the public good. Placing the statue in a private viewing area and charging admission misses the point of a monument. This feature makes it difficult for private individuals to collect enough funds to provide public goods. The fact that people can choose to enjoy public goods without paying for them is called the **free-rider** problem, and it is one reason economists often recommend that the public sector take a role in providing public goods.

3   When the private market fails to allocate resources efficiently, there is a potential role for government action. For example, when a public good such as a traffic light is needed, the government is the natural choice to provide it. When negative externalities are present, such as pollution, the government may be able to discourage them. The income distribution produced by private markets may be unacceptable, and the government may be able to redistribute it. Governments are large organizations, however, and policies do not always work as intended.

4   The existence of market failures prompts the call for more government intervention. **Government failures** justify calls for less intervention. Often what is needed is different, better government action, which harnesses market incentives to bring about a better allocation of resources.

SELF-TEST

True or False

1   Most western European economies are mixed economies that rely primarily on private markets.

2   Government's role in the economy has remained essentially unchanged since the early 1900s.

3   Services, such as police and fire protection, education, and parks, are provided mostly by central and local governments.

4   Adam Smith's "invisible hand" refers to the role of government in correcting market failures.

5   Government action is distinguished from private sector action in that government always has better information.

6   While markets often are efficient producers of wealth, they do not necessarily distribute that wealth equally.

7   Externalities are present whenever an individual or a firm can take an action without bearing all the costs or benefits.

8   The marginal cost of an additional consumer is zero for a public good.

9   The marginal cost of production is zero for a public good.

10   It is very costly to exclude those who do not pay from consuming private goods.

11   Markets for new inventions fail if those who benefit from new inventions do not pay the inventor.

12   The free-rider problem implies that private markets may not provide public goods efficiently.

13   If the private market provides too little of some good or service, then government can increase the quantity provided by subsidising the good or service.

14   Even though markets may fail to allocate resources efficiently, government action may make matters worse.

15   Civil service rules and political pressures create incentive problems that may lead to public failures.

Multiple Choice

1   Which of the following is *not* one of the four basic questions an economy must answer?

    a   What is produced, and in what quantities?
    b   How are goods and services produced?
    c   For whom are the goods and services produced?
    d   Who makes the decisions?
    e   None of the above.

2   Private institutions, such as business firms and not-for-profit organizations, are distinguished from government in that

    a   private decision makers are rational.
    b   government decision makers have adaptive expectations.

c government decision makers are elected or appointed by someone who is elected.

d government has certain powers of coercion.

e *c* and *d*.

3 In his book *The Wealth of Nations,* Adam Smith argued that the public interest is best promoted by

a government control of the economy.

b the benevolence of well-meaning citizens.

c individuals pursuing their own self-interest.

d adherence to time-honoured traditions.

e all of the above.

4 Which of the following is *not* a legitimate role of government?

a Solving the problem of scarcity

b Redistributing income

c Stabilising the level of economic activity

d Correcting market failures

e None of the above

5 Which of the following is an example of market failure?

a Housing is expensive.

b The poor often cannot afford adequate housing.

c Ostentatious displays of wealth by the rich and famous are offensive.

d Periodic episodes of high unemployment trouble market economies.

e All of the above.

6 Which of the following is an example of direct action?

a Taxation

b Nationalisation

c Subsidies

d Incentives

e All of the above

7 Which of the following is *not* an example of an externality?

a Environmental pollution

b Research and development

c Restoring buildings in decaying areas

d Contributions to philanthropic organizations

e None of the above

8 When farmers irrigate their crops with water provided by the government at subsidised prices, there is

a an externality.

b a public good.

c a market.

d a patent.

e none of the above.

9 Which of the following is (are) true of pure public goods?

a The marginal cost of an additional individual using the good is zero.

b It is impossible to exclude people from receiving the good.

c They are efficiently provided through the interaction of supply and demand.

d All of the above.

e *a* and *b*.

10 Private markets have difficulty supplying public goods because

a of the free-rider problem.

b of the government.

c the level of private activity fluctuates.

d the income distribution is inequitable.

e all markets are efficient.

11 One advantage that government has in the provision of public goods is that it

a is not subject to scarcity.

b does not face uncertainty about the demand for public goods.

c can coerce citizens to pay for them.

d need not always be rational.

e none of the above.

12 The free-rider problem refers to the idea that

a public transport systems always make a loss.

b when people can enjoy a public good without paying for it, they often do not contribute.

c markets fail to allocate resources efficiently when there are externalities.

d the marginal cost of an additional consumer enjoying a pure public good is zero.

e none of the above.

13 Which of the following is *not* an example of direct government action to correct market failure?

a A country nationalises its banking system.

b Tax breaks are offered for exploring for new deposits of oil.

c A large city builds shelters for the homeless.

d The army purchases tanks from a private firm.

e None of the above.

14 Which of the following is *not* an example of legal enforcement of private sector action?

a Tuna trawlers are required to use nets with larger openings so that captured dolphins can escape.

b Power stations are required to install air filters in chimneys.

c Road haulers are required to pay a petrol tax.

d All of the above.

e *a* and *b*.

15 Consumer sovereignty means that

a individuals are the best judge of what is in their own interest.

b there is no role for government in product-safety regulations.

c consumers always have good information.

d consumers are rational decision makers.

e *a* and *c*.

16 Which of the following is *not* a reason for government failure?

a Imperfect information

b Government waste

c Incentives of public administrators.

d Missing markets.

e None of the above

17 Which of the following is *not* a reason for market failure?

a Externalities

b Public goods

c Missing markets

d Lack of competition

e None of the above

18 Private markets may not provide information efficiently because

a information is scarce.

b information is costly to produce.

c certain types of information are public goods.

d the principle of consumer sovereignty does not apply to information.

e private markets are not regulated.

19 Market failure occurs when there are

a positive externalities.

b negative externalities.

c positive or negative externalities.

d no externalities.

e none of the above.

20 Government can provide incentives to produce more of some good by

a taxing it.

b subsidising it.

c banning its production.

d redistributing it.

e using the "invisible hand."

Completion

1 The failure of private markets to produce economic efficiency is called _____.

2 When an individual or firm can take an action without bearing the full costs and benefits, there is said to be an _____.

3 Goods for which it costs nothing extra to have an additional individual enjoy are called _____.

4 Because it is difficult to exclude those who do not pay from benefiting from public goods, the private markets do a poor job of providing public goods. This is the _____ problem.

5 If the government seeks to encourage some activity, such as recycling, it can _____ the activity.

6 The sale of state-owned assets to individual and institutional shareholders is called _____.

7 When resources are idle, the economy is operating _____ its production possibilities curve.

8 Three legitimate economic roles of government are to redistribute income, stabilise the economy, and _____.

9 During the 1980s and 1990s British and other Western European governments reduced or eliminated many regulations in the telephone, gas, electricity, and financial sectors. This process is an example of _____.

10 Three instruments of government for economic purposes are taking direct action, enforcing private action, and providing _____ to the private sector through taxes and subsidies.

Answers to Self-Test

True or False

1	T	4	F	7	T	10	F	13	T
2	F	5	F	8	T	11	T	14	T
3	T	6	T	9	F	12	T	15	T

Multiple Choice

1	e	6	b	11	c	16	d
2	e	7	e	12	b	17	e
3	c	8	a	13	b	18	c
4	a	9	e	14	c	19	c
5	d	10	a	15	a	20	b

Completion

1 market failure

2 externality

3 public goods

4 free-rider

5 subsidise

6 privatization

7 inside

8 reallocate resources

9 deregulation

10 incentives

Tools and Practice Problems

When an activity causes positive externalities, or external benefits, the government can often improve matters through subsidies. This section explores two questions. First, how do subsidies encourage more of the subsidised activity? Our analysis will be very much like the treatment of the economic effects of taxation in Chapter 5. The other issue is why decisions are likely to be inefficient when there are externalities. This is an application of the technique of balancing marginal benefits and marginal costs introduced in Chapter 2.

SUBSIDIES

Many goods and services receive subsidies from various levels of government. Sometimes, as in the case of home ownership, the demanders benefit directly. In other cases, as with the railways, the subsidies are paid directly to the suppliers. Subsidies achieve their effects by shifting supply or demand curves, bringing about new equilibrium quantities. Tool Kit 7.1 shows how to analyse the impacts of subsidies.

Tool Kit 7.1 Using Supply and Demand to Determine the Effects of Subsidies

If subsidies are paid directly to demanders, the demand curve shifts. If subsidies are paid directly to suppliers, the supply curve shifts. The remainder of the analysis parallels the basic method of supply and demand. Follow these steps.

Step one: Start with a no-subsidy equilibrium in the appropriate market.

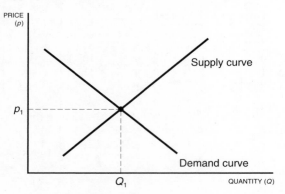

Step two: Identify the magnitude of a subsidy and whether it is paid directly to the demanders or suppliers.

Step three: If the subsidy is paid to demanders, shift the demand curve up (vertically) by exactly the amount of the subsidy. If the subsidy is paid to suppliers, shift the supply curve down by exactly the amount of the subsidy.

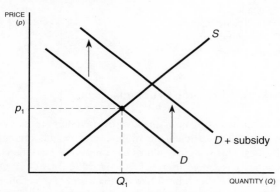

Step four: Find the new equilibrium and compare it with the original equilibrium.

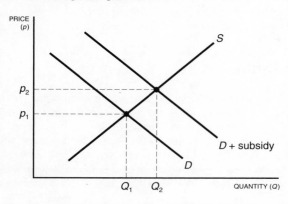

1 (Worked problem: effects of subsidies) Home ownership was treated very favourably by the U.K. tax system, and the interest paid on mortgages used to be tax deductible. To see how the subsidy affects the housing market, consider the market for three-bedroom bungalows in Little Spoon. The market demand and supply curves without the subsidy are given in Table 7.1.

Table 7.1

Demand		Supply	
Price	Quantity	Price	Quantity
£125,000	10	£125,000	50
£100,000	14	£100,000	42
£ 90,000	25	£ 90,000	31
£ 80,000	28	£ 80,000	28
£ 70,000	31	£ 70,000	20

a Find the equilibrium price and quantity.
b The tax advantages accruing to the home owner amount to £20,000 over the life of the occupancy. Calculate the demand curve with the subsidy included.
c Find the equilibrium price and quantity with the subsidy in place. How does the subsidy change the number of bungalows sold in Little Spoon?

Step-by-step solution

Step one (a): Start with a no-subsidy equilibrium in the appropriate market. The price is £80,000; the market clears with 28 houses sold. This is the answer to part *a*.

Step two (b): Identify the magnitude of the subsidy and whether it is paid directly to the demanders or suppliers. The subsidy is £20,000, paid to demanders.

Step three: Because it is paid to demanders, the subsidy causes the demand curve to shift vertically by £20,000. To calculate this, add £20,000 to each entry in the price column of the demand curve. The new demand curve is given in Table 7.2, which is the answer to part *b*.

Table 7.2

Demand	
Price	Quantity
£145,000	10
£120,000	14
£110,000	25
£100,000	28
£ 90,000	31

Step four (c): Find the new equilibrium and compare it with the original equilibrium. The new equilibrium price is £90,000, and the market clears at 31 houses sold. The subsidy has increased the number of home owners in Little Spoon from 28 to 31. The price is £10,000 higher, so the £20,000 subsidy makes home owners only £10,000 better off. Suppliers share in the benefits with a £10,000 higher price. The solution is illustrated in the diagram.

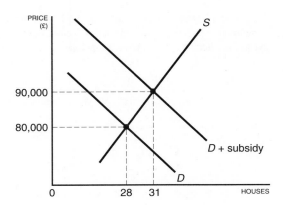

2 (Practice problem: effects of subsidies) Research shows that child care subsidies are a vote winner. The government has proposed child care grants of £10,000 per family. The demand and supply curves for child care services (measured in days) are given in Table 7.3.

Table 7.3

Demand		Supply	
Price (thousands)	Quantity (days)	Price (thousands)	Quantity (days)
£50	50,000	£50	100,000
£45	60,000	£45	80,000
£40	70,000	£40	70,000
£35	80,000	£35	60,000
£30	100,000	£30	50,000

a Find the equilibrium price and quantity without the subsidy.
b Calculate the demand with the subsidy.
c Find the equilibrium price and quantity with the subsidy. Compare the equilibria, and explain the effects of the subsidy.

3 (Practice problem: effects of subsidies) To promote conversion to renewable sources of energy, the government has offered various tax deductions and subsidies for the purchase and installation of solar water heaters. The effective subsidy to a typical taxpayer is £3,000. The supply and demand curves for solar water heaters are given in Table 7.4.

Table 7.4

Demand		Supply	
Price	Quantity	Price	Quantity
£8,000	1,000	£8,000	10,000
£7,000	3,000	£7,000	9,000
£6,000	5,000	£6,000	8,000
£5,000	7,000	£5,000	7,000
£4,000	9,000	£4,000	6,000
£3,000	11,000	£3,000	5,000

a Find the equilibrium price and quantity without the subsidy.

b Calculate the demand with the subsidy.
c Find the equilibrium price and quantity with the subsidy. Compare the equilibria, and explain the effects of the subsidy.

POSITIVE EXTERNALITIES

Individuals make decisions by balancing their private benefits and costs at the margin, but efficiency requires that all benefits and costs, not only the private ones, be included in the decision. Thus, when there are externalities, there are costs or benefits ignored by the individual making the decision, and this fact leads to inefficient decisions. This tool kit focuses on positive externalities and the inefficiencies that result.

Tool Kit 7.2 Showing How Positive Externalities Lead to Inefficiencies

Positive externalities occur when decision makers ignore some benefits of their actions. Follow these steps to see how this leads to inefficient decisions.

Step one: Find the private marginal benefits and costs of the relevant activity.

Step two: Find the equilibrium level of the activity, which is the level at which private marginal benefits equal marginal cost.

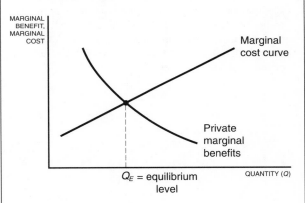

Step three: Calculate the social marginal benefits by adding the external benefit to the private marginal benefit at each level of the activity.

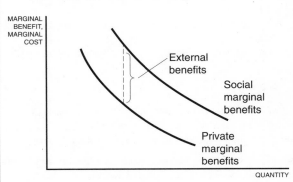

Step four: Find the efficient level of the activity, which is the level at which social marginal benefits equal marginal cost.

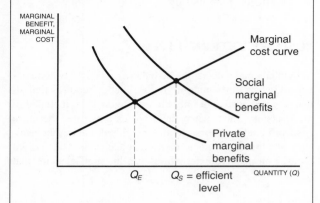

Step five: Compare the equilibrium and efficient levels of the activity.

4   (Worked problem: positive externalities) An important example of an activity that generates positive externalities is worker training. When firms train their employees, the employees not only become more productive in the job, they can also earn higher wages elsewhere. This increase in earning power is a positive externality. The QXV Corporation is considering sending some of its white-collar employees on a computer training programme. The cost is £1,000 per week, and the private marginal benefits to QXV are given in Table 7.5. Also, the value of the external benefit is £500 per week.

Table 7.5

Weeks at school	Private marginal benefits
1	£1,500
2	£1,250
3	£1,000
4	£ 750
5	£ 500
6	£ 250

a How many weeks of computer training will the company provide?
b Find the social marginal benefits of computer training.
c What is the efficient number of weeks of training?

Step-by-step solution

Step one (a): Find the private marginal benefits and costs of the relevant activity. The private marginal benefits are in Table 7.5; the private marginal cost is £1,000 per week.

Step two: Find the equilibrium level of the activity. Private marginal benefits equal £1,000 at 3 weeks.

Step three (b): Calculate the social marginal benefits by adding the external benefit to the private marginal benefit at each level of the activity. The answer is in Table 7.6.

Table 7.6

Weeks of training	Private marginal benefits	Social marginal benefits
1	£1,500	£2,000
2	£1,250	£1,750
3	£1,000	£1,500
4	£ 750	£1,250
5	£ 500	£1,000
6	£ 250	£ 750

Step four (c): Find the efficient level of the activity. Social marginal benefits equal marginal cost at 5 weeks.

Step five: Compare the equilibrium and efficient levels of the activity. The equilibrium number of weeks is 3, which is less than the efficient number, which is 5. The number of weeks provided is too low because the firm ignores the externality.

5   (Practice problem: positive externalities) ZZZX Pharmaceuticals is considering how many scientists to put to work researching a new drug for flu. Each scientist, complete with equipment and assistance, costs £200,000. The research will bring profits to ZZZX, but it will also bring about advances in viral research that other companies may build on in their own research. The private benefits are given in Table 7.7. The external marginal benefits are £150,000.

Table 7.7

Scientists	Private benefits
1	£400,000
2	£600,000
3	£700,000
4	£750,000
5	£750,000

a How many scientists will the company use? (Hint: First find the private marginal benefits.)
b Find the social marginal benefits of research scientists.
c What is the efficient number of scientists?

6   (Practice problem: positive externalities) Hillside County farmers have been advised to erect earthen dikes for erosion control. Each dike costs £2,000. The private marginal benefits are given in the second column of Table 7.8, but they do not include the external benefit that one farmer's erosion control efforts provide to her neighbors. The external benefits appear in the third column of the table.

Table 7.8

Dikes	Private marginal benefits	External marginal benefits
1	£3,000	£8,000
2	£2,000	£7,000
3	£1,500	£6,000
4	£1,000	£5,000
5	£ 500	£4,000
6	£ 0	£3,000
7	£ 0	£2,000

a How many dikes will each farmer erect?
b Find the social marginal benefits of a farmer's dikes.
c What is the efficient number of dikes?

Answers to Problems

2 a Price = £40; quantity = 70,000.
   b The new demand is given in Table 7.9.

Table 7.9

Demand with subsidy	
Price (thousands)	Quantity (days)
£60	50,000
£55	60,000
£50	70,000
£45	80,000
£40	100,000

c The new equilibrium price is £45,000, and the quantity is 80,000. The subsidy increases the quantity from 70,000 to 80,000. Consumers are better off by £5,000 (£10,000 subsidy – £5,000 increase in price), and firms are better off by £5,000, which is the increase in price.

3 a Price = £5,000; quantity = 7,000.
   b The new demand curve is given in Table 7.10.

Table 7.10

Demand with subsidy	
Price	Quantity
£11,000	1,000
£10,000	3,000
£ 9,000	5,000
£ 8,000	7,000
£ 7,000	9,000
£ 6,000	11,000

c The new equilibrium price is £7,000, and the quantity is 9,000. The subsidy increases the quantity from 7,000 to 9,000. Consumers are better off by £1,000 (£3,000 subsidy – £2,000 increase in price), and firms are better off by £2,000, which is the increase in price.

5 a 2 scientists.
   b The social marginal benefits are given in Table 7.11.

Table 7.11

Scientists	Private benefits	Private marginal benefits	Social marginal benefits
1	£400,000	£400,000	£550,000
2	£600,000	£200,000	£350,000
3	£700,000	£100,000	£250,000
4	£750,000	£ 50,000	£200,000
5	£750,000	£ 0	£150,000

c The efficient number is 4 scientists. The company chooses only 2 because it ignores the externality.

6 a 2 dikes.
   b The social marginal benefits are given in Table 7.12.

Table 7.12

Dikes	Private marginal benefits	External marginal benefits	Social marginal benefits
1	£3,000	£8,000	£11,000
2	£2,000	£7,000	£ 9,000
3	£1,500	£6,000	£ 7,500
4	£1,000	£5,000	£ 6,000
5	£ 500	£4,000	£ 4,500
6	£ 0	£3,000	£ 3,000
7	£ 0	£2,000	£ 2,000

c The efficient number of dikes is 7. Farmers only erect 2 because they ignore the external benefits.

Part Two

_____

PERFECT MARKETS

Chapter 8

THE CONSUMPTION DECISION

Chapter Review

The detailed study of microeconomics, the branch that focuses on the behavior of individuals and firms and builds up to an understanding of markets, begins in this chapter and continues throughout Parts Two and Three of the text. The basic competitive model of the private economy developed here is one you'll use throughout this course. Chapters 8 to 13 build on this model, exploring first the decisions individuals make—how much to consume, save, invest, and work—and then the decisions firms take—what and how much to produce and by what method. The entire model is put together in Chapter 13.

ESSENTIAL CONCEPTS

1   The consumer's decisions about how much of each good to purchase—the demand for each—are made in a two-step procedure. First, the consumer finds how much can be consumed given the amount of money available. This step is the construction of the **opportunity set,** the outer edge of which is the **budget constraint.** Second, he chooses the best alter-

native along the budget constraint. Figure 8.1 depicts a budget constraint.

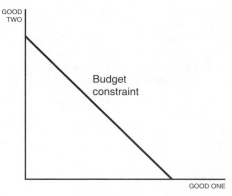

Figure 8.1

2   The budget constraint shows how much of each good can be purchased with the money available. The **slope** of the budget constraint is the **relative price** of the good measured on the horizontal axis. This relative price indicates the **trade-off:** how much of one good must be forgone to consume one more unit of the other.

3   The benefit or utility that a consumer derives from a good is measured by how much she is willing to pay. Consumers focus on the margin (the next unit) and continue to purchase more of the good until the *marginal benefit equals the price.*

4   When income increases, the budget constraint shifts out, but its slope does not change. Consumers buy more normal goods. Goods that people buy less of as income increases are called inferior goods, but these are the exceptions. The **income elasticity of demand** measures how much the quantity demanded changes as income changes. It is positive for **normal goods** and negative for **inferior goods.**

5   When price changes, the budget constraint rotates, becoming steeper if the price of the good on the horizontal axis rises and flatter if it falls. Introduced in Chapter 5, the **price elasticity of demand** measures how much the quantity demanded changes as price changes.

6   Price changes cause substitution and income effects. Suppose the price of a good rises. Because the good is relatively more expensive, the principle of substitution says that consumers will shift some of their consumption to other goods. This change is the **substitution effect.** At the same time, when the price is higher, the consumer is worse off and tends to buy less if the good is normal but more if the good is inferior. This change is the **income effect.**

7   *Utility* is the term economists use for the benefits that individuals receive for consuming goods. As people consume more of a particular good, they get smaller increments of utility. In other words, there is **diminishing marginal utility.** When the consumer has chosen the best bundle of goods, her utility is maximised and the marginal utility of each good equals its price.

8   **Consumer surplus** equals the difference between what the consumer is willing to pay for goods and the price (what she has to pay). Figure 8.2 shows a demand curve for apples, which also represents what the consumer is willing to pay for apples. When the price is 25 pence, the consumer purchases 8 apples. The consumer surplus, shown as the area between the demand curve and the price, measures the consumer's gain from trade.

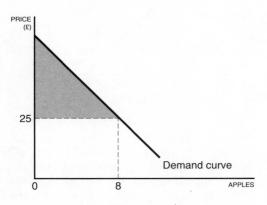

Figure 8.2

BEHIND THE ESSENTIAL CONCEPTS

1   The budget constraint shows which quantities of goods are affordable. If you know the prices of goods and an individual's income, you can draw her budget constraint. As you might expect, people who have the same income and must pay the same prices have the same budget constraint. As price changes, each individual's budget constraint changes in the same way. The budget constraint indicates opportunities; it says nothing about the value that the consumer places on the goods. Individual tastes only come into the picture when the actual choices are made.

2   The slope of the budget line depends only upon prices, not upon income. Therefore, changes in income cannot change the slope of the budget line. Changes in income bring about a parallel shift in the budget constraint. Price changes, on the other hand, do change the slope. The budget constraint rotates when price changes.

3   Economists measure the responsiveness of quantity to income or price changes by using elasticities. In this chapter, there are two elasticities: the income elasticity of demand and the price elasticity of demand. Elasticities are relative percentage changes. The income elasticity equals the percentage that the quantity demanded changes when income changes by 1 percent. The price elasticity equals the percentage change in quantity demanded as the result of a 1 percent change in price.

4   The distinction between substitution and income effects is important, and it will reappear in the next chapter and throughout the course. Two points are key here. First, income effects are small in the consumption decision. Suppose that the price of milk rises by 10 percent. If you were spending £10 per month on milk, now you must spend £1 more to buy the same amount of milk. This makes you worse off by approximately £1, not a very important change in my well-being. The income effect captures how much extra milk can be bought with £1 of extra income. The second point is that the relatively more important substitution effect governs many important issues concerning the response to price changes, such as how elastic are demand curves, whether goods are substitutes or complements, and why taxes may lead to inefficiencies.

5   The basic economic model says that individuals balance the benefits and costs of their decisions. It emphasises choice at the margin, for the next unit of a good or service. Individuals continue buying until the marginal benefit equals the marginal cost. For the consumer, the marginal benefit (called the marginal utility) is just how much she is willing to pay for another unit. The marginal cost is the price. When marginal utility equals price, the consumer has realised all the possible gains from the purchase of the good.

6   There are two important diagrams in this chapter: the budget constraint and the demand curve. Although each is downward sloping, they should not be confused. The budget constraint drawn in Figure 8.1 shows the combinations of goods that a person can afford. Quantities of

goods are measured on each axis. The demand curve drawn in Figure 8.2 shows how much of *one* good will be purchased at each price. The quantity of the good is measured on the horizontal axis, and the price is measured on the vertical axis.

SELF-TEST

True or False

1   The budget constraint indicates that in the absence of borrowing, the amount spent on goods cannot exceed after-tax income.

2   The slope of the budget constraint shows the trade-off between two goods.

3   Income determines the slope of the budget constraint.

4   The amount that an individual is willing to pay for coffee is called the marginal utility of coffee.

5   The amount that an individual is willing to pay for an extra cup of coffee is called the marginal utility of coffee.

6   A rational individual will increase her consumption of a good until the marginal utility equals the price.

7   When income increases, the budget constraint rotates, becoming flatter.

8   When income increases, the consumer demands more of inferior goods.

9   If an individual demands more of a good when income falls, the good is a complement.

10   If the income elasticity is less than zero, then the good is an inferior good.

11   The long-run income elasticity of demand is greater than the short-run income elasticity of demand.

12   If when the price of one good rises the demand for another also rises, the goods are substitutes.

13   If when the price of one good falls the demand for another also falls, the goods are complements.

14   When the price of a good falls, the substitution effect encourages more consumption of that good.

15   When the price of a normal good falls, the income effect encourages more consumption of that good.

Multiple Choice

1   Assuming that there is no saving or borrowing and a consumer's income is fixed, his budget constraint

   a   defines his opportunity set.
   b   indicates that total expenditures cannot be greater than total income.
   c   shows that marginal utility is decreasing.
   d   all of the above.
   e   *a* and *b*.

2   Suppose that the price of a cinema ticket is £5 and the price of a pizza is £10. The trade-off between the two goods is

   a   one pizza for one cinema ticket.
   b   two cinema tickets for one pizza.
   c   two pizzas for one cinema ticket.
   d   £2 per cinema ticket.
   e   none of the above.

3   The marginal utility of a good indicates

   a   that the usefulness of the good is limited.
   b   the willingness to pay for an extra unit.
   c   that the good is scarce.
   d   that the slope of the budget constraint is the relative price.
   e   none of the above.

4   Diminishing marginal utility means that

   a   the usefulness of the good is limited.
   b   the willingness to pay for an extra unit decreases as more of that good is consumed.
   c   the good is less scarce.
   d   the slope of the budget constraint is flatter as more of that good is consumed.
   e   none of the above.

5   If Fred is willing to pay £100 for one espresso maker and £120 for two, then the marginal utility of the second espresso maker is

   a   £20.
   b   £120.
   c   £100.
   d   £60.
   e   £50.

6   When the income of a consumer increases, her budget constraint

   a   shifts outward parallel to the original budget constraint.
   b   rotates and becomes steeper.
   c   rotates and becomes flatter.
   d   shifts inwards parallel to the original budget constraint.
   e   none of the above.

7   The percentage change in quantity demanded brought about by a 1 percent increase in income is

   a   1.
   b   greater than zero.
   c   the income elasticity of demand.
   d   the price elasticity of demand.
   e   none of the above.

8   If the share of income that an individual spends on a good decreases as her income increases, then the income elasticity of demand is

   a   greater than 1.
   b   between 0 and 1.
   c   0.
   d   less than 1.
   e   less than 0.

9   In the long run, the

   a   price elasticity of demand is greater than in the short run.

b   income elasticity of demand is greater than in the short run.

c   price elasticity of demand is less than in the short run.

d   income elasticity of demand is less than in the short run.

e   *a* and *b*.

10   When the price of a good (measured along the horizontal axis) falls, the budget constraint

a   rotates and becomes flatter.

b   rotates and becomes steeper.

c   shifts out parallel to the original budget constraint.

d   shifts in parallel to the original budget constraint.

e   none of the above.

11   If demand for a good falls as income rises, then the

a   good is a normal good.

b   good is an inferior good.

c   income elasticity is less than 0.

d   income elasticity is between 0 and 1.

e   *b* and *c*.

12   When the price of a good falls, the substitution effect

a   encourages the individual to consume more of the good.

b   encourages the individual to consume less of the good.

c   leads to more consumption if the good is an inferior good, but less if the good is a normal good.

d   leads to less consumption if the good is an inferior good, but more if the good is a normal good.

e   *a* and *c*.

13   When the price of a good falls, the income effect

a   encourages the individual to consume more of the good.

b   encourages the individual to consume less of the good.

c   leads to more consumption if the good is an inferior good, but less if the good is a normal good.

d   leads to less consumption if the good is an inferior good, but more if the good is a normal good.

e   *a* and *c*.

14   The rational consumer chooses her purchases for each good so that the

a   utility equals total expenditure.

b   marginal utility equals price.

c   consumer surplus equals 0.

d   marginal utility is diminishing.

e   income elasticity equals 1.

15   The difference between what the consumer is willing to pay for an item and what she has to pay is called

a   marginal utility.

b   the substitution effect.

c   consumer surplus.

d   the income effect.

e   the price elasticity of demand.

16   In general, the price elasticity of demand is greater when

a   the good is an inferior good.

b   there are good, close substitutes available.

c   there are good, close complements available.

d   the income elasticity of demand is less.

e   none of the above.

17   For normal goods, when income rises,

a   the budget constraint shifts out, parallel.

b   the demand curve shifts to the right.

c   quantity demanded increases.

d   more money is spent on the good.

e   all of the above.

18   For normal goods, as price rises,

a   the substitution effect encourages less consumption.

b   the income effect encourages less consumption.

c   the quantity demanded falls.

d   the demand for substitute goods increases.

e   all of the above.

19   For inferior goods, as price rises, the

a   substitution effect encourages less consumption.

b   income effect encourages less consumption.

c   income effect encourages more consumption.

d   quantity demanded rises.

e   *a* and *c*.

20   The slope of the budget constraint depends on

a   the relative price of the goods.

b   the income of the consumer.

c   the availability of substitute goods.

d   whether the good is normal or inferior.

e   *a* and *b*.

Completion

1   The opportunity set for the consumer is defined by the _____, which says that in the absence of borrowing, expenditures cannot exceed income.

2   The slope of the budget line equals the _____ of the two goods.

3   The benefits of consumption are called _____.

4   The willingness to pay for an extra unit of a good is its _____.

5   When income increases, the budget constraint shifts outwards in a _____ way.

6   The _____ of demand measures how consumption of a good changes in response to a change in income.

7   When the price of a good changes, the budget constraint _____.

8   The _____ of demand measures how consumption of a good changes in response to a change in price.

9   When the price of a good falls, the _____
effect always encourages more consumption of the
good.

10 The difference between what the consumer is willing
to pay for an item and what she has to pay is called

_____ .

Answers to Self-Test

True or False

1	T	4	F	7	F	10	T	13	F
2	T	5	T	8	F	11	T	14	T
3	F	6	T	9	F	12	T	15	T

Multiple Choice

1	e	6	a	11	e	16	b
2	b	7	c	12	a	17	e
3	b	8	d	13	d	18	e
4	b	9	e	14	b	19	e
5	a	10	a	15	c	20	a

Completion

1   budget constraint
2   relative price
3   utility
4   marginal utility
5   parallel
6   income elasticity
7   rotates
8   price elasticity
9   substitution
10 consumer surplus

Tools and Practice Problems

The most important model in this chapter is the opportunity
set for the consumer: the budget constraint. This section will
first review how to construct the budget constraint and then
explain how the budget constraint changes when price and
income change. A somewhat more advanced topic follows—
the substitution and income effects of price changes. Next,
there are some applications: in-kind transfers and tax-
subsidy schemes. Finally, we turn to marginal utility.

THE BUDGET CONSTRAINT

Because we have limited income, we must limit our purchases. The budget constraint shows what combinations of
goods are affordable. Tool Kit 8.1 shows how to plot the
budget constraint. After some practice problems, we study
the effects of income and price changes. The basic technique
is to draw first the budget constraint using the original income and price and then a new budget constraint using the
new income and prices. Finally, we compare the old and new
budget constraints.

Tool Kit 8.1 Plotting the Budget Constraint

The budget constraint shows what combinations of
goods can be purchased with a limited amount of
money. Constructing the budget constraint is one of
the essential techniques needed in Part Two. Follow
these four steps.

Step one: Draw a set of coordinate axes. Label the
horizontal axis as the quantity of one good consumed
and the vertical axis as the quantity of a second good
consumed.

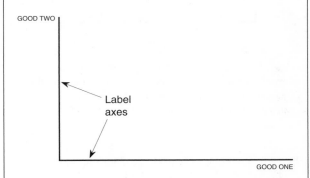

Step two: Calculate the quantity of the good measured
on the horizontal axis that can be purchased if all the
consumer's money is spent on it. Plot this quantity
along the horizontal axis.

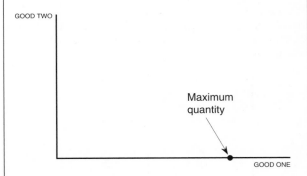

Step three: Calculate the quantity of the good measured on the vertical axis that can be purchased if all
the consumer's money is spent on it. Plot this quantity
along the vertical axis.

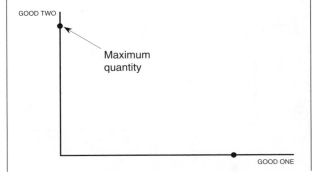

Step four: Draw a line segment connecting the two points. This line segment is the budget constraint.

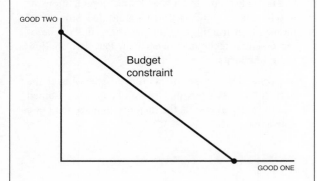

Step five: Verify that the slope of the budget constraint is (minus) the price of the good measured on the horizontal axis divided by the price of the good measured on the vertical axis.

1   (Worked problem: budget constraint) Richard has a budget of £500 to decorate the rooms in his new house. The price of enough paint for 1 room is £25; the price of wallpaper is £50 per room. Draw Richard's budget constraint.

Step-by-step solution

Step one: Draw a set of coordinate axes, and label the horizontal one "Rooms painted" and the vertical one "Rooms wallpapered." (There is no rule as to which good goes on which axis. It is fine either way.)

Step two: Calculate how many rooms can be painted with the entire £500. This number is £500/£25 = 20 rooms. Plot this quantity along the horizontal axis.

Step three: Calculate how many rooms can be wallpapered with the entire £500. This number is £500/£50 = 10 rooms. Plot this quantity along the vertical axis.

Step four: Draw a line segment connecting these two points. This line segment is the budget constraint.

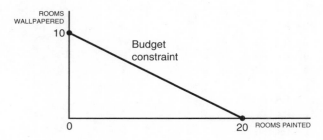

Step five: Verify the slope. The slope of the budget constraint is 10/20 = 1/2. The price ratio is £25/£50 = 1/2.

2   (Practice problem: budget constraint) The computing services department of a well-known university wants to buy new computer desks and new software. The department has a budget of £1,000. Each computer desk costs £50 and each software licence costs £40. Plot the department's budget constraint and verify that the slope is the relative price.

3   (Practice problem: budget constraint). Draw the following budget constraints.

a   Budget for hiring gardeners = £100,000; price of a full-time employee = £20,000; price of a part-time employee = £8,000.

b   Budget for food = £250; price of microwave snacks = £2.0. (Plot expenditures on all other food on the vertical axis.)

c   Budget for landscaping = £2,000; price of rose bushes = £50; price of cherry trees = £80.

d   Budget for library acquisitions = £50,000; price of books = £40; price of journal subscriptions = £100.

4   (Worked problem: budget constraint with income and price changes) Bill Smith has decided to take a course on English literature. Many books are recommended on the reading list, and all are available in the abridged "Fred's Notes" versions at £8 each. The unabridged versions cost £3 each. Bill has £72 to spend.

a   Plot his budget constraint.

b   Show how it changes when Bill finds that he has another £24 (for a total of £96).

Step-by-step solution

Step one (a): Plot Bill's budget constraint using the procedure outlined above. He can afford £72/£8 = 9 abridged and £72/£3 = 24 unabridged notes. Note that the slope is 9/24 = £3/£8, which is the ratio of the prices.

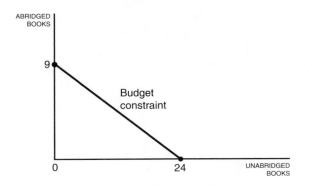

Step two (b): Plot Bill's budget constraint with £96 to spend. He can now afford £96/£8 = 12 abridged and £96/£3 = 32 unabridged notes.

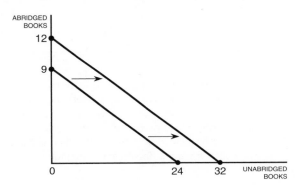

Step three: Verify that the shift in the budget constraint is parallel. The slope is 12/32 = £3/£8, which is the ratio of the prices. Because the prices have not changed, the slope has not changed. The income increase causes a parallel shift.

5   (Practice problem: budget constraint with income and price changes) Helen is nervous about her end of year exams. She is considering hiring a tutor at £10 per hour. Another possibility is purchase study guides at £15 each. She has £90.

  a   Plot her budget constraint.
  b   Oops! Unexpectedly stuck with the bill at Ernie's Pizza Parlour, Helen now has only £60 to spend. Plot her new budget constraint.

6   (Worked problem: budget constraint with income and price changes) Dissatisfied with his social life, Horatio has budgeted £400 for self-improvement. He is considering elocution lessons at £25 per hour and ballroom dancing classes at £10 each.

  a   Plot Horatio's budget constraint.
  b   Good news! A new elocution school offers lessons at the introductory price of £20. Plot his new budget constraint.

Step-by-step solution

Step one (a): Plot the budget constraint at the £25 price. Horatio can afford £400/£25 = 16 elocution lessons or £400/£10 = 40 classes. Note that the slope is 40/16 = £25/£10, which is the ratio of the prices.

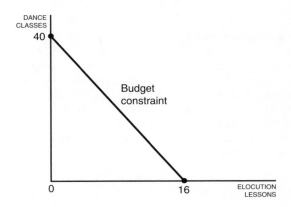

Step two (b): Plot the budget constraint at the £20 price. Horatio can now afford £400/£20 = 20 elocution lessons, which is 4 more, but he still can only buy 40 dance lessons.

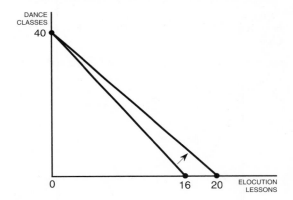

Step three: Verify that the budget constraint rotates. The slope is now 40/20 = £20/£10, which is the ratio of the new prices and is flatter. The price decrease rotated the budget constraint. The point at 0 elocution lessons and 40 dance classes does not change, because when no elocution lessons are purchased, the price change makes no difference.

7   (Practice problem: budget constraint with income and price changes) With some of her extra cash (£100 each month), Sho-Yen buys meals and blankets and donates them to the nearby shelter for the homeless. The meals cost £2 each, and the blankets £5 each.

  a   Plot her budget constraint.
  b   The supplier of meals cuts the price to £1. Plot the new budget constraint.

8   (Practice problem: budget constraint with income and price changes) For each of these problems, draw the budget constraints before and after the change. Plot "Expenditure on other goods" on the vertical axis.

  a   Income = £400; price of potatoes = £1 per sack; price of potatoes rises to £2 per sack.

b   Income = £5,000; price of concert tickets = £100; income rises to £6,000.

c   Income = £450; price of housecleaning = £45; income falls to £225.

d   Income = £100; price of pizzas = £5; price increases to £10.

Substitution and Income Effects

Price changes rotate the budget constraint and bring about two effects, substitution and income. The substitution effect indicates that consumers buy more when the price falls and less when it rises. The income effect, on the other hand, is not necessarily in the opposite direction of the price change. Tool Kit 8.2 uses the budget constraint to distinguish substitution and income effects.

Tool Kit 8.2 Distinguishing between Substitution and Income Effects

When the price of a good changes, there are two effects: substitution and income. These can be illustrated using the budget constraint. This technique clarifies the point that while the substitution effect is always in the opposite direction to the price change, the income effect may go either way. Follow these steps.

Step one: Draw the budget line with the original price.

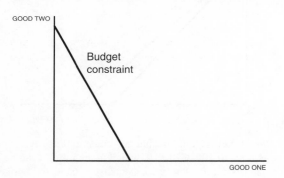

Step two: Find the chosen quantities along the budget line. Label this point *A*.

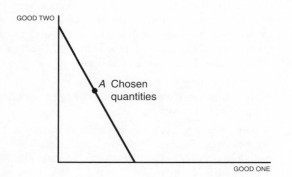

Step three: Draw the budget line with the new price.

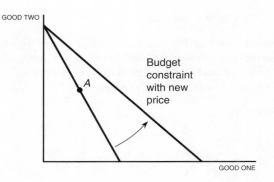

Step four: Draw a dashed line through point *A* and parallel to the *new* budget line.

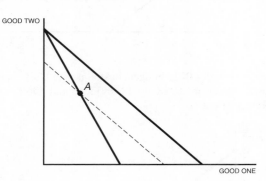

Step five: Darken the portion of the dotted-line segment that lies above the original budget line. The points along this darkened segment represent the quantities made possible by the substitution effect of the price change. The income effect shifts this line out parallel to the new budget line drawn in step three.

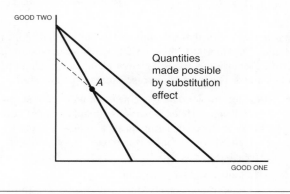

---

9   (Worked problem: substitution and income effects) In order to keep in touch with her family and friends, Louise puts aside £30 per month for postage and phone calls. A long-distance phone call costs her £2 on average, and the price of a stamped envelope is 30 pence. She makes 6 calls and posts 60 letters each month.

a   Plot her budget constraint, and label the point that she has chosen.

b   Headline news! The price of a stamped envelope falls to 20 pence. Illustrate the substitution and income effects of the price change.

Step-by-step solution

Step one (a): Draw the original budget constraint. The maximum quantity of calls is £30/£2 = 15, and the maximum quantity of letters is £30/£.30 = 100.

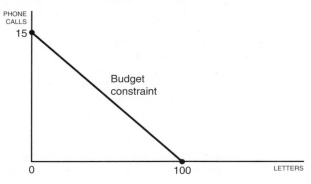

Step two: Plot and label the chosen point (6 phone calls, 60 letters). Note that this is on the budget constraint because (6 × £2) + (60 × 30 pence) = £30. Label this point *A*.

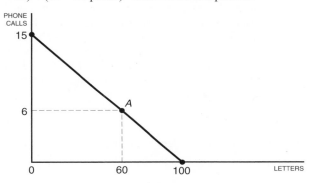

Step three (b): Draw the new budget constraint. The maximum quantities are 15 phone calls and 30/£.2 = 150 letters.

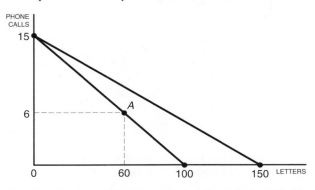

Step four: Draw a dashed line segment through *A* parallel to the new budget constraint.

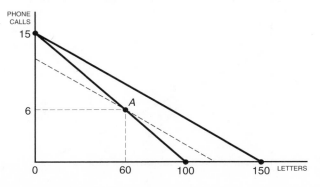

Step five: Darken the portion of the dashed line segment that lies above the original budget constraint. Notice that the substitution effect would lead Louise to choose a point like *B* along this segment, where the quantity of letters is greater. We say that the substitution effect of a price decrease is always to increase the quantity demanded. The income effect moves this darkened segment out to the new budget constraint. Louise would write more letters if letters were a normal good, but she would write fewer if letters were an inferior good. The income effect can go either way in principle, although most goods are normal.

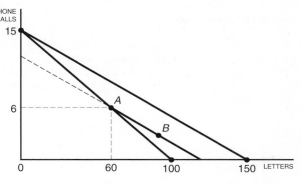

10 (Practice problem: substitution and income effects) Yves loves to wear whites for tennis. He sends his outfits to the cleaners at a price of £3.60 each. Playing tennis also requires new balls, which cost £2. Yves' tennis budget is £36 per week, which allows him his current consumption levels of 8 cans of balls and 5 clean outfits.

a Plot his budget constraint, and show his current consumption choice.

b The price of tennis balls has risen to £4.50. Illustrate the substitution and income effects of this price increase.

11 (Practice problem: substitution and income effects) For each of the following, illustrate the substitution and income effects of the price change. Plot "Expenditure on other goods" on the vertical axis, and pick any point on the original budget line as the quantities consumed before the price change.

a Income = £100; price of bricks = 10 pence each; price changes to 20 pence.

b Income = £1,000; price of haircuts = £20; price changes to £25.

c Income = £500; price of pies = £5; price changes to £4.

d Income = £10; price of chocolate bars = 50 pence; price changes to 25 pence.

APPLICATIONS

Now that you have mastered plotting the budget constraint and analysing how it changes when price or income changes, you are ready for some applications. The following problems look at how the budget constraint is affected by transfer payments, such as social security benefits and tax changes. These latter problems illustrate the relationship between the substitution effect and tax distortions.

12   (Worked problem: applications) Some social security benefits are targeted. For example, the housing benefit can only be used to rent accommodation. Economists often argue that cash transfers are better. The typical housing benefit recipient has £200 per week in income in addition to £80 per week in housing benefit.

   a   Draw the budget constraint.
   b   One proposal is to substitute £80 in cash for the housing benefit. Draw the budget constraint that results from this proposal.
   c   Which would the recipient prefer? Why?

Step-by-step solution

Step one (a): Draw the budget constraint with housing benefit. Label the axes "Housing (£)" and "Other goods (£)." The slope is 1 because £1 less spent on other goods means £1 spent on housing. Note that no more than £200 can be spent on other goods.

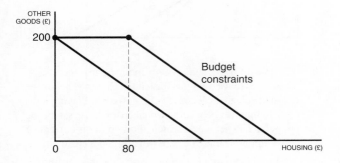

Step two (b): Draw the budget constraint with the cash grants replacing the housing benefit.

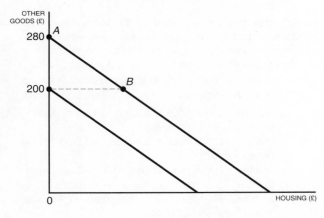

Step three (c): Compare. The difference is that the cash grant allows the recipient to choose the points between *A* and *B*. Many recipients would not choose these low levels of housing consumption anyway; so there would be no difference. Some might, however, and these people would prefer the cash.

13   (Practice problem: applications) The city of Leicester recently planted 1 tree (worth £40) outside every house. The typical Leicester resident has £4,000 in disposable income this summer.

   a   Plot the budget constraint with the in-kind transfer of 1 tree.

   b   Plot the budget constraint with the £40 refunded through the tax system.
   c   Which opportunity set is preferred? How could the tree planting be justified?

14   (Worked problem: applications) When less consumption of some good or service is needed, economists often recommend putting a tax on the good or service. One objection is that the taxes lead to higher prices, which make people worse off. If the tax revenue is refunded, however, people can be approximately as well off, yet still face higher prices for the good or service. In essence, it is possible to put the substitution effect to work and reduce consumption of the good or service without reducing the well-being of consumers very much. The city of Pleasantville is running out of space at its refuse sites. The typical resident has an income of £100 per week and purchases 6 rubbish bags weekly at 10 pence each.

   a   Plot the budget constraint for the typical resident, and show the current consumption choice.
   b   In an effort to encourage recycling and discourage disposal, the city institutes a user fee of £1.90 per rubbish bag. (Rubbish bags now cost £2.) The city council members vote to combine the user fee with a tax refund. Each resident receives a tax refund of £1.90 × 6 = £11.40. Plot the new budget constraint.
   c   Discuss the user fee–tax refund plan.

Step-by-step solution

Step one (a): Plot the budget constraint with neither a user

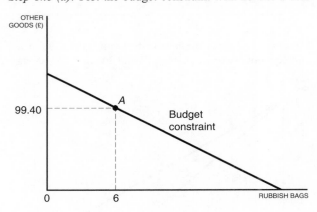

fee nor a tax refund. Label the resident's chosen point *A*.
Step two (b): Plot the budget constraint with the user fee and tax refund.

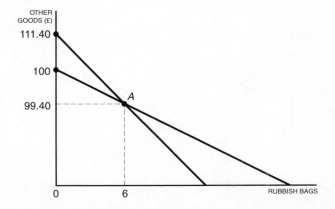

Step three (c): We see that the net effect of the entire user fee–tax refund scheme is only the substitution of the increase in the price of bags to £2. The resident is no worse off (because he can still consume as he did before the user fee), but he will be motivated to use fewer bags. (One minor flaw in the program is that as people substitute away from rubbish bags, they will pay less in user fees than is needed to finance the tax relief.)

15   The government is concerned about pollution and has decided to impose a tax on petrol that raises the price of petrol from £1 to £2 per litre. The government also proposes to refund the petrol tax revenue through an income tax cut large enough to allow consumers to buy the same amount of petrol as before the tax.

  a   Plot the budget constraint with no petrol tax.
  b   Plot the budget constraint with the petrol tax and the refund.
  c   Journalist Jim Greenley writes, "This plan will have no effect. The government takes money away with one hand and gives it back with the other." Is he right? Why or why not?

UTILITY AND PREFERENCES

The first step in the consumption decision is to determine what is affordable—to plot the budget constraint. The second step is to choose the best bundle of goods from all those which lie along the budget constraint. Economists say that the best bundle is the one that provides the greatest utility. When the consumer has chosen the best bundle, the marginal utility (what she would be willing to pay for another unit) equals the price. Tool Kit 8.3 shows how to use marginal utility to interpret the consumption decision and also calculate consumer surplus.

Tool Kit 8.3 Using Marginal Utility
to Choose the Best Bundle of Goods

The rational consumer demands the quantity of a good for which marginal utility equals price. The difference between what she is willing to pay and her expenditure is consumer surplus. Follow these steps to see how it works.

Step one: Identify the product price and utility (willingness to pay) for each quantity of the good.

Step two: Compute marginal utility for each quantity of the good.

Marginal utility = change in utility
= utility of 1 fewer unit – utility.

Step three: Choose the quantity for which marginal utility equals price.

Step four: Compute her expenditure.

Expenditure = price × quantity.

Step five: Calculate consumer surplus.

Consumer surplus = utility – expenditure.

---

16   (Worked problem: marginal utility) Table 8.1 gives Charles's willingness to pay (utility) for various hours of on-line access to the Internet per week. On-line time is priced at 12 pence per hour.

  a   Compute his marginal utility for each hour.
  b   How many hours will Charles purchase?
  c   Compute his consumer surplus for this good.

Table 8.1

Number of on-line hours	Utility (willingness to pay, pence)
0	0
1	20
2	38
3	54
4	68
5	80
6	90
7	98
8	104

Step-by-step solution

Step one: Identify the utility for each quantity and the price. The price is 12 pence and the utility is given in Table 8.1.

Step two: Compute the marginal utility. The first unit raises utility from 0 pence to 20 pence. The marginal utility is then 20 pence – 0 pence = 20 pence. Similarly, marginal utility for the second unity equals 38 pence – 20 pence = 18 pence. Continuing, we have the following table. Notice that marginal utility diminishes as quantity increases.

Table 8.1A

Number of on-line hours	Utility (willingness to pay, pence)	Marginal utility (pence)
0	0	
1	20	20
2	38	18
3	54	16
4	68	14
5	80	12
6	90	10
7	98	8
8	104	6

Step three: Choose the quantity for which marginal utility equals price. The price (12 pence) equals the marginal utility when 5 hours are purchased.

Step four: Calculate expenditure. Expenditure is 12 pence × 5 = 60 pence.

Step five: Calculate consumer surplus. His utility is 80 pence when he buys 5 hours. Consumer surplus is 80 pence – 60 pence = 20 pence.

17   Table 8.2 gives Maria's willingness to pay for concert tickets. The price of a concert ticket is £20.

a Compute the marginal utility for a ticket.
b How many tickets will Maria purchase?
c Compute her consumer surplus.

Table 8.2

Number of tickets	Utility (willingness to pay)
0	£ 0
1	£ 35
2	£ 65
3	£ 90
4	£110
5	£125
6	£135
7	£140

18 Table 8.3 gives Charles's consumer surplus for tennis balls, which sell for £2 a can.

a Compute his marginal utility for each can.
b How many cans will Charles purchase?
c Compute his consumer surplus for this good.

Table 8.3

Number of cans of tennis balls	Utility (willingness to pay)
0	£ 0
1	£10
2	£16
3	£20
4	£22
5	£23
6	£23.50
7	£23.75

Answers to Problems

2

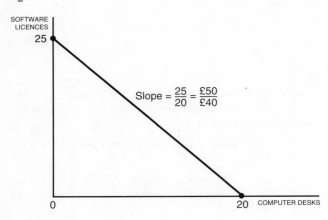

3 *a*

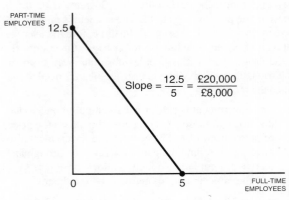

b

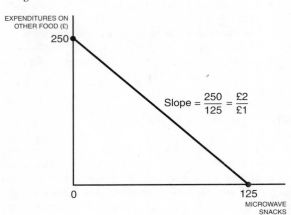

c

d

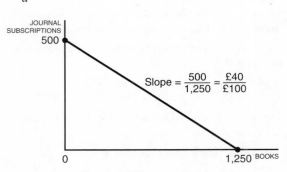

5

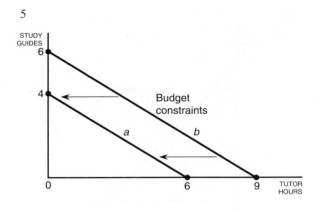

7

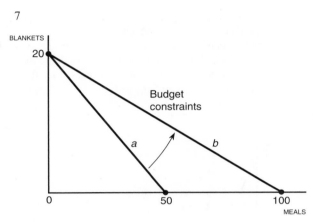

8   *a*

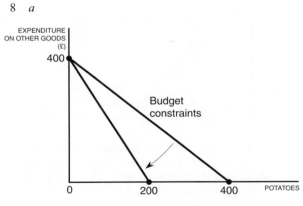

b

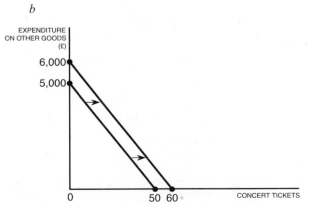

c

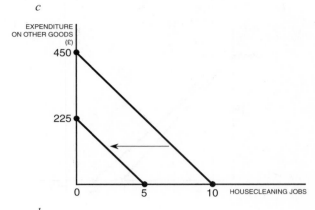

d

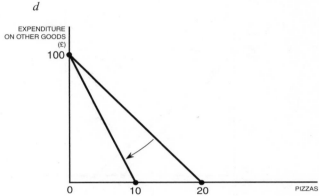

10

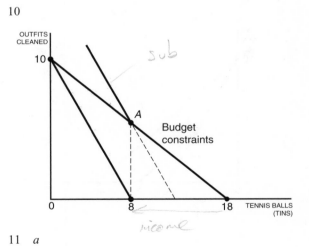

11   *a*

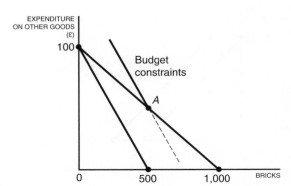

b

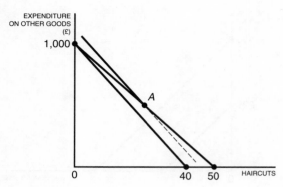

c

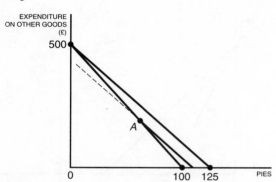

d

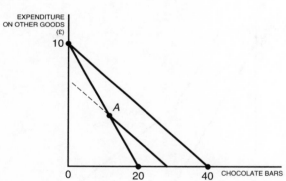

13   *a*

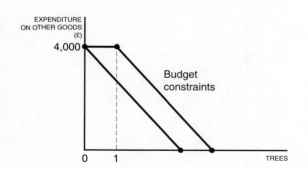

b

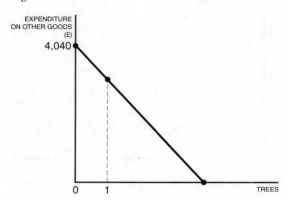

c   The budget constraint with the tax refund, which is shown in part *b*, is preferred because it allows more choices. If desired, the resident can spend as much as £4,040 on other goods, and with the in-kind transfer of one tree, she can spend a maximum of £4,000 on other goods.

15   *a* and *b*

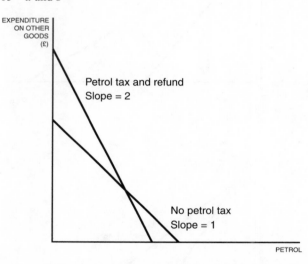

c   He is wrong. The petrol tax and refund program results in a budget constraint with more alternatives that involve less petrol consumption. It motivates individuals to substitute other goods for petrol.

17   *a*

Table 8.2

Number of tickets	Utility (willingness to pay)	Marginal Utility
0	£ 0	
1	£ 35	£35
2	£ 65	£30
3	£ 90	£25
4	£110	£20
5	£125	£15
6	£135	£10
7	£140	£ 5

b   4.

c   £110 − (£20 × 4) = £30.

18 *a*

Table 8.3

Number of cans of tennis balls	Utility (willingness to pay)	Marginal Utility
0	£ 0	
1	£10	£10
2	£16	£ 6
3	£20	£ 4
4	£22	£ 2
5	£23	£ 1
6	£23.50	£ 0.50
7	£23.75	£ 0.25

b. 4.
c. £22 − (£2 × 4) = £14.

Chapter 9

LABOUR SUPPLY AND SAVINGS

Chapter Review

Chapter 8 explored the individual's decision to spend her income. This chapter continues the discussion of household decision making. First, it examines the labour supply decision, the choice between leisure and the income needed for consumption. As with the consumption decision in Chapter 8, the individual chooses the best alternative along the budget constraint. The chapter examines how much labour time to offer, which level of education to pursue, and when to retire. Next comes the savings decision, where the trade-off pits current versus future consumption.

ESSENTIAL CONCEPTS

1   The decision to supply labour is primarily a time allocation problem. Individuals have only so much time available, and they must divide their time between working and other activities. Any time not devoted to working and earning money, whether it is spent in recreation, sleep, or housework and other unpaid chores, is called leisure. The income earned while working is available for consumption; therefore, the *trade-off* is between

leisure and **consumption,** between consuming time and consuming goods.

2   The chapter focuses on the budget constraint between leisure and consumption, shown here in Figure 9.1. The slope is the wage rate, and changes in the wage rate rotate the budget constraint, causing income and substitution effects. When an individual's wage increases, leisure becomes more expensive; thus, the *substitution*

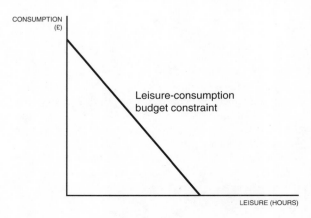

Figure 9.1

effect encourages less leisure and more work. On the other hand, the *income effect* leads the individual to want to consume more leisure; this results in less work. Because the income and substitution effects work in opposite directions, the supply curve for labour may slope upwards or even bend backwards.

3   There are more dimensions to labour supply than hours worked. Individuals choose whether to participate in the workforce. They must also decide how much education and training to acquire and when to retire. Each of these decisions can be understood as the choice of the best alternative within an appropriately specified budget constraint.

4   Government policy also affects labour supply. Taxation reduces the consumption that a given amount of labour will yield. The national pension system affects the decision to retire through the earnings limit, by discouraging the elderly from participating in the labour force. Both the substitution and income effects of the welfare system encourage recipients to work less or not at all. Each of these policies is analysed in terms of how it alters the leisure-consumption budget constraint.

5   According to **human capital** theory, individuals invest in education and training to acquire human capital, or skills that increase their productivity and wages. Another view is that education signals to employers which potential workers are innately more productive. This signal leads to credentials competition, the process by which people gather degrees, not for any learning that takes place but rather to show that they will be productive if hired.

6   The **savings decision** is basically a decision about *when* to consume; households choose whether to spend all of their income now, or to save it for future consumption. The **two-period budget constraint** employs the techniques we learned in Chapter 8 to show which combinations of consumption in the present and consumption in the future are affordable, given present and future incomes and the interest rate. As in Chapter 8, the slope of the budget constraint indicates the *trade-off,* and it equals the relative price. Since current consumption is measured on the horizontal axis, the slope is the **relative price of current consumption,** which is **1 plus the interest rate.**

7   When the interest rate changes, the budget constraint rotates, becoming steeper if the interest rate increases and flatter if it decreases. In exactly the same manner as Chapter 8's analysis of the consumption decision, the change in the budget constraint causes income and substitution effects. Higher interest rates make savers better off, and because current consumption is a normal good, the *income effect* makes them want to consume more today, thus reducing savings. On the other hand, higher interest rates lower the relative price of future consumption. The resulting *substitution effect* increases savings. In the decision to save, the substitution and income effects work in opposite directions.

8   There are several motives for saving. People save during their working lives to provide for retirement. This is called **life-cycle savings.** People set aside **precautionary savings** to guard against the chance of accident or illness. The **bequest motive** leads people to save for their heirs. People save to meet a particular goal, such as buying a house or starting a business. We call this motive **target savings.** Furthermore, government policies affect savings; some encourage saving, others do not. For example, increases in state pensions tend to reduce life-cycle savings because people do not feel as compelled to save for retirement. Taxes on interest lower the after-tax rate of interest and thus provide less incentive to save.

BEHIND THE ESSENTIAL CONCEPTS

1   The basic diagram for the first part of the chapter is the budget constraint for leisure and consumption. It is important to understand that this diagram is very much like the consumer's budget constraint in Chapter 8. Each shows which combinations are affordable. The slopes are the relative prices; in this case, the relative price of leisure is the wage rate. If the individual wants to consume another hour of leisure, the opportunity cost is the money that could be earned in that hour. Changes in nonwage income, such as investment returns, bring about a parallel shift in the budget constraint, but changes in the wage rate rotate it. Again, this is very similar to the Chapter 8 budget constraint.

2   Changes in the wage rate rotate the budget constraint and cause substitution and income effects. The income effect leads to more leisure (less work) when the wage rate increases. The substitution effect, on the other hand, causes less leisure (more work) when the wage rate increases. As with the savings decision, the substitution and income effects of wage changes work in opposite directions. For consumption, however, they work in the same direction. Thus, while the demand curves for goods and services are downward sloping the supply curves for savings and labour may be upward sloping or backward bending.

3   Table 9.1 summarises the substitution and income effects.

Table 9.1

If the wage rate rises,
The *substitution* effect leads to more work because leisure is more expensive.
The *income* effect leads to less work because the worker is better off and demands more leisure.
If the wage rate falls,
The *substitution* effect leads to less work because leisure is less expensive.
The *income* effect leads to more work because the worker is worse off and demands less leisure.

4   Be sure not to confuse the budget constraint with the labour supply curve. The budget constraint shows the

combinations of leisure and consumption the individual can afford given the wage rate and any nonwage income. The labour supply curve shows the quantity of labor she supplies at each wage rate. As usual, it is important to pay attention to what is measured along each axis.

5   The basic diagram in the second part of this chapter is the two-period budget constraint shown in Figure 9.2. It is important to see how similar this diagram is to the consumer's budget constraint of Chapter 8. There, the trade-off was between consuming different goods. Here, the trade-off involves consuming at different time periods. In each case, the slope is the relative price. When the relative price changes, there are substitution and income effects. Price changes rotate the budget constraint, but income changes bring about a parallel shift. This basic approach will also be used later for the labour supply decision and for other issues throughout the course.

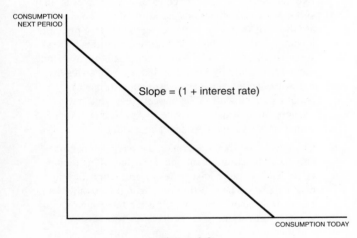

CONSUMPTION NEXT PERIOD

Slope = (1 + interest rate)

CONSUMPTION TODAY

Figure 9.2

6   Think about the slope of the two-period budget constraint. If an individual desires to consume more in the future, he can save today. One pound saved today results in (1 plus the interest rate) pounds of consumption in the future. That is, he can buy $(1 + r)$ pounds of future consumption at an opportunity cost of only 1 pound today. Conversely, when he buys 1 more pound of current consumption, he must give up $(1 + r)$ pounds of future consumption. The relative price of current consumption is, then, 1 plus the interest rate.

7   One plus the interest rate is also the slope of the budget constraint; therefore, only changes in the interest rate can change its slope. If the interest rate rises, the budget constraint becomes steeper. If the interest rate falls, the budget constraint becomes flatter. Income changes, either now or in the future, only shift the budget constraint in a parallel way.

8   Table 9.2 summarises the substitution and income effects.

Table 9.2

If the interest rate rises,
   The *substitution* effect leads to more savings because current consumption is relatively more expensive.
   The *income* effect leads to less savings because the saver is better off and desires to consume more today.
If the interest rate falls,
   The *substitution* effect leads to less savings because current consumption is relatively less expensive.
   The *income* effect leads to more savings because the saver is worse off and desires to consume less today.

SELF-TEST

True or False

1   The percentage change in hours worked resulting from a 1 percent change in the real wage is the elasticity of supply of labour.

2   The income effect of a decrease in wages is to increase the quantity of labour supplied.

3   The substitution effect of a decrease in wages is to increase the quantity of labour supplied.

4   Investment in education is an example of human capital.

5   An increase in nonwage income rotates the budget constraint.

6   An increase in social security benefits leads people, on average, to retire later.

7   The labour force participation of women has increased since World War II.

8   According to human capital theory, education increases the productivity of students, enabling them to earn more in the labour market.

9   The slope of the budget constraint equals the rate of interest.

10   As the interest rate increases, the income effect leads individuals with savings to save less.

11   As the interest rate increases, the substitution effect leads people to save less.

12   As the interest rate increases, the budget constraint shifts out in a parallel way.

13   An increase in social security benefits will increase national savings.

14   When the interest rate changes, the income and substitution effects work in the same direction.

15   A cut in interest taxes matters because people are concerned with the after-tax rate of interest.

Multiple Choice

1   If a person can earn £10 per hour, then the slope of the leisure-consumption budget constraint is

a   1.
b   10.
c   .01.
d   .10.
e   none of the above.

2   If nonwage income increases, the budget constraint

a   rotates, becoming steeper.
b   rotates, becoming flatter.
c   shifts out parallel.
d   shifts in parallel.
e   none of the above.

3   If the wage increases, the budget constraint

a   rotates, becoming steeper.
b   rotates, becoming flatter.
c   shifts out parallel.
d   shifts in parallel.
e   none of the above.

4   An increase in nonwage income will usually lead to

a   a decrease in the quantity of labour supplied through the substitution effect.
b   a decrease in the quantity of labour supplied through the income effect.
c   an increase in the quantity of labour supplied through the substitution effect.
d   an increase in the quantity of labour supplied through the income effect.
e   none of the above.

5   The substitution effect of a wage increase leads to

a   a decrease in the quantity of the labour supplied.
b   an increase in the quantity of the labour supplied.
c   a decrease in leisure.
d   a parallel shift in the budget constraint.
e   *b* and *c*.

6   A decrease in the marginal income tax rate will

a   cause a big increase in the quantity of labour supplied because the income effect is weaker than the substitution effect.
b   cause a big decrease in the quantity of labour supplied because the substitution effect is weaker than the income effect.
c   lead to little change in the quantity of labour supplied.
d   have no effect on the quantity of labour supplied because taxes do not affect the budget constraint.
e   none of the above.

7   Currently in the United Kingdom, the elasticity of female labour supply is

a   higher than the elasticity of male labour supply.
b   lower than the elasticity of male labour supply.
c   equal to the elasticity of male labour supply.
d   perfectly elastic.
e   irrelevant, because few women work.

8   Under a progressive income tax regime, taxing married couples on the basis of their joint income means that the effective tax rate for the secondary earner is

a   higher than for the primary earner.
b   the same as for the primary earner.
c   lower than for the primary earner.
d   irrelevant, because only one spouse works.
e   none of the above.

9   Increased lifetime wealth leads to

a   earlier retirement through the income effect.
b   later retirement through the substitution effect.
c   earlier retirement through the substitution effect.
d   later retirement through the income effect.
e   *a* and *c*.

10   Which of the following is *not* an example of investment in human capital?

a   Formal education
b   On-the-job learning
c   Technical training
d   Plant and equipment
e   None of the above

11   The opportunity costs of attending university do *not* include

a   tuition fees.
b   costs of materials and books.
c   room and board.
d   forgone earnings while attending university and studying.
e   any of the above.

12   Investment in human capital in Britain has

a   significantly increased since 1945.
b   significantly decreased since 1945.
c   stayed constant throughout the postwar period.
d   risen as more people have entered full-time education.
e   *a* and *d*.

13   Using the budget constraint to analyse the savings decision underscores the fact that the individual is really deciding

a   when to consume.
b   what the slope of the budget constraint should be.
c   without knowing what the future will bring.
d   what the interest rate should be.
e   none of the above.

14   The slope of the intertemporal budget constraint

a   equals 1 plus the interest rate.
b   shows the trade-off between consuming now and waiting to consume.
c   indicates the relative price of current and future consumption.
d   all of the above.
e   *a* and *b*.

15   If the interest rate falls, the budget constraint

a   shifts to the left in a parallel way.
b   shifts to the right in a parallel way.
c   rotates, becoming steeper.
d   rotates, becoming flatter.
e   none of the above.

16   If the interest rate falls, the substitution effect

   a   encourages people to consume more in the future, because the relative price of future consumption is less.
   b   increases savings.
   c   decreases savings.
   d   encourages people to consume less in the future, because the relative price of current consumption is lower.
   e   c and d.

17   If the interest rate rises, the income effect for people who are saving

   a   encourages people to consume more in the future, because the relative price of future consumption is less.
   b   leads people to want to consume more both now and in the future.
   c   increases savings.
   d   decreases savings.
   e   b and d.

18   If the interest rate rises, the substitution effect increases life-cycle savings because

   a   the relative price of future consumption is higher.
   b   people are better off and want to consume more today.
   c   the budget constraint rotates, becoming flatter.
   d   people are worse off and want to consume more today.
   e   none of the above.

19   In Britain, as the proportion of people over retirement age has increased relative to the total population,

   a   the National Insurance pension scheme has become increasingly costly.
   b   the National Insurance pension scheme has been allowed to fall relative to wages.
   c   the use of private pension plans and other savings has grown.
   d   all of the above.
   e   none of the above.

20   An increase in the National Insurance pension

   a   reduce national savings.
   b   increase national savings.
   c   have no effect on the national savings rate.
   d   raise savings through the income effect but reduce savings through the substitution effect.
   e   reduce savings through the income effect but increase savings through the substitution effect.

Completion

1   The decision concerning how much labour to supply is a choice between _____ and _____.

2   The slope of the budget line is equal to (minus) the _____.

3   When the nonwage income of an individual decreases, his labour supply _____.

4   The _____ effect of a wage decrease leads individuals to decrease their labour supply.

5   If an individual's labour supply is backward bending, then the _____ effect is stronger.

6   The labour supply of women is usually _____ elastic than the labour supply of men.

7   The relative price of consumption today and consumption tomorrow is 1 plus the _____.

8   If the interest rate increases, the budget constraint for the savings decision becomes _____.

9   The income effect of higher interest rates _____ savings.

10   The effect of an increase in state pensions is to increase _____ and reduce _____.

True or False

1	T	4	T	7	T	10	T	13	F
2	T	5	F	8	T	11	F	14	F
3	F	6	F	9	F	12	F	15	T

Multiple Choice

1	b	6	c	11	c	16	e
2	c	7	a	12	e	17	e
3	a	8	a	13	a	18	e
4	b	9	a	14	d	19	d
5	e	10	d	15	d	20	a

Completion

1   leisure, consumption
2   wage
3   increases
4   substitution
5   income
6   more
7   interest rate
8   steeper
9   reduces
10   consumption, savings

Tools and Practice Problems

LABOUR SUPPLY

The most important model in the first part of this chapter is the opportunity set for the labour supply decision: the leisure-consumption budget constraint. In this section, we first review how to construct the budget constraint. We then see how the budget constraint changes when the wage rate or non-wage income changes. As in Chapter 8, the substitution and income effects of wage changes can be illustrated using the budget constraint. Finally, there are some applications.

THE LEISURE-CONSUMPTION BUDGET CONSTRAINT

We work in order to earn money for consumption, but we give up time that could be used for leisure. Economists see the labour supply decision as involving a trade-off between leisure and consumption. The basic tool for analysing labour supply is the budget constraint. Tool Kit 9.1 shows how to construct the leisure-consumption budget constraint.

Tool Kit 9.1 Plotting the Leisure-Consumption Budget Constraint

The budget constraint shows what combinations of leisure and consumption can be afforded given the wage rate and the amount of nonwage income. To plot the budget constraint, follow this five-step procedure.

Step one: Draw a set of coordinate axes. Label the horizontal axis as the quantity of leisure consumed and the vertical axis as the consumption level.

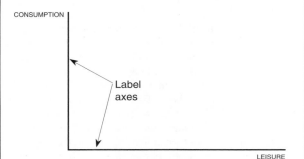

Step two: If an individual chooses to do no work, leisure equals the total time available, and consumption is equal to the nonwage income. Plot this point.

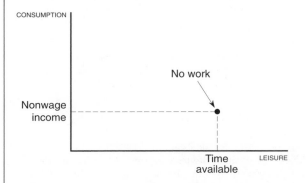

Step three: Calculate the maximum earnings if the individual consumes no leisure. Add this amount to the nonwage income, and plot this quantity along the vertical axis.

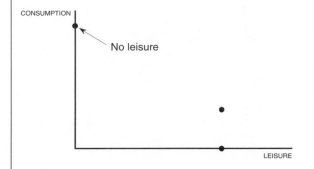

Step four: Draw a line segment connecting the two points. This line segment is the leisure-consumption budget constraint.

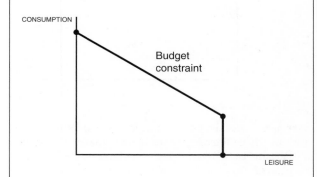

Step five: Verify that the slope of the budget constraint is (minus) the wage rate.

---

1 (Worked problem: leisure-consumption budget constraint) In his spare time, Mike, a student at Big City University, referees varsity football matches. Each game pays £7, and if he could stand the abuse, Mike could referee as many as 60 each month. On average, each game takes 1 hour. This is not Mike's only source of income; each month his parents send him £200 for maintenance.

  a Construct Mike's budget constraint.
  b Suppose that Mike chooses to referee 20 matches. Label his chosen alternative, and indicate his total income, income from refereeing, hours worked, and leisure.

Step-by-step solution

Step one (a): Draw the two axes, and label the vertical one "Consumption" and the horizontal one "Leisure."

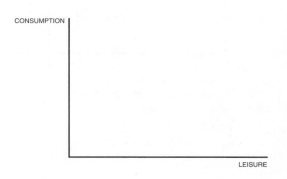

Step two: Plot the no-work consumption point. If Mike referees no matches, he consumes all 60 hours as leisure. This leaves him £200 (from his parents) for consumption. Plot this point.

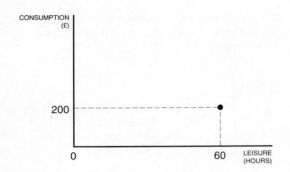

Step three: Calculate total income if Mike works all the time available. If he referees the maximum number of matches, 60, he earns £420 from refereeing and retains the £200 from his parents. This leaves him with £620 for consumption but no time for leisure. Plot this point.

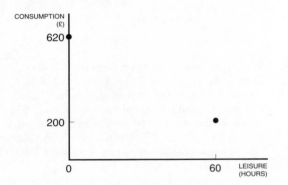

Step four: Draw a line segment between the two plotted points. This is the budget constraint.

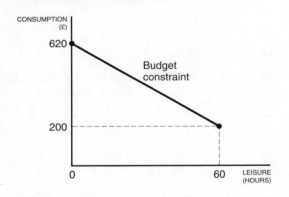

Step five: The slope of the budget constraint is (620 − 200)/60 = 7, which is the wage.

Step six (b): If Mike referees 20 matches, then he is left with 40 hours of leisure, and he earns £140 in wage income for a total of £340. Plot the point, and label it appropriately.

2   (Practice problem: leisure-consumption budget constraint) University professors can earn extra cash by reviewing papers for journals. Editors pay around £50 per paper for an academic opinion about whether it should be accepted for publication. Reviewing a paper takes 1 hour. Professor Cavendish has 15 hours available each month for outside work such as reviewing.

He earns £3,000 monthly from Brunswick University, and that is his only other source of income.

a   Plot Cavendish's budget constraint.
b   Suppose that he reviews 6 papers in March. Plot and label his chosen alternative.

3   (Practice problem: leisure-consumption budget constraint) For each of the following, draw a budget constraint. Also, choose a point along the budget constraint, and show the corresponding amount of leisure, work, nonwage income, and wage income.

	Wage	Total time	Nonwage income
a	£25/hour	80 hours	£ 1,000
b	£200/day	30 days	£ 0
c	£1,000/week	50 weeks	£15,000
d	£5/hour	100 hours	£ 0

4   (Worked problem: leisure-consumption budget constraint) When either nonwage income or the wage rate changes, the budget constraint moves. The basic technique here is to draw the budget constraint using the original nonwage income and wage rate, following the procedure shown above. Then draw a new budget constraint using the new nonwage income and wage rate. Compare the two budget constraints, and verify that the shift is parallel when nonwage income changes, but the budget constraint rotates when the wage rate changes. Art supplements his pension by repairing cash dispencing machines. Each service call takes 1 hour, and he receives £50 per call. His pension and other nonwage income is £200 per week. Art has 30 hours available and can work as much as he likes.

a   Plot Art's budget constraint.
b   His pension fund has done well with its investments and increases Art's nonwage income to £300. Plot his new budget constraint.
c   How will Art change his work effort?

Step-by-step solution

Step one (a): Plot his budget constraint in the usual way. If he consumes all 30 hours as leisure, Art can consume £200. If he works all 30 hours, he can consume £200 + (£50 × 30) = £1,700. Note that the slope is (1,700 − 200)/30 = 50, which is the wage.

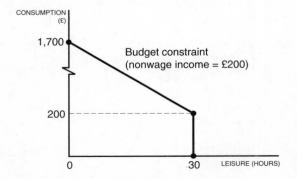

Step two (b): Plot his budget constraint with nonwage income equal to £300. His nonwork consumption is now £300 + (30 × £50) = £1,800 if he works all of the available time. Note that the nonwage income increase brings about a parallel shift.

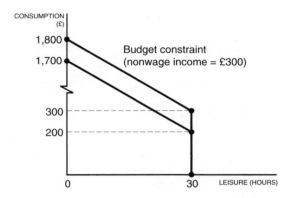

Step three (c): The change in the budget constraint is an income effect. The income effect reduces work effort when income rises. Art will work less.

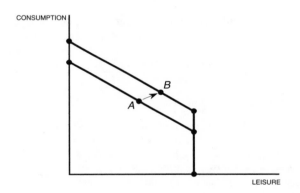

5   (Practice problem: leisure-consumption budget constraint) Liza's job as a broker requires making unsolicited, or "cold," calls to potential clients in an attempt to persuade them to put their portfolio in her hands. On average, cold calls earn Liza £10 each. She can make 4 per hour, and she can work as much as 80 hours per week. Her basic salary (nonwage income) is £100 per week.

   a   Plot her budget constraint.
   b   Suppose that the firm offers her an increase in her basic salary to £150 per week. Plot her new budget constraint.
   c   Will Liza make more or fewer cold calls? Why?

6   (Practice problem: leisure-consumption budget constraint) Sara is offered a position as a tour guide for a local museum. She can conduct 2 tours per hour and earn £10 each. She has no nonwage income, but she must pay 25 percent of her salary in tax. The museum will allow her to work as much as 20 hours each week.

   a   Plot her budget constraint.
   b   The tax rate is reduced to 20 percent. Plot her budget constraint.

7   (Practice problem: leisure-consumption budget constraint) Theodore tutors some of his fellow students in economics for £10 per hour. He also receives £2,000 for maintenance per term from his scholarship. He can work as much as 100 hours per term.

   a   Plot his budget constraint.
   b   Students realise that there is a plethora of semi-intelligent postgraduate students who will tutor for less pay. Theodore now only receives £8 per hour. Plot his new budget constraint.

8   (Practice problem: leisure-consumption budget constraint) For each of the following, plot the budget constraint before and after the change.

   a   Nonwage income = £100; wage = £20 hour; total time available = 40 hours; nonwage income changes to £0.
   b   Nonwage income = £0; wage = £500 per week; total time available = 52 weeks; wage changes to £300/week.
   c   Nonwage income = £10,000; wage = £40 per hour; total time available = 50 hours; available time increases to 60 hours.
   d   Nonwage income = £500; wage = £200 per week; total time available = 52 weeks; wage changes to £400 per week.

SUBSTITUTION AND INCOME EFFECTS

As in the case of Chapter 8's budget constraint, price changes cause two kinds of effects: substitution and income. When the wage increases, the substitution effects motivate households to supply more labour, but the income effects indicate that they supply less labour. These concepts show how the labour supply curve can bend backwards. Tool Kit 9.2 uses the budget constraint to distinguish between substitution and income effects.

Tool Kit 9.2 Distinguishing between Substitution and Income Effects of Wage Changes

When the wage rate changes, there are two effects: substitution and income. These can be illustrated using the leisure-consumption budget constraint. This technique clarifies the fact that, as in the case of savings, the substitution and income effects work in opposite directions.

Step one: Draw the budget line with the original wage.

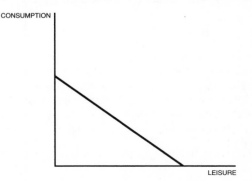

Step two: Find the chosen point along this budget line. Label this point *A*.

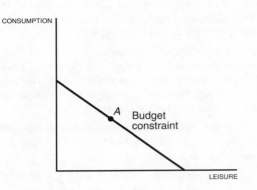

Step three: Draw the budget line with the new wage.

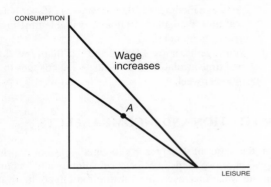

Step four: Draw a dotted line segment through point *A* and parallel to the *new* budget line.

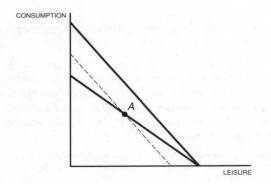

Step five: Darken the portion of the dotted line segment that lies above the original budget line. The points along this darkened segment represent the new alternatives made possible by the substitution effect of the wage change. The income effect shifts this line parallel out to the new budget line drawn in step three.

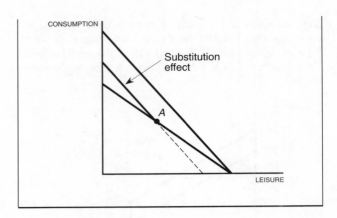

9   (Worked problem: wage changes/applications) John currently works 45 hours per week tuning pianos at a wage of £20 per hour. This is his only income. He is offered a raise to £30 per hour. He has 80 hours available for work each week.

a   Draw his budget constraint at £20 per hour. Label his chosen alternative along this budget line.
b   Draw his budget constraint at £30 per hour.
c   Show the substitution effect of the wage increase. Why must the substitution effect lead John to work no less at the new, higher wage?

Step-by-step solution

Step one (a): Draw the budget constraint at the original wage. We label the horizontal axis "Leisure" and the vertical axis "Consumption." If John does not work, he has 80 hours of leisure and no consumption. If he works all 80 hours (leisure = 0), he consumes £1,600. Draw John's budget constraint connecting the two points.

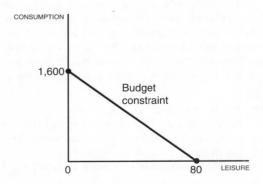

Step two: Find the chosen point along this budget line. John chooses $80 - 45 = 35$ hours of leisure, which give him $45 \times £20 = £900$. Label this point *A*, and note that it does lie along the budget constraint.

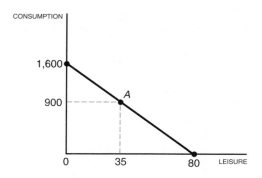

Step three (b): Draw the budget constraint when the wage is £30. The no-work alternative still offers consumption equal to £0, but now if John works the 80 hours available, he consumes £30 × 80 = £2,400. Plot and connect the two endpoints.

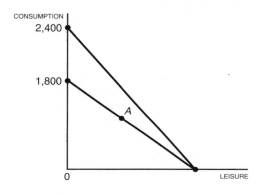

Step four (c): Draw a dotted line parallel to the £30 budget constraint through point *A*.

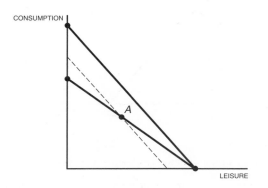

Step five: Darken the portion that lies above the budget constraint drawn in step one. These are the alternatives made possible by the substitution effect of the wage increase. All of these points involve more work than at point *A*, the alternative chosen when the wage is £20.

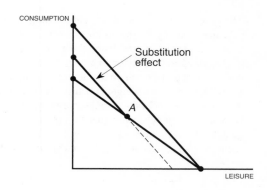

10   (Practice problem: applications) Arna loves her job as a design consultant. She can earn £60 per hour and has been able to work as much as she likes up to 50 hours per week. She has no nonwage income. She is currently working 15 hours per week.

  a   Plot her budget constraint. Find her chosen alternative, and label the point *A*.
  b   A new income tax of 10 percent is passed. Arna now takes home only £54 per hour. Plot her new budget constraint.
  c   Show the substitution effect of the wage decrease.

11   (Practice problem: substitution and income effects) For each of the following, draw the budget constraint with the wage in the first column and a new budget line with the wage in the second column. Pick an alternative along the first budget constraint, and show the substitution effect. There is no nonwage income.

	Old wage	New wage	Total time
a	£25/hour	£ 50/hour	80 hours
b	£200/day	£ 100/day	30 days
c	£1,000/week	£1,500/week	50 weeks
d	£5/hour	£ 4/hour	100 hours

APPLICATIONS OF THE LEISURE-CONSUMPTION BUDGET CONSTRAINT

The following applications use the leisure-consumption budget constraint. We analyse social security benefits, overtime pay, and even divorce arrangements. The basic technique is to draw the budget constraint without the policy in question, draw another budget constraint with the policy in place, and compare the two using substitution and income effects.

12   The social security system provides benefit payments to the unemployed and those on low income. Unemployed workers receive £100 per week in unemployment benefit, and those on low income can receive up to £100 per week in income support but any earnings are deducted *pro rata*. For example, someone earning £60 per week would only receive £40 in income support. The minimum wage for those in work is £4 per hour and the maximum working week is 80 hours.

  a   Draw the budget constraint for a social security claimant.

b   The government is considering substituting an employment subsidy for the social security system. Under the employment subsidy the government pays nothing to those who do not work and 50 pence per pound earned up to a total payment of £100. Draw the new budget constraint and compare it with the one under the social security system.

c   Do you think the government's employment subsidy proposal is an improvement on the social security system? What other factors are involved?

Step-by-step solution

Step one (a): Draw a set of axes labeled "Leisure (hours)" and "Consumption (£)." If the claimant does no work, she consumes £100. Plot this point, and label it *A*.

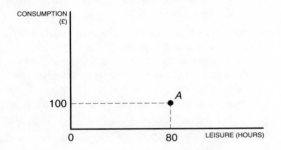

Step two: If the recipient earns £100, she loses all of her benefits and still consumes £100. At £4 per hour, £100 is earned in £100/£4 = 25 hours, which leaves 80 − 25 = 55 hours of leisure. Plot the point (100, 55). Label this point *B*.

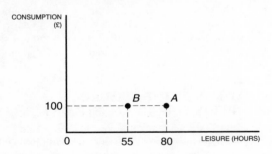

Step three: If the recipient works all 80 hours, she consumes £4 × 80 = £320. Plot this point, and label it *C*.

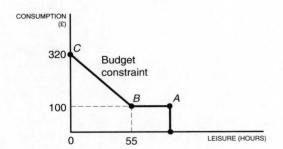

Step four: Draw line segments connecting points *A* and *B* and points *B* and *C*. This is the budget constraint under the social security system.

Step five (b): With the employment subsidy, if the person works no hours, he consumes nothing. Plot the point (0, 80). Label it *D*.

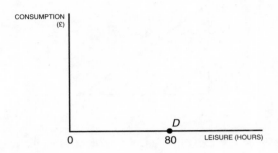

Step six: If the person earns £200, he receives the maximum subsidy, which is £100. The total consumption is then £300. To earn £200 (and consume £300) takes £200/£4 = 50 hours of work, leaving 80 − 50 = 30 hours of leisure. Plot the point (300, 30), and label it *E*.

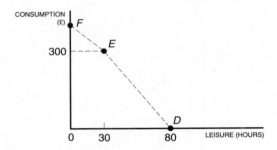

Step seven: If the person works all 80 hours, he consumes £100 + (80 × £4) = £420. Plot the point (420, 0), and label it *F*.

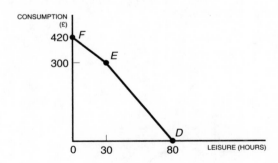

Step eight: Draw line segments connecting *DEF*. This is the budget constraint with the employment subsidy.

13   (Practice problem: applications) The management at Acme Manufacturing is disturbed that although the typical factory worker is required to work 250 days each year, most only work 230. It proposes a £100 bonus for any employee who works more than 240 days each year. The wage of the typical factory worker is £120 per day.

a   Draw the budget constraint without the attendance bonus.

b   Draw the budget constraint with the attendance

bonus. How is attendance likely to change for the typical factory worker?

c   Suppose that the company simply gives each worker $100. How is the opportunity set different from the one with the attendance bonus?

d   Under which scheme will the typical worker work more? Why?

14   (Practice problem: applications) The Quantity Bakery Company has paid its workers £6 per hour to make doughnuts, cakes, and pies. There are always sweets to make, and the workers can work as many hours as they choose up to 80 hours per week. Recently, the company union won a new contract that keeps the wage at the same level but now allows for overtime pay of "time and a half" for any hours worked in excess of 40 per week.

a   Draw the budget constraint under the old contract with no provision for overtime pay.

b   Draw the budget constraint with the overtime pay.

c   What is likely to happen to the number of hours that Quantity Bakery workers work under the new contract? Explain.

15   Under the current tax regime, earnings below £20,000 are taxed at 15 percent. Any earnings above £20,000 incur a 28 percent tax rate. Linda Weale, a freelance journalist, earns £800 per week and has 50 weeks per year available for work.

a   Draw her budget constraint if she pays no taxes.

b   Draw her budget constraint under the schedule described above. How do progressive income taxes shape the budget constraint.

16   (Practice problem: applications) Harry Gold makes £5,000 by working 20 days each month as a solicitor. His wage is £250 per day, and he can work as many as 30 days each month (except February, of course). The income tax rate for Harry is 20 percent. Also, he pays £1,000 monthly in National Insurance contributions. His nonwage income is £4,000 per month. (Hint: Review the solutions to problems 15 and 16 of Chapter 8.)

a   What is Harry's net wage after tax and National Insurance contributions?

b   Draw his budget constraint.

c   The government considers eliminating income tax and increasing National Insurance. Harry figures that his National Insurance contributions will rise to £2,000. Draw his budget constraint under the proposed tax changes.

d   Will Harry work more or less under the new proposals? Why?

e   Is Harry better off under the new tax proposals? Why or why not?

17   (Practice problem: applications) After 10 miserable years, John and Norma Bennet are getting a divorce. They have agreed that Norma will have custody of their two children. John makes £50 per hour from his job as a marriage counselor, and this is his only income. Although he could work as many as 40 hours, he currently only works 20 hours per week. The court has ruled that he must pay £250 per week in child support regardless of his earnings. (Hint: Review the solutions to problems 15 and 16 of Chapter 8.)

a   Draw John's (postdivorce) leisure-consumption budget constraint.

b   Suppose the government passes a law that requires noncustodial parents to pay 25 percent of their income per child. Draw John's budget line for this child care payment.

c   Under which plan will John work more? Why?

SAVINGS

Now we turn to the saver's opportunity set: the two-period budget constraint. Given the wealth or income of the household and the interest rate, we can construct the two-period budget constraint. We see how the budget constraint is altered when income (either present or future) and interest rates change. We show the substitution and income effects by using the rotation and shift technique introduced in the last chapter. Finally, we learn some applications: different borrowing and lending interest rates, individual retirement, tax exempt savings accounts, and how social security benefits affect savings.

The Two-Period Budget Constraint

When we save money, we forgo current consumption in order to increase consumption at some later date. The trade-off involves current and future consumption. Tool Kit 9.3 shows how to plot the two-period budget constraint, which is the economist's basic tool for analysing savings.

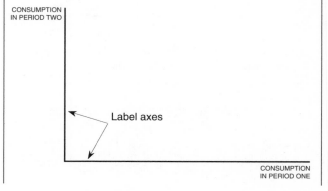

Tool Kit 9.3 Plotting the Two-Period Budget Constraint

The two-period budget constraint shows which combinations of consumption in each period are possible, given the income and interest rate. Follow the steps.

Step one: Draw a set of coordinate axes. Label the horizontal axis "Consumption in period one" and the vertical axis "Consumption in period two."

CONSUMPTION IN PERIOD TWO

Label axes

CONSUMPTION IN PERIOD ONE

Step two: Calculate the maximum possible consumption in period one. (This quantity is the present discounted value of income.) Plot this quantity along the horizontal axis.

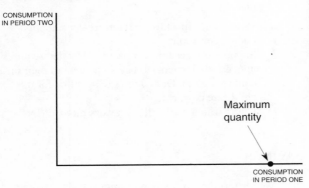

Step three: Calculate the maximum possible consumption in period two. (This quantity is the future value of income.) Plot this quantity along the vertical axis.

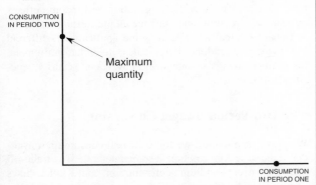

Step four: Draw a line segment connecting the two points. This line segment is the two-period budget constraint.

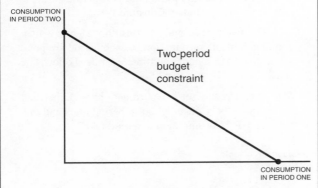

Step five: Verify that the slope of the budget constraint is (minus) $1 + r$, where r is the interest rate.

18 (Worked problem: two-period budget constraint) Patricia won the lottery! It is only £5,000, but that seems a lot to someone earning £18,000 per year. Her interest rate is 6 percent, and the capital market is perfect. Plot her two-period budget constraint.

Step-by-step solution

Step one: Draw coordinate axes, labeling the horizontal axis "Consumption now" and the vertical axis "Consumption next year."

Step two: The maximum consumption today is the present discounted value of all income. Make the following table, and compute and plot the amount along the horizontal axis.

Year	Income	Discount factor	Present discounted value
Now	£23,000	1	£23,000
Next year	£18,000	1/(1.06)	£16,980

Present discounted value = £39,980.

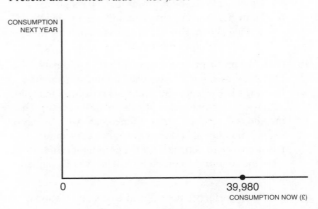

Step three: The maximum consumption next year is

$$£23,000 \, (1 + .06) + £18,000 = £42,380.$$

Plot this point.

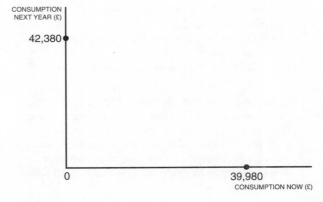

Step four: Draw a line segment connecting the two points.

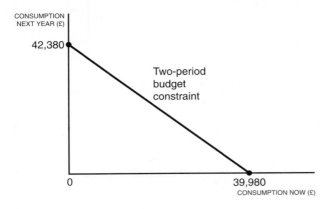

Step five: Verify that the slope equals 1 plus the interest rate. It is $42,380/39,980 = 1.06 = 1 + r$.

19 (Practice problem: two-period budget constraint) Current income is £40,000. Retirement income is £15,000. The interest rate for the period between now and retirement is 150 percent. Plot the two-period budget constraint.

20 (Practice problem: two-period budget constraint) Plot the two-period budget constraints for the following.

	Interest rate	Present income	Future income
a	100%	£100,000	£ 25,000
b	50%	£ 40,000	£ 10,000
c	250%	£ 20,000	£ 0
d	80%	£ 0	£150,000

21 (Worked problem: two-period budget constraint) When the interest rate, current income, or future income changes, the two-period budget constraint moves. The basic technique here is to draw the two-period budget constraint using the original income and interest rate, and then draw a new two-period budget constraint using the new incomes and interest rate. Compare the two budget constraints and verify that the shift is parallel when either current or future income changes, but the budget constraint rotates when the interest rate changes. Michael is earning £25,000 as a secretary and expects to earn the same in the future. His interest rate is 5 percent.

a   Plot his two-period budget constraint.
b   He learns that his aunt is sick and has one year to live. She plans to leave him £50,000. Plot his two-period budget constraint.

Step-by-step solution

Step one (a): Follow the procedure to plot the two-period budget constraint. The slope is $1 + r = 1.05$, and it passes through the point £25,000 now and £25,000 next year.

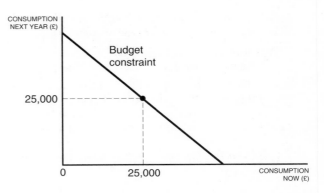

Step two (b): Plot the new budget constraint. Because the interest rate is the same, the slope does not change. The new budget constraint passes through the point £25,000 now and £75,000 next year.

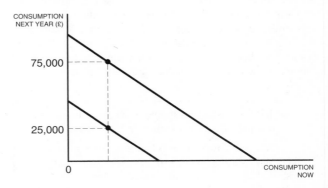

22 (Practice problem: two-period budget constraint) Boris currently takes home £45,000 as a skilled lathe operator. His union contract guarantees him the same salary next year. The credit union at the factory pays 8 percent interest.

a   Plot his two-period budget constraint.
b   Boris's employer is experiencing low profits this year. He proposes that Boris accept £35,000 this year and £55,000 next year. Plot his two-period budget constraint. Does the offer shift the budget constraint? How?

23 (Practice problem: two-period budget constraint) Monica plans to retire in 20 years. She now takes home £40,000 and expects £20,000 in retirement income. The interest rate for the 20 years is 180 percent.

a   Plot her budget constraint.
b   A new broker promises her a 20-year return of 250 percent. She believes him. Plot her new budget constraint.

24 (Practice problem: two-period budget constraint) The Coddingtons now take home £375,000 per year, but they have no retirement income planned. Their portfolio will earn them 100 percent over the 12 years left until retirement.

a   Plot their budget constraint.
b   Tax increases reduce their after-tax return to 60 percent. Plot their new budget constraint.

25   (Practice problem: two-period budget constraint) Plot the budget constraints before and after the change.

	Current income	Future income	Interest rate	Change
a	£100,000	£ 0	40%	Interest rate = 60%
b	£100,000	£ 0	40%	Future income = £100,000
c	£ 0	£50,000	10%	Current income = £25,000
d	£ 60,000	£80,000	50%	Interest rate = 20%

SUBSTITUTION AND INCOME EFFECTS

As in the case of the other budget constraints that you have studied, price changes cause two kinds of effects: substitution and income. When the interest rate increases, the substitution effects motivate households to save more, but the income effects indicate that they save less. These concepts show why the supply curve of savings may bend backwards. Tool Kit 9.4 uses the budget constraint to distinguish between substitution and income effects of changes in interest rates.

Tool Kit 9.4 Distinguishing between Substitution and Income Effects of Changes in Interest Rates

When the interest rate changes, there are two effects: substitution and income. These effects can be illustrated by using the two-period budget constraint. Follow this procedure.

Step one: Draw the two-period budget line with the original interest rate.

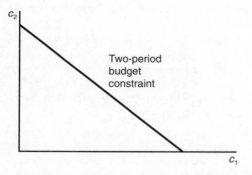

Step two: Find the chosen current and future consumption level along this budget line. Label this point A.

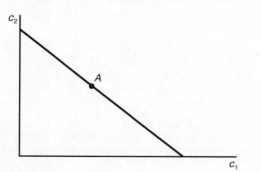

Step three: Draw the two-period budget line with the new interest rate.

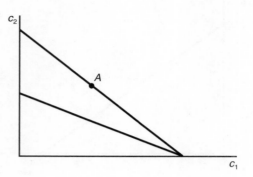

Step four: Draw a dotted line segment through point A and parallel to the *new* budget line.

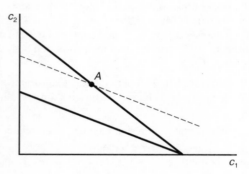

Step five: Darken the portion of the dotted line segment that lies above the original budget line. The points along this darkened segment represent the quantities made possible by the substitution effect of the interest rate change. The income effect shifts this line out in a parallel way to the new budget line drawn in step three.

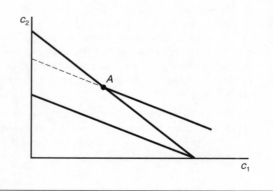

26   (Worked problem: substitution and income effects) Show the substitution and income effects of the change in the rate of return for Monica's portfolio in problem 23. She is currently saving £5,000 per year.

Step-by-step solution

Step one: Draw the two-period budget constraint with the interest rate equal to 180 percent. It must pass through the point (£40,000, £20,000).

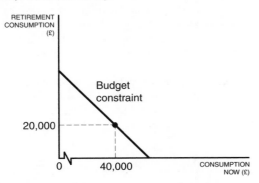

Step two: Label Monica's current consumption (£40,000 − £5,000 = £35,000) point *A*.

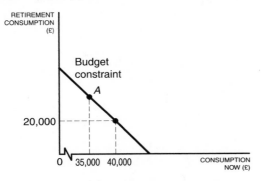

Step three: Draw the two-period budget constraint with the interest rate equal to 250 percent. It also must pass through the point (£40,000, £20,000).

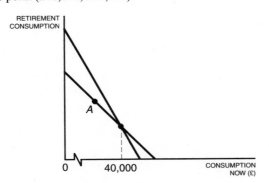

Step four: Draw a dotted line with a slope of 1 + 2.50 = 3.50 through *A*.

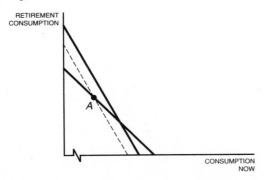

Step five: Darken the portion of the dotted line that lies above the original budget constraint drawn in step one. These are the alternatives made possible by the substitution effect of the interest rate change. All of these involve more savings; thus, the substitution effect of an increase in the interest rate is an increase in savings. The income effect shifts this darkened line segment out parallel to the budget constraint drawn in step two and reduces savings.

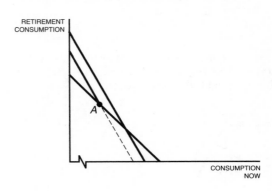

27 (Practice problem: substitution and income effects) Show the substitution and income effects for the change in the Coddingtons' after-tax interest rate in problem 24. Currently they have no savings.

28 (Practice problem: substitution and income effects) Show the substitution and income effects for parts *a* through *d* in problem 25. In each case, savings equal £10,000 before the interest rate changes.

APPLICATION OF THE TWO-PERIOD BUDGET CONSTRAINT

The following applications show how the two-period budget constraint can be used to analyze imperfect capital markets, social security, and government policies that affect savings incentives. Again, the procedure is to draw budget constraints with and without the feature of interest and compare them using substitution and income effects.

29 (Worked problem: applications) If the capital market were perfect, then the interest rates for borrowing and lending would be the same. The rates for borrowing, however, are higher. David and Maria take home £40,000 each year. They can earn 4 percent on any savings, but they must borrow at 14 percent. Plot their two-period budget constraint.

Step-by-step solution

This is an application of the opportunity set with multiple constraints introduced in Chapter 2.

Step one: Plot the budget constraint with the 4 percent interest rate. The slope is 1.04, and it passes through the point £40,000 now and £40,000 next year.

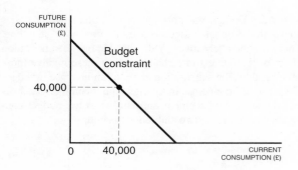

Step two: Plot the budget constraint with the 14 percent interest rate. The slope is 1.04, and it passes through the point £40,000 now and £40,000 next year.

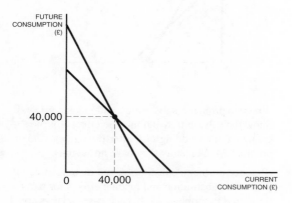

Step three: Darken the portion of each budget constraint that lies under the other constraint.

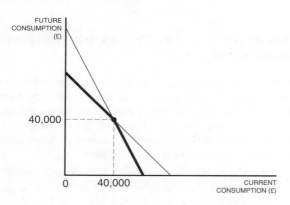

30   (Practice problem: applications) Bob takes home £20,000 this year, but he anticipates taking home £30,000 next year. He can earn 8 percent on savings, but he has a poor credit rating and must pay 19 percent to borrow. Plot his two-period budget constraint.

31   (Worked problem: applications) Concern about low savings rates has prompted a number of proposals for tax-exempt savings accounts. The Davidsons take home £100,000 per year after taxes. David, their son, will enter university in three years. The Davidsons can earn a 25 percent real rate of return before taxes over the three-year period.

a   Draw their two-period budget constraint.
b   The Davidsons face a 40 percent marginal tax rate. Draw their budget constraint with the tax on interest. (Hint: What is their after-tax real rate of return on savings?)
c   A new savings account is proposed that offers parents an opportunity to deposit up to £3,000 in a special tax-exempt account. Draw their two-period budget constraint if the plan becomes law.
d   Before the plan, the Davidsons were saving £3,500 each year. Use the concepts of substitution and income effects to explain how their savings will be affected by the savings account.

Step-by-step solution

Step one (a): Plot the two-period budget constraint. The slope is $1 + 0.25 = 1.25$, and the budget constraint must pass through the point where current and future income are each £100,000.

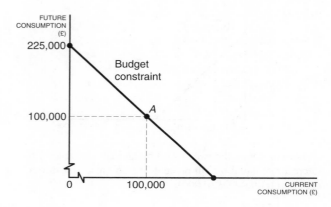

Step two (b): Plot the two-period budget constraint with the tax on interest. Taxes take 40 percent of the interest, so their after-tax interest rate for the three years is 15 percent. The slope is now 1.15. Interest taxes make the budget constraint flatter.

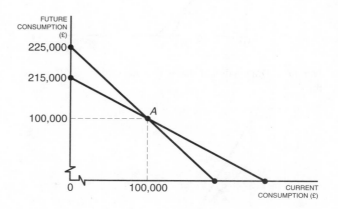

Step three (c): The savings account allows the Davidsons to save along the tax-free budget constraint, where the slope is 1.25 until their savings reach £3,000. At that point (*B*), there is a kink, and the slope of the budget constraint returns to the flatter after-tax slope of 1.15.

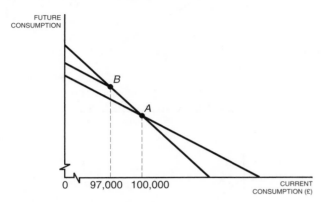

Step four (d): Since the Davidsons save more than £3,000, the account will have only an income effect. The account will not change their after-tax marginal rate of return, because only the first £3,000 of savings is tax exempt.

32 (Practice problem: applications) The Reeds do not know where they will find the money to send their children to university in five years. They make £26,000 per year and have been unable to save. Their marginal tax rate is 20 percent, and they could earn 40 percent interest on savings over the five-year period.

    a   Plot the Reeds' two-period budget constraint, ignoring the tax on interest.

    b   Plot their two-period budget constraint, including the tax on interest.

    c   Plot their two-period budget constraint under the tax-exempt savings account spelled out in problem 31.

    d   Use the concepts of substitution and income effects to explain how their savings will be affected by the tax-exempt savings account.

33 (Worked problem: applications) National Insurance reduces the incentives that individuals have to save for retirement. Melissa is already fantasizing about retirement, even though it is forty years away. She estimates that a dollar deposited today will return £3.50 in interest when she retires. She currently takes home £25,000 after paying taxes, including £3,250 annually in National Insurance contributions, and expects to draw a national insurance pension of £14,625. Although she is thinking about retirement, Melissa has no savings.

    a   Calculate the present discounted value of Melissa's National Insurance pension.

    b   Draw her two-period budget constraint, and label her levels of consumption now and in the future.

    c   Suppose that the entire National Insurance contributions system is eliminated. Draw her two-period budget constraint.

    d   How much does Melissa save?

Step-by-step solution

Step one (a): The present discounted value of her National Insurance pension is £14,625/(1 + r) = £3,250, which is exactly her National Insurance contribution.

Step two (b): Draw Melissa's two-period budget constraint. Label the axes "Current consumption (£)" and "Consumption 40 years in the future (£)." The slope is 1 + r, and the interest rate for the forty-year period is 350 percent. Also, the budget constraint must pass through her current choice: £25,000 now and £14,625 in forty years.

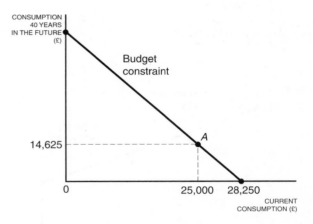

Step three (c): Eliminating the National Insurance pension reduces her future income to £0, but because she no longer pays National Insurance contributions, her current after-tax income rises to £28,250. Because the present discounted value of her two-period income does not change, the budget constraint does not change. (In general, the National Insurance system shifts the budget constraint out for low-income people and shifts it in for high-income people.)

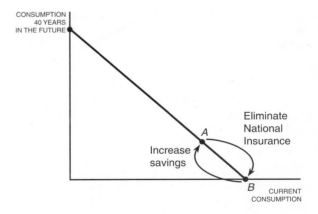

Step four (d): Because Melissa has the same budget constraint, she chooses the same point. This means that she must save £3,250 (which returns £14,625 in forty years), which is exactly the amount she now pays in National Insurance. Eliminating National Insurance would (for Melissa) lead to the same consumption but greater national savings.

34 (Practice problem: applications) Melissa's uncle is only ten years from retirement. He can expect to re-

ceive £1 in interest for every £1 saved for retirement. He takes home £50,000 annually, saves £10,000, and expects a National Insurance pension of £20,000 when he retires.

a   Plot his two-period budget constraint.
b   Suppose that the government increases state pensions by 50 percent. National Insurance contributions also rise, so that the budget constraint of Melissa's uncle does not change. How will his earnings change? How will his consumption now and during retirement change?

Answers to Problems

2

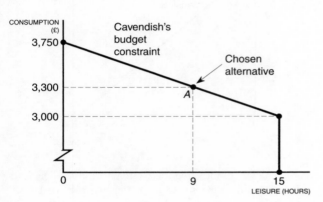

3   *a*

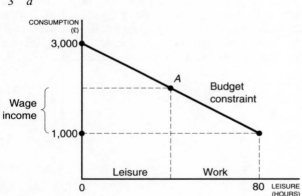

b

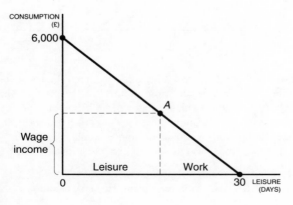

c

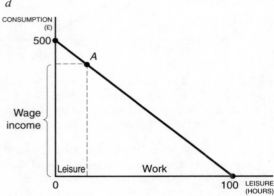

d

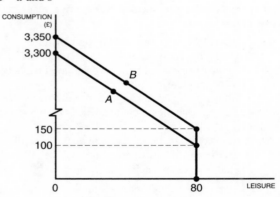

5   *a* and *b*

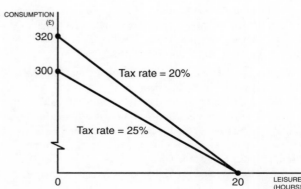

c   Liza will make fewer cold calls; she will consume more leisure when her income increases, as shown by the movement from point *A* to point *B*.

6

7

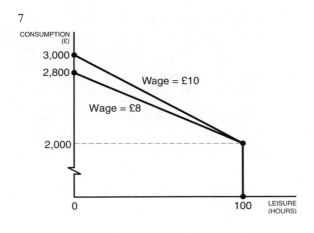

8   *a*

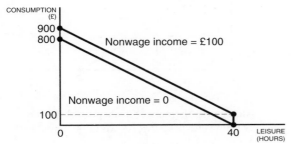

b

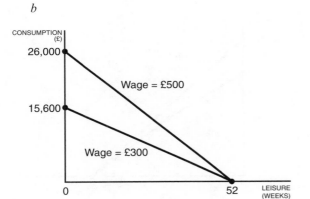

c

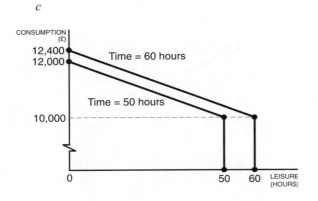

d

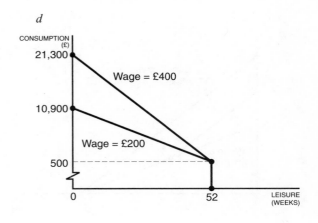

10

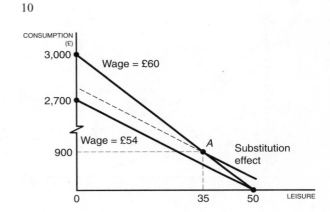

11   *a*

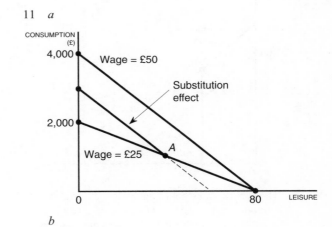

b

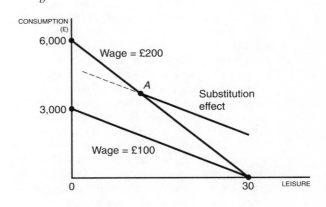

c

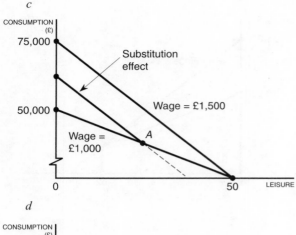

d

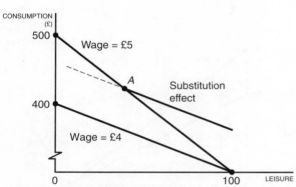

13   *a, b,* and *c*

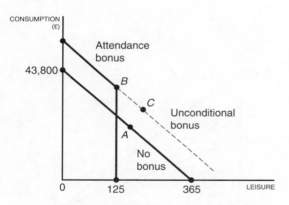

a   The vertical intercept of the budget constraint
without bonus is £43,800 (maximum income at-
tainable if a worker works 365 days at a daily wage
of £120). The horizontal intercept is 365 days. The
budget constraint without attendance bonus joins
these two points.

b   The attendance bonus shifts the budget constraint
up in a parallel way when workers work more than
240 days per year (equivalent to 125 days leisure).
For points to the right of 125 days leisure, the old
budget constraint applies. The typical factory worker is likely to increase the number of days worked.

c   The budget constraint for an unconditional bonus
is shown by an upward parallel shift in the budget
contraint regardless of days worked. It includes the
dotted segment that is unattainable under the attendance bonus. It increases the opportunity set.

d   An unconditional bonus of £100 simply shifts the
budget constraint up in a parallel way, causing an
income effect. The typical worker consumes more
leisure at point *C*. The attendance bonus does not
offer the points along the dashed budget constraint. Point *B* or another point involving even
more work will be chosen. Clearly, there is a
greater incentive to work with the attendance
bonus.

14   *a* and *b*

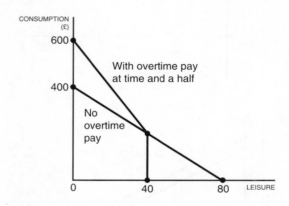

c   All the new alternatives made possible by the
overtime provision involve working more than 40
hours. Work time probably will increase.

15   *a* and *b*

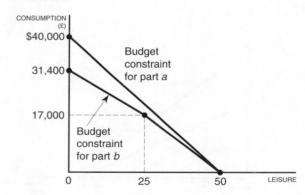

16

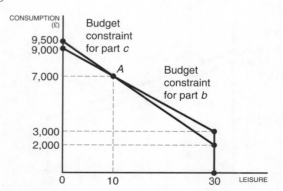

a   £200/day.

d   He will work more because the tax change offers
him new alternatives with more work. In effect it

leaves him with the substitution effect's of a wage
increase, with the income effect's being canceled
by the property tax increase.

e   He is better off because he can continue to
choose point *A*, but he also has some new
alternatives.

17

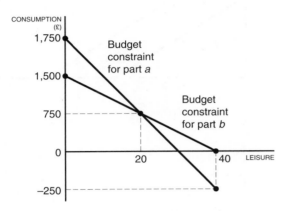

c   John will likely work more under the lump-sum
child care requirement. The other system leaves
him with the substitution effect of a wage decrease.

19   *a*

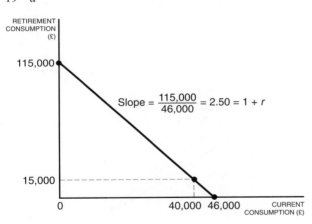

20

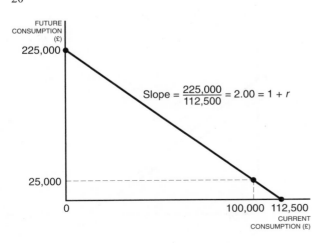

b

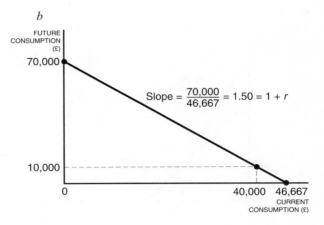

c

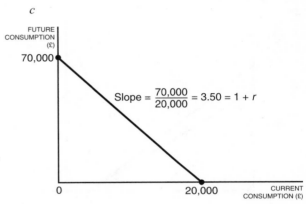

d

22

23

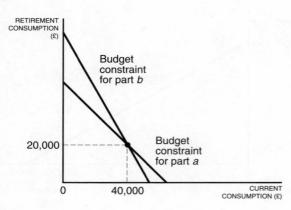

c

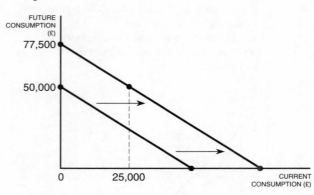

24

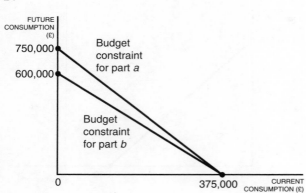

d

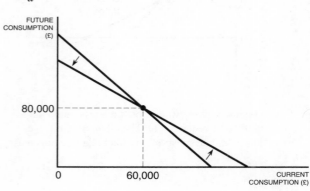

25   *a*

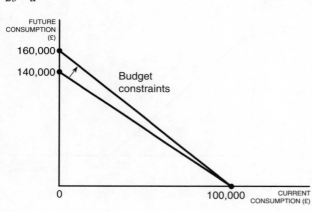

27

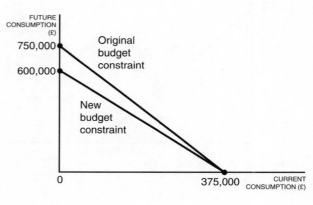

b

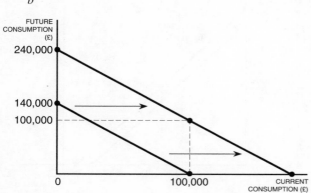

28   *a*

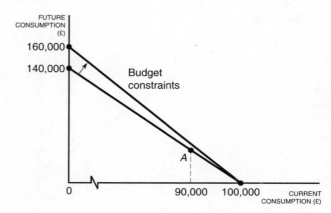

b

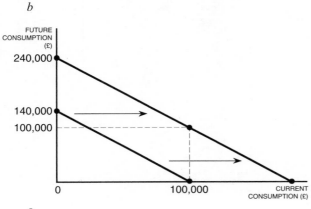

c

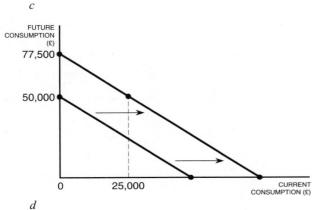

d

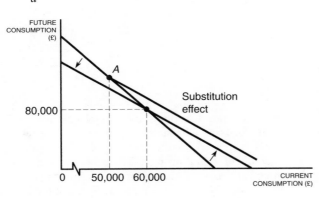

30

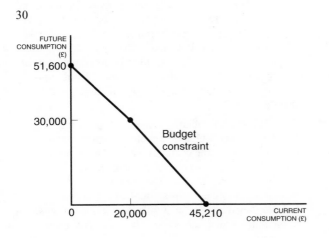

32

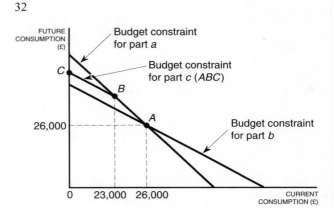

d If the Reeds save less than £3,000, the tax exempt savings account has both substitution and income effects. If they save more than £3,000, there is only an income effect.

34 *a*

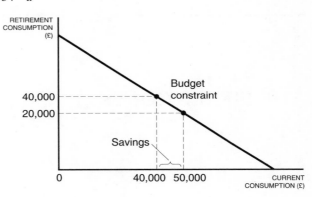

b

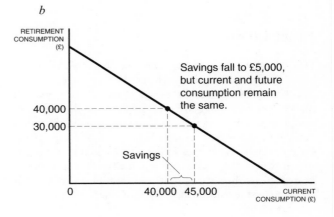

Chapter 10

THE FIRM'S COSTS

Chapter Review

One side of the competitive model, the household's, is complete. Business enterprises—firms—occupy the other side. This chapter begins the discussion of the role of firms in a market-based economy. We learn about the production function, which summarises the relationship between the inputs that the firm demands (especially in the labour market) and the outputs that it supplies in the product market. Payments to purchase inputs make up most of the firm's costs, and this chapter treats these costs in depth. How the costs are balanced against revenue is the subject of Chapter 11.

ESSENTIAL CONCEPTS

1 In the basic competitive model, the firm's objective is to maximize its market value. Because the value of the firm depends on its profit-making potential, another way to put this is to say the firm's objective is to maximise its (long-term) profits. **Profits** equal revenue minus costs, and revenue is simply price times quantity.

2 The **production function** shows the relationship between inputs and outputs. The increase in output resulting from a small increase in the use of an input is called the **marginal product.** The **principle of diminishing returns** states that as more of one input is used, holding other inputs fixed, the marginal product declines. While diminishing returns represent the usual case, some production functions exhibit **increasing returns,** where the marginal product increases as more of an input is used. If doubling the input doubles the output, then there are **constant returns.** Inputs that do not change as output changes are called **fixed inputs;** inputs that do change with output are called **variable inputs.**

3 There are costs associated with each type of input: either **fixed costs,** which do not change when output changes, or **variable costs,** which do. The important concept to grasp is how the various measures of costs change as output changes. The **average cost** curve is typically U-shaped; the **marginal cost** curve lies below it when average cost falls, equals average cost at the minimum, and lies above it when average cost increases.

4   The **principle of substitution** says that as the price of an input increases, firms substitute other inputs. The firm always chooses the least-cost production technique. In the long run, all inputs are variable; the firm has more choices. The **long-run average cost curve** is the lower boundary of all possible short-run average cost curves.

5   In the long run, firms can increase inputs in the same proportion: there are **constant returns to scale** if output increases in the same proportion. If output increases by less, there are **diminishing returns to scale**. **Increasing returns to scale** imply that output increases by a greater proportion than inputs do. **Economies of scope** refer to the cost savings from producing several goods together rather than separately.

BEHIND THE ESSENTIAL CONCEPTS

Of the many diagrams in this chapter, there are four that you should master. Each is explained below. Notice how the economic idea (such as diminishing returns or increasing returns to scale) determines the shape of the curves.

1   The first diagram to master is the production function (Figure 10.1, which is similar to Figure 10.4 in the text). The production function indicates how output (measured on the vertical axis) changes as the quantity of the variable input (measured on the horizontal axis) changes. There are two important facts to know. The first is that the shape indicates whether the production function has diminishing, constant, or increasing returns. Figure 10.1 shows diminishing returns. Also, the slope of the line from the origin to the curve is equal to the average product.

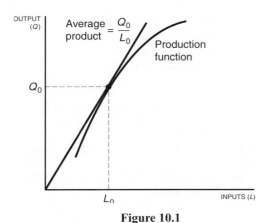

Figure 10.1

2   The second diagram is the total cost curves, shown in Figure 10.2 (which summarises Figure 10.5A, B, and C of the text). Output is measured along the horizontal axis, and cost along the vertical one. Again, there are two important features to observe. First, total cost is the sum of fixed and variable costs. Because by definition

fixed costs don't change, the difference between the parallel variable and total cost curves equals fixed costs. The second feature is that the total cost curve inherits its shape from the production function. This will be explored in the analysis part of this chapter.

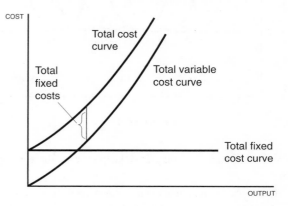

Figure 10.2

3   Third, there is the average cost–marginal cost diagram, shown in Figure 10.3 (which duplicates Figure 10.6 in the text). The important concept here is the relationship between the marginal and average cost curves. The average cost curve is typically U-shaped. When marginal cost is below average cost, average cost is downward sloping. Marginal cost equals average cost at the minimum of average cost, and marginal cost is above average cost when average cost is upward sloping. Average cost falls as fixed costs are spread over more units. Average cost rises because diminishing returns drive the marginal cost curve above the average cost curve.

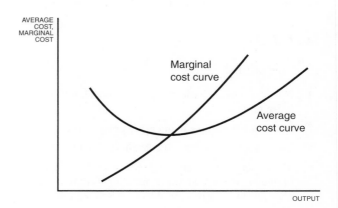

Figure 10.3

4   Finally, there is the long-run average cost curve. For every production process, there are fixed inputs and an associated average cost curve. The long-run average cost curve is the lower boundary, as shown in Figure 10.4 (which duplicates Figure 10.14 in the text). The curve is drawn flat, which represents constant returns of scale.

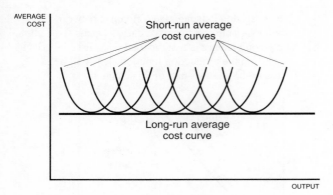

Figure 10.4

In reviewing these four diagrams, keep in mind three pointers.

1   Remember to note what is measured along each axis. It's easy to make the mistake of memorizing the shapes of the curves while forgetting how to label the axes.

2   Note the relationships among the curves, especially the marginal cost and average cost relationship.

3   The shapes of the curves illustrate the economic properties. It's important to be able to recognize economic properties like diminishing returns and economies of scale in the diagrams of production functions and cost curves.

Diminishing returns refer to production processes in which some but not all inputs are variable. Diminishing returns imply that the marginal product decreases as more inputs are used. Economists add the words *to scale* when describing a production process in which all inputs are variable. Thus, decreasing returns to scale mean that as all inputs are increased in a certain proportion, output increases by less.

SELF-TEST

True or False

1   According to the basic competitive model, firms maximise profits.

2   Firms in competitive markets are price takers.

3   The marginal product is the last unit of output.

4   The principle of diminishing returns says that as more of one input is added, while other inputs remain unchanged, the marginal product of the added input diminishes.

5   With constant returns, if all inputs are increased by one-third, then output increases by one-third.

6   Costs associated with inputs that change as output changes are called variable costs.

7   Total costs are the sum of average and marginal costs.

8   If labour is the only variable input, then marginal cost equals the wage divided by the marginal product.

9   The average variable cost curve lies below the average total cost curve.

10   The marginal cost curve intersects the average cost curve at the minimum of the marginal cost curve.

11   If the price of an input rises, the firm will substitute other inputs to some extent, but its cost curves will still shift up.

12   Short-run average cost curves are typically U-shaped.

13   If there are economies of scale, the long-run average cost curve slopes downwards.

14   The long-run average cost curve is the lower boundary of all short-run average cost curves.

15   Economies of scope imply that producing a set of goods is cheaper than producing each of them singly.

Multiple Choice

1   In the basic competitive model, a firm that charges more than the going price

   a   will lose some of its customers slowly over time.
   b   will lose all its customers.
   c   may keep its customers if its goods are of higher quality than those of its competitors.
   d   will lose no customers if its price equals its marginal cost.
   e   none of the above.

2   The statement that firms in competitive markets are price takers means that

   a   firms accept the price set by the market.
   b   firms maximise profits.
   c   production has constant returns.
   d   marginal cost is upward sloping.
   e   average cost equals marginal cost at the minimum of average cost.

3   Profits equal

   a   fixed costs minus average cost.
   b   revenue minus fixed costs.
   c   revenue minus variable costs.
   d   price minus average cost.
   e   revenue minus total cost.

4   The marginal product of an input is

   a   the cost of producing 1 more unit of output.
   b   the extra output that results from hiring 1 more unit of the input.
   c   the cost required to hire 1 more unit of the input.
   d   output divided by the number of inputs used in the production process.
   e   *a* and *c*.

5   According to the principle of diminishing returns,

   a   as more of one input is added, the marginal product of the added input diminishes.
   b   as more of one input is added, holding other inputs unchanged, the marginal product of the added input diminishes.
   c   as more of the output is produced, the cost of production diminishes.

d   as more of the output is produced, the marginal
   cost of production diminishes.

e   none of the above.

6   If the production function exhibits increasing returns,

a   the marginal product of all input increases with the
   amount produced.

b   the marginal cost increases with output.

c   productivity is higher.

d   the production function is downward sloping.

e   *a* and *d*.

7   If, when the total quantity of all inputs is doubled, output
exactly doubles, the production function exhibits

a   constant returns.

b   diminishing returns.

c   increasing returns.

d   economies of scale.

e   none of the above.

8   Fixed inputs are inputs that

a   cannot be moved.

b   can be purchased in only one fixed configuration.

c   can be purchased at a fixed price.

d   do not depend on the level of output.

e   none of the above.

9   Fixed costs

a   are the costs associated with fixed inputs.

b   do not change with the level of output.

c   include payment to some variable factors.

d   all of the above.

e   *a* and *b*.

10   The relationship between the marginal product of labor
and the marginal cost of output is that marginal cost

a   is the inverse of marginal product.

b   equals the wage divided by the marginal product.

c   is downward sloping when marginal product is
   downward sloping.

d   is constant but marginal product is subject to
   diminishing returns.

e   *b* and *d*.

11   The principle of diminishing returns implies that

a   marginal product diminishes as more of the input
   is hired.

b   marginal cost increases with the level of output.

c   productivity is higher in large firms.

d   all of the above.

e   *a* and *b*.

12   Total cost equals

a   the sum of fixed and variable costs.

b   the product of fixed and variable costs.

c   the ratio of fixed and variable costs.

d   the sum of average cost and average variable cost.

e   none of the above.

13   When the marginal cost curve is above the average
cost curve, the

a   average cost curve is at its minimum.

b   marginal cost curve is at its maximum.

c   marginal cost curve is downward sloping.

d   average cost curve is downward sloping.

e   average cost curve is upward sloping.

14   According to the principle of substitution,

a   marginal cost equals average cost at the minimum
   of average cost.

b   an increase in the price of an input will lead the
   firm to substitute other inputs.

c   a decrease in the price of an input will lead the
   firm to substitute other inputs.

d   if the firm does not know its marginal cost curve,
   it can substitute its average cost curve.

e   none of the above.

15   The difference between the long and the short run
is

a   that there are constant returns in the short run,
   but not in the long run.

b   that in the long run, all inputs can be varied.

c   three months.

d   that the average cost is decreasing in the short
   run, but increasing in the long run.

e   *a* and *b*.

16   In the short run, the typical average cost curve is

a   upward sloping.

b   downward sloping.

c   U-shaped.

d   horizontal.

e   none of the above.

17   The long-run average cost curve is

a   the sum of the short-run average cost curves.

b   the lower boundary of the short-run average cost
   curves.

c   the upper boundary of the short-run average cost
   curves.

d   horizontal.

e   none of the above.

18   The long-run average cost curve

a   may slope down because of overhead costs.

b   may eventually slope up because of managerial
   problems.

c   always exhibits increasing returns to scale.

d   *a* and *c*.

e   *a* and *b*.

19   The concept of increasing returns to scale means
that

a   it is more expensive to produce a variety of goods
   together than to produce them separately.

b   it is more expensive to produce a large quantity
   than a small quantity.

c   the average cost of production is lower when a
   larger quantity is produced.

d   the marginal cost curve is downward sloping.

e   *a* and *b*.

20   The concept of economies of scope means that

a   it is less expensive to produce a variety of goods
   together than to produce them separately.

b   it is more expensive to produce a large quantity
    than a small quantity.
c   the average cost of production is lower when a
    larger quantity is produced.
d   the marginal cost curve is downward sloping.
e   a and b.

Completion

1   The relationship between the inputs used in production
    and the level of output is called the _____.

2   The increase in output that results from using 1 more
    unit of an input is the _____.

3   The principle of _____ says that as more and
    more of one input is added, while other inputs remain
    unchanged, the marginal product of the added input
    diminishes.

4   Costs that do not depend upon output are called
    _____, or overhead costs.

5   The _____ is the extra cost of producing 1 more
    unit of output.

6   The marginal cost curve intersects the average cost
    curve at the _____ of the _____ cost
    curve.

7   If marginal costs are above average costs, then pro-
    ducing an additional unit will _____ the
    average.

8   An increase in the price of one input will lead a firm
    to substitute other inputs. This is a statement of the
    _____.

9   If the average cost is lower when the firm produces a
    larger quantity, then there are economies of
    _____.

10 If it is less expensive to produce a variety of goods to-
    gether than to produce each good separately, then there
    are economies of _____.

Answers to Self-Test

True or False

1	T	6	T	11	T
2	T	7	F	12	T
3	F	8	T	13	T
4	T	9	T	14	T
5	T	10	F	15	T

Multiple Choice

1	b	6	a	11	e	16	c
2	e	7	a	12	a	17	b
3	e	8	d	13	e	18	e
4	b	9	e	14	b	19	c
5	b	10	b	15	b	20	a

Completion

1   production function
2   marginal product

3   diminishing returns
4   fixed
5   marginal cost
6   minimum, average
7   raise
8   principle of substitution
9   scale
10 scope

Tools and Practice Problems

There is quite a bit of technical detail in this chapter, including production functions and a host of cost curves. First, we
will explore the production function, calculating the marginal and average product and plotting the curves. It is important to understand how the shape of the production function
exhibits diminishing, constant, or increasing returns. Next,
we turn our attention to the cost curves; we calculate the
various cost concepts and plot the curves. Again, it is important to understand the relationships between the curves and
the economic meaning of the shapes of the curves.

THE PRODUCTION FUNCTION

The relationship between inputs and outputs is given by the
production function. It shows how much output will result
from the efficient use of each possible quantity of the inputs.
Economists are interested also in the marginal product, the
extra returns brought about by using one additional unit of an
input, and the average product, output per input. In order to
understand the decisions of firms, you must understand the
production function and its relationship to marginal and average product. Table 10.1 lists the key facts and Tool Kit 10.1
shows how to calculate and graph the key concepts.

Table 10.1
Production Function

The marginal product is the slope of the production
    function:

$$\text{Marginal product} = \frac{\text{change in output}}{\text{change in number of units of inputs}}.$$

The average product is the slope of a line from the origin
    to the production function:

$$\text{Average product} = \frac{\text{output}}{\text{input}}.$$

If returns are diminishing,
    The marginal product is decreasing.
    The slope of the production function is becoming flatter.
If returns are constant,
    The marginal product is constant.
    The slope of the production function is constant.
If returns are increasing,
    The marginal product is increasing.
    The slope of the production function is becoming steeper.

Tool Kit 10.1 Calculating and Graphing Marginal and Average Products

The production function summarises the relationship between inputs and outputs. It is important to understand its relationship with the marginal and average products, which can be calculated from the information in the production function and can also be derived from the graph of the production function. Here is how it is done.

Step one: Identify and graph the production function.

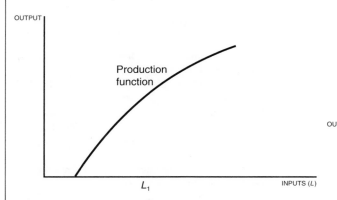

Step two: Calculate the average product, which is output per unit of the input:

Average product = output/number of units of inputs.

The average product is the slope of a line from the origin to the production function.

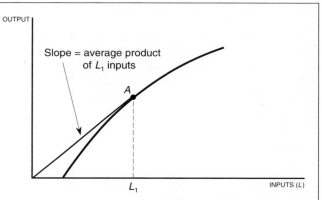

Step three: Calculate the marginal product, which is the extra output resulting from the use of 1 more unit of the input:

Marginal product = change in output/change in input.

The marginal product equals the slope of the production function.

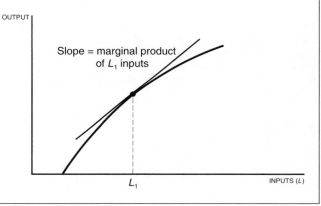

1 (Worked problem: marginal and average products) Table 10.2 gives the production function for keyboards at Tek-Tek computer products.

Table 10.2

Number of workers	Output	Average product	Marginal product
1	80		
2	150		
3	210		
4	260		
5	300		

a Compute the average and marginal product, and fill in the table.
b Plot the production function. For each point, verify that the slope of the line from the origin to the production function equals the average product.
c Between each two adjacent points on the production function, verify that the slope equals the marginal product.

d Does the production function exhibit diminishing, constant, or increasing returns?

Step-by-step solution

Step one (a): Identify and graph the production function. This is given in Table 10.2.

Step two: Calculate and graph the average product. The average product is output divided by the number of workers. If output is 80, the average product is 80/1 = 80. Enter this number. If output is 150, the average product is 150/2 = 75. Complete the average product column. The result is given in Table 10.3.

Table 10.3

Number of workers	Output	Average product	Marginal product
1	80	80	80
2	150	75	70
3	210	70	60
4	260	65	50
5	300	60	40

Step three: Calculate the marginal product. The marginal product is the extra output resulting from using one additional unit of input. The marginal product of the first worker is 80. Enter this number. When the second worker is used, output rises to 150. The marginal product of this worker is 150 − 80 = 70. Enter this number. Complete the marginal product column. Table 10.3 gives the result.

Step four (b): Plot the production function.

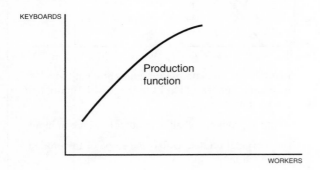

Step five: Choose a point on the production function, and verify that the slope of a line from the origin to that point is equal to the average product. Choose the point labeled *A,* where output is 210 and the number of workers is 3. Draw a line from the origin to point *A.* The slope is rise/run = 210/3 = 70, which is the average product.

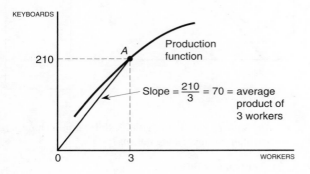

Step six (c): Verify that the slope of the production function is the marginal product. The slope of the production function between *A* and *B,* where output is 300 and the number of workers is 5, is (300 − 260)/(5 − 4) = 40, which is the marginal product of the fourth worker.

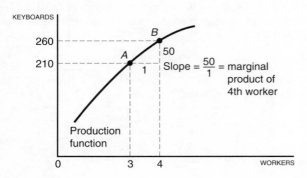

Step seven (d): The marginal product is decreasing; this indicates diminishing returns.

2   (Practice problem: marginal and average products) Table 10.4 gives the production function for the insect spray Nobeetle at Insectout Pesticide Company.

Table 10.4

Number of workers	Output	Average product	Marginal product
1	1,200		
2	2,200		
3	3,000		
4	3,600		
5	4,000		

a   Compute the average and marginal products, and fill in the table.
b   Plot the production function. For each point, verify that the slope of the line from the origin to the production function equals the average product.
c   Between each two adjacent points on the production function, verify that the slope equals the marginal product.
d   Does the production function exhibit diminishing, constant, or increasing returns?

3   (Practice problem: marginal and average products) For the following production functions, answer parts *a* through *d* in problem 2.

a   Bedford Waterbeds

Number of workers	Output	Average product	Marginal product
1	24		
2	42		
3	57		
4	68		
5	75		

b   Worry-Free Insurance

Number of sellers	Policies	Average product	Marginal product
10	200		
20	500		
30	700		
40	800		
50	850		

COST

A firm's costs are its payments to inputs. Some of these inputs are fixed and some are variable. We are interested in the total cost curves and also in average and marginal costs. Thus we have many cost curves. Table 10.5 summarises the important information about cost curves and Tool Kit 10.2 shows how to calculate and graph the key concepts.

Tool Kit 10.2 Calculating and Graphing Cost Measures

There are two sets of cost curves: the total curves (total costs, fixed costs, and variable costs), and the average and marginal curves (average cost, marginal cost). It is important to be able to calculate each of the cost concepts and also to recognize their relationships on the graphs. Follow along.

Step one: Identify and graph the total cost curve.

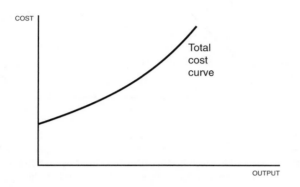

Step two: Calculate and graph the variable cost curve:

Variable cost = total cost − fixed cost.

The variable cost curve is parallel to the total cost curve, lying below it by the amount of fixed costs.

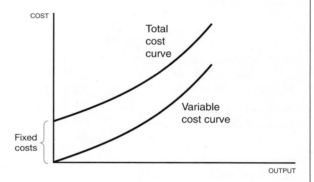

Step three: Calculate and graph the average cost curve: average cost = total cost/output.

Average cost equals the slope of a line from the origin to the total cost curve.

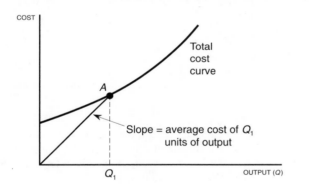

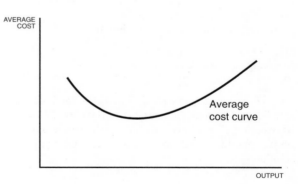

Step four: Calculate and graph the marginal cost curve: marginal cost = change in cost/change in output.

Marginal cost is the slope of the total cost curve.

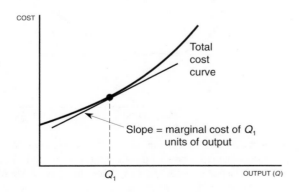

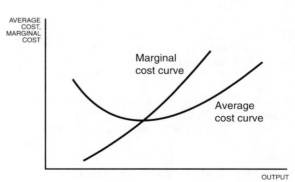

Table 10.5 summarizes the key information about cost curves.

Table 10.5
Cost Curves

The variable cost curve is parallel to the total cost curve, and below it by the amount of fixed costs:
Variable cost = total cost − fixed cost.

The marginal cost is the slope of the total cost curve:

$$\text{Marginal cost} = \frac{\text{change in total cost}}{\text{change in output}}.$$

Average cost is the slope of the line from the origin to the total cost curve:

$$\text{Average cost} = \frac{\text{total cost}}{\text{output}}.$$

If returns are diminishing,
   The marginal cost is increasing.
   The slope of the total cost curve is becoming steeper.

If returns are constant,
   The marginal cost is constant.
   The slope of the total cost curve is constant.

If returns are increasing,
   The marginal cost is decreasing.
   The slope of the total cost curve is becoming flatter.

If marginal cost is below average cost,
   The average cost curve is decreasing.

If marginal cost equals average cost,
   The average cost curve is at its minimum.

If marginal cost is above average cost,
   The average cost curve is increasing.

---

4   (Worked problem: cost curves) The total fixed costs at Stay-Bright Cleaning Company are £100,000. Table 10.6 gives their total costs for different levels of output measured in truckloads of Stay-Bright Cleaning Solution.

Table 10.6

Output	Total costs	Variable costs	Average cost	Marginal cost
1,000	£180,000			
2,000	£280,000			
3,000	£420,000			
4,000	£600,000			
5,000	£800,000			

a   Compute variable, average, and marginal costs, and enter them in the table.
b   Plot the total cost and variable cost curves on one diagram, and verify the relationships given in Table 10.5.
c   Plot the average cost and marginal cost curves, and verify the marginal-average relationship.
d   Do the cost curves exhibit increasing, constant, or diminishing returns?

Step-by-step solution

Step one (a): Identify and graph the total cost curve.

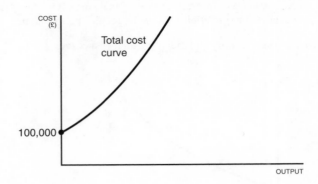

Step two: Calculate and graph the variable cost curve. Variable cost is just the difference between total cost and total fixed cost. The variable cost of 1,000 units is £180,000 − £100,000 = £80,000. Enter this number. Complete the variable cost column.

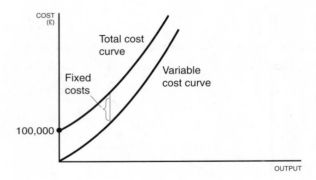

Step three: Calculate and graph the average cost curve. Average cost is total cost divided by output. The average cost of 1,000 units is £180,000/1,000 = £180. Enter this number. Complete the average cost column.

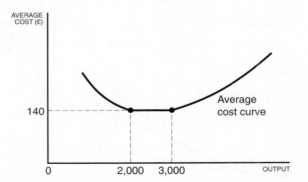

Step four: Calculate and graph the marginal cost curve. Marginal cost is the extra cost of producing one more unit. The marginal cost per unit for the first 1,000 units is £80,000/1,000 = £80. Enter this number, and continue to fill in the column. The complete information appears in Table 10.7.

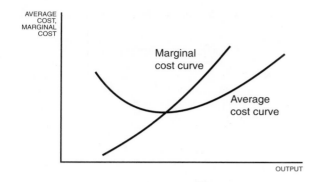

is rising; they are equal at *B,* which is the minimum of average cost; and marginal cost is above average cost at *C,* where average cost is rising.

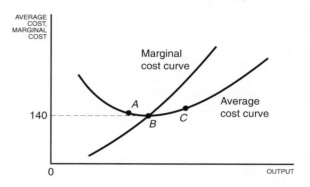

Table 10.7

Output	Total costs	Variable costs	Average cost	Marginal cost
1,000	£180,000	£ 80,000	£180	£ 80
2,000	£280,000	£180,000	£140	£100
3,000	£420,000	£320,000	£140	£140
4,000	£600,000	£500,000	£150	£180
5,000	£800,000	£700,000	£160	£200

Step five (b): Choose a point on the total cost curve, and verify the relationships.

The variable cost curve is parallel to the total cost curve. For example, between *A* and *B,* the slope of the total cost curve is (£600,000 − £420,000)/(4,000 − 3,000) = 180. The slope of the variable cost curve for the same levels of output is (£500,000 − £320,000)/(4,000 − 3,000) = 180.

The variable cost curve lies below the total cost curve by the amount of fixed costs. The difference all along the curves is £100,000, which is fixed costs.

The slope of the total cost curve equals marginal cost. Between *A* and *B,* the slope is 180, which is the marginal cost at 4,000 workers.

The slope of a line from the origin to the total cost curve equals average cost. Between the origin and point *A,* the slope of the line is £420,000/3,000 = 140, which is average cost.

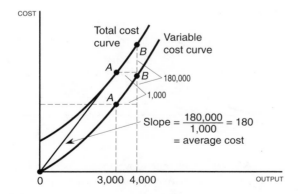

Step six (c): Plot the average and marginal cost curves, and verify the average-marginal relationship. As you can see, marginal cost is above average cost at *A,* where average cost

Step seven: The cost curves exhibit diminishing returns. Marginal cost is increasing, and total cost is becoming steeper.

5 (Practice problem: cost curves). The fixed costs at Pestle Mortar Company are £50,000. Table 10.8 gives their costs for different levels of output measured in mortars.

Table 10.8

Output	Total costs	Variable costs	Average cost	Marginal cost
1,000	£ 250,000			
2,000	£ 500,000			
3,000	£ 800,000			
4,000	£1,200,000			
5,000	£1,800,000			

a Compute variable, average, and marginal costs, and enter them in the table.
b Plot the total cost and variable cost curves on one diagram, and verify the relationships given in Table 10.5.
c Plot the average cost and marginal cost curves, and verify the marginal-average relationship.
d Do the cost curves exhibit increasing, constant, or diminishing returns?

6 (Practice problem: cost curves) For the following cost data, answer parts *a* through *d* in question 5.

a Fixed costs are £1,000.

Output	Total costs	Variable costs	Average cost	Marginal cost
10	£1,500			
20	£2,200			
30	£3,000			
40	£4,000			
50	£6,000			

b   Fixed costs are £0.

Output	Total costs	Variable costs	Average cost	Marginal cost
100	£1,000			
200	£1,800			
300	£2,400			
400	£2,800			
500	£3,200			
600	£3,600			

c   Fixed costs are £80,000.

Output	Total costs	Variable costs	Average cost	Marginal cost
1	£140,000			
2	£180,000			
3	£220,000			
4	£260,000			
5	£300,000			
6	£340,000			

Answers to Problems

2   *a*   The marginal and average products are given in Table 10.9.

Table 10.9

Number of workers	Output	Average product	Marginal product
1	1,200	1,200	1,200
2	2,200	1,100	1,000
3	3,000	1,000	800
4	3,600	900	600
5	4,000	800	400

b   The production function is drawn in the figure below. The average product for 3 workers, which is 1,000, is shown as the slope of the line from the origin to point *B*.

c   The marginal product of the 4th worker, which is 600, is shown as the slope between points *B* and *C*.

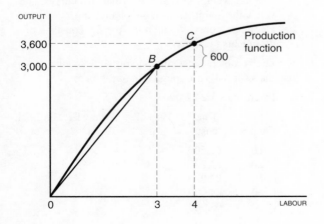

d   The production function exhibits diminishing returns.

3   *a*   Bedford Waterbeds—diminishing returns

Number of workers	Output	Average product	Marginal product
1	24	24	24
2	42	21	18
3	57	19	15
4	68	17	11
5	75	15	7

b   Worry-Free Insurance—diminishing returns

Number of sellers	Policies	Average product	Marginal product
10	200	20.0	20
20	500	25.0	30
30	700	23.3	20
40	800	20.0	10
50	850	17.0	5

5   *a*   The completed table is given in Table 10.10.

Table 10.10

Output	Total costs	Variable costs	Average cost	Marginal cost
1,000	£ 250,000	£ 200,000	£250	£200
2,000	£ 500,000	£ 450,000	£250	£250
3,000	£ 800,000	£ 750,000	£267	£300
4,000	£1,200,000	£1,150,000	£300	£400
5,000	£1,800,000	£1,750,000	£360	£600

b   The diagram below shows the total cost and variable cost curves. The variable cost curve is parallel to and lies below the total cost curve by £50,000, which is the amount of fixed costs.

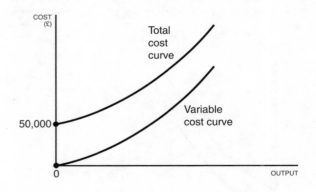

c   The following diagram shows the average and marginal cost curves. Average and marginal costs are equal at £250, which is the minimum of the average cost curve. Average cost rises after this point, while marginal cost hovers above.

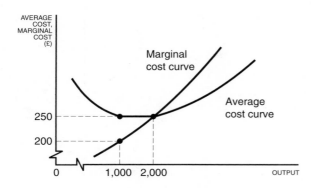

d   The cost curves exhibit diminishing returns.

6   The completed cost tables appear below.

a   These cost curves show diminishing returns.

Output	Total costs	Variable costs	Average cost	Marginal cost
10	£1,500	£ 500	£150	£ 50
20	£2,200	£1,200	£110	£ 70
30	£3,000	£2,000	£100	£ 80
40	£4,000	£3,000	£100	£100
50	£6,000	£5,000	£120	£200

b   These cost curves show increasing returns.

Output	Total costs	Variable costs	Average cost	Marginal cost
100	£1,000	£1,000	£10.00	£10
200	£1,800	£1,800	£ 9.00	£ 8
300	£2,400	£2,400	£ 8.00	£ 6
400	£2,800	£2,800	£ 7.00	£ 4
500	£3,200	£3,200	£ 6.50	£ 4
600	£3,600	£3,600	£ 6.00	£ 4

c   These cost curves show increasing returns until output equals 2, and constant returns thereafter.

Output	Total costs	Variable costs	Average cost	Marginal cost
1	£140,000	£ 60,000	£140,000	£60,000
2	£180,000	£100,000	£ 90,000	£40,000
3	£220,000	£140,000	£ 73,333	£40,000
4	£260,000	£180,000	£ 65,000	£40,000
5	£300,000	£220,000	£ 60,000	£40,000
6	£340,000	£260,000	£ 56,667	£40,000

Chapter 11

PRODUCTION

Chapter Review

This chapter moves the discussion from the firm's costs to decisions firms must make regarding production. In the process, it shows the role of the firm in the competitive model. The firm is a supplier in product markets and a demander in input markets, especially in labour markets. The chapter also explains why and when new firms will enter an industry and why and when existing firms will shut down. Each of these issues requires carefully distinguishing opportunity costs from sunk costs, and profits from rents. This close examination of the firm's production decision completes the discussion of all the individual parts of the basic competitive model that began in Chapter 8. What remains is to put them together and evaluate how the model works. This is done in Chapter 12.

ESSENTIAL CONCEPTS

1 Firms choose output to **maximise profits.** Profit is the difference between total revenue and total costs. The output decision can be illustrated in two ways. One way, shown in Figure 11.1A, is to draw the total revenue and total cost curves and find the quantity where the total revenue curve is above the total cost curve by the greatest amount. At this point, the curves are parallel and their slopes are equal. The second way, shown in panel B, uses the marginal revenue curve. The slope of the total revenue curve is marginal revenue, which for the competitive firm equals the price of its product. The slope of the total cost curve is marginal cost. Therefore, at this point, marginal revenue (price) equals marginal cost, and profit maximization can be shown by the intersection of these two curves.

2 If the market price for a good or service exceeds the minimum average cost, then it pays new firms to enter the market. In deciding whether to *exit* the market, however, a firm must pay attention to those costs it cannot recover. Costs that the firm must pay whether or not it leaves the market are called **sunk costs.** The firm should stay in the market whenever it can earn revenue greater than all the costs not sunk. If all the fixed costs are nonrecoverable sunk costs, then the firm will exit when price falls below minimum average variable cost.

3 The *supply curve of the firm* is the marginal cost curve above the minimum price needed to keep the firm from exiting. The *market supply curve* is the sum of the quantities supplied of all firms in the market, and it takes into account both the adjustments made by existing

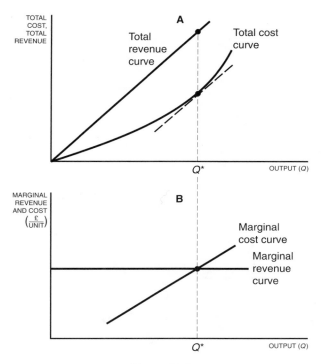

Figure 11.1

firms and the new entrants attracted to the market as the price rises. This curve is more elastic in the long run than in the short run, because existing firms have time to adjust to the lowest-cost production techniques and new firms have time to enter the market and produce.

4   When the going price in a competitive industry exceeds the minimum of the average cost, new firms will enter. The reason is that they will be able to earn higher profits in this industry than elsewhere in the economy. (Recall that the normal rate of return to capital is included in average cost.) Competition thus forces all firms to produce at minimum cost and drives any inefficient firms out of the market. In a similar vein, the theory of **contestable markets** argues that if there are no sunk costs, the threat of entry alone will compel a firm to earn zero profits even if it is the only one in the industry.

5   Firms exit an industry when they can no longer earn enough revenue to cover their costs, but the focus is on recoverable costs. Sunk costs are ignored in making the exit decision. The existence of significant sunk costs breaks down the theory of contestable markets. The threat of entry is not so strong if the entrant risks losing its investment.

6   The firm's demand for inputs follows from its decision about how much to produce. More formally, the demand for an input is the **value of its marginal product,** which equals its marginal product (how much extra output the marginal input produces) times the product price (how much revenue the firm receives in selling the output). Again, the market demand is just the sum of the quantities demanded by all firms in the market. Because labour is by far the most important input in production,

it is used as the main example of an input in the text. Nevertheless, the demand for any input is the value of its marginal product.

BEHIND THE ESSENTIAL CONCEPTS

1   It is important that cost include all opportunity costs of production borne by the firm. Not only are such explicit costs as wages, energy, raw materials, and interest included, but also more subtle *opportunity costs* are taken into account, such as the value of the entrepreneur's time or the alternative earnings on the equity invested by the owners of the firm. These are considered opportunity costs because if the firm did not produce, the entrepreneur would devote time to some other activity, and the owners would take their investment capital elsewhere.

When a firm is making zero *economic* profits, its revenues is sufficient to cover all costs, including normal returns on the invested financial capital. An economist would say that the firm is only making enough to compensate the owners for the opportunity cost of putting their money into the firm. An accountant would view the situation differently, saying that a firm earning normal returns was actually making positive accounting profits.

2   Another difference between the way economists and accountants view profits concerns rent. **Rent** is the return to anything that is supplied inelastically. For example, suppose a firm's superior location enables it to earn 50 percent more than its competitors. An accountant would say that this firm's profits are 50 percent higher. An economist would call this extra return a rent, because the firm's earnings are higher than the minimum necessary to induce it to stay in its location. Although land is a good example, the concept of rent applies to any payment to a factor of production above the minimum necessary to bring that factor onto the market.

3   Sunk costs and fixed costs are distinct ideas. *Sunk costs* cannot be recovered no matter what the firm does. The firm can shut down production, even go out of business and sell off all its assets, but it cannot recover its sunk costs. *Fixed costs* do not change as output changes, but they may be recoverable if the firm exits the industry. For example, the firm may own a plant, and the alternative earnings (the opportunity cost) of its plant do not depend on whether the firm produces a little or a great deal of output. If the firm can sell the factory when it exits the industry, then the costs of the plant are fixed but not sunk.

4   There is only one way to maximise profits. If the firm produces goods for the least cost and sets price equal to marginal cost, then it must set the input price equal to the value of the marginal product of that input. Thus, the profit-maximising demand for labour is just the other side of the coin of the profit-maximising supply of output. This fact is illustrated in Figure 11.2, where in panel A the firm sets the product price equal to marginal cost and produces Q^* units of output. (Note that this is

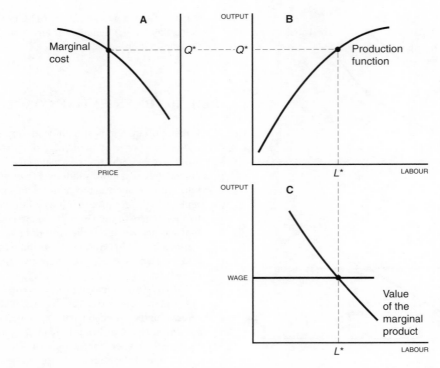

Figure 11.2

the usual diagram turned on its side.) The production function, drawn in panel B, shows that this level of output requires L^* hours of labour. Finally, panel C shows that when the firm sets the wage equal to the value of the marginal product of labour, it chooses exactly L^* hours of labour.

5   The competitive firm has four basic decisions to make: when to enter, when to exit, how much to produce, and how many inputs to hire. Table 11.1 summarises the decision rules.

Table 11.1

Entry	Enter when price > minimum average cost.
Exit	Exit when revenue < nonrecoverable costs.
Supply	Produce the quantity of output for which price equals marginal cost.
Demand	Hire the quantity of inputs for which the input price equals the value of the marginal product.

SELF-TEST

True or False

1   The firm is choosing the profit-maximising level of output when price equals marginal cost.

2   The firm is choosing the profit-maximising level of any input when the input price equals the value of the marginal product.

3   The value of the marginal product equals the marginal product divided by the wage.

4   In the competitive model, marginal revenue is less than price because increasing output leads to a decrease in price.

5   All fixed costs are sunk, but not all sunk costs are fixed.

6   Accounting profits are always less than economic profits.

7   In the long run in a competitive industry, economic profits are zero for any potential entrant.

8   Firms exit the industry when price falls below the minimum of the average cost.

9   A firm will enter an industry if the price is above the minimum average variable cost.

10   Economic rent is any payment to an input in excess of that needed to keep the input in its current use.

11   Land is the only input that can earn economic rent.

12   The long-run supply is more elastic than the short-run supply for the industry but not for the individual firm.

13   The long-run supply curve is the sum of the supply curves of individual firms, including those that enter at high prices.

14   Even if a firm's supply curve is upward sloping in the short run, it may be perfectly elastic in the long run.

15   Correctly measured, total cost should include all opportunity costs of operating.

Multiple Choice

1   Marginal revenue

   a   is less than price for the competitive firm because as it sells more output, it must lower the price.
   b   equals price for the competitive firm.
   c   is the revenue that the firm receives for selling another unit of output.
   d   is the extra profit that the firm receives from selling another unit of output, after accounting for all opportunity costs.
   e   b and c.

2   The firm supplies the profit-maximising level of output when

   a   marginal revenue equals price.
   b   marginal revenue equals marginal cost.
   c   economic profits are zero.
   d   accounting profits are zero.
   e   sunk costs equal fixed costs.

3   The extra cost of producing an additional unit of output is called

   a   marginal cost.
   b   fixed cost.
   c   overhead cost.
   d   sunk cost.
   e   marginal revenue.

4   It pays a firm to enter a market whenever

   a   the market price is greater than the minimum average cost at which the firm can produce.
   b   the firm can earn revenue greater than any non-recoverable costs.
   c   price is greater than the minimum of the average variable cost curve.
   d   price equals marginal cost.
   e   marginal revenue equals marginal cost.

5   The firm should exit the market whenever

   a   it cannot earn revenue equal to at least its non-recoverable costs.
   b   price is less than marginal cost.
   c   price is less than the minimum of the average cost curve.
   d   price is less than minimum average variable cost.
   e   all of the above.

6   Sunk costs are

   a   costs that do not change when output changes.
   b   the costs of starting the business.
   c   nonrecoverable costs.
   d   variable costs.
   e   opportunity costs.

7   Which of the following is true?

   a   Accounting costs are always greater than economic costs.
   b   Economic costs are always greater than accounting costs.
   c   Accounting profits are always greater than economic profits.
   d   Economic profits are always greater than accounting profits.
   e   None of the above.

8   The firm's economic costs include

   a   the opportunity cost of the time of the entrepreneur.
   b   the revenue that could be earned in alternative uses by the assets that the firm owns.
   c   the return on the equity invested in the firm by the owners.
   d   depreciation on company-owned buildings and machinery.
   e   all of the above.

9   The long-run supply curve for the industry is

   a   perfectly elastic.
   b   more elastic than the short-run supply curve.
   c   less elastic than the short-run supply curve.
   d   the lower boundary of the short-run supply curves.
   e   the sum of the short-run supply curves.

10   Economic rent refers to

   a   economic profit minus sunk cost.
   b   any payment to an input above the minimum needed to keep the input in its present use.
   c   payments from tenants to landlords.
   d   the wages of especially skilled labour.
   e   revenue received by efficient firms.

11   In the basic competitive model, profits are driven to zero. This means that

   a   revenue is just enough to cover all nonrecoverable costs.
   b   revenue is just enough to cover all costs, including the opportunity cost of invested financial capital.
   c   price equals the minimum of the average variable cost curve.
   d   accounting profits are equal to zero.
   e   b and d.

12   When price is greater than minimum average variable cost, the firm

   a   enters the market.
   b   exits the market.
   c   may continue or exit depending upon the magnitude of sunk costs.
   d   shuts down production but does not exit.
   e   enters the market only if overhead costs are zero.

13   The market supply curve is

   a   the sum of the quantities of the supply curves of all the firms.
   b   less elastic than the supply curves of all the firms.
   c   the marginal cost curve of the last firm to enter the market.

d   always horizontal.

e   none of the above.

14   The value to the firm of hiring one more worker is

    a   equal to marginal cost.

    b   equal to marginal revenue.

    c   equal to the marginal product of labour.

    d   equal to the marginal product of labour multiplied by the product price.

    e   equal to the marginal product of labour multiplied by the wage.

15   The value of the marginal product is

    a   the revenue that the firm receives for the last unit of output.

    b   the revenue that the firm receives for entering the market.

    c   the marginal product multiplied by the wage.

    d   the marginal product multiplied by the product price.

    e   none of the above.

16   The market demand for labour equals

    a   the market supply of output.

    b   the sum of the demands for labour of all the firms.

    c   the wage.

    d   the marginal product of labour.

    e   none of the above.

17   If all of a firm's fixed costs are sunk, then it shuts down when

    a   price is less than marginal cost.

    b   price is less than the minimum of the average cost curve.

    c   price is less than the minimum of the average variable cost curve.

    d   accounting profits fall below zero.

    e   economic profits fall below zero.

18   If none of a firm's fixed costs are sunk, then it shuts down when

    a   price is less than marginal cost.

    b   price is less than the minimum of the average cost curve.

    c   price is less than minimum average variable cost.

    d   economic profits fall below zero.

    e   *b* and *d*.

19   If a firm with a U-shaped short-run average cost curve doubles its output by doubling its number of plants and keeps its average cost the same, then the long-run supply is

    a   perfectly elastic.

    b   perfectly inelastic.

    c   upward sloping.

    d   downward sloping.

    e   none of the above.

20   The real product wage is equal to the

    a   value of the marginal product of labour.

    b   marginal cost.

    c   product price.

d   wage divided by the marginal product.

e   wage divided by the product price.

Completion

1   The extra revenue that a firm receives for selling another unit of output is the _____.

2   In the basic competitive model, the marginal revenue equals the _____.

3   The extra cost that the firm bears for producing another unit of output is the _____.

4   The level of output that maximises profits is found by setting _____ equal to _____.

5   The supply curve of the competitive firm is the same as the _____ curve when price is high enough to keep the firm in the market.

6   Costs that are not recoverable are called _____ costs.

7   Economic profits equal revenue received in excess of all _____ costs of operating the firm.

8   The demand for inputs is the _____ of the _____.

9   New firms enter the industry whenever price is greater than the minimum of the _____ curve.

10   The value of the marginal product is found by multiplying the _____ by the _____.

Answers to Self-Test

True or False

1	T	4	F	7	T	10	T	13	T
2	T	5	F	8	F	11	F	14	T
3	F	6	F	9	F	12	F	15	T

Multiple Choice

1	*e*	6	*c*	11	*b*	16	*b*
2	*b*	7	*e*	12	*c*	17	*c*
3	*a*	8	*e*	13	*a*	18	*e*
4	*a*	9	*b*	14	*d*	19	*a*
5	*a*	10	*b*	15	*d*	20	*e*

Completion

1   marginal revenue

2   price

3   marginal cost

4   price, marginal cost

5   marginal cost

6   sunk

7   opportunity

8   value, marginal product

9   average cost

10   marginal product, product price

Tools and Practice Problems

The firm's decision of how much output to supply requires marginal benefit and marginal cost reasoning. So does the firm's demand for labour or any other input. In this section, we will do problems involving the profit-maximising quantity of output and corresponding quantities of inputs. Next, we will investigate the entry and exit decisions, reviewing opportunity and sunk costs. A good understanding of costs allows us to derive the entire supply curve of output. Finally, we will tackle a capstone problem that integrates the production function, cost curves, entry decision, exit decision, supply curve, and demand curve for the competitive firm.

SUPPLY OF OUTPUT

Firms must decide how much output to offer for sale. This supply decision involves balancing marginal revenue and marginal cost. Competitive firms are price takers, so marginal revenue equals price. All this implies that price must equal marginal cost, and this is the rule for profit maximization in the supply of output. Tool Kit 11.1 shows how to solve the problem of how much output to supply.

Tool Kit 11.1 Finding the Quantity of Output to Supply

The quantity of output that maximises the firm's profits is found by setting marginal revenue equal to marginal cost. When the firm is a price taker, the marginal revenue equals the product price. The rule is then to find the quantity for which price equals marginal cost.

Step one: Calculate the marginal cost for each unit of output.

Step two: Identify the market price.

Step three: Find the greatest level of output for which price equals marginal cost. This is the quantity supplied.

---

1   (Worked problem: quantity supplied) Barbara's Carpet Cleaners has fixed costs of £100 per month and a total cost curve as given in Table 11.2. Output is the number of carpets cleaned.

Table 11.2

Output	Total costs
10	£ 200
20	£ 320
30	£ 460
40	£ 620
50	£ 800
60	£1,000

a   The current price for cleaning a carpet is £18. How many carpets must be cleaned to maximise profits? What will the profit be?
b   Suppose that the price falls to £14. Calculate the profit-maximising output and the total profits.

Step-by-step solution

Step one (a): Marginal cost is the extra cost of cleaning another carpet. When output is increased from 0 to 10, total costs increase by £200 – £100 = £100; therefore, the marginal cost is £100/10 = £10. Derive the marginal cost schedule shown in Table 11.3.

Table 11.3

Output	Total costs	Marginal cost
10	£ 200	£10
20	£ 320	£12
30	£ 460	£14
40	£ 620	£16
50	£ 800	£18
60	£1,000	£20

Step two: Identify the market price. It is £18.

Step three: Find the greatest level of output for which price equals marginal cost. The £18 price equals marginal cost when output is 50.

Step four: Calculate profits. Profits equal revenue minus costs. Revenue equals £900 (50 × £18); profits equal £900 – £800 = £100. So the firm makes profits equal to £100.

Step five (b): If the price falls to £14, then price equals marginal cost at 30 units. Profits = (30 × £14) – £460 = –£40, and the firm loses £40.

2   (Practice problem: quantity supplied) The fixed costs for Martin Block, is £10,000. The company's cost schedule is given in Table 11.4.

Table 11.4

Output	Total costs	Marginal cost
10,000	£21,000	
20,000	£32,100	
30,000	£43,300	
40,000	£54,600	
50,000	£66,000	
60,000	£77,500	

a   The current price for blocks is £1.12. Find the profit-maximising quantity of blocks to produce. What will the profit be?
b   Suppose that the price rises to £1.15. Calculate the profit-maximising output and the total profits.

3   (Practice problem: quantity supplied) For each of the following, find the profit-maximising output level, and calculate total profits.

a   Fixed costs = £40,000; price = £600.

Output	Total costs	Marginal cost
100	£ 80,000	
200	£120,000	
300	£170,000	
400	£230,000	
500	£300,000	
600	£380,000	
700	£470,000	

b   Fixed costs = £900; price = £3.00.

Output	Total cost	Marginal cost
1,000	£ 1,900	
2,000	£ 2,900	
3,000	£ 4,600	
4,000	£ 6,600	
5,000	£ 9,400	
6,000	£12,400	
7,000	£16,000	
8,000	£20,000	

c   Fixed costs = £0; price = £80.

Output	Total cost	Marginal cost
1	£ 40	
2	£ 90	
3	£150	
4	£210	
5	£280	
6	£360	
7	£450	
8	£550	

DEMAND FOR INPUTS

Profits are always maximised by setting marginal revenue equal to marginal cost. When the firm is a price taker in both product and input markets, the marginal revenue from hiring another input is the value of the marginal product, which is the marginal product of that input multiplied by the product price. The marginal cost of hiring another input is the input price. In the case of labour, the input price is the wage. Tool Kit 11.2 shows how to solve for the input demand.

Tool Kit 11.2 Finding the Quantity of
an Input to Demand

The demand for an input is its value of the marginal product. This is found by multiplying the marginal product by the product price. Follow this five step procedure to determine the profit-maximising quantity of an input.

Step one: Calculate the marginal product for each level of the input.

Step two: Identify the product price.

Step three: Compute the value of the marginal product by multiplying the marginal product by the product price for each level of the input:

Value of the marginal product
= Marginal product × product price.

Step four: Identify the input price. (In the case of labour, this is the wage.)

Step five: Find the level of the input for which the value of the marginal product equals the input price. This is the quantity demanded.

---

4   (Worked problem: quantity demanded) The new company The Hair Cuttery is ready to start employing stylists. The price of haircuts is £8, and the production function is given in Table 11.5.

Table 11.5

Stylists	Haircuts per day	Marginal product	Value of the marginal product
1	8		
2	16		
3	23		
4	29		
5	34		
6	38		

a   The wage paid to hair stylists is £40 per day. Find the profit-maximising number of hair stylists to hire.

b   Suppose that the wage rises to £64 per day. Find the number of hair stylists that maximises profits.

Step-by-step solution

Step one (a): The marginal product is the extra output that results from hiring one more input. When the first hair stylist is hired, output rises from 0 to 8. The marginal product is 8. Enter this number. When the second hair stylist is hired, output rises from 8 to 16. The marginal product is 16 − 8 = 8; enter this number and continue. The marginal product column is given in Table 11.6.

Table 11.6

Stylists	Haircuts per day	Marginal product	Value of the marginal product
1	8	8	
2	16	8	
3	23	7	
4	29	6	
5	34	5	
6	38	4	

Step two: The product price is £8.

Step three: The value of the marginal product equals the product price multiplied by the marginal product. The value of the marginal product of the first worker is 8 × £8 = £64. Continue to enter the results in the appropriate column. The completed information is given in Table 11.7.

Table 11.7

Stylists	Haircuts per day	Marginal product	Value of the marginal product
1	8	8	£64
2	16	8	£64
3	23	7	£56
4	29	6	£48
5	34	5	£40
6	38	4	£32

Step four: The wage is £40 per day.

Step five: Profits are maximised when the wage is set equal to the value of the marginal product. The wage is £40, which equals the value of the marginal product when 5 hair stylists are hired.

Step six (b): When the wage is £64, it equals the value of the marginal product if 2 stylists are employed.

5   (Practice problem: quantity demanded) Moe's Lawn Service mows lawns for £20 each. Moe's production schedule is given in Table 11.8. Output is measured as the number of lawns mowed.

Table 11.8

Workers	Output per day	Marginal product	Value of the marginal product
1	5.0		
2	9.0		
3	13.0		
4	16.5		
5	19.5		
6	22.0		
7	24.0		

Moe pays his lawn mowers £40 per day.

a   Find the profit-maximising number of mowers to hire.
b   Suppose that the wage rises to £70 per day. Find the profit-maximising number of mowers to hire.

6   (Practice problem: quantity demanded) For each of the following, complete the table and find the profit-maximising number of inputs.

a   Product price = £10; wage = £100 per day.

Workers	Output per day	Marginal product	Value of the marginal product
10	200		
20	360		
30	500		
40	620		
50	720		
60	800		

b   Product price = £10,000; wage = £10,000 per month.

Workers	Output per day	Marginal product	Value of the marginal product
10	20		
20	40		
30	55		
40	65		
50	70		
60	70		

c   Product price = £5; input price = £40.

Workers	Output per day	Marginal product	Value of the marginal product
1,000	10,000		
2,000	18,000		
3,000	25,500		
4,000	31,500		
5,000	36,000		
6,000	40,000		

ENTRY AND EXIT

A firm should seize the opportunity and enter an industry whenever it can make positive (or at least zero) economic profits. This occurs when price is greater than minimum average cost. A firm should give up and exit an industry whenever it can no longer earn revenue in excess of its nonrecoverable costs. If all fixed costs are recoverable, then the firm exits whenever price falls below the minimum of the average cost curve. If none of the fixed costs are recoverable, then the firm exits when price falls below the minimum of the average *variable* cost curve. If some costs are recoverable, the exit price lies somewhere in between. Tool Kit 11.3 explores this idea.

Tool Kit 11.3 Determining Entry and Exit Prices

Firms enter the market when the price rises above the minimum average cost. They exit when the price falls below the minimum average recoverable cost. Follow this procedure to find these prices.

Step one: Calculate the average cost for each level of output.

Step two: Find the minimum average cost; this is the entry price. When the price is greater than or equal to the minimum average cost, then the firm should enter the market.

Step three: Identify all costs that are not sunk (nonrecoverable).

Step four: Calculate the average of the costs that are not sunk.

Step five: Find the minimum average nonsunk cost; this is the exit price. When the price falls below this level, the firm should exit the market.

---

7   (Worked problem: entry and exit prices) Let's return to Barbara's Carpet Cleaners in problem 1. The total cost schedule is given in Table 11.9.

Table 11.9

Output	Total cost
10	£ 200
20	£ 320
30	£ 460
40	£ 620
50	£ 800
60	£1,000

a   Find the entry price, which is the minimum price that will induce the firm to enter the market.

b   Assume that all the fixed costs are sunk. Find the exit price, which is the maximum price that will induce the firm to exit the market.

c   Now assume that £50 of the fixed costs is recoverable. Find the exit price.

Step-by-step solution

Step one (a): Calculate the average cost for each level of output, and enter it in the table. The average cost at 10 carpets is £200/10 = £20. Continue to fill in the column as in Table 11.10.

Table 11.10

Output	Total costs	Average cost
10	£ 200	£20.00
20	£ 320	£16.00
30	£ 460	£15.33
40	£ 620	£15.50
50	£ 800	£16.00
60	£1,000	£16.66

Step two: The minimum of the average cost curve is £15.33, and this is the entry price. This is the answer to part *a*.

Step three (b): Identify the costs that are not sunk. If all fixed costs are sunk, then only the variable costs can be recovered. In this case, the exit price is the minimum average variable cost. First, compute variable cost by subtracting fixed costs from total costs. The variable costs for 10 units of output is £200 − £100 = £100. Continue to fill in this column as in Table 11.11.

Table 11.11

Output	Total costs	Variable costs
10	£ 200	£100
20	£ 320	£220
30	£ 460	£360
40	£ 620	£520
50	£ 800	£700
60	£1,000	£900

Step four: Compute average variable cost. For 10 carpets, the average variable cost is £100/10 = £10. Enter the results as given in Table 11.12.

Table 11.12

Output	Total cost	Variable cost	Average variable cost
10	£ 200	£100	£10
20	£ 320	£220	£11
30	£ 460	£360	£12
40	£ 620	£520	£13
50	£ 800	£700	£14
60	£1,000	£900	£15

Step five: The minimum average variable cost is £10; therefore, the firm should exit when the price falls below £10. This is the answer to part *b*.

Step six (c): Only £50 is sunk; thus, the firm exits when revenues fall below variable costs plus £50. To find the recoverable costs, simply add £50 to the variable costs. Next, find the average of these numbers, and the minimum of these averages is the exit price. The results appear in Table 11.13.

Table 11.13

Output	Variable costs	Recoverable costs	Average recoverable cost
10	£100	£150	£15.00
20	£220	£270	£13.50
30	£360	£410	£13.66
40	£520	£570	£14.25
50	£700	£750	£15.00
60	£900	£950	£15.83

The minimum of the average recoverable cost column is £13.50, which is the exit price. When the price is £13.50, the firm loses £50, which means that revenue covers all but the nonrecoverable costs.

8   (Practice problem: entry and exit prices) Now let's return to Martin Block in problem 2. The total cost schedule is reprinted in Table 11.14. Fixed costs equal £10,000.

Table 11.14

Output	Total cost
10,000	£21,000
20,000	£32,100
30,000	£43,300
40,000	£54,600
50,000	£66,000
60,000	£77,500

a   Find the entry price, which is the minimum price that will induce the firm to enter the market.

b   Assume that all of the fixed costs are sunk. Find the exit price, which is the maximum price that will induce the firm to exit the market.

9   (Practice problem: entry and exit prices) Find the entry price and the exit price for the firms in problem 3. Assume that all the fixed costs are sunk.

10 (Worked problem: applications) The competitive firm is a price taker in product and input markets. It has a production function and a level of fixed costs. Given this information, we can derive all the firm's cost curves, its supply curve, its demand curve, and the price at which it will enter or exit the industry. Remo's Repos recovers cars from borrowers who default on loan repayments. Local banks pay it £50 per car recovered. Remo hires workers at £100 per night to

repossess the cars. He runs a low-budget operation with fixed costs of only £500. The production function is given in Table 11.15, where output is measured as the number of cars repossessed.

a   Complete the table below, and calculate the profit-maximising number of workers to hire.

Table 11.15

Agents	Output	Marginal product	Value of the marginal product
1	8		
2	15		
3	21		
4	26		
5	30		
6	33		
7	35		
8	36		
9	37		

b   Complete the cost table below, and calculate the profit-maximising number of cars to repossess.

Output	Total costs	Variable costs	Average cost	Average variable cost	Marginal cost

c   Verify that the number of workers hired repossesses the quantity of output produced.
d   Find the entry price.
e   Assume that the fixed costs are sunk, and find the exit price.

Step-by-step solution

Step one (a): Follow the solution to problem 4, and complete the table given above. The results are given in Table 11.16.

Table 11.16

Agents	Output	Marginal product	Value of the marginal product
1	8	8	£400
2	15	7	£350
3	21	6	£300
4	26	5	£250
5	30	4	£200
6	33	3	£150
7	35	2	£100
8	36	1	£ 50
9	37	1	£ 50

Step two: Set the input price (£100) equal to the value of the marginal product, which is £100 when 7 workers are hired.

Step three (b): Compute the cost for each output level in the production function. For 8 cars repossessed, 1 worker is

hired at £100 and fixed costs are £500; therefore, total costs equal £100 + £500 = £600. Enter this number. For 15 cars, 2 workers at £100 each added to the £500 gives total costs of £700. Continue and complete the total cost column. The result is given in Table 11.17.

Table 11.17

Output	Total cost
8	£ 600
15	£ 700
21	£ 800
26	£ 900
30	£1,000
33	£1,100
35	£1,200
36	£1,300
37	£1,400

Step four: Follow the solution to problems 1 and 7, and complete the table. Be careful with marginal cost. For example, the marginal cost at 8 cars is (£600 − £500)/8 = £12.50. The marginal cost at 15 cars is (£700 − £600)/(15 − 8) = £14.29. The complete information is given in Table 11.18.

Table 11.18

Output	Total costs	Variable costs	Average cost	Average variable cost	Marginal cost
8	£ 600	£100	£75.00	£12.50	£ 12.50
15	£ 700	£200	£46.66	£13.33	£ 14.29
21	£ 800	£300	£38.09	£14.28	£ 16.66
26	£ 900	£400	£34.61	£15.38	£ 20.00
30	£1,000	£500	£33.33	£16.66	£ 25.00
33	£1,100	£600	£33.33	£18.18	£ 33.33
35	£1,200	£700	£34.28	£20.00	£ 50.00
36	£1,300	£800	£36.11	£22.22	£100.00
37	£1,400	£900	£37.83	£24.32	£100.00

Step five: Set price equal to marginal cost. The price is £50, which equals marginal cost when 35 cars are repossessed.

Step six (c): Check the production function to make sure that when 7 workers are hired, 35 cars are repossessed.

Step seven (d): The entry price is the minimum average cost, which is £33.33. Note that marginal cost equals average cost at the minimum average cost.

Step eight (e): The exit price for the case in which all fixed costs are sunk is the minimum average variable cost, which is £12.50. Again, note that at the minimum average variable cost, it is equal to marginal cost.

11   (Practice problem: applications) Perry's Perfect Pet Place hires people to groom dogs. Perry pays the groomer £20 per day and charges the dogs £10 per treatment. His fixed costs are £50. The production function is given in Table 11.19.

a   Complete the table below, and calculate the profit-maximising number of groomers to hire.

Table 11.19

Groomers	Treatments	Marginal product	Value of the marginal product
1	6		
2	11		
3	15		
4	18		
5	20		
6	21		

b   Complete the cost table below, and calculate the profit-maximising number of dogs to groom.

Output	Total costs	Variable costs	Average cost	Average variable cost	Marginal cost

c   Verify that the number of groomers hired does give the profit-maximising number of treatments.
d   Find the entry price.
e   Assume that the fixed costs are sunk, and find the exit price.

Answers to Problems

2   *a*   The marginal costs are given in Table 11.20.

Table 11.20

Output	Total costs	Marginal cost
10,000	£21,000	—
20,000	£32,100	£1.11
30,000	£43,300	£1.12
40,000	£54,600	£1.13
50,000	£66,000	£1.14
60,000	£77,500	£1.15

When the price is £1.12, output is 30,000, and profits equal (£1.12 × 30,000) − £43,300 = −£9,400.

b   When the price is £1.15, output is 60,000, and profits equal (£1.15 × 60,000) − £77,500 = −£8,500.

3   *a*   The marginal cost are given in Table 11.21.

Table 11.21

Output	Total costs	Marginal cost
100	£ 80,000	£400
200	£120,000	£400
300	£170,000	£500
400	£230,000	£600
500	£300,000	£700
600	£380,000	£800
700	£470,000	£900

Output = 400; profits = (£600 × 400) − £230,000 = £10,000.

b   The marginal costs are given in Table 11.22.

Table 11.22

Output	Total costs	Marginal cost
1,000	£ 1,900	£1.00
2,000	£ 2,900	£1.00
3,000	£ 4,600	£1.70
4,000	£ 6,600	£2.00
5,000	£ 9,400	£2.80
6,000	£12,400	£3.00
7,000	£16,000	£3.60
8,000	£20,000	£4.00

Output = 6,000; profits = (£3.00 × 6,000) − £12,400 = £5,600.

c   The marginal costs are given in Table 11.23.

Table 11.23

Output	Total costs	Marginal cost
1	£ 40	£ 40
2	£ 90	£ 50
3	£150	£ 60
4	£210	£ 60
5	£280	£ 70
6	£360	£ 80
7	£450	£ 90
8	£550	£100

Output = 6; profits = (6 × £80) − £360 = £120.

5   The values of the marginal product are given in Table 11.24.

Table 11.24

Workers	Output per day	Marginal product	Value of the marginal product
1	5.0	5.0	£100
2	9.0	4.0	£ 80
3	13.0	4.0	£ 80
4	16.5	3.5	£ 70
5	19.5	3.0	£ 60
6	22.0	2.5	£ 50
7	24.0	2.0	£ 40

a   When the wage is £40, it equals the value of the marginal product if 7 are employed.
b   When the wage is £70, it equals the value of the marginal product if 4 are employed.

6   *a*   The values of the marginal product are given in Table 11.25. The quantity demanded is 50 workers.

Table 11.25

Workers	Output per day	Marginal product	Value of the marginal product
10	200	20	£200
20	360	16	£160
30	500	14	£140
40	620	12	£120
50	720	10	£100
60	800	8	£ 80

b   The value of the marginal product is given in Table 11.26. The quantity demanded is 40 workers.

Table 11.26

Workers	Output per day	Marginal product	Value of the marginal product
10	20	2.0	£20,000
20	40	2.0	£20,000
30	55	1.5	£15,000
40	65	1.0	£10,000
50	70	0.5	£ 5,000
60	70	0	£ 0

c   The value of the marginal product is given in Table 11.27. The quantity demanded is 2,000 workers.

Table 11.27

Workers	Output per day	Marginal product	Value of the marginal product
1,000	10,000	10.0	£50.00
2,000	18,000	8.0	£40.00
3,000	25,500	7.5	£37.50
4,000	31,500	6.0	£30.00
5,000	36,000	4.5	£22.50
6,000	40,000	4.0	£20.00

8   The cost measures are given in Table 11.28.

Table 11.28

Output	Total costs	Average cost	Variable costs	Average variable cost
10,000	£21,000	£2.10	£11,000	£1.10
20,000	£32,100	£1.61	£22,100	£1.11
30,000	£43,300	£1.43	£33.300	£1.11
40,000	£54,600	£1.37	£44,600	£1.12
50,000	£66,000	£1.32	£56,000	£1.12
60,000	£77,500	£1.29	£67,500	£1.13

a   Entry price = £1.29.
b   Exit price = £1.10.

9   *a*   The cost measures appear in Table 11.29.

Table 11.29

Output	Total costs	Average cost	Variable costs	Average variable cost
100	£ 80,000	£800	£ 40,000	£400
200	£120,000	£600	£ 80,000	£400
300	£170,000	£567	£130,000	£433
400	£230,000	£575	£190,000	£475
500	£300,000	£600	£260,000	£520
600	£380,000	£633	£340,000	£567
700	£470,000	£671	£430,000	£614

Entry price = £567; exit price = £400.

b   The cost measures appear in Table 11.30.

Table 11.30

Output	Total costs	Average cost	Variable costs	Average variable cost
1,000	£ 1,900	£1.90	£ 1,000	£1.00
2,000	£ 2,900	£1.45	£ 2,000	£1.00
3,000	£ 4,600	£1.53	£ 3,700	£1.23
4,000	£ 6,600	£1.65	£ 5,700	£1.43
5,000	£ 9,400	£1.88	£ 8,500	£1.70
6,000	£12,400	£2.07	£11,500	£1.92
7,000	£16,000	£2.29	£15,100	£2.16
8,000	£20,000	£2.50	£19,100	£2.39

Entry price = £1.45; exit price = £1.00.

c   The cost measures appear in Table 11.31.

Table 11.31

Output	Total costs	Average cost	Variable costs	Average variable cost
1	£ 40	£40.00	£ 40	£40.00
2	£ 90	£45.00	£ 90	£45.00
3	£150	£50.00	£150	£50.00
4	£210	£52.50	£210	£52.50
5	£280	£56.00	£280	£56.00
6	£360	£60.00	£360	£60.00
7	£450	£64.29	£450	£64.29
8	£550	£68.75	£550	£68.75

Entry price = £40; exit price = £40.

11   *a*   The complete information is given in Table 11.32.

Table 11.32

Groomers	Treatments	Marginal product	Value of the marginal product
1	6	6	£60
2	11	5	£50
3	15	4	£40
4	18	3	£30
5	20	2	£20
6	21	1	£10

Perry should hire 5 groomers.

b   The completed cost information appears in Table 11.33.

Table 11.33

Output	Total costs	Variable costs	Average cost	Average variable cost	Marginal cost
6	£ 70	£ 20	£11.67	£3.33	£ 3.33
11	£ 90	£ 40	£ 8.18	£3.64	£ 4.00
15	£110	£ 60	£ 7.33	£4.00	£ 5.00
18	£130	£ 80	£ 7.22	£4.44	£ 6.33
20	£150	£100	£ 7.50	£5.00	£10.00
21	£170	£120	£ 8.10	£5.71	£20.00

Perry should sell 20 treatments.

c   5 groomers complete 20 treatments.

d   Entry price = £7.22.

e   Exit price = £3.33.

COMPETITIVE EQUILIBRIUM

Chapter Review

The elements of the basic competitive model have been presented over the last six chapters of the text. In Chapter 12, these elements—from individuals and their decisions regarding consumption, savings, investment, and work, to firms and their choices regarding production and costs—are brought together in the general equilibrium model. The focus of the model is on the interdependencies of the product, labour, and capital markets. Another major topic is a normative one: how well does the competitive economy perform? The notion of Pareto efficiency provides a tool with which economists can evaluate how well the market economy answers the basic economic questions. This chapter completes the presentation of the competitive model and closes Part Two. In Part Three, attention shifts to imperfect markets.

ESSENTIAL CONCEPTS

1   Partial equilibrium analysis looks at one market in isolation. This kind of analysis can be inappropriate if changes in the market under consideration cause disturbances in the rest of the economy, which then feed back in an important way to the original market. General equilibrium analysis takes into account the relationships among different markets and keeps track of the interactions.

2   The basic competitive three-market model is a relatively simple general equilibrium model and is very good for analysing the interactions among markets. The three markets are the labour, capital, and product markets. They are interdependent in that as the price changes in one market, demand and supply curves shift in the others. In general equilibrium, the three prices (wage, interest rate, and product price) are set so that each market clears.

   a   Demand equals supply in the labour market.
   b   Demand equals supply in the capital market.
   c   Demand equals supply in the goods market.

3   Another view of the general equilibrium of the economy is given by the circular flow model. The simple version given in Figure 12.1 shows that households supply labour and financial capital to firms and demand products. Firms demand labour and capital and supply products. The flows of funds balance. For example, the revenue that firms receive for the sale of their goods equals the payments to labour as wages and to capital as divi-

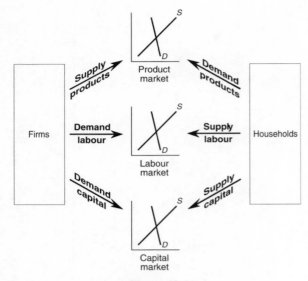

Figure 12.1

dends and interest. The circular flow model can be expanded to keep track of flows between one country and the rest of the world and between the private sector and the government.

4   The concept of efficiency used by economists is called **Pareto efficiency.** An allocation of resources is Pareto efficient if there is no way to reallocate resources to make anyone better off without making someone else worse off. The equilibrium of the competitive economy is Pareto efficient. There is **exchange efficiency** because the goods and services produced by the economy are distributed efficiently among individuals, **production efficiency** because the economy is on its production possibilities curve, and **product-mix efficiency** because the mix of goods matches consumers' tastes.

5   Free-market economists take the view that the basic competitive model provides a good description of the world, and they see a quite limited role for government. Imperfect-market economists, on the other hand, take the competitive model as an important base but move beyond its boundaries to investigate situations where the economy is inefficient. Although they see a role for government in market failures, all economists caution that this does not necessarily imply that any particular government intervention will improve matters. Effective government intervention requires careful consideration of the reasons for market inefficiencies and the design of the remedy.

BEHIND THE ESSENTIAL CONCEPTS

1   The interdependencies of markets demonstrate another facet of the principle of substitution. When the price of one good rises, the demand for its substitutes rises, while the demand for its complements falls. When the

price of one input rises, firms substitute other inputs. A change in the capital market affects the wealth of consumers and the costs of firms. The economy is a spider's web, and a movement in any one part reverberates throughout the whole.

2   Even though there are connections among all markets, in many cases the effects beyond a single market may be small. When this is true, it is sufficient to concentrate on the one market, that is, to employ partial equilibrium analysis and ignore any general equilibrium repercussions. The art of economic analysis is to bring to light the important general equilibrium considerations and leave aside the portion of the economy that remains relatively unaffected.

3   If a firm produces several goods and there exists a way to rearrange its production and increase the output of one good without reducing the output of any other, an economist would say that this firm is inefficient. The firm is wasting inputs, because it is not getting the maximum output from the inputs. The output of the economy is the satisfaction (the utility) of its members. Therefore, if the economy is doing things one way, and there exists another way to do things that increases the utility of one individual (makes her better off) without reducing the utility of anyone else, then, just like the firm above, the economy is inefficient. Pareto efficiency is a natural definition of efficiency for the economy, the important output of which is ultimately not goods and services but human satisfaction.

SELF-TEST

True or False

1   A general equilibrium analysis takes into account all the important interactions among markets.

2   A partial equilibrium analysis focuses on one market only.

3   General equilibrium and partial equilibrium analyses always differ quite dramatically.

4   For the most part, in the capital market, firms are demanders and households are suppliers.

5   In the product market, firms are demanders and households are suppliers.

6   In the labor market, firms are demanders and households are suppliers.

7   The economy is in equilibrium when most of its markets clear.

8   In the circular flow model, the flows to households must equal the flows from households.

9   In the circular flow model, exports plus funds lent abroad must equal imports plus money borrowed from abroad.

10   The allocation of resources is Pareto efficient in competitive equilibrium.

11 The allocation of resources is equal in competitive equilibrium.

12 Pareto efficiency means that everyone can be made better off by some reallocation of resources.

13 Imperfect-market economists despair of the market's ability to produce efficient outcomes and advocate government control over the economy.

14 All points along the production possibilities curve are Pareto efficient.

15 Pareto efficiency requires exchange efficiency, production efficiency, and product-mix efficiency.

Multiple Choice

1 When an analysis focuses on the interactions between markets, it is called

  a   partial equilibrium analysis.
  b   interactive equilibrium analysis.
  c   disequilibrium analysis.
  d   general equilibrium analysis.
  e   none of the above.

2 When an analysis looks only at the changes in one market, it is called

  a   partial equilibrium analysis.
  b   interactive equilibrium analysis.
  c   disequilibrium analysis.
  d   general equilibrium analysis.
  e   none of the above.

3 In a general equilibrium model, the supply of labour depends upon

  a   product prices.
  b   the wage.
  c   interest rates.
  d   all of the above.
  e   *a* and *b*.

4 In a general equilibrium model, the supply of products depends upon the wage and interest rates because

  a   these input prices affect costs.
  b   household income is affected by changes in the wage and interest rates.
  c   households can substitute leisure or future consumption for current products.
  d   the demand for capital depends upon the wage rate.
  e   all of the above.

5 Which of the following is *not* necessarily true when the economy is in full, general equilibrium?

  a   The supply of labour equals the demand.
  b   The supply of products equals the demand.
  c   The supply of capital equals the demand.
  d   The distribution of income is fair.
  e   None of the above.

6 An increase in immigration will shift the supply of

  a   labour to the left, decreasing wages.
  b   labour to the right, decreasing wages.

  c   products to the right, decreasing prices.
  d   products to the left, increasing prices.
  e   *b* and *c*.

7 In general equilibrium, a tax on business profits will be paid by individuals through

  a   increases in product prices.
  b   decreases in wages.
  c   decreases in dividends.
  d   capital losses on share ownership.
  e   all of the above.

8 An increase in the tax rate on commercial property will

  a   have no effect on the returns to other forms of capital investment.
  b   cause financial capital to flow from commercial property to other forms of capital investment, reducing the average return to capital.
  c   have no effect on the allocation of financial capital.
  d   have no effect on the returns to capital because all investments must be equally profitable in equilibrium.
  e   *a* and *c*.

9 If the allocation of resources is Pareto efficient,

  a   the distribution of income is fair.
  b   there is a way to reallocate resources and make everyone better off.
  c   there is a way to reallocate resources and make some people better off without making others worse off.
  d   there is no way to reallocate resources and make anyone better off without making someone else worse off.
  e   none of the above.

10 In the basic circular flow model,

  a   households demand goods and services.
  b   firms supply goods and services.
  c   households supply labour and financial capital.
  d   firms demand labour and financial capital.
  e   all of the above.

11 The circular flow model shows that

  a   some taxes are paid by businesses and some by households.
  b   all taxes are paid by businesses through lower product prices, higher wages, or higher costs of capital.
  c   all taxes are paid by households through higher product prices, lower wages, or lower returns to capital.
  d   the government pays all taxes.
  e   none of the above.

12 Which of the following probably does *not* require a general equilibrium analysis?

  a   A change in corporate taxes
  b   A ban on foreign investment
  c   A change in value-added tax

d   Elimination of trade restrictions

e   None of the above

13   Which of the following probably requires only a partial equilibrium analysis?

a   An increase in the supply of green beans

b   Stricter anti-pollution regulations

c   A reduction in the size of the military by one-half

d   An end to agricultural price supports

e   All of the above

14   According to the circular flow model, if personal income tax is cut, then

a   government borrowing increases.

b   some other tax is increased.

c   government spending decreases.

d   all of the above.

e   Either *a, b,* or *c,* or some combination of each.

15   Free-market economists believe that

a   market outcomes are usually efficient.

b   the market's determination of the distribution of income is just.

c   markets cannot be relied upon to produce efficient outcomes.

d   the market brings about production efficiency but not exchange efficiency.

e   the market brings about exchange efficiency but not production efficiency.

16   Imperfect-market economists believe that

a   market outcomes are usually efficient.

b   the market's determination of the distribution of income is just.

c   markets cannot be relied upon to produce efficient outcomes.

d   the market brings about production efficiency but not exchange efficiency.

e   the market brings about exchange efficiency but not production efficiency.

17   Exchange efficiency means that

a   the distribution of the goods and services that the economy produces is efficient.

b   the distribution of the goods and services that the economy produces is equitable.

c   the economy is operating along its production possibilities curve.

d   all of the above.

e   *a* and *b*.

18   Production efficiency means that

a   the mix of goods and services that the economy produces reflects the preferences of consumers.

b   the economy is operating along its production possibilities curve.

c   the distribution of what the economy produces is efficient.

d   the distribution of what the economy produces is equitable.

e   all of the above.

19   Which of the following is *not* implied by Pareto efficiency?

a   Exchange efficiency

b   Production efficiency

c   Efficiency of the product mix

d   All individuals share equally in the decisions that the economy makes

e   None of the above.

20   If the competitive model is an accurate depiction of the economy, then

a   the allocation of resources is Pareto efficient.

b   the distribution of income may be quite unequal.

c   the economy is operating on the production possibilities curve.

d   the economy is operating on the utility possibilities curve.

e   all of the above.

Completion

1   Focusing on a single market while ignoring any spillover effects on other markets is called _____ analysis.

2   _____ analysis takes into account all the interactions and interdependencies between various parts of the economy.

3   In the simple circular flow model of the economy, households _____ labour and savings (financial capital) to firms and _____ goods and services.

4   In the simple circular flow model of the economy, firms _____ labour and financial capital from households and _____ goods and services.

5   When there is no way to make anyone better off without making someone else worse off, the allocation of resources is _____.

6   _____ requires that the economy's output of goods and services be distributed efficiently among its consumers.

7   When the economy is productively efficient, it is operating on its _____ curve.

8   The view that the basic competitive model gives a good description of the world is held by _____.

9   _____ believe that there are many examples of market failure and that well-designed government intervention can improve matters.

10   Environmental degradation and unemployment are examples of _____.

Answers to Self-Test

True or False

1	T	4	T	7	F	10	T	13	F
2	T	5	F	8	T	11	F	14	F
3	F	6	T	9	F	12	F	15	T

Multiple Choice

1	*d*	6	*e*	11	*c*	16	*c*
2	*a*	7	*e*	12	*e*	17	*a*
3	*d*	8	*b*	13	*a*	18	*b*
4	*a*	9	*d*	14	*e*	19	*d*
5	*d*	10	*e*	15	*a*	20	*e*

Completion

1   partial equilibrium
2   General equilibrium
3   supply, demand
4   demand, supply
5   Pareto efficient
6   Exchange efficiency
7   production possibilities
8   free-market economists
9   Imperfect-market economists
10 market failure

Tools and Practice Problems

The skill in general equilibrium analysis lies in choosing which interdependencies are important and which can be left aside. In this problem set, we first use the three-market model to analyse the effects of major changes in the economy: the introduction of a sales or value-added tax, an important technological advance, and an increase in savings. Finally, there are a few problems that focus on the connections between two markets. We consider corporate taxation, compensating differentials, and natural resource prices.

Tool Kit 12.1 Using General Equilibrium Analysis

When doing general equilibrium analysis, keep the following procedure in mind.

Step one: Identify the relevant markets.

Step two: Start with an equilibrium in each market, as in the figure.

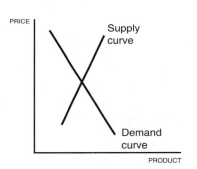 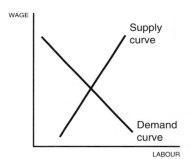 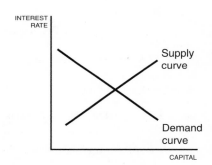

Step three: Identify a change, and determine which curves shift as a direct result of the change. In the second row of the figure, the demand for labour shifts outwards.

Step four: Shift the curves, and find the new equilibrium. In the general equilibrium model, this is only a temporary equilibrium because there are second-round effects to be accounted for. Observe which prices have changed. In the diagram, wages increase.

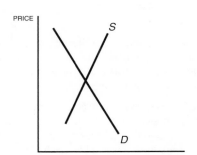 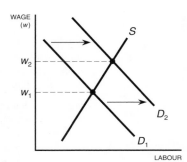 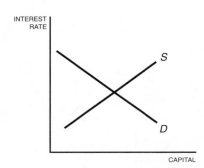

Step five: Determine which curves shift as a result of the price changes observed in step four.

Step six: Shift the curves, as shown here by lower supply in the product market and higher demand in the capital market, and find the new equilibrium.

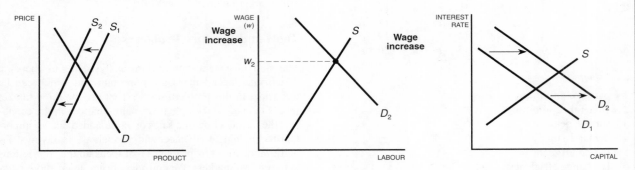

Step seven: Stop. Usually a second round is enough to identify the direction of changes in related markets. Compare the new equilibrium with that in step two.

---

1   (Worked problem: general equilibrium analysis) There are three major markets: labour, capital, and product. They are interrelated in that the prices in other markets cause the demand curves and supply curves to shift. Because of this interdependence, there will be important second-round effects in the three-market model. Most European countries have value-added taxes, a type of sales tax.

a   Use the three-market model to evaluate the effects of a value-added tax.

b   Who pays the value-added tax?

Step-by-step solution

Step one (a): Identify the relevant markets. We will use the labour, capital, and product markets.

Step two: Start with an equilibrium in each market.

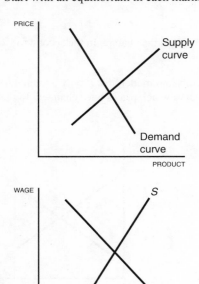

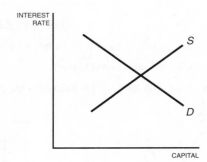

Step three: The value-added tax shifts the product market supply curve up by the amount of the tax. (This step is exactly like the analysis of the effects of taxes in Chapter 5.)

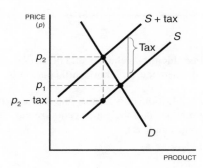

Step four: Find the new (temporary) equilibrium. Note that some of the tax is paid by consumers in the form of higher product prices. On the other hand, firms also receive less after the tax. This completes the first round.

Step five: Determine which curves shift as a result of the price changes observed in step four. The lower net of tax product prices observed in step four implies that the value of the marginal product of inputs is lower. This means that the demand curve for labour and the demand curve for capital must shift to the left.

Step six: Shift the curves, and find the new equilibrium.

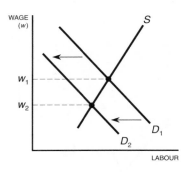

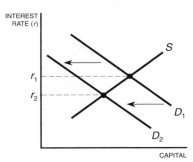

Step seven: Compare the new equilibrium with that in step two. We see that the wage and the interest rate are lower.

Step eight (b): The value-added tax is paid for in three ways. First, it is shifted forwards to consumers in the form of higher product prices. Second, it is shifted backwards to workers through lower wages. Third, it is shifted backwards to savers in terms of lower interest rates. A vital lesson of the general equilibrium approach is that all taxes are ultimately paid by individuals. A partial equilibrium treatment in the product market alone would imply that firms pay some of the tax. The full general equilibrium analysis reveals that the producers' share of the tax is passed backwards to workers and savers.

2   (Practice problem: general equilibrium analysis) A substantial share in the growth of developed countries is accounted for by technological advance, by improvements in how goods and services are produced, and by the introduction of new and better products. The hope for continued economic progress rests on technological advance in production. Use the three-market model to analyse the effects of a major technological advance.

a   Start with an equilibrium in the three markets.
b   Better technology increases the marginal products of labour and capital. Which curves are shifted? (Hint: Remember the formula for the value of the marginal product and the relationship between marginal product and marginal cost.)
c   In the second round, how does the equilibrium change?

3   (Practice problem: general equilibrium analysis) Many people are concerned about the low savings rate. One cause for optimism is that the aging of the relatively large baby boom generation will lead to more savings. Suppose that households decrease their consumption and increase their savings. Trace through the effects using the three-market model.

4   (Worked problem: general equilibrium analysis) Often when a change occurs in one market, there is another market closely linked to the first. In these cases, both markets must be included in the analysis. Investors seeking the highest possible returns can choose to buy shares in quoted companies or to invest their money in unquoted companies. If the returns were higher in the quoted sector of the economy, then no one would invest in the unquoted sector. If the returns were higher in the unquoted sector, all money would flow out of the quoted sector. In equilibrium, then, the rate of return must be equal in the two sectors.

a   Illustrate an equilibrium in the markets for quoted and unquoted investment.
b   In Britain, companies must pay taxes on their income. Corporatation tax is in addition to the taxes paid by investors on their dividend income. Show how a corporation tax on quoted companies affects the market for investment in the quoted sector.
c   Show how the investment in unquoted companies will adjust to restore both markets to equilibrium.
d   Who pays the tax on quoted companies?

Step-by-step solution

Step one (a): Start with an equilibrium. In this case, not only must supply and demand be equal in each market, but also each market must pay the same returns.

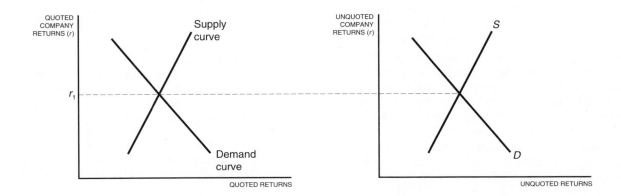

Step two (b): Determine which curve shifts. The quoted company tax is paid by the demanders (quoted companies); therefore, the demand curve in the market for quoted company investment shifts down.

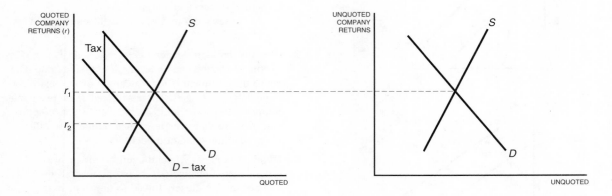

Step three: The (temporary) equilibrium in the market for quoted investment has a lower rate of return than in the market for unquoted investment.

Step four (c): Determine the effects in the unquoted investment market. Because they can earn higher after-tax returns in the unquoted sector, investors in quoted companies will move their money. The supply of quoted investment will shift left, and the supply of unquoted investment will shift right, until the returns are equal.

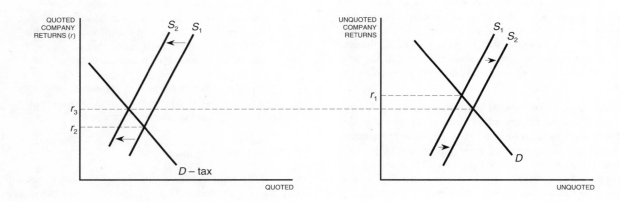

Step five (d): Find the new equilibrium and compare. In the new equilibrium, the returns are equal in each sector, but overall the returns are lower. We conclude that the quoted company tax is paid by both quoted and unquoted investors.

5   (Practice problem: general equilibrium analysis) Differences in wages that reflect differences in the characteristics of jobs are called compensating differentials. Long-distance lorry drivers are paid more than those who work on local routes. Suppose that the difference is £50 per week in equilibrium.

   a   Start with an equilibrium in the markets for local and long-distance drivers. Be sure that the difference in wages is £50 per week.

   b   A new policy, agreed upon by both union and management, specifies that each driver must earn the same amount. Explain how the markets will adjust.

6   (Practice problem: general equilibrium analysis) Many people are concerned about the possible exhaustion of the limited supplies of natural resources, such as oil. To understand the economics of this issue, consider a two-period problem. Known reserves of oil equal 100,000 barrels. The oil can be sold now or be saved and sold in the future period. The discount rate is 50 percent over the time between the periods. The demand is the same now and in the future, and it is given in Table 12.1.

Table 12.1

Price	Quantity	Present discounted value of the future price
£50	20,000	
£45	30,000	
£40	40,000	
£35	55,000	
£30	70,000	
£25	80,000	
£20	90,000	
£10	100,000	

a   Calculate the present discounted value of each of the prices for the future demand. This is the current value of waiting to sell at the future price.

b   If the current price is greater than the present discounted value of the future price, all the oil will be sold today. If the reverse is true, the oil will be sold in the future. In equilibrium, current price must equal the present discounted value of the future price, and the total quantity sold in both periods must equal 100,000 barrels. Find the equilibrium price today, the price in the future, and the quantity sold in each period.

Answers to Problems

2 a   The initial equilibrium price is p_1, the wage is w_1, and the interest rate is r_1, as in figure **a.**

b   The technical advance shifts the demands for labour and capital to the right because both factors are made more productive, and it shifts the supply of products to the right because costs are lower. The product price falls to p_2, the wage rises to w_2, and the interest rate rises to r_2, as in figure **b.**

c   In the second round, the supply curve for products shifts left (mitigating the effects of the original shift) because wages and interest rates are higher. The demand curves for labour and capital shift back to the left (offsetting somewhat the effects of the original shift) because product prices are lower. (Recall that the demand for a factor of production is the value of the marginal product, which is price

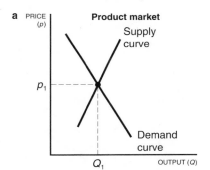
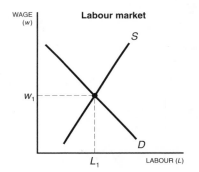
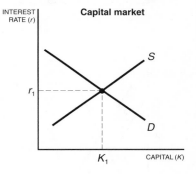
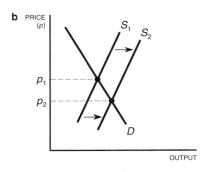
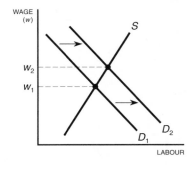
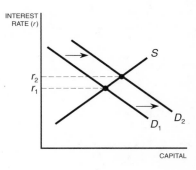
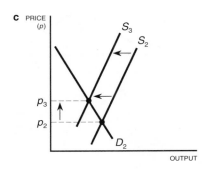
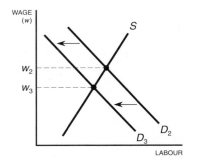
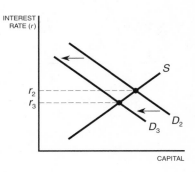

multiplied by marginal product.) The ultimate price is p_3, which is higher than p_1 but lower than p_2, because of the general equilibrium repercussions. Similarly, w_3 is greater than w_1 and r_3 is greater than r_1, as in figure **c.** But the changes are less great than a partial equilibrium analysis would imply.

3   a   The initial equilibrium price is p_1, the wage is w_1, and the interest rate is r_1, as in figure **a.**

b   As people consume less, the demand for output falls. As they save more, the supply shifts to the right in the capital market. Product prices and interest rates fall as a result, as in figure **b.**

c   In the second round, the fall in interest rates shifts the supply of output to the right and further reduces product prices. The fall in product prices, observed in part b, reduces the demand for capital and leads to a further decrease in the interest rate. In the labour market, demand shifts up because of lower interest rates but shifts down because of lower product prices, as in figure **c.** The ultimate impact on the wage is not certain.

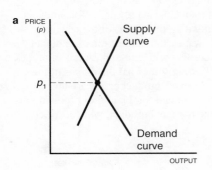
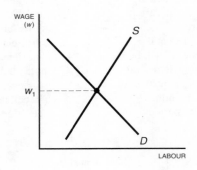
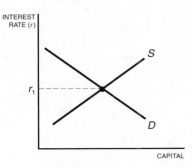

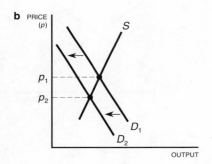
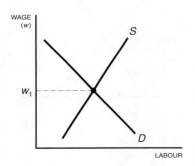
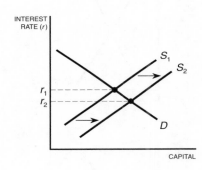

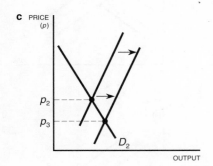
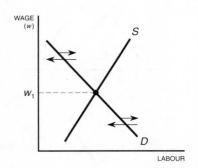
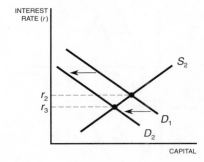

5   *a*   In the initial equilibrium, both markets clear, and the weekly wage is £50 higher in the long-distance market.

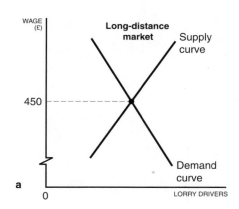 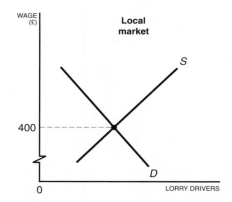

b   When the same wage is paid in the two markets, there is a shortage of long-distance drivers, and a surplus of drivers in the local market.

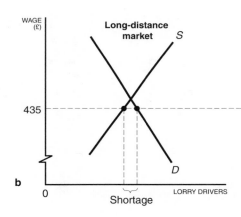 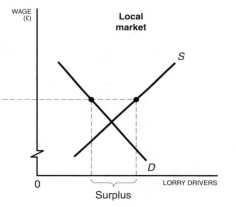

6   *a*   The present discounted value of the future price is given in Table 12.2.

Table 12.2

Price	Quantity	*Present discounted value of the future price*
£50	20,000	£50/(1 + £.50) = £33.33
£45	30,000	£30.00
£40	40,000	£26.67
£35	55,000	£23.33
£30	70,000	£20.00
£25	80,000	£16.67
£20	90,000	£13.33
£10	100,000	£ 6.67

b   The current price is £30, and 70,000 barrels are sold. The future price is £45, and 30,000 barrels are sold. The total is 70,000 + 30,000 = 100,000. The present discounted value of the future price is £30, which is the current price.

Part Three

IMPERFECT MARKETS

Chapter 13

MONOPOLIES AND IMPERFECT COMPETITION

Chapter Review

With the detailed study of perfect competition completed in Part Two, this chapter begins the study of imperfect competition. The real world differs from the basic competitive model in many important ways, and these differences shape the remainder of the text.

The first difference involves setting prices. While the competitive firm must accept the market price as a given fact, most firms in the real world have some control over their prices. How prices are set in monopolies, where there is only one seller, is the first topic taken up in the textbook chapter. The chapter then turns to a discussion of barriers to entry, which keep new firms from competing in an established industry, and competition among many firms producing similar but not identical products. Chapters 14, 15, 16, 17, and parts of Chapter 19 consider related problems and build on this chapter's techniques for analyzing imperfect competition.

ESSENTIAL CONCEPTS

1 There are four important types of **market structure: perfect competition, monopoly, monopolistic competition**, and **oligopoly**. A monopoly has a single seller.

Under monopolistic competition there are many firms, each selling a distinct product. Few firms dominate the industry in oligopolies. The essential differences are summarized in Table 13.1.

Table 13.1

Market structure	Firm's demand curve	Entry	Product differentiation	Examples
Perfect competition	Horizontal	Free entry	Homogenous products	Wheat, corn
Monopoly	Downward sloping	Barriers to entry	Only one firm	Premier league football, holders of patents
Monopolistic competition	Downward sloping	Free entry	Differentiated products	Restaurants, designer clothing
Oligopoly	Downward sloping	Barriers to entry	Either homogenous or differentiated products	Aluminium manufacturers, car manufacturers

2 Like all firms, monopolies maximise profit by setting marginal cost equal to marginal revenue. Unlike for

competitive firms, for monopolies marginal revenue is less than price. This fact is shown by the following formula: Marginal revenue = price (1 − 1/elasticity of demand). Barriers to entry allow monopolists to earn above-normal profits (also called monopoly rents). Finally, as price makers, monopolists can sometimes profitably charge different prices to different customers, a practice known as **price discrimination.**

3   Monopolistic competition and oligopoly are two special types of imperfect competition. In these industries firms have market power, which means that they can raise price without losing all of their sales. **Market power** is greater when the number of firms is lower and when there is more product differentiation. When products are more differentiated, there are more distant substitutes and firms' demands are less elastic. The characteristics of products, locations of sellers, and information and perceptions of buyers cause products to differ.

4   Factors that prevent entry into markets are called **barriers to entry.** Government policies such as licence requirements and patents create barriers to entry. The cost structure of the industry can also be a barrier, specifically the fraction of market demand accounted for by the output at the minimum of the firm's average cost curve. If one firm can produce the entire market demand for less than it could if it shared the market, the structure is called a **natural monopoly.** A monopoly can be sustained if a firm has control over an essential resource or if the firm has information advantages. Finally, strategies of existing firms can create barriers if they can credibly convince potential competitors that entry would be met with fierce competition.

5   Monopolistic competition describes the market structure made up of many firms, each ignoring the reactions of the others. The demand curves facing the firms slope down (thus, price is above marginal cost), but new firms enter when there are profit opportunities (thus, in equilibrium, price equals average cost). New entrants produce close substitutes to the products of existing firms. Each entry shifts the demand curves facing existing firms to the left, reducing their profits.

BEHIND THE ESSENTIAL CONCEPTS

1   One important idea in the theory of imperfect competition is the relationship between marginal revenue and price. Marginal revenue is the extra revenue that the firm takes in when it sells another unit. In perfect competition, this amount is the price. But in imperfect competition, the price falls as more output is sold. Thus, there are two effects on revenue, shown in Figure 13.1. The firm is initially selling 10 units for £10 each. If it chooses to produce and sell 11 units, the price falls to £9.50. The first effect on revenue is that the firm sells more units at £9.50. This is shown as the area with pluses. If the demand curve facing the firm were horizontal, as under perfect competition,

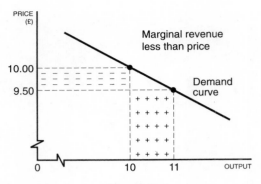

Figure 13.1

this would be the end of the story: the extra revenue would be price times the extra quantity sold. However, the downward-sloping demand curve makes the price drop in order to sell one extra unit. This is the second effect. It means that the firm loses revenue on all its existing sales (because the price is lower for all units). This effect is shown as the area with minuses, and it makes marginal revenue less than the simple price-times-quantity calculation.

2   All imperfectly competitive firms face a downward-sloping demand curve. Thus, their profit-maximising price is greater than marginal cost. In monopoly, there are barriers to entry, which allow monopolies to earn pure profits without attracting new competition. Monopoly prices are greater-than-average costs. In monopolistic competition, however, new entry drives economic profits to zero. When profits are zero, price equals average cost. To sum up,

Downward-sloping demand implies that price is greater than marginal cost.
Barriers to entry imply that price is greater than average cost.

3   Monopoly and monopolistic competition are similar in that each firm faces a downward-sloping demand curve and sets marginal revenue equal to marginal cost, which is less than price. The similarities stop here, however, because in a monopoly no new firm can enter even though a firm may earn pure profits. In monopolistically competitive industries, new firms enter, produce close substitutes, and capture customers. This entry shifts demand to the left until price equals average cost. The basic difference in the equilibria is that monopolies earn pure profits.

4   Monopolies are inefficient because price (which equals the marginal benefit of the good to consumers) is greater than marginal cost. Producing another unit would benefit customers more than it would cost. In monopolistic competition, things are not so simple. If all firms produce more goods, there are gains to both consumers and firms because price is greater than marginal cost and also because average cost falls. (Remember that the monopolistically competitive firm produces along the downward-sloping part of average cost.) On

the other hand, the overall industry demand is only so large, and if the firms become bigger, there will be room for fewer firms. Fewer firms mean fewer types of goods, so there is a trade-off between costs and variety.

SELF-TEST

True or False

1 The demand curve facing the firm is downward sloping in perfect competition.

2 The demand curve facing the firm is downward sloping in monopolistic competition.

3 When the demand curve facing the firm is downward sloping, marginal revenue is less than price.

4 Marginal revenue is less than price because price must fall for output to increase.

5 An industry with a single seller is a monopoly.

6 The demand curve facing a monopolist is the same as the industry demand curve.

7 Price is greater than marginal cost in monopoly.

8 Price is greater than marginal cost in monopolistic competition.

9 Compared to perfect competition, monopolies produce more but charge higher prices.

10 If there is a barrier to entry, firms may continue to earn pure profits.

11 Product differentiation is caused by barriers to entry.

12 In a natural monopoly, one firm can produce at a lower average cost than it could if it shared the market with other firms.

13 In equilibrium in monopolistic competition, price is greater than average cost.

14 The extent of a firm's market power is measured by how steeply the industry demand curve slopes downwards.

15 The more elastic the demand, the more price exceeds marginal cost in monopolies.

Multiple Choice

1 In the competitive model,

    a marginal revenue for the firm equals the market price.
    b if the firm raises its price above that charged by its competitors, it will lose all its customers.
    c the demand curve facing the firm is horizontal.
    d the firm is a price taker.
    e all of the above.

2 If a single firm supplies the entire market, the market structure is

    a perfect competition.
    b oligopoly.
    c monopoly.
    d monopolistic competition.
    e none of the above.

3 If the market is dominated by several firms, its market structure is

    a perfect competition.
    b oligopoly.
    c monopoly.
    d monopolistic competition.
    e none of the above.

4 Monopolistic competition is distinguished from oligopoly by the fact that

    a in monopolistic competition, firms do not worry about the reactions of their rivals.
    b there is no competition in oligopoly.
    c oligopoly is a form of imperfect competition.
    d the demand curve facing the firm is downward sloping in monopolistic competition.
    e price is above marginal cost in an oligopoly.

5 When there is imperfect competition the demand curve facing the firm,

    a equals the market demand curve.
    b is horizontal.
    c is downward sloping.
    d is upward sloping.
    e is vertical.

6 When the demand curve facing the firm is downward sloping, marginal revenue is less than price

    a because of the principle of diminishing returns.
    b in the short run but not in the long run.
    c because as output increases, the price must fall on all units.
    d because taxes must be paid.
    e none of the above.

7 "Marginal cost equals price" is the rule for maximising profits for firms in which of the following market structures?

    a Perfect competition
    b Monopolistic competition
    c Monopoly
    d Oligopoly
    e All of the above

8 Compared to competition, a monopoly

    a charges a higher price.
    b sells more output.
    c charges a lower price.
    d sells less output.
    e *a* and *d*.

9 The market demand curve is the same as the demand curve facing the firm when the market structure is

    a perfect competition.
    b monopoly.

c   oligopoly.
d   monopolistic competition.
e   all of the above.

10   A monopoly increases price above marginal cost by a greater amount when the demand is

a   more elastic.
b   more inelastic.
c   unitary elastic.
d   perfectly elastic.
e   none of the above.

11   Because they are single sellers, monopolies can earn

a   pure economic profits.
b   pure accounting profits.
c   zero profits.
d   the normal rate of return on invested capital.
e   c and d.

12   The measure of a firm's market power is

a   the number of employees it has.
b   the size of its capital stock.
c   the market price of its stock shares.
d   the extent to which the demand curve it faces is downward sloping.
e   all of the above.

13   How much the demand curve facing the firm slopes downwards is determined by the

a   number of firms in the industry.
b   extent to which its product is differentiated from those of its competitors.
c   size of its capital stock.
d   minimum of its average cost curve.
e   a and b.

14   The five-firm concentration ratio measures the

a   number of firms in the industry.
b   elasticity of industry demand.
c   extent to which production is concentrated among a few firms.
d   extent to which foreign firms dominate the industry.
e   average elasticity among the five largest firms.

15   Product differentiation is caused by

a   differences in the characteristics of products produced by different firms.
b   differences in the location of firms.
c   perceived differences, often induced by advertising.
d   imperfect information about price and availability.
e   all of the above.

16   When the products sold in one industry are differentiated, if one firm raises its price,

a   it will lose all of its customers.
b   it will lose none of its customers.
c   it will lose some but not all of its customers.
d   it will go out of business.
e   its profits will rise.

17   Barriers to entry

a   are factors that prevent new firms from entering the market.
b   are illegal.
c   allow firms in the industry to continue to earn economic profits.
d   imply that marginal revenue is greater than marginal cost.
e   a and c.

18   In the equilibrium of monopolistic competition,

a   firms make zero economic profits.
b   price equals average cost.
c   marginal revenue equals marginal cost.
d   price is greater than marginal cost.
e   all of the above.

19   The practice of charging different prices to different customers is called

a   product differentiation.
b   price discrimination.
c   predatory pricing.
d   limit pricing.
e   natural monopoly.

20   Economies of scale refer to

a   lower average cost as output is increased.
b   charging different prices to different customers.
c   any factor that erects barriers to the entry of new competitors.
d   lower average cost as different goods are produced with the same plant and equipment.
e   charging low prices for a limited time in order to drive competitors from the market.

Completion

1   The way in which an industry is organised is called its _____.

2   A few firms dominate an industry in _____.

3   An industry with a single seller is called _____.

4   In monopolistic competition, there are enough firms that each firm _____ the reactions of rivals.

5   In industries where the characteristics of products are different, there is said to be _____.

6   In imperfect competition, marginal revenue is _____ than price.

7   Any factor that prevents new firms from coming into an industry is called a _____.

8   If the market demand curve intersects the average cost curve for the firm at a point where it is decreasing, the industry is a _____.

9   In monopolistic competition, there is a trade-off between lower prices and more _____.

10   In equilibrium in monopolistic competition, price _____ average cost.

Answers to Self-Test

True or False

1	F	6	T	11	F
2	T	7	T	12	T
3	T	8	T	13	F
4	T	9	F	14	F
5	T	10	T	15	F

Multiple Choice

1	e	6	c	11	a	16	c
2	c	7	a	12	d	17	e
3	b	8	e	13	e	18	e
4	a	9	b	14	c	19	b
5	c	10	b	15	e	20	a

Completion

1 market structure
2 oligopoly
3 monopoly
4 ignores
5 product differentiation
6 less
7 barrier to entry
8 natural monopoly
9 variety
10 equals

Tools and Practice Problems

In this section, we start with two basic topics and several applications. First, we calculate marginal revenue and find the profit-maximising price and quantity for the monopolist. The second topic is price discrimination, which is the practice of firms in imperfectly competitive markets charging different prices to different consumers in order to raise profits. The applications that follow include the effects of taxes and price controls in monopoly markets and a couple of puzzles. Artists, entertainers, and authors are often paid a percentage of revenue. Also, they generally prefer lower prices than their producers and publishers. Two problems toward the end of this problem set show why this is true. Other problems explore the effects of taxes and price ceilings in monopoly markets and show that the monopolist always produces along the elastic portion of the demand curve.

MARGINAL REVENUE

The key idea that distinguishes perfect from imperfect competition is that for the latter, marginal revenue is less than price. This is because price must be lowered on all units in order to sell more. Tool Kit 13.1 shows how to calculate marginal revenue from the demand schedule.

Tool Kit 13.1: Calculating Marginal Revenue

The first step in solving the monopolist's problem is to calculate marginal revenue.

Step one: Make a table with four column headings: "Price," "Quantity," "Total revenue," and "Marginal revenue." Enter the demand curve in the first two columns.

Price   Quantity   Total revenue   Marginal revenue

Step two: Calculate revenue for each point on the demand curve, and enter the result in the table. Total revenue is price multiplied by quantity:

$$\text{Total revenue} = \text{price} \times \text{quantity}.$$

Step three: Calculate marginal revenue for each interval along the demand curve, and enter the result in the table. Marginal revenue is the change in total revenue divided by the change in quantity:

Marginal revenue
= change in total revenue/change in quantity.

After calculating marginal revenue, choose the price and quantity for which marginal revenue equals marginal cost.

---

1 (Worked problem: marginal revenue) As the only cement producer within 200 kilometres, Sam's Cement faces a downward-sloping demand curve, which is given in Table 13.2.

Table 13.2

Price	Quantity (tonnes)
£4.00	400
£3.50	800
£3.00	1,400
£2.50	2,800
£2.00	4,000

Sam's marginal cost is £2.00 per tonne, and he has fixed costs of £1,000.

a Calculate total revenue and marginal revenue, and insert these in two columns of the table.
b Find the profit-maximising price and quantity.
c Compute Sam's costs and profits at this price.
d Suppose that Sam's fixed costs fall to £500. What is his profit-maximising price and quantity, and how much does he earn in profits?
e Illustrate your answer with a diagram.

Step-by-step solution

Step one (a): Make a table.

Price   Quantity   Total revenue   Marginal revenue

Step two: Calculate total revenue for each point on the demand curve. When the price is £4, total revenue is £4 × 400 = £1,600. Continuing, we derive Table 13.3.

Table 13.3

Price	Quantity	Total revenue	Marginal revenue
£4.00	400	£1,600	
£3.50	800	£2,800	
£3.00	1,400	£4,200	
£2.50	2,800	£7,000	
£2.00	4,000	£8,000	

Step three: Calculate marginal revenue for each interval along the demand curve. For the first 400 units, total revenue rises from £0 to £1,600. Thus, marginal revenue is £1,600/400 = £4. As output is increased to 800, total revenue grows from £1,600 to £2,800. Marginal revenue is (£2,800 − £1,600)/(800 − 400) = £3. Complete the marginal revenue column as shown in Table 13.4.

Table 13.4

Price	Quantity	Total revenue	Marginal revenue
£4.00	400	£1,600	£4.00
£3.50	800	£2,800	£3.00
£3.00	1,400	£4,200	£2.33
£2.50	2,800	£7,000	£2.00
£2.00	4,000	£8,000	£0.83

Step four (b): To find the monopoly output and price, set marginal revenue equal to marginal cost. This occurs when the price is £2.50 and output is 2,800.

Step five (c): To find total costs, add fixed costs, which are £1,000, and total variable costs. Each unit costs £2, and 2,800 units are produced. Total costs equal £1,000 + (£2 × 2,800) = £6,600. Profits equal revenues minus costs. Total revenue is £7,000, so profits equal £7,000 − £6,600 = £400.

Step six (d): If fixed costs fall, marginal cost does not change. The profit-maximising price is still £2.50, but total profits now equal £7,000 − (£500 + £5,600) = £900. Unless the firm decides to shut down, fixed costs do not affect the output and pricing decisions.

Step seven (e): The solution is illustrated in the diagram.

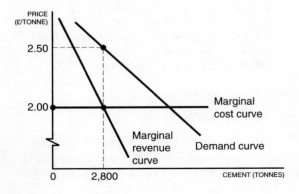

2   (Practice problem: marginal revenue) Strikers United is the only professional football team within several hundred kilometres. The marginal cost of admitting another fan is £1. Fixed costs, which include player salaries, are £100,000. The demand curve is given in Table 13.5. The quantity column gives the season's attendance.

Table 13.5

Price	Quantity	Total revenue	Marginal revenue
£8	100,000		
£7	150,000		
£6	200,000		
£5	250,000		
£4	300,000		
£3	350,000		
£2	400,000		

a   Compute marginal revenue, and complete the column.
b   Find the profit-maximising price and quantity.
c   Compute United's costs and profits at this price.
d   Suppose that transfers fees are abolished and the consequent increase in salaries raises fixed costs to £150,000. What is United's profit-maximizing price and quantity, and how much profit does the team earn?
e   Illustrate your answer with a diagram.

3   (Practice problem: marginal revenue) For each of the following firms, find the profit-maximizing price and quantity and total profits earned.

a   Fixed costs = £0; marginal cost = £8.

Price	Quantity	Total revenue	Marginal revenue
£10	1		
£ 9	2		
£ 8	3		
£ 7	4		
£ 6	5		
£ 5	6		
£ 4	7		

b   Fixed costs = £50,000; marginal cost = 10 pence.

Price	Quantity	Total revenue	Marginal revenue
50p	500,000		
45p	600,000		
40p	700,000		
35p	800,000		
30p	900,000		

c   Compute marginal cost from the table.

Price	Quantity	Total revenue	Marginal revenue	Total costs	Marginal cost
£20	400			£ 5,000	
£18	800			£ 7,000	
£16	1,200			£ 9,400	
£14	1,600			£12,600	
£12	2,000			£16,200	
£10	2,400			£21,000	

d   Compute marginal cost from the table.

Price	Quantity	Total revenue	Marginal revenue	Total costs	Marginal cost
£1.00	1,000			£ 200	
£0.90	2,000			£ 300	
£0.80	3,500			£ 450	
£0.70	5,500			£ 650	
£0.60	8,000			£ 900	
£0.50	11,000			£1,230	
£0.40	15,000			£1,730	
£0.30	20,000			£2,355	

PRICE DISCRIMINATION

When it is possible to do so, an imperfectly competitive firm can improve profits by charging different prices to different consumers. This is called price discrimination. The idea is to segment the market and set marginal revenue equal to marginal cost in each market and charge the corresponding price.

4   (Worked problem: price discrimination) Although the sale of the product is illegal, a drug ring operates according to sound business practices. It sells addictive designer drugs to two types of customers: non-addicted experimenters and addicts (former experimenters). The demands for each type of customer are given in Table 13.6. The drug has no fixed costs and has marginal cost equal to £10 per dose.

Table 13.6

	Nonaddicts				Addicts		
Price	Quantity	Total revenue	Marginal revenue	Price	Quantity	Total revenue	Marginal revenue
£50	100			£50	500		
£40	300			£40	700		
£30	500			£30	1,050		
£20	1,000			£20	1,650		

a   Calculate marginal revenue for each demand curve.
b   Find the profit-maximising price and quantity for each type of consumer.
c   Calculate total profits.

Step-by-step solution

Step one (a): Follow the procedure outlined above to calculate marginal revenue. The result should look like Table 13.7.

Table 13.7

	Nonaddicts				Addicts		
Price	Quantity	Total revenue	Marginal revenue	Price	Quantity	Total revenue	Marginal revenue
£50	100	£ 5,000	£50	£50	500	£25,000	£50.00
£40	300	£12,000	£35	£40	700	£28,000	£15.00
£30	500	£15,000	£15	£30	1,050	£31,500	£10.00
£20	1,000	£20,000	£10	£20	1,650	£33,000	£ 2.50

Step two (b): Find the profit-maximising price in each market. Marginal cost, which is £10, equals marginal revenue for non-addicts at a price of £20 and a quantity of 1,000. For addicts, marginal revenue equals marginal cost at a price of £30 and a quantity of 1,050.

Step three (c): Calculate total profits. Total revenue is £20,000 from the non-addicts and £31,500 from the addicts. Costs are £10 × (1,000 + 1,050) = £20,500; so profits equal £51,500 – £20,500 = £31,000.

5   (Practice problem: price discrimination) A common instance of price discrimination is dumping, which occurs when a firm faces less competition in its home market than abroad. In these cases, it will pay the company to charge different prices in the two markets. Fibre-Tech sells carpet fibres in the foreign and domestic markets. Its marginal cost is £1 per spool, and it has fixed costs of £5,000. The domestic and foreign demands are given in Table 13.8.

Table 13.8

	Home market				Foreign market		
Price	Quantity	Total revenue	Marginal revenue	Price	Quantity	Total revenue	Marginal revenue
£10	2,000			£10	2,000		
£ 9	2,500			£ 9	3,000		
£ 8	3,000			£ 8	4,000		
£ 7	3,500			£ 7	5,000		
£ 6	4,000			£ 6	6,000		
£ 5	4,500			£ 5	7,000		
£ 4	5,000			£ 4	8,000		

a   Calculate marginal revenue for each demand curve.
b   Find the profit-maximising price and quantity for each type of consumer.
c   Calculate total profits.

6   (Practice problem: price discrimination) Convenience Stores is one of the few chains that has not closed its local High Street shops. Convenience has expanded to the out of town shopping centres, but faces more competition there. An example of a product sold in both markets is hamburgers, which have a marginal cost equal to £1. The space required to sell hamburgers costs Convenience about £100, and the demand curves in the shopping centres and High Street are given in Table 13.9.

Table 13.9

	Shopping centres				High Street		
Price	Quantity	Total revenue	Marginal revenue	Price	Quantity	Total revenue	Marginal revenue
£4.00	200			£4.00	100		
£3.50	400			£3.50	120		
£3.00	600			£3.00	140		
£2.50	800			£2.50	160		
£2.00	1,000			£2.00	180		
£1.50	1,200			£1.50	200		

a   Calculate marginal revenue for each demand curve.

b   Find the profit-maximising price and quantity for each type of consumer.

c   Calculate total profits.

APPLICATIONS

The following problems apply the idea of marginal revenue and monopoly decision making to the percentage of gross revenue contracts, tax incidence, price controls, and elasticity. Simply follow the procedure outlined in Tool Kit 13.1.

8   (Worked problem: marginal revenue) After the surprising success of her first novel, Imelda has negotiated a deal in which she receives 20 percent of the revenue from the sale of her second novel. The demand curve is given in Table 13.10. The publisher has fixed costs of £20,000, and the marginal cost of printing and distributing each book printed is £20.

Table 13.10

Price	Quantity	Total revenue	Marginal revenue	Imelda's revenue
£40	10,000			
£35	20,000			
£30	30,000			
£25	40,000			
£20	50,000			

a   Calculate marginal revenue, and enter in the table.

b   Find the profit-maximising price and quantity.

c   Compute Imelda's revenue for each price, and enter in the table.

d   What price maximises Imelda's revenue?

e   Draw a diagram illustrating your answer.

Step-by-step solution

Step one (a): Calculate marginal revenue. Follow the usual procedure. The answer is in Table 13.11.

Table 13.11

Price	Quantity	Total revenue	Marginal revenue	Imelda's revenue
£40	10,000	£ 400,000	£40	
£35	20,000	£ 700,000	£30	
£30	30,000	£ 900,000	£20	
£25	40,000	£1,000,000	£10	
£20	50,000	£1,000,000	£ 0	

Step two (b): Find the profit-maximising price and quantity. Marginal cost equals marginal revenue for the publisher at a price of £30, where the quantity sold is 30,000.

Step three (c): Calculate Imelda's revenue. She receives 20 percent of the total. At a price of £40, she receives 0.20 × £400,000 = £80,000. Continue to calculate, and enter the results. They are given in Table 13.12.

Table 13.12

Price	Quantity	Total revenue	Marginal revenue	Imelda's revenue
£40	10,000	£ 400,000	£40	£ 80,000
£35	20,000	£ 700,000	£30	£140,000
£30	30,000	£ 900,000	£20	£180,000
£25	40,000	£1,000,000	£10	£200,000
£20	50,000	£1,000,000	£ 0	£200,000

Step four (d): Imelda prefers a price of £25 or £20, which earns her £200,000, more than the £180,000 that she earns at the publisher's preferred price.

Step five (e): Draw a diagram. Note that the publisher sets marginal revenue equal to marginal cost. Imelda is only concerned with revenue, so she prefers the point where marginal revenue equals zero.

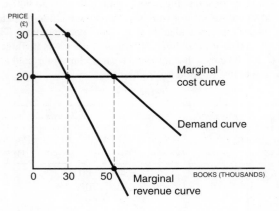

9   (Practice problem: marginal revenue) Magdalena, a budding female recording artist, has just completed her first album. She will receive 25 percent of the revenue. The record company reports that its demand curve is as given in Table 13.13, and its marginal costs are £6 per CD.

Table 13.13

Price	Quantity	Total revenue	Marginal revenue	Magdalena's revenue
£20	20,000			
£18	25,000			
£16	30,000			
£14	35,000			
£12	40,000			
£10	48,000			

a   Calculate marginal revenue, and enter in the table.

b   Find the profit-maximising price and quantity.

c   Compute Magdalena's revenue for each price, and enter it in the table.
d   What price maximises Magdalena's revenue?
e   Draw a diagram illustrating your answer.

10 (Practice problem: marginal revenue) Like most cities, South Potato is a one-newspaper town. The *South Potato Truth is* distributed for a marginal cost of 10 pence. The demand curve is given in Table 13.14.

Table 13.14

Price	Total quantity	Revenue	Marginal revenue
£1.00	30,000		
£0.95	40,000		
£0.90	50,000		
£0.85	60,000		
£0.80	70,000		
£0.75	80,000		
£0.70	90,000		
£0.65	100,000		
£0.60	110,000		
£0.55	120,000		

a   Calculate marginal revenue, and enter in the table.
b   Find the profit-maximising price and quantity.
c   Suppose that a tax of 10 pence per paper is instituted. The tax will be paid by the newspaper company. Find the new profit-maximising price and quantity.
d   How much of the tax is paid by consumers?
e   Draw a diagram illustrating your answer.

11 (Practice problem: marginal revenue) In competitive markets, price ceilings lower price and reduce the quantity sold. This is not true in monopoly markets. The demand for cable subscriptions in New Town is given in Table 13.15. The marginal cost, including payments to cable programming providers, is £15.

Table 13.15

Price	Quantity	Total revenue	Marginal revenue
£45	60,000		
£40	80,000		
£35	100,000		
£30	120,000		
£25	140,000		

a   Calculate marginal revenue, and enter in the table.
b   Find the profit-maximising price and quantity of subscriptions.
c   Now suppose that the town sets a price ceiling

equal to £25. How much will the company charge, and how many subscriptions will be sold?
d   Draw a diagram illustrating your answer.

12 (Practice problem: marginal revenue) Because a monopoly is a single seller of a good, it has no competition. Since price elasticity is generally lower when consumers have little opportunity to find substitutes, you might think that the demand for the monopolist's product is always inelastic. Nevertheless, it is true that the monopolist always produces on the elastic portion of its demand curve. To see this, compute elasticity along the demand curve given in question 3a. Show that at the chosen price and quantity, the price elasticity of demand is greater than 1.

Answers to Problems

2   a   Marginal revenue appears in Table 13.15.

Table 13.16

Price	Quantity	Total revenue	Marginal revenue
£8	100,000	£ 800,000	—
£7	150,000	£1,050,000	£5
£6	200,000	£1,200,000	£3
£5	250,000	£1,250,000	£1
£4	300,000	£1,200,000	−£1
£3	350,000	£1,050,000	−£3
£2	400,000	£ 800,000	−£5

b   Profits are maximized when the price is £5 and the number of fans is 250,000.
c   Costs = £100,000 + (250,000 × £1) = £350,000; profits = £1,250,000 − £350,000 = £900,000.
d   The price and quantity remain as in part a, but profits fall to £1,250,000 − £400,000 = £850,000.
e   The solution is illustrated in the diagram.

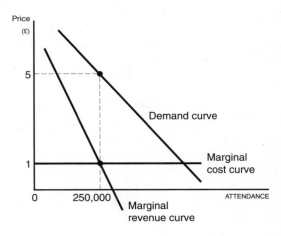

3   a   Marginal revenue appears in Table 13.17.

Table 13.17

Price	Quantity	Total revenue	Marginal revenue
£10	1	£10	—
£ 9	2	£18	£8
£ 8	3	£24	£6
£ 7	4	£28	£4
£ 6	5	£30	£2
£ 5	6	£30	£0
£ 4	7	£28	–£2

Price = £9; quantity = 2; profits = £18 – (£8 × 2) = £2.

b   Marginal revenue appears in Table 13.18.

Table 13.18

Price	Quantity	Total revenue	Marginal revenue
£0.50	500,000	£250,000	—
£0.45	600,000	£270,000	£0.20
£0.40	700,000	£280,000	£0.10
£0.35	800,000	£280,000	£0
£0.30	900,000	£270,000	–£0.10

Price = £0.40; quantity = 700,000; profits = £280,000 – [£50,000 + (700,000 × £0.10)] = £160,000.

c   The complete table appears in Table 13.19.

Table 13.19

Price	Quantity	Total revenue	Marginal revenue	Total costs	Marginal cost
£20	400	£ 8,000	—	£ 5,000	—
£18	800	£14,400	£16	£ 7,000	£ 5
£16	1,200	£19,200	£12	£ 9,400	£ 6
£14	1,600	£22,400	£ 8	£12,600	£ 8
£12	2,000	£24,000	£ 4	£16,200	£ 9
£10	2,400	£24,000	£ 0	£21,000	£12

Price = £14; quantity = 1,600; profits = £22,400 – £12,600 = £9,800.

d   The completed table appears in Table 13.20.

Table 13.20

Price	Quantity	Total revenue	Marginal revenue	Total costs	Marginal cost
£1.00	1,000	£1,000	—	£ 200	—
£0.90	2,000	£1,800	£0.80	£ 300	£0.10
£0.80	3,500	£2,800	£0.67	£ 450	£0.10
£0.70	5,500	£3,850	£0.52	£ 650	£0.10
£0.60	8,000	£4,800	£0.38	£ 900	£0.10
£0.50	11,000	£5,500	£0.23	£1,230	£0.11
£0.40	15,000	£6,000	£0.12	£1,730	£0.12
£0.30	20,000	£6,000	£0	£2,355	£0.14

Price = £0.40; quantity = 15,000; profits = £4,270.

5   a   The marginal revenue figures appear in Table 13.21.

Table 13.21

	Home market				Foreign market		
Price	Quantity	Total revenue	Marginal revenue	Price	Quantity	Total revenue	Marginal revenue
£10	2,000	£20,000	—	£10	2,000	£20,000	—
£ 9	2,500	£22,500	£5	£ 9	3,000	£27,000	£7
£ 8	3,000	£24,000	£3	£ 8	4,000	£32,000	£5
£ 7	3,500	£24,500	£1	£ 7	5,000	£35,000	£3
£ 6	4,000	£24,000	–£1	£ 6	6,000	£36,000	£1
£ 5	4,500	£22,500	–£3	£ 5	7,000	£35,000	–£1
£ 4	5,000	£20,000	–£5	£ 4	8,000	£32,000	–£3

b   Home market price = £7; quantity = 3,500. Foreign market price = £6; quantity = 6,000.

c   Profits = £24,500 + £36,000 – [(3,500 + 6,000) × £1] – £5,000 = £46,000.

6   a   The completed table appears in Table 13.22.

Table 13.22

	Shopping Centres				High Street		
Price	Quantity	Total revenue	Marginal revenue	Price	Quantity	Total revenue	Marginal revenue
£4.00	200	£ 800	—	£4.00	100	£400	—
£3.50	400	£1,400	£3	£3.50	120	£420	£1
£3.00	600	£1,800	£2	£3.00	140	£420	£0
£2.50	800	£2,000	£1	£2.50	160	£400	–£1
£2.00	1,000	£2,000	£0	£2.00	180	£360	–£2
£1.50	1,200	£1,800	–£1	£1.50	200	£300	–£3

b   Shopping centre price = £2.50; quantity = 800. High Street price = £3.50; quantity = 120.

c   Profits = £2,000 + £420 – [(800 + 120) × £1] – £100 = £1,400.

9   a and c   The marginal revenues and Magdalena's revenues are given in Table 13.23.

Table 13.23

Price	Quantity	Total revenue	Marginal revenue	Magdalena's revenue
£20	20,000	£400,000	—	£100,000
£18	25,000	£450,000	£10	£112,500
£16	30,000	£480,000	£ 6	£120,000
£14	35,000	£490,000	£ 2	£122,500
£12	40,000	£480,000	–£ 2	£120,000
£10	48,000	£480,000	£ 0	£120,000

b and d   The profit-maximising price is £16 and the quantity is 30,000, but Magdalena's revenue is maximised at a price of £14, where 35,000 CDs are sold.

e The solution is illustrated in the diagram.

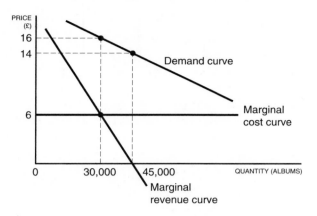

10 *a* Marginal revenue is given in Table 13.24.

Table 13.24

Price	Quantity	Total revenue	Marginal revenue
£1.00	30,000	£30,000	—
£0.95	40,000	£38,000	£0.80
£0.90	50,000	£45,000	£0.70
£0.85	60,000	£51,000	£0.60
£0.80	70,000	£56,000	£0.50
£0.75	80,000	£60,000	£0.40
£0.70	90,000	£63,000	£0.30
£0.65	100,000	£65,000	£0.20
£0.60	110,000	£66,000	£0.10
£0.55	120,000	£66,000	£0

b Price = £0.60; quantity = 110,000.
c The tax increases marginal cost to £0.20. The price becomes £0.65 and the quantity, 100,000.
d Consumers pay £.05 of the tax.
e The solution is illustrated in the diagram.

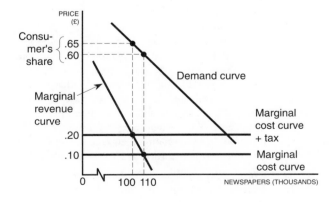

11 *a* Marginal revenue is given in Table 13.25.

Table 13.25

Price	Quantity	Total revenue	Marginal revenue
£45	60,000	£2,700,000	—
£40	80,000	£3,200,000	£25
£35	100,000	£3,500,000	£15
£30	120,000	£3,600,000	£ 5
£25	140,000	£3,500,000	–£ 5

b Price = £35; quantity = 100,000.
c Price = £25; quantity = 140,000.
d The solution is illustrated in the diagram.

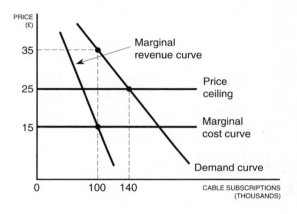

12 The elasticity for each point on the demand curve is given in Table 13.26.

Table 13.26

Price	Quantity	Total revenue	Marginal revenue	Elasticity
£10	1	£10	—	—
£ 9	2	£18	£8	19/3
£ 8	3	£24	£6	17/5
£ 7	4	£28	£4	15/7
£ 6	5	£30	£2	13/9
£ 5	6	£30	£0	11/11
£ 4	7	£28	–£2	9/11

Along the elastic portion of the demand curve, which is where price exceeds £5, marginal revenue is positive. Marginal revenue equals marginal cost at a price of £9, which is on the elastic portion.

Chapter 14

OLIGOPOLIES

Chapter Review

Chapters 13 and 14 present the three imperfect competitive market structures: monopoly, monopolistic competition, and oligopoly. Chapter 13 dealt with the first two; this chapter rounds out the study with a look at oligopoly.

Oligopolies are industries in which only a few firms dominate. Each firm watches its competitors closely, because each firm's best price, output level, or strategy depends upon what its rivals choose. The European car industry is a perfect example of an oligopolistic market. Even today, with foreign firms competing in the European market, it is still easy to see how the leading European manufacturers respond to one another with competing discount schemes, lower prices, or cheap financing. The chapter introduces the Prisoner's Dilemma models to examine the possibilities and motives for collusion. Chapter 15 builds upon the insights of this chapter and Chapter 13 to explore government policy towards imperfect competition.

ESSENTIAL CONCEPTS

1   In **oligopoly**, a few firms dominate the industry. If any one firm changes its price, produces more, or adopts a new strategy, then the other firms in the oligopoly will notice the change and react to it. It is essential, then, that oligopolists pay careful attention and try to anticipate the reactions of their rivals. This strategic interaction is the essential feature of oligopolies, and it makes the study of oligopolies both difficult and fascinating.

2   Because total profits are lower when firms compete, oligopolists have the incentive to form a cartel and to collude, fix prices, and share the market. This behaviour is not only illegal under U.K. and European competition law, it is also difficult to sustain. First, individual firms are tempted to cheat and take advantage of the higher prices charged by others by undercutting their prices. Further, as demand and costs change over time, oligopolies have trouble renegotiating their tacit agreements. Finally, the pure profits earned by successful colluders attract entry and new competition.

3   The conflict between collusion and competition is at the heart of oligopoly. The combined profits of firms are highest if they collude. Collectively, their incentives are to fix prices and share the market. But each individual firm is tempted by its own self-interest. If its rivals keep their prices high, a firm can undercut and capture the market. The **Prisoner's Dilemma** summarises this conflict and shows how collusion might work. If the game

is played only once and self-interest quickly takes over, all firms cheat and the equilibrium is competition. If the game is played repeatedly for an indefinite period of time, firms may be able to threaten cheaters with competitive price wars and motivate one another to continue colluding.

4 Certain **restrictive practices** help sustain collusion. These include dealership arrangements that assign local monopolies to suppliers in particular geographic areas, for example, car distributers, exclusive dealing at retail outlets, and insisting upon tie-in arrangements that force a customer who buys one product to buy an additional product. These practices can reduce competition by increasing the costs of capturing the customers of rival firms. Firms also facilitate cooperation through such practices as matching low-price offers of rivals.

5 There are three important models of competition in oligopolies.

   a If firms are committed to producing a given amount of output, as is the case in industries where fixed costs are high and changing capacity is very expensive, there is quantity or **Cournot competition.** One such example is the steel industry. Setting up a factory to commence or expand production is very expensive, so the firm gets locked in at certain capacities. It tries to select capacities corresponding to a price where profits will be maximised.

   b If the costs of increasing capacity are low, then price or **Bertrand competition** reigns. An example of this is the catalogue marketing industry. Setting up a mail-order firm is inexpensive, and the firm can vary the size of its orders from suppliers. It selects a price corresponding to a quantity where profits will be maximized.

   c The **kinked demand curve** model shows that if firms expect rivals to match a price cut but not a price increase, then they are unlikely to change price or quantity.

BEHIND THE ESSENTIAL CONCEPTS

1 The world of perfect competition is simple and precise. The firm cannot affect the market of any competitor; it simply chooses its quantity to maximise profits. The world of oligopoly is rich and varied. Firms try to limit competition and promote collusion. They have a wealth of strategies to choose from: price and quantity, of course, but also such practices as matching offers of rivals and threatening price wars with new entrants or existing firms who cheat on tacit agreements to limit price competition. Oligopoly is an area in which economics has made much progress in the last ten or fifteen years.

2 As a group, firms in an oligopoly want to cooperate, charge high prices, and share monopoly profits, but they always run up against the problem of self-interest. Each individual firm would like to cheat while the others abide by the cooperative strategy. It is this noncooperative behavior by individual firms that promotes economic efficiency, because it keeps the oligopolists from cooperating to gouge customers with high prices. It is ironic that if firms were more cooperative, the economy would not work so well.

SELF-TEST

True or False

1 An oligopolist considering lowering its price must anticipate the reactions of its rivals.

2 A cartel is a group of firms engaging in price competition.

3 Competition law allow cartels to negotiate openly to fix prices.

4 Tacit collusion is an implicit understanding among oligopolists that their profits will be higher if they do not compete too vigorously.

5 Offers to match prices charged by rivals result in more price competition.

6 A price leader can help a cartel adjust to changing conditions.

7 One difficulty that cartels have is that when they succeed in raising price, their members are tempted to undercut the cartel price.

8 If the possibility of entry keeps prices competitive, the market is said to be contestable.

9 The Prisoner's Dilemma is a simple game that shows how parties can overcome their self-interest to achieve the benefits of cooperation.

10 Certain restrictive practices such as resale price maintenance and dealership arrangements help oligopolies reduce competition and increase profits.

11 Although restrictive practices such as exclusive dealing help oligopolists collude, they also promote economic efficiency.

12 In an oligopoly, firms must worry about the reactions of rivals.

13 In Cournot competition, oligopolists choose their quantity expecting that their rivals will produce the same quantity as themselves.

14 In Bertrand competition, firms choose their price expecting their rivals to keep price constant.

15 If the firm perceives a kinked demand curve, there is a jump in marginal revenue at the current output.

Multiple Choice

1 Unlike firms operating in monopolistically competitive markets, oligopolists

   a face downward-sloping demand curves.

   b are price takers.

c   must worry about how rivals will react to their decisions.

d   set price above marginal cost.

e   *a* and *d*.

2   A group of companies that act jointly to divide the industry and maximise profits is called

a   a monopoly.

b   a monopsony.

c   a cartel.

d   an antitrust.

e   none of the above.

3   One difficulty cartels have is that individual firms may cheat and

a   charge less than the agreed price.

b   sell more than the agreed quantity.

c   charge more than the agreed price.

d   *a* and *b*.

e   *b* and *c*.

4   In the Prisoner's Dilemma,

a   both prisoners act in their own self-interest. this leads to the best alternative from their combined standpoint.

b   both prisoners cooperate to bring about the best alternative.

c   acting in their own self-interest, the prisoners bring about the worst alternative.

d   it is impossible to say what happens because each prisoner must worry about the reactions of the other.

e   none of the above.

5   Collusion is difficult in practice because

a   competition law makes explicit price-fixing agreements illegal.

b   individual firms are tempted to cheat and undercut their rivals.

c   as demand and cost conditions change, it is difficult to renegotiate tacit agreements.

d   all of the above.

e   none of the above.

6   When oligopolists publicly offer to match any price charged by any other firm, there will be

a   more price competition.

b   the same amount of price competition.

c   less price competition.

d   trouble because matching offers are illegal.

e   none of the above.

7   In contestable markets,

a   firms can successfully collude to share monopoly profits.

b   firms are unable to collude because cartel members cheat on tacit agreements.

c   potential competition ensures competitive pricing.

d   price returns to the competitive level but only after entry.

e   firms deter the entry of new competition by carrying excess capacity.

8   A tie-in is

a   a requirement that firms offer the same price as their rivals.

b   an agreement among cartel members to match price cuts but not price increases.

c   a requirement that any customer who buys one product must buy another.

d   a practice whereby the prices of the followers are tied to the leader's price.

e   a threat to meet new entry with resistance.

9   Competition law

a   prohibits collusive behavior.

b   requires that firms in an oligopoly charge the same price.

c   punishes firms for cheating on collusive agreements.

d   promotes collusion by raising rival's costs.

e   bars entry into oligopolies.

10   In an oligopoly the price leader

a   sets the industry's highest price.

b   sets the industry's price and the other firms follow.

c   deters entry by threatening to lower price.

d   ensures cooperation among all firms by threatening to lower price.

e   offers to match the industry's lowest price.

11   In oligopolies firms often share inventories or combine research and development efforts. These practices

a   are illegal under competition law.

b   can facilitate cooperation because firms that cheated on the collusive price agreement may be excluded.

c   are examples of predatory pricing.

d   only exist in contestable markets.

e   are examples of tie-ins.

12   The Prisoner's Dilemma shows the

a   power of competition law.

b   effectiveness of facilitating practices.

c   impact of potential competition.

d   difficulty of sustaining collusive arrangements.

e   importance of the kinked demand curve.

13   In Cournot competition, the firms

a   compete by choosing quantity, given some conjecture about the quantity that the rival will produce.

b   compete by choosing price, given some conjecture about the price that the rival will charge.

c   match price cuts by rivals but not price increases.

d   collude to fix prices and earn monopoly profits.

e   divide the market in an orderly way.

14   In Bertrand competition, the firms

a   compete by choosing quantity, given some conjecture about the quantity that the rival will produce.

b   compete by choosing price, given some conjecture about the price that the rival will charge.

c   match price cuts by rivals but not price increases.

d   collude to fix prices and earn monopoly profits.

e   divide the market in an orderly way.

15 In laboratory experiments economists have found that

    a participants evolve simple strategies to bring about collusion if the game is repeated a number of times.

    b collusion is nearly impossible.

    c collusion requires the ability to write firm contracts to enforce it.

    d complicated strategies are used by most participants.

    e none of the above.

16 Restrictive practices restrict competition. These include

    a resale price maintenance.

    b exclusive dealing.

    c vertical restrictions.

    d horizontal restrictions.

    e all of the above.

17 Marginal revenue for the firm with a kinked demand curve

    a is greater than in monopoly.

    b is less than in monopoly.

    c is the same as in monopoly.

    d has a jump at the level of current output.

    e none of the above.

18 Resale price maintenance is a practice whereby retailers are required to

    a compete vigorously with other retailers.

    b sell only to certain customers.

    c also sell a specific tie-in product.

    d carry no competing products.

    e sell at the list price.

19 Restrictive practices, such as exclusive dealing and vertical restraints, may

    a reduce economic efficiency.

    b restrict competition.

    c raise costs for rivals.

    d raise price.

    e all of the above.

20 If rivals match price cuts but do not match price increases, the demand curve facing the firm

    a is kinked at the current output level.

    b has a jump at the current output level.

    c is horizontal at the current price.

    d is vertical at the current output level.

    e either *c* or *d*.

Completion

1 In an oligopoly, there are so few firms that each must consider how its rival will _____ to any change in strategy.

2 A group of companies operating jointly as if they were a monopoly is called a _____.

3 Collusive behavior is prohibited by _____.

4 The _____ is a game that illustrates the problem cartels have in enforcing collusive behaviour.

5 Markets in which the threat of competition impels firms to charge the competitive price are called _____.

6 A firm that insists that any other firm selling its products refrain from selling those of its rivals is engaging in _____.

7 _____ was an arrangement whereby retailers agreed to sell at the list price.

8 Restrictive practices aimed at wholesalers and retailers selling a producer's goods are called _____.

9 If a firm believes that its rivals will match its price cuts but not its price increases, then it will perceive its demand curve to be _____ at the current price.

10 Firms that conjecture that their rival's quantity is fixed are engaging in _____.

Answers to Self-Test

True or False

1	T	6	T	11	F
2	F	7	T	12	T
3	F	8	T	13	F
4	T	9	F	14	T
5	F	10	T	15	T

Multiple Choice

1	*c*	6	*c*	11	*b*	16	*e*
2	*c*	7	*c*	12	*d*	17	*d*
3	*a*	8	*c*	13	*a*	18	*e*
4	*c*	9	*a*	14	*b*	19	*e*
5	*d*	10	*b*	15	*a*	20	*a*

Completion

1 react
2 cartel
3 competition law
4 Prisoner's Dilemma
5 contestable
6 exclusive dealing
7 Resale price maintenance
8 vertical restrictions
9 kinked
10 Cournot competition

Tools and Practice Problems

This section looks at three issues pertaining to oligopoly. First, we consider collusion and the difficulty that cartels have in enforcing their tacit agreements. We see not only how two firms can divide a market and share monopoly profits but also how difficult it is to maintain a cartel. The cartel's success in restricting output and raising prices tempts each of the cartel members to cheat by producing more than their assigned amounts and undercutting the cartel's price. One way to lessen the incentives to cheat is to assign exclusive dealership arrangements. We look at collusion and cheating in several problems before turning to some simple game theory problems, using the Prisoner's Dilemma framework to investigate collusion.

CARTELS, COLLUSION, AND CHEATING

Many firms can secretly organise and agree to cooperate to share monopoly profits. Tool Kit 14.1 shows how they might do this. The following problems use this insight to show how individual firms have incentives to cheat and produce more than they agreed. Tool Kit 14.2 shows that when there is quantity competition (Cournot), the same incentive problem arises. This is developed and extended to price competition in the problems.

Tool Kit 14.1 Organizing a Cartel of Many Price-Taking Firms

To organize a cartel of many firms, one must find the monopoly output and price. Then each firm must be assigned its quota. The following steps show how to proceed.

Step one: Identify and add the supply curves of the individual firms. The result is the cartel's marginal cost curve.

Step two: Identify the market demand curve, and find its marginal revenue.

Step three: Find the profit-maximising price and quantity for the cartel by setting marginal revenue equal to marginal cost.

Step four: Determine each firm's output by evenly dividing the cartel's output among its members.

---

1 (Worked problem: collusion and cheating) The European Water Group is a cartel of 1,000 mineral water producers. The demand for mineral water and the supply curve of one typical producer are given in Table 14.1. The quantity represents litres.

Table 14.1

Market demand		Firm's supply	
Price (pence)	Quantity (litres)	Price (pence)	Quantity (litres)
100	10,000	100	60
90	15,000	90	55
80	20,000	80	50
70	25,000	70	45
60	30,000	60	40
50	35,000	50	35
		40	30
		30	25
		20	20

a   Find the profit-maximising price for the cartel as a whole. How many litres will be sold at this price: How many must each firm produce to sustain this price?

b   If the cartel charges the price computed in part *a*, how many units would the individual firm like to produce?

c   Now suppose that all firms cheat and the market becomes competitive. Find the equilibrium price and quantity.

Step-by-step solution

Step one (a): Add the individual supplies. Since there are 1,000 firms, the market supply is simply the quantity supplied by the firm multiplied by 1,000. The market supply is given in Table 14.2.

Table 14.2

Firm's supply		Market supply	
Price (pence)	Quantity (litres)	Price (pence)	Quantity (litres)
100	60	100	60,000
90	55	90	55,000
80	50	80	50,000
70	45	70	45,000
60	40	60	40,000
50	35	50	35,000
40	30	40	30,000
30	25	30	25,000
20	20	20	20,000

Step two: Derive the marginal revenue curve. First find total revenue and enter it in the appropriate column. Marginal revenue is the change in total revenue divided by the change in quantity. The answer is given in Table 14.3.

Table 14.3

Market demand		Total revenue (£)	Marginal revenue (pence)
Price (pence)	Quantity (litres)		
100	10,000	1,000	
90	15,000	1,350	70
80	20,000	1,600	50
70	25,000	1,750	30
60	30,000	1,800	10
50	35,000	1,750	–10

Step three: Find the profit-maximising price for the cartel. The market supply curve is the cartel's marginal cost. Marginal cost equals marginal revenue when the quantity is 25,000. The corresponding price is 70 pence. Each firm produces 25 litres.

Step four (b): Find how much the firm would like to supply at the cartel price. At a price of 70 pence, the firm would like to produce 45 units (this number is read off the firm's supply curve), which is 20 more than it is assigned.

Step five (c): If all firms cheat, then the market will become a competitive market and will clear at a price of 50 pence, where each firm produces 35 litres.

2   (Practice problem: collusion and cheating) The 500 mail-order computer equipment suppliers are (discreetly) forming a cartel. The market demand curve and the supply curve of a typical equipment supplier are given in Table 14.4. The quantity represents the number of computers.

Table 14.4

Market demand		Total revenue	Marginal revenue
Price	Quantity		
£1,000	300,000		
£ 900	400,000		
£ 800	500,000		
£ 700	600,000		
£ 600	700,000		
£ 500	800,000		
£ 400	900,000		
£ 300	1,000,000		

Firm's supply		Market supply	
Price	Quantity	Price	Quantity
£1,000	4,000		
£ 900	3,500		
£ 800	3,000		
£ 700	2,400		
£ 600	2,000		
£ 500	1,600		
£ 400	1,000		
£ 300	500		
£ 200	100		

a   Derive the marginal revenue for the computer equipment supplier market.
b   Add the 500 individual firm supplies to derive the market supply.
c   Find the profit-maximising price for the cartel as a whole. How many computers will be sold at this price? How many must each firm sell to sustain this price?
d   If the cartel charges the price computed in part c, how many units would the individual firm like to sell?
e   Now suppose that all firms cheat and the market becomes competitive. Find the equilibrium price and quantity.

Tool Kit 14.2 Finding the Profit-Maximising Output in Quantity Competition between Duopolists

In some industries, such as steel or aluminum, the fixed costs of plant and equipment are such a large share of total costs that firms have little discretion in changing output once the machinery is in place. In this case, the competition is over quantity, and the price will be whatever clears the market of the quantities that firms have collectively decided to produce.

Step one: Identify the market demand, marginal cost, and output of the opponent firm.

Step two: Subtract the output of the opponent firm from the market demand. The difference is called the **residual demand curve**:

Residual demand
   = market demand – opponent's output.

Step three: Find the marginal revenue for the residual demand curve.

Step four: Choose the output for which marginal revenue equals marginal cost.

3   (Worked problem: quantity competition) The New Chairs for Old Company shares the furniture-refinishing market with the Like New Company. Each uses enormous vats of chemicals, which are expensive to set up but cheap to operate. One vat will permit the refinishing of 10 pieces of furniture per day. The marginal cost for each firm is constant and equal to £4. Table 14.5 gives the market demand.

Table 14.5

Price	Quantity
£7.50	0
£7.00	10
£6.50	20
£6.00	30
£5.50	40
£5.00	50
£4.50	60
£4.00	70

a   Suppose that the two firms try to operate as a cartel and share the market equally. Find the profit-maximising quantity for each.
b   Now look at the problem from the point of view of the owner of New Chairs for Old. She conjectures that her rival is commited to the quantity solved for in part a. Find the profit-maximising quantity.

Step-by-step solution

Step one (a): We follow the usual procedure for the monopolist: find the marginal revenue and set marginal revenue equal to marginal cost. Table 14.6 gives the marginal revenue.

Table 14.6

Price	Quantity	Total revenue	Marginal revenue
£7.50	0	£ 0	—
£7.00	10	£ 70	£7
£6.50	20	£130	£6
£6.00	30	£180	£5
£5.50	40	£220	£4
£5.00	50	£250	£3
£4.50	60	£270	£2
£4.00	70	£280	£1

Marginal revenue equals marginal cost when the total quantity is 40. Each firm then buys two vats and refinishes 20 pieces of furniture.

Step two (b): Identify the market demand, marginal cost, and output of the opponent firm. The market demand is given in Table 14.5, the marginal cost is £4, and Like New is expected to produce 20.

Step three: Subtract the output of the opponent firm from the market demand, as shown in Table 14.7.

Table 14.7

Price	Quantity
£7.00	0
£6.50	20 – 20 = 0
£6.00	30 – 20 = 10
£5.50	40 – 20 = 20
£5.00	50 – 20 = 30
£4.50	60 – 20 = 40
£4.00	70 – 20 = 50

Step four: Find the marginal revenue for the residual demand curve, as given in Table 14.8.

Step five: Choose the output for which marginal revenue equals marginal cost. When output is 30, marginal revenue and marginal cost both equal £4.

Table 14.8

Price	Quantity	Total revenue	Marginal revenue
£7.00	0	0	—
£6.50	0	0	—
£6.00	10	£ 60	£6
£5.50	20	£110	£5
£5.00	30	£150	£4
£4.50	40	£180	£3
£4.00	50	£200	£2

4 (Practice problem: quantity competition) The Davis Lead Company competes with its rival Anderson Lead. Because the plant and equipment are so expensive and because marginal production costs are so low (only £5 per tonne) until capacity is reached, the two firms compete by choosing quantity. The market demand is given in Table 14.9.

Table 14.9

Price	Quantity (tonnes)
£22.50	0
£20.00	100
£17.50	200
£15.00	300
£12.50	400
£10.00	500
£ 7.50	600

a   Suppose that the two firms try to operate as a cartel and share the market equally. Find the profit-maximising quantity for each.
b   Now look at the problem from the point of view of the owner of Davis. The owner conjectures that the rival firm is commited to the quantity solved for in part *a*. Find the profit-maximising quantity.

5 (Worked problem: price competition) There are two dry-cleaning establishments in Mudville: Jay's Cleaners and Fay's Cleaners. Although they hate each other personally, the two owners have decided to form a cartel. This is illegal, of course, but they meet discreetly. Each faces a marginal cost of £1 per item. Consumers always patronise the lower-price establishment; therefore, either Jay or Fay can capture the entire market by pricing below the other. One additional fact is that in Mudville people only carry 50 pence pieces, so the price must be a multiple of 50 pence. Table 14.10 gives the market demand.

Table 14.10

Price	Quantity
£3.00	1,500
£2.50	3,000
£2.00	4,500
£1.50	6,000
£1.00	7,500

a   Derive the marginal revenue curve, and enter in the table.
b   Find the profit-maximising price. If they divide the market equally, how many items will each clean?
c   Compute the profits for each firm.
d   Suppose that Fay decides to undercut Jay and capture the market. What price will Fay charge? How many will Fay sell? Compute Fay's profits.

Step-by-step solution

Step one (a): Derive marginal revenue. Follow the usual procedure, as in Table 14.11.

Table 14.11

Price	Quantity	Total revenue	Marginal revenue
£3.00	1,500	£4,500	£3
£2.50	3,000	£7,500	£2
£2.00	4,500	£9,000	£1
£1.50	6,000	£9,000	£0
£1.00	7,500	£7,500	–£1

Step two (b): Find the profit-maximising price. Marginal cost equals marginal revenue at a price of £2.

Step three (c): At a price of £2, there are 4,500 items cleaned. If each does one-half, then each cleans 2,250. The profits for each are £2 – £1 = £1 per unit, so each earns £2,250.

Step four (d): Fay can capture the market by charging the next-lower price, which is £1.50. Fay will sell 6,000 units. Fay's profit will be £1.50 – £1.00 = £0.50 per unit for a total of £3,000. Fay gains £750 by cheating on their agreement.

6 (Practice problem: price competition) Yuppie Company and its rival Buppie Company sell dark green and grey wool jumpers through catalogues. They buy the jumpers from supplier firms for £10 each. The market demand is given in Table 14.12.

Table 14.12

Quantity (jumpers)	Price
0	£27.50
100	£25.00
200	£22.50
300	£20.00
400	£17.50
500	£15.00
600	£12.50

a Derive marginal revenue, and enter it in the table.
b Find the profit-maximising price. If the companies divide the market equally, how many items will each clean?
c Compute the profits for each firm.
d Suppose that Yuppie decides to undercut Buppie and capture the market. What price will it charge? How many will it sell? Compute its profits.

PRISONER'S DILEMMA

The Prisoner's Dilemma is one of the most important models in social science. It shows why groups may have difficulty inducing their members to cooperate and act in the group interest. In this section our interest is in the ability of oligopolists to collude. Tool Kit 14.3 shows how to use this model.

Tool Kit 14.3 Using the Prisoner's Dilemma

The Prisoner's Dilemma highlights the conflict between what is good for the cartel as a whole and what is best for the individual firm. Follow these steps to represent this conflict as a game.

Step one: Draw a box with four cells, and label it as shown.

Step two: Identify the payoff for each party if both cooperate, and enter it in the appropriate cell.

Step three: Identify the payoff for each party if both compete, and enter it in the appropriate cell.

Step four: Identify the payoffs for each party if one competes while the other cooperates, and enter them in the corresponding cells.

Step five: In the classic one-shot Prisoner's Dilemma, competing is always the best strategy, whatever the opponent chooses. Show that competition is the equilibrium.

7   (Worked problem: Prisoner's Dilemma) Chiaravelli and Fiegenshau are the only two lawyers in Plainville. They have been colluding, sharing the market and earning monopoly profits of £100,000 each for several years. Fiegenshau is considering reducing his price. He estimates that if Chiaravelli keeps his price at current levels, Fiegenshau would earn £150,000, although Chiaravelli's earnings would fall to £25,000. There is also the possibility that Chiaravelli would compete with Fiegenshau. The resulting price war would reduce the earnings of each to £40,000.

   a   Represent this market as a Prisoner's Dilemma game.
   b   Explain why the equilibrium might be achieved when both lawyers compete.

Step-by-step solution

Step one (a): Draw a box with four cells, and label it as shown.

	CHIARAVELLI	
	Cooperate	Compete
FIEGENSHAU Cooperate		
Compete		

Step two: Identify the payoff for each party if both cooperate, and enter it in the appropriate cell. If both cooperate, they each earn £100,000.

	CHIARAVELLI	
	Cooperate	Compete
FIEGENSHAU Cooperate	C = £100,000 F = £100,000	
Compete		

Step three: Identify the payoff for each party if both compete, and enter it in the appropriate cell. If both compete, they each earn £40,000.

	CHIARAVELLI	
	Cooperate	Compete
FIEGENSHAU Cooperate	C = £100,000 F = £100,000	
Compete		C = £40,000 F = £40,000

Step four: Identify the payoffs for each party if one competes while the other cooperates, and enter them in the corresponding cells. In this case, the lawyer who competes earns £150,000, and the other is left with £25,000.

	CHIARAVELLI	
	Cooperate	Compete
FIEGENSHAU Cooperate	C = £100,000 F = £100,000	C = £150,000 F = £ 25,000
Compete	C = £ 25,000 F = £150,000	C = £40,000 F = £40,000

Step five (b): Show that competition is the equilibrium. For each party, competition is always the best alternative. If Chiavarelli cooperates, then Fiegenshau can earn more by competing (£150,000 > £100,000). If Chiavarelli competes, again Fiegenshau earns more by competing (£40,000 > £25,000). The same is true for Chiavarelli. So both choose to compete.

8   (Practice problem: Prisoner's Dilemma) City Airlines and Northern Airways share the market from London to Amsterdam. If they cooperate, they can extract enough monopoly profits to earn £400,000 each, but unbridled competition can reduce profits to £50,000 each. If one is foolish enough to cooperate in its pricing policy while the other undercuts it, the cooperating firm would earn £0, and the competing firm would earn £800,000.

   a   Represent this market as a Prisoner's Dilemma game.
   b   Explain why the equilibrium might be that both firms would compete.

9   (Practice problem: Prisoner's Dilemma) Rosewood Athletic Club and Elmwood Athletic Club are the best athletic clubs in the region. Each prides itself on the strength of its team. If neither offers scholarships for promising athletes, then obviously the cost of scholarships will be zero. For £20,000 in scholarships, either could attract the best athletes (if the other did not offer scholarships), win the championship, and attract at least £50,000 in donations and funding. In this case, however, donations and funding at the losing club would fall by £30,000. On the other hand, if both offered scholarships, there would be no advantage, no extra donations, and each would have spent £20,000 for nothing.

   a   Represent this situation as a Prisoner's Dilemma game.
   b   Explain why the equilibrium might be achieved when both clubs compete.

FACILITATING AND RESTRICTIVE PRACTICES

Oligopolists can use certain practices to facilitate collusion and restrict competition. These practices may enable them to get around the incentive to cheat on collusive arrangements. These problems illustrate how dividing the market into exclusive territories and promising to match competitors' low prices can promote collusion.

10   (Worked problem: facilitating and restrictive practices) This problem builds upon problem 3. Having accumulated several years of experience with the unpleasant

results of competition, the two furniture-refinishing firms decide to try a new method of collusion. Henceforth, the New Chairs for Old Company will specialise in refinishing chairs, and the Like New Company will take care of the table share of the market. It so happens in Southpoint that exactly half of the business involves tables and half involves chairs. Their marginal costs remain at £4.

a   Compute the profit-maximising quantity of chairs and tables and the corresponding prices for both companies.
b   Compare the answer to the answer to part *a* of problem 3.

Step-by-step solution

Step one (a): Divide the market into chair and table markets. The result is given in Table 14.13.

Table 14.13

Price	Quantity of chairs	Quantity of tables
£7.50	0	0
£7.00	5	5
£6.50	10	10
£6.00	15	15
£5.50	20	20
£5.00	25	25
£4.50	30	30
£4.00	35	35

Step two: Compute the marginal revenue for each firm. These are shown in Table 14.14. Note that since the demands are exactly the same, so are the marginal revenue curves. Only one is shown.

Table 14.14

Price	Quantity of chairs	Quantity of tables	Total revenue	Marginal revenue
£7.50	0	0	£ 0	—
£7.00	5	5	£ 35	£7
£6.50	10	10	£ 65	£6
£6.00	15	15	£ 90	£5
£5.50	20	20	£110	£4
£5.00	25	25	£125	£3
£4.50	30	30	£135	£2
£4.00	35	35	£140	£1

Step three (b): Marginal revenue equals marginal cost at a quantity of 20 for each. The market price will be £5.50, which is exactly the outcome that was solved for in part *a* of problem 3. Dividing the market promotes collusion.

11   (Practice problem: facilitating and restrictive practices) This problem builds upon problem 4. The Davis and Anderson companies have come up with a scheme to promote collusion. From now on, Davis will advertise

and take orders from customers in the west, leaving the eastern half of the market to Anderson. They divide the market so that exactly half of the customers will go to each firm. The marginal cost remains at £5 per tonne, and the market demand is as given in Table 14.9.

a   Compute the profit-maximising quantity and price for each firm.
b   Compare with the collusive price and quantity solved for in part *a* of problem 4.

12   (Worked problem: facilitating and restrictive practices) Let's return to Mudville and problem 5, where Fay is considering undercutting Jay.

a   Compute profits if she reduces her price by £50 below the collusive price and Jay matches the price cut. Assume that customers divide themselves equally between the firms charging the same price.
b   Derive Fay's demand curve under the assumption that Jay will match any price cuts but no price increases. Draw a diagram illustrating your answer.

Step-by-step solution

Step one (a): The collusive price is £2, and Fay's profits are £2,250. If she cuts price to £1.50 and Jay matches the cut, then the quantity demanded is 6,000, and Fay will serve 3,000 of them.

Step two: Fay earns (£1.50 – £1.00) × 3,000 = £1,500. Because this number is less than collusive profits, the offer to match price cuts by Jay will deter Fay from undercutting him.

Step three (b): To find the demand if Jay matches price cuts (below £2) but not price increases, simply divide the market evenly at prices of £2 or below and give all the customers to Jay for higher prices. Table 14.15 gives the result. Notice the kink at a price of £2.

Table 14.15

Price	Quantity
£3.00	0
£2.50	0
£2.00	2,250
£1.50	3,000
£1.00	3,750

13   (Practice problem: facilitating and restrictive practices) Return to problem 6 and the competition between Yuppie and Buppie. Suppose that each agree to match price offers of the other.

a   Compute Yuppie's profits if it cuts price by £2.50 below the collusive price and its cut is matched by Buppie. Assume that customers divide themselves equally between firms charging the same price.
b   Derive Yuppie's demand curve assuming that Buppie will match price cuts (below the collusive price) but not price increases.

Answers to Problems

2   *a,b* The marginal revenue and the market supply appear in Table 14.16.

Table 14.16

Market demand		Total revenue	Marginal revenue
Price	Quantity		
£1,000	300,000	£300,000,000	—
£ 900	400,000	£360,000,000	£600
£ 800	500,000	£400,000,000	£400
£ 700	600,000	£420,000,000	£200
£ 600	700,000	£420,000,000	£ 0
£ 500	800,000	£400,000,000	−£200
£ 400	900,000	£360,000,000	−£400
£ 300	1,000,000	£300,000,000	−£600

Firm's supply		Market supply	
Price	Quantity	Price	Quantity
£1,000	4,000	£1,000	2,000,000
£ 900	3,500	£ 900	1,750,000
£ 800	3,000	£ 800	1,500,000
£ 700	2,400	£ 700	1,200,000
£ 600	2,000	£ 600	1,000,000
£ 500	1,600	£ 500	800,000
£ 400	1,000	£ 400	500,000
£ 300	500	£ 300	250,000
£ 200	100	£ 200	50,000

c Cartel price = £800; market quantity = 500,000; each firm's quantity = 1,000.

d 3,000.

e Price = £500; quantity = 800,000.

4   *a* Marginal revenue for the market demand is given in Table 14.17.

Table 14.17

Price	Quantity (tonnes)	Revenue	Marginal revenue
£22.50	0	£ 0	
£20.00	100	£2,000	£20
£17.50	200	£3,500	£15
£15.00	300	£4,500	£10
£12.50	400	£5,000	£ 5
£10.00	500	£5,000	£ 0
£ 7.50	600	£4,500	−£ 5

Price = £12.50; market quantity = 400; each firm sells 200 tonnes.

b The residual demand is found by subtracting 200 from the market demand. This and marginal revenue appear in Table 14.18.

Table 14.18

Price	Quantity (tonnes)	Revenue	Marginal revenue
£22.50	0	£ 0	
£20.00	0	£ 0	
£17.50	0	£ 0	
£15.00	100	£1,500	£15
£12.50	200	£2,500	£10
£10.00	300	£3,000	£ 5
£ 7.50	400	£3,000	£ 0

Davis will produce 300. The market quantity will be 200 + 300 = 500, and the price will be £10 per tonne.

6   *a* Marginal revenue for the market demand is given in Table 14.19.

Table 14.19

Price	Quantity (jumpers)	Revenue	Marginal revenue
£27.50	0	£ 0	—
£25.00	100	£2,500	£25
£22.50	200	£4,500	£20
£20.00	300	£6,000	£15
£17.50	400	£7,000	£10
£15.00	500	£7,500	£ 5
£12.50	600	£7,500	£ 0

b Cartel price = £17.50; market quantity = 400; each firm sells 200.

c Profits = (200 × £17.50) − (200 × £10) = £1,500.

d Yuppie's price = £15; quantity = 500; profits = (£15 × 500) − (£10 × 500) = £2,500.

8   *a*

		City	
		Cooperate	Compete
Northern	Cooperate	C = £400,000 N = £400,000	C = £800,000 N = £50
	Compete	C = £0 N = £800,000	C = £50,000 N = £50,000

b If Northern competes, City prefers to compete (£800,000 > £400,000). If Northern cooperates, City still prefers to compete (£50,000 > £0). If City competes, Northern prefers to compete (£800,000 > £400,000). If City cooperates, Northern still prefers to compete (£50,000 > £0) Since both always prefer competition, the equilibrium is that both compete and profits are £50,000 each.

9   *a*

		Elmwood	
		Cooperate	Compete
Rosewood	Cooperate	E = £0 R = £0	E = £30,000 R = −£30,000
	Compete	E = −£30,000 R = £30,000	E = −£20,000 R = −£20,000

b   If Rosewood cooperates and does not offer scholarships, Elmwood prefers to compete and offer them (£30,000 > £0). If Rosewood competes and offers scholarships, Elmwood still prefers to offer them (–£20,000 > –£30,000). If Elmwood cooperates and does not offer scholarships, Rosewood prefers to offer them (£30,000 > £0). If Elmwood competes and offers scholarships, Rosewood still prefers to offer them (–£20,000 > –£30,000). Since both always prefer competition, the equilibrium is that both compete, offer scholarships, and lose £20,000 each.

11   The demand for each firm's share of the market and the corresponding marginal revenue appear in Table 14.20.

Table 14.20

Price	Quantity (tonnes)	Total revenue	Marginal revenue
£22.50	0	£ 0	—
£20.00	50	£1,000	£20
£17.50	100	£1,750	£15
£15.00	150	£2,250	£10
£12.50	200	£2,500	£ 5
£10.00	250	£2,500	£ 0
£ 7.50	300	£2,250	–£ 5

a   Each firm charges £12.50 and sells 200.
b   The price and quantity are the same as under monopoly.

13   a   If both reduce price by £2.50 to £15.00, the market quantity will equal 500, which implies that each will sell 250. Profits will equal (£15 × 250) – (£10 × 250) = £1,250, which is less than the £1,500 they earn by charging £17.50.
b   Points on a yuppie's demand curve if price cuts below £17.50 are matched but price increases are not is given in Table 14.21.

Table 14.21

Price	Quantity (jumpers)
£27.50	0
£25.00	0
£22.50	0
£20.00	0
£17.50	200
£15.00	250
£12.50	300

Chapter 15

GOVERNMENT POLICIES TOWARDS COMPETITION

Chapter Review

Monopolies and oligopolies, explored in Chapters 13 and 14, produce too little output and charge inefficiently high prices. This chapter of the text returns to the role government plays in the economy, this time examining government policies to promote competition. Another important topic is government responses to natural monopolies. Natural monopolies occur in markets like home electric service, where a single firm can produce the good more cheaply than multiple firms can. In Chapter 16, the focus shifts to how firms compete to introduce new products and discover better ways of producing.

ESSENTIAL CONCEPTS

1   Competitive industries allocate resources efficiently. Monopolies and other imperfectly competitive industries, however, often operate inefficiently. Economists study four types of inefficiency.

   a   Monopolies restrict output below what it would be if the industry were competitive. The lower output results in higher prices and a transfer of wealth from consumers to the monopoly. There is an additional loss in consumer surplus, because output is below the level at which all gains from trade are realized. This loss is called the deadweight loss of monopoly.

   b   Although monopoly profits are higher when their costs are lower, monopolies are not forced to produce at the lowest cost. There is some room for **managerial slack,** which allows monopolies to be inefficient.

   c   Although there are examples of monopolies that engage in effective **research and development,** the incentives are less under monopoly.

   d   Because monopolies earn rents (profits above the level necessary to compensate investors), resources are expended to acquire and retain these existing rents. This type of activity is called **rent seeking** and is socially wasteful.

2   In some industries, where there are high fixed and low marginal costs, the lowest cost of production occurs when there is only one firm. Such an industry is called a **natural monopoly.** Figure 15.1 shows that the average cost curve for a natural monopoly is falling and that marginal cost always lies below average cost. Governments sometimes nationalise and operate natural monopolies. In both the nationalised and regulated cases pricing decisions are not entirely free from political in-

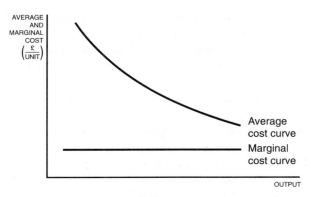

Figure 15.1

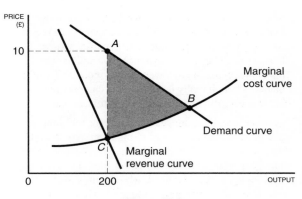

Figure 15.2

fluence: products may be sold below cost in some markets and above cost in others. This practice is called cross subsidization. More recently, governments have tended to move away from nationalization and have chosen to privatise and regulate natural monopolies. In Britain regulatory agencies set prices according to the RPI-X rule, where X represents cost reductions associated with productivity growth. In so doing, the regulatory offices aim to ensure that cost savings are passed onto consumers in the form of lower prices. However, it has been argued that this policy encourages firms to engage in wasteful expenditure on unnecessary costs, such as excessive salary increases for top managers. In the United States regulators aim to ensure that firms do not make excessive returns on their investment by using rate of return regulation. This has the effect of encouraging firms to overinvest.

3   A final way of dealing with natural monopolies is to increase competition. Examples include the deregulation of telephone, gas, and electricity supply to allow more than one producer to supply these services. In the United Kingdom, privatization of these services was followed (not always immediately) by deregulation and the introduction of competition. Competition provides firms with incentives to innovate and reduce costs, and can eliminates cross subsidization. On the other hand, for a given level of demand with more firms in the industry, each firm produces less, that is, chooses a point higher up the average cost curve.

4   In the United Kingdom the government uses **competition policy** to promote competition. Competition policy consists of two main elements: (1) monopolies and mergers policy and (2) policies to prevent anticompetitive practices by groups of firms or single firms. Important pieces of legislation in the United Kingdom include the Fair Trading Act, the Restrictive Practices Act, and the 1980 Competition Act. The Fair Trading Act aims to control monopolies and mergers. The Restrictive Practices Act aims to prevent collusion and other anticompetitive practices carried out by two or more firms. The 1980 Competition Act aims to prevent anticompetitive behaviour by individual firms. In addition, the European Union aims to promote competition in Europe via Articles 85 and 86 of the Treaty of Rome and European merger policy. In November 1998 the United Kingdom

government introduced the Competition Act 1998 which aims to bring United Kingdom policy more in line with European competition policy. This act became fully operational in 2000.

BEHIND THE ESSENTIAL CONCEPTS

1   The problem of deadweight loss lies at the heart of economic arguments about making exchange efficient. As an example, look at Figure 15.2, which shows a monopoly output equal to 200. The firm sets the price at £10 and maximises its profits. Notice, however, that at this point the marginal benefit to consumers of one or more unit (measured, as usual, by the price they're willing to pay) is greater than the marginal cost. This means that producing and selling additional units would create value—there would be gains from trade. The total possible additional gains equal the area of triangle ABC. But these gains are not realised, and therefore they are called the deadweight loss of monopoly.

   The idea that exchange creates value and that any reduction in the amount of exchange below the competitive level leads to a deadweight loss (as seen in Figure 15.2) is very important in economics.

2   Firms desiring greater profits seek them in two different ways. First, they offer better products or devise better ways of producing and doing business. These activities do make profits, and they create value and enhance efficiency as well. Firms can also try to convince government to protect them against competition or devise strategies to deter entry. Practices of this type do not create anything, they only redistribute money and reduce economic efficiency. The latter behaviour is called rent seeking.

3   In competitive industries, firms are forced to produce at the lowest possible cost. If they do not, new firms will enter the market, undercut the price, and drive existing firms out. In a monopoly, however, whether it is private, nationalised, or regulated, the firm can get away with some slack. It can pay its workers a little more than the going wage, it can postpone adopting the most efficient production techniques, or it can overlook the low-cost suppliers. You can probably see how this could happen in an unregulated monopoly, where there are extra profits,

or in a nationalised industry, where the government makes up any losses, but it is also possible in a regulated monopoly because regulators do not always know the lowest cost. The firm has an incentive and the ability to make the regulators believe that it is more costly to do business than it really is. Regulators can prevent fraud, but it is very difficult to find and eliminate waste.

4   In order to determine whether a merger will inhibit competition, the number of firms in an industry and their size relative to the market need to be determined. The geographic size of the market should be considered, as some industries are local, while many have become international. For example, the gold market is a world market. The cement industry, on the other hand, is local. The product is very expensive to transport, and only nearby firms could merge. The similarity of the products also needs to be considered. Is plastic wrap in the same industry as aluminium foil? If so, does a single producer of plastic wrap have a monopoly, or is it simply another firm in the food-wrapping industry? Economists look at the cross-price effect to determine the extent to which firms are competing. How much does a price decrease by one firm reduce another's demand?

5   Monopolies and mergers policy is concerned with prohibiting market domination. This begs the question of what it means to dominate the market. First there is the issue of the bounds of the market. Which product belongs in which market? Economists look at the effect of an increase in the price of one good on the demand for another good. If demand rises significantly, then the goods are part of the same market. Under United Kingdom competition law a firm is deemed to have potential monopoly power if it controls more than 25 percent of a market. Mergers that would lead to the newly merged firm controlling 25 percent or more of a market may be referred by the director general of fair trading to the Competition Commission (the former Monopolies and Mergers Commission, renamed in 1999) for investigation. If the commission's inquiry concludes that the merger would operate against the public interest the secretary of state for trade and industry has powers to block the proposed merger.

SELF-TEST

True or False

1   Monopolies produce less output than would be produced if the industry were competitive.

2   Monopolies must produce at the lowest cost.

3   Rent seeking refers to anything done in pursuit of monopoly profits.

4   Monopolies have stronger incentives to undertake research and development than competitive firms do.

5   In a natural monopoly, the cost of production is higher because of the lack of competition.

6   Cross subsidization refers to the practice of selling below cost in one market and above cost in another.

7   Regulated natural monopolies are usually forced to charge a price equal to marginal cost.

8   Subjecting a natural monopolist to competition can be an effective strategy if the average cost curve is not too steep.

9   In a horizontal merger, a firm acquires an upstream supplier.

10 Vertical mergers are illegal *per se* in the European Union.

11 In Britain, competition law is the exclusive domain of the British government.

12 One important goal of monopolies and mergers is to limit the absolute size of firms.

13 In the United Kingdom a merger may be blocked by the government if it is deemed to be against the public interest.

14 The Restrictive Practices Act prohibited specific anticompetitive practices, such as collusion.

15 In the United Kingdom the burden of proof in monopolies and mergers policy rests with firms.

Multiple Choice

1   Monopolists set the price

   a   equal to marginal cost.
   b   equal to average cost.
   c   above marginal cost.
   d   below marginal cost.
   e   below average cost.

2   Monopoly output is

   a   the same as competitive output.
   b   less than competitive output.
   c   more than the competitive output.
   d   sometimes more and sometimes less than competitive output.
   e   determined by setting marginal revenue equal to price.

3   The deadweight loss caused by monopoly is

   a   the difference between consumer surplus under the monopoly and what consumer surplus would have been if the industry were competitive.
   b   the amount of monopoly profits.
   c   the increase in cost brought about by managerial slack.
   d   the total of rent-seeking expenditure.
   e   the difference between consumer surplus under the monopoly and what consumer surplus would have been if the industry were competitive minus the transfer from consumers to the monopolist.

4   Managerial slack refers to

   a   the lack of efficiency in some monopolies.
   b   activities designed to protect a monopoly position.
   c   the loss in consumer surplus as a result of restricted output.
   d   the lessened incentives for research and development under monopoly.
   e   the failure of antitrust policies.

5 Among the problems of monopolies are

   a restricted output.
   b managerial slack.
   c reduced incentives for research and development.
   d rent seeking to protect the monopoly position.
   e all of the above.

6 Which of the following is not a type of rent seeking?

   a Research aimed at reducing the cost of production
   b Lobbying the legislature for protection against foreign competition
   c Contributions to political campaigns for candidates who support regulations favoured by the monopoly
   d Entry-deterring activities
   e Designing the product to be incompatible with competitors' products

7 If the cost of production is lowest when there is only one firm, then the industry is a

   a trust.
   b natural oligopoly.
   c natural monopoly.
   d horizontal merger.
   e vertical merger.

8 In a natural monopoly, marginal cost

   a equals price.
   b equals average cost.
   c is less than average cost.
   d is greater than average cost.
   e is greater than price.

9 Cross-subsidization involves selling

   a below cost in some markets and above cost in others.
   b at cost in all markets.
   c above cost in each market.
   d below cost in each market.
   e *a* and *b*.

10 Cross subsidization

   a occurs in nationalised monopolies but not in regulated monopolies.
   b occurs in regulated monopolies but not in nationalised monopolies.
   c occurs in neither regulated nor nationalised monopolies.
   d occurs in both regulated and nationalised monopolies.
   e never occurs.

11 Regulation of the utilities in the United Kingdom, such as gas, electricity, water, and telecommunications, is done using

   a rate of return regulation.
   b recommended retail prices.
   c profit targets.
   d the RPI-X price capping rule.
   e an output-related tax levy.

12 Natural monopolies regulated by rate of return regulation often

   a invest too much.
   b invest too little.

   c hire too much labour.
   d hire too few workers.
   e sell too much output.

13 In the United Kingdom a proposed merger may be referred to the Competition Commission if

   a the newly merged firm would control 25 percent or more of a market.
   b the firms involved have combined assets of £70 million.
   c the firms operate in vertically related markets.
   d the newly merged firm would control at least 20 percent or more of the market.
   e *a* or *b*.

14 Which of the following is an example of a horizontal merger?

   a One steel producer buys another steel producer.
   b A meat-packing firm buys a large cattle farm.
   c A maker of chalk buys a pizza delivery firm.
   d A foreign company buys a British company.
   e A U.K. company buys a foreign company.

15 Which of the following is an example of a vertical merger?

   a One steel producer buys another steel producer.
   b A meat-packing firm buys a large cattle farm.
   c A maker of chalk buys a pizza delivery firm.
   d A foreign company buys a British company.
   e A U.K. company buys a foreign company.

16 Which of the following is *not* a goal of competition policy?

   a Limiting anticompetitive practices
   b Preventing market domination
   c Limiting the absolute size of firms
   d Preventing collusive agreements
   e None of the above

17 Under British law the director general of fair trading has powers to

   a refer mergers for investigation if it appears that a monopoly would be created.
   b prohibit a merger that the Competition Commission has found to be against the public interest.
   c prohibit a merger without reference to the Competition Commission.
   d prohibit a merger that has been deemed to operate against the public interest.
   e *a* and *b*.

18 The act that made it illegal for two or more firms in the United Kingdom to enter into agreements to limit or distort competition was the

   a Restrictive Practices Act.
   b Fair Trading Act.
   c Sherman Act.
   d Office of Fair Trading Act.
   e Monopolies nd Mergers Act.

19 The hypothesis that regulators eventually serve the interests of the industry that they regulate and not the customers is called

a   the antitrust hypothesis.
b   the rent-seeking hypothesis.
c   the regulatory capture hypothesis.
d   the natural monopoly hypothesis.
e   none of the above.

20   In the United Kingdom the Secretary of State for Trade and Industry can only block a proposed merger if the

a   newly merged firm would account for more than 25 percent of the market.
b   firms involved have combined assets of more than £10 million.
c   Competition Commission finds that the merger would operate against the public interest.
d   merger is a horizontal merger.
e   merger is a vertical merger.

Completion

1   Monopolies restrict output and cause a loss in consumer surplus, part of which is a transfer to the monopolist, and the remainder is called the _____.

2   The fact that, shielded from competition, monopolists may not produce for the lowest costs is called _____.

3   Political contributions and lobbying expenses for the purpose of winning regulations to restrict competition are examples of _____.

4   Regulated or nationalised firms may sell below cost in some markets and above cost in others, a practice known as _____.

5   In a _____, the cost of production is lowest if there is only one firm in the industry.

6   Government policy to promote competition by restricting anticompetitive tactics or opposing mergers is called _____.

7   When a firm buys a competitor that was producing a competing product, it is called a _____.

8   The purchase by one firm of an upstream supplier or downstream distributor is called a _____.

9   The _____ was designed to control mergers in the United Kingdom.

10   The _____ brings United Kingdom competition law closer to European Union Law.

Answers to Self-Test

True or False

1	T	6	T	11	F
2	F	7	F	12	F
3	F	8	T	13	T
4	F	9	F	14	T
5	F	10	F	15	F

Multiple Choice

1	c	6	a	11	d	16	c
2	b	7	c	12	a	17	a
3	e	8	c	13	a	18	a
4	a	9	a	14	a	19	c
5	e	10	d	15	b	20	c

Completion

1   deadweight loss
2   managerial slack
3   rent seeking
4   cross subsidization
5   natural monopoly
6   competition policy
7   horizontal merger
8   vertical merger
9   Fair Trading Act
10   Competition Act 1998

Tools and Practice Problems

One of the important costs that monopolies impose on the economy is the deadweight loss, which reflects the losses resulting from the fact that monopolies restrict output. Here, we study how to compute the deadweight loss and then move on to consider the regulation of natural monopolies.

DEADWEIGHT LOSS

When a monopoly controls an industry, it can increase its profits by restricting output below the level where price equals marginal cost. By doing so, the monopoly reduces the number of mutually beneficial trades. Because these trades do not occur, there is a loss in consumer surplus, and this loss is called the deadweight loss. (Consumer surplus falls still further because of the higher price that the monopoly charges, but this loss in consumer surplus is only a transfer from consumers to the monopolist and is not part of the deadweight loss.) Tool Kit 15.1 shows how to compute deadweight loss.

Tool Kit 15.1 Finding the Deadweight Loss of Monopoly

When price is set above marginal cost, the market contracts and there is a deadweight loss. Follow these five steps to compute it.

Step one: Identify the demand and marginal cost curves.

Step two: Calculate marginal revenue.

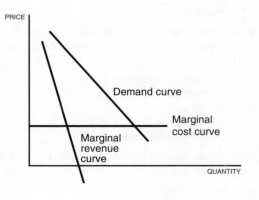

Step three: Find the monopoly output (Q_m) and price (p_m) by choosing the quantity for which marginal revenue equals marginal cost (MC_m).

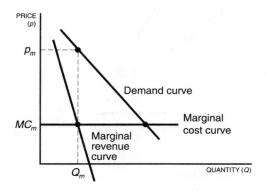

Step four: Find the competitive quantity (Q_c) by choosing the quantity for which demand equals marginal cost.

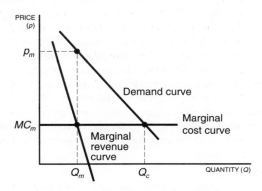

Step five: Compute the deadweight loss as the area between the demand and marginal cost curves:

Deadweight loss = ½ ($Q_c - Q_m$) × ($p_m - MC_m$).

(This formula exactly measures the area only when demand is a straight line.)

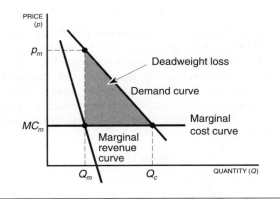

1 (Worked problem: deadweight loss) The West India Tea Company has been granted the sole franchise to sell green tea in Greenville. Its marginal cost is £5 per box. Demand is given in Table 15.1. Solve for its output and price and the deadweight loss.

Table 15.1

Price	Quantity
£10	10,000
£ 9	15,000
£ 8	20,000
£ 7	25,000
£ 6	30,000
£ 5	35,000

Step-by-step solution

Step one: Identify the demand and marginal cost curves. The demand curve is given in Table 15.1; marginal cost is constant and equal to £5.

Step two: Calculate marginal revenue. Follow the usual procedure outlined in Tool Kit 15.1. The marginal revenue for the West India Tea Company is given in Table 15.2.

Table 15.2

Price	Quantity	Total revenue	Marginal revenue
£10	10,000	£100,000	—
£ 9	15,000	£135,000	£7
£ 8	20,000	£160,000	£5
£ 7	25,000	£175,000	£3
£ 6	30,000	£180,000	£1
£ 5	35,000	£175,000	−£1

Step three: Find the monopoly output by choosing the quantity for which marginal revenue equals marginal cost. Marginal revenue equals marginal cost when price is £8 and 20,000 boxes are sold.

Step four: Find the competitive quantity by choosing the quantity for which demand equals marginal cost. The competitive price is £5, and the quantity is 35,000.

Step five: Compute the deadweight loss as the area between the demand and marginal cost curves.

$$\text{Deadweight loss} = ½ (Q_c - Q_m) \times (p_m - MC_m)$$
$$= ½ (35,000 - 20,000) \times (£8 - £5)$$
$$= £22,500.$$

2 (Practice problem: deadweight loss) Although its marginal cost is only £4 for each ride, the Calloway Cab Company has bribed the city council to grant it monopoly status at the local airport. The demand for rides is given in Table 15.3.

Table 15.3

Price	Quantity
£7.50	0
£7.00	10
£6.50	20
£6.00	30
£5.50	40
£5.00	50
£4.50	60
£4.00	70

Solve for the company's output and price and the deadweight loss.

3 (Practice problem: deadweight loss) As all football fans know, there is only one team in Mudville. The marginal cost of another fan in the park is £1, and the demand is given in Table 15.4.

Table 15.4

Price	Quantity
£3.00	1,500
£2.50	3,000
£2.00	4,500
£1.50	6,000
£1.00	7,500

Solve for the team's output and price and the deadweight loss.

NATURAL MONOPOLY

Natural monopolies are industries with high fixed costs and low marginal costs. Costs in these industries are lowest when there is only one firm. In the United Kingdom, the United States, and many other countries, so-called natural monopolies, such as public utilities, cable television companies, and telephone companies, are often regulated by government agencies to control the entry of competitors and prevent firms from charging excessive prices or making excessive profits. In the United Kingdom regulators use RPI-X regulation to encourage firms to reduce prices over time. Rate of return regulation is used in the United States. Tool Kit 15.2 shows how to set price according to the RPI-X formula. The tool kit also shows how to set price in a regulated monopoly to ensure that the firm only makes a normal rate of return.

Tool Kit 16.2 Finding the price for a Regulated Natural Monopoly

Regulation to ensure a normal rate of return

In the United Kingdom public utility commissioners often regulate natural monopolies so that they make a normal rate of return. This implies that price must equal average cost. Follow these steps.

Step one: Identify the demand curve, marginal cost, and fixed costs.

Step two: Compute the average cost by dividing total cost by quantity:

Average cost = total cost/quantity.

Step three: Find the price for which average cost crosses the demand curve. This is the price for a regulated natural monopoly.

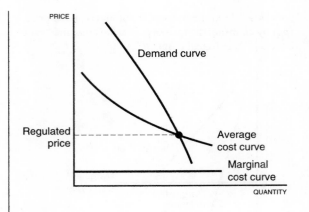

1 RPI – X regulation

In the United Kindgom many so-called natural monopolies are regulated using variants of the RPI-X rule. In this formula RPI denotes the general rate of price inflation and X reflects the rate of productivity growth or cost savings in the regulated industry. To set the regulated price, the regulator needs to know the general rate of inflation, RPI, and the rate of productivity growth (or required cost savings) in the regulated industry. The regulator then calculates the required change in price as the difference between RPI and X using the RPI-X formula. For example, if the general rate of inflation is 5 percent and technical progress means that costs in the regulated industry fall by 3 percent, then the regulator will require the firm to limit its price increase to 2 percent as follows:

RPI – X =
    percentage price change in regulated industry

which in the above case equals

5 percent – 3 percent = 2 percent.

This formula ensures that cost savings are passed onto consumers in the form of lower prices. Note that if cost savings occur, the price of the regulated industry must fall relative to the general price level.

4 (Worked problem: natural monopoly) Cutthroat Cable Company is the only provider of cable television services in Kings. Most of its costs are access fees and maintenance expenses, and these fixed costs, which do not vary with the number of customers, total £760,000 monthly. The marginal cost of another subscriber is only £1 per month. The company's demand curve is given in Table 15.5.

Table 15.5

Price (per month)	Number of subscribers
£50	10,000
£40	20,000
£30	30,000
£20	40,000
£10	50,000
£ 1	100,000

The Kings Borough Regulatory Agency regulates the price of cable services and wants to set the price so that Cutthroat makes a normal rate of return. What price should it mandate?

Step-by-step solution

Step one: Identify the demand curve, marginal cost, and fixed costs. Demand is given in Table 15.5; marginal cost is £1, and fixed costs are £760,000.

Step two: Compute average cost. When price is £50, there are 10,000 subscribers, and total costs are £760,000 + (10,000 × £1) = £770,000. Average cost is £770,000/10,000 = £77. Continuing this procedure, we derive Table 15.6.

Table 15.6

Price	Number of subscribers	Total costs	Average cost
£50	10,000	£770,000	£77.00
£40	20,000	£780,000	£39.00
£30	30,000	£790,000	£26.33
£20	40,000	£800,000	£20.00
£10	50,000	£810,000	£16.20
£ 1	100,000	£860,000	£ 8.60

Step three: Find the price for which average cost crosses the demand curve. This price is £20, and it is the price that the regulatory agency will choose.

5 (Practice problem: natural monopoly) The new big-cat exhibit at the Potter Park Zoo is proving popular with the public. Demand is given in Table 15.7. The zoo costs the park service only £1 per visitor, but its fixed costs equal £12,000. The governor has declared that no public funds will be used to support zoos, so Potter Park must charge a price just high enough to cover its costs. What price will do this?

P=AC

MC=MR

MC=P

Table 15.7

Price	Number of visitors
£8	1,000
£7	2,000
£6	3,000
£5	4,000
£4	5,000
£3	6,000
£2	7,000
£1	8,000

6 (Practice problem: natural monopoly) Over the past eight years the In-Touch Telephone Company has experienced productivity growth and associated cost savings as shown by column X in Table 15.8. The table also shows the general rate of inflation (RPI).

For each year calculate the change in price mandated by the regulator.

Table 15.8

Year	RPI (%)	X (%)	Mandatory price change (%)
1	5	3	
2	3	4	
3	6	2	
4	4	2	
5	4	4	
6	5	4	
7	4	2	
8	5	3	

Answers to Problems

2 The marginal revenue is given in Table 15.9.

Table 15.9

Price	Quantity	Revenue	Marginal revenue
£7.50	0	£ 0	—
£7.00	10	£ 70	£7
£6.50	20	£130	£6
£6.00	30	£180	£5
£5.50	40	£220	£4
£5.00	50	£250	£3
£4.50	60	£270	£2
£4.00	70	£280	£1

The monopoly output and price are 40 and £5.50, respectively. The competitive output and price would be 70 and £4, respectively. The deadweight loss is

$$\tfrac{1}{2} (70 - 40) \times (£5.50 - £4.00) = £22.50.$$

3 The marginal revenue is given in Table 15.10.

Table 15.10

Price	Quantity	Revenue	Marginal revenue
£3.00	1,500	£4,500	£3
£2.50	3,000	£7,500	£2
£2.00	4,500	£9,000	£1
£1.50	6,000	£9,000	£0
£1.00	7,500	£7,500	−£1

The monopoly price and output are £2 and 4,500, respectively. The competitive price and output would be £1 and 7,500, respectively. The deadweight loss is

$$\tfrac{1}{2} \times (7,500 - 4,500) \times (£2 - £1) = £1,500.$$

5 Average cost is given in Table 15.11.

Table 15.11

Price	Number of visitors	Total costs	Average cost
£8	1,000	£13,000	£13.00
£7	2,000	£14,000	£ 7.00
£6	3,000	£15,000	£ 5.00
£5	4,000	£16,000	£ 4.00
£4	5,000	£17,000	£ 3.40
£3	6,000	£18,000	£ 3.00
£2	7,000	£19,000	£ 2.70
£1	8,000	£20,000	£ 2.50

The price that allows Potter Park to cover its costs is £3.

Not 7=7

3 has lower AC for consumer.

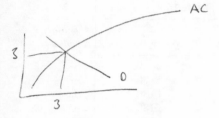

6   The maximum mandatory price change set by the regulator is given in Table 15.12.

Table 15.12

Year	RPI (%)	X (%)	Mandatory price change (%)
1	5	3	2
2	3	4	−1
3	6	2	4
4	4	2	2
5	4	4	0
6	5	4	1
7	4	2	2
8	5	3	2

Note that if the rate of cost savings in the industry exceeds the general rate of price inflation, the price of the regulated industry falls, as is the case in year 2.

Chapter 16

TECHNOLOGICAL CHANGE

Chapter Review

Think back once again to the history of the car in Chapter 1. At the beginning of this century, the car had not been invented, much less produced in any quantity or in the form we know it today. The enormous technological change in the car industry during this century is astounding. Yet the basic model of perfect competition assumes that the goods produced and the technology used to produce them do not change. In this chapter, the emphasis shifts to firms as they actively compete to discover new products and new ways of producing. Although many firms may be involved, the race for new ideas brings with it many of the aspects of imperfect competition covered in Chapters 13 to 15.

The most important point made in this chapter is that imperfect competition is not all bad. It brings with it the positive benefits of technological advance. Government policy to promote technological change includes granting patents, subsidising research and development (R & D), and occasionally protecting infant industries.

ESSENTIAL CONCEPTS

1 In the basic competitive model, there is one lowest-cost way of producing, and all firms adopt this technology.

The entry of new firms into the market soon drives away any profits, and all firms settle down to produce at the minimum of the average cost curve. The world of **technological change,** however, is vastly different. Firms compete aggressively to develop new products or production processes so that they can earn monopoly profits, at least for a while. For various reasons, the study of technological change must focus on imperfect competition.

2 A **patent** is a property right to an idea, and it gives the owner monopoly status and the opportunity to earn monopoly profits for the duration of the patent. Firms compete in **patent races**, a winner-take-all system in which the first firm with a discovery is awarded that patent, and its competitors get nothing. Because not all ideas are patentable and because to obtain a patent, the firm must disclose details of the idea, firms sometimes forgo applying for one and keep the idea a **trade secret.** In this case, the firm earns monopoly profits until its competitors discover the idea or a better one.

3 Patent policy involves two types of trade-offs:

   a The first issue is the **life** of the patent. Longer patents offer greater rewards for winning the race, and at the same time they promote research and development. On the other hand, for the duration of the patent, the firm sells at the monopoly price, which is above marginal cost, and so causes short-run inefficiencies, that is, deadweight losses.

   b The second issue is the **breadth** of the patent. Should patents be given for the narrowly defined idea or something more general? More broadly defined patents increase the rewards for R & D; however, access to the idea is restricted, and this restriction inhibits any subsequent innovative activity that might build on the patented idea.

4 Several features of research and development encourage large-sized firms.

   a First, R & D is a *fixed cost,* in the sense that once discovered, an idea can be used many times without additional cost. Fixed costs increase the efficient scale of the firm.

   b Second, the **learning curve** shows that costs fall with experience. The more the firm learns, the more it produces, and thus learning by doing encourages firms to increase their size.

   c Third, firms have difficulty borrowing to finance R & D. Larger firms with more retained earnings can finance more of their own research.

5 **Basic research** on the nature of fundamental ideas generates such widespread external benefits that it has the two characteristics of **public goods:** Basic research produces knowledge, and it is difficult (not to mention undesirable) to exclude others from learning and taking advantage of new knowledge. Also, the marginal cost of giving another user access to new knowledge is certainly zero. Because basic research has the characteristic features of public goods, the government has an important role to play in providing funding for such work.

6 Because R & D creates external benefits not captured through patents, most economists advocate additional government policies to encourage it. Tax credits for increased R & D spending are one form of subsidy used in the United States. Also, the **infant industry argument for protection** says that new industries require protection against foreign competition until they move down the learning curve and acquire sufficient expertise to compete effectively. Further, competition policy can be relaxed to allow for joint ventures.

BEHIND THE ESSENTIAL CONCEPTS

1 Most of microeconomics sings the praises of perfect competition, especially to the extent that it allocates resources efficiently given the existing production technology. But does a perfectly competitive economy always find the best way to generate more-advanced technologies of production, better products, and new ways of doing things? This chapter suggests that the answer is no. In order to encourage R & D, the government set up the patent system to motivate firms towards innovation by rewarding the winner with a period of freedom from competition. Perhaps paradoxically, government creates monopoly to encourage competition.

2 Technological advance is a vital engine of economic growth. Because it is so important, government promotes it with a wide range of complementary policies. Longer-lived and more broadly defined patents increase the rewards for R & D, while tax subsidies reduce the cost. Government also provides direct funding for basic research.

3 Economists generally consider the infant industry argument for protection to be valid but to carry some risks. Sometimes the protected industry gains expertise through experience and becomes a world-class competitor; other times the industry becomes inefficient and requires constant government support to survive. The difficulty is determining which industries will thrive and which will not.

4 You learned the basic logic of externalities in Chapter 7: whenever costs or benefits of some decision are not borne entirely by the decision maker, there is inefficiency. Most important to note in this chapter are the external benefits not captured by the firm that invests in R & D. These positive externalities include the fruits of subsequent R & D following an initial discovery, the gains after the expiration of the patent, and the consumer surplus arising from the application of the new idea. The firm ignores these externalities and thus undervalues the true social benefit of the R & D. Government policy can improve matters by promoting additional research efforts.

SELF-TEST

True or False

1 Firms engage in R & D expenditures so that they can participate in competitive markets.

2 A patent confers the exclusive right to produce and market an innovation for a limited period of time.

3 Patents and copyrights are both forms of intellectual property.

4 The firm that finishes second in a patent race wins nothing.

5 Holders of patents set the price of their goods equal to marginal cost.

6 Patents promote dynamic efficiency at the expense of short-run inefficiency.

7 The length of patents is set to balance the costs of monopoly pricing by patent holders against the incentives to innovate.

8 Defining a patent more broadly might reduce the rate of innovation by denying access to previous innovations.

9 Any firm eligible for a patent will surely apply for one.

10 R & D is a variable cost of production.

11 The learning curve shows how fixed costs decline with experience.

12 One advantage that smaller firms have in R & D is their better access to capital markets.

13 Venture capital firms specialise in assessing the prospects of R & D ventures and providing capital to innovating firms.

14 The market is unlikely to provide enough basic research because basic research is a public good.

15 Competition law inhibits firms from engaging in joint ventures.

Multiple Choice

1 Capitalism is a process of

  a   steady and smooth growth in the living standards of every individual.
  b   stagnation, in which the same goods are produced in the same way and distributed to the same people.
  c   creative destruction, in which new products and technologies continually destroy existing jobs, firms, and even entire industries.
  d   efficient allocation of resources in the short run, without any incentives for technological advance.
  e   b and d.

2 Firms engage in research and development expenditures in order to

  a   destroy their rivals.
  b   provide beneficial externalities to society.
  c   advance knowledge, which is a public good.
  d   gain market power and charge prices above costs.
  e   promote perfect competition.

3 Research and development refers to expenditures intended to

  a   discover new ideas and products.
  b   discover new technologies.
  c   develop products and bring them to market.
  d   all of the above.
  e   a and b.

4 A patent is

  a   a property right to an idea.
  b   the right to produce and sell an invention or innovation for all time.
  c   the right to produce and sell an invention or innovation for a limited time.
  d   a and b.
  e   a and c.

5 Patents

  a   promote short-run efficiency by encouraging firms to set price equal to marginal cost.
  b   stimulate research and innovation and promote dynamic efficiency.
  c   are awarded to the firm that has devoted the most resources to researching and developing the idea.
  d   are given for advances in basic knowledge.
  e   all of the above.

6 In Europe, the typical patent life is 20 years. The length involves a trade-off between

  a   short-run inefficiency and incentives to innovate.
  b   greater incentives to innovate and stimulation of subsequent innovation through greater access to past innovations.
  c   promoting research and fostering new product development.
  d   the profits of innovators and those of rivals.
  e   all of the above.

7 The breadth of patent coverage involves a trade-off between

  a   short-run inefficiency and incentives to innovate.
  b   greater incentives to innovate and stimulation of subsequent innovation through greater access to past innovations.
  c   promoting research and fostering new product development.
  d   the profits of innovators and those of rivals.
  e   all of the above.

8 Direct rewards from R & D are given

  a   in proportion to R & D expenditures.
  b   in proportion to market share.
  c   on the basis of how many positive externalities are generated.
  d   on a winner-take-all basis.
  e   equally to all who entered the race.

9 A patent might not be awarded for an innovation if

  a   the innovator chose not to apply for the patent, preferring to hide the advance as a trade secret.
  b   the idea was too broad to be patentable.
  c   other firms had tried harder to find this particular innovation.
  d   too many jobs would be destroyed if the patent were awarded.
  e   a and b.

10 When patent holders raise price above marginal cost, there is a sacrifice of

  a   trade secrets.
  b   dynamic efficiency.
  c   infant industries.
  d   public goods.
  e   short-run efficiency.

11 R & D expenditures is

  a   variable costs.
  b   fixed costs.
  c   marginal cost.
  d   U-shaped average cost.
  e   none of the above.

12 Which of the following is true?

  a   Large firms have advantages in R & D because they may have better access to capital markets.
  b   Large firms have advantages in R & D because they can reap the cost savings on sales of more units.

c   Small firms have advantages in R & D because of the bureaucratic environment in large corporations.

d   All of the above.

e   *a* and *b*.

13   Learning by doing refers to

a   the fact that education only signals higher productivity. it does not increase productivity.

b   the idea that as firms gain experience from production, their costs fall.

c   the fact that R & D is wasteful because firms must produce products before they can innovate.

d   the fact that R & D is the only way to lower costs.

e   none of the above.

14   The learning curve

a   shows the trade-off between short-run and dynamic efficiency.

b   shows the trade-off between providing incentives to innovate and allowing access to previous innovations.

c   shows that patents lead to monopoly profits.

d   shows how marginal cost declines as cumulative experience increases.

e   disproves the infant industry argument.

15   According to the infant industry argument,

a   firms that have higher costs than their foreign rivals should be protected in order to save jobs.

b   firms should be protected if foreign labour costs are so low that the domestic firm cannot compete.

c   firms that have higher costs than their foreign rivals should be protected until they move down the learning curve.

d   free trade is efficient.

e   *a, b,* and *c*.

16   Which of the following is *not* true?

a   Competition drives firms that do not innovate from the market.

b   Competition inhibits innovation by eliminating profits that could be used to finance R & D.

c   Competition leads firms to imitate innovations, eroding returns.

d   Competition spurs R & D by making it clear that the principal way to earn profits is to innovate and capture market power.

e   All of the above.

17   The market will not supply enough R & D because

a   firms that win patent races do not have to pay for the patents.

b   the benefits of R & D spill over to others not directly involved.

c   firms that lose patent races cannot market the innovation.

d   firms that win patent races set price higher than marginal cost.

e   all of the above.

18   Which of the following is *not* a property of public goods?

a   It is difficult to exclude anyone from the benefits.

b   The marginal cost of an additional user is close to zero.

c   The market is likely to supply too few public goods.

d   All of the above are properties of public goods.

e   *a* and *b*.

19   Which of the following types of R & D is most likely to be a public good?

a   Basic research

b   Product development

c   Applied research

d   The costs of marketing new goods and services

e   All of the above

20   When firms share research and development efforts, they

a   are in violation of competition.

b   forgo the right to patent their innovations.

c   may restrict access to their discoveries, thereby creating an entry barrier.

d   forgo the right to ask for government subsidies.

e   undermine dynamic efficiency.

Completion

1   As new products and technologies drive older jobs, technologies, and industries from the market, capitalism, in the words of Joseph Schumpeter, is a process of _____.

2   Expenditures designed to discover new ideas, products, and technologies and bring them to market are called _____.

3   The exclusive right to produce and sell an invention or innovation is a _____.

4   The fact that the rewards of research and development are given on a winner-take-all basis makes R & D a _____.

5   Rather than seek a patent, an innovator may try to hide the new knowledge as a _____.

6   _____ refers to the idea that as firms gain experience, their costs fall.

7   The curve showing how marginal costs of production decline as total experience increases is called the _____.

8   The benefits of research and development spill over to others not directly involved and generate positive _____.

9   Basic research produces knowledge from which it is difficult to exclude potential users and which can be used by others at no cost to the producers; therefore, it is an example of a _____.

10 The hope that an industry not currently able to compete with foreign firms may in time acquire the experience to move down the learning curve is called the _____ argument for protection.

Answers to Self-Test

True or False

1	F	6	T	11	F
2	T	7	T	12	F
3	T	8	T	13	T
4	T	9	F	14	T
5	F	10	F	15	T

Multiple Choice

1	c	6	a	11	b	16	e
2	d	7	b	12	d	17	b
3	d	8	d	13	b	18	d
4	e	9	e	14	d	19	a
5	b	10	e	15	c	20	c

Completion

1   creative destruction
2   research and development
3   patent
4   patent race
5   trade secret
6   Learning by doing
7   learning curve
8   externalities
9   public good
10 infant industry

Tools and Practice Problems

Firms undertake research and development in order to market new products or to find new and less costly ways of producing. They compete to win patents or secure trade secrets that will allow them to enjoy some protection against competition and to earn above-normal profits. In this section we study the rewards that motivate R & D. First, several problems explore the value of new product patents and trade secrets. Next, we study innovations that result in lower production costs and consider whether incumbent monopolies have as much incentive to innovate as do potential entrants.

PATENTS

The incentive to undertake research and development is the expectation of future profits. Patents allow firms to earn these profits by conferring monopoly status for the duration of the patent. Tool Kit 16.1 shows how to compute the value of a patent and thus the reward for successful innovation.

Tool Kit 16.1 Calculating the Value of a Patent

The developer of a new product may be able to win a patent, which in Europe grants the exclusive right to market the product for 20 years. The value of the patent is then the present discounted value of monopoly profits for the duration of the patent. Follow these steps to compute the value of a patent.

Step one: Compute monopoly profits resulting from the patent.

Step two: Find the present discounted value of 20 years of profits. This number is the value of the patent:

Value of the patent = profits + [profits] $\times 1/(1 + r)^1$]
$+ [profits \times 1/(1 + r)^2] + \cdots$
$+ [profits \times 1/(1 + r)^{19}]$.

(The variable r stands for the real rate of interest. In the problems below, we will set r equal to 3 percent. A shortcut for step two is to multiply profits by 15.32.)

1   (Worked problem: patents) Nu Products, plc, has come up with another winning idea—a rubberised surface for high-capacity, no-injury playgrounds. The company wins the patent. Demand for resurfacings is given in Table 16.1, and costs are £20,000 per park. Calculate the value of the patent.

Table 16.1

Price	Playgrounds resurfaced
£60,000	10
£50,000	20
£40,000	30
£30,000	40
£20,000	50

Step-by-step solution

Step one: Compute the monopoly profits resulting from the patent. Table 16.2 gives the marginal revenue for resurfacings.

Table 16.2

Price	Playgrounds resurfaced	Total Revenue	Marginal revenue
£60,000	10	£ 600,000	£60,000
£50,000	20	£1,000,000	£40,000
£40,000	30	£1,200,000	£20,000
£30,000	40	£1,200,000	£ 0
£20,000	50	£1,000,000	–£20,000

Marginal cost equals marginal revenue when price is £40,000 and 30 playgrounds are resurfaced. Profits then equal (£40,000 × 30) – (£20,000 × 30) = £600,000.

Step two: Find the present discounted value of 20 years of profits. This number is the value of the patent.

Value of the patent $= £600,000 + [(£600,000) \times 1/(1 + r)^1]$
$+ [(£600,000) \times 1/(1 + r)^2] +$
$+ \ldots [(£600,000) \times 1/(1 + r)^{19}]$
$= £600,000 \times 15.32 = £9,192,000.$

2   (Practice problem: patents) No Fungicide, plc, has discovered a new product that kills potato blight bugs. It wins the patent. The firm's economics department computes that it can expect to earn £100,000 for the length of the patent. Compute the value of the patent.

3   (Practice problem: patents) New Steel, plc, has developed a new procedure for making steel sheet. They have decided not to apply for a patent, but rather to keep the technique secret. They expect that others will be able to duplicate the procedure in four years and that the resulting competition will allow only a normal rate of return thereafter. Their costs are £5,000 per steel sheet, and they estimate that the demand curve is as given in Table 16.3.

Table 16.3

Price	Quantity
£30,000	20
£25,000	30
£20,000	40
£15,000	50
£10,000	60
£ 5,000	70

The real interest rate is expected to remain at 5 percent over the period. Find the value of the trade secret.

THE ENTRANT VERSUS THE INCUMBENT

A firm that discovers and patents a new, lower-cost production technique will be able to earn above-normal profits for the duration of the patent. If the firm is already a monopoly, then it merely takes advantage of the lower costs. If the firm is a potential entrant, it can undercut the existing firm, drive it from the market, and take its place as the incumbent monopolist. Here, we compare the incentives that incumbent and entrant firms have to innovate, and demonstrate that monopolists do have lower incentives to innovate, as we learned in Chapter 15. Tool Kit 16.2 shows how to predict the outcome of competition between a new entrant and the incumbent monopolist. The following problems use this idea to compare incentives to innovate.

Tool Kit 16.2 Finding Equilibrium with an Incumbent Monopolist and a Potential Entrant

When a firm discovers how to produce for less, it is in position to take over an industry. It can set price just below the average cost of its rival and capture all sales. Follow these steps.

Step one: Identify the incumbent's costs, the potential entrant's costs, and the demand curve.

Step two: Find the equilibrium. The incumbent sets price equal to the entrant's average cost and captures the entire market. (Actually, the price must be 1 penny less than the average cost of the entrant, but we will round up in the problems below.)

---

4   (Worked problem: monopolist and potential entrant) Computerise, plc, has had the monopoly in the market for computerising dental offices in Rosetown. While other firms could set up a computer system for £20,000, Computerise's costs are only £15,000. Demand is given in Table 16.4.

Table 16.4

Price	Offices computerised
£30,000	20
£25,000	30
£20,000	40
£15,000	50
£10,000	60

a   Find the equilibrium.
b   Suppose that a new innovation in programming would lower costs to £10,000. Assume that the incumbent, Computerise, discovers and patents the innovation first. Find the new equilibrium and the incumbent's profits. How much is the innovation worth to Computerise?
c   Now assume that a potential entrant discovers and patents the innovation first. Find the new equilibrium and the entrant's profits.
d   Who has stronger incentives to innovate?

Step-by-step solution

Step one (a): Identify the incumbent's costs, the potential entrant's costs, and the demand curve. The incumbent, Computerise, has an average cost of £15,000; the entrant has an average cost of £20,000. The demand appears in Table 16.4.

Step two: Find the equilibrium. The incumbent sets price equal to the entrant's average cost, which is £20,000, and captures the entire market of 40 offices. Its profits are $(£20,000 \times 40) - (£15,000 \times 40) = £200,000$.

Step three (b): If it discovers the innovation and wins the patent, Computerise is still the low-cost firm. It captures the entire market with the same price of £20,000 and earns profits of $(£20,000 \times 40) - (£10,000 \times 40) = £400,000$.

Step four (c): If a potential entrant discovers the patent first, it becomes the low-price firm. It sets price equal to COmputerise's average cost, which is £15,000, and captures the entire market of 50 offices. Its profits are $(£15,000 \times 50) - (£10,000 \times 50) = £250,000$.

Step five (d): The gain to innovation for Computerise is the difference between its profits before and after the innovation, which equal £400,000 – £200,000 = £200,000. The entrant gains £250,000 by innovating and thus has stronger incentives.

5   (Practice problem: monopolist and potential entrant) Blackdare has patented its unique process for extinguishing oil fires. It can put out a typical well fire for £150,000, but its competitors, without access to the patented process, have average costs equal to £200,000. The demand for extinguishing oil fires is given in Table 16.5.

Table 16.5

Price	Fires
£400,000	10
£350,000	12
£300,000	14
£250,000	16
£200,000	18
£150,000	20
£100,000	22

a   Find the equilibrium price and quantity and profits.
b   Suppose that a new innovation in firefighting would lower costs to £100,000. Assume that the incumbent, Blackdare, discovers and patents the innovation first. Find the new equilibrium and the incumbent's profits. How much is the innovation worth to Blackdare?
c   Now assume that a potential entrant discovers and patents the innovation first. Find the new equilibrium and the entrant's profits.
d   Who has the stronger incentives to innovate?

6   (Practice problem: monopolist and potential entrant) PhXXX Pharmaceuticals has a monopoly on the treatment of Rubinski's Trauma, an obscure ailment of the saliva glands. The average cost of curing a patient is £2,000 for PhXXX. The only other treatment available costs £5,000. Demand for the treatment of Rubinski's Trauma is given in Table 16.6.

Table 16.6

Price	Treatments
£8,000	100
£7,000	200
£6,000	300
£5,000	400
£4,000	500
£3,000	600
£2,000	700
£1,000	800

a   Find the equilibrium price and quantity.
b   Suppose that a new genetically engineered drug would lower treatment costs to £1,000. Assume that the incumbent, PhXXX, discovers and patents the new drug first. Find the new equilibrium and the incumbent's profits. How much is the innovation worth to PhXXX?
c   Now assume that a potential entrant discovers and patents the innovation first. Find the new equilibrium and the entrant's profits.
d   Who has the stronger incentives to innovate?

Answers to Problems

2   Value of patent = £100,000 × 15.32 = £1,532,000.

3   Marginal revenue is given in Table 16.7.

Table 16.7

Price	Quantity	Total revenue	Marginal revenue
£30,000	20	£600,000	—
£25,000	30	£750,000	£15,000
£20,000	40	£800,000	£ 5,000
£15,000	50	£750,000	–£ 5,000
£10,000	60	£600,000	–£15,000
£ 5,000	70	£350,000	–£25,000

Marginal revenue equals marginal cost at a price of £20,000, where 40 units are supplied. Profits = (£20,000 × 40) – (£5,000 × 40) = £600,000. The value of the trade secret is £600,000 + £600,000 × 1/(1.05) + £600,000 × 1/(1.05)^2 + £600,000 × 1/(1.05)^3 = £2,209,380.

5   a   Price = £200,000; quantity = 18; profits = £900,000.
    b   Price = £200,000; quantity = 18; profits = £1,800,000.
    c   Price = £150,000; quantity = 20; profits = £1,000,000.
    d   The entrant would gain £1,000,000, while Blackdare would only gain £1,800,000 – £900,000 = £900,000. The entrant has stronger incentives.

6   a   Price = £5,000; quantity = 400; profits = £1,200,000;
    b   Price = £5,000; quantity = 400; profits = £1,600,000;
    c   Price = £2,000; quantity = 700; profits = £700,000.
    d   The entrant would gain £700,000, while PhXXX would only gain £1,600,000 – £1,200,000 = £400,000. The entrant has stronger incentives.

IMPERFECT INFORMATION IN THE PRODUCT MARKET

Chapter Review

Chapter 17 begins the exploration of the economics of information with a look at information problems in the product market. Why can't customers always be sure of the quality of a good? Why do customers sometimes pay a higher price for a good than the good is worth? This chapter explains the various ways in which the economy attempts to solve these problems. In doing so, the chapter deviates from the basic competitive model to introduce a fascinating world of signaling, reputation, search, and advertising. Imperfect information causes markets to look a lot like the imperfect competition models discussed in Chapters 13 to 15 (on monopoly and oligopoly). Chapters 18 and 19 will take up imperfect information as well, in the labour and capital markets.

ESSENTIAL CONCEPTS

1   The basic competitive model assumes that information is perfect, that households are well informed about the prices, quality, and availability of goods and services, and that firms know all input and output prices and the best available technology. Economists now believe that there are important aspects of the economy's performance that are the result of **imperfect information.** For instance, mutually beneficial trades may not occur if customers cannot judge accurately a product's quality.

If there were such a thing as a market for information, it would not solve the problem. There would be no way for a customer to evaluate information before buying it, and if she already had the information, she would have no need to buy it.

2   **Asymmetric information** exists when one side of the market knows something that the other does not. For example, the seller of a used car may know more about its reliability than the buyer. Asymmetric information can cause the demand curve to be upward sloping, because buyers reason that only low-quality cars would be sold at low prices and that quality increases with price. This odd situation can lead to more than one possible equilibrium and can cause markets to be thin or nonexistent in spite of potential gains from trade.

3   One way to send buyers a message in a market with asymmetric information is called **signaling.** For example, a seller of quality used cars can distinguish his product by offering warranties or by building expensive showrooms. Buyers will reason that a seller of defective

cars (or what Americans term lemons) could not afford the expenses of honoring the warranty and will conclude that this seller's used cars are reliable. The seller can also charge higher prices, another potentially informative signal. Buyers understand that only lemons would be sold at low prices, and thus they judge the quality according to the price.

4   If buyers can observe the quality of what is sold, then they can provide sellers with good incentives by basing pay on quality. For example, an employer can pay a typist according to the number of errors made. When buyers do not know the quality of goods before purchasing them, markets do not provide built-in incentives for firms to produce high-quality merchandise. Two possible solutions to this incentive problem are **contracts** and **reputations.**

   a   Contracts typically include **contingency clauses,** which make payment depend on the quality of the service. For example, a contract might specify that the service must be performed by a certain date unless there is a strike or bad weather. Spelling out contingencies provides incentives and shares the risk, but it makes contracts complicated. When the terms of a contract are violated, one party is said to be in breach, but if the reasons for the breach are ambiguous, contract enforcement becomes an issue. Certainly, contracts help, but they provide only an imperfect solution to the incentive problems accompanying trade in the presence of asymmetric information.

   b   By repeatedly providing quality goods and service, a firm establishes a reputation, which enables it to earn extra profits. To preserve its valuable reputation, the firm must continue to provide quality. Reputations thus provide firms with incentives to perform well.

5   Because quality is uncertain and also because the same good may be sold at different prices in different locations (**price dispersion**), customers spend time and money in **search.** Rational search balances the benefits (finding better goods at lower prices) against the costs. Customers usually stop searching even though there is more to learn. **Information intermediaries** are firms that gather information to make customer search easier and more effective. Department stores and travel agents are examples of information intermediaries.

6   Firms try to influence customers' purchasing decisions through **informative** and **persuasive advertising.** The goal of advertising is to shift the demand curve to the right and so enable the firm to raise prices and sell more goods. Advertising may also serve as a signal. Customers may reason that only a high-quality product with good sales would justify a large expenditure on advertising.

7   Concern for poorly informed consumers and deceptive advertising has led to **consumer protection legislation,** which attempts to stop misleading advertising. Such legislation includes disclosure requirements. For exam-

ple, the Stock Exchange requires firms whose shares are listed on it to disclose financial information. Even so, distinguishing between illegal misleading advertising and its legal counterparts (confusing and persuasive advertising) is difficult.

BEHIND THE ESSENTIAL CONCEPTS

1   Markets do not necessarily fail when information is imperfect. The market for assets is an example of a very efficient market. Uncertainty in these markets exists, but the uncertainty is symmetric. Neither side knows the ultimate value of the assets they are trading. Efficiency problems arise, however, when information is asymmetric, that is, when one side of the market knows something that the other does not. Many mutually beneficial exchanges do not take place because buyers cannot be sure about quality, and they fear that sellers may exploit their informational advantage and sell lemons.

2   In the basic competitive model, customers ask simple questions, such as "Is the good worth its price?" In the presence of asymmetric information and, especially, signaling, customers must be more sophisticated. The seller of a quality item wants to signal that his goods have value. He could just say, "My goods are great!" but few customers would believe him. If he provides a guarantee and builds an expensive shop, customers may be more confident that he would be there to honor his word should the product fail. The customer infers from the warranty and the shop that the seller's goods are quality goods.

3   The information problems discussed in this chapter lead the market structure away from perfect competition, creating two possible situations: **barriers to entry** and firms with **downward-sloping demand curves.**

   a   Customers who cannot know the quality of goods buy from businesses with good reputations. Because a reputation is built up over time, firms that would otherwise enter an industry will not be able to justify the investment necessary to establish a good reputation. In this scenario, reputation becomes a barrier to entry and results in less competition.

   b   Because customers must search to learn about price and quality, it becomes cheaper for them to shop at familiar stores. Although the goods themselves may be identical, the stores are different in the eyes of the customer because he knows about some stores and is ignorant of others. Thus, a firm faces a downward-sloping demand curve, where high demanders are those who have information about the firm and low demanders do not as yet.

4   Information problems in the product market run parallel to the problems in the insurance market discussed in Chapter 6. Again, there are two types of information problems.

a In the insurance market, when the price of insurance is high, only the risky customers buy insurance. The mix of customers is adversely selected when the price rises. Adverse selection also appears in the market for lemons. Customers reason that as the price rises, more quality cars are offered for sale, and the fraction of lemons declines. In other words, there is *adverse selection* in the average quality of used cars when the price falls.

b *Moral hazard* troubles the insurance market because people who have insurance tend to be less cautious. They lose their incentives to be careful when they are protected against loss. Similarly, in this chapter, we see that suppliers must be given incentives to live up to the terms of their contracts. There is a moral hazard that the other party may not fulfill his promise and instead give some excuse that cannot be verified.

5 Although this chapter is about information problems, you should also keep in mind that markets do economise on the need for gathering information. In deciding what to produce and in what quantities and the method of production, firms do not need to know the preferences or incomes of households, the production techniques of other firms, or the overall quantities of inputs available. They only need to know the price. Similarly, households do not need to know others' tastes or anything about firms. Price conveys all relevant information, a great advantage of markets.

SELF-TEST

True or False

1 In the basic competitive model, individuals know their opportunity sets.

2 In the basic competitive model, firms know the opportunity sets of individuals.

3 Markets for information do not work well because once the consumer has enough information to evaluate the worth of the information, she no longer has the incentive to pay for it.

4 In the lemons model, demand may slope upwards if average quality increases as price increases.

5 Supply and demand may cross more than once if customers do not know the quality of the goods they are asked to buy.

6 Lemons markets have adverse selection in that as the price falls, the mix of goods offered for sale contains more low-quality goods.

7 Customers may believe that a product that carries a warranty is reliable because if the product were not reliable, the firm would incur costs honoring the warranty.

8 Even if customers judge the quality of goods by their price, the market always clears in equilibrium.

9 In the car hire market, there is an incentive problem because customers have less reason to drive carefully.

10 Contracts attempt to provide incentives through contingency clauses that specify what each party agrees to do in different situations.

11 Problems of specifying and enforcing quality make it difficult to overcome the incentive problems with contracts.

12 The reputation of a firm may persuade customers that its goods are of high quality because if the firm were to lose its reputation, its profits would fall.

13 The reputations of existing firms attract new competitors to the market because these firms earn higher profits.

14 Markets where customers must search to learn price are characterised by perfect competition.

15 Information intermediaries reduce the search costs of firms and customers.

Multiple Choice

1 In the basic competitive model, households are assumed to know

a their opportunity set.
b the prices of all goods and services offered for sale.
c the characteristics of all goods and services.
d their preferences.
e all of the above.

2 In the basic competitive model, firms are assumed to know

a the best available technology.
b the productivity of each job applicant.
c all input prices from every possible supplier.
d the present and future prices for their outputs.
e all of the above.

3 In the basic competitive model, firms are assumed to know

a the preferences of individual consumers.
b the costs of production for their suppliers.
c the overall quantities of available inputs.
d all of the above.
e none of the above.

4 Markets for information do not work well because

a no firm would be willing to sell information.
b consumers are not willing to pay for information.
c consumers cannot know what they are buying before they actually buy the information.
d markets only work to allocate material goods.
e all of the above.

5 In the lemons model,

a customers know the quality of the goods but sellers do not.

    b   sellers know the quality of the goods but customers do not.

    c   neither customers nor sellers know the quality of the goods.

    d   both customers and sellers know that the quality of the goods is low.

    e   none of the above.

6   In the lemons model, average quality

    a   rises as price falls.

    b   falls as price falls because sellers know the quality, and owners of lower-quality goods are willing to sell at lower prices.

    c   does not change as price falls because consumers know quality and will not buy lower-quality goods.

    d   may rise or fall as price falls.

    e   none of the above.

7   In the lemons model,

    a   demand is downward sloping.

    b   supply is upward sloping.

    c   demand may slope up or down.

    d   supply may slope up or down.

    e   *b* and *c*.

8   Which of the following involve(s) adverse selection?

    a   Consumers sometimes make mistakes and select inferior products.

    b   Consumers may not be able to find the lowest-price supplier.

    c   As the price falls, the fraction of used cars that are lemons increases.

    d   As car insurance premiums increase, those least likely to have an accident drop out of the market.

    e   *c* and *d*.

9   In markets with imperfect information,

    a   firms are price takers.

    b   firms set prices, taking into account the effect that price has as a signal of quality.

    c   price plays no role because consumers are uncertain about quality.

    d   markets clear for the usual reasons.

    e   there is a uniform market price per unit of quality, but the goods of different firms sell for different prices.

10   Which of the following are examples of information signals?

    a   The seller claims that her goods are high quality.

    b   The seller offers a warranty.

    c   The seller constructs an expensive showroom.

    d   All of the above.

    e   *b* and *c*.

11   In markets with imperfect information, the incentive problem arises because firms

    a   have no incentive to pay lower prices since they do not know quality.

    b   have limited incentive to produce good-quality items if they cannot convince consumers.

    c   can raise price above the consumer's willingness to pay.

    d   have no incentive to produce quality items unless they can be patented.

    e   have no incentive to build reputations.

12   Provisions in contracts that specify what each of the parties must do in certain situations are called

    a   signals.

    b   adverse selection.

    c   contingency clauses.

    d   reputations.

    e   none of the above.

13   When a party to a contract violates its terms, he

    a   is in adverse selection.

    b   writes a contingency clause.

    c   creates price dispersion.

    d   is an information intermediary.

    e   is in breach.

14   In some markets, the reputations of firms help persuade customers that their products are high quality. In these markets,

    a   price remains above the cost of production.

    b   firms earn reputation rents.

    c   the reputations of existing firms act as a barrier to the entry of new competitors.

    d   all of the above.

    e   *a* and *b*.

15   A firm with a reputation for high-quality goods might not cut its price because

    a   cutting price would attract more customers.

    b   customers might infer that at the low price, the firm will not have enough incentive to maintain its reputation.

    c   lower prices would attract new competitors.

    d   the firm cannot set its price; it is a price taker.

    e   *a* and *b*.

16   When customers do not have perfect information about price, there may be price dispersion, which means

    a   the same good is sold at different prices.

    b   the expenses of searching eliminate the gains from trade.

    c   customers will search for the best value.

    d   all of the above.

    e   *a* and *c*.

17   When search is costly for customers,

    a   the demand curves for a firm's products will be downward sloping.

    b   firms will be price takers.

    c   the firm will lose all its customers if it raises its price above the prices of its competitors.

d the firm will gain all its competitors' business if it charges lower prices.

e *c* and *d*.

18 Markets in which customers must search to learn prices and qualities are best described by the

a competitive model.

b pure monopoly model.

c monopolistic competition model.

d *a* or *b*.

e none of the above.

19 An information intermediary

a helps bring together buyers and sellers.

b cannot make money because markets for information do not work well.

c writes contracts for buyers and sellers.

d eliminates the need for advertising.

e *c* and *d*.

20 Advertising

a provides price information to potential customers.

b informs customers about which products are available.

c attempts to persuade customers to buy certain products.

d all of the above.

e *a* and *b*.

Completion

1 In the market for _____, customers do not know the quality of the goods being sold.

2 Actions taken by sellers to convince buyers of the high quality of their goods are called _____.

3 The _____ arises when the individual is not rewarded for what she does or when she does not have to pay the full costs of what she does.

4 Clauses in contracts that make the payment depend on precisely how the service is performed are called _____.

5 Someone who brings buyers and sellers together is called an _____.

6 The reputations of existing firms act as a _____ against new competition.

7 When the same good is sold at different prices, there is _____.

8 When customers must search for price and quality information, competition is _____.

9 Advertising that conveys information about price, product availability, and quality is called _____ advertising.

10 Advertising may _____ to customers that the product is of high quality because if the quality were poor, the firm would soon lose its new customers and would have wasted its advertising expenses.

Answers to Self-Test

True or False

1	T	6	T	11	T
2	F	7	T	12	T
3	T	8	F	13	F
4	T	9	T	14	F
5	T	10	T	15	T

Multiple Choice

1	*e*	6	*b*	11	*b*	16	*e*
2	*e*	7	*e*	12	*c*	17	*a*
3	*e*	8	*e*	13	*e*	18	*c*
4	*c*	9	*b*	14	*d*	19	*a*
5	*b*	10	*e*	15	*b*	20	*d*

Completion

1 lemons
2 signals
3 incentive problem
4 contingency clauses
5 information intermediary
6 barrier to entry
7 price dispersion
8 imperfect
9 informative
10 signal

Tools and Practice Problems

Three topics are discussed in this section. First, we look at the important **lemons model,** where average quality is higher as price increases. In this situation, we may see upward-sloping demand curves, which may cause markets to fail to exist or may create the possibility of more than one equilibrium. Also, when firms are able to set prices in this model, there is the possibility of excess supply. Second, we turn to price dispersion and search. We explore the benefits and costs of searching and see why the consumer will likely stop searching before the lowest price is found. Finally, we study how advertising increases profits.

LEMONS

When consumers do not know the quality of a good until after they make the purchase, there is asymmetric information in the product market. Firms that produce low-quality goods (lemons) can sell their goods in the high-quality market. If information were perfect, there would be two markets; now there is one. In figuring out their own demand, consumers must estimate how average quality changes as the market expands. Tool Kit 17.1 shows how to derive the demand curve under these circumstances and that it may slope upwards, and some problems explore the consequences.

Tool Kit 17.1 Deriving the Demand Curve When Consumers Do Not Know the Quality of the Good

If they cannot observe the quality of a good at the time of purchase, customers must estimate and base their demand on the average quality available on the market. Follow this four-step procedure.

Step one: Add the supplies of low- and high-quality goods to find the market supply curve.

Price	Quantity supplied
p_1	$Q_{low} + Q_{high}$
p_2	$Q_{low} + Q_{high}$
Etc.	

Step two: Find the fractions of high- and low-quality goods at each point on the supply curve.

Fraction of high-quality goods = $Q_{high}/(Q_{low} + Q_{high})$.

Fraction of low-quality goods = $Q_{low}/(Q_{low} + Q_{high})$.

Step three: Find the average value at each point. This number is what consumers are willing to pay; therefore, it is the demand price.

Average value = demand price
= (fraction of high quality ×
value of high quality)
+ (fraction of low quality ×
value of low quality).

Step four: Construct the demand curve.

Price = average value	Quantity demanded
p_1	$Q_{low} + Q_{high}$
p_2	$Q_{low} + Q_{high}$
Etc.	

1 (Worked problem: lemons) Many firms sell 50-kilo packages of meat at the local farmers' market. Customers place a value of £20 per package on fatty, low-quality beef, and they place a value of £50 per package on lean, good-quality beef. The beef is wrapped and frozen, so at the time of purchase, customers cannot distinguish the quality of beef they are buying. The supply curves for low- and high-quality beef appear in Table 17.1.

Table 17.1

Low quality		High quality	
Price	Quantity	Price	Quantity
£15	1,000	£15	0
£20	2,000	£20	0
£25	3,000	£25	1,000
£30	4,000	£30	4,000
£35	5,000	£35	10,000
£40	6,000	£40	12,000
£45	7,000	£45	14,000
£50	8,000	£50	16,000

a Derive the demand curve for beef.
b Find the market-clearing price (or prices) and quantity (or quantities).
c For purposes of comparison, suppose that consumers could tell the difference and that there were separate markets for the two types of beef. Find the equilibrium price and quantity for each type of beef. How does the asymmetric information about quality affect the market for high-quality beef?

Step-by-step solution

Step one (a): Add the supplies to find the market supply. For example, if the price is £325, there will be 5,000 low-quality packages of beef and 10,000 high-quality packages for a total of 15,000. Proceeding in this way gives the market supply as shown in Table 17.2.

Table 17.2

Price	Quantity (both high and low quality)
£15	1,000
£20	2,000
£25	4,000
£30	8,000
£35	15,000
£40	18,000
£45	21,000
£50	24,000

Step two: Find the fractions of the total that are high and low quality at each point. For example, if the price is £35, there are 10,000 high-quality packages. The total number of packages is 15,000. The fraction is $(10,000/15,000) \times 100 = 2/3$. Enter the number and continue. The corresponding fraction of low-quality goods is then 1/3. The complete information appears in Table 17.3.

Table 17.3

Price	Low-quality quantity	High-quality quantity	Fraction high	Fraction low
£15	1,000	0	0	1
£20	2,000	0	0	1
£25	3,000	1,000	1/4	3/4
£30	4,000	4,000	1/2	1/2
£35	5,000	10,000	2/3	1/3
£40	6,000	12,000	2/3	1/3
£45	7,000	14,000	2/3	1/3
£50	8,000	16,000	2/3	1/3

Step three: Compute the average value for each price. For example, when the price is £35, there are 5,000 packages valued at £20 and 10,000 valued at £50. The average value is [(£20 × 5,000) + (£50 × 10,000)]/15,000 = £40. Continue and complete the table as shown in Table 17.4. Note that average value increases with price. This is because at a higher price, the percentage of packages that are high quality is greater.

Table 17.4

Price	Low-quality quantity	High-quality quantity	Fraction high	Average value
£15	1,000	0	0	£20.00
£20	2,000	0	0	£20.00
£25	3,000	1,000	1/4	£27.50
£30	4,000	4,000	1/2	£35.00
£35	5,000	10,000	2/3	£40.00
£40	6,000	12,000	2/3	£40.00
£45	7,000	14,000	2/3	£40.00
£50	8,000	16,000	2/3	£40.00

Step four: Construct the demand curve shown below using the data in Table 17.5. The price column is the average value, and the quantity column is the sum of the low- and high-quality quantities.

Table 17.5

Price	Quantity
£20.00	1,000
£20.00	2,000
£27.50	4,000
£35.00	8,000
£40.00	15,000
£40.00	18,000
£40.00	21,000
£40.00	24,000

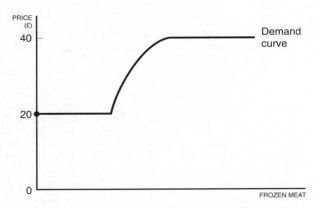

Step five (b): Find the market-clearing prices and quantities. The market clears at a price of £20, where the quantity demanded equals the quantity supplied at 2,000. At this equilibrium, there are no high-quality packages sold. Also, the market clears at a price of £40, where the quantity demanded and the quantity supplied equal 18,000. At this equilibrium, there are 6,000 low-quality and 12,000 high-quality packages. The two equilibria are shown in the diagram.

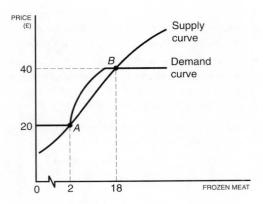

Step six (c): If consumers had perfect information about quality, then there would be a separate low-quality market with 2,000 sold at a price of £20 and a high-quality market with a price of £50 and 16,000 units sold. The asymmetric information destroys the high-quality market in equilibrium *A*. In equilibrium *B*, the high-quality market survives, but the quantity is smaller than it would be with perfect information.

$$P = AV$$

2   (Practice problem: <u>lemons</u>) Trying to appear better educated, many people are buying abbreviated guides to culture—lists of novels, operas, and works of art an educated person should know. The guides also include a paragraph or two of witty things to say. The consumers of these books, obviously, cannot judge the quality until they say the wrong thing at the next important social function. The supply curves of low- and high-quality guides are given in Table 17.6. The value of a high-quality guide (complete with video tapes and workbooks) is £300. Low-quality guides are worthless.

Table 17.6

Price	Low-quality guides	High-quality guides
£ 50	1,000	0
£100	2,000	1,000
£150	4,000	6,000
£200	8,000	16,000
£250	12,000	36,000
£300	16,000	48,000

a   Derive the demand curve for guides.
b   Find the market-clearing price (or prices) and quantity (or quantities).
c   For the purposes of comparison, suppose that consumers could tell the difference and that there were separate markets for the two types of guides. Find the equilibrium price and quantity for each type of guide. How does the asymmetric information about quality affect the market for high-quality guides?

3   (Practice problem: lemons) Several new varieties of tomatoes are coming on to the market. Each promises tasty tomatoes with long shelf lives, and a tomato plant that fulfilled this promise would be worth £4. Consumers cannot observe the quality until the end of the growing season, but they suspect that the new hybrids are no better or worse than existing ones valued at £1 per plant. The supply curves of low- and high-quality tomato plants are given in Table 17.7.

Table 17.7

Price	Low-quality tomato plants	High-quality tomato plants
£1.00	10,000	0
£1.50	20,000	5,000
£2.00	30,000	20,000
£2.50	40,000	60,000
£3.00	50,000	100,000
£3.50	60,000	300,000
£4.00	70,000	500,000

a   Derive the demand curve for tomato plants.
b   Find the market-clearing price (or prices) and quantity (or quantities).
c   For the purposes of comparison, suppose that consumers could tell the difference and that there were separate markets for each of the two types of plants. Find the equilibrium price and quantity for each type of plant. How does the asymmetric information about quality affect the market for high-quality plants?

Judging Quality by Price

Because it is more expensive to produce high-quality goods than low, consumers may reason that at low prices only the poor-quality items are offered for sale and that as price increases, so does average quality. If firms understand this sort of reasoning, they will set price so that quality per dollar is as high as possible, even though this price may not be the market-clearing price. It is possible that shortages will occur, and yet no firm will reduce its price because it knows that it will not gain customers, who believe that lower prices imply lower quality. This is a profound result. In normal competitive markets, the role of prices is only to clear the market. In markets where customers do not know quality, however, price acts as a signal of quality. The price that does the best job of signaling quality may not clear the market. Tool Kit 17.2 shows how price is set in this case.

Tool Kit 17.2 Finding the Price That Maximises Quality per Pound

If customers judge quality by price, firms will set price to maximise quality per dollar. Follow these steps to find the right price.

Step one: Identify and plot the relationship between quality and price.

Step two: For each price, find the quality-price ratio: quality-price ratio = quality/price.

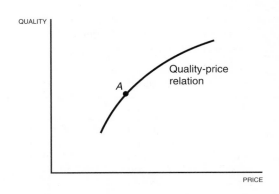

Step three: Choose the highest quality-price ratio. Label this point *A*.

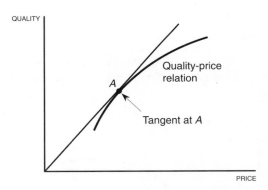

Step four: Draw a line from the origin to point *A*. It should be tangent to the quality-price curve, and its slope equals the maximum quality-price ratio.

4   (Worked problem: quality and price) Consumers of 12-litre fire extinguishers care deeply about the quality of the item, but they cannot distinguish effective and ineffective goods at the time of purchase. The quality of the fire extinguisher only matters if and when it is used. Consumers may reason that at low prices, firms could not afford the quality-control procedures necessary to ensure effective operation. Suppose consumers believe that the relationship between quality and price is as given in Table 17.8.

Table 17.8

Price	Quality (litres of fire retardant released)
£ 5	0
£10	1.0
£15	4.5
£20	7.0
£25	10.0
£30	11.0
£35	12.0
£40	12.0

a   Find the price that maximises quality per pound.

b   Suppose that demand and supply are as given in Table 17.9. Find the equilibrium price. Does it clear the market? Why or why not?

Table 17.9

Price	Demand	Supply
£40	10,000	28,000
£35	12,000	25,000
£30	14,000	21,000
£25	16,000	20,000
£20	17,000	19,000
£15	19,000	17,000
£10	21,000	11,000

Step-by-step solution

Step one (a): Identify and plot the relationship between quality and price. It is given in Table 17.8 and drawn in the diagram.

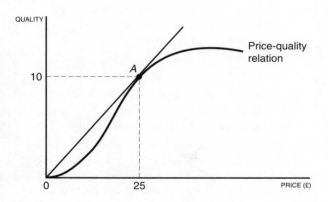

Step two: For each price, find the quality-price ratio. When the price is £40, the quality-price ratio is 12/£40 = 0.30. Continuing, we derive Table 17.10.

Table 17.10

Price	Quality	Quality-price ratio
£ 5	0	—
£10	1.0	0.10
£15	4.5	0.30
£20	7.0	0.35
£25	10.0	0.40
£30	11.0	0.37
£35	12.0	0.34
£40	12.0	0.30

Step three: Choose the highest quality-price ratio. It is 0.40, which occurs at a price of £25.

Step four: Draw a line from the origin to point *A*. It should be tangent to the quality-price curve, and its slope should equal the maximum quality-price ratio, as shown in the diagram.

Step five (b): At a price of £25, the quantity demanded is 16,000, and the quantity supplied is 20,000. Even though there is a surplus of 4,000, firms do not reduce the price. They know that customers would interpret the lower price as a signal of lower quality.

5   (Practice problem: quality and price) Tourists come to South Sea for the prawns. Dozens of small establishments offer prawns, but tourists have little ability to judge the quality before eating. They reason, however, that at low prices the firms cannot afford to ensure that the prawns are tasty. Suppose consumers believe that the relationship between quality and price is as given in Table 17.11.

Table 17.11

Price (dozen prawns)	Quality (percentage of tasty prawns)
£1	10
£2	30
£3	60
£4	70
£5	80
£6	85

a   Find the price that maximises quality per pound.

b   Suppose that demand and supply are as given in Table 17.12. Find the equilibrium price. Does it clear the market? Why or why not?

Table 17.12

Price	Demand	Supply
£6	2,000	6,000
£5	2,500	5,500
£4	3,000	5,000
£3	3,500	4,500
£2	4,000	4,000
£1	6,000	3,000

6   (Practice problem: quality and price) The boom in home exercise equipment continues, but there are many purchasers who have given up the quest for the perfect body. These purchasers offer their used equipment for sale. The market also includes those who are selling used lemons, worthless devices that do not perform as advertised. Consumers of used exercise equipment judge that the relationship between price and quality is as given in Table 17.13.

Table 17.13

Price	Quality (calories burned per hour)
£100	100
£200	500
£300	1,100
£400	1,600
£500	1,750

Find the price that maximises quality per pound.

SEARCH

In imperfectly competitive markets, different firms may offer the same good for sale at different prices. This situation, called price dispersion, means that consumers must not only decide which goods to purchase, they also must expend time and effort to locate lower price offers and decide which offer to accept. The optimal amount to search is the subject of these problems. As usual, the solution involves carefully balancing benefits and costs. Tool Kit 17.3 shows how.

Tool Kit 17.3 Searching for Lower Prices

When there is price dispersion, customers must search. These steps show how to balance the benefits and costs of searching for lower prices.

Step one: Identify the marginal cost of search and the relationship between search effort and price.

Step two: Calculate the marginal benefits of search:

$$\text{marginal benefits} = \frac{\text{change in lowest price}}{\text{change in search effort}}.$$

Step three: Find the amount of search for which the marginal benefits equal the marginal cost.

Step four: Draw a diagram illustrating the solution.

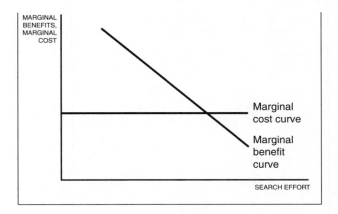

7   (Worked problem: search) Jennifer would like to buy a garden shed for her new house's garden. She has in mind the type she would like and is considering sending away for catalogues offering shed kits. Each catalogue costs £5. The relationship between the lowest appropriate shed kit price and the number of catalogues is given in Table 17.14.

Table 17.14

Number of catalogues ordered	Lowest price found	Marginal benefits
1	£250	
2	£225	
3	£210	
4	£205	
5	£202	
6	£200	

a   What is the optimal number of catalogues for Jennifer to order?

b   What price does she expect to pay for a shed kit?

c   Draw a diagram illustrating your solution.

Step-by-step solution

Step one (a): Identify the marginal cost of search and the relationship between search effort and price. The marginal cost is £5, and the relationship appears in Table 17.14.

Step two: Calculate the marginal benefit of search. The expected price is £250 from the first catalogue and £225 from the second. The marginal benefit is thus £25. Continuing, we derive the marginal benefits as shown in Table 17.15.

Table 17.15

Number of catalogues ordered	Lowest price found	Marginal benefits
1	£250	—
2	£225	£25
3	£210	£15
4	£205	£ 5
5	£202	£ 3
6	£200	£ 2

Step three: Find the amount of search for which the marginal benefits equal the marginal cost. This is 4 catalogues, which is the answer to part *a*.

Step four (b): The expected lowest price is £205, when she buys 4 catalogues.

Step five (c): The solution appears in the diagram.

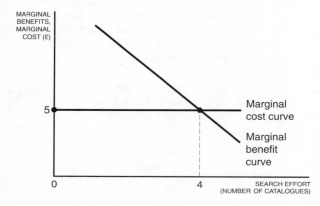

8   (Practice problem: search) Paul wants to refinish his floors. This type of home improvement project is very popular in his neighborhood, and appointments for estimates must be made and paid for weeks in advance. Estimates cost £25, and Paul guesses that the relationship between the number of estimates and the lowest price is as given in Table 17.16.

Table 17.16

Number of estimates	Expected lowest price
1	£800
2	£650
3	£550
4	£500
5	£475
6	£465
7	£460

a   What is the optimal number of estimates for Paul to schedule?
b   What price does he expect to pay for refinishing his floors?
c   Draw a diagram illustrating your solution.

9   (Practice problem: search) The Melling Forging Company needs a new robotic lathe. Several companies offer the lathes, but Melling's management feels there is enough variety that an on-site inspection is needed for each. Time is short, so the company plans to send engineers simultaneously to the plants of some of the firms that sell robotic lathes. The company would like to visit all robotic lathe producers, but a plant visit costs the company £1,000. The relationship between the number of visits and the profits that the new system will earn is given in Table 17.17.

Table 17.17

Number of visits	Expected maximum profitability
1	£18,000
2	£23,000
3	£26,000
4	£27,000
5	£27,500

How many engineers should Melling send?

10   (Practice problem: advertising) Advertising is designed to shift the demand curve to the right. This allows a firm to charge higher prices on the goods that it sells and to adjust the quantity to the profit-maximising level along the new demand curve. To see how profits change with a successful advertising program, simply follow the procedure outlined in Chapter 13 for deriving marginal revenue and finding the monopoly price and quantity.

Fay's Cleaners has been advertising its new service, which offers customers the opportunity to leave and pick up their dry cleaning at the commuter train station. The demand curves before and after the advertising campaign are given in Table 17.18. Quantity measures suits cleaned and pressed. The marginal cost of each item is £1. Fixed costs equal £1,000.

Table 17.18

Before advertising		After advertising	
Price	Quantity	Price	Quantity
£5.00	100	£5.00	500
£4.50	200	£4.50	1,000
£4.00	300	£4.00	1,500
£3.50	400	£3.50	2,000
£3.00	500	£3.00	2,500
£2.50	600	£2.50	3,000
£2.00	700	£2.00	3,500

a   Find the profit-maximising price and quantity and level of profits before the advertising campaign.

b Find the profit-maximising price and quantity and level of profits after the advertising campaign.

c How much is the advertising campaign worth to Fay's Cleaners?

11 (Practice problem: advertising) The West Side Harriers, a minor league football team, is evaluating its advertising program. The demand curves before and after the advertising campaign are given in Table 17.19. Quantity measures the attendance. The marginal cost of another supporter at the ground is £0.50. Fixed costs are £50,000.

Table 17.19

Before advertising		After advertising	
Price	Quantity	Price	Quantity
£10.00	15,000	£10.00	20,000
£ 9.50	17,500	£ 9.50	30,000
£ 9.00	20,000	£ 9.00	40,000
£ 8.50	22,500	£ 8.50	50,000
£ 8.00	25,000	£ 8.00	60,000
£ 7.50	27,500	£ 7.50	70,000
£ 7.00	30,000	£ 7.00	80,000
£ 6.50	32,500	£ 6.50	90,000
£ 6.00	35,000	£ 6.00	100,000
£ 5.50	37,500	£ 5.50	110,000

a Find the profit-maximising price and quantity and level of profits before the advertising campaign.

b Find the profit-maximising price and quantity and level of profits after the advertising campaign.

c How much is the advertising campaign worth to the West Side Harriers?

Answers to Problems

2 *a* The market demand and supply curves appear in Table 17.20.

Table 17.20

Price	Low-quality guides	High-quality guides	Total market quantity	Demand price
£ 50	1,000	0	1,000	£ 0
£100	2,000	1,000	3,000	£100
£150	4,000	6,000	10,000	£180
£200	8,000	16,000	24,000	£200
£250	12,000	36,000	48,000	£225
£300	16,000	48,000	64,000	£225

b The market clears at a price of £100, with 1,000 high- and 2,000 low-quality guides. Another market-clearing price is £200, where high-quality guides number 16,000 and low-quality, 8,000.

c If there were perfect information, there would be no low-quality guides, 48,000 high-quality guides, and an equilibrium price equal to £300.

3 *a* The market demand and supply curves appear in Table 17.21.

Table 17.21

Price	Low-quality tomato plants	High-quality tomato plants	Total market quantity	Demand price
£1.00	10,000	0	10,000	£1.00
£1.50	20,000	5,000	25,000	£1.60
£2.00	30,000	20,000	50,000	£2.20
£2.50	40,000	60,000	100,000	£2.80
£3.00	50,000	100,000	150,000	£3.00
£3.50	60,000	300,000	360,000	£3.50
£4.00	70,000	500,000	570,000	£3.63

a The market clears at a price of £1.00, where 10,000 low-quality plants are sold, and also at a price of £3.00, where 50,000 low- and 100,000 high-quality plants are sold.

c The equilibrium price of low-quality plants would be £1.00 with 10,000 sold. In the high-quality market, the price would equal £4.00, and 500,000 would be sold.

5 *a* The quality-price ratio appears in Table 17.22.

Table 17.22

Price (dozen prawns)	Quality (percentage of tasty prawns)	Quality-price ratio
£1	10	10.0
£2	30	15.0
£3	60	20.0
£4	70	17.5
£5	80	16.0
£6	85	14.2

b Firms choose a price of £3. This results in a surplus of 4,500 − 3,500 = 1,000.

6 The quality-price ratio appears in Table 17.23.

Table 17.23

Price	Quality (calories burned per hour)	Quality-price ratio
£100	100	1.00
£200	500	2.50
£300	1,100	3.67
£400	1,600	4.00
£500	1,750	3.50

8 The marginal benefits of searching appear in Table 17.24.

Table 17.24

Number of estimates	Expected lowest price	Marginal benefits
1	£800	—
2	£650	£150
3	£550	£100
4	£500	£ 50
5	£475	£ 25
6	£465	£ 10
7	£460	£ 5

a Paul should get 5 estimates.   MC = £25
b He expects to pay £475.
c

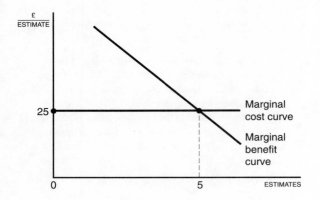

9   The marginal benefits of search appear in Table 17.25.

Table 17.25

Number of visits	Expected maximum profitability	Marginal benefits
1	£18,000	—
2	£23,000	£5,000
3	£26,000	£3,000
4	£27,000	£1,000
5	£27,500	£ 500

The company should send 4 engineers and expect to earn £27,000.

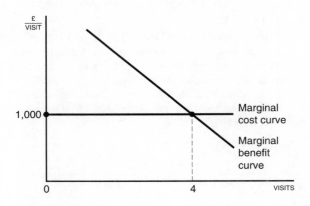

10 a   Price = £3; quantity = 500; profits = £3 × 500 – £1 × 500 – £1,000 – £0.
    b   Price = £3; quantity = 2,500; profits = £3 × 2,500 – £1 × 2,500 – £1,000 = £4,000.
    c   The advertising campaign increases profits by £4,000 –£0 = £4,000.

11 a   Price = £6; quantity = 32,500; profits = £7 × 30,000 – £0.50 × 30,000 – £50,000 = £145,000.
    b   Price = £5.50; quantity = 110,000; profits = £5.50 × 110,000 – £0.50 × 110,000 – £50,000 = £500,000.
    c   The advertising campaign increases profits by £500,000 – £145,000 = £355,000.

Chapter 18

IMPERFECTIONS IN THE LABOUR MARKET

Chapter Review

This chapter of the text returns to the labor market and applies the lessons of imperfect competition from Chapter 13 and imperfect information from Chapter 17. The chapter first explores labor unions and compares them to monopolies in the context of the labor they supply to the firm. Next the chapter examines reasons for wage differences. Finally, it takes up the problems of motivating and selecting employees. Particular attention is paid to how different compensation schemes affect incentives.

ESSENTIAL CONCEPTS

1 Employees band together in **unions** to negotiate better working conditions and higher wages. After increasing for decades, trade union membership in Britain peaked in 1979 and has since declined. Reasons for the decline include a decrease in employment in sectors of the economy that are highly unionised, an increase in employment in the service sector where unionization is lower, an increase in the employment of women and part-time workers, the introduction of legislation that

has curbed the power of trade unions, and more competitive product markets.

2 Unions can be thought of as *monopolies* in the supply of labour to the firm. As such, they raise the wage and allow employment to fall. When the employer firm makes monopoly profits in its own product market, however, it is possible for unions to secure higher wages without reduced employment, at least for a while. Overall, higher union wages probably result in somewhat lower wages for nonunion workers and lower union employment in the long run. Unions also promote job security, health and safety regulations, minimum wages, and general conditions of employment. In some European countries, such as Sweden, the Netherlands, and Germany, unions have successfully cooperated in a tripartite social partnership between unions, employers, and government.

3 Whether they are represented by a union or not, current employees or insiders are often in a strong position compared to outsiders. This is because insiders have specialist knowledge of all aspects of their work and because firms incur costs in hiring and firing workers. These costs include the training costs for new workers and redundancy payments to current workers. Insider-outsider theory explains why the wages and employment

conditions of current workers may not be responsive to labour market conditions outside the firm. Even in periods of unemployment, the bargaining power of insiders may protect them from competition from unemployed workers.

4   Because of imperfect information and other factors, labour is somewhat immobile, and wage differentials exist. Wage differentials may be caused by several factors:

   a   **Compensating differentials** are wage differences that reflect characteristics of the job. For example, a police officer may earn more than a firefighter; this reflects the greater danger of police work.

   b   **Information-based differentials** reflect a worker's imperfect information. Workers must search for job offers. A worker currently receiving a low wage may not be able to convince another employer to offer a higher wage because the prospective employer will not know the quality of the worker. This is the lemons model from Chapter 17 applied to the labour market. The difficulty that workers have in moving from job to job gives firms some market power and leads to lower wages.

   c   **Productivity wage differentials** simply account for differences in abilities to produce output.

5   **Discrimination** reduces the wages of certain groups. This may involve outright prejudice or just **statistical discrimination**, which results from the use of screening devices (such as degrees from well-established universities) that unintentionally sort out certain classes of workers from the hiring pool. In Britain there are laws that make racial and sexual discrimination illegal. However, these laws are relatively weak because they carry no direct penalties for discrimination. European laws are arguably more effective because they may impose compensation payments. In the United States the government has a policy of a **affirmative action** that requires firms to actively seek out minorities and women and include them in the applicant pool.

6   Employers must **motivate** workers to perform the task for which they were hired. When the marginal product of a worker is observable, a firm can base pay on output. Thus, **piece-rate systems** provide strong incentives to workers but can subject them to substantial risk. Again, there is a risk-incentive trade-off. When there is concern for quality, piece-rate systems may fail to give good incentives.

7   Especially when a worker's output is difficult for the employer to observe, the employer may want to **monitor** workers. Also, paying relatively high **efficiency wages** gives workers incentives to work hard and be more productive. Employers can reduce turnover (and training costs) by letting pay and fringe benefits increase with seniority.

8   Sometimes the employer may not know whether output is high because the employees are working hard and well or because the demand for the product is high. In this case, one option is to set up **contests** where workers are paid according to how well they do relative to their peers. Also, basing pay on team performance can encourage workers to monitor and help each other.

BEHIND THE ESSENTIAL CONCEPTS

1   The most important idea to keep in mind when thinking about the labour market is that it is a market. Many of the same models that explained aspects of imperfect product markets appear in the labour market. Consider the following.

   a   Just as the firm may be a monopoly in the product market, a union has monopoly power over the labour supply to the firm. In each case, the price (wage) is set above marginal cost (supply curve of labour), and the quantity (employment) is less.

   b   Consumers must search for price and quality information, while workers must search for job offers. In the product market, there is price dispersion; in the labour market, there are information-based wage differentials.

   c   Firms need incentives to produce quality products just as workers need incentives to be productive. There is always the risk-incentive trade-off. Contracts and reputations create incentives in product markets. Monitoring, efficiency wages, seniority benefits, contests, and team rewards create incentives in labour markets.

2   Not only is information imperfect, but exactly what the employer does not know is important. On the basis of what she does not know, the employer must choose a means of selecting and motivating her workers. For example:

   a   If the employer does not know the productivity of a job applicant, she may rely on signals. A low wage in the current job may indicate low productivity. A university degree may indicate innate abilities.

   b   If the employer can observe the marginal productivity of his workers, then he may offer a piece-rate schedule of wages, but this scheme may expose the employee to substantial risk.

   c   If the employer cannot observe the effort of her workers, she can monitor them and pay above-market efficiency wages. High wages make the job valuable and make fear of losing the job motivate the worker.

   d   If the employer thinks that the worker has other employment opportunities, the employer may offer higher wages and better working conditions to discourage more senior workers from quitting. This becomes especially important if the employer must pay to train new workers.

   e   If the employer does not know whether the output of her workers is due to their productivity or to market conditions, she may set up contests that reward workers who do relatively better.

   f   If the employer cannot observe the productivity of his employees but thinks that his employees are aware of one another's productivity, he can reward good performance by a team; this induces employees to motivate one another.

SELF-TEST

True or False

1 In Britain laws passed in 1980, 1982, 1984, 1988, and 1993 were designed to reduce the power of trade unions.

2 In Sweden, the Netherlands, and Germany, there has been a spirit of cooperation between unions, employees, and government.

3 One reason for the decline in the percentage of the work force in the private sector that belongs to unions is that consumers have shifted their demand towards more manufacturing and fewer services.

4 Unions act like monopolies in the supply of labour to the firm.

5 Unions' power is limited by threats of replacing striking workers and also by unemployment.

6 Wage differentials resulting from differences in job characteristics are called compensating differentials.

7 Imperfect information will not lead to wage differentials if workers search for job opportunities.

8 Employers may be reluctant to offer jobs to workers who currently earn low wages if they believe that current wages signal low productivity.

9 Statistical discrimination results from overt prejudice.

10 Insiders have less bargaining power than outsiders.

11 Under a piece-rate system, workers are insured against any risk related to the overall success of the business.

12 Piece-rate systems do not work well if the firm cannot easily and accurately measure the marginal product of workers.

13 Paying higher efficiency wages may motivate workers to be more productive because they perceive that the high-wage job is worth keeping.

14 Firms that are unsure about a task's difficulty can motivate workers by using contests.

15 When pay depends upon team performance, workers have incentives to cooperate, work together, and monitor each other's effort.

Multiple Choice

1 In Britain, laws introduced in the 1980s

  a strengthened the power of trade unions.
  b made it easier for a firm to sack its workforce and hire a new one.
  c reduced the power of trade unions.
  d ended secondary picketing.
  e b, c, and d.

2 Insiders have more bargaining power than outsiders because

  a they have specialist knowledge of the job and the firm.
  b there are costs involved in hiring and firing workers.
  c they are often needed to train new workers.
  d all of the above.
  e none of the above.

3 Reasons for the decline in the percentage of the workforce that belongs to unions include which of the following?

  a Employment has fallen in sectors of the economy that are highly unionised.
  b Consumer demand has shifted towards relatively less unionised sectors, such as services.
  c Increased competition and labour market legislation have curbed the power of trade unions.
  d All of the above.
  e None of the above.

4 In negotiating wages with firms, unions are most like

  a monopolies.
  b monopsonies.
  c competitive firms.
  d individual consumers.
  e none of the above.

5 Unless the firm is making monopoly profits in its product market, the higher wages negotiated by a union must

  a increase the level of employment at the firm.
  b have no effect on the level of employment at the firm.
  c reduce the level of employment at the firm.
  d lead the firm to substitute labour for capital.
  e a and d.

6 Higher wages for union labour

  a increase the supply of nonunion labour.
  b decrease the supply of nonunion labour.
  c reduce wages received by nonunion labour.
  d a and c.
  e b and c.

7 In a labour-management negotiation, the bargaining surplus refers to

  a the fact that although the firm can hire other workers and workers can find other jobs, both sides can gain by reaching agreement.
  b the costs of negotiation in lawyers' and arbitrators' salaries.
  c the strike funds built up by the firms and unions in anticipation of possible work stoppages.
  d the extra workers that the union forces management to hire.
  e b and d.

8 Compensating differentials are wage differences resulting from

  a the fact that workers must search to find job offers and learn of alternative wages.

b   the fact that employers are unlikely to make offers to workers who currently earn low wages, inferring that these workers may be less productive.

c   differences in job characteristics.

d   wage differences that compensate for differences in productivity.

e   a and b.

9   Jobs that are similar in all respects

a   must pay the same wage, because no worker would take the lower-paying job when higher-paying ones are available.

b   can have different wages according to the theory of compensating differentials.

c   may pay different wages if it takes time and effort for workers to learn about the alternative job possibilities.

d   may pay different wages because employers can pay whatever they want and workers must accept it.

e   none of the above.

10   Wage differences that are due to differences in ability to produce output are called

a   compensating differentials.

b   information-based differentials.

c   statistical discrimination.

d   productivity differentials.

e   affirmative action.

11   When workers are not aware of alternative job possibilities,

a   firms may take advantage of their information-based market power and raise wages.

b   information-based wage differentials may occur.

c   workers can earn compensating differentials.

d   all similar workers must earn the same wage for jobs with the same characteristics.

e   none of the above.

12   Statistical discrimination refers to

a   wage differences based on statistical measures of productivity differentials.

b   requirements that firms keep statistics on the number of employees in each ethnic group.

c   requirements that firms actively seek out women and minorities for hiring and promotion.

d   the use of screening devices that unintentionally sort out members of certain groups.

e   paying lower wages to workers who have little statistical information about the labour market and alternative job possibilities.

13   Affirmative action refers to

a   wage differences based on statistical measures of productivity differentials.

b   requirements that firms keep statistics on the number of employees in each ethnic group.

c   requirements that firms actively seek out women and minorities for hiring and promotion.

d   the use of screening devices that unintentionally sort out members of certain groups.

e   paying lower wages to workers who have little statistical information about the labour market and alternative job possibilities.

14   The system of payment in which a worker is paid for each item produced is called

a   a compensating differential system.

b   an adverse selection system.

c   a signaling system.

d   monopsony.

e   a piece-rate system.

15   One difficulty with basing workers' pay on their output is that

a   although workers are given appropriate incentives to work hard, they bear considerable risk.

b   although they bear the appropriate amount of risk, workers are given little incentive to work hard.

c   piece-rate schemes are illegal under the European Union employment law.

d   a and c.

e   none of the above.

16   Most workers are not paid on a piece-rate basis, because

a   piece-rate pay is too expensive.

b   workers are risk lovers.

c   it is often difficult to measure the quantity and quality of an individual worker's output.

d   all of the above.

e   none of the above.

17   If the employer cannot observe the contribution to output of each worker, she can

a   monitor each worker's effort.

b   pay higher wages to increase the cost to the worker of being fired.

c   set up a piece-work system.

d   all of the above.

e   a and b.

18   Efficiency wages

a   reduce job turnover.

b   attract more productive job applicants.

c   motivate workers to put forth more effort.

d   increase payments to workers.

e   all of the above.

19   When workers are paid on the basis of relative performance, as in contests,

a   they are given incentives to be productive, even though management does not know their job's difficulty.

b   they are better off because they bear less risk.

c   they receive efficiency wages and thus work hard.

d   turnover is reduced.

e   all of the above.

20   When pay is based on team performance,

a   workers are motivated to monitor each other's efforts.

b   workers are motivated to help each other.

c   promotions go the those workers who have been more productive.

d all of the above.

e *a* and *b*.

Completion

1 Unions can raise wages because they have a
_____ on the supply of labour to the firm.

2 _____ sets a floor to the wage rate.

3 _____ are differences in wages that reflect different job characteristics, such as working conditions or advancement possibilities.

4 _____ results from firms using screening devices that unintentionally sort out members of certain groups from the applicant pool.

5 The system of payment in which a worker is paid for each item produced or each task performed is called a _____ system.

6 The theory that paying higher wages leads to a more productive work force is called _____ theory.

7 Some compensation schemes, such as bonuses for the top sales representatives, base pay on _____ performance.

8 Incumbent employees are in a stronger bargaining position than _____.

9 _____ can explain the persistence of unemployment.

10 The "glass ceiling" that prevents the promotion of women to higher management is an example of _____ discrimination.

Answers to Self-Test

True or False

1	T	6	T	11	F
2	T	7	F	12	T
3	F	8	T	13	T
4	T	9	F	14	T
5	T	10	F	15	T

Multiple Choice

1	e	6	d	11	b	16	c
2	d	7	a	12	d	17	e
3	d	8	c	13	c	18	e
4	a	9	c	14	e	19	a
5	c	10	d	15	a	20	e

Completion

1 monopoly
2 The minimum wage
3 Compensating differentials
4 Statistical discrimination
5 piece-work
6 efficiency wage
7 relative
8 Outsiders
9 Hysteresis
10 job

Tools and Practice Problems

A successful union forms a monopoly in the supply of labour to a firm or industry. We apply the tools of monopoly to study the behaviour of unions in several problems in this section. Then we move to compensating differentials, an important source of wage differences among workers. In accepting a job offer, a worker also buys a list of job characteristics, such as safety, advancement potential, training, and the aesthetics of the workplace. We use the budget constraint to show how the labour market offers a choice among job characteristics and establishes an implicit market price for them.

THE WAGE-EMPLOYMENT TRADE-OFF

If a union is able to force the signing of a contract, guaranteeing that only union members will be hired, it is in the position of a monopolist in the supply of labour. Unions may control the supply of labour to an industry, a craft, or an individual firm. The problems here focus on the latter case. Usually unions set wages and let management choose the quantity of labour to hire. In this case, the firm's demand for labour, which is the marginal revenue product, includes all the combinations of wages and employment that the union can achieve. These combinations, in turn, show the trade-off faced by the union. Tool Kit 18.1 shows how to construct the demand for labour and some possible choices that a union might make.

Tool Kit 18.1 Constructing the Union's Trade-off between Wages and Employment

Higher wages usually bring about reduced employment. Follow this procedure to construct the trade-off.

Step one: Identify the production function and the price of the product, and set up a table as follows.

Workers	Output	Revenue	Marginal revenue product

Step two: Find the revenue corresponding to each level of labor use by multiplying the output level by price, and enter the results in the table:

Revenue = output × price.

Step three: Compute the marginal revenue product, which is the change in revenue divided by the change in labour, and enter the results in the table:

$$\text{Marginal revenue product} = \frac{\text{change in revenues}}{\text{change in output}}.$$

Step four: Plot the marginal revenue product. This is the curve of the of possible wage and employment levels.

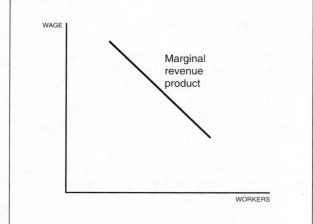

1   (Worked problem: unions) The miners of Davis Lead are represented by the Lead Workers Union, which is considering its stance for the upcoming contract negotiations. The union's economist has estimated a production function for lead, as given in Table 18.1. Its current price is £10 per tonne.

Table 18.1

Workers	Output (tonnes per month)
10	20,000
20	40,000
30	60,000
40	75,000
50	85,000
60	90,000
70	90,000

a   Calculate the marginal revenue product, plot it, and interpret it as a schedule of wage and employment possibilities.
b   What is the maximum wage? How much employment would result at this wage?
c   Workers can earn £5,000 elsewhere. What is the maximum level of employment?

Step-by-step solution

Step one (a): Identify the production function and the price of the product. The production function is given in Table 18.1, and the price of lead is £10 per tonne.

Step two: Find the revenue corresponding to each level of labor use. We multiply output by £10, which is the price of lead. When there are 10 workers, output is 20,000, and revenue is 20,000 × £10 = £200,000. Continuing, we derive Table 18.2.

Table 18.2

Workers	Output	Total revenue
10	20,000	£200,000
20	40,000	£400,000
30	60,000	£600,000
40	75,000	£750,000
50	85,000	£850,000
60	90,000	£900,000
70	90,000	£900,000

Step three: Compute the marginal revenue product, which is the change in revenue divided by the change in labour. The marginal revenue product for the first 10 workers is £200,000/10 = £20,000. Continuing, we derive Table 18.3.

Table 18.3

Workers	Output	Total revenue	Marginal revenue product
10	20,000	£200,000	£20,000
20	40,000	£400,000	£20,000
30	60,000	£600,000	£20,000
40	75,000	£750,000	£15,000
50	85,000	£850,000	£10,000
60	90,000	£900,000	£ 5,000
70	90,000	£900,000	£ 0

Step four: Plot the marginal revenue product.

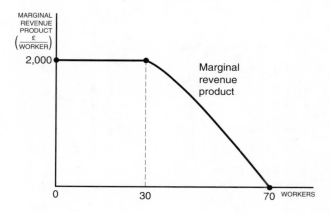

Step five (b): The maximum possible wage is £20,000 per month, and 30 workers will have jobs at this wage.

Step six (c): If the company pays £5,000, which is the alternative wage, there will be 60 workers hired.

2   (Practice problem: unions) The staff at Rosewood Training Centre has voted to join the union to bargain for higher wages and better working conditions. The production function is given in Table 18.4. Training fees bring the centre an income of £1,000 per trainee after all expenses (except staff salaries) are deducted.

Table 18.4

Staff	Trainees
20	100
30	600
40	1,000
50	1,300
60	1,500
70	1,600
80	1,600

a Calculate and plot the marginal revenue product schedule. Interpret it as a schedule of salary and employment possibilities.

b What is the maximum salary that the union could negotiate? Keep in mind that the training centre receives a subsidy from the government, so it would not close down even if it lost money.

c The alternative salary for a typical Rosewood employee is £20,000. What is the maximum level of employment?

3 (Practice problem: unions) The cherry pickers at Bingley's Cherry Orchard have won an agreement that the owner will only hire union workers. The production function is given in Table 18.5, and cherries sell for £2 per punnet.

Table 18.5

Pickers	Cherries (punnets per day)
1	24
2	64
3	96
4	120
5	136
6	144
7	148
8	150

a Calculate and plot the marginal revenue product. Interpret it as a schedule of wage and employment possibilities.

b What is the maximum wage? Will the orchard shut down if labour is its only nonsunk cost?

c The workers have an alternative wage of £16 per day. What is the maximum level of employment?

COMPENSATING DIFFERENTIALS

A job offer brings with it a promised wage and a bundle of job characteristics. Workers may not accept the highest-paying job, preferring a lower wage alternative if it offers more attractive nonwage benefits. The additional wage that accompanies a job with some undesirable nonwage aspect is called the compensating differential. The budget constraint allows us to identify and study the trade-off between wages and job characteristics. Tool Kit 18.2 shows the technique.

Tool Kit 18.2: Using Budget Constraints to Analyze Compensating Differentials

When an individual has several job offers, she faces a trade-off between higher wages and other desirable job characteristics. These steps show how to illustrate the trade-off with a budget constraint.

Step one: Draw a set of axes with the wage measured on the vertical axis and the nonwage characteristic on the horizontal.

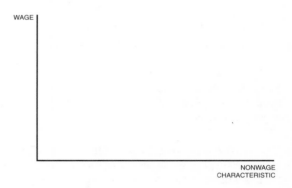

Step two: Plot a point corresponding to each job offer.

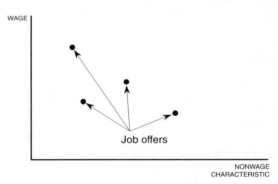

Step three: Cancel the dominated offers, offers of jobs with both lower wages and less-attractive job characteristics.

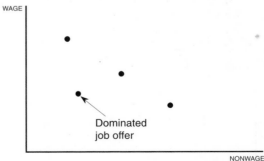

Step four: Draw a smooth curve through the undominated job offers. These are the ones that include higher wages and/or more attractive job characteristics. This curve is the budget constraint, reflecting the alternative combinations of wages and job characteristics available to the worker.

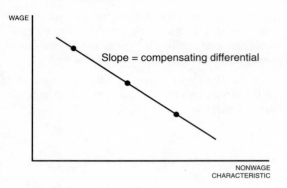

Step five: Identify the trade-off between several points on the budget constraint. The slope is the compensating differential.

4   (Worked problem: compensating differentials) Many parents in two-earner families worry about day care for infants. Recognizing this concern, some progressive companies offer on-site day care, although the facilities vary greatly in quality. Table 18.6 lists some local firms, the entry-level salaries for management trainees, and the expenditure per child for the day care facility.

Table 18.6

Firm	Salary	Expenditure per child
ALX Corp.	£30,000	£5,000
ABX Corp.	£35,000	£3,000
PBX Corp.	£37,000	£4,000
APX Corp.	£46,000	£ 0
AXX Corp.	£40,000	£1,000

a   Represent the salaries and day care expenditures as an opportunity set.
b   Are there any dominated offers?
c   What is the compensating differential for reducing day care expenditures from £5,000 to £4,000? From £1,000 to £0?

Step-by-step solution

Step one (a): Draw a set of axes.

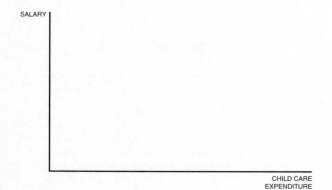

Step two: Plot a point corresponding to each job offer.

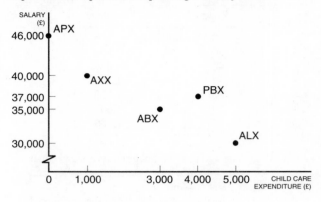

Step three (b): Cancel the dominated offers. The ABX offer, which entails less money and child care expenditure, is dominated by the PBX offer.

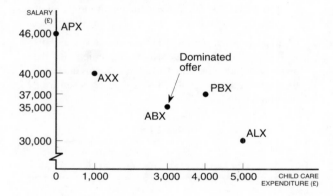

Step four: Draw a smooth curve through the undominated job offers.

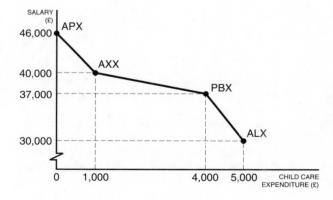

Step five (c): Identify the trade-offs between several points on the budget constraint. As the day care expenditure falls from £5,000 to £4,000, salary rises by £37,000 − £30,000 = £7,000. The compensating differential for a decrease from £1,000 to £0 is £46,000 − £40,000 = £6,000.

5   (Practice problem: compensating differentials) John Day is looking for a job. The alternatives, the corresponding annual salaries, and some data on accidental deaths are given in Table 18.7. John has offers for each

type of job, he is qualified for each, and he considers them equally satisfying except for the risk of death.

Table 18.7

Job	Salary	Deaths per 100,000
Night guard	£16,000	2
Shoe seller	£15,000	1 (irate customer)
Bank clerk	£24,000	5
Taxi driver	£19,000	6
Security guard	£22,000	3

  a Represent the job offers as an opportunity set.

  b Without knowing anything about John's willingness to risk death, can you say if there is a job offer he will definitely refuse? Explain.

  c What is the compensating differential for increasing the annual death risk from 1 to 2 deaths per 100,000 workers? What is the compensating differential for increasing the annual death risk from 3 to 5 deaths per 100,000 workers?

6 (Practice problem: compensating differentials) The banking industry in Rosewell offers a wide variety of salaries and vacation days. Table 18.8 gives entry salaries and holidays offered to new hires.

Table 18.8

Bank	Salary	Holidays (days)
First One	£20,000	5
Bank One	£25,000	8
First Bank	£32,000	5
Premier Bank	£30,000	6
Second Bank	£28,000	7

  a Represent the salaries and vacation days as an opportunity set.

  b Are there any dominated offers?

  c What is the compensating differential for reducing holidays from 8 to 7? From 6 to 5?

Answers to Problems

2 *a* The marginal revenue product schedule is given in Table 18.9.

Table 18.9

Staff	Trainees	Total revenue	Marginal revenue product
20	100	£ 100,000	—
30	600	£ 600,000	£50,000
40	1,000	£1,000,000	£40,000
50	1,300	£1,300,000	£30,000
60	1,500	£1,500,000	£20,000
70	1,600	£1,600,000	£10,000
80	1,600	£1,600,000	£ 0

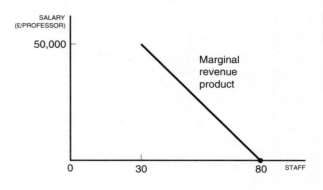

  b The maximum wage is £50,000, at which 30 staff will be employed.

  c The maximum employment occurs at a wage of £20,000, with 60 staff.

3 *a* The marginal revenue product schedule is given in Table 18.10.

Table 18.10

Pickers	Cherries	Total revenue	Marginal revenue product
1	24	£ 48	£48
2	64	£128	£80
3	96	£192	£64
4	120	£240	£48
5	136	£272	£32
6	144	£288	£16
7	148	£296	£ 8
8	150	£300	£ 4

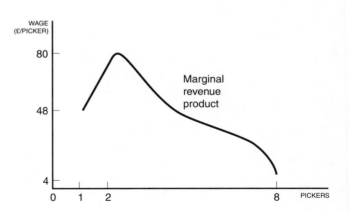

  b The maximum wage is £80, at which there will be 2 pickers.

  c The maximum employment is 6, where the wage equals £16.

5   *a*

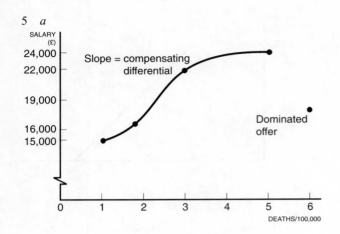

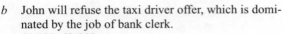

b   John will refuse the taxi driver offer, which is dominated by the job of bank clerk.

c   £1,000, £2,000.

6   *a*

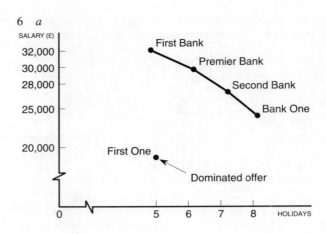

b   First One.

c   £3,000, £2,000.

Part Four

POLICY ISSUES

Chapter 19

EXTERNALITIES AND THE ENVIRONMENT

Chapter Review

Of the three major economic players—individuals, firms, and government—the first two have been centre stage so far in the text, while the third has mainly stood silently at the side. Government has been the central focus only of Chapters 7 and 15. This is appropriate, because the critical points for you to understand are where markets succeed at answering the main economic questions, where they fail, and how.

Where markets fail, government may have an economic role to play. This chapter wraps up some loose ends with respect to government's role. You have already seen problems of competition, information, and technological change that interfere when private markets are used to answer economic questions. Another major category of market failure is externalities, a concept first introduced in Chapter 7. As you may remember, externalities can be positive or negative. The distinguishing characteristic of externalities is that, positive or negative, they represent benefits or costs that are not captured in the market price. The first example studied here is pollution. The chapter then moves on to consider natural resources, where the focus is on whether correct incentives exist to conserve.

ESSENTIAL CONCEPTS

1   A market transaction is a voluntary exchange between two parties. Any costs or benefits not captured by market transactions are called **externalities. Positive externalities** are benefits received by others. Markets produce too few activities that generate positive externalities, such as research and development or on-the-job training. Other affects, such as pollution, noise, or congestion, confer costs on others that often do not figure into the market price. Markets create too many of these **negative externalities.**

2   Markets require clearly defined *property rights* in order to allocate resources efficiently. **Coase's theorem** says that any externality problem could be solved if the government would assign property rights for the externalities. For example, direct pollution of a privately owned lake would not occur unless the owner judged that the benefits exceeded the costs. General environmental pollution is a serious problem because the environment is commonly, not privately, owned.

3   Externalities lead to **market failures** because resources are not allocated efficiently. Individuals consider only their private costs and benefits and ignore the larger so-

cial costs and benefits. Potential governmental solutions to the problems fall into two categories: **command and control regulations** and market-like devices such as taxes, subsidies, and **marketable permits.** For example, in the case of pollution, governments can issue regulations requiring pollution-control equipment or banning the use of hazardous materials. Alternatively, they can employ more market-oriented policies, such as taxes on pollution emissions, subsidies for pollution abatement, or even creating a market for pollution permits.

4   Private property and the price system enhance the conservation of natural resources. If all is well, current prices reflect the value of natural resources used today and expected future prices equal their expected value in the future. Seeking the highest value for his property, the natural resource owner sells today if the current price exceeds the present discounted value of the future price. If not, he conserves. Thus, private owners make socially efficient decisions.

5   There are two problems surrounding private incentives for natural resource conservation. First, property rights may not be secure, especially in resource-rich developing countries. If an owner sees a risk of confiscation, she will likely use her resource at a faster than efficient rate. In the same vein, governments often make poor guardians of commonly owned public lands. Second, if capital markets impose borrowing constraints on resource owners, they may substitute faster extraction for borrowing and thereby foil conservation.

BEHIND THE ESSENTIAL CONCEPTS

1   Individuals and firms make efficient decisions when they bear the full costs and benefits of their choice. When externalities are present, some benefit or cost is ignored, and the decision becomes inefficient. The missing ingredient is property rights. Coase's theorem says that if property rights are clearly assigned, decisions will be efficient. The logic can best be understood with an example.

Suppose that your neighbour in university halls of residence likes to play the stereo very loudly each evening while you are reading this book. Clearly, there is an externality. You complain to the hall manager, and there are two possible reactions. The manager may say that playing the stereo is a right of all students, in effect giving the property right (to make noise) to your neighbour. Or the manager may insist on quiet and give the property right (to silence) to you. According to Coase's theorem, either way of assigning property rights will do. If your neighbour has the right, then you can buy the right to silence by paying your neighbour to be quiet. If you have the right, she must buy your permission to play the music. Of course, you would prefer the latter; nevertheless, in either case, the externality is eliminated and replaced by a market transaction. (Any reader who lives in a university hall of residence can judge how realistic it is to apply Coase's theorem to externalities.)

2   Pollution is an example of a negative externality. It is a cost ignored by the polluter and borne by others. The inefficiency can be corrected by raising the polluter's private marginal opportunity cost of pollution to the level of the social marginal cost. There are three market-like ways to do this: taxes on pollution, subsidies for pollution abatement, and marketable pollution permits. Here is how they work.

   a   Suppose that the firm must pay a *tax* of £10 per unit of pollution. Clearly, any pollution now has a private marginal cost of £10, because the tax must be paid.

   b   Suppose that the government pays a *subsidy* of £10 per unit of pollution abatement. Again, the marginal opportunity cost of the pollution is £10, because if the pollution is emitted, it is not abated and the subsidy is not received.

   c   Under the marketable permits scheme, pollution requires a permit, which must be purchased. The purchase price of the permit is the marginal cost of the pollution. All three market-like policies put a price on pollution and encourage polluters to find economical ways to reduce emissions.

3   Whether we are using our limited natural resources efficiently and whether we are likely to run out of these resources are important economic questions. The key aspects in the answer to these questions are property rights and markets.

   a   For those resources, such as oil, minerals, and arable farmland, that are *privately owned,* markets provide good incentives for conservation. Future shortages mean high prices in the future. The profit opportunities from future sales motivate owners to conserve resources for the future.

   b   For those resources, such as the ozone layer and endangered species, that are not privately owned, there is no reason for optimism. Since there are *no markets* for these resources, there is no financial incentive to conserve.

SELF-TEST

True or False

1   When there is no government interference, markets will always produce efficient outcomes.

2   The market failures approach assigns to government the task of improving matters when markets allocate resources inefficiently.

3   Markets fail because too many people are motivated by greed.

4   The market will supply too many goods for which there are positive externalities.

5   The social marginal cost is greater than the private marginal cost for a good that generates negative externalities.

6   Coase's theorem contends that externality problems require government intervention.

7   Reassigning property rights can sometimes correct a market failure.

8   Because pollution is an example of a negative externality, economists recommend taxing pollution abatement.

9   Goods for which there are negative externalities should be taxed so that the price captures more of the social costs.

10   The regulation requiring catalytic converters on cars is an example of the command and control approach.

11   Marketable permits give no incentive to reduce pollution, because firms that want to pollute can simply buy the permits.

12   Because pollution is a negative externality, it should be eliminated on efficiency grounds.

13   We are using up our limited supply of natural resources because they are sold without concern for the needs of potential future users.

14   Both current and future property rights are essential to provide private owners with incentives to conserve natural resources.

15   If natural resource owners face borrowing constraints, they may conserve more of natural resources than is socially efficient.

Multiple Choice

1   The market failures approach to the role of government in the economy says that

   a   because markets fail, governments must do as much as they can afford.
   b   governments have a role to play when markets fail to produce efficient outcomes.
   c   government is less likely to fail than markets.
   d   Coase's theorem is correct about the role of property rights in producing efficient market outcomes.
   e   marketable prices will fail to give incentives for natural resource conservation.

2   Examples of market failures include

   a   externalities.
   b   a lack of sufficient competition.
   c   information problems.
   d   insufficient technological innovation.
   e   all of the above.

3   The costs of environmental pollution are examples of

   a   positive externalities.
   b   public goods.
   c   negative externalities.
   d   private costs.
   e   diminishing returns.

4   Social marginal cost includes

   a   all marginal costs borne by all individuals in the economy.

   b   only those marginal costs not included in private marginal cost.
   c   only those marginal costs included in private marginal cost.
   d   total revenue minus total private costs.
   e   marginal revenue minus marginal cost.

5   Coase's theorem claims that

   a   market outcomes are always efficient.
   b   when markets fail to produce efficient outcomes, the government should allocate resources.
   c   negative externalities should be subsidised.
   d   reassigning property rights can solve externality problems.
   e   the decisions made by a majority of voters may be inconsistent.

6   Which of the following is *not* an example of a negative externality?

   a   CFC gases destroy some of the ozone layer.
   b   Carbon dioxide emissions bring about global warming.
   c   Industrial smoke emissions increase lung cancer rates.
   d   Customers must pay more when the prices of natural resources are increased.
   e   Seepage of pesticides pollutes streams and rivers.

7   Which of the following is an example of command and control regulations?

   a   Subsidies for the production of goods with positive externalities
   b   Taxation of goods with negative externalities
   c   Regulations limiting the allowable level of pollution emissions
   d   Assigning property rights to victims of environmental pollution
   e   Nonrivalrous consumption

8   To reduce emissions of pollution, the government can

   a   tax pollution abatement.
   b   subsidise pollution abatement.
   c   subsidise the sale of polluting goods, such as steel and chemicals.
   d   reassign to polluters the property rights to pollute.
   e   take over the production facilities of firms.

9   Under the marketable permits approach to curbing pollution,

   a   firms purchase permits from the government.
   b   permits allow firms to emit a certain amount of pollution.
   c   a market for pollution permits exists for firms to buy and sell the permits.
   d   firms have strong incentives to reduce pollution.
   e   all of the above.

10   The market system encourages conservation because

   a   the price of a natural resource, such as an oil field, equals the present discounted value of potential future uses.

b   wasteful exploitation is punished by fines or imprisonment.

c   markets always allocate resources efficiently.

d   permits from the government are required before natural resources may be sold.

e   there is such an abundance of natural resources.

11   Private owners may undervalue future demand for natural resources if

a   there are negative externalities associated with the current use of the resource.

b   there are positive externalities associated with the current use of the resource.

c   property rights are not secure.

d   owners may face limited borrowing opportunities.

e   b, c, and d.

12   The view that there is a role for government when markets do not produce efficient outcomes is called

a   Coase's theorem.

b   the market failure approach.

c   marketable permits.

d   the command and control approach.

e   none of the above.

13   How does Coase's theorem recommend that the European Union solve the problem of overgrazing public lands?

a   The EU should put a tax on fishing.

b   The government should sell fishing areas to private owners.

c   The government should subsidize fishing.

d   The government should issue regulations mandating how many fishing boats can fish each season.

e   Coase's theorem allows no role for government.

14   Which of the following is not an example of a problem with command and control regulations of environmental pollution?

a   Firms cannot afford to clean up their pollution.

b   Regulations do not allow for variations in circumstances among firms.

c   The least-cost cleanup technology may not be the mandated one.

d   There are limited incentives for technological advance in pollution abatement.

e   All of the above are problems with command and control regulations.

15   Which of the following methods can reduce environmental pollution?

a   Taxes on pollution emissions

b   Subsidies for pollution abatement

c   Marketable permits

d   Command and control regulations

e   All of the above

16   When the social marginal cost of an activity exceeds its private marginal cost, it should be

a   subsidised.

b   taxed.

c   outlawed.

d   all of the above.

e   a or b.

17   If the government uses the marketable permits policy, firms

a   must purchase permits from the government.

b   may sell their permits to the government but not to other firms.

c   may buy their permits from the government but not from other firms.

d   may sell their unused permits but may not buy additional permits.

e   may buy or sell permits as they choose.

18   The marketable permits system specifies that firms

a   purchase permits in order to pollute.

b   may buy permits from other firms.

c   may sell unused permits to other firms.

d   all of the above.

e   none of the above.

19   The production of too many goods with negative externalities is an example of

a   paternalism.

b   consumer sovereignty.

c   public failure.

d   market failure.

e   the voting paradox.

20   In deciding when to extract and sell a mineral deposit, the private owner compares

a   the present and expected future prices.

b   the present net return and the discounted present value of the future net return.

c   the discounted present value of future costs and prices.

d   the expected value of future costs and prices.

e   present costs and price.

Completion

1   The _____ approach to the role of government calls upon the government when markets fail to produce efficient outcomes.

2   The extra costs and benefits not captured by market transactions are called _____.

3   The _____ cost of pollution is borne entirely by the polluter, while the _____ cost includes all costs borne by individuals in the economy.

4   _____ claims that externality problems can be solved by reassigning property rights.

5   Regulatory measures that set limits on pollution emissions and mandate the use of specific types of pollution-control technologies are examples of the _____ approach.

6   The _____ approach issues to firms permits, which allow them to emit a certain amount of pollution and which can be traded.

7   Government can bring about a reduction in pollution emissions by subsidising _____.

8   When social marginal costs exceed private marginal costs there is a _____ externality.

9   High expected future prices motivate private owners to _____ natural resources.

10 When there are negative externalities associated with a good, the market will produce too _____.

Answers to Self-Test

True or False

1	F	6	F	11	F
2	T	7	T	12	F
3	F	8	F	13	F
4	F	9	T	14	T
5	T	10	T	15	F

Multiple Choice

1	b	6	d	11	e	16	b
2	e	7	c	12	b	17	e
3	c	8	b	13	b	18	a
4	a	9	e	14	a	19	d
5	d	10	a	15	e	20	b

Completion

1   market failure
2   externalities
3   private, social
4   Coase's theorem
5   command and control
6   marketable permits
7   pollution abatement
8   negative
9   conserve
10 much

Tools and Practice Problems

The first topic of this section is how taxes and subsidies can be used to encourage an activity for which there are positive externalities. We see how firms can be induced to emit less pollution by engaging in pollution abatement. Next, we turn to markets for goods that generate negative externalities such as noise, congestion, and pollution. A few problems show situations in which market equilibrium levels are too high and investigate how taxes can be used to make the market more efficient. The last topic focuses directly on the market for pollution and the marketable permits system brings about efficient use of the environment.

POLLUTION ABATEMENT

Like other decisions made by firms, the question of the level of pollution abatement involves marginal benefit and cost reasoning. If the government taxes pollution emissions, then abating pollution saves the tax. If the government subsidises pollution abatement, then abating pollution earns the sub-

sidy. In each case, the marginal benefit of pollution abatement is determined by the government's policy. Tool Kit 19.1 demonstrates this.

Tool Kit 19.1 Determining the Level of Pollution Abatement

Pollution abatement is encouraged by taxing pollution or subsidising abatement. Each raises the marginal cost of polluting. Follow these steps to find the resulting level of abatement.

Step one: Identify the cost of pollution emission and abatement.

Step two: Calculate the marginal abatement costs:

$$\text{Marginal abatement cost} = \frac{\text{change in cost}}{\text{change in level of pollution abatement}}.$$

Step three: Determine the marginal benefit of pollution abatement.

Step four: Set the marginal benefit of pollution abatement equal to its marginal cost.

---

1   (Worked problem: pollution abatement) Pollution from the Pb Lead Mine has raised lead levels in the Freshwater River. The current level of lead effluent is 10 kilos per month. A filtering technology would enable the company to reduce its effluent. The abatement costs are given in Table 19.1.

Table 19.1

Pollution emitted (kilos/month)	Pollution abated (kilos/month)	Total cost	Marginal cost
10	0	£ 0	—
9	1	£ 10	
8	2	£ 25	
7	3	£ 45	
6	4	£ 70	
5	5	£100	
4	6	£135	
3	7	£175	
2	8	£225	
1	9	£290	
0	10	£400	

a   Suppose that a pollution tax (or fine) of £40 is assessed per kilogram of lead emitted. How much will the company emit? What quantity of pollution will be abated?

b   Suppose that rather than a tax, a subsidy of £40 is given per unit of pollution abated. How much will the company emit? What quantity of pollution will be abated?

c   The firm's profits from the production and sale of lead total £10,000. Compare its profits under the tax with its profits under the subsidy plan.

Step-by-step solution

Step one (a): The cost of pollution emission and abatement is given in Table 19.1.

Step two: Calculate the marginal abatement cost. The marginal abatement cost is the extra cost incurred in reducing pollution emissions by 1 more unit. For example, reducing pollution from 10 to 9 units raises costs from £0 to £10; therefore, the marginal abatement cost is £10 for the first unit. The remainder of the schedule is given in Table 19.2.

Table 19.2

Pollution emitted	Pollution abated	Total costs	Marginal cost
10	0	£ 0	—
9	1	£ 10	£ 10
8	2	£ 25	£ 15
7	3	£ 45	£ 20
6	4	£ 70	£ 25
5	5	£100	£ 30
4	6	£135	£ 35
3	7	£175	£ 40
2	8	£225	£ 50
1	9	£290	£ 65
0	10	£400	£110

Step three: Determine the marginal benefit of abatement. Each unit of pollution emitted incurs a tax of £40; thus, the marginal benefit of abatement is £40.

Step four: Set the marginal benefit of pollution abatement equal to its marginal cost. This results in 3 kilos of lead emitted and 7 kilos abated.

Step five (b): When the policy is to subsidise abatement, the marginal benefit is the subsidy, which is £40. Setting £40 equal to the marginal abatement cost again gives 3 pounds of lead emitted and 7 kilos abated. The answer is the same as for part a. Notice that under the subsidy scheme, each unit emitted still costs the firm £40, in the sense that any unit emitted is a unit not abated and a subsidy not received.

Step six (c): Profits under the tax equal £10,000 less the abatement cost and the tax, or

Profits = £10,000 − £175 − £40 (3) = £9,705.

Under the subsidy, however,

Profits = £10,000 − £175 + £40 (7) = £10,105.

Notice that the difference in profits is £10,105 − £9,705 = £400, which is the magnitude of the tax/subsidy multiplied by the number of units that the firm emits with no regulation. It is the total value of the property right to pollute.

2   (Practice problem: pollution abatement) The Sea Tuna Fishing Company kills 20 dolphins during an average catch. It has various options for reducing the number of dolphins killed, and the costs are given in Table 19.3.

Table 19.3

Dolphins killed	Dolphins saved	Total costs	Marginal cost
20	0	£ 0	—
18	2	£ 100	
16	4	£ 240	
14	6	£ 400	
12	8	£ 600	
10	10	£ 1,000	
8	12	£ 1,500	
6	14	£ 2,200	
4	16	£ 3,000	
2	18	£ 5,000	
0	20	£10,000	

a   Suppose that a tax (or fine) of £100 is assessed per dolphin killed. How many dolphins will be killed? What number of dolphins will be saved?

b   Suppose that rather than a tax, a subsidy of £100 per dolphin is granted for reductions in the dolphin kill. How many will the company kill? How many will be saved?

c   With no tax or subsidy, the company's profits are £10,000. Compute its profits with the tax and with the subsidy.

3   (Practice problem: pollution abatement) Flying Goose Air Transport has its hub in Sleepy Village. Dozens of planes land and take off each night, causing considerable noise. By muffling engines or other more-advanced techniques, the company can reduce its noise. The costs are given in Table 19.4.

Table 19.4

Average level of noise (decibels)	Total costs	Marginal cost
1,000	£ 0	—
900	£ 50	
800	£ 150	
700	£ 300	
600	£ 500	
500	£ 750	
400	£1,100	

a   Suppose that a pollution tax (or fine) of £2.50 is assessed per decibel of noise created. How much noise will the company still create? What quantity of noise will be abated?

b   Suppose that rather than a tax, a subsidy of £2.50 is granted per unit of noise abated. How much noise will the company create now? What quantity of noise will be abated?

c   With no tax or subsidy, the company's profits are £5,000. Compute its profits with the tax and with the subsidy.

MARKETS AND EXTERNALITIES

When there are negative externalities, such as pollution, noise, and congestion, market outcomes will be inefficient. Specifically, there will be more negative externalities than the socially efficient amount. The socially efficient level just balances the social marginal costs with the marginal benefits. But markets ignore the externality and focus only on the private marginal benefits. Tool Kit 19.2 shows how to distinguish private and social benefits and how to compare the market and socially efficient levels.

Tool Kit 19.2 Finding the Efficient Quantity in Markets with Negative Externalities

The production and consumption of many goods causes negative externalities. In these cases, markets bring about too much production and consumption of these negative externalities. Follow these steps to compare market with efficient levels.

Step one: Determine the market equilibrium at the intersection of the supply and demand curves.

Step two: Add the marginal external cost to the supply curve, which is the private marginal cost, to determine the social marginal cost curve.

Step three: Find the efficient quantity at the intersection of the demand curve and the social marginal cost curve.

Step four: Compare the market equilibrium with the efficient quantities.

---

4 (Worked problem: negative externalities) Pollution from intensive farming is polluting local lakes and rivers. The negative externality per head of cattle is £100. The demand and supply curves for cattle are given in Table 19.5.

Table 19.5

Demand		Supply	
Price	Quantity	Price	Quantity
£200	350	£200	1,100
£180	500	£180	1,000
£160	650	£160	900
£140	800	£140	800
£120	950	£120	700
£100	1,100	£100	600
£ 80	1,300	£ 80	500

a Find the market equilibrium quantity and price.
b Calculate the social marginal cost, and determine the efficient quantity of cattle.

Step-by-step solution

Step one (a): Find the market equilibrium quantity and price. At a price of £140, the market clears with 800 sold.

Step two (b): Find the social marginal cost curve. We add the marginal external cost, which is £100, to the supply curve, which is the private marginal cost. Table 19.6 gives the solution.

Table 19.6

Quantity	Social marginal cost
500	£180
600	£200
700	£220
800	£240
900	£260
1,000	£280
1,100	£300

Step three: Find the efficient quantity at the intersection of the demand curve and the social marginal cost curve. This occurs at a quantity of 500 and a price of £180.

Step four: Compare the market equilibrium and efficient quantities. Notice that the efficient quantity is only 500, while the market produces 800. Incorporating the external cost into the supply curve would raise the price and reduce the quantity to the efficient level.

5 (Practice problem: negative externalities) The private flying lessons at Daredevil Airport cause noise that disturbs local residents. The residents are also uneasy about the occasional crashes. One estimate of the magnitude of the negative externalities is £15 per flight. The market supply and demand curves for flight lessons are given in Table 19.7.

Table 19.7

Demand		Supply	
Price	Quantity	Price	Quantity
£75	10	£75	100
£70	20	£70	80
£65	30	£65	60
£60	40	£60	40
£55	50	£55	20
£50	60	£50	0

a Find the market equilibrium price and quantity.
b Calculate the social marginal cost, and find the efficient quantity.

6 (Practice problem: negative externalities) New developments of townhouses are springing up in the suburbs around Westhampton. The supply and demand curves for new townhouses are given in Table 19.8.

Table 19.8

Demand		Supply	
Price	Quantity	Price	Quantity
£140,000	100	£140,000	900
£130,000	200	£130,000	800
£120,000	300	£120,000	700
£110,000	400	£110,000	600
£100,000	500	£100,000	500
£ 90,000	600	£ 90,000	400
£ 80,000	700	£ 80,000	300

a   Find the market equilibrium quantity of townhouses and the corresponding price.

b   The new developments impose costs on other current residents for sewage, transportation, and congestion. An estimate of the magnitude of these negative externalities is £20,000 per townhouse. Find the efficient level of townhouse production and the corresponding price.

MARKETABLE PERMITS

The problem of pollution (and other negative externalities) can be attacked more directly by considering the "market" for pollution itself. The polluters are the demanders for pollution, and their demand curve is just the marginal abatement cost curve. If it costs a firm £40 to clean up a tonne of sludge from its emissions, then that firm is willing to pay £40 to be given the right to emit the sludge. The efficient level of pollution occurs where the demand curve intersects the social marginal cost curve, which is the marginal damage done by the pollution. These problems explore the issue of the efficient level of pollution and how a marketable permit scheme can bring about this outcome. Use Tool Kit 19.3.

Tool Kit 19.3 Using Marketable Permits to Bring About the Efficient Level of Pollution

The marketable permit policy sells permits to pollute. The market price for these permits gives firms incentives to reduce pollution. The following procedure shows how to find the number of permits to sell and the market price.

Step one: Identify the demand for pollution (the sum of all the marginal abatement cost curves) and the social marginal cost curve.

Step two: Find the efficient level of pollution, which is at the intersection of the demand for pollution and the marginal abatement cost curve.

Step three: Determine how many permits to sell. This quantity is the efficient level of pollution found in step two.

Step four: Find the market price for the permits. Read this price off the demand curve.

---

7   (Worked problem: marketable permits) Discharges from factories, farmlands, and many other activities pollute the Northern Lakes. The pollution could be reduced, but any reduction would involve expensive abatement procedures. The marginal abatement cost schedule is given in Table 19.9 along with the social marginal cost of the pollution. (BOD means biochemical oxygen demand).

Table 19.9

Pollution (millions of kilos/BOD)	Marginal abatement cost	Social marginal cost
100	£1,200	£ 0
200	£1,000	£ 0
300	£ 900	£ 150
400	£ 800	£ 300
500	£ 700	£ 450
600	£ 600	£ 600
700	£ 500	£ 800
800	£ 300	£1,000

Find the efficient level of pollution, and explain how a marketable permits scheme can achieve an efficient outcome.

Step-by-step solution

Step one: Identify the demand for pollution and the social marginal cost curve. The demand is the marginal abatement cost curve given in Table 19.9, which also includes the social marginal cost curve.

Step two: Find the efficient level of pollution. The intersection of the demand for pollution and the marginal abatement cost curve occurs at 600 parts/million.

Step three: Determine how many permits to sell. This number is 600, and each permit entitles the holder to emit 1 part/million of pollution.

Step four: Find the market price for the permits. If 600 permits are offered for sale, their market price will be £600. This price is read off the marginal abatement cost curve at 600 units.

8   (Practice problem: marketable permits) The marginal abatement cost and social marginal cost of pollution in the Northwest Air Shed are given in Table 19.10. Find the efficient level of pollution, and explain how a marketable permits scheme can achieve an efficient outcome. Pollution is measured as metric tonnes of sulphur oxide.

Table 19.10

Pollution	Marginal abatement cost	Social marginal cost
10	£100	£ 0
20	£ 80	£ 0
30	£ 60	£ 5
40	£ 50	£10
50	£ 40	£20
60	£ 30	£30
70	£ 15	£50

9   (Practice problem: marketable permits) Pesticides, engine oil, chemicals, and other pollutants are finding their way into the groundwater. Abatement is possible but expensive. The marginal abatement cost and social marginal cost of this type of pollution are given in Table 19.11. Find the efficient level of pollution, and explain how a marketable permits scheme can achieve it.

Table 19.11

Pollution	Marginal abatement cost	Social marginal cost
100	£10,000	£ 10
150	£ 8,000	£ 100
200	£ 6,000	£ 1,000
250	£ 5,000	£ 5,000
300	£ 4,000	£10,000
350	£ 3,000	£20,000

Answers to Problems

2   The marginal abatement cost for reducing the dolphin kill is given in Table 19.12.

Table 19.12

Dolphins killed	Dolphins saved	Total cost	Marginal cost
20	0	£ 0	—
18	2	£ 100	£ 50
16	4	£ 240	£ 70
14	6	£ 400	£ 80
12	8	£ 600	£ 100
10	10	£ 1,000	£ 200
8	12	£ 1,500	£ 250
6	14	£ 2,200	£ 350
4	16	£ 3,000	£ 400
2	18	£ 5,000	£1,000
0	20	£10,000	£2,500

a   The firm reduces the number of dolphins killed by 8 for a total of 12 killed.
b   Again, the firm reduces its dolphin kill by 8 for a total of 12 killed.
c   Profits under the tax = £10,000 – 12 × £100 = £8,800; profits under the subsidy = £10,000 + 8 × £100 = £10,800.

3   The marginal abatement cost for noise is given in Table 19.13.

Table 19.13

Average level of noise (decibels)	Total costs	Marginal cost
1,000	£ 0	—
900	£ 50	£0.50
800	£ 150	£1.00
700	£ 300	£1.50
600	£ 500	£2.00
500	£ 750	£2.50
400	£1,100	£3.50

a   The firm will emit 500 decibels (abating 500).
b   The firm will abate 500 decibels (emitting 500).
c   Profits under tax = £5,000 – 500 × £2.50 = £3,750; profits under subsidy = £5,000 + 500 × £2.50 = £6,250.

5   a   Market equilibrium quantity = 40; price = £60;
    b   The social marginal cost is given in Table 19.14.

Table 19.14

Quantity	Social marginal cost
0	£65
20	£70
40	£75
60	£80
80	£85
100	£90

Efficient quantity = 20; price = £70.

6   a   Market equilibrium quantity = 500; price = £100,000.
    b   The social marginal cost is given in Table 19.15.

Table 19.15

Quantity	Social marginal cost
300	£100,000
400	£110,000
500	£120,000
600	£130,000
700	£140,000
800	£150,000
900	£160,000

Efficient quantity = 400; price = £110,000.

8   Efficient level = 60. If 60 permits are sold, the market price will be £30 each, 60 permits will be purchased, and the level of pollution will be 60.

9   Efficient level = 250. If 250 permits are sold, the market price will be £5,000 each, 250 permits will be purchased, and the level of pollution will be 250.

TAXES, TRANSFERS, AND REDISTRIBUTION

Chapter Review

Chapter 20 is about why governments redistribute income and how they do so. It begins with the basic argument of why markets may not provide a satisfactory answer to the question of for whom goods are produced. It looks separately at the tax, transfer, and social security and welfare systems and at social insurance and asks how each promotes a more equitable distribution of the economy's output. The chapter examines the fundamental trade-off between efficiency and equality and discusses various current public-policy controversies.

ESSENTIAL CONCEPTS

1   While the idea of market failure justifies many government policies aimed at improving the efficiency of the economy, the case for **redistribution** of the economy's output depends upon overriding social values relating to equality. Markets allocate too small a share of output to those at the lower end of the economic spectrum and too much to those at the upper end, and the distribution has grown more unequal in the last twenty years. Redistribution programs often interfere with economic efficiency, so it is important to pay attention to their design.

2   A good tax system has five important characteristics, the first of which is **fairness.** Economists have emphasised two principles of fairness. **Horizontal equity** says that individuals in the same circumstances should pay the same tax, and **vertical equity** says that taxes should be based on ability to pay. By the standard of vertical equity, the tax system should be **progressive;** this means that the fraction of income paid in taxes should be larger for those with more income.

3   The second characteristic of a good tax system is **efficiency.** The system should change the economy's resource allocation decisions as little as possible and also impose few extra costs on taxpayers. Taxes discourage the consumption and production of goods and services, encourage their consumption and production. For example, excise duties on petrol, beer, wines, spirits, and tobacco discourage consumption and production, while subsidies for mortgage tax relief (which is gradually being phased out in Britain) encourage people to buy their own home rather than to rent. Other characteristics of a good tax system include **administrative simplicity, flexibility,** and **transparency;** transparency means that it should be clear who is paying how much of each tax.

4   The current system of transfer programs in Britain has its roots in the welfare state established after the Second World War by the Labour government of Clement Atlee following the recommendations of the Beveridge Re-

port. The aim was to ensure that everyone had access to free education and health care and was protected from poverty caused by low pay or unemployment. Under this system, much of which still survives today, government programs for welfare fall into three main categories: universal programs, such as health and education; National Insurance programs, such as state pensions and unemployment benefits, where benefits paid out are called **contributory benefits** because they are based on National Insurance contributions (or payroll taxes); and finally **noncontributory benefits,** such as income support. Noncontributory benefits are often means tested, as is the case with income support, but this is not always the case. For example, child benefit is a fixed amount per child payable to households irrespective of income. Over time some elements of the welfare state in Britain have been eroded. For example, charges have been introduced for some types of health care, such as prescriptions, dental services, and eyesight tests (although these services are still free for pensioners and those on low income). Similarly, university tuition fees are no longer fully subsidised by the state. Also there has been a gradual erosion in the value of unemployment benefits and pensions relative to average earnings and the link between National Insurance contributions and the amount paid out in benefits has become rather weak.

5   One of the problems of the current benefit system in Britain is the **poverty trap.** The poverty trap arises when members of a household who are unemployed and receive benefits find that if they started employment, they would lose benefits, such as income support, housing benefit, free dental care, medical prescription, and school meals for children. For some levels of income, the increase in income from employment would be less than the loss in income from benefits, and the household would face an effective tax rate of over 100 percent. As a result, there is little point in members of the household looking for work unless they can find a job with a rate of pay after tax that exceeds their income from benefits. Hence, the poverty trap provides a barrier to employment. The poverty trap arises because unemployed workers face very high marginal tax rates. A negative income tax scheme would alleviate the problem. The working families tax credit introduced in October 1999 is a move towards such a scheme.

6   Any program or tax provision that promotes equality may reduce efficiency. This basic **equity-efficiency trade-off** must be faced in making choices about social security and tax reforms. Overall, income equality in the United Kingdom, as shown by the **Lorenz curve,** is reduced somewhat by taxation and government programs, but it has been increasing in recent decades.

BEHIND THE ESSENTIAL CONCEPTS

1   You can judge the U.K. tax system on how well it meets the five criteria outlined in the text. The following are some arguments.

a   Fairness: The marginal tax rate, which is the tax paid out of the extra pound of income, is higher for higher incomes. This aspect together with payments to those on low income makes the income tax system mildly progressive, although the progressivity is offset somewhat by a variety of provisions that have helped higher-income households, such as mortgage tax relief. Moreover, some people in the poverty trap face very high marginal tax rates. National Insurance contributions are only progressive at lower ranges of the income scale where the average contribution rises with earnings. Once the fixed ceiling on National Insurance contributions is reached, this tax becomes regressive as earnings rise. Taken together, National Insurance contributions and income tax produce a total tax system that is not very progressive. Also, the shift from direct to indirect taxation in the 1980s has made the system even less progressive.

b   Efficiency: During the 1980s there was a shift from direct to indirect taxation as the Conservative government cut income tax and increased the rate of value-added tax. This switch was justified by the government on the basis that high marginal rates of income tax, particularly for the most-qualified, able, and highly paid workers, acted as a disincentive to work. There is little objective evidence to support this claim. High rates of taxation may also encourage people to exploit (legal) tax loopholes or to undertake do-it-yourself work that is not taxable. High indirect tax rates may also encourage the growth of the informal economy whereby people work for cash and do not declare earnings to the government.

c   Administrative simplicity: Reducing the number of individuals who pay tax makes the system easier and cheaper to administer. In the United Kingdom, the switch from rates (a property-based tax on households) to the community charge, or poll tax (a tax on virtually all adults), led to administrative complexity. Under the poll tax, many more people were tax payers than under the old rates system and keeping track of individuals, rather than property, proved complex. The tax became difficult to collect and was replaced by a new property tax—the council tax.

d   Flexibility: The U.K. government has considerable freedom to change taxes. The budget is announced annually by the chancellor of the Exchequer in November and is usually agreed in law with little amendment. This is in contrast to the situation in the United States where tax changes often open up debate between Congress and the president.

e   Transparency: For some taxes, such as the corporation tax and the value-added tax, it is difficult to determine the actual tax burden.

2   The equity-efficiency trade-off is similar to the risk-incentive trade-off you studied in earlier chapters. You learned that an employer who pays commissions, for example, will provide stronger incentives to her sales force than another who pays a fixed salary. The result of the strong incentives, however, is risk for the em-

ployees. The risk is not only that incomes may be high in some months and low in others, but also that some employees may earn more than others. Just as an employer can have strong incentives at a cost of risk for the employees, an economy can have efficiency at a cost of inequality. Social security measures that alleviate poverty also reduce the incentives to earn income. Similarly, progressive income taxation pays for social security but discourages effort.

SELF-TEST

True or False

1 Redistribution is necessary to promote a more efficient allocation of resources than the market provides.

2 Horizontal equity says that upper-income individuals should pay a larger fraction of income in taxes.

3 Vertical equity says that people in similar situations should pay the same tax.

4 A tax system is progressive if upper-income individuals pay a larger fraction of income in taxes.

5 Income tax in the United Kingdom is an example of a progressive tax.

6 The U.K. income tax system is quite flexible and can respond relatively quickly to changes in economic circumstances.

7 The community charge reduced administrative complexity and made local taxes easier to collect.

8 Corporation tax is an example of a transparent tax in that it is easy to see how much each person effectively pays.

9 The poverty trap describes a situation where those on low income face high marginal tax rates if they gain employment.

10 Contributory benefits are related to National Insurance payments.

11 The Gini coefficient equals twice the area between the Lorenz curve and the 45-degree line.

12 The burden of National Insurance contributions is the same whether they are paid by workers or their employers.

13 Noncontributory benefits in the United Kingdom are always means tested.

14 The Lorenz curve illustrates the efficiency of the economy.

15 Income inequality in the United Kingdom has been increasing.

Multiple Choice

1 Which of the following is *not* an excise tax?

  a the cigarette tax
  b the tax on alcohol
  c the petrol tax
  d the tax on air travel
  e corporation tax

2 Horizontal equity means that

  a people in the same economic situation should pay the same amount in tax.
  b richer individuals should pay a larger fraction of their income in taxes.
  c richer individuals should pay a larger monetary amount in taxes.
  d the marginal tax rate should be higher for higher-income individuals.
  e the tax schedule should be flat.

3 Vertical equity means that

  a people in the same economic situation should pay the same amount in taxes.
  b richer individuals should pay a larger fraction of their income in taxes.
  c richer individuals should pay a larger monetary amount in taxes.
  d the marginal tax rate should be higher for higher-income individuals.
  e the tax schedule should be flat.

4 If lower-income individuals pay a larger fraction of their income in tax, the system is

  a progressive.
  b regressive.
  c transparent.
  d efficient.
  e flexible.

5 Mortgage interest tax relief is an example of a

  a tax subsidy.
  b tax incidence.
  c excise tax.
  d tax burden.
  e means-tested benefit.

6 The marginal tax rate is

  a the tax rate on an additional pound of income.
  b the amount of tax expenditure on an additional pound of income.
  c the amount of tax subsidy on an additional pound of income.
  d the ratio of taxes to taxable income.
  e all of the above.

7 The burden of a tax refers to

  a how many people must pay it.
  b how difficult it is to determine how much is paid.
  c who really bears the burden of the tax, taking into account its economic repercussions.
  d who sends the money to the tax authority.
  e how much the tax distorts economic decisions.

8 An efficient tax system

  a distorts economic decisions as little as possible.
  b collects its revenue with as little additional cost to taxpayers as possible.
  c is flexible.

d all of the above.

e *a* and *b*.

9 Which of the following is *not* an attribute of a good tax system?

a Efficiency

b Vertical equity

c Horizontal equity

d Transparency

e None of the above

10 Which of the following is *not* an important issue in welfare reform?

a Making value judgements about equity versus efficiency

b Job training

c Job search training

d Administrative simplicity

e None of the above

11 The poverty trap describes a situation where

a households face extremely high marginal tax rates.

b unemployed members of a household have little incentive to find a job.

c gaining employment can reduce household income.

d the tax and benefit systems provide a barrier to employment.

e all of the above.

12 Assuming that labour supply is inelastic, the effect of National Insurance contributors is to

a reduce wages by the amount that the worker pays.

b reduce wages by the amount that the employer pays.

c reduce wages by the total amount of the tax regardless of who pays.

d leave wages unchanged.

e increase wages somewhat.

13 A subsidy that is provided to low-wage workers is

a the job seeker allowance.

b income support.

c the minimum wage.

d National Insurance.

e *b* and *d*.

14 In Britain state pensions have traditionally been financed primarily by

a noncontributory benefits.

b means testing.

c the value-added tax.

d National Insurance payments.

e excise duties.

15 The welfare state and social security system in Britain

a have no redistribution effect.

b are purely redistributive.

c provide insurance and also redistribute from higher- to lower-income households.

d are financed by taxes that have disincentive effects.

e *c* and *d*.

16 Government programs that redistribute income to the poor with money raised by taxes are examples of

a the equity-efficiency trade-off.

b regressive taxes.

c market failures.

d consumer sovereignty.

e none of the above.

17 Economists represent inequality using the

a Lorenz curve.

b Stiglitz curve.

c redistribution curve.

d equity-efficiency trade-off.

e market failure approach.

18 The Gini coefficient measures inequality by

a the slope of the Lorenz curve.

b twice the area between the Lorenz curve and the 45-degree line.

c the area between the Lorenz curve and the 45-degree line.

d one half the area between the Lorenz curve and the 45-degree line.

e the curvature of the Lorenz curve.

19 The incidence of National Insurance payments falls

a evenly between the employer and the employee.

b entirely on the employee.

c entirely on the employer.

d on upper-income salaried workers.

e on the self-employed.

20 The government's role in redistribution is primarily motivated by

a market failure.

b social values concerning those unable to sustain a minimum standard of living.

c imperfect information.

d distrust of consumer sovereignty.

e noncompetitive markets.

Completion

1 The idea that individuals who are in identical situations should pay the same tax is called _____.

2 The idea that people who have more income or wealth should pay more tax is called _____.

3 A tax system in which individuals pay a larger fraction of income as income increases is called _____.

4 In Britain, the state pension is an example of a _____ benefit.

5 A good tax system has the characteristics of _____; this means that it is clear what each person is paying in taxes.

6 The rate of tax incurred on an additional pound of income is the _____.

7 The _____ of a tax refers to who actually bears its economic burden.

8 In Britain, child support is an example of a _____ benefit.

9   The _____ measures economic inequality as twice the area between the 45-degree line and the Lorenz curve.

10   The _____ shows the fraction of income earned by the poorest 10 percent, 20 percent, and so on.

Answers to Self-Test

True or False

1	F	6	T	11	T
2	F	7	F	12	T
3	F	8	F	13	F
4	T	9	T	14	F
5	T	10	T	15	T

Multiple Choice

1	*e*	6	*a*	11	*e*	16	*a*
2	*a*	7	*c*	12	*c*	17	*a*
3	*b*	8	*e*	13	*b*	18	*b*
4	*b*	9	*e*	14	*d*	19	*b*
5	*a*	10	*e*	15	*e*	20	*b*

Completion

1   horizontal equity
2   vertical equity
3   progressive
4   contributory
5   transparency
6   marginal tax rate
7   burden
8   noncontributory
9   Gini coefficient
10   Lorenz curve

Tools and Practice Problems

One way to measure inequality is with the Lorenz curve. It shows how the cumulative percentage of income (or wealth) varies with the population as we move up the income scale. Complete equality implies that the Lorenz curve is a 45 degree line. Tool Kit 20.1 shows how to plot it.

Tool Kit 20.1 Plotting the Lorenz Curve

The Lorenz curve is a convenient way to represent graphically the inequality in income (or any other economic variable). It shows what percentage of income is earned by the lowest 10 percent of the population, the lowest 20 percent, and so on. Here is how to plot it.

Step one: Order the groups from lowest income to highest.

Step two: Make a table with headings as follows.

Group	Percentage population	Cumulative percentage population	Percentage income	Cumulative percentage income

Step three: Compute the percentage of income for each group, and enter it in the table.

Step four: Compute the percentage of the population for each group, and enter it in the table.

Step five: Compute the cumulative percentage of income for each group by adding its percentage to all percentages of the lower-income groups, and enter it in the table.

Step six: Compute the cumulative percentage of the population for each group by adding its percentage to all percentages of the lower-income groups, and enter it in the table.

Step seven: Draw coordinate axes. Label the horizontal one "Cumulative percentage of population" and the vertical one "Cumulative percentage of income."

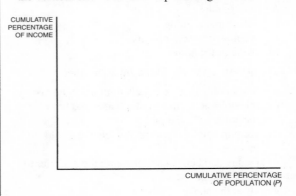

Step eight: Plot points corresponding to each group.

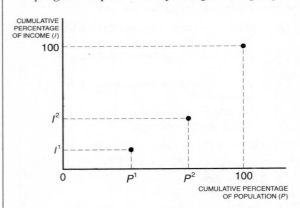

Step nine: Draw a curve connecting the points. This curve is the Lorenz curve.

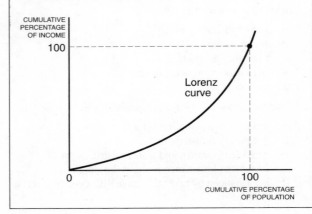

1   (Worked problem: Lorenz curve) In Tweadle Village there are four types of households: farmers, professionals, shopkeepers, and business owners. The population of each group (in millions) and the income (in pound equivalent) of each are given in Table 20.1.

Table 20.1

Income		Population (millions)
Farmers	£ 5,000	40
Professionals	£50,000	20
Shopkeepers	£10,000	30
Business owners	£80,000	10

Plot the Lorenz curve.

Step-by-step solution

Step one: Order the groups from lowest income to highest.

Farmers	£ 5,000	40
Shopkeepers	£10,000	30
Professionals	£50,000	20
Business owners	£80,000	10

Step two: Make a table.

Group	Percentage population	Cumulative percentage population	Percentage income	Cumulative percentage income
Farmers				
Shopkeepers				
Professionals				
Business owners				

Step three: Compute the percentage of income for each group, and enter it in the table. For farmers, it is 40 × £5,000/40 × £5,000 + 30 × £10,000 + 20 × £50,000 + 10 × £80,000 = 14 percent. The completed column is given in Table 20.2.

Step four: Compute the percentage of the population for each group, and enter in the table. For peasant farmers, it is 40/(40 + 30 + 20 + 10) = 40 percent. Continue, and complete the column, which is given in Table 20.2.

Table 20.2

Group	Percentage population	Cumulative percentage population	Percentage income	Cumulative percentage income
Farmers	40		14	
Shopkeepers	30		21	
Professionals	20		7	
Business owners	10		57	

Step five: Compute the cumulative percentage of income for each group by adding its percentages to all the percentages of the lower-income groups, and enter it in the table. For farmers, it is simply 9 percent. For shopkeepers, it is 14 + 21 = 35 percent. Continue.

Step six: Compute the cumulative percentage of the population for each group by adding its percentage to all the percentages of the lower-income groups, and enter it in the table. For farmers, it is simply 40 percent. For shopkeepers, it is 40 + 30 = 70 percent. Continue. The complete information appears in Table 20.3.

Table 20.3

Group	Percentage population	Cumulative percentage population	Percentage income	Cumulative percentage income
Farmers	40	40	14	14
Shopkeepers	30	70	21	35
Professionals	20	90	7	42
Business owners	10	100	57	100

Step seven: Draw coordinate axes. Label the horizontal one "Cumulative percentage of population" and the vertical one "Cumulative percentage of the income."

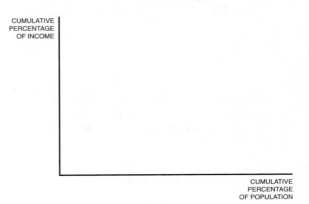

Step eight: Plot points corresponding to each group.

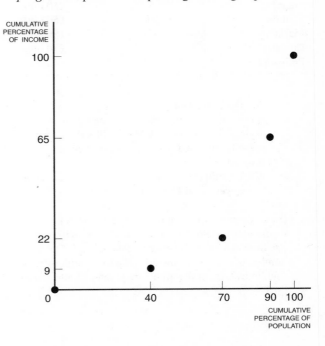

Step nine: Draw a curve connecting the points. This curve is the Lorenz curve.

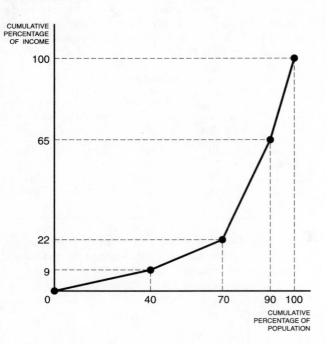

2   (Practice problem: Lorenz curve) Red Brick University is reconsidering the equity of its pay structure. The number of professors in each department and their salaries are given in Table 20.4.

Table 20.4

Department	Number of professors	Salary
Sociology	8	£50,000
Economics	10	£60,000
Marketing	2	£80,000
Literature	16	£30,000
Philosophy	4	£40,000

a   Plot the Lorenz curve.
b   An organization of faculty members proposes paying each professor £50,000. Plot the Lorenz curve for the faculty if this proposal were adopted.
c   What would the Lorenz curve look like if each professor were paid £80,000?

3   (Practice problem: Lorenz curve) Newton, a pleasant town outside Belle City, is populated by factory workers, bureaucrats, civil servants, and retirees. The number of each, their income, and the wealth of each individual in the group are given in Table 20.5.

Table 20.5

Career	Number	Income	Wealth of each
Factory workers	100	£30,000	£ 30,000
Civil servants	100	£40,000	£ 40,000
Professionals	100	£80,000	£ 80,000
Retirees	100	£50,000	£350,000

a   Plot the Lorenz curve for income.
b   Plot the Lorenz curve for wealth.
c   Compare the two. Is there more inequality in income or in wealth?

Answers to Problems

2   a   The Lorenz curve appears in Table 20.6 and the diagram.

Table 20.6

Department	Percentage population	Cumulative percentage population	Percentage income	Cumulative percentage income
Literature	40	40	40	40
Philosophy	10	50	10	50
Sociology	20	70	20	70
Economics	25	95	25	95
Marketing	5	100	5	100

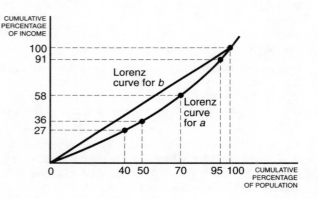

b   The complete information is given in Table 20.7. The Lorenz curve is the 45-degree line if there is equality.

Table 20.7

Department	Percentage population	Cumulative percentage population	Percentage income	Cumulative percentage income
Literature	40	40	40	40
Philosophy	10	50	10	50
Sociology	20	70	20	70
Economics	25	95	25	95
Marketing	5	100	5	100

c The answer does not depend upon the magnitude of income, only upon its distribution. The answer is the same as for part *b*.

3 *a* The Lorenz curve for income is given in Table 20.8 and the diagram.

Table 20.8

Career	Percentage population	Cumulative percentage population	Percentage income	Cumulative percentage income
Factory workers	25	25	15	15
Civil servants	25	50	20	35
Retirees	25	75	25	60
Professionals	25	100	40	100

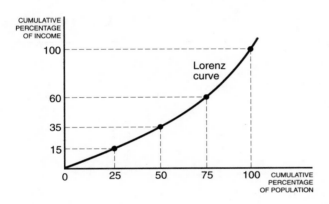

b The Lorenz curve for wealth is given in Table 20.9 and the diagram.

Table 20.9

Career	Percentage population	Cumulative percentage population	Percentage income	Cumulative percentage income
Factory workers	25	25	6	6
Civil servants	25	50	8	14
Retirees	25	75	16	30
Professionals	25	100	70	100

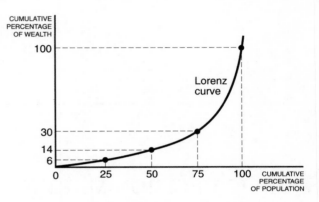

c Wealth is distributed more unequally than income. The Lorenz curve for wealth is farther from the diagonal (45-degree line) than is the Lorenz curve for income.

Chapter 21

PUBLIC DECISION MAKING

Chapter Review

The economic theory of government, which is called public choice, fills this chapter. In previous chapters we have asked when and how government can improve the economy's resource allocation. Here, the subject concerns how actual governments allocate resources. The focus is on voting, lobbying, and the functioning of bureaucracies. Reasons why governments may fail to work efficiently are explored and discussed.

ESSENTIAL CONCEPTS

1   According to the economic approach, government is not a coordinated, benign decision maker, but rather a collection of rational individuals playing a variety of roles. There are voters, candidates, interest groups, and bureaucrats. Economists focus on their choices and on the outcome of the political process.

2   An important way of making public decisions is majority voting. The **voting paradox** illustrates one problem: a majority of the electorate may not hold consistent views as to desirable policies. When it comes to such

matters as deciding how much to spend on education, on the other hand, the median voter model demonstrates that government responds to the preferences of the voter who stands between equal numbers of voters desiring more spending or less spending.

3   The incentives facing interest groups and bureaucrats may stand in the way of efficient public decisions. The **rent-seeking** activities of interest groups may lead to inefficient policies that benefit their members at the expense of the relatively poorly organized general electorate. Further, once a policy is set, there is the principal-agent problem, which inhibits the ability to motivate those charged with implementing policy to act in the public interest.

4   Although there are many examples of efficient government enterprises and helpful programs, government often allocates resources wastefully. Reasons for **public failures** include improper incentives attributable to the constraints of the legislative process, inability to make long-term commitments, and political pressures. Also budgetary and spending problems such as soft budget constraints, the annual round of negotiations for departmental budgets, and inflexible cost containment restrictions like competitive bidding requirements undermine efficiency. In addition, there is the general problem of

unintended consequences and unforeseen incentives and behavior brought about by the interaction of government policy and the very complex economy. In Britain the Conservative governments of the 1980s and 1990s followed a program of privatization and contracting out of services provided by the public sector. New organizational and incentive structures were introduced in a range of services including education and health care. Many of the changes represented attempts to introduce transparency and competition into the provision of public services and reduce the extent of political control. However, the changes have been controversial and only clearly successful in a few cases. They have also led to the establishment of "Quangos"—quasi-autonomous nongovernmental organizations—that have no clear responsibility to elected politicians. In many cases, the incentive structures facing the newly created Quangos are obscure. Overall the effects of many of these changes on organization and efficiency are unclear.

5   In Britain, until very recently, there has been a tendency towards centralization of government. Central government, based in London, has wide-ranging tax and expenditure powers while local government is severely constrained in the extent to which it can design policy and raise local taxes. Local taxation—the council tax—raises only a small part of local government expenditure; the remainder is financed from central government. The Labour government elected in 1997 ended the long trend towards increasing centralization and initiated a move away from centralised government with devolution of powers to the newly established Scottish parliament and Welsh assembly. As yet, little power has been devolved to the English regions and a truly federal structure in Britain looks some way off.

BEHIND THE ESSENTIAL CONCEPTS

1   It is important to understand what the voting paradox is and what is is not. It tells us that in certain circumstances majority voting may not be able to make consistent choices or even rank alternatives. This implies that even if all citizens are rational, when they act collectively, they may not be. The voting paradox does not say that every public decision is irrational or inconsistent.

2   One example of a situation where majority voting is consistent is that where the decision concerns a single variable for which each individual voter has a preferred level and also favors alternatives closer to this level than others further away. Examples include funding levels for local public goods such as parks and education. In these cases, **median voter theory** says that public decisions will reflect the preferences of the median voter. Assuming that the median voter is consistent, public decisions will be consistent. (Nothing in median voter theory implies that public decisions will be efficient, only that they will be consistent.)

3   The principal-agent problem helps us understand why governments may not be able to design and implement the policies they would like to pursue. In order to govern, the government must employ civil servants to run its departments and implement policy. But often civil servants have access to information not known by government politicians and may use this information asymmetry to influence the design and implementation of policy to serve their own ends. As a result, policies reflect not only the desires of politicians but also those of civil servants.

4   You can understand certain constraints placed on government decision making as imperfect solutions to larger problems. For example, the lack of clear performance targets and clear means of measuring the performance of government departments, in terms of service provision, makes it difficult to monitor government performance. In addition, government decision making is often based on imperfect information. In the case of Quangos, there is a lack of clear lines of responsibility to government and clear incentive structures. As a result Quangos face only weak constraints to meet government policy objectives efficiently. The time horizon of governments may often be short term, while more effective decision making requires long-term commitments. The government's inability to make long-term commitments does lead to inefficiencies, but it also limits the ability of the current legislature to impose undue burdens on future generations.

5   When you think about the federalism (or subsidiarity) question—which tasks should be assigned to which level of government—you may relate it to the broad issue of decentralised decision making within organizations. As we have seen in other chapters, decentralised decision making has the advantage of better coordination. Decentralised decision making also means that local governments and local communities have more of a say in how their affairs are run. Experience of federalism in the United States shows that decentralization often leads to greater experimentation and innovation—the states of the United States are often referred to as "laboratories of democracy." Thus we can expect the devolution of power in Britain to lead to new ways of dealing with policy problems.

SELF-TEST

True or False

1   Economists focus on the voting behaviour of rational individuals and on the public choices that are the outcome of the political process.

2   The voting paradox shows that majority vote cannot result in a determinate political outcome, and thus it argues for dictatorship.

3   The voting paradox states that political parties will advocate the alternative most preferred by the average voter.

4   Median voter theory shows that when there is a vote over a single issue, individuals have a most-preferred alternative and they vote for alternatives closest to it;

the outcome of a majority vote reflects the preferences of the median voter.

5   The median voter in a community is the person who earns the average income.

6   Rent seeking refers to activities and expenditures designed to secure special favors from government.

7   Due to the realities of the principal-agent problem, civil servants may not act in the interest of the electorate.

8   Public enterprises are always less efficient than their private counterparts.

9   Imperfect information means that government decision making may be inefficient.

10   The inability to make long-term commitments can undermine the efficiency of public agencies.

11   Quangos increase the transparency and accountability of government decision making and policy implementation.

12   Decentralization of government decision making means that local communities have more say in how their affairs are run.

13   When government bears some of the risk of public investment projects, private contractors and governments have misaligned incentives.

14   Devolution refers to a process whereby powers are transferred to lower levels of government.

15   Devolution in Britain has resulted in a purely federal system of government.

Multiple Choice

1   In their study of public decision making, economists focus on

a   coalition formation.
b   the media.
c   voting behaviour and the outcomes of the political process.
d   biographies of great political leaders.
e   all of the above.

2   The voting paradox refers to the

a   tendency of democratic governments to make inconsistent choices.
b   reasons for market failure.
c   reasons for public failure.
d   principle that political parties gravitate toward the political center.
e   principal agent problem as applied to motivating bureaucrats.

3   Which of the following voting systems did Kenneth Arrow show to be troubled by potential inconsistencies?

a   Simple majority voting
b   Weighted majority voting
c   Two-thirds majority voting
d   Three-fourths majority voting
e   All of the above

4   Which of the following is *not* a characteristic of a public choice described by the median voter theory?

a   The vote concerns a single variable.
b   Individual voters have a most-preferred outcome.
c   Voters vote for an alternative on the basis of how close it is to their most-preferred outcome.
d   Only two alternatives are considered.
e   None of the above.

5   On issues such as education finance, where people have different views about the desirable level of public support, median voter theory predicts that the majority vote will result in

a   inconsistent decisions.
b   no money allocated to education because everyone cannot agree.
c   the preferences of the median voter determining the level of funding.
d   property rights' being reassigned.
e   inefficient public decisions as a result of imperfect information.

6   Consider a majority vote to decide how much land to set aside for a local park. The median voter

a   earns the average level of income.
b   desires less park land than half of the voters and more park land than half of the voters.
c   lives an average distance from the park.
d   neither likes nor dislikes parks.
e   is governed by the voting paradox.

7   Which of the following best describes the relationship between the voting paradox and median voter theory?

a   Political scientists believe in the voting paradox, but economists argue that median voter theory more closely describes public decision making in a democracy.
b   Median voter theory resolves the voting paradox.
c   Inconsistencies in democratic decision making are inevitable. therefore the median voter is an interesting, but incorrect description.
d   Inconsistencies in democratic decision-making are not inevitable. Median voter theory explains one type of situation where choices are consistent.
e   While economists once believed in the voting paradox, now they only use the median voter model to study public choices in a democracy.

8   Economic rents are

a   moneys paid to landlords.
b   returns enjoyed by a factor of production that go beyond those required to elicit its supply.
c   political contributions.
d   inefficient public decisions resulting from lobbying for special favours from government.
e   activities, such as lobbying and political contributions, designed to promote the agenda of special interests.

9   Rent seeking refers to

a   advertising by landlords.
b   returns enjoyed by a factor of production that go beyond those required to elicit its supply.

c   special favors from government, such as subsidies and protection from foreign competition.

d   inefficient public decisions resulting from lobbying for special favors from government.

e   activities, such as lobbying and political contributions, designed to promote the agenda of special interests.

10   Civil servants may not actively pursue the agenda of the electorate because of

a   the voting paradox.

b   the principal-agent problem.

c   the free-rider problem.

d   unintended consequences problem.

e   public choice theory.

11   Which of the following is *not* an example of the principal-agent problem as it applies to the administration of government policy?

a   Bureaucrats may act in a risk-averse manner.

b   Public managers may seek to advance their careers by expanding their spheres of influence.

c   Special interests lobby politicians for favors, such as subsidies and protection from competition.

d   Performance of public administrators may be judged by how they conform to procedures.

e   None of the above.

12   The "Citizen's Charter" in Britain was an attempt to

a   give citizens a greater say in how the country was run.

b   include citizens in government decision making.

c   raise the quality of government services.

d   decentralise decision making and policy design.

e   none of the above.

13   The interests of small groups of voters may have undue influence on government policy because

a   elected politicians face incentives to serve their own interests and not those of the general public.

b   elected politicians have a desire to be reelected.

c   small groups of voters may be able to tip the scales in an election.

d   there are median voter effects.

e   *a, b,* and *c.*

14   Problems of efficiency in the public sector arise because

a   government departments and agencies may have monopoly positions.

b   the incentives that public sector workers face do not always lead them to pursue the interests of the public.

c   there is imperfect information.

d   there is a principal-agent problem.

e   all of the above.

15   Public enterprises and public investment projects may make losses because of

a   soft budget constraints.

b   government underwriting of risk.

c   imperfect information.

d   the principal-agent problem.

e   all of the above.

16   The concept of public failures refers to

a   inefficient decisions by government.

b   inefficient allocations of resources by market.

c   a socially unacceptable distribution of income.

d   the voting paradox.

e   the free-rider problem.

17   When government subsidies increase demand and raise costs, it is an example of

a   soft budget constraints.

b   unintended consequences.

c   due process.

d   externalities.

e   market failure.

18   Which of the following are sources of government failure?

a   Due process regulations limit flexibility.

b   Governments have limited ability to make long-term commitments.

c   Expenditures are appropriated on an annual basis.

d   Rigid procurement rules impose excessive costs.

e   All of the above.

19   Which of the following concerns argues for provision of government goods and services at the regional or local level?

a   Some government activities are national public goods.

b   Some government activities generate externalities on neighboring jurisdictions.

c   Regions and localities can have more say in how their communities are run.

d   Left to itself, the market may not yield a socially acceptable distribution of income.

e   None of the above.

20   In the European Union, the European Commission

a   is made up of civil servants.

b   takes a leading role in the formulation of policy.

c   is subject to a principal-agent problem.

d   is elected in European elections.

e   *a, b,* and *c.*

Completion

1   The _____ illustrates the tendency for public decisions to be inconsistent.

2   _____ predicts that in certain cases public decisions will reflect the preferences of the voters whose most-preferred alternative lies in the middle of the distribution of voters, with an equal number of voters desiring more or less of the public good.

3   Activities, such as lobbying and political contributions, designed to secure tax breaks or subsidies are called _____.

4   The notion that the self-interest of public managers may not coincide with the will of the electorate is an example of the _____.

5   The principal-agent problem arises because of _____.

6   Due to _____, government enterprises and public investment can suffer financial losses with the deficit funded out of government revenues.

7   The program of federally guaranteed student loans in the United States which gave students a strong incentive to declare themselves bankrupt, is an example of _____.

8   _____ refers to inefficient decisions by governments.

9   _____ have no clear responsibility to politicians but continue to receive and spend public funds to deliver services.

10   _____ describes a process whereby powers are transferred to lower levels of government.

Answers to Self-Test

True or False

1	T	6	T	11	F
2	F	7	T	12	T
3	F	8	T	13	T
4	T	9	T	14	T
5	F	10	T	15	F

Multiple Choice

1	c	6	b	11	c	16	a
2	a	7	d	12	c	17	b
3	e	8	b	13	e	18	e
4	d	9	e	14	e	19	c
5	c	10	b	15	e	20	e

Completion

1   voting paradox
2   Median voter theory
3   rent seeking
4   principal agent problem
5   asymmetric information
6   soft budget constraints
7   unforeseen responses
8   Public failures
9   Quangos
10 Devolution

Tools and Practice Problems

Public choice theory analyses the voting behaviour of rational individuals and the collective choices that result from the political process. Two important models are the voting paradox and median voter theory. Together they show that majority voting sometimes but not always leads to a determinate outcome. Some problems explore these ideas.

VOTING PARADOX

The voting paradox can arise when people vote to choose among at least three alternatives. If the outcome of majority voting cannot provide a ranking or even pick out unambiguously the best alternative, it reveals a voting paradox. Of course, this may not always occur. Tool Kit 21.1 shows how to use the majority voting model to discover inconsistencies arising from the voting paradox.

Tool Kit 21.1 Finding the Voting Paradox

When at least three individuals must choose among at least three alternatives, the outcome of their majority vote may lead to inconsistencies. Follow this procedure to discover voting paradoxes.

Step one: Identify the alternatives, the voters, and their preferences.

Step two: Choose two alternatives and hold a majority election. Conclude that the winner is chosen over the loser.

Step three: Conduct similar majority votes for each pair of alternatives. (For three alternatives there will be three elections, four alternatives six.)

Step four: Rank the alternatives on the basis of the outcome of the elections. If the alternative cannot be ranked unambiguously, there is a voting paradox.

---

1   (Worked problem: voting paradox) Alice, Bob, and Colleen are considering lunch at one of three local restaurants: Xerxes, Yellowfoot, and Zeke's. Their preferences are given in Table 21.1.

Table 21.1

Voter	Most preferred	Second best	Worst
Alice	Xerxes	Yellowfoot	Zeke's
Bob	Yellowfoot	Zeke's	Xerxes
Colleen	Zeke's	Xerxes	Yellowfoot

a   Suppose that they decide by majority vote. Can they rank the three alternatives?
b   Is there a most-preferred alternative?

Step-by-step solution

Step one: Identify the alternatives (Xerxes, Yellowfoot, and Zeke's), the voters (Alice, Bob, and Colleen), and their preferences (given in the table).

Step two: Choose two alternatives and hold a majority vote election. Let's vote on Xerxes versus Yellowfoot. Alice votes for Xerxes. Bob votes for Yellowfoot. Colleen votes for Xerxes. Xerxes wins 2 to 1. therefore Xerxes is preferred to Yellowfoot.

Step three: Conduct similar majority votes for every pair. Continuing as in step two, Yellowfoot is preferred to Zeke's (Alice and Bob vote for Yellowfoot, defeating Colleen, who votes for Zeke's). Finally, Zeke's wins a majority vote over Xerxes.

Step four: Rank the alternatives. The outcome of the vote is as follows. Xerxes is preferred to Yellowfoot. Yellowfoot is preferred to Zeke's. But Zeke's is preferred to Xerxes. There is an inconsistency, and there is no single most-preferred alternative. This is an example of the voting paradox.

2 (Practice problem: voting paradox) Representatives of the three halls of residence at Large Town University are meeting to vote on how to allocate the trustee's grant. There are three alternatives: library expansion, football scholarships, and campus beautification. The preferences are given in Table 21.2.

Table 21.2

Hall of residence	Most preferred	Second best	Worst
North Towers	Football	Library	Beautification
Shady Acres	Library	Football	Beautification
Cement Block	Library	Beautification	Football

a Does majority voting give an unambiguous ranking of the three alternatives?
b Does majority voting select a single best alternative?

3 (Practice problem: voting paradox) The city council consists of three voting members, who must decide among four alternative sources of funds to make up the budget shortfall. The alternatives are a council tax increase, an increase in the price of some council services, a cut in recreation funding, and reduced payments into the retirement fund for city council members. Their preferences are given in Table 21.3.

Table 21.3

Member	First choice	Second	Third	Fourth
Hammer-mesh	Property	Price	Recreation	Retirement
Menchik	Price	Recreation	Property	Retirement
Davidson	Recreation	Property	Price	Retirement

a Does majority voting give an unambiguous ranking of the four alternatives?
b Does majority voting select a single best alternative?

MEDIAN VOTER THEORY

Many votes in local and central government involve the choice of a single variable: how much to spend or tax. Usually, voters will have a most-preferred alternative and will vote for the proposal closest to their liking. In this case median voter theory predicts that the outcome will reflect the preferences of the median voter, who is the one preferring the level in the middle of the distribution of voters. Half of the voters prefer more and half prefer less. This theory has

been used extensively to analyze funding for local public goods and many other issues decided by voting. Tool Kit 21.2 shows how to find the median voter and predict the outcome of majority voting.

Tool Kit 21.2 Using Median Voter Theory

When the vote concerns the magnitude of a single variable about which people have a most preferred level and always vote for alternatives closer to that level, the preferences of the median voter will determine the outcome. That is the majority vote will choose the level most preferred by the median voter.

Step one: Identify the variable subject to vote, the voters, and their most-preferred level.

Step two: Order the voters from highest to lowest according to their most-preferred level of the variable.

Step three: Find the median voter. This is the voter in the middle of the list constructed in step two. If there is an odd number of voters, there will be an equal number of voters preferring more than the median voter and an equal number preferring less. If there is an even number of voters, then take an average of the two in the middle.

Step four: Predict the outcome of the vote. According to median voter theory, it is the level preferred by the median voter found in step three.

---

4 (Worked problem: median voter theory) Grove City Council is about to vote on the level of funding for the City's Library bond issue. The voters and their preferred (per student) level of funding are given in Table 21.4.

Table 21.4

Voter	Preferred funding
Kowalski	£5,000
Stokowski	£4,000
Litovsk	£3,500
Stanislav	£6,200
Jones	£8,000

a Who is the median voter?
b Find the outcome of the election according to median voter theory.

Step-by-step solution

Step one: Identify the variable subject to vote, the voters, and their most-preferred level. The variable is library funding. The voters and their preferred levels are given above in Table 21.4.

Step two: Order the voters. From high to low, the ordering appears in Table 21.5.

Table 21.5

Voter	Preferred funding
Jones	£8,000
Stanislav	£6,200
Kowalski	£5,000
Stokowski	£4,000
Litovsk	£3,500

Step three: Find the median voter. He is Kowalski. Jones and Stanislav want more; an equal number of voters, Stokowski and Litovsk, want less.

Step four: Predict the outcome. Kowalski, the median voter, desires £5,000 per student. According to median voter theory the outcome will be £5,000 per student.

5 Suppose that four additional councillors are elected. Their names and preferences are given in Table 21.6.

Table 21.6

Voter	Preferred funding
Cheong	£7,500
Davis	£8,000
Samuels	£7,000
Biddle	£8,000

   a Who is the median voter now?

   b Find the outcome of the election according to median voter theory.

6 Frightened of the recent surge in crime, a council committee vows to increase the size of the local police force. There are five voters, and their preferences and names are given in Table 21.7.

Table 21.7

Voter	Preferred number of police officers
Davis	1
Lee	1
Gaudin	2
Stevens	1
Mathews	4

   a Who is the median voter?

   b Find the outcome of the election according to median voter theory.

Answers to Problems

2 *a* Yes. Football is preferred to beautification. The library is preferred to football. The library is preferred to beautification. There is a ranking: library, football scholarships, campus beautification. In this case there is no voter's paradox.

   b Yes. Library expansion is the most-preferred alternative.

3 *a* No. Property tax increase defeats price increase, price increase defeats recreation cut, and recreation cut defeats property tax.

   b No, there is no single best alternative.

5 *a* Samuels is the median voter.

   b The preferred funding will be £7,000.

6 *a* Davis, Lee, or Stevens is the median voter.

   b The preferred number of officers is 1.

Part Five

FULL-EMPLOYMENT MACROECONOMICS

Chapter 22

MACROECONOMIC GOALS AND MEASURES

Chapter Review

Macroeconomics is concerned with the characteristics of the economy as a whole. This chapter of the text introduces three central macroeconomic variables: the unemployment rate, the inflation rate, and gross domestic product, which is the standard measure of the economy's output. We learn how to measure each variable and discover how each is related to the major goals for the performance of the economy: full employment, price stability, and a high rate of economic growth.

ESSENTIAL CONCEPTS

1   Macroeconomics is concerned with the performance of the economy as a whole. The three important indicators—the level of **unemployment**, the **inflation rate**, and the rate of **economic growth**—are related to the three major markets. High unemployment occurs when demand does not equal supply in the labour market. When demand and supply in product markets are not consistent with a stable price level, there is inflation. Low growth results, in part, when the capital market does not allocate enough funds for investment.

2   The **gross domestic product**, or GDP, measures the output of the economy. It is the money value of the goods and services produced within a country in a year. Adjusting the number for inflation gives real GDP. The rate of increase in the real GDP is the primary measure of economic growth. Although the U.K. rate averaged around 3 percent per year from 1950 to 1973, it has fallen to about 1 percent per year since.

3   GDP can be measured in three equivalent ways. The **final goods approach** computes the market value of goods sold to their ultimate consumers. The **value-added approach** adds up the additional market value created at each step in the process from production to market. The **income approach** adds the total income received by all individuals and profits retained by firms. Another important measure is **net domestic product**, which subtracts depreciation from the GDP.

4   The **labour force** includes those individuals who are either employed or actively seeking employment. The fraction of the labour force that is without work is called the **unemployment rate.** Unemployment is a persistent phenomenon in the United Kingdom: from 8.8 to 10.4 percent of the labour force was unemployed in the early 1990s. This represents an enormous waste of a resource, and it can be devastating personally for

the unemployed and also for communities with high unemployment.

5 Economists distinguish among four types of unemployment. **Seasonal unemployment** occurs when the jobs are available for only part of the year. People who are between jobs make up **frictional unemployment. Structural unemployment,** which is more long-term, arises because the skills of the current labour force do not match the skills required by the available jobs. Finally, **cyclical unemployment** is due to a slowdown in the overall level of economic activity. One of the important tasks of macroeconomics is to understand and reduce cyclical unemployment.

6 The **inflation rate** is the rate of increase in the general level of prices. It is measured using **price indices** such as the retail price index, or RPI. The annual percentage change in the RPI indicates the increase in the cost of living from one year to the next. Inflation in the United Kingdom was under 10 percent between 1945 and 1973 but rose rapidly to about 25 percent in 1975. Between 1980 and 1995 inflation ranged between 10 and 2.5 percent. Inflation hurts people on fixed incomes because it erodes their purchasing power. When variable, inflation makes borrowing and lending riskier, and it is generally disruptive of the economy.

BEHIND THE ESSENTIAL CONCEPTS

1 If you have a job or are looking for one, then economists count you as a member of the labour force. The unemployment rate is the fraction of the labour force that does not have a job. But the unemployment rate is difficult to measure and different definitions are used to calculate official statistics. In the United Kingdom prior to 1998, the main measure of unemployment was the "claimant count" based on the number of people claiming unemployment-related benefits. However, this measure excludes people who are not eligible for benefits but looking for work and includes people who only say they are looking for work in order to claim benefits or who are holding out for an unrealisitically high wage. The definition of unemployment used in the U.K. claimant count figures was frequently changed (as the rules governing benefits changed), and many people felt it was underestimating the true unemployment rate. In the United States, unemployment statistics are based on surveys which ask households whether any members are seeking work. This has the advantage of decoupling the measure of unemployment from the system of benefits. However, there are still some disadvantages. For example, the measure includes people who say they are looking for work when, in fact, they are not and excludes **discouraged workers** who have given up looking for a job because the prospects of gaining employment are so poor. A discouraged worker would be part of the usual decline in the **labour force participation rate** during recessions. In 1998, the United Kingdom adopted a new survey-based measure of unemployment that meets internationally agreed standards using the definition of unemployment used by the International Labor Office (ILO).

2 Economists use the price index, which is constructed by comparing the cost of a particular basket of goods in different years, to measure inflation. The retail price index measures your cost of living only if you consume exactly what is in the market basket. It also gives an inexact measure of quality changes and sometimes underestimates the importance of sale items.

3 Similarly, GDP does not quite measure all the output in the economy. It ignores nonmarketed goods, such as the services of unpaid spouses, and it can only be adjusted imperfectly to capture changes in the quality of goods and the value of nonmarketed government services.

SELF-TEST

True or False

1 Productivity refers to output per capita.

2 The gross domestic product measures the money value of goods and services produced within a country during a specific time period.

3 Nominal GDP is real GDP adjusted for inflation.

4 Gross domestic product is the sum of consumption, investment, government expenditure, and net exports.

5 There are three equally valid ways to compute gross domestic product: final goods, value added, and income.

6 Value added is computed by subtracting a firm's purchases of inputs from its revenues.

7 The unemployment rate measures the percentage of the working-age population that is unemployed.

8 The labour force includes the entire working-age population.

9 Structural unemployment includes those unemployed who have skills that do not match the skills required for currently available jobs.

10 When the economy is on an upswing, cyclical unemployment declines.

11 The price index for the base year equals 100.

12 The wholesale price index is based upon a market basket of goods sold by wholesalers to retailers.

13 The producer price index is based upon a market basket of goods sold by wholesalers to producers.

14 Inflation reduces the purchasing power of people living on fixed incomes.

15 Variable rates of inflation increase the riskiness of borrowing and lending.

Multiple Choice

1 Which of the following is *not* an important macroeconomic goal?

a   Price stability

b   Full employment

c   Perfect competition

d   Rapid growth

e   None of the above

2   The money value of all goods and services produced within a country in a year is the

a   gross national product.

b   gross domestic product.

c   net domestic product.

d   depreciation index.

e   producer price index.

3   Inflation-adjusted gross domestic product is called

a   gross national product.

b   net domestic product.

c   nominal gross domestic product.

d   real gross domestic product.

e   nominal gross national product.

4   If the price level has risen recently, the real GDP is

a   greater than the nominal GDP.

b   less than the nominal GDP.

c   equal to the nominal GDP.

d   greater than the GNP.

e   less than the GNP.

5   A leading indicator is

a   a misleading measure of economic activity.

b   a variable that signals the onset of a boom.

c   a variable that signals the onset of a recession.

d   *b* and *c*.

e   none of the above.

6   The final goods approach to GDP

a   adds the differences between the revenues and costs of intermediate goods.

b   adds all income received by individuals and governments in the economy.

c   subtracts the inflation rate from the nominal GDP.

d   adds the value of goods, services, and the environment.

e   adds the total money value of goods and services purchased by their ultimate users.

7   The value-added approach to GDP

a   adds the differences between final revenues and the costs of intermediate goods.

b   adds all income received by individuals and governments in the economy.

c   subtracts the inflation rate from the nominal GDP.

d   adds the value of goods, services, and the environment.

e   adds the total money value of goods and services purchased by their ultimate users.

8   Gross domestic product divided by the number of hours worked equals

a   net domestic product.

b   real GNP.

c   real GDP.

d   productivity.

e   NDP.

9   The total labour force comprises all

a   individuals of working age who are employed.

b   individuals of working age who are unemployed.

c   individuals of working age.

d   heads of households.

e   individuals of working age who are either employed or unemployed.

10   The costs of unemployment include

a   underutilization of the economy's resources.

b   personal difficulties for unemployed individuals.

c   financial troubles for communities with high unemployment.

d   exacerbated racial and ethnic divisions.

e   all of the above.

11   The unemployment rate is the ratio of the number of unemployed to the

a   number of employed.

b   total labour force.

c   inflation rate.

d   gross domestic product.

e   adult working-age population.

12   The U.S. Department of Labor survey probably

a   underestimates the true unemployment rate in that some discouraged workers have given up hope of finding a job.

b   overestimates the true unemployment rate in that some discouraged workers have given up hope of finding a job.

c   underestimates the true unemployment rate in that some individuals who respond that they are actively seeking work are not.

d   overestimates the true unemployment rate in that some individuals who respond that they are actively seeking work are not.

e   *a* and *d*.

13   Those individuals who are unemployed because they work in seasonal jobs make up

a   seasonal unemployment.

b   frictional unemployment.

c   structural unemployment.

d   cyclical unemployment.

e   discouraged-worker unemployment.

14   Those individuals who are temporarily between jobs make up

a   seasonal unemployment.

b   frictional unemployment.

c   structural unemployment.

d   cyclical unemployment.

e   discouraged-worker unemployment.

15   When the skills required by available jobs are not the same as the skills of the unemployed, there is

a   seasonal unemployment.

b   frictional unemployment.

c   structural unemployment.

d   cyclical unemployment.
e   discouraged-worker unemployment.

16   In recessions, the level of economic activity declines and there is an increase in

a   seasonal unemployment.
b   frictional unemployment.
c   structural unemployment.
d   cyclical unemployment.
e   discouraged-worker unemployment.

17   If prices and wages rise at the same rate, the purchasing power of typical workers

a   increases.
b   decreases.
c   remains the same.
d   doubles.
e   falls to zero.

18   When the inflation rate rises and falls unpredictably,

a   lenders gain at the expense of borrowers.
b   borrowers gain at the expense of lenders.
c   there is no appreciable impact on borrowing and lending.
d   borrowing and lending become riskier.
e   lending increases, but borrowing falls.

19   The producer price index includes in its market basket a representative bundle of goods

a   purchased by consumers.
b   sold by wholesalers to retailers.
c   sold by producers to wholesalers.
d   purchased by government.
e   sold by wholesalers to consumers.

20   The price index used to calculate the real gross domestic product is

a   the retail price index.
b   the producer price index.
c   the weighted average of the producer and retail price indices.
d   the GDP deflator.
e   an index of raw material prices.

Completion

1   The money value of all final goods and services produced within a country in a year is called the _____.

2   Dividing nominal GDP by the price level gives _____.

3   A variable that signals changes in economic activity is called a _____.

4   A firm's revenue minus the costs of intermediate goods equal its _____.

5   _____ is calculated by dividing GDP by the number of hours worked.

6   The unemployment rate is the ratio of the number of unemployed to the _____.

7   People who are temporarily between jobs make up part of _____ unemployment.

8   _____ unemployment is due to a mismatch between the skills of those without jobs and the skills needed to perform the available jobs.

9   _____ unemployment rises in recession and falls in booms.

10   The percentage increase in the price level from one year to the next is called the _____.

Answers to Self-Test

True or False

1	T	6	T	11	T
2	T	7	F	12	T
3	F	8	F	13	F
4	T	9	T	14	T
5	T	10	T	15	T

Multiple Choice

1	*c*	6	*e*	11	*b*	16	*d*
2	*b*	7	*a*	12	*e*	17	*c*
3	*d*	8	*d*	13	*a*	18	*d*
4	*b*	9	*e*	14	*b*	19	*b*
5	*d*	10	*e*	15	*c*	20	*d*

Completion

1   gross domestic product
2   real GDP
3   leading indicator
4   value added
5   Productivity
6   labour force
7   frictional
8   Structural
9   Cyclical
10   inflation rate

Tools and Practice Problems

In this section, we will explore how economists measure economic performance. After learning how to calculate the rate of inflation, we use this technique to construct the price index and to distinguish real and nominal GDP. Finally, we calculate GDP by the final goods, value-added, and income approaches, verifying that the three techniques give equivalent answers. Although the examples are simplified, you should realise that the government agencies responsible for computing inflation and GDP perform their calculations in the same way.

Inflation

Inflation refers to a general increase in the price level. It is calculated by computing the increase in the cost of purchasing a fixed market basket of goods. The U.K. government has several inflation measures, including the retail price index, the producer price index, and the GDP deflator. In these problems we focus on the computation of the retail price index (RPI). Tool Kit 22.1 shows how it is done.

Tool Kit 22.1 Calculating the Inflation Rate

The inflation rate is the percentage increase in the cost of purchasing a predetermined basket of goods. Follow this procedure to calculate the inflation rate.

Step one: Identify the quantities of each good in the market basket:

Quantity of good 1 =
Quantity of good 2 =
Quantity of good 3 =

Step two: Calculate the cost of purchasing the quantities in the market basket at year 1 prices:

Quantity of good 1 × price in year 1
+ quantity of good 2 × price in year 1
+ quantity of good 3 × price in year 1
= cost of living at year 1 prices.

Step three: Calculate the cost of purchasing the quantities in the market basket at year 2 prices:

Quantity of good 1 × price in year 2
+ quantity of good 2 × price in year 2
+ quantity of good 3 × price in year 2
= cost of living at year 2 prices.

Step Four: Find the percentage change in the two costs of living by using

$$\left(\frac{\text{Cost of living at year 2 prices}}{\text{Cost of living at year 1 prices}} - 1 \right) \times 100 = \text{inflation rate.}$$

1   (Worked problem: inflation rate) There are three goods consumed in Dangerville: fast cars, parachute jumps, and hang gliders. The prices and quantities for each in 1990 and the prices in 1991 are given below.

Goods	1990 Prices	Quantities	1991 Prices
Fast cars	£20,000	20	£30,000
Parachute jumps	£ 100	2,500	£ 80
Hang gliders	£ 500	400	£ 800

The market basket comprises the 1990 quantities. Calculate the inflation rate.

Step-by-step solution:

Step one: Identify the quantities in the market basket. There are 20 fast cars, 2,500 parachute jumps, and 400 hang gliders.

Step two: Calculate the cost of purchasing the market basket at 1990 prices:

(£20,000 × 20) + (£100 × 2,500) + (£500 × 400) = £850,000.

Step three: Calculate the cost of purchasing the market basket at 1991 prices:

(£30,000 × 20) × (£80 × 2,500) + (£800 × 400) = £1,120,000.

Step four: Find the percentage change:

(£1,120,000/£850,000 – 1) × 100 = 32 percent.

The inflation rate is 32 percent.

2   (Practice problem: inflation rate) In order to determine how to adjust stipends for disabled workers, the Paper Profits Company wants to compute the inflation rate. It has identified a market basket for stipend recipients. This is given below, along with the prices in 1980 (the year of the last adjustment) and in 1990.

Good or service	Quantity	1980 Prices	1990 Prices
Prepared meals	7	£ 5	£ 6
Housecleaning	1	£25	£30
Physical therapy	3	£50	£75
Compact discs	4	£10	£10

Compute the inflation rate.

3   (Practice problem: inflation rate) A recent graduate of Large Town University, Lamont has dozens of job offers. He has narrowed his search to jobs in two cities: Bigville and Smallville. In order to compare the offers, he must compute the relative costs of living in the two cities. His market basket and prices are given below.

Good or service	Quantity	Gotham price	Smallville price
2-bedroom apartment	1	£1,500	£300
Pickup truck	1	£ 600	£400
Meals	90	£ 10	£ 5

How much more expensive (in percent) is the cost of living in Bigville than in Smallville?

Inflation Adjustment

The distinction between real and nominal values is essential in macroeconomics. Real values are adjusted for inflation; that is, they measure what would have occurred if the pound maintained its purchasing power. While the technique is appropriate for any pound value, in these problems we focus on adjusting nominal GDP. Tool Kit 22.2 shows how to adjust for inflation.

Tool Kit 22.2 Adjusting for Inflation

The money value of all goods and services purchased during a year is the nominal GDP. To get a better idea of how actual output changes from year to year, it is important to adjust this number for inflation. Real GDP is nominal GDP adjusted for inflation, and it gives the value of output measured in base year pounds. Follow this procedure to calculate real GDP.

Step one: Calculate this year's price index. Multiply last year's price index by 1 plus the inflation rate:

Last year's price index × (1 + inflation rate)
= current year's price index.

Step two: Calculate this year's real GDP. Divide current nominal GDP by the price index and multiply by 100. The result is current real GDP expressed in base year pounds. (To express real GDP in any other year's pounds, simply multiply by the price index in the desired year and divide by 100.)

(Nominal GDP/price index) × 100 = real GDP.

4   (Worked problem: adjusting for inflation) The nominal GDP in Monrovia was £2 billion during 1992. The price index for 1991 was 210, and 1992 saw an inflation rate of 30 percent.

   a   Calculate the price index in 1992.
   b   Calculate real GDP for 1992. Express it in base year pounds.
   c   Express real GDP in 1991 pounds.

Step-by-step solution

Step one (a): Calculate the price index for the current year (1992). The price index for 1991 was 210. The inflation rate was 30 percent. The price index for 1992 is

$$210 × 1.30 = 273.$$

Step two (b): Calculate this year's real GDP. The current nominal GDP is £2 billion. The 1992 real GDP is

$$(£2 \text{ billion}/273) × 100 = £732.6 \text{ million.}$$

Step three (c): Real GDP in 1991 pounds is

$$(£732.6 × 210)/100 = £1,538 \text{ million.}$$

5   (Practice problem: adjusting for inflation) Suppose that nominal GDP in 1992 is £4 trillion, the 1991 price index is 352, and the 1992 inflation rate is 95 percent.

   a   Calculate the price index in 1992.
   b   Calculate real GDP for 1992. Express it in base year dollars.
   c   Express real GDP in 1991 pounds.

6   (Practice problem: adjusting for inflation) Suppose that sales of new homes total £30 billion in 1992. The 1992 price index is 222. Express the total sales of new homes in base year pounds.

Gross Domestic Product

The market value of all goods and services produced in a year is the gross domestic product. In the macroeconomics section of this book, when we measure the economy's output we will be looking at GDP. It is very important to realise that GDP equals national income; thus it can also be measured by adding all income earned in the economy. Finally, the value added at each step along the production chain gives another equivalent approach to calculating GDP. Tool Kit 22.3 shows how to calculate GDP.

Tool Kit 22.3 Calculating GDP

Gross domestic product is the money value of all goods and services as purchased by their ultimate users. It can be calculated by adding the money value of all final products, the values added by all firms, or the incomes received by all individuals.

Final goods approach

Step one: Determine which goods are purchased by their ultimate users.

Step two: Add the money values (price × quantity) of these goods:

GDP = money value of good 1
                 + money value of good 2 + · · ·

Value-added approach

Step one: For each firm, compute the value added by subtracting any payments to other firms from its receipts:

Value added = receipts − purchases from other firms.

Step two: Sum the values added of each firm:

GDP = value added at firm 1
                 + value added at firm 2 + · · ·

Income approach

Step one: Find the total wages, total dividends, total interest, and any other form of income for all individuals in the economy.

Step two: Add the totals of each kind of income:

GDP = wages + dividends + interest.

---

7   (Worked problem: calculating GDP) Suppose that the economy produces three goods: wheat, flour, and bread. All of the wheat is sold to millers. All of the flour is sold to bakers. Consumers buy the bread from the bakers. The income and expenditure accounts for each of the three industries are given in Table 22.1.

Table 22.1

	Expenditures (billions)	Receipts (billions)
Wheat industry		
Wages	£ 40	£ 50
Dividends	£ 0	
Interest	£ 10	
Flour industry		
Wages	£ 30	£110
Purchases of wheat	£ 50	
Dividends	£ 15	
Interest	£ 15	
Bread industry		
Wages	£ 60	£200
Purchases of flour	£110	
Dividends	£ 30	
Interest	£ 0	

a Calculate (nominal) GDP using the final goods approach.
b Calculate (nominal) GDP using the value-added approach.
c Calculate (nominal) GDP using the income approach.
d Compare the three answers.

Step-by-step solution

Step one (a): Determine which goods are purchased by their ultimate users. Only bread is a final output.

Step two: Add the money value of these goods. The value of bread is £200. The GDP thus equals £200.

Step three (b): Find the value added for each firm or industry.

Value added in wheat = £50 – £0 = £50;
Value added in flour = £110 – £50 = £60;
Value added in bread = £200 – £110 = £90.

Step four: Sum the value-added numbers.

GDP = £50 + £60 + £90 = £200.

Step five (c): Find the total wages, dividends, and interest.

Total wages = £40 + £30 + £60 = £130;
Total dividends = £0 + £15 + £30 = £45;
Total interest = £10 + £15 + £0 = £25.

Step six: Add the totals of each income type.

GDP = £130 + £45 + £25 = £200.

Step seven (d): Compare. Note that the GDP equals £200 billion according to each method.

8 (Practice problem: calculating GDP) The economy of Literaria cuts down trees in order to make paper and uses all its paper for books. The expenditure and income accounts for each of the three industries are given in Table 22.2.

Table 22.2

	Expenditures (billions)	Receipts (billions)
Tree industry		
Wages	£ 80	£100
Dividends	£ 20	
Interest	£ 0	
Paper industry		
Wages	£100	£250
Purchases of trees	£100	
Dividends	£ 40	
Interest	£ 10	
Book industry		
Wages	£150	£500
Purchases of paper	£250	
Dividends	£ 50	
Interest	£ 50	

a Calculate (nominal) GDP using the final goods approach.
b Calculate (nominal) GDP using the value-added approach.
c Calculate (nominal) GDP using the income approach.
d Compare the three answers.

9 (Practice problem: calculating GDP) in Computavia, they produce chips, all of which are used in the production of computer hardware. Half of the hardware is purchased by consumers, and half is sold to the software industry. Consumers purchase all of the software. The expenditure and income accounts for each of the three industries are given in Table 22.3.

Table 22.3

	Expenditures (billions)	Receipts (billions)
Chip industry		
Wages	£ 600	£1,000
Dividends	£ 400	
Interest	£ 0	
Hardware industry		
Wages	£ 600	£2,000
Purchases of chips	£1,000	
Dividends	£ 200	
Interest	£ 200	
Software industry		
Wages	£ 600	£2,000
Purchases of hardware	£1,000	
Dividends	£ 0	
Interest	£ 400	

a Calculate (nominal) GDP using the final goods approach.
b Calculate (nominal) GDP using the value-added approach.
c Calculate (nominal) GDP using the income approach.
d Compare the three answers.

Answers to Problems

2 [(42 + 30 + 225 + 40)/(35 + 25 + 150 + 40)] – 1] × 100 = 30 percent.

3 [(1,500 + 600 + 900)/(300 + 400 + 450)] – 1] × 100 = 161 percent.

5 a 1992 price index = 352 × 1.95 = 686.4.
   b 1992 real GDP (base year pounds) = (4/686.4) × 100 = £0.58 trillion.
   c 1992 real GDP (1991 pounds) = (0.58 × 352)/100 = £2.042 trillion.

6 (30/222) × 100 = £14 billion.

8 *a* £500 (books).

   b Value added in tree industry = £100 – 0 = £100;
        value added in paper industry = £250 – £100 = £150;
        value added in book industry = £500 – £250 = £250;
        total value added = £100 + £150 + £250 = £500.

   c Wages = £80 + £100 + £150 = £330;
        dividends = £20 + £40 + £50 = £110;
        interest = £0 + £10 + £50 = £60;
        total income = £330 + £110 + £60 = £500.

   d Each answer is £500, which is the GDP.

9 *a* Hardware purchased by consumers = £2,000/2 = £1,000;
        software purchased by consumers = £2,000;
        total final goods = £1,000 + £2,000 = £3,000.

   b Value added in chip industry = £1,000 – £0 = £1,000;
        value added in hardware industry = £2,000 – £1,000 = £1,000;
        value added in software industry = £2,000 – £1,000 = £1,000;
        total value added = £1,000 + £1,000 + £1,000 = £3,000.

   c Wages = £600 + £600 + £600 = £1,800;
        dividends = £400 + £200 + £0 = £600;
        interest = £0 + £200 + £400 = £600;
        total income = £1,800 + £600 + £600 = £3,000.

   d Each answer is £3,000, which is the GDP.

Chapter 23

THE FULL-EMPLOYMENT MODEL

Chapter Review

The full-employment model describes the performance of the economy in the long run, after prices and wages have had time to adjust. Equilibrium in the product, labour, and capital markets combines with a balance in international transactions to bring the economy to full-employment production at the level of its productive capacity or potential GDP. This chapter lays out the essentials of the model, and the following one delves into several of its uses.

ESSENTIAL CONCEPTS

1 This chapter's model is the basic competitive model in which households and firms interact in product, labour, and capital markets. Households supply labour to firms for use in producing goods, and they provide savings that finance firms' investments in plant and equipment. Receiving their wages, interest, and dividends, households purchase the goods in the product market. Wages, interest rates, and product prices adjust to equate supply and demand in each market. The markets are interdependent in the sense that what occurs in any one market affects each of the others.

2 The labour market governs job creation and employment. The demand for labour depends upon the productivity of workers, and it slopes downwards because as the real wage falls, firms hire labour to substitute for capital and to produce additional output. Households determine their supply of labour, which is assumed to be inelastic. As shown in Figure 23.1, the real wage adjusts to the level at which demand and supply are equal.

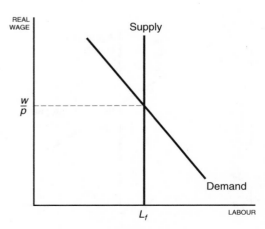

Figure 23.1

An increase in labour supply shifts the supply curve to the right, increasing employment and reducing the real wage. An increase in the demand for labour (due to improved technology or additional investment) shifts demand to the right, bidding up wages.

3 The capacity of the economy, also called its **potential gross domestic product** or **full-employment output**, depends upon the available technology, its stock of capital, and the supply of labour. With a given capital stock and technology, the **short-run production function** shows how potential output varies with different quantities of labour. Figure 23.2 illustrates the short-run production function and its property of diminishing returns. It is related to the aggregate supply curve shown in Figure 23.3. Notice that aggregate supply does not depend upon product price. An increase in labour supply represents a movement along the short-run production function and a rightward shift in aggregate supply. An increase in the capital stock or a technological advance also shifts aggregate supply to the right.

4 **Aggregate demand** includes consumption, investment, government expenditure, and net exports. It slopes downwards as shown in Figure 23.3, chiefly because as the price level falls, the real value of money and other pound denominated assets rises and people consume more. In equilibrium the price level adjusts to the intersection of aggregate demand and aggregate supply, and output equals its full-employment level.

5 The savings of households depend upon their disposable income and interest rates. Panel A of Figure 23.4 shows the supply of funds sloping slightly upward; panel B shows it as vertical. The demand for funds, also called the investment function, results from firms' intentions to invest in plant and capital equipment. It depends upon their expectations of future profitability and the real interest rate. In equilibrium, savings equals investment. A rightward shift in investment raises the interest rate. It increases investment only if the supply of funds is elastic (panel A).

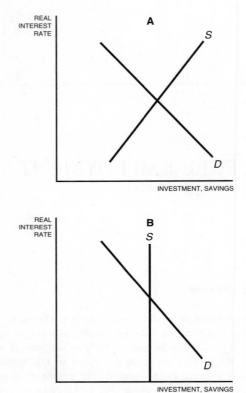

Figure 23.4

6 In the economy's general equilibrium, all markets clear. There is full employment because the real wage adjusts to bring the demand for labour equal to the supply. At the equilibrium price level, aggregate demand equals aggregate supply in the product market, and the economy produces its potential GDP. Finally, the real interest rate finds its equilibrium level where savings equal investment.

7 The general equilibrium model provides a coherent way to view the effects of various changes as they work their way through the three markets. Here are some examples.

a The introduction of personal computers raises the productivity of workers, shifting the demand for

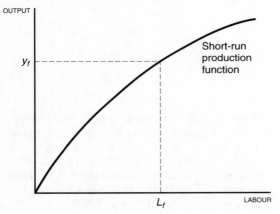

Figure 23.2

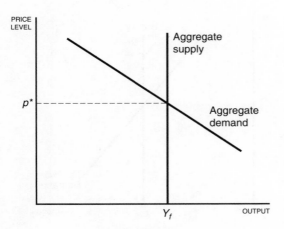

Figure 23.3

labour to the right and increasing real wages. In the product market this new technology manifests itself as a rightward shift in aggregate supply. A look at the capital market shows an increase in savings (because households have more income) and an increase in investment.

b   Government expenditure and taxation affect the composition of output. An equal increase in spending and taxes reduces savings and drives up the interest rate. The economy's aggregate supply will not shift, but it will comprise less consumption and investment, offsetting the extra government spending.

c   When the economy is at full employment, money is neutral. This means that an increase in the supply of money shifts aggregate demand to the right, increasing the price level, but the real wage, real interest rate, real output, and real investment remain unchanged.

8   Trade affects the goods market, because net exports is one of the four components of aggregate demand, and affects the capital market, because foreign households provide an additional source of funds. In a **small open economy**, such as Switzerland, the real interest rate is fixed (determined on international capital markets); therefore any change in domestic savings cannot affect investment. In a large open economy, such as the United States, changes in savings affect interest rates and investment. Also, the world capital market is not fully integrated, a fact that makes investment quite sensitive to changes in savings in a large open economy.

BEHIND THE ESSENTIAL CONCEPTS

1   While the basic competitive model employed in this chapter is the same basic competitive model studied in microeconomics, there is a difference in interpretation. In macroeconomics we study the behaviour of aggregates: total output, total employment, the price level, and so on. We proceed as if all firms produced a single good and as if there were only one kind of labour. This simplification directs attention away from the complexity of the economy and allows us to see the major forces involved in the movements of broad measures of economic performance.

2   Remember that the real wage refers to the amount of goods that an hour of work will buy. When you decide to take a part-time job, you focus on what your earnings will allow you to purchase, not simply on the amount of money you receive. Similarly, in the capital market the real interest rate governs savings and investment decisions. Households put aside funds in order to consume additional goods at some future date. It is the real increase in purchasing power that motivates savings. The price level, on the other hand, is the nominal price level. Aggregate demand affects this price level, but because aggregate supply is vertical at full employment, the economy's output is not affected by aggregate demand. Shifts in aggregate demand, whether brought about by changes in the money supply or anything else, affect only the price level, leaving real wages, real interest rates, real investment, and output unchanged. This is an essential feature of the full-employment economy.

3   When the price of croissants falls, people consume more croissants. They substitute croissants for scrambled eggs, cereal, or other breakfast foods. When the price level falls, however, there is no comparable opportunity to substitute. Why then does aggregate demand slope down? The answer has to do with households' wealth. A fall in the price level makes your cash worth more. The same number of pounds now buys more goods. When you experience an increase in wealth, you spend some. The same is true of any asset (such as a government bond) that is not indexed for inflation. A lower price level means greater real wealth and more consumption.

4   When the interest rate rises, you have an incentive to save more. The reason is, of course, that a given amount of savings results in more goods in the future. This idea is called the **substitution effect:** at higher interest rates people save more, in effect substituting future for current consumption. Why is the supply of funds so insensitive to changes in the interest rate? The reason is the other factor, the **income effect.** As the interest rate increases, savers have more lifetime wealth. As we have seen, when people experience an increase in wealth, they increase their consumption. This extra consumption means that savings fall. This income effect counteracts the substitution effect, leaving the supply of funds almost inelastic.

5   In competitive markets firms are price takers. The usual reason is that they are too small relative to the market to affect the price. Any barley farmer who tried to charge above market prices would find no customers. Charging less simply gives away profits for no gain. It is the same with countries in the international capital market. A small country, such as Belgium, Botswana, or Paraguay, simply does not borrow or lend enough funds to affect world interest rates.

6   Study the structure of the full-employment model with care. The basic division of the economy into the three markets and the channels through which the markets affect each other are constants in macroeconomics. Later in the book, we look at unemployment macroeconomics, where prices are at first rigid and then adjust slowly. Although these other models have quite different implications, their basic structures mirror the one studied in this chapter. Furthermore, it is important that you understand them in terms of their difference with the full-employment model. If you think about it, it is economical to learn one model well and to use that knowledge as a base for learning the others.

SELF-TEST

True or False

1   In the basic competitive model all markets are interdependent.

2   Macroeconomics focuses on the behavior of aggregate measures such as total employment.

3   An increase in the supply of labour causes the real wage to increase.

4   Like most supply curves, aggregate supply slopes upwards.

5   The full-employment level of output is the same as potential GDP.

6   The short-run production function exhibits diminishing returns.

7   When the interest rate rises, the income effect motivates savers to increase their savings.

8   The investment function refers to financial investment.

9   In general equilibrium all markets clear.

10 Computerization in industry will cause the supply of labour to shift to the left.

11 An equal increase in government spending and taxation will reduce private investment and consumption.

12 The neutrality of money in the full-employment economy means that an increase in the supply of money increases the price level but has no real effects on output, employment, or investment.

13 In a small open economy, interest rates are fixed because they are determined on international capital markets.

14 Switzerland is a small open economy.

15 Most economists agree that money is neutral when the economy is at full employment.

Multiple Choice

1   In the labour market

    a   households supply labour.
    b   the real wage adjusts to clear the market.
    c   firms use the labour supplied by households to produce output.
    d   labour supply is assumed to be inelastic.
    e   all of the above.

2   An increase in the supply of labour causes

    a   an increase in both the real wage and employment.
    b   a decrease in both the real wage and employment.
    c   an increase in the real wage and a decrease in employment.
    d   a decrease in the real wage and an increase in employment.
    e   no change in the real wage because supply is assumed to be inelastic.

3   An increase in investment most likely will shift

    a   the demand for labour to the right.
    b   the supply of labour to the right.
    c   the demand for labour to the left.
    d   the supply of labour to the left.
    e   both the supply and demand for labour to the right.

4   The real wage must be

    a   greater than the nominal wage.
    b   equal to the nominal wage when there is full employment.
    c   less than the nominal wage when interest rates are high.
    d   less than the nominal wage if there is income tax.
    e   none of the above.

5   In this chapter labour supply is assumed to be perfectly inelastic. This means that an increase in the real wage

    a   increases the quantity of labour supplied.
    b   decreases the quantity of labour supplied.
    c   causes no change in the quantity of labour supplied.
    d   causes the nominal wage to fall.
    e   causes no change in the nominal wage.

6   The relationship between employment and output, holding the technology and capital stock fixed, is called the

    a   short-run production function.
    b   full-employment gross domestic product.
    c   short-run aggregate supply.
    d   investment function.
    e   labour supply curve, which is assumed to be inelastic.

7   The short-run production function exhibits diminishing returns. This means that as more labour is used in production, output

    a   diminishes due to overcrowding.
    b   increases at an increasing rate.
    c   decreases at an increasing rate.
    d   increases at a decreasing rate.
    e   decreases at a decreasing rate.

8   Which of the following is *not* a synonym?

    a   Full-employment level of output
    b   Potential gross domestic product
    c   Productive capacity
    d   Aggregate supply
    e   Aggregate demand

9   If the labour force grows,

    a   aggregate supply shifts to the right.
    b   aggregate demand shifts to the right.
    c   both aggregate supply and aggregate demand shift to the right.
    d   aggregate supply does not shift because it does not depend upon price.
    e   the real wage rises.

10 Aggregate demand slopes downwards because as the price level falls,

    a   households substitute among goods.
    b   the real value of money and other assets rises and households increase consumption.
    c   households fear inflation and stock up on necessities.
    d   firms reduce their quantity supplied.

    e Aggregate demand does not slope down. it is assumed to be inelastic.

11 The income effect of an increase in the real interest rate causes savers to

    a reduce savings because they are better off and want to consume more now.

    b increase savings because consumption in the future is cheaper.

    c reduce savings because they can meet their target level with less savings.

    d increase savings because they are better off and want to consume more in the future.

    e choose no change in the level of savings.

12 The substitution effect of an increase in the real interest rate causes savers to

    a reduce savings because they are better off and want to consume more now.

    b increase savings because consumption in the future is cheaper.

    c reduce savings because they can meet their target level with less savings.

    d increase savings because they are better off and want to consume more in the future.

    e choose no change in the level of savings.

13 The supply of funds depends upon

    a the interest rate.

    b expectations about future profitability.

    c disposable income.

    d all of the above.

    e *a* and *c*.

14 The demand for funds depends upon

    a the interest rate.

    b expectations about future profitability.

    c disposable income.

    d all of the above.

    e *a* and *b*.

15 The relationship between the real interest rate and the level of investment is called the

    a short-run production function.

    b investment function.

    c aggregate supply.

    d potential GDP.

    e aggregate demand.

16 An equal increase in government spending and taxes

    a increases investment because the government spending adds to aggregate demand.

    b decreases investment because the increased taxes reduce aggregate demand.

    c decreases investment because the increased taxes reduce disposable income and households save less.

    d increases investment because the real interest rate falls.

    e increases investment because the price level rises.

17 An increase in the money supply

    a increases the price level.

    b increases the real wage.

    c increases the real interest rate.

    d all of the above.

    e *a* and *c*.

18 The neutrality of money in the full-employment economy refers to the idea that changes in the supply of money do not change

    a investment.

    b output.

    c the real wage.

    d the real interest rate.

    e any of the above.

19 In a small open economy,

    a interest rates are determined on international capital markets.

    b interest rates adjust to equate the domestic demand and supply of funds.

    c the supply of savings is perfectly inelastic.

    d the demand for funds is perfectly inelastic.

    e savings do not depend upon the interest rate.

20 In the U.S. economy,

    a investment does not depend upon domestic savings.

    b interest rates are fixed, determined on international capital markets.

    c domestic savings affect interest rates and investment.

    d domestic savings affect investment but not interest rates.

    e savings are perfectly inelastic.

Completion

1 In the labour market the _____ adjusts to equate the supply and demand for labour.

2 For a given technology and capital stock the relationship between employment and output is called the _____.

3 The aggregate supply curve shows how much output the economy can produce when it is at _____.

4 Aggregate demand is composed of consumption, investment, government expenditure, and _____.

5 When the interest rate rises, households are motivated to save less because of the _____ effect.

6 When government spending and taxes rise in the same amount, the interest rate _____, crowding out private investment and consumption.

7 When there is full employment, an increase in the money supply will increase the _____ but will have no effect on output or any other real variable.

8 The _____ of money refers to the idea that at full employment increases in the money supply have no real effects.

9 In a _____ interest rates are fixed, determined on international capital markets.

10 The United States is a _____ open economy.

Answers to Self-Test

True or False

1	T	6	T	11	T
2	T	7	F	12	T
3	F	8	F	13	T
4	F	9	T	14	T
5	T	10	F	15	T

Multiple Choice

1	e	6	a	11	a	16	c
2	d	7	d	12	b	17	a
3	a	8	e	13	e	18	e
4	e	9	a	14	e	19	a
5	c	10	b	15	b	20	c

Completion

1 real wage
2 short-run production function
3 full employment
4 net exports
5 income
6 increases
7 price level
8 neutrality
9 small open economy
10 large

Tools and Practice Problems

The full-employment model occupies a central place in modern economics because in many areas the economy behaves according to its predictions. For example, the long-run performance of the economy corresponds quite closely to the full-employment model. In this chapter we study the full-employment model in four steps. First, we look at the relationship between the short-run production function and the demand for labour. Next, we consider the links between the labour and product markets. Third, we study how the capital and product markets interrelate before we put it all together with some applications. The focus here is on the structure of the full-employment model. Master this subject and unemployment macroeconomics will go smoothly. (The chapter also covers the open economy, but we will defer the study of that model until Chapter 24.)

The Short-Run Production Function and the Demand for Labour

The short-run production function shows how much output results from using various amounts of labour, holding the level of capital input and the technology fixed. From this function we can compute the marginal product of labour, which is the extra output resulting from one more unit of the input labour. This curve is the demand for labour. Tool Kit 23.1 shows how to make the derivation.

Tool Kit 23.1 Deriving the Demand for Labour from the Short-Run Production Function

Firms employ workers to produce output. The additional output that one more worker produces is called the marginal product of labour. The marginal product schedule is also the demand for labour, in the sense that firms choose the amount of labour to employ by setting the marginal product equal to the real wage. Follow these steps to derive the demand for labour.

Step one: Identify and plot the short-run production function.

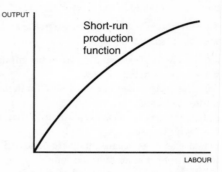

Step two: Compute the marginal product for each level of labour. The marginal product equals

$$\text{Marginal product} = \frac{\text{change in output}}{\text{change in labour}}.$$

Step three: Plot the marginal product.

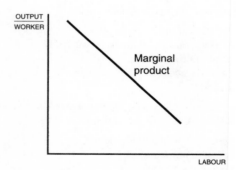

Step four: Identify the real wage. To find the quantity demanded of labour, find the quantity for which the real wage equals the marginal product.

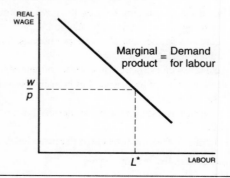

1   (Worked problem: demand for labor) This problem looks at Costa Guano, whose currency is the guano. The short-run production function is given in Table 23.1.

a   Find the marginal product schedule.
b   Suppose, for example, that the real wage is 300 guanos per year. How much labour is demanded?

Table 23.1

Quantity of labour (million person years)	Output (millions of guanos)
0	0
1	600
2	1,100
3	1,500
4	1,800
5	2,000
6	2,100
7	2,150

Step-by-step solution

Step one: Identify and plot the short-run production function. See Table 23.1.

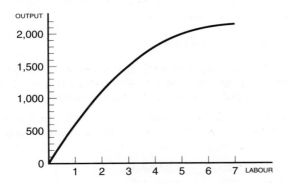

Step two: Compute the marginal product for each level of labour. When the first million workers are used, output rises from 0 to 600 million; therefore the marginal product of this worker is 600. When the second is added, output rises from 600 to 1,100; therefore the second worker's marginal product is 1,100 − 600 = 500. Continuing in the same manner gives the entire marginal product schedule.

Quantity of labour (million person years)	Marginal product of labour
1	600
2	500
3	400
4	300
5	200
6	100
7	50

Step three: Plot the marginal product curve.

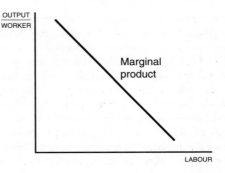

Step four: Find the quantity for which the real wage equals the marginal product. The real wage is 300, which equals marginal product when the quantity of labour is 4.

2   (Practice problem: demand for labour) The short-run production function is given in Table 23.2.

a   Find the marginal product schedule.
b   Suppose that the real wage is 3,000 dorals. How much labour is demanded?

Table 23.2

Quantity of labour (million person years)	Output (billions of dorals)
0	0
1	25
2	45
3	60
4	70
5	75
6	78
7	80
8	81

3   (Practice problem: demand for labour) In the land of Erehwemos the short-run production function is as given in Table 23.3. The currency is called the wemo.

a   Find the marginal product schedule.
b   Suppose that the real wage is 3,000 wemos per year. How much labour is demanded?

Table 23.3

Quantity of labour (million person years)	Output (billions of wemos)
0	0
1	5
2	9
3	12
4	14
5	15
6	15.5

The Labour Market and the Product Market

The labour market and product market are linked by the short-run production function. The marginal product of labour, derived from the short-run production function, is the demand for labour, which, together with the supply of labour, determines the real wage. We will assume that the supply of labour is perfectly inelastic, an assumption that is not far from the truth. The short-run production function shows how much output will be produced by the supply of labour, and this quantity of output is the aggregate supply in the product market. Note the direction of influence: from the labour market to the product market. The labour market determines the labour supply and, with the production function, it determines the level of output. Changes in the product market have no impact upon the labour market. Tool Kit 23.2 illustrates this linkage.

Tool Kit 23.2 Deriving Aggregate Supply from the Labour Market and Short-Run Production Function

With the supply of labour and the short-run production function, we can find the economy's aggregate supply, which is also called potential GDP, full-employment output, or capacity. The labour market gives the real wage and the production function gives the aggregate supply. Follow these steps.

Step one: Identify the supply of labour and the short-run production function.

Step two: Find the demand for labour. Follow the steps of Tool Kit 23.1.

Step three: Find the equilibrium real wage. This is the real wage that clears the labour market.

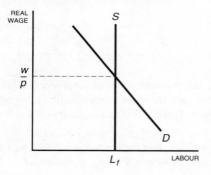

Step four: Find the economy's full employment output. This is the output corresponding to the equilibrium level of labour.

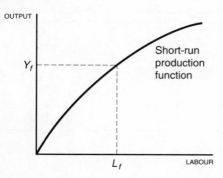

Step five: Plot the aggregate supply curve. This is a vertical line drawn with output equal to its full-employment level.

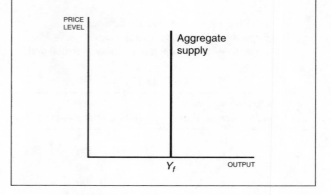

4   (Worked problem: aggregate supply) We continue with Costa Guano, whose production function is given in Table 23.1. The labour supply is inelastic, equal to 5 million.

   a   Calculate the marginal product schedule.
   b   Find the equilibrium real wage. Draw a diagram of the labour market.
   c   Find the economy's potential GDP. Draw the aggregate supply curve.

Step-by-step solution

Step one: Identify the supply of labour and the short-run production function. The production function is given in Table 23.1 and the labour supply equals 5 million.

Step two: Find the demand for labour. The demand for labour is as follows. Notice that it is the same as the marginal product schedule.

Quantity of labour (person years)	Real wage (guanos)
1	600
2	500
3	400
4	300
5	200
6	100
7	50

Step three: Find the equilibrium real wage. Demand equals supply (5 million) when the wage equals 200.

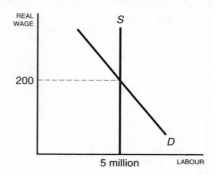

Step four: Find the economy's full-employment output. From the production function, output at 5 million person years equals 2,000 million guanos.

Step five: Plot the aggregate supply curve. Note that output equals 2,000 for each price level.

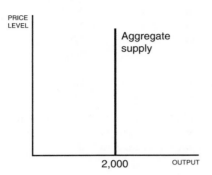

5   (Practice problem: aggregate supply) We continue with the analysis of El Dorado from problem 2. Suppose that the production function is given in Table 23.2 and that the labour supply is inelastic, equal to 3,000 person years.

   a   Find the demand for labour.
   b   Find the equilibrium real wage. Draw a diagram of the labour market.

   Find the economy's potential GDP. Draw the aggregate supply curve.

6   (Practice problem: aggregate supply) We continue with the country of Erehwemos, where the production function is given in Table 23.3. Suppose that the labour supply is inelastic, equal to 5 million.

   a   Find the demand for labour.
   b   Find the equilibrium real wage. Draw a diagram of the labour market.

   Find the economy's potential GDP. Draw the aggregate supply curve.

The Product Market and the Capital Market

The capital market determines the quantity of investment. Recall that the real interest rate adjusts to balance the demand and supply of funds. The product market is affected in that investment is one of the four components of aggregate demand. In this case the effects go both ways because the product market affects the capital market through the link between output (which equals income) and savings. For example, an increase in the level of the economy's output will lead households to increase their savings. Tool Kit 23.3 illustrates these linkages.

Tool Kit 23.3 Linking the Product and Capital Markets

The product market determines the economy's output, which equals its income. The capital market is affected because households save a fraction of their income. That fraction is the average propensity to save. The capital market then determines the level of investment, which is one of the components of aggregate demand. You can keep this two-way influence straight with the following procedure.

Step one: Identify aggregate supply, aggregate demand (excluding investment), the investment function, and the average propensity to save.

Step two: Find the savings supply (assumed to be inelastic). First, observe that aggregate supply equals output and output equals income. Next, multiply income by the average propensity to save. The product is total savings.

Total savings = income × average propensity to save.

Step three: Find the equilibrium real interest rate and investment level by equating the investment function with total savings.

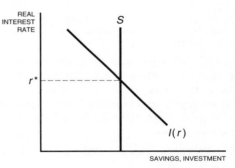

Step four: Find aggregate demand by adding investment to the aggregate demand (excluding investment).

Step five: Find the equilibrium price level by equating aggregate demand and aggregate supply.

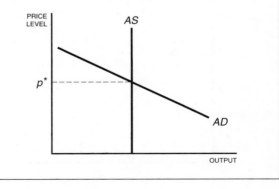

7   (Worked problem: product and capital markets) Continuing the analysis of Costa Guano, recall that the short-run production function is given in Table 23.1 and output equals 2,000 million guanos. Costa Guanoans save 10 percent of their income. The invest-

ment function and aggregate demand (excluding investment) are given in Table 23.4.

a   Compute total savings.
b   Find the equilibrium real interest rate. Draw a diagram of the capital market.
c   Find aggregate demand.
d   Find the equilibrium price level. Draw a diagram of the product market.

Table 23.4

Investment function		Aggregate demand (excluding investment)	
Investment (millions of guanos)	Real interest rate	Aggregate demand (millions of guanos)	Price level
50	10	1,000	280
75	9	1,200	260
100	8	1,400	240
125	7	1,600	220
150	6	1,800	200
175	5	2,000	180
200	4	2,200	160
225	3	2,400	140

Step one: Identify aggregate supply, aggregate demand (excluding investment), the investment function, and the average propensity to save. See Table 23.4 for the investment function and aggregate demand (excluding investment). Aggregate supply is 2,000 (from problem 4) and the average propensity to save is 0.1.

Step two: Find the savings supply (assumed to be inelastic). Total savings = 2,000 × 0.1 = 200.

Step three: Find the equilibrium real interest rate and investment level by equating the investment function with total savings. The capital market clears when the real interest rate equals 4 percent. Equilibrium investment is then 200.

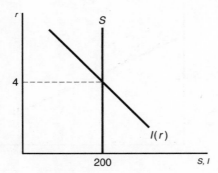

Step four: Find aggregate demand by adding investment to aggregate demand (excluding investment). Adding investment, which equals 200, to aggregate demand gives the following.

Aggregate demand = investment + aggregate demand (exclusive investment) (millions of guanos)	Price level
1,200	280
1,400	260
1,600	240
1,800	220
2,000	200
2,200	180
2,400	160
2,600	140

Step five: Find the equilibrium price level by equating aggregate demand and aggregate supply. The product market clears at a price level equal to 200.

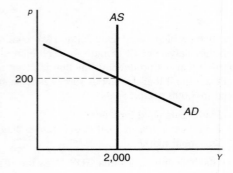

8   (Practice problem: product and capital markets) Continuing the analysis of El Dorado, recall that the short-run production function is given in Table 23.2 and output equals 60 billion dorals. Households save one-sixth of their income in El Dorado. The investment function and the aggregate demand curve (excluding investment) are given in Table 23.5.

a   Compute total savings.
b   Find the equilibrium real interest rate. Draw a diagram of the capital market.
c   Find aggregate demand.
d   Find the equilibrium price level. Draw a diagram of the product market.

Table 23.5

Investment function		Aggregate demand (excluding investment)	
Investment (billions of dorals)	Real interest rate	Aggregate demand (billions of dorals)	Price level
3	9	45	200
4	8	50	190
5	7	55	180
6	6	60	170
8	5	65	160
10	4	70	150
15	3	75	140
20	2	80	130

9 Continue with the analysis of Erehwemos, the production function of which is given in Table 23.3. Households save one-third of their income. The investment function and the aggregate demand (excluding investment) are given in Table 23.6. National income equals 15 billion wemos.

    a Compute total savings.

    b Find the equilibrium real interest rate. Draw a diagram of the capital market.

    c Find aggregate demand.

    d Find the equilibrium price level. Draw a diagram of the product market.

Table 23.6

Investment function		Aggregate demand (excluding investment)	
Investment (billions of wemos)	Real interest rate	Aggregate demand (billions of wemos)	Price level
1	10	7	330
2	9	8	320
3	8	9	310
4	7	10	300
5	6	11	290
6	5	12	280
7	4	13	270
8	3	14	260
9	2	15	250

The Labour Market and the Capital Market

The investment function gives the level of investment for each interest rate. It represents firms' judgments about the profitability of potential investments. Since these profits come in the future, the chief determinant of the investment function is business expectations. It also depends upon costs and thus is linked to the labour market through the real wage and to technology. We will not do a separate set of problems here, but keep in mind that the investment function shifts up when technology improves or the real wage falls, and it shifts down in the opposite cases.

The Full-Employment Model

Now we are ready to put the pieces together and use the entire full-employment model to show the effects of various exogenous changes, including shifts in the supply of labour, the short-run production function, the supply of savings, the demand for savings, the money supply, and the size of government. There will be a worked problem and a practice problem for each. As usual, the basic method involves starting with an equilibrium, identifying an exogenous change, shifting curves, finding the new equilibrium, and comparing. This general equilibrium model is complicated because adjustment in one market affects the others, and these effects must be traced through. We will pay special attention to these linkages.

Tool Kit 23.4 Using the Full-Employment Model

The full-employment model is a general equilibrium model. This means that when there is an exogenous change, it starts a process that reverberates through all three markets. To avoid confusion proceed in this step-by-step fashion.

Step one: Start with an equilibrium in the product, labour, and capital markets.

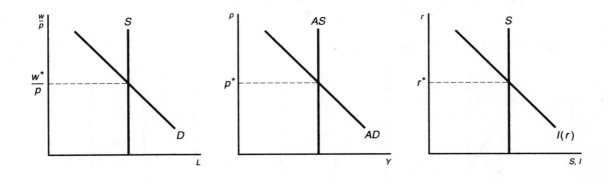

Step two: Identify an exogenous change and determine which curve shifts.

Step three: Shift the curve.

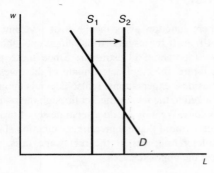

Step four: Find the new (partial) equilibrium in the market where the curve shifted.

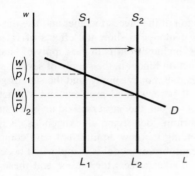

Step five: Trace through the links of the change to the related markets and shift the relevant curves.

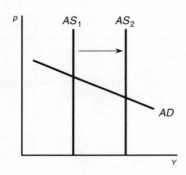
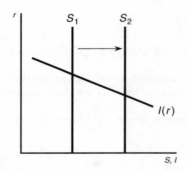

Step six: Find the new general equilibrium and compare.

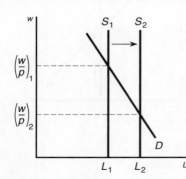
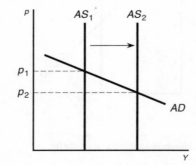
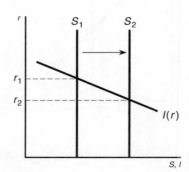

THE FULL-EMPLOYMENT MODEL

10 (Worked problem: full-employment model) Review problems 1, 4, and 7. This problem continues the analysis of Costa Guano.

a Draw a diagram illustrating the general equilibrium in the Costa Guano economy as solved for in the answers to problems 1, 4, and 7. In the following always begin with this equilibrium.

b Suppose that the money supply increases by 10 percent. Trace through the impact of this change in the economy. Show on the diagrams.

c Now suppose that the demand for investment rises by 50 million guanos at each interest rate. Trace through the impact of this change in the economy. Show on the diagrams.

d Now suppose that savings falls by 25 million. Of course, consumption will also increase by this same amount. Trace through the impact of this change in the economy. Show on the diagrams.

e Government expenditure and taxes increase by 50 million. Trace through the impact of this change in the economy. Show on the diagrams.

f The short-run production function doubles for each level of labor input.

g The supply of labour decreases to 3 million.

Step-by-step solution

Step one (a): Start with equilibrium in the product, labour, and capital markets.

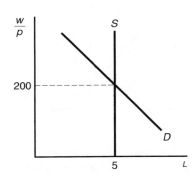

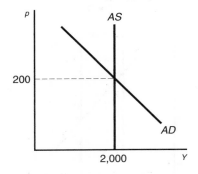

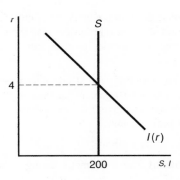

Step two (b): Identify an exogenous change and determine which curve shifts. Aggregate demand shifts up. The new aggregate demand schedule is as follows. Note that the price level has increased 10 percent for each level of output; for example, $280 + 0.1\,(280) = 308$.

Aggregate demand (millions of guanos)	Price level
1,200	308
1,400	296
1,600	264
1,800	242
2,000	220
2,200	198
2,400	176
2,600	154

Step three: Shift the curve.

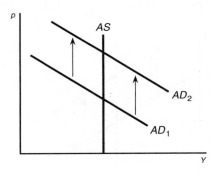

Step four: Find the new (partial) equilibrium in the market where the curve shifted. The new equilibrium price level is 220, which is 10 percent higher.

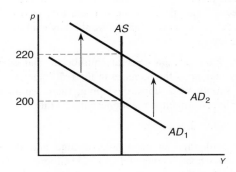

Step five: Trace through the links of the change to the related markets and shift the relevant curves. There are no other effects. Changes in the price level do not affect the capital and labour markets.

Step six: Find the new general equilibrium and compare. The only change is a 10 percent increase in the price level. No real magnitudes change; thus we conclude that the money supply increase is neutral.

Step one (c): Same as above.

Step two: Identify an exogenous change and determine which curve shifts. The investment function shifts up by 50 million at each real interest rate.

Step three: Shift the curve. The new investment function is given below.

Investment function

Investment (millions of guanos)	Real interest rate
100	10
125	9
150	8
175	7
200	6
225	5
250	4
275	3

Step four: Find the new (partial) equilibrium in the market where the curve shifted. The real interest rate rises to 6 percent. Because in this example the supply of savings is inelastic, there is no change in the level of investment.

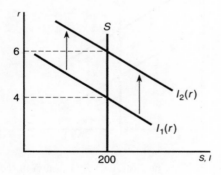

Step five: Trace through the links of the change to the related markets and shift the relevant curves. There are no other real effects. Aggregate demand may shift down because of the interest rate increase, but this would only lead to a fall in the price level.

Step six: Find the new general equilibrium and compare. The only change is the increase in the real interest rate. (If savings supply were upward sloping, there would be an increase in investment at the higher interest rate.)

Step one (d): Same as above.

Step two: Identify an exogenous change and determine which curve shifts. Savings falls to 175 million, and savings supply shifts to the left in the capital market. But the accom-

panying increase in consumption shifts aggregate demand to the right in the product market.

Step three: Shift the curves. The new aggregate demand is below.

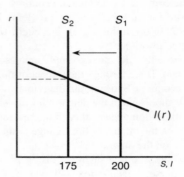

Aggregate demand (millions of guanos)	Price level
1,175	280
1,375	260
1,575	240
1,775	220
1,975	200
2,175	180
2,375	160
2,575	140

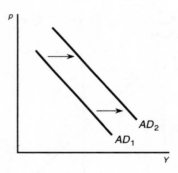

Step four: Find the new (partial) equilibrium in the market where the curve shifted. The real interest rate rises to 5 percent, and investment falls to 175 million. In the product market the price level increases.

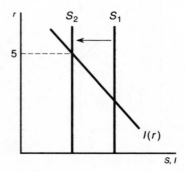

Step five: Trace through the links of the change to the related markets and shift the relevant curves. Aggregate demand must fall by the amount of the decrease in investment. This exactly offsets the increase in consumption; thus the price level returns to its original 200.

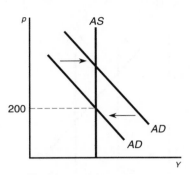

Step six: Find the new general equilibrium and compare. The new equilibrium has the same total output, although its composition is different. There is less investment (now only 175) and more consumption. Note how capital market changes do not affect current output. Of course, as time passes the changes in investment will affect the economy's growth rate.

Step one (e): Same as above.

Step two: Identify an exogenous change and determine which curve shifts. The increase in taxes reduces consumption. This shifts aggregate demand to the left. Because households save 10 percent of their income and consume 90 percent, consumption must fall by 45 million. The increase in government expenditure shifts aggregate demand to the right by 50 million. The net effect is a 5 million increase. In the capital market the supply shifts to the left by 5 million.

Step three: Shift the curves.

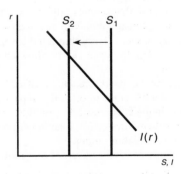

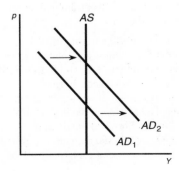

Step four: Find the new (partial) equilibrium in the market where the curve shifted. The real interest rate rises by less than 1 percent, and investment falls by the reduction in savings, which is 5 million. In the product market the price level increases slightly.

Step five: Trace through the links of the change to the related markets and shift the relevant curves. Aggregate demand must fall by the amount of the decrease in investment. This exactly offsets the 5 million increase in step three; thus the price level returns to its original 200.

Step six: Find the new general equilibrium and compare. The new equilibrium has the same total output, although its composition is different. There is less investment (now only 195), less consumption, and more government expenditure.

Step one (f): Same as above.

Step two: Identify an exogenous change and determine which curve shifts. The technological advance shifts the short-run production function up. Usually, this will shift the demand for both capital and labor to the right. In this case, we can calculate the new demand for labour by following the steps sketched in Tool Kit 23.1. Also, because the same amount of labour now produces more output, aggregate supply will shift to the right.

Step three: Shift the curves. The new production function and demand for labour are as follows.

Quantity of labour (million person years)	Output (millions of guanos)	Real wage (same as marginal product)
0	0	
1	1,200	1,200
2	2,200	1,000
3	3,000	800
4	3,600	600
5	4,000	400
6	4,200	200
7	4,300	100

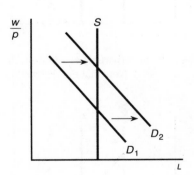

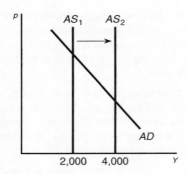

Step four: Find the new (partial) equilibrium in the market where the curve shifted. Labour supply, which equals 5 million, equals labour demand at a real wage of 400. Output increases to 4,000.

Step five: Trace through the links of the change to the related markets and shift the relevant curves. The shift to the right in aggregate supply reduces the price level.

Step six: Find the new general equilibrium and compare. Both output and the real wage double. Also, as firms anticipate higher returns from the better technology, the investment function will shift out, increasing the real interest rate.

Step one (g): Same as above.

Step two: Identify an exogenous change and determine which curve shifts. Labour supply shifts to the left to 3 million.

Step three: Shift the curve.

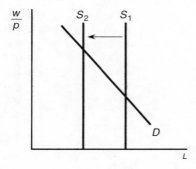

Step four: Find the new (partial) equilibrium in the market where the curve shifted. Note that the real wage increases to 400.

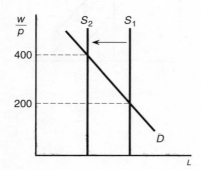

Step five: Trace through the links of the change to the related markets and shift the relevant curves. The reduction in labour reduces output to 1,500 million; thus aggregate supply shifts to the left, increasing the price level. In the capital market, the demand for investment probably falls as firms anticipate higher labour costs.

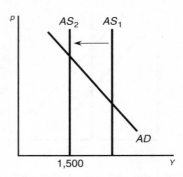

Step six: Find the new general equilibrium and compare.

11 (Practice problem: full-employment model) Review problems 2, 5, and 8. This problem continues the analysis of El Dorado.

   a   Draw a diagram illustrating the general equilibrium in the El Dorado economy as solved for in the answer to problems 2, 5, and 8. In the following always begin with this equilibrium.

   b   Suppose that the money supply increases by 20 percent. Trace through the impact of this change in the economy. Show on the diagram.

   c   Now suppose that the demand for investment rises by 5 billion dorals at each interest rate. Trace through the impact of this change in the economy. Show on the diagrams.

   d   Now suppose that savings fall by 5 billion dorals. Of course, consumption will also increase by this same amount. Trace through the impact of this change in the economy. Show on the diagrams.

   e   Government expenditure and taxes increase by 30 billion dorals. Trace through the impact of this change in the economy. Show on the diagrams.

   f   The short-run production function doubles for each level of labour input.

   g   The supply of labour increases to 5 million.

12 (Practice problem: full-employment model) Review problems 3, 6, and 9. This problem continues the analysis of Erewhemos.

   a   Draw a diagram illustrating the general equilibrium in the Erewhemos economy as solved for in the answer to problems 3, 6, and 9. In the following always begin with this equilibrium.

   b   Suppose that the money supply increases by 10 percent. Trace through the impact of this change in the economy. Show on the diagrams.

   c   Now suppose that the demand for investment rises by 3 billion wemos at each interest rate. Trace through the impact of this change in the economy. Show on the diagrams.

d   Now suppose that savings fall by 1 billion. Of course, consumption will also increase by this same amount. Trace through the impact of this change in the economy. Show on the diagrams.

e   Government expenditure and taxes fall by 3 billion. Trace through the impact of this change in the economy.

f   The short-run production function doubles for each level of output.

g   The supply of labour decreases to 4 million.

Answers to Problems

2   a   The marginal product schedule is as follows.

Quantity of labour (million person years)	Marginal product
1	25
2	20
3	15
4	10
5	5
6	3
7	2
8	1

b   The quantity of labour demanded is 6 thousand person years of labour.

3   a   The marginal product schedule is as follows.

Quantity of labour (million person years)	Marginal product
1	5,000
2	4,000
3	3,000
4	2,000
5	1,000
6	500

b   The quantity of labour demanded is 3 million person years.

5   a   The demand for labour is as follows.

Quantity of labour (million person years)	Real wage (dorals per year)
1	25
2	20
3	15
4	10
5	5
6	3
7	2
8	1

b   Real wage = 15; output = 60.

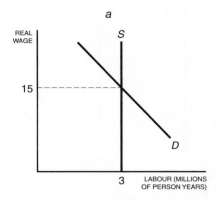

a

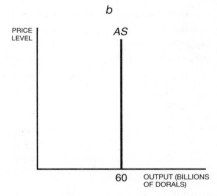

b

6   a   The demand for labour is as follows.

Quantity of labour (million person years)	Real wage (wemos per year)
1	5,000
2	4,000
3	3,000
4	2,000
5	1,000
6	500

b   Real wage = 1,000 wemos per year; output = 15,000.

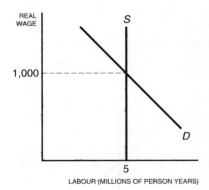

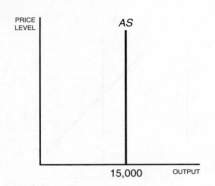

8   a   Total savings = 10 billion dorals.

     b   Real interest rate = 4 percent. Investment = 10 billion dorals.

     c   Aggregate demand

(billions of dorals)	Price level
55	200
60	190
65	180
70	170
75	160
80	150
85	140
90	130

     d   Equilibrium price level = 190.

9   a   Total savings = 1/3 × 15 = 5 billion wemos.

     b   Real interest rate = 6 percent; investment = 5 billion.

     c   Aggregate demand

(billions of wemos)	Price level
12	330
13	320
14	310
15	300
16	290
17	280
18	270
19	260
20	250

     d   Price level = 300.

11   a   General equilibrium is shown below.

b   Aggregate demand shifts up by 20 percent. The new price level equals 228, but there are no other changes. Money is neutral in the full-employment model.

c   The real interest rate rises to 7 percent. Because the supply of funds is inelastic, the level of investment remains at 10 billion dorals. There are no other changes. If the supply of funds sloped upwards, investment would increase and aggregate demand would shift out, driving up the price level. This would result in less consumption to offset the increase in investment.

d   The real interest rate rises to 7 percent. Investment falls to 5 billion dorals. In the product market the increase in consumption shifts aggregate demand to the right by 5 billion dorals, but this is offset by the decrease in investment. The price level remains constant. There are no other changes.

e   The increase in taxes reduces disposable income by 30 billion dorals. Since the average propensity to save is one-sixth, savings fall by 5 billion dorals and consumption falls by 25 billion dorals. The supply of savings shifts left and the real interest rate rises to 7 percent. Investment falls by 5 billion dorals. Aggregate demand shifts right by the 30 billion doral increase in government expenditure, but it shifts left by the 5 billion doral fall in investment plus the 25 billion doral fall in consumption. The net effect is no shift in aggregate demand. The price level remains the same and there are no other changes.

f   The real wage doubles to 30, and output increases to 120. Aggregate supply shifts right to 120 and the price level falls. Savings increase because national income doubles. Also, the demand for investment increases.

g   The supply of labour shifts to the right, driving the real wage down to 5 dorals. Output increases to 75; therefore aggregate supply shifts to the right. The increase in national income increases savings and the supply of funds shifts to the right.

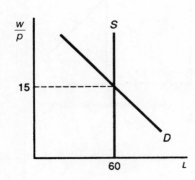

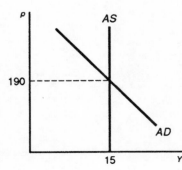

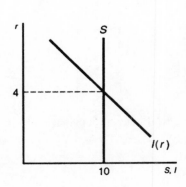

12   *a*   General equilibrium is shown below.

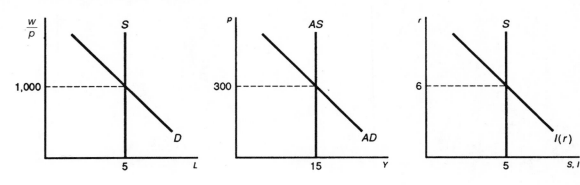

b   Aggregate demand shifts up by 10 percent. The new price level equals 330, but there are no other changes. Money is neutral in the full-employment model.

c   The real interest rate rises to 9 percent. Because the supply of funds is inelastic, the level of investment remains at 5 billion wemos. There are no other changes. If the supply of funds sloped upward, investment would increase and aggregate demand would shift out, driving up the price level. This would result in less consumption to offset the increase in investment.

d   The real interest rate rises to 7 percent. Investment falls by 1 billion wemos. In the product market the increase in consumption shifts aggregate demand to the right by 1 billion wemos, but this is offset by the decrease in investment. The price level remains constant. There are no other changes.

e   The decrease in taxes increases disposable income by 3 billion wemos. Since the average propensity to save is one-third, savings rise by 1 billion wemos and consumption rises by 2 billion wemos. The supply of savings shifts right and the real interest rate falls to 5 percent. Investment rises by 1 billion wemos. Aggregate demand shifts left by the 3 billion wemos decrease in government expenditure, but it shifts right by the 1 billion wemos rise in investment plus the 2 billion wemos rise in consumption. The net effect is no shift in aggregate demand. The price level remains the same and there are no other changes.

f   The real wage doubles to 2,000 wemos, and output increases to 30. Aggregate supply shifts right to 30 and the price level falls. Savings increase because national income doubles. Also, the demand for investment would increase.

g   The supply of labour shifts to the left, driving the real wage up to 2,000 wemos. Output decreases to 14 billion; therefore aggregate supply shifts to the left. The decrease in national income decreases savings and the supply of funds shifts to the left.

Chapter 24

USING THE FULL-EMPLOYMENT MODEL

Chapter Review

The full-employment model, developed in Chapter 23, is put to use analysing the budget deficit, the trade deficit, and the causes of economic growth. The center of attention is the capital market and the openness of the economy to international trade and investment. Considerable use is made of two identities: the basic trade identity and the savings-investment identity. With this chapter the discussion of full-employment macroeconomics draws to a close. The next chapter begins the analysis of unemployment macroeconomics.

ESSENTIAL CONCEPTS

1   The **budget deficit** is the difference between what the government receives in taxes and its expenditure.

2   National savings are the sum of private savings and government savings. When the government runs a deficit, government savings are negative. Thus, an increase in the deficit reduces national savings and shifts the supply of funds in the capital market to the left. In a closed economy this shift raises interest rates and reduces investment. In a small open economy interest rates are set on international capital markets. Because interest rates are fixed, investment will not change. The reduction in national savings will lead to increased borrowing from abroad.

3   The difference between imports and exports in a given year is the **trade deficit** which, according to the basic trade identity, must equal the inflows of foreign capital. The exchange of currencies for imports, exports, and capital flows is governed by the exchange rate, which is the relative price of two currencies. The **exchange rate** adjusts to bring into balance the demands and supplies of all currencies.

4   In an open economy the **savings-investment identity** says that investment equals total savings, which comprises private savings, government savings (the budget deficit), and foreign inflows of capital. Thus if the budget deficit is increased and private savings and investment remain unchanged, capital flows from abroad (which equal the trade deficit) must also increase. Trade deficits are a problem because the foreign borrowing that finances them accumulates into foreign indebtedness, which reduces the future standard of living. Policies to reduce the trade deficit focus on increasing private savings or reducing the budget deficit. Either would shift the supply of savings to the right.

5   Growth requires a more productive labour force, more and better capital, and technological advances. Investments in human capital, plant and equipment, and research and development enhance economic growth. These investments can be stimulated through the use of investment tax credits or accelerated depreciation. Another approach is to increase savings through individual retirement accounts or tax breaks on investment income. The net effect of these policies must balance the gain in private savings with the increased budget deficit caused by the loss in tax revenue. Finally, reduced government expenditure narrows the budget deficit, but reduced government investment may counteract the increased private investment.

BEHIND THE ESSENTIAL CONCEPTS

1   The connection between budget and trade deficits can be seen by examining two identities: the **basic trade identity** and the **savings-investment identity** for an open economy.

   a   The basic trade identity is

   Trade deficit = imports – exports = capital inflows.

   This means that if foreign capital flows into the United Kingdom (in greater amounts than U.K. capital flows abroad), then the United Kingdom runs a trade deficit.

   b   The savings-investment identity for an open economy is

   Private savings + capital inflows
                = investment + federal budget deficit.

   This identity says that unless investment falls and savings rise by enough to finance the budget deficit, the deficit results in capital inflows, which the basic trade identity says must equal the trade deficit.

   National debt is the cumulative amount that the government owes. The role of government deficits and national debt was highlighted by the Maastricht Treaty and Economic Monetary Union in Europe. The treaty set maximum conditions for both the government deficit and the national debt as percentages of GDP for entry into the Monetary Union. The conditions for entry into European Monetary Union stipulated a maximum government deficit of 3 percent of GDP and a maximum national debt of 60 percent of GDP. In Britain, the government deficit exceeded the critical limit in some years in the 1990s, but by the late 1990s it had been brought within the 3 percent limit. Despite meeting the criteria, Britain chose not to join the European Monetary Union in 1999.

2   Historically the U.K. national debt to GDP ratio rose dramatically during the two world wars as governments borrowed to finance expenditures associated with the war effort. After falling between 1945 and 1980, the national debt as a percentage of GDP in Britain followed a more cyclical pattern, rising in the first half of the 1980s, falling between 1986 and 1990, and rising again between 1990 and 1996. Despite this, in 1995 Britain's debt to GDP ratio was relatively low by international standards. In contrast, Britain's **trade deficit** has been rising for much of the postwar period although North Sea Oil improved the trade balance in the late 1970s and early 1980s. Trade deficits and fiscal deficits may sometimes be related, and in the United States in the mid-1980s there was much talk of the "twin deficits" problem.

3   Government borrowing can affect future generations in three ways. First, the burden can be shifted directly to the future generation by increasing taxes after the current generation has retired. Second, borrowing drives up interest rates and crowds out private investment. Finally, since much of the borrowing comes from abroad and foreign investors are attracted by higher U.K. interest rates, current borrowing increases foreign indebtedness. Repayment of foreign debt then requires reduced future living standards.

4   *In the federal U.S. government budget deficit caused the trade deficit* in the following way. Government borrowing to finance the budget deficit drove up interest rates and attracted capital flows from abroad. The increased foreign demand for dollars to lend and invest in the United States led to an appreciation of the dollar. The higher exchange rate made U.S. imports cheaper and U.S. exports more expensive. Foreigners bought fewer of the relatively expensive U.S. exports, while Americans bought more of the relatively cheaper imports, and the trade deficit skyrocketed.

5   The currency market is where different currencies are traded in order to make international transactions. Its price is called the exchange rate, and it is governed by supply and demand in a manner similar to other markets. There is a special language to this market, however. When the price of a country's currency rises, we say that its exchange rate *appreciates;* when it falls, we say that the currency *depreciates*. When the price is high, we say that the currency is strong. A weak currency simply means that the price is low.

SELF-TEST

True or False

1   The national debt is the difference between what the government receives in taxes and what it spends.

2   The Maastricht Treaty stipulated minimum criteria regarding government deficits and national debt as percentages of GDP as entry conditions into the European Monetary Union.

3   In a closed economy investment equals private savings.

4   Increased budget deficits reduce national savings.

5   In a small open economy increasing the budget deficit shifts supply to the left, increasing the interest rate and reducing investment.

6   The trade deficit always equals capital inflows from abroad.

7   The exchange rate is the relative price of two currencies.

8   When the price of a country's currency rises, it is said to appreciate.

9   According to the savings-investment identity, investment equals the sum of private savings, government savings, and capital flows from abroad.

10 Although it has run large trade deficits for more than a decade, the United States is still a creditor nation.

11 The trade deficit can be reduced by reducing investment or increasing savings.

12 The main keys to increased growth are improving the productivity of labour, adding capital, and advancing technology.

13 Human capital is the result of investment in education and training the labour force.

14 The interest elasticity of savings is quite high, indicating that an increase in the after-tax rate of return will increase savings substantially.

15 In a large open economy like the United States, savings and investment tend to move together.

Multiple Choice

1   Which of the following is true of the U.K. government budget deficit or national debt?

   a   By the late 1990s the government budget deficit exceeded the criterion laid out in the Maastricht Treaty.
   b   By the late 1990s the government budget deficit met the criterion laid out in the Maastricht Treaty.
   c   In the late 1990s the national debt was within the criterion laid out in the Maastricht Treaty.
   d   In the late 1990s the national debt exceeded the criterion laid out in the Maastricht Treaty.
   e   *a* and *c*.

2   In 1995 the debt to GDP ratio in Britain was about

   a   10 percent.
   b   20 percent.
   c   30 percent.
   d   40 percent.
   e   50 percent.

3   During much of the 1980s, the United States ran

   a   federal budget deficits and trade surpluses.
   b   federal budget surpluses and trade deficits.
   c   federal budget and trade surpluses.
   d   federal budget and trade deficits.
   e   balanced federal budgets and trade accounts.

4   In a closed economy investment equals

   a   private savings.
   b   private savings minus government savings.
   c   government savings.
   d   private savings minus government savings minus the budget deficit.
   e   the trade deficit.

5   In a closed economy an increase in the budget deficit

   a   reduces the interest rate and investment.
   b   does not change the interest rate or investment.
   c   increases the interest rate and investment.
   d   increases the interest rate but reduces investment.
   e   decreases the interest rate but increases investment.

6   In a small open economy an increase in the budget deficit

   a   reduces the interest rate and investment.
   b   does not change the interest rate or investment.
   c   increases the interest rate and investment.
   d   increases the interest rate but reduces investment.
   e   decreases the interest rate but increases investment.

7   When a German buys a U.S. government bond, the transaction is an example of

   a   imports.
   b   exports.
   c   capital inflows.
   d   capital outflows.
   e   currency exchange.

8   The basic trade identity says that

   a   imports must equal exports.
   b   imports must equal capital flows from abroad.
   c   exports must equal capital flows from abroad.
   d   the trade deficit must equal capital flows from abroad.
   e   capital flows from abroad must equal capital flows to overseas economies.

9   If a country invests more overseas than foreign countries invest in it, then

   a   its trade account must be in balance.
   b   it must run a trade surplus.
   c   it must run a trade deficit.
   d   it must balance its government budget.
   e   its government deficit must equal the net flow of capital to other countries.

10 The exchange rate is

   a   the trade deficit between two countries.
   b   a country's net inflow of capital.
   c   the relative price of two currencies.
   d   the rate of appreciation of a country's currency.
   e   the rate of depreciation of a country's currency.

11 In an open economy, the savings-investment identity says that private savings

   a   must equal private investment.
   b   plus capital flows from abroad must equal investment.
   c   plus capital flows from abroad must equal investment plus the government deficit.
   d   plus capital flows from abroad must equal the government deficits plus the trade deficit.
   e   plus capital flows from abroad must equal the government deficit plus the trade deficit plus investment.

12 According to the savings-investment identity for an open economy, investment may be financed from

   a   private savings.
   b   government savings.
   c   capital flows from abroad.
   d   all of the above.
   e   *a* and *c*.

13 Typically, developing economies

   a   borrow less than mature economies.

   b   borrow while mature economies lend.

   c   lend while mature economies borrow.

   d   neither borrow nor lend.

   e   borrow or lend at the same rates as mature economies.

14 In Britain, which of the following is true of exports or imports?

   a   Imports have grown as a proportion of GDP.

   b   Exports have grown as a proportion of GDP

   c   In 1995 imports counted for around 30 percent of GDP.

   d   In 1995 exports accounted for just under 30 percent of GDP.

   e   All of the above.

15 To reduce the trade deficit, a country can

   a   shift the investment function to the left or the savings curve to the right.

   b   shift the investment function to the right or the savings curve to the left.

   c   shift either the investment function or the savings curve to the right.

   d   shift either the investment function or the savings curve to the left.

   e   restrict the importation of foreign goods.

16 To increase investment in a closed economy,

   a   shift the investment function to the left or the savings curve to the right.

   b   shift the investment function to the right or the savings curve to the left.

   c   shift either the investment function or the savings curve to the right.

   d   shift either the investment function or the savings curve to the left.

   e   negotiate with foreign counties to reduce world interest rates.

17 Policies to enhance growth include

   a   investment in human capital.

   b   investment in plant and equipment.

   c   investment in research and development.

   d   public investments.

   e   all of the above.

18 A depreciation allowance

   a   allows firms to offset the annual depreciation of capital equipment against tax.

   b   is loosely dependent on the length of life of the machine.

   c   stimulates investment.

   d   is a once-off investment subsidy.

   e   *a, b,* and *c.*

19 Tax breaks for approved pension schemes, dividends, and capital gains

   a   increase savings because households have a greater incentive to save.

   b   decrease savings because smaller tax collection increases the budget deficit.

   c   may increase or decrease savings depending upon the relative magnitude of increased household savings and increased budget deficits.

   d   reduce savings because households have a greater incentive to save.

   e   increase savings because smaller tax collection increases the budget deficit.

20 Tax incentive schemes for savings may

   a   increase the total amount of savings.

   b   divert savings to tax exempt schemes.

   c   increase investment.

   d   all of the above.

   e   none of the above.

Completion

1 The _____ is the cumulative amount that the government owes.

2 The difference between government expenditures and revenues is the _____.

3 The basic trade identity says that the trade deficit must equal _____.

4 In an open economy, private savings plus capital flows from abroad must equal investment plus the _____.

5 The relative price of two currencies is called the _____.

6 When the price of a country's currency rises, it is said to _____.

7 The trade deficit equals the sum of the _____ deficits.

8 Investments in education and training produce _____.

9 An _____ allows firms to subtract the estimated costs of annual wear and tear of capital equipment from their taxes.

10 The measure of how much private savings increase when the after-tax interest rate falls is called the _____.

Answers to Self-Test

True or False

1	F	6	T	11	T
2	T	7	T	12	T
3	T	8	T	13	T
4	T	9	T	14	F
5	F	10	F	15	T

Multiple Choice

1	e	6	b	11	c	16	c
2	e	7	c	12	d	17	e
3	d	8	d	13	b	18	e
4	a	9	b	14	e	19	c
5	d	10	c	15	a	20	d

Completion

1   national debt
2   budget deficit
3   capital inflows from abroad
4   budget deficit
5   exchange rate
6   appreciate
7   government and private sector
8   human capital
9   investment depreciation allowance
10 interest elasticity of savings

Tools and Practice Problems

The discussion of the three major topics of this chapter—budget deficits, trade deficits, and growth—centers on the capital market. Government finances budget deficits by borrowing funds on the capital market. Trade deficits, through the basic trade identity, result in flows of foreign capital to the capital market. The engine of growth is investment in research, human capital, and capital equipment, and this investment must be financed with capital obtained on the capital market. An essential aspect of the capital market is its openness to international borrowing and savings. We first look at the model of a small open economy and then study the model of a large open economy. Throughout the discussion, the trade and savings investment identities will play an important role.

Small Open Economy

The international capital market is so huge that a small country's borrowing and lending have no effect on interest rates. Thus, a small open economy can borrow and lend on international markets at a fixed interest rate. Because its investment equals its quantity demanded at that fixed interest rate, domestic savings have no effect on investment. This separation of savings and investment implies that the most important effects of budget deficits concern flows of foreign capital. Another implication identifies trade deficits as a result of domestic savings and investment decisions. Tool Kit 24.1 shows how the small open economy model works.

Took Kit 24.1 Using the Small Open
Economy Model

For a small open economy the interest rate is fixed, determined on international capital markets that are large relative to the size of the economy. If the interest rate clears the domestic market, the trade account is balanced. Higher interest rates imply a trade surplus; lower interest rates imply a trade deficit. Follow these steps to analyse the working of the capital market for a small open economy.

Step one: Identify the world interest rate, the demand, and the supply of funds.

Step two: Find the level of investment. This is the quantity demanded, and it is read off the demand curve at the world interest rate.

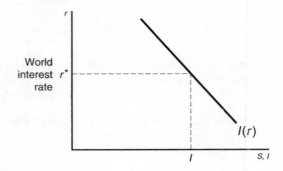

Step three: Find the level of savings. This is the quantity supplied, and it is read off the supply curve at the world interest rate.

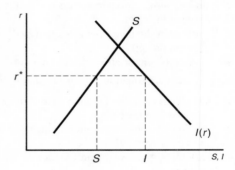

Step four: Find the level of capital inflows or outflows. If the quantity demanded exceeds the quantity supplied, then the country imports capital. Otherwise capital is exported.

Capital inflows from abroad
   = quantity demanded – quantity supplied (if positive).

Capital outflows to abroad
   = quantity supplied – quantity demanded (if positive).

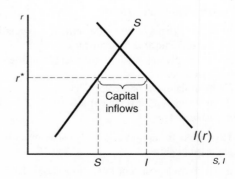

Step five: Find the trade deficit or surplus. If there are capital inflows, the country runs a trade deficit. If there are capital outflows, the country runs a trade surplus.

Trade deficit = inflows of foreign capital.

Trade surplus = outflows of foreign capital.

1 (Worked problem: small open economy) Costa Guano is a small open economy facing a world interest rate equal to 10 percent. Its domestic demand and supply of funds are given in Table 24.1.

a   Find the level of investment.
b   Find the level of savings.
c   Find the level of capital inflows or outflows.
d   Does the country run a trade deficit or surplus? How much is it?

Table 24.1

Interest rate (percent)	Demand for funds (millions of guanos)	Supply of funds (millions of guanos)
15	100	100
14	110	90
13	120	80
12	130	70
11	140	60
10	150	50
9	160	40
8	170	30

Step-by-step solution

Step one: Identify the world interest rate, the demand, and the supply of funds. The world interest rate is 10 percent and the demand and supply of funds are given in Table 24.1.

Step two: Find the level of investment. When the interest rate is 10 percent, the demand for funds (investment) equals 150 million guanos.

Step three: Find the level of savings. At an interest rate equal to 10 percent, savings (supply of funds) equals 50 million guanos.

Step four: Find the level of capital inflows or outflows. The quantity demanded exceeds the quantity supplied, so the country imports capital.

Capital inflows from abroad
   = quantity demanded – quantity supplied
   = 150 – 50 = 100 million guanos.

Step five: Find the trade deficit or surplus. If there are capital inflows, the country runs a trade deficit.

Trade deficit = inflows of foreign capital
   = 100 million guanos.

2 (Practice problem: small open economy) El Dorado is a small open economy facing a world interest rate equal to 9 percent. Its domestic demand and supply of funds are given in Table 24.2.

a   Find the level of investment.
b   Find the level of savings.
c   Find the level of capital inflows or outflows.
d   Does the country run a trade deficit or surplus? How much is it?

Table 24.2

Interest rate (percent)	Demand for funds (millions of dorals)	Supply of funds (millions of dorals)
11	200	400
10	225	350
9	250	300
8	275	250
7	300	200
6	325	150
5	350	100

3 (Practice problem: small open economy) Erehwemos is a small open economy facing a world interest rate equal to 15 percent. Its domestic demand and supply of funds are given in Table 24.3.

a   Find the level of investment.
b   Find the level of savings.
c   Find the level of capital inflows or outflows.
d   Does the country run a trade deficit or surplus? How much is it?

Table 24.3

Interest rate (percent)	Demand for funds (millions of wemos)	Supply of funds (millions of wemos)
20	50	50
19	60	45
18	70	40
17	80	35
16	90	30
15	100	25
14	110	20

Large Open Economy

The United States is a large open economy. This means that domestic savings affect interest rates and the level of investment. Approximately 80 percent of additional savings is invested in the United States. The remaining savings flows abroad. We can analyse large open economies by distinguishing between the domestic and total supply of funds. Tool Kit 24.2 shows how this is done.

Tool Kit 24.2 Using the Large Open Economy Model

   Unlike the small open economy model, where foreign savings are perfectly elastic, for the large open economy foreign savings are upward sloping. The interest rate is determined where the total savings supply intersects the domestic demand for funds. Follow these steps.

Step one: Identify the foreign supply of savings, the domestic supply of savings, and the domestic demand for funds (investment function).

Step two: Calculate the total savings supply curve. For each interest rate add the quantity of foreign and domestic savings.

   Total savings = foreign savings + domestic savings.

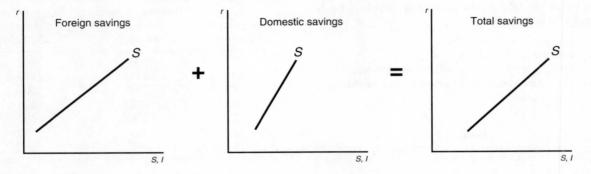

Step three: Find the interest rate that clears the market.

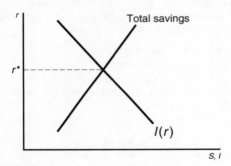

Step four: Find the level of investment. This is the quantity demanded at the equilibrium interest rate.

Step five: Find the level of domestic savings. This is read off the domestic supply of funds at the equilibrium interest rate.

Step six: Calculate the level of capital flows. Recall that this is also the level of the trade deficit.

   Capital inflows from abroad = trade deficit = quantity demanded – quantity supplied (if positive).

   Capital outflows to abroad = trade surplus = quantity supplied – quantity demanded (if positive).

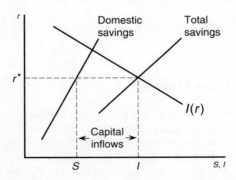

4   (Worked problem: large open economy) Table 24.4 gives the foreign supply of funds, the domestic supply of funds, and the demand for funds (investment function) for a large open economy such as in the United States.

a   Calculate the total supply of funds.
b   Find the equilibrium interest rate.
c   Does this country import or export capital? How much?
d   What is the size of the trade deficit or surplus?

Table 24.4

Interest rate (percent)	Foreign supply (billions of dollars)	Domestic supply (billions of dollars)	Domestic demand (billions of dollars)
12	10,000	15,000	13,000
11	9,000	13,000	16,000
10	8,000	11,000	19,000
9	7,000	9,000	22,000
8	6,000	7,000	25,000
7	5,000	5,000	30,000

Step-by-step solution

Step one: Identify the foreign supply of savings, the domestic supply of savings, and the domestic demand for funds. They are given in Table 24.4.

Step two: Calculate the total savings supply curve. For each interest rate, add the quantity of foreign and domestic savings.

Total savings = foreign savings + domestic savings.

At 12 percent, total savings = $10,000 + $15,000 = $25,000 billion. At 11 percent, total savings = $9,000 + $13,000 = $22,000 billion. Continuing, we get the total supply.

Interest rate (percent)	Total supply (billions of dollars)
12	10,000 + 15,000 = 25,000
11	9,000 + 13,000 = 22,000
10	8,000 + 11,000 = 19,000
9	7,000 + 9,000 = 16,000
8	6,000 + 7,000 = 13,000
7	5,000 + 5,000 = 10,000

Step three: Find the interest rate that clears the market. Supply and demand are equal at $19,000 billion when the interest rate is 10 percent.

Step four: Find the level of investment. This is the quantity demanded at the equilibrium interest rate, and it equals $19,000 million.

Step five: Find the level of domestic savings. This is read off the domestic supply of funds at the equilibrium interest rate. At 10 percent the domestic supply is $11,000 billion.

Step six: Calculate the level of capital flows. Recall that this is also the level of the trade deficit. Since demand exceeds supply, there will be inflows of capital.

Capital inflows from abroad = trade deficit

= quantity demanded – quantity supplied

= 19,000 – 11,000 = $8,000 million.

5   (Practice problem: large open economy) Table 24.5 gives the foreign supply of funds, the domestic supply of funds, and the demand for funds (investment function) for a large open economy.

a   Calculate the total supply of funds.
b   Find the equilibrium interest rate.
c   Does this country import or export capital? How much?
d   What is the size of the trade deficit or surplus?

Table 24.5

Interest rate (percent)	Foreign supply (billions of dollars)	Domestic supply (billions of dollars)	Domestic demand (billions of dollars)
15	1,000	500	900
14	800	400	1,200
13	600	300	1,500
12	400	200	1,800
11	200	100	2,100
10	100	50	2,500

6   (Practice problem: the United States, a large open economy) Table 24.6 gives the foreign supply of funds, the domestic supply of funds, and the demand for funds (investment function) for a large open economy.

a   Calculate the total supply of funds.
b   Find the equilibrium interest rate.
c   Does this country import or export capital? How much?
d   What is the size of the trade deficit or surplus?

Table 24.6

Interest rate (percent)	Foreign supply (billions of dollars)	Domestic supply (billions of dollars)	Domestic demand (billions of dollars)
8	200	50	100
7	180	45	110
6	160	40	130
5	140	35	140
4	120	30	150
3	100	25	160
2	80	20	170

Answers to Problems

2   a   Investment = 250 million dorals.
    b   Savings = 300 million dorals.
    c   Capital outflows = 50 million dorals.
    d   Trade surplus = 50 million dorals.

3   a   Investment = 100 million wemos.
    b   Savings = 25 million wemos.

c   Capital inflows = 75 million wemos.

d   Trade surplus = 75 million wemos.

5   *a*

Interest rate (percent)	Total supply (billions of dollars)
15	1,000 + 500 = 1,500
14	800 + 400 = 1,200
13	600 + 300 = 900
12	400 + 200 = 600
11	200 + 100 = 300
10	100 + 50 = 150

b   Interest rate = 14 percent.

c   Capital inflows = $1,200 − $400 = $800 billion.

d   Trade deficit = $800.

6   *a*

Interest rate (percent)	Total supply (billions of dollars)
8	200 + 50 = 250
7	180 + 45 = 225
6	160 + 40 = 200
5	140 + 35 = 175
4	120 + 30 = 150
3	100 + 25 = 125
2	80 + 20 = 100

b   Interest rate = 4 percent.

c   Capital inflows = $150 − $30 = $120 billion.

d   Trade deficit = $120 billion.

Part Six

UNEMPLOYMENT MACROECONOMICS

Chapter 25

OVERVIEW OF UNEMPLOYMENT MACROECONOMICS

Chapter Review

Beginning the unemployment part of the course, this chapter sketches how the full-employment model is modified to study downturns in the economy when there is excess capacity and unemployment persists at a high rate. The discussion of the consequences of fixed wages and price for the labour, product, and capital markets provides the framework for the remainder of this part. (In Part Four we see how wages and prices adjust slowly, leading to the investigation of dynamics.) The chapter concludes by applying this framework to recent macroeconomic history.

ESSENTIAL CONCEPTS

1   Slow adjustment of wages to changes in the supply and demand for labour is the basic explanation for the high levels of unemployment that periodically trouble the economy. This chapter and the others in Part Three develop the model of the economy under the assumptions that wages and prices are rigid and that there is no net change in the capital stock. While this is a simplification, it does expose the basic structure of the economy and gives results that mirror the behaviour of labour and product markets in the short run.

2   The aggregate labour market includes all of the workers and jobs in the economy. If the wages settle at the market-clearing level, the economy would be at full employment. Anyone willing to work at the going wage could find a job. In reality, this is not the case, because wages are somewhat inflexible. When the demand for labour shifts to the left and the wage fails to adjust downwards, unemployment exists. The key to understanding unemployment lies in three questions: what causes shifts in the demand for labour, why do wages fail to adjust, and why does the shortage take the form of unemployment rather than a shared reduction in hours among workers? The latter questions are postponed until Part Seven; shifts in labour demand are the focus here.

3   In the product market the vertical aggregate supply curve intersects with the downward-sloping aggregate demand curve. If prices settle at the market-clearing level, the economy would produce its potential GDP. Prices are costly to change, however, and in the short run may be rigid. In this case, if demand shifts to the left, for example, the economy's output will fall to the quantity demanded, which is less than aggregate supply. There is excess capacity.

4   Any **demand shock**, such as economic downturns abroad or a loss in business confidence, can bring about

a demand shock and production level below the economy's capacity. When there is excess capacity, government may use fiscal policy to shift aggregate demand to the right, restoring full employment without waiting for the slow adjustment of wages and prices. On the other hand, supply shifts have no impact on output when there is excess capacity.

5   The central bank uses monetary policy to affect interest rates. This can also shift aggregate demand in that lower interest rates may stimulate investment. Central banks are also interested in controlling inflation by limiting aggregate demand. Given their primary concern with monetary variables, such as inflation and interest rates, central banks may be too aggressive in raising interest rates and push the economy into recession. In Britain, the newly established Monetary Policy Committee, chaired by the governor of the Bank of England, sets interest rates to meet government inflation targets.

6   Examples of the effects of fiscal and monetary policies include the Barber "dash for growth" based on tax cuts and a very expansionary fiscal policy that, by chance, happened to coincide with the quadrupling of the oil price in 1973. The level of unemployment fell in response to the dash for growth but quickly rose again in response to the rise in the price of oil, the increase in the value of imports, and the associated fall in the value of the pound. Inflation, fueled by higher oil prices and fiscal expansion, rose from 7.1 percent in 1972 to 9.2 percent in 1973 and to 24.3 percent in 1975. In contrast to the Barber dash for growth, Mrs. Thatcher's government used tight monetary and fiscal policies to try to reduce inflation. These policies had the effect of raising unemployment to 11.1 percent of the work force in 1986. Although inflation did fall, it was more as a result of reduced aggregate demand associated with high unemployment than through effective control of the money supply.

BEHIND THE ESSENTIAL CONCEPTS

1   The supply of labour is quite inelastic, but not perfectly so. If the wage rises, more people are willing to work. If the wage that you could currently earn rose high enough, you might get a part-time job, increase the hours at the part-time job you already have, or even drop out of college to get a full-time job. It follows that if the wage falls, individuals voluntarily leave the labour force. Involuntary unemployment, however, differs from voluntary unemployment. If the wage is stuck above the market-clearing level, there is an excess supply of workers, each of whom would like a job at the going wage. Because there is a shortage of jobs, these individuals are involuntarily unemployed.

2   The basic structure of the model developed in this chapter is the same as the full-employment model studied in Chapters 23 and 24. The economy divides into three markets: product, labour, and capital. Further, the various supplies and demands have essentially the same interpretation, and the markets are interdependent. The key difference is that here we assume that price and

wages are rigid, whereas in the full-employment version, prices adjust to clear the markets. The reason for the two approaches is that the economy behaves in the long run as the full-employment model predicts. This is natural because prices and wages have time to adjust in the long run. However, in the short run, before there is time for adjustment, the fixed price approach works better.

3   While aggregate demand plays a minor role in full-employment macroeconomics, it takes center stage in unemployment macroeconomics. With fixed prices the short side of the product market determines the output level. When demand exceeds supply, supply is the short side and output is at full employment, but there is upward pressure on prices. When demand falls short of supply, demand is the short side, and output is set at the intersection of demand and the price level. According to this model economic downturns result from insufficient demand.

4   In microeconomics we often look at one market at a time. Macroeconomics, however, is a general equilibrium discipline. We must keep an eye on product, labour, and capital markets. The fundamental lesson from general equilibrium analysis is that markets are linked. The key link between the product and labour market is that shifts in output bring about shifts in the demand for labour. The key link between the capital and product market is that interest rates affect investment and consumption, the two chief components of aggregate demand.

SELF-TEST

True or False

1   The basic explanation for unemployment is that wages do not adjust quickly to their market-clearing levels.

2   The focus of this chapter is the short run, when prices and wages are rigid and the net change in the capital stock is small.

3   Involuntary unemployment results when the demand for labour shifts to the right and wages fail to adjust.

4   If reductions in the demand for labour were shared equally among workers, there would not be unemployment, but rather underemployment.

5   The supply curve for labour is quite elastic.

6   If the labour supply curve is upward sloping and wages adjust, then any reduction in the number of jobs represents involuntary unemployment.

7   Most economists agree that the primary causes of disturbance in the labour market are shifts in the demand curve.

8   In the model of the product market prices are assumed to be rigid.

9   A rightward shift in aggregate demand leads to excess capacity and involuntary unemployment.

10   When the economy experiences excess capacity, a rightward shift in aggregate supply increases output.

11   When the economy experiences excess capacity, a

rightward shift in aggregate demand increases output.

12 Lower interest rates encourage investment, shifting aggregate demand to the right.

13 The Barber dash for growth was an example of an expansionary fiscal policy.

14 Tight monetary and fiscal policies under the Thatcher government in the early 1980s were intended to shift the aggregate supply curve to the left.

15 Tight monetary and fiscal policies under the Thatcher government in the early 1980s had the effect of shifting the aggregate demand curve to the left and raising unemployment.

Multiple Choice

1 Unemployment macroeconomics deals with the short run, a period of time when

    a product prices are rigid.
    b nominal wages are rigid.
    c real wages are rigid.
    d the net change in the capital stock is small.
    e all of the above.

2 The basic model of the labour market in this chapter is based on the assumption that

    a wages are fixed.
    b product prices are fixed.
    c interest rates and product prices are fixed.
    d wages and product prices are fixed.
    e wages, interest rates, and product prices are fixed.

3 In modern economies, the labour supply curve is

    a perfectly elastic.
    b relatively flat.
    c horizontal.
    d relatively inelastic.
    e downward sloping.

4 Suppose that the demand for labor increases. If the supply of labour is perfectly inelastic, then

    a wages increase.
    b employment increases.
    c both wages and employment increase.
    d wages decrease.
    e both wages and employment decrease.

5 If the wage is the market-clearing wage, then

    a any unemployment is involuntary.
    b any unemployment is voluntary.
    c unemployment is voluntary at low wages and at high wages.
    d the supply of labour is relatively elastic.
    e none of the above.

6 If every worker who wants a job at prevailing wages has one, then there is

    a full employment.
    b no voluntary unemployment.
    c no inflation.
    d all of the above.
    e *b* and *c*.

7 Suppose the demand curve for labour shifts to the left. Then

    a there is full employment if wages are flexible.
    b if wages are inflexible, there is involuntary unemployment.
    c there is unemployment if the supply of labor is relatively inelastic.
    d the supply of labor will also shift to the left.
    e a and b.

8 Suppose the demand curve for labour shifts to the left. If wages are rigid, then

    a most workers work fewer hours.
    b wages rise.
    c most workers work more hours.
    d most workers work the same number of hours, some individuals will not be able to find employment.
    e most workers work more hours, but some job vacancies will not be filled.

9 The aggregate supply curve is

    a vertical.
    b relatively flat at low levels of output but relatively steep at higher levels of output.
    c relatively steep at low levels of output but relatively flat at higher levels of output.
    d relatively inelastic.
    e horizontal.

10 The aggregate demand and supply model of the product market presented in this chapter is based on the assumption that

    a wages are fixed.
    b product prices are fixed.
    c interest rates and product prices are fixed.
    d wages and product prices are fixed.
    e wages, interest rates, and product prices are fixed.

11 There is excess capacity when

    a aggregate supply is to the left of aggregate demand at the fixed price level.
    b aggregate demand is to the left of aggregate supply at the fixed price level.
    c the price level is fixed above its market clearing level.
    d the demand for labour is elastic.
    e interest rates are set on international capital markets.

12 When there is excess capacity

    a an increase in aggregate demand has no effect on output.
    b an increase in aggregate supply puts upward pressure on prices.
    c a decrease in aggregate supply puts upward pressure on prices.
    d an increase in aggregate demand increases output with little effect on prices.
    e an increase in aggregate supply increases output and reduces the price level.

13 When there is excess demand,

    a output is below the economy's potential GDP.
    b output is above the economy's potential GDP.

c   output equals the economy's potential GDP.

d   there is downward pressure on prices.

e   *a* and *d*.

14   When there is excess demand,

a   an increase in aggregate demand has no effect on output.

b   an increase in aggregate supply puts upward pressure on prices.

c   a decrease in aggregate supply puts upward pressure on prices.

d   an increase in aggregate demand increases output with little effect on prices.

e   none of the above.

15   When the government increases defence spending in order to shift aggregate demand to the right, this is an example of

a   monetary policy.

b   fiscal policy.

c   supply restrictions.

d   protectionism.

e   monetary stimulus.

16   Central banks and, in the case of the United Kingdom, the Monetary Policy Committee have the power to change

a   taxes.

b   subsidies.

c   fiscal policy.

d   interest rates.

e   minimum wage rates.

17   Monetary policy affects aggregate demand through its effect on

a   capacity.

b   unemployment.

c   interest rates.

d   real wages.

e   the price level.

18   The oil price shock in 1973–74 caused

a   the aggregate demand curve to shift to the left.

b   the aggregate demand curve to shift to the right.

c   the aggregate supply curve to shift to the left.

d   the aggregate supply curve to shift to the right.

e   inflation to fall and employment to increase.

19   The oil price shocks of the early 1970s caused

a   aggregate demand to shift to the left.

b   aggregate supply to shift to the left.

c   aggregate demand to shift to the right.

d   aggregate supply to shift to the right.

e   no change in either aggregate supply or demand.

20   The onset of the 1991 recession was due in part to

a   overaggressive monetary policy.

b   the Gulf War inspired oil price shock.

c   a weak banking system in the aftermath of the savings and loan crisis.

d   all of the above.

e   none of the above.

Completion

1   When employers pay the market-clearing wage, any unemployment is _____.

2   If the demand for labour shifts to the left and there is no adjustment in wages, unemployment _____.

3   If the price level is greater than the level at which aggregate demand equals aggregate supply, then there is an excess _____ of goods.

4   Leftward shifts in aggregate demand that lead to downturns in the economy are called _____.

5   When the government increases its expenditures in order to shift aggregate demand to the right and eliminate excess capacity it is performing _____.

6   In Britain interest rate changes are made by _____.

7   During a period of excess capacity, a rightward shift in _____ leaves output unchanged.

8   When there is full employment, a rightward shift in _____ puts upward pressure on prices.

9   The Barber dash fro growth shifted the aggregate demand curve to the _____.

10   In the early 1980s in Britain, Thatcher's tight monetary policy shifted the aggregate demand curve to the _____.

Answers to Self-Test

True or False

1	T	6	F	11	T
2	T	7	T	12	T
3	T	8	T	13	T
4	T	9	F	14	F
5	F	10	F	15	T

Multiple Choice

1	e	6	a	11	b	16	d
2	e	7	e	12	d	17	c
3	d	8	d	13	c	18	c
4	a	9	a	14	a	19	b
5	b	10	d	15	b	20	d

Completion

1   voluntary

2   increases

3   supply

4   demand shocks

5   fiscal policy

6   the Monetary Policy Committee

7   aggregate supply

8   aggregate demand

9   right

10   left

Tools and Practice Problems

In the aggregate labour market, the economy's levels of employment, unemployment, and real wages are determined. Unemployment results from the failure of wages to adjust to the market-clearing level, and several problems explore this relationship between sticky wages and unemployment. The output of the economy is determined in the product market, but with rigid prices it may not be clear. The key to analysing how low output is affected by changes in the economy is to find out whether the initial equilibrium is at the intersection of aggregate demand and supply or one of excess demand or supply. Several problems study this issue.

Unemployment and Rigid Wages

When real wages remain stuck above market-clearing levels, the number of workers willing to work at the going wage exceeds the number of jobs available. This excess supply of labour is involuntary unemployment and is part of the overall unemployment rate. In this section we calculate the real

---

Tool Kit 25.1 Determining the Unemployment Rate

Above-market-clearing real wages lead to unemployment. The level of unemployment is the amount of excess supply in the labour market. Follow these steps to see this relationship.

Step one: Identify the demand curve, the supply curve, and the nominal wage and price level.

Step two: Find the real wage by adjusting the nominal wage for inflation:

real wage = (nominal wage/price index) × 100.

Step three: Use the demand schedule to find the quantity demanded at this real wage. This is the number of jobs available.

Step four: Use the supply schedule to find the quantity supplied at this real wage. This is the number of workers willing to work at the going wage.

Step five: Find the quantity of unemployment by subtracting the quantity demanded from the quantity supplied:

Unemployment
= quantity supplied – quantity demanded.

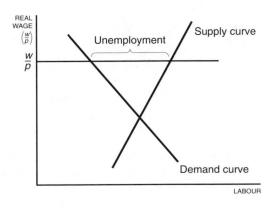

---

wage by adjusting the nominal wage for inflation and then determine the level of unemployment. Tool Kit 25.1 shows how to proceed.

1   (Worked problem: unemployment rate) The nominal wage level equals £2,400 per month, and the price index equals 120. Table 25.1 gives the demand and supply of labour. Find the level of unemployment.

Table 25.1

Real wage	Demand	Supply
£2,400	6,000	18,000
£2,200	7,000	16,000
£2,000	8,000	14,000
£1,800	9,000	12,000
£1,600	10,000	10,000
£1,400	11,000	8,000
£1,200	12,000	6,000

Step-by-step solution

Step one: Identify the demand curve, the supply curve, and the nominal wage and price level. The demand and supply are given in Table 25.1, the nominal wage is £2,400, and the price index equals 120.

Step two: Find the real wage by adjusting the nominal wage for inflation:

Real wage = (£2,400/120) × 100 = £2,000.

Step three: Substitute the real wage into the demand curve, and find the quantity demanded. It is 8,000.

Step four: Substitute the real wage into the supply curve, and find the quantity supplied. It is 14,000.

Step five: Find the quantity of unemployment by subtracting the quantity demanded from the quantity supplied:

Unemployment = 14,000 – 8,000 = 6,000.

2   (Practice problem: unemployment rate) Suppose that the nominal wage level remains at £2,400, as in problem 1, and the demand and supply curves remain as given in Table 25.1 but the price level increases to 150. Find the new level of unemployment.

3   (Practice problem: unemployment rate) Suppose that the nominal wage is £3,300, the price index is 150, and the demand and supply curves are as given in Table 25.1. Find the level of unemployment.

4   (Practice problem: unemployment rate) For each of the following, find the level of unemployment given the demand and supply of labour shown in Table 25.2.

a   Nominal wage = £50,000; price level = 100.
b   Nominal wage = £50,000; price level = 125.
c   Nominal wage = £50,000; price level = 167.
d   Nominal wage = £60,000; price level = 120.

Table 25.2

Real wage	Demand	Supply
£60,000	8,000	26,000
£55,000	10,000	25,000
£50,000	12,000	24,000
£45,000	14,000	23,000
£40,000	16,000	22,000
£35,000	18,000	21,000
£30,000	20,000	20,000
£25,000	22,000	19,000

The Labour Market with Rigid Wages

When either the demand or supply of labour shifts and wages fail to adjust to the market-clearing level, there is unemployment. In modern economies, wages exhibit downward rigidity, although they do adjust upwards when conditions warrant. In the following problems real wages are assumed to be inflexible downwards, but flexible upwards. Tool Kit 25.2 shows how to analyse labour markets under these conditions.

Tool Kit 25.2 Analyzing the Labour Market with Rigid Real Wages and Unemployment

If the labour market is at its market-clearing equilibrium and demand or supply shifts, it may not move to the new market-clearing equilibrium if the real wage does not adjust. Follow these steps to analyse a labour market in which the real wage is rigid when market conditions call for it to fall.

Step one: Start with a market-clearing equilibrium in the labour market.

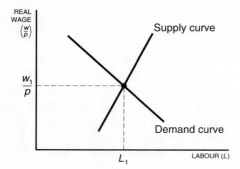

Step two: Identify a cause, and determine which curve shifts.

Step three: Shift the supply or demand curve.

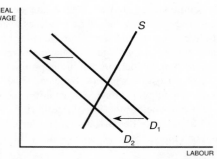

Step four: Find the new equilibrium. If there is excess demand, increase the real wage to the market-clearing level. If there is excess supply, keep the real wage constant.

Step five: Show the level of unemployment as the difference between quantity demanded and quantity supplied.

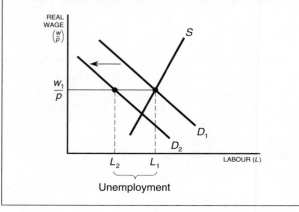

5   (Worked problem: rigid wages) Suppose a deep recession strikes the economy. Show the effect on real wages, unemployment, and the labour market.

Step-by-step solution

Step one: Start with an equilibrium.

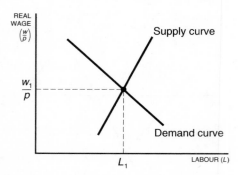

Step two: Identify a cause, and determine which curve shifts. The economy's output falls in a recession, and this reduces the demand for labour.

Step three: Shift the demand curve. It shifts left.

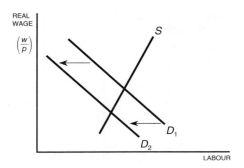

Step four: Find the new equilibrium. Although there is an excess supply of labour, wages do not adjust downward, because they are assumed rigid.

Step five: Show the level of unemployment.

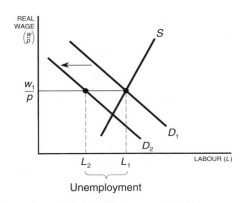

Unemployment

6   (Practice problem: rigid wages) Improvements in child care provision make it easier for single parents to enter the labour market. Show the effect on real wages and unemployment assuming rigid wages.

7   (Practice problem: rigid wages) For each of the following, show the effect on real wages, unemployment, and the labour market.

  a   The economy booms, and its output increases.
  b   Changes in equal opportunities policy make it easier for women to enter the labour market.
  c   The demand for U.S. exports soars, and the economy's output expands to meet the demand.
  d   The baby boom generation has already reached working age, and the number of new entrants declines.
  e   Recession overseas reduces the demand for U.K. exports, and the economy falls into a recession.

The Product Market with Rigid Prices

When prices are rigid, the economy may not reach equilibrium at full employment. In this case the short-run equilibrium will occur where the rigid price level meets the short side of the market. If aggregate demand is less than aggregate supply, the economy will have excess capacity. If aggregate demand at this price level exceeds aggregate supply, the economy will produce at capacity, but the price level

will remain below the intersection. In these two cases the economy responds differently to shifts in aggregate demand or supply. Tool Kit 25.3 shows how to analyse the product market with rigid prices.

Tool Kit 25.3 Using Aggregate Demand and Supply When Prices Are Rigid

When prices are rigid, aggregate demand and supply shift for the same reasons they shift when prices are flexible. Table 25.3 lists some important causes of these shifts. The difference is that output must adjust to the short side of the market. These steps show how to find the short-run equilibrium when prices are rigid.

Table 25.3

Shifts in aggregate demand: changes in consumption, investment, government spending, or net exports

Shifts in aggregate supply: increases in capacity (aggregate supply shifts right) or changes in import prices (aggregate supply shifts up or down)

Step one: Start with an equilibrium. This may be at the intersection of aggregate supply and demand or not.

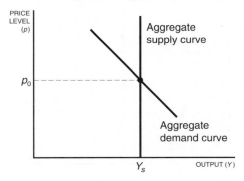

Step two: Identify an exogenous cause and determine which curve shifts and in what direction.

Step three: Shift the curve.

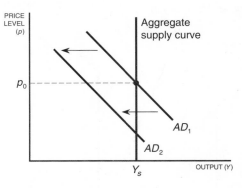

Step four: Find the new equilibrium level of output. This will occur at the intersection of the rigid price level and the short side of the market; that is the lesser of aggregate demand or supply.

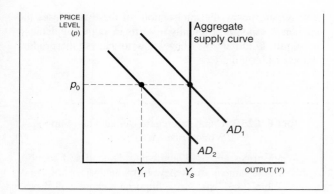

8   (Worked problem: aggregate demand and supply) The
    economy is in deep recession with high unemployment
    and a great deal of excess capacity. The government
    increases depreciation allowances to 100 percent, and
    firms respond with larger levels of private investment.
    Show the effect on equilibrium output.

Step-by-step solution

Step one: Start with an equilibrium. Because the economy is
in deep recession, this will be on the flat portion of the aggregate supply curve.

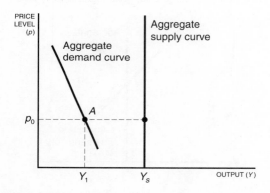

Step two: Identify a cause, and determine which curve shifts
and in what direction. The increase in investment shifts aggregate demand to the right.

Step three: Shift the curve.

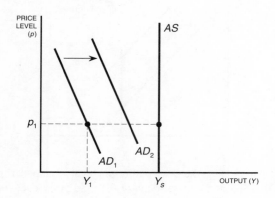

Step four: Find the new equilibrium, and compare the output
and price levels. Output increases with little or no change in
the price level.

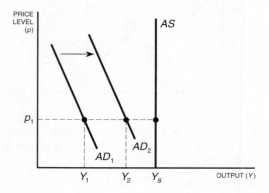

9   (Practice problem: aggregate demand and supply) The
    economy is brimming with activity. Although unem-
    ployment and idle production capacity are at ten-year
    lows, foreign demand for U.K. exports surges still
    higher. Show the effect on equilibrium output.

10 (Practice problem: aggregate demand and supply) For
    each of the following, show the effect on equilibrium
    output.

    a   The economy is in equilibrium at the intersection
          of aggregate demand and aggregate supply. Tight
          monetary policy raises interest rates, and this caus-
          es a dramatic decline in new investment.
    b   The economy is in deep recession, and the govern-
          ment stimulates private consumption with a tax
          cut.
    c   The economy is at maximum capacity, and the
          government increases its spending.
    d   The economy is in equilibrium at the intersection
          of aggregate demand and aggregate supply. The
          government increases income taxes.
    e   The economy is in deep recession, and foreign
          demand for exports falls still further.
    f   The economy is in equilibrium at the intersection
          of aggregate demand and aggregate supply. The
          price of imported oil rises by 50 percent.
    g   The economy is in deep recession, and the price of
          imported oil rises by 50 percent.
    h   The economy is at maximum capacity. There is
          excess demand. Capacity expands.

Answers to Problems

2   Real wage = (£2,400/150) × 100 = £1,600;
    unemployment = 10,000 − 10,000 = 0.

3   Real wage = (£3,300/150) × 100 = £2,200;
    unemployment = 16,000 − 7,000 = 9,000.

4   *a*   Real wage = (£50,000/100) × 100 = £50,000;
          unemployment = 24,000 − 12,000 = 12,000.
    b   Real wage = (£50,000/125) × 100 = £40,000;
          unemployment = 22,000 − 16,000 = 6,000.
    c   Real wage = (£50,000/167) × 100 = £30,000;

unemployment = 20,000 − 20,000 = 0.

d Real wage = (£60,000/120) × 100 = £50,000;
unemployment = 24,000 − 12,000 = 12,000.

6 The supply curve shifts to the right, and the wage fails
to adjust downwards; this results in unemployment
equal to $L_s - L_1$.

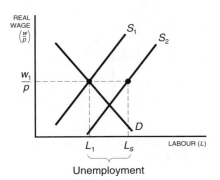

7 *a* The demand curve shifts to the right, and wages
adjust upwards to clear the market.

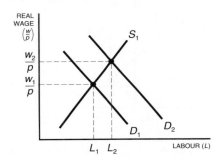

b The supply curve shifts to the right, and the wage
fails to adjust downwards; this results in unemployment equal to $L_s - L_1$.

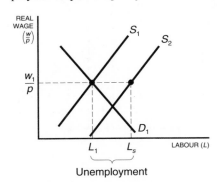

c The demand curve shifts to the right, and wage adjusts upwards to clear the market.

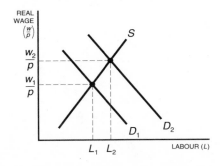

d The supply curve shifts to the left, and the wage
adjusts upwards to clear the market.

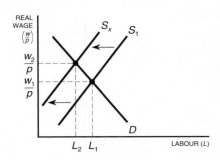

e The demand curve shifts to the left, and the wage
fails to adjust downwards; this results in unemployment equal to $L1 - L_s$.

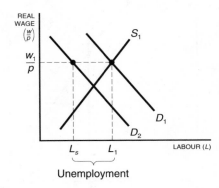

9 Aggregate demand shifts to the right; this leaves
output unchanged.

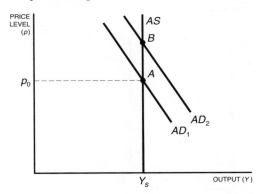

10 *a* Aggregate demand shifts to the left and decreases
output.

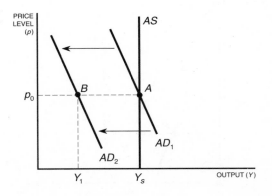

b   Aggregate demand shifts to the right; this increases output.

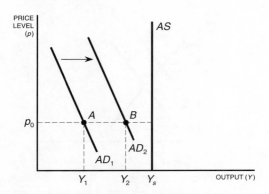

c   Aggregate demand shifts to the right; this leaves output unchanged.

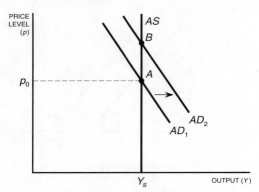

d   Aggregate demand shifts to the left and decreases output.

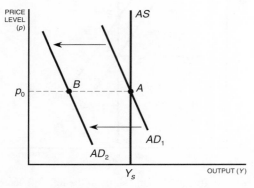

e   Aggregate demand shifts to the left; this decreases output.

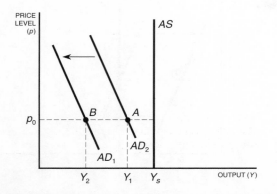

f   Aggregate supply shifts to the left; this decreases output.

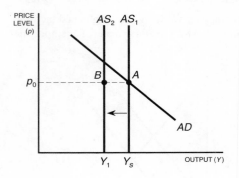

g   Aggregate supply shifts to the left; this leaves output unchanged.

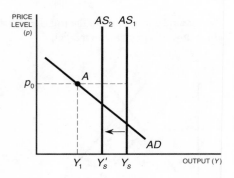

h   Aggregate supply shifts to the right; this increases output.

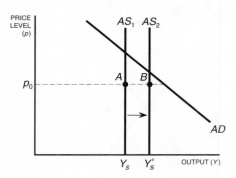

Chapter 26

AGGREGATE DEMAND

Chapter Review

Chapter 25 showed how in the short run the economy's level of output is governed by aggregate demand. This chapter takes a look behind aggregate demand and explains what it is composed of and how it is determined. Income-expenditure analysis is used to show how the economy reaches an equilibrium on the demand side and why the equilibrium changes. The multiplier process, by which changes in spending ripple through the economy, is explained.

ESSENTIAL CONCEPTS

1   **Income-expenditure analysis** starts with the assumption that the price level is fixed. Aggregate expenditure then depend upon national income, and the **aggregate expenditures schedule,** drawn in Figure 26.1, shows how aggregate expenditures increase as national income increases. Because national income equals national output (GDP), the horizontal axis also measures output. Aggregate expenditure equals output where the aggregate expenditures schedule crosses the 45-degree line. This is the equilibrium, and at this point all of the economy's output is purchased.

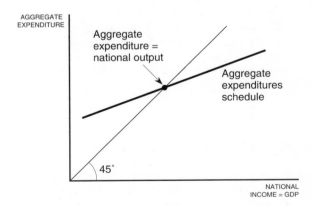

Figure 26.1

2   Aggregate expenditure comprises consumption, investment, government purchases, and net exports, as shown by the equation

$$AE = C + I + G + E.$$

Changes in any of the components of expenditure shift the aggregate expenditures schedule up or down and cause equilibrium output to change. In Figure 26.2 AE shifts up and output increases.

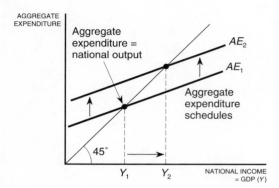

Figure 26.2

3 The **consumption function** describes the relationship between income and consumption. The additional consumption resulting from a one-pound increase in income is the **marginal propensity to consume** (*MPC*), which is the slope of the consumption function. The **marginal propensity to save** (*MPS*) is the additional amount saved out of a one-pound increase in income.

4 The **investment multiplier** shows that when aggregate expenditure shifts, the change in output is greater than the change in spending. It works as follows. Suppose investment increases. This investment causes incomes to rise and, through the marginal propensity to consume, causes a second round of extra consumption spending. This extra round of consumption further increases incomes and generates a third round of spending. The process continues, and the ultimate increase in output equals the multiplier times the initial change in spending. The formula for the multiplier is $1/(1 - MPC)$.

5 Income taxation makes the consumption function flatter because some of the extra income is taken in taxes, rather than spent. Similarly, in an open economy, some spending leaves the economy for imported goods, further flattening the aggregate expenditures schedule. Both taxes and imports cause the multiplier to be smaller.

BEHIND THE ESSENTIAL CONCEPTS

1 You might wonder why we need an entire chapter on aggregate demand. Although it appears simple (just another downward-sloping demand), the aggregate demand curve masks some complexity. Income-expenditure analysis shows that the amount of aggregate demand at any given price level is an equilibrium, where desired spending is brought into equality with output. Like most equilibria in the economy, this one requires some adjustment time as inventories rise or fall towards their appropriate level and as successive rounds of spending work their way through the economy. For some purposes we may be satisfied with limiting our attention to the aggregate demand curve. Other purposes require the deeper look given by the income-expenditure approach.

2 You might wonder what role prices play in income-expenditure analysis. Prices are determined by supply and demand, but here we are concerned only with the demand side. At this level of analysis, prices are fixed; one way of thinking about this is that the economy is operating on the flat portion of the aggregate supply curve.

3 How does the economy reach equilibrium without price adjustment? **Inventories** play the key role.

   a If GDP is below equilibrium, then households and firms want to buy more than the economy produces. Firms notice this when they sell the goods they have on inventory. Firms produce more to restore inventories, and GDP increases.

   b If GDP is above equilibrium, the story is reversed. Households and firms buy less than the economy produces, inventories of unsold goods accumulate, and firms cut back on production. GDP falls.

4 A helpful way to understand the multiplier process and why the multiplier is smaller when there are taxes and trade is to think in terms of injections and leakages. Suppose that the economy gets an injection of new spending, say an increase in exports. Some people will receive this money, and they will save some and spend some. We say that the money that is saved "leaks" out of the system. The money that is spent becomes other people's income; they in turn save some and spend some, and the process continues. The total amount of spending generated is a multiple of the initial injection. But any leakage reduces the total amount of spending. Clearly, taxes go to the government. That is a leakage. Money spent on imports goes abroad—another leakage. More leakages mean less spending and a smaller multiplier.

SELF-TEST

True or False

1 Aggregate expenditures include what households, firms, and government spend on goods and services.

2 As income increases by one pound, aggregate expenditure increases by less than one pound.

3 The statement that national income equals national output is an example of an equilibrium relationship.

4 The statement that aggregate expenditure equals national output is an example of an equilibrium relationship.

5 Unplanned inventories equal zero in equilibrium.

6 The aggregate expenditures schedule gives total desired spending at each price level.

7 Aggregate expenditure equals consumption plus investment plus government purchases plus net exports.

8 Net exports equal imports minus exports.

9   The relationship between a household's income and its consumption is called its consumption function.

10   Disposable income equals national income plus taxes.

11   The marginal propensity to consume equals the marginal propensity to save.

12   The multiplier equals 1 divided by the marginal propensity to consume.

13   An increase in investment causes equilibrium output to increase by more than the change in investment.

14   A higher tax rate on income means that the multiplier is larger.

15   Imports increase as income increases.

Multiple Choice

1   This chapter focuses on the case where
   a   aggregate demand equals aggregate supply.
   b   aggregate demand is greater than aggregate supply.
   c   aggregate demand is less than aggregate supply.
   d   prices are fully flexible.
   e   the economy's capacity is fully utilized.

2   The aggregate expenditures schedule traces out the relationship between the economy's total expenditures and national income,
   a   keeping output fixed.
   b   at a given price level.
   c   as price changes to clear the product market.
   d   holding consumption fixed.
   e   holding net exports fixed.

3   As income increases, aggregate expenditures
   a   increase.
   b   decrease.
   c   remain the same.
   d   increase or decrease depending upon how product prices change.
   e   increase or decrease depending upon events in the capital market.

4   The marginal propensity to consume gives the
   a   fraction of extra income that will be consumed.
   b   ratio of consumption to income.
   c   fraction of extra consumption that comes from wage income.
   d   fraction of extra consumption that comes from interest and dividends.
   e   ratio of consumption out of wage income to consumption out of interest and dividend income.

5   The aggregate expenditures schedule
   a   is horizontal.
   b   is horizontal for low levels of output, upward sloping for intermediate levels of output, and steep at high levels of output.
   c   is upward sloping.
   d   is downward sloping.
   e   is a 45-degree line.

6   If national income were zero, consumption would
   a   be zero.
   b   be positive because people would borrow or consume out of savings.
   c   equal autonomous consumption.
   d   b and c.
   e   none of the above.

7   The statement that national income is equal to national output is an example of
   a   an equilibrium relationship.
   b   an identity.
   c   a behavioural relationship.
   d   a hypothesis.
   e   an assumption.

8   The statement that aggregate expenditure equals aggregate output is an example of
   a   an equilibrium relationship.
   b   an identity.
   c   a behavioural relationship.
   d   a hypothesis.
   e   an assumption.

9   In equilibrium, it is true that
   a   the output of the economy must be purchased.
   b   aggregate expenditure equals national output.
   c   aggregate expenditure equals what households, firms, and government want to spend at the equilibrium level of national income.
   d   unplanned inventories equal zero.
   e   all of the above.

10   An upward shift in the aggregate expenditures schedule occurs when
   a   households, firms, and government decide to spend more at each level of income.
   b   households, firms, and government decide to spend less at each level of income.
   c   households, firms, and government decide to spend less at each price level.
   d   households, firms, and government decide to spend more at each price level.
   e   the economy is in recession.

11   Which of the following is *not* a component of aggregate expenditure?
   a   Consumption
   b   Investment
   c   Government purchases
   d   Net exports
   e   Taxes

12   The household's consumption function traces out the relationship between its consumption and its
   a   investment.
   b   income.
   c   taxes.
   d   inflation rate.
   e   total expenditure.

13   The slope of the aggregate expenditures schedule equals

a   zero.
b   the average propensity to save.
c   the marginal propensity to save.
d   the average propensity to consume.
e   the marginal propensity to consume.

14   The marginal propensity to save equals

a   the marginal propensity to consume.
b   1 plus the marginal propensity to consume.
c   1 minus the marginal propensity to consume.
d   the reciprocal of the marginal propensity to consume.
e   none of the above.

15   Autonomous consumption is

a   the extra consumption out of an additional pound of income.
b   the ratio of consumption to disposable income.
c   that part of consumption that does not depend upon disposable income.
d   the extra savings out of an additional pound of income.
e   the level of consumption when desired inventories equal zero.

16   When investment increases, equilibrium output

a   increases by more than the change in investment.
b   increases by less than the change in investment.
c   increases by the same amount as the change in investment.
d   decreases by less than the change in investment.
e   decreases by more than the change in investment.

17   In the simple model without taxes, the multiplier equals

a   1 divided by the marginal propensity to save.
b   the marginal propensity to save.
c   the marginal propensity to consume.
d   1 divided by the marginal propensity to consume.
e   zero.

18   Adding taxes to the income-expenditure model causes

a   disposable income to be less than national income.
b   the aggregate expenditures schedule to be flatter.
c   the multiplier to be smaller.
d   the aggregate consumption function to be flatter.
e   all of the above.

19   The amount of each extra pound of disposable income spent on imports is the marginal propensity to

a   import.
b   consume.
c   save.
d   export.
e   invest.

20   Adding international trade to the income-expenditure model causes

a   the multiplier to be larger.
b   the aggregate expenditures schedule to be flatter.
c   the aggregate expenditures schedule to be steeper.
d   the equilibrium level of output to be lower.
e   *a* and *c*.

Completion

1   The relationship between the economy's total expenditures and national income is summarised by the _____.

2   The _____ traces the relationship between consumption and disposable income.

3   The portion of consumption that does not depend upon income is called _____.

4   The fraction of additional income that is consumed is called the _____.

5   National output increases by more than the amount of a given increase in investment by a factor called the _____.

6   When firms cannot sell all that they produce, they experience an increase in _____.

7   The relationship between national income and imports is summarised by the _____.

8   The additional imports purchased as a result of a one-pound increase in income is called the _____.

9   An economy actively engaged in international trade and investment is called an _____.

10   The difference between imports and exports equals a _____.

Answers to Self-Test

True or False

1	T	6	F	11	F
2	T	7	T	12	F
3	F	8	F	13	T
4	T	9	T	14	F
5	T	10	F	15	T

Multiple Choice

1	c	6	d	11	e	16	a
2	b	7	b	12	b	17	a
3	a	8	a	13	e	18	e
4	a	9	e	14	c	19	a
5	c	10	a	15	c	20	b

Completion

1   aggregate expenditures schedule
2   consumption function
3   autonomous consumption
4   marginal propensity to consume
5   multiplier
6   unplanned inventories
7   import function
8   marginal propensity to import
9   open economy
10   trade deficit

Tools and Practice Problems

The topic of this section is income-expenditure analysis. We begin with an explanation of the tools needed and follow with problems involving economies with no taxes or imports. For each, we find the consumption function, calculate the aggregate expenditures schedule, and solve for the economy's equilibrium output. We then study the multiplier process, which shows how a change in spending brings about a larger change in equilibrium output. Finally, we consider progressively more complicated problems with income taxes and imports, where the net export function must be calculated. An important lesson of these latter problems concerns how taxes and imports affect the multiplier and the stability of the economy.

Tool Kit 26.1 Finding the Aggregate
Consumption Function

Aggregate expenditure equals the sum of consumption, investment, government spending, and net exports. The first step is to find the aggregate consumption function, which shows the level of consumption that corresponds to each level of national income.

Step one: Identify the marginal propensity to consume (*MPC*), autonomous consumption, and the income tax rate.

Step two: Calculate the aggregate consumption function by substituting various values of national income into the following formula:

Aggregate consumption
  = autonomous consumption
    + [national income (1 − tax rate)] *MPC*.

(Note that the term in square brackets is disposable income, which equals national income when the tax rate is zero.)

Tool Kit 26.2 Finding the Net Export Function

In an open economy, net exports must be included in aggregate expenditure. The **net export function** shows the level of net exports that corresponds to each level of national income.

Step one: Identify the marginal propensity to import (*MPI*), the tax rate, and the level of exports.

Step two: Calculate the import function by substituting various levels of national income into the following formula:

Imports = [national income (1 − tax rate)] *MPI*.

Step three: Find the net export function by subtracting imports from exports for every level of national income:

Net exports = exports − imports.

Tool Kit 26.3 Finding the Aggregate
Expenditures Schedule

With the aggregate consumption and net export functions in place, the aggregate expenditures schedule can be calculated. The aggregate expenditures schedule shows the level of aggregate spending corresponding to each level of national income.

Step one: Identify the aggregate consumption function, the level of investment spending, the level of government spending, and the net export function.

Step two: Calculate the aggregate expenditures schedule by summing consumption, investment, government spending, and net exports for each level of national income:

$$AE = C + I + G + X.$$

Tool Kit 26.4 Using Income-Expenditure Analysis
to Determine the Equilibrium

We find the equilibrium level of output and national income (which are always equal), where the aggregate expenditures schedule crosses the 45-degree line. At this point, consumers, firms, government, and foreigners spend just enough to purchase the economy's output.

Step one: Identify the aggregate expenditures schedule.

Step two: Choose a level of national income, and find the corresponding level of aggregate expenditure. If they are equal, stop. This is the equilibrium level of output.

Step three: If aggregate expenditure exceeds national income, then inventories will fall, firms will increase production, and output will expand. Choose a greater level of national income, and repeat step one. If aggregate expenditure is less than national income, then inventories will rise, firms will cut back production, and output will decrease. Choose a lower level of national income, and repeat step one.

Step four: Continue until the equilibrium is found.

Tool Kit 26.5 Using Multiplier Analysis to Find the
Ultimate Change in Output Caused by an Initial
Change in Spending

The great lesson of income-expenditure analysis is that an initial change in spending ripples through the economy and ultimately results in a larger change in output. The process by which this happens is the multiplier process, and the multiplier itself shows how much larger than the initial change in spending is the ultimate change in output.

Step one: Identify the marginal propensity to consume, the tax rate, the marginal propensity to import, and the initial change in spending.

Step two: Calculate the multiplier. Use the appropriate formula:

No taxes or imports	$1/(1 - MPC)$
Income taxes	$1/[1 - MPC(1 - \text{tax rate})]$
Open economy (no taxes)	$1/[1 - (MPC + MPI)]$
Open economy with taxes	$1/[1 - (MPC - MPI)(1 - \text{tax rate})]$

Step three: Calculate the ultimate change in output by multiplying the initial change in spending by the multiplier:

Change in output = change in spending × multiplier.

Step four: Verify the result in step three by adding the change in spending to the original aggregate expenditures schedule and solving for the new equilibrium level of output.

1 (Worked problem: income-expenditure analysis) For years, Costa Guano has remained closed to foreign trade and investment. The government of the isolated country spends no money and collects none in taxes. Autonomous consumption is 300 million guanos (the currency of Costa Guano), and the marginal propensity to consume equals 0.8. Finally, domestic private investment equals 100 million guanos.

a Find the aggregate consumption function.
b Find the aggregate expenditures schedule.
c Calculate equilibrium output and national income.
d Brimming with confidence, Costa Guano's firms increase their investment spending by 100 million guanos (for a total of 200 million guanos). Calculate the multiplier and the ultimate change in output brought about by this increase in investment.

Step-by-step solution

Step one (a): Find the aggregate consumption function. Identify the MPC, autonomous consumption, and the tax rate. The MPC is 0.8 and autonomous consumption is 300 million guanos, but the tax rate is zero.

Step two: Calculate the aggregate consumption function. When national income equals zero, aggregate consumption equals autonomous consumption (300 million). At 500 million guanos in national income, consumption equals 300 + 0.8 (500) = 700 million guanos. Continuing, we derive Table 26.1.

Table 26.1

National income (millions of guanos)	Aggregate consumption (millions of guanos)
0	300
500	700
1,000	1,100
1,500	1,500
2,000	1,900
2,500	2,300
3,000	2,700

Step one (b): Find the aggregate expenditures schedule. Identify the aggregate consumption function, investment, government spending, and the net export function. The aggregate consumption function is given in Table 26.1, and investment equals 100 million guanos. Government spending and net exports equal zero.

Step two: Calculate the aggregate expenditures schedule adding investment and consumption, as shown in Table 26.2.

Table 26.2

National income	Aggregate consumption	Investment	Aggregate expenditure
	(millions of guanos)		
0	300	100	400
500	700	100	800
1,000	1,100	100	1,200
1,500	1,500	100	1,600
2,000	1,900	100	2,000
2,500	2,300	100	2,400
3,000	2,700	100	2,800

Step one (c): Calculate equilibrium output and national income. Identify the aggregate expenditures schedule. It appears in Table 26.2.

Step two: Choose a level of national income. When national income is 2,000 million guanos, aggregate expenditure equals 2,000 million guanos. Consumers and firms purchase exactly the economy's output of 2,000 million.

Step one (d): Calculate the multiplier and the ultimate change in output brought about by this increase in investment of 100 million (from 100 to 200). Identify the marginal propensity to consume, the tax rate, the marginal propensity to import, and the initial change in spending. The MPC is 0.8, the initial change in spending is 100 million guanos. There are no taxes or imports.

Step two: Calculate the multiplier. Because there are no taxes or imports, the multiplier equals

$1/(1 - MPC) = 1/(1 - 0.8) = 1/0.2 = 5.$

Step three: Calculate the ultimate change in output:

Change in output = 100 × 5 = 500 million.

Step four: Verify the result in step three by adding the change in spending to the original aggregate expenditures schedule and solving for the new equilibrium level of output. The new aggregate expenditures schedule is given in Table 26.3.

Table 26.3

National income	Aggregate consumption	Investment	Aggregate expenditure
(millions of guanos)			
0	300	200	500
500	700	200	900
1,000	1,100	200	1,300
1,500	1,500	200	1,700
2,000	1,900	200	2,100
2,500	2,300	200	2,500
3,000	2,700	200	2,900

The new equilibrium level of output is 2,500 million guanos, which is 500 million guanos more than originally. It checks!

2 (Practice problem: income-expenditure analysis) El Dorado, an insular economy closed to foreign trade and investment, has no income-based taxes, and its government spends nothing. The marginal propensity to consume is 0.9, autonomous consumption is 5 billion dorals (the currency of El Dorado), and private investment totals 1 billion dorals. (Hint: Choose national income in intervals of 10 billion; that is, 0, 10, 20, and so on.)

a Find the aggregate consumption function.
b Find the aggregate expenditures schedule.
c Calculate equilibrium output and national income.
d After a period of stability, investment in El Dorado jumps to 2 billion dorals. Calculate the multiplier and the ultimate change in output brought about by this increase in investment.

3 (Practice problem: income-expenditure analysis) In Erehwemos, there is no taxation and also no government spending. The economy is closed to the outside world. All investment is undertaken by private domestic firms, and the total is 2 billion wemos (the Erehwemosian currency). The marginal propensity to consume is 0.75, and autonomous consumption is 2 billion wemos. (Hint: Choose national income levels in intervals of 4 billion; that is, 0, 4, 8, 12, and so on.)

a Find the aggregate consumption function.
b Find the aggregate expenditures schedule.
c Calculate equilibrium output and national income.
d Investment climbs to 4 billion. Calculate the multiplier and the ultimate change in output brought about by this increase in investment.

4 (Worked problem: income-expenditure analysis) This problem builds on problem 1. Recognising the need for infrastructure investment, the government of Costa Guano institutes an income tax with a flat rate of 25 percent and spends 300 million guanos. Private investment continues at 200 million guanos, the marginal propensity to consume is 0.8, and autonomous consumption equals 300 million guanos. The economy remains closed to foreign trade.

a Find the consumption function.
b Find the aggregate expenditures schedule.

c Find the equilibrium level of output.
d Suppose that the government raises its spending by 200 million guanos (for a total of 500 million). Calculate the multiplier, and solve for the ultimate change in output brought about by the increase in government spending.

Step-by-step solution

Step one (a): Identify the marginal propensity to consume, autonomous consumption, and the income tax rate. The *MPC* is 0.8, autonomous consumption equals 300 million guanos, and the income tax rate is 25 percent.

Step two: Calculate the aggregate consumption function. When national income equals zero, aggregate consumption equals autonomous consumption (300 million guanos). At 500 million guanos in national income, aggregate consumption = $300 + 500(1 - 0.25) \times 0.8 = 600$ million guanos. Continuing, we derive Table 26.4.

Table 26.4

National income (millions of guanos)	Aggregate consumption (millions of guanos)
0	300
500	600
1,000	900
1,500	1,200
2,000	1,500
2,500	1,800
3,000	2,100

Step one (b): Identify the aggregate consumption function, investment, government spending, and the net export function. The aggregate consumption function is given in Table 26.4, investment equals 200 million guanos, and government spending equals 300 million guanos. Net exports remain zero.

Step two: Calculate the aggregate expenditures schedule by adding consumption, investment, and government spending, as shown in Table 26.5.

Table 26.5

National income	Aggregate consumption	Investment	Government spending	Aggregate expenditures
(millions of guanos)				
0	300	200	300	800
500	600	200	300	1,100
1,000	900	200	300	1,400
1,500	1,200	200	300	1,700
2,000	1,500	200	300	2,000
2,500	1,800	200	300	2,300
3,000	2,100	200	300	2,600

Step one (c): Identify the aggregate expenditures schedule. It appears in Table 26.5.

Step two: Choose a level of national income. When national income is 2,000 million guanos, aggregate expenditure equals 2,000 million guanos. Consumers and firms purchase exactly the economy's output of 2,000 million guanos.

Step one (d): Identify the marginal propensity to consume, the tax rate, the marginal propensity to import, and the initial change in spending. The *MPC* is 0.8, and the initial change in spending is 200 million guanos. The tax rate is 25 percent, but there are no imports.

Step two: Calculate the multiplier. Because there is an income tax but no imports, the multiplier equals

$$1/[1 - MPC\,(1 - \text{tax rate})] = 1/[1 - 0.8\,(1 - 0.25)]$$
$$= 1/(1 - 0.6) = 1/0.4 = 2.5.$$

(In problem 1, there was no income tax and the multiplier equaled 5. Here, the income tax reduces the multiplier to 2.5.)

Step three: Calculate the ultimate change in output:

Change in output = 200 × 2.5 = 500 million guanos.

Step four: Verify the result in step three by adding the change in spending to the original aggregate expenditures schedule and solving for the new equilibrium level of output. The new aggregate expenditures schedule is given in Table 26.6.

Table 26.6

National income	Aggregate consumption	Investment	Government spending	Aggregate expenditure
		(millions of guanos)		
0	300	200	500	1,000
500	600	200	500	1,300
1,000	900	200	500	1,600
1,500	1,200	200	500	1,900
2,000	1,500	200	500	2,200
2,500	1,800	200	500	2,500
3,000	2,100	200	500	2,800

The new equilibrium level of output is 2,500 million guanos, which is 500 million more than originally. It checks. The economy is more stable with the income tax, for it took a 200-million change in spending to change output by 500 million guanos in problem 1, where there was no tax.

5   (Practice problem: income-expenditure analysis) This problem builds on problem 2. An income tax system is passed by El Dorado's Council of Ministers. The flat tax rate is 1/9 on all income, and the government plans to spend 3 billion dorals. The marginal propensity to consume remains at 0.9, autonomous consumption is 5 billion dorals, and private investment continues at 2 billion dorals.

a   Find the consumption function.
b   Find the aggregate expenditures schedule.
c   Find the equilibrium level of output.
d   Suppose that the government raises its spending by 4 billion dorals (for a total of 7 billion dorals). Calculate the multiplier, and solve for the ultimate change in output brought about by the increase in government spending.

6   (Practice problem: income-expenditure analysis) This problem builds on problem 3. Erehwemos institutes an income tax with a flat rate of 1/3. The government

spends 2 billion wemos. The marginal propensity to consume remains at 0.75, autonomous consumption equals 2 billion wemos, and private investment equals 4 billion wemos.

a   Find the aggregate consumption function.
b   Find the aggregate expenditures schedule.
c   Calculate equilibrium output and national income.
d   Responding to the war threat from neighboring Erehwon, the government doubles spending. The increase in government spending is 2 billion wemos (for a total of 4 billion wemos). Calculate the multiplier and the ultimate change in output brought about by this increase in government spending.

7   (Worked problem: income-expenditure analysis) This problem builds on problems 1 and 4. Costa Guano has opened its economy to foreign trade. It exports 500 million guanos in world markets. Its citizens have developed tastes for foreign goods, however, and their marginal propensity to import is 1/3. Autonomous consumption remains at 300 million guanos, investment equals 200 million guanos, government spending has returned to 300 million guanos, the marginal propensity to consume is 0.8, and the tax rate is 25 percent.

a   Find the aggregate consumption function.
b   Find the net export function.
c   Find the aggregate expenditures schedule.
d   Find the equilibrium level of output.
e   Suppose that exports increase by 325 million (for a total of 825 million guanos). Calculate the multiplier, and solve for the ultimate change in output brought about by the increase in exports.

Step-by-step solution

Step one (a and b): The aggregate consumption function is the same as in problem 4 and is given in Table 26.4. Identify the marginal propensity to import, the tax rate, and the level of exports. The *MPI* equals 1/3, the tax rate is 25 percent, and the level of exports equals 500 million guanos.

Step two: Calculate the import function. When national income is zero, so are imports. When national income is 500 million guanos, imports = 500(1 − 0.25) × 1/3 = 125 million guanos. Continuing, we derive the import function in Table 26.7.

Table 26.7

National income (millions of guanos)	Imports (millions of guanos)
0	0
500	125
1,000	250
1,500	375
2,000	500
2,500	625
3,000	750

Step three: Find the net export function. When national income is zero, net exports are 500 − 0 = 500 million guanos.

When national income is 500 million guanos, net exports are 500 − 125 = 375 million guanos. Continuing, we derive the net export function in Table 26.8.

Table 26.8

National income	Exports	Imports	Net exports
	(millions of guanos)		
0	500	0	500
500	500	125	375
1,000	500	250	250
1,500	500	375	125
2,000	500	500	0
2,500	500	625	−125
3,000	500	750	−250

Step one (c): Identify the aggregate consumption function, investment, government spending, and the net export function. The aggregate consumption function is given in Table 26.4, investment equals 200 million guanos, government spending is 300 million guanos, and the net export function appears in Table 26.8.

Step two: Calculate the aggregate expenditures schedule by adding consumption, investment, government spending, and net exports. Table 26.9 gives the results.

Table 26.9

National income	Aggregate consumption	Invest-ment	Govern-ment spending	Net exports	Aggregate expenditure
		(millions of guanos)			
0	300	200	300	500	1,300
500	600	200	300	375	1,475
1,000	900	200	300	250	1,650
1,500	1,200	200	300	125	1,825
2,000	1,500	200	300	0	2,000
2,500	1,800	200	300	−125	2,175
3,000	2,100	200	300	−250	2,350

Step one (d): Identify the aggregate expenditures schedule. It is given in Table 26.9.

Step two: Choose a level of national income. When national income equals 2,000 million guanos, aggregate expenditure equals 2,000 million guanos, and this is the equilibrium level of output.

Step one (e): Identify the marginal propensity to consume, the tax rate, the marginal propensity to import, and the initial change in spending. The *MPC* is 0.8, the tax rate is 25 percent, the *MPI* equals 1/3, and exports increase by 325 million guanos.

Step two: Calculate the multiplier.

Multiplier = 1/[1 − (*MPC* − *MPI*)(1 − tax rate)]

= 1/[1 − (0.8 − 1/3)(1 − 0.25)] = 20/13 = 1.54.

Note that in the open economy, the multiplier is smaller than in the closed economy of problem 4.

Step three: Calculate the ultimate change in output:

Change in output = 325 × 20/13 = 500 million guanos.

Step four: Verify the result in step three by adding the change in exports to the original aggregate expenditures schedule (Table 26.9) and solving for the new equilibrium level of output. The new aggregate expenditures schedule is given in Table 26.10. (Note that the increase in exports increases net exports by 325 million guanos.)

Table 26.10

National income	Aggregate consumption	Invest-ment	Govern-ment spending	Net exports	Aggregate expenditure
		(millions of guanos)			
0	300	200	300	825	1,625
500	600	200	300	700	1,800
1,000	900	200	300	575	1,975
1,500	1,200	200	300	450	2,150
2,000	1,500	200	300	325	2,325
2,500	1,800	200	300	200	2,500
3,000	2,100	200	300	75	2,825

The new equilibrium level of output is 2,500 million guanos, which is 500 million more than originally. It checks. The open economy is yet more stable because it took a 325 million guanos change in spending to change output by 500 million guanos.

8 (Practice problem: income-expenditure analysis) This problem builds on problems 2 and 5. The new economics minister wins the day with a brilliant argument against protectionism, and El Dorado opens its economy. Its exports surge to 14 billion dorals. The marginal propensity to import is 9/40, the marginal propensity to consume remains at 0.9, autonomous consumption is 5 billion dorals, private investment is 2 billion dorals, and the government spends 3 billion dorals.

a Find the consumption function.
b Find the net export function.
c Find the aggregate expenditures schedule.
d Find the equilibrium level of output.
e Suppose that exports increase by 4 billion (for a total of 18 billion dorals). Calculate the multiplier, and solve for the ultimate change in output brought about by the increase in exports.

9 (Practice problem: income-expenditure analysis) This problem builds on problems 3 and 6. With peace at hand, the Erehwemos economy is opened to foreign trade and investment. Exports equal 8/3 (2.67) billion wemos, and the marginal propensity to import is 0.25. Government spending has returned to 2 billion wemos, but private investment remains at 4 billion wemos. Autonomous consumption is also 2 billion wemos, and the marginal propensity to consume remains at 0.75. Finally, the tax rate is 1/3.

a Find the aggregate consumption function.
b Find the net export function.

c   Find the aggregate expenditures schedule.
d   Calculate the equilibrium output and national income.
e   Exports increase to 16/3 (5.33) billion wemos. Calculate the multiplier and the ultimate change in output brought about by this increase in exports.

Answers to Problems

2   Table 26.11 gives

a   The aggregate consumption function
b   The aggregate expenditures schedule

Table 26.11

National income	Aggregate consumption	Investment	Aggregate expenditure
(billions of dorals)			
0	5	1	6
10	14	1	15
20	23	1	24
30	32	1	33
40	41	1	42
50	50	1	51
60	59	1	60
70	68	1	69
80	77	1	78
90	86	1	87
100	95	1	96

c   Equilibrium output is 60 billion dorals.
d   The multiplier is $1/(1 − 0.9) = 10$. The change in output is $1 × 10 = 10$ billion dorals. Table 26.12 shows that when investment increases to 2 billion dorals, equilibrium output grows to 70 billion dorals. It verifies that equilibrium output increases by 10 billion dorals (from 60 to 70 billion), as indicated above.

Table 26.12

National income	Aggregate consumption	Investment	Aggregate expenditure
(billions of dorals)			
0	5	2	7
10	14	2	16
20	23	2	25
30	32	2	34
40	41	2	43
50	50	2	52
60	59	2	61
70	68	2	70
80	77	2	79
90	86	2	88
100	95	2	97

3   Table 26.13 gives

a   The aggregate consumption function
b   The aggregate expenditures schedule

Table 26.13

National income	Aggregate consumption	Investment	Aggregate expenditure
(billions of dorals)			
0	2	2	4
4	5	2	7
8	8	2	10
12	11	2	13
16	14	2	16
20	17	2	19
24	20	2	22
28	23	2	25

c   Equilibrium output is 16 billion wemos.
d   The multiplier is $1/(1 − MPC) = 1/(1 − 0.75) = 4$. The change in output is $2 × 4 = 8$ billion wemos. This is verified by Table 26.14, which shows that the new equilibrium output is 24 billion wemos.

Table 26.14

National income	Aggregate consumption	Investment	Aggregate expenditure
(billions of dorals)			
0	2	4	6
4	5	4	9
8	8	4	12
12	11	4	15
16	14	4	18
20	17	4	21
24	20	4	24
28	23	4	27

5   Table 26.15 shows

a   The aggregate consumption function
b   The aggregate expenditures schedule

Table 26.15

National income	Aggregate consumption	Investment	Government spending	Aggregate expenditure
(billions of dorals)				
0	5	2	3	10
10	13	2	3	18
20	21	2	3	26
30	29	2	3	34
40	37	2	3	42
50	45	2	3	50
60	53	2	3	58
70	61	2	3	66
80	69	2	3	74
90	77	2	3	82
100	85	2	3	90

c   The equilibrium level of output is 50 billion dorals.
d   The multiplier is $1/[1 − MPC (1 − t)] = 1/[1 − 0.9(1 − 1/9)] = 5$. The change in output is $4 × 5 = 20$ billion dorals. Table 26.16 shows that when gov-

ernment spending is 7 billion dorals, the new equilibrium output is 70 billion dorals, which represents an increase of 20 billion dorals.

Table 26.16

National income	Aggregate consumption	Investment	Government spending	Aggregate expenditure
		(billions of dorals)		
0	5	2	7	14
10	13	2	7	22
20	21	2	7	30
30	29	2	7	38
40	37	2	7	46
50	45	2	7	54
60	53	2	7	62
70	61	2	7	70
80	69	2	7	78
90	77	2	7	86
100	85	2	7	94

6   Table 26.17 gives

  a   The aggregate consumption function
  b   The aggregate expenditures schedule

Table 26.17

National income	Aggregate consumption	Investment	Government spending	Aggregate expenditure
		(billions of wemos)		
0	2	4	2	8
4	4	4	2	10
8	6	4	2	12
12	8	4	2	14
16	10	4	2	16
20	12	4	2	18
24	14	4	2	20
28	16	4	2	22

  c   Equilibrium output is 16 billion wemos.
  d   The multiplier is

$$1/[1 - MPC(1 - t)] = 1/[1 - 0.75(1 - 1/3)] = 2.$$

The change in equilibrium output is $2 \times 2 = 4$ billion wemos, as is verified by Table 26.18, which shows that the new equilibrium output is 20 billion wemos.

Table 26.18

National income	Aggregate consumption	Investment	Government spending	Aggregate expenditure
		(billions of wemos)		
0	2	4	4	10
4	4	4	4	12
8	6	4	4	14
12	8	4	4	16
16	10	4	4	18
20	12	4	4	20
24	14	4	4	22
28	16	4	4	24

8   Table 26.19 shows

  a   The aggregate consumption function
  b   The net export function
  c   The aggregate expenditures schedule

Table 26.19

National income	Aggregate consumption	Investment	Government spending	Net exports	Aggregate expenditure
			(billions of dorals)		
0	5	2	3	14	24
10	13	2	3	12	30
20	21	2	3	10	26
30	29	2	3	8	42
40	37	2	3	6	48
50	45	2	3	4	54
60	53	2	3	2	60
70	61	2	3	0	66
80	69	2	3	-2	72
90	77	2	3	-4	78
100	85	2	3	-6	84

  d   Equilibrium output is 60 billion.
  e   The multiplier is

$$1/[1 - (MPC - MPI)(1 - t)]$$

$$= 1/[1 - (0.9 - 9/40)(1 - 1/9)] = 2.5.$$

The change in output is $4 \times 2.5 = 10$ billion dorals. Table 26.20 shows that the new equilibrium output is 70 billion dorals, which indicates an increase of 10 billion dorals.

Table 26.20

National income	Aggregate consumption	Investment	Government spending	Net exports	Aggregate expenditure
			(billions of dorals)		
0	5	2	3	18	28
10	13	2	3	16	34
20	21	2	3	14	40
30	29	2	3	12	46
40	37	2	3	10	52
50	45	2	3	8	58
60	53	2	3	6	64
70	61	2	3	4	70
80	69	2	3	2	76
90	77	2	3	0	82
100	85	2	3	-6	84

9   Table 26.21 shows

  a   The aggregate consumption function
  b   The net export function
  c   The aggregate expenditures schedule

Table 26.21

National income	Aggregate consumption	Invest-ment	Govern-ment spending	Net exports	Aggregate expenditure
			(billions of dorals)		
0	2	4	2	2⅔	10⅔
4	4	4	2	2	12
8	6	4	2	1⅓	13⅓
12	8	4	2	⅔	14⅔
16	10	4	2	0	16
20	12	4	2	−⅔	17⅓
24	14	4	2	−1⅓	18⅔
28	16	4	2	−2	20

Table 26.22

National income	Aggregate consumption	Invest-ment	Govern-ment spending	Net exports	Aggregate expenditure
			(billions of dorals)		
0	2	4	2	5⅓	13⅓
4	4	4	2	4⅔	14⅔
8	6	4	2	4	16
12	8	4	2	3⅓	17⅓
16	10	4	2	2⅔	18⅔
20	12	4	2	2	20
24	14	4	2	1⅓	21⅓
28	16	4	2	⅔	22⅔

d Equilibrium output equals 16 billion dorals.

e The multiplier is

$$1/[1 - (MPC - MPI)(1 - t)]$$
$$= 1/[1 - (0.75 - 0.25)(1 - ⅓)] = 1.5.$$

The change in output is $(8/3) \times 1.5 = 4$ billion dorals. Table 26.22 shows that the new equilibrium output equals 20 billion dorals, which is an increase of 4 billion dorals.

Chapter 27

CONSUMPTION AND INVESTMENT

Chapter Review

This chapter moves behind aggregate expenditures and takes a deeper look at two of its components—consumption and investment. The important issues involve how consumption and investment are determined and the causes of shifts in the consumption and investment functions. This chapter concludes the discussion of income-expenditure analysis. The next three chapters move on to the topics of money and monetary policy.

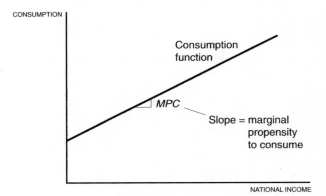

Figure 27.1

ESSENTIAL CONCEPTS

1   What determines **consumption** expenditure? The basic building block is the **Keynesian consumption function,** which gives the relationship between consumption and current income. Figure 27.1 shows that as current income increases by one dollar, consumption increases by the marginal propensity to consume. Other, more future-oriented theories of consumption are the **life-cycle hypothesis** and the **permanent income hypothesis.** These hypotheses shift the focus away from current in-come to expected future income, interest rates, and prices.

2   The life-cycle hypothesis asserts that individuals plan their consumption over their entire lifetime. Thus, people save during their working years when income is high in order to provide for consumption during retirement. Because savings play such an important role, cur-

rent and expected future interest rates as well as expected future income have significant effects on the level of consumption. The life-cycle hypothesis is a future-oriented explanation. It implies that the relationship between consumption and current income would be quite flat, as shown in Figure 27.2.

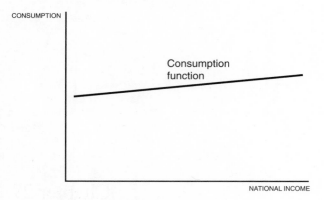

Figure 27.2

3   The permanent income hypothesis also argues that people rationally plan their present and future consumption, saving in good years to provide extra consumption in bad years. Again, the focus is on both current and future income, interest rates, and prices. The permanent income hypothesis reconciles the discrepancy between the aggregate and the individual: over time, aggregate consumption increases in the same proportion as income, while for individuals, consumption increases by a smaller proportion than income.

4   In reality, the relationship between current income and consumption is not as flat as the future-oriented theories suggest. Two explanations of why consumption seems to be more dependent on current income involve **durable goods consumption** and **credit rationing.** When incomes fall during recessions, individuals postpone purchases of durable goods. Because they are uncertain when and if good times will return, they take the safer alternative of making do with old durable goods. Further, when incomes fall, individuals find borrowing more difficult than the permanent income hypothesis asserts. Banks also are unsure of the future incomes of borrowers and are reluctant to lend money to the unemployed. It is safer for banks to lend money to those who do not need it!

5   **Investment** includes firms' purchases of new plant and equipment and inventories, and households' purchases of new houses, which are durable goods. Business investment in plant and equipment is based on the expectation that future profits from the investment will more than outweigh the current investment expenditure. Of course, the firm must discount future revenues and costs; therefore, the interest rate is important. The investment schedule gives the total value of investment at each rate of interest. Lower interest rates increase the present value of profits and lead to more investment.

6   Firms face technological risks and market risks, and they demand compensation, the size of which depends upon the size of the risks, their ability to share the risks, and their willingness to bear the risks themselves. The other important factor is the availability of funds. During recessions the investment schedule shifts to the left because expectations of profits decrease, risks appear larger, risk-sharing opportunities diminish, firms grow less willing to bear risks, and available funds dry up.

7   Firms hold inventories of inputs in order to **facilitate production;** a firm can be sure that the inputs will be there when needed. Firms may hold inventories of output in order to **smooth production;** that is, the firm can produce at a steady rate and always have enough to meet a highly variable consumer demand. Nonetheless, inventories are much more variable than output and contribute to the instability of the economy. During downturns, for example, it is less risky for firms to cut production and sell off inventories than to continue to produce in the hope that good times will return.

BEHIND THE ESSENTIAL CONCEPTS

1   The marginal propensity to consume out of current income is quite high, and thus the consumption function slopes up rather steeply. Why, then, do we study the future-oriented theories of consumption, which stress the future and predict a flat consumption function? The answer is that the life-cycle and permanent income hypotheses provide a deeper understanding of consumption, especially of which factors cause the Keynesian consumption function to shift and which factors lead to its stability. For example, in recessions, people become pessimistic about future incomes and postpone durable goods purchases, shifting the consumption function and aggregate expenditures down. Remember that the central questions in macroeconomics involve the fluctuations in the economy; therefore, it is vital to understand the causes of the changes.

2   The life-cycle and permanent income hypotheses involve borrowing and saving; thus, they teach us the importance of capital markets. If you were always able to obtain credit, your consumption would not vary much. You could borrow in low-income years (such as during college), live well, and repay during high-income years. But capital markets are not perfect; credit rationing suggests that banks are reluctant to let you borrow against future earnings. When your income is less during recessions and you need money, the best available option is to postpone major purchases. Imperfect capital markets make consumption more variable, and thus they are at the center of the discussion about economic ups and downs.

3   To see why business investment is volatile and why it fluctuates over the business cycle, put yourself in the shoes of a business owner. The economy is in recession, and customers are not buying your products. Profits are

down, and you have little retained earnings to spend on investment. The bank will not lend to you because it perceives your precarious financial position. Even if you could obtain funds, a recession is not the time to take risks. During good times, a failed investment may only mean lower profits; during bad times, it may mean bankruptcy. The safest option is to postpone purchases of new plant and equipment, cut production, and sell off inventories.

4 While modern macroeconomists of every school think that a firm microeconomic foundation for their theories is essential, the differences between microeconomics and macroeconomics are interesting. Microeconomics focuses largely on prices. In the basic competitive model, prices always adjust and clear the market. Even when imperfect competition is the subject, economists focus on the failure of prices to capture all costs and benefits or to find the right level. In macroeconomics, especially the new Keynesian approach, prices do not do their job, and markets do not always clear. Consumption is driven by income, not so much by prices. There is still an equilibrium, but it is one in which income, not price, adjusts until desired aggregate spending equals output.

SELF-TEST

True or False

1 The Keynesian consumption function describes the relationship between consumption and permanent disposable income.

2 According to the life-cycle hypothesis, people save during working years to provide for consumption during retirement.

3 According to the permanent income hypothesis, people save during good years to offset low income during bad years.

4 Future-oriented theories of consumption imply that the consumption function is relatively flat.

5 Future-oriented theories of consumption imply that the multiplier is large.

6 Future-oriented theories of consumption imply that current income is relatively less important than wealth.

7 Spending on durable goods is less variable than spending on nondurable goods.

8 A borrower is credit rationed if she cannot afford the interest rate at which banks are willing to lend.

9 Consumption depends more upon current disposable income than the future-oriented theories of consumption imply.

10 The investment spending relevant for aggregate expenditures includes purchases of capital equipment by firms and purchases of shares by individuals.

11 Almost all of the volatility in investment is explained by variations in real interest rates.

12 Firms finance most investment out of retained earnings.

13 Firms usually perceive that investment is riskier during recessions.

14 Opportunities to share risk increase during recessions.

15 In the U.K. economy, inventories fluctuate less than output because firms try to smooth production and produce at a steady rate.

Multiple Choice

1 The view that current disposable income determines current consumption is consistent with the
a Keynesian consumption function.
b life-cycle hypothesis.
c permanent income hypothesis.
d all of the above.
e b and c.

2 The idea that individuals save during working years in order to provide for consumption during retirement is called the
a Keynesian consumption function.
b life-cycle hypothesis.
c permanent income hypothesis.
d all of the above.
e b and c.

3 The theory that people save in good years to provide for extra consumption in bad years is called the
a Keynesian consumption function.
b life-cycle hypothesis.
c permanent income hypothesis.
d all of the above.
e b and c.

4 Which of the following emphasize(s) that expected future income affects current consumption?
a The Keynesian consumption function
b The life-cycle hypothesis
c The permanent income hypothesis
d All of the above
e b and c

5 Which of the following imply(ies) that a temporary tax cut will significantly increase current consumption?
a The Keynesian consumption function
b The life-cycle hypothesis
c The permanent income hypothesis
d All of the above
e b and c

6 According to the future-oriented consumption theories, the multiplier is
a quite small.
b zero.
c large.
d small in recessions but large in booms.
e large in recessions but small in booms.

7   If the price of an asset that an individual owns rises, then that individual is said to receive

   a   human capital.
   b   capital gains.
   c   retained earnings.
   d   temporary income.
   e   disposable income.

8   Which of the following are reasons why consumption depends more upon current income than the future-oriented theories might suggest?

   a   Individuals can postpone purchases of durable goods when current income falls.
   b   Banks are reluctant to lend money to people whose current income is low.
   c   Individuals can see through the corporate veil and so reduce their consumption when profits fall.
   d   Government tax and spending policies do not affect individual consumption.
   e   a and b.

9   An individual is credit rationed if

   a   he cannot afford the interest charged on a loan.
   b   banks charge a higher rate of interest to reflect their perception of the risk that he will not repay on schedule.
   c   he is unable to borrow even though he is willing to pay the interest, and the interest rate reflects the risk of lending to him.
   d   he has no savings.
   e   he has no current income.

10   The component of aggregate expenditures that is most variable is probably

   a   investment.
   b   consumption.
   c   government expenditures.
   d   net exports.
   e   all the above; they are equally variable.

11   For aggregate expenditure calculation, which of the following is *not* included in investment spending?

   a   Purchases of new industrial plant and buildings
   b   Inventories accumulated in anticipation of sales
   c   Purchases of raw materials for immediate use
   d   Purchases of vehicles and machinery used by firms
   e   None of the above

12   Before investing, businesses must

   a   predict future revenues.
   b   predict future costs.
   c   adjust future revenues and costs for inflation.
   d   compute the present value of profits using the real interest rate.
   e   all of the above.

13   The investment function describes the total value of investment at each

   a   price level.
   b   level of disposable income.
   c   level of national income.

   d   level of GDP.
   e   rate of interest.

14   Real interest rates

   a   are quite volatile, reflecting instability in the capital market.
   b   vary enough to provide a good explanation of short-term variations in investment.
   c   vary little.
   d   are irrelevant to the investment decision.
   e   change very little but lead to large changes in the level of investment because investment demand is quite elastic.

15   The compensation that firms require to justify the risk of investment depends upon

   a   their ability to share the risks.
   b   their willingness to bear the risks.
   c   the magnitude of the risks.
   d   all of the above.
   e   none of the above.

16   Most investment is financed

   a   out of retained earnings.
   b   by borrowing at the real interest rate.
   c   by issuing new shares.
   d   by selling bonds.
   e   by raising product prices.

17   Firms invest less during recessions because

   a   retained earnings fall as revenue declines faster than expenses.
   b   as individual firms cut back on investment and inventories, national output falls owing to the multiplier effect, further reducing the profitability of investment.
   c   banks are less willing to lend because they foresee a greater risk that the loans will not be repaid.
   d   firms' forecasts of the profitability of investment become more pessimistic.
   e   all of the above.

18   The theory that investment is more volatile than output because firms try to keep a constant ratio of their capital stock to output is called

   a   the investment accelerator.
   b   Tobin's q.
   c   the investment multiplier.
   d   production-facilitating theory.
   e   production-smoothing theory.

19   Which of the following correctly states the correlation between inventories and output according to the two theories of inventory investment?

   a   Both production smoothing and production facilitating imply that output and inventories are negatively correlated.
   b   Both production smoothing and production facilitating imply that output and inventories are positively correlated.
   c   Production smoothing implies that output and in-

ventories are negatively correlated, but production facilitating implies that they are positively correlated.

d Production smoothing implies that output and inventories are negatively correlated, but production facilitating implies that they are positively correlated.

e Neither theory implies anything about the correlation.

20 Ways of stimulating investment include

a increasing business confidence by maintaining high output and full employment.

b tax breaks for investment, such as accelerated depreciation allowances.

c increasing the availability of credit through monetary policy.

d direct government lending programs such as loan guarantee schemes.

e all of the above.

Completion

1 The present discounted value of expected future wages is called _____.

2 According to the _____ hypothesis, people save during their working years in order to increase consumption after retirement.

3 The _____ hypothesis argues that people save during good earning years to provide extra consumption during bad years.

4 The Keynesian consumption function stresses the relationship between consumption and _____.

5 Future-oriented theories of consumption, such as the permanent income and life-cycle hypotheses, imply that the aggregate expenditure schedule is

_____.

6 The ability to postpone purchases of durable goods and the fact that it is difficult to borrow against future earnings make consumption _____ dependent on current income.

7 Changes in the level of _____ are the principal reason for the economy's instability.

8 Most firms finance most of their investment through

_____.

9 Inventories generally _____ during recessions.

10 The _____ theory explains why inventories would decrease during recessions.

Answers to Self-Test

True or False

1	F	6	T	11	F
2	T	7	F	12	T
3	T	8	F	13	T
4	T	9	T	14	F
5	F	10	F	15	F

Multiple Choice

1	a	6	a	11	c	16	a
2	b	7	b	12	e	17	e
3	c	8	e	13	e	18	a
4	e	9	c	14	c	19	c
5	a	10	a	15	d	20	e

Completion

1 human capital
2 life-cycle
3 permanent income
4 current income
5 relatively flat
6 more
7 investment
8 retained earnings
9 increase
10 production facilitating

Tools and Practice Problems

Using income-expenditure analysis is the first subject in this section. We see how factors that cause changes in consumption and investment bring about shifts in the aggregate expenditure schedule and new equilibrium levels of output. Next, we look carefully at the notion of Ricardian equivalence and study how government fiscal policies may be offset by private savings and borrowing, leaving consumption unchanged. In the real world, consumption is affected by government tax and spending policies. One important explanation involves the cost and availability of credit. Several problems show how imperfect capital markets lead to the failure of Ricardian equivalence.

INCOME-EXPENDITURE ANALYSIS

Income-expenditure analysis can be used to answer such questions as "What is the effect on output of a change in interest rates?" In general, when some economic event causes a change in consumption or investment, the aggregate expenditure schedule will shift and bring about a change in the equilibrium level of output. Table 27.1 lists some important factors that change consumption and investment.

Tool Kit 27.1 Using Income-Expenditure Analysis

Changes in consumption or investment will shift the aggregate expenditure curve and bring about a change in output. The change in output will be a multiple of the initial change in spending. Follow these steps.

Table 27.1

Shifts in Aggregate Expenditure
  Changes in consumption, which are related to changes in wealth, real interest rates, credit availability, or estimates of future earnings
  Changes in investment, which are related to changes in real interest rates, stock prices, credit availability, retained earnings, expectations of profitability, perceptions of risk, or willingness to bear risk

Step one: Start with an equilibrium.

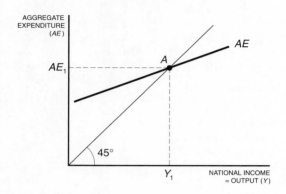

Step two: Identify a cause, and determine its effect on consumption, investment, or both.

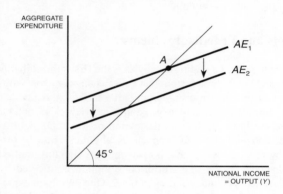

Step three: If consumption or investment increases, shift the aggregate expenditures schedule up; if either decreases, shift the schedule down.

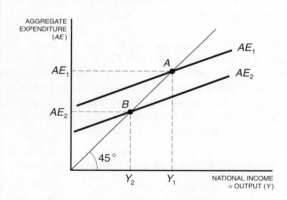

Step four: Find the new equilibrium level of output, and compare.

1 (Worked problem: income-expenditure analysis) Use income-expenditure analysis to explain the impact of a boom in the stock market.

  Step-by-step solution

Step one: Start with an equilibrium.

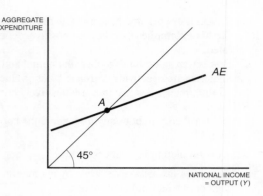

Step two: Identify a cause, and determine its effect on consumption, investment, or both. The increase in stock prices makes individuals wealthier, inducing them to increase consumption. Firms can finance more investment by issuing new shares; thus, investment increases.

Step three: Shift the aggregate expenditures schedule. Because both consumption and investment increase, it shifts up.

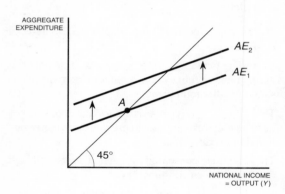

Step four: Find the new equilibrium, and compare. In the new equilibrium, output is greater. The increase in stock prices has brought about an increase in the economy's output.

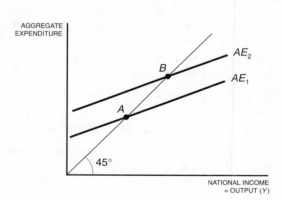

2 (Practice problem: income-expenditure analysis) Use income-expenditure analysis to determine the impact of an increase in real interest rates.

3 (Practice problem: income-expenditure analysis) Use income-expenditure analysis to determine the impact of each of the following.

a   Firms anticipate an economic downturn accompanied by lower profits.

b   The economy has fallen into recession, and because bankruptcies threaten, firms are less willing to bear risk.

c   Believing that the defence budget will be cut, consumers fear involuntary redundancies.

d   Retained earnings reach a four-year high.

e   Tight monetary policy has limited the availability of credit for households and firms.

f   Real interest rates fall by 2 percent.

g   Uncertain about the consequences of the free-trade negotiations with non-EU countries, European firms perceive a risky future.

h   Loose monetary policy increases the availability of credit.

THE BARRO-RICARDO ARGUMENT

When the government increases spending without a tax increase, it finances its deficit by selling bonds. Today's bonds must be repaid, however. This means that future taxpayers are liable for the debts incurred to finance current spending. The notion of Barro and Ricardo says that households will save now in order to be able to pay the future tax liability, and these savings will completely offset the effects of government deficit finance. In this section, we see how this might be true if capital markets were perfect, and several reasons why private savings do not offset government deficits in the real world: credit constraints and different interest rates for borrowing and lending. The lesson is that imperfect capital markets are an important reason why fiscal policy can be effective.

Tool Kit 27.2 Exploring the Barro-Ricardo Argument

The household's budget constraint shows what combinations of current and future consumption are possible given expectations of current and future income and interest rates. We can use it to analyse the Barro-Ricardo argument that private savings offset budget deficits and thus fiscal policy is ineffective. Follow this procedure.

Step one: Draw the two-period budget constraint for the typical household. (Follow the procedure outlined in Chapter 2.)

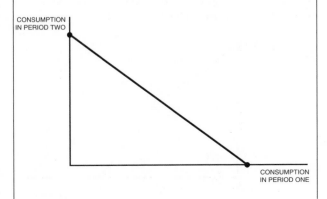

Step two: Choose a point that reflects the household's consumption and savings decisions. Label it *A*.

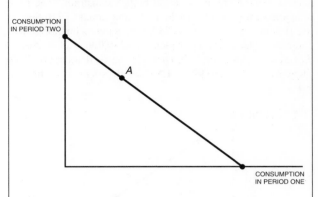

Step three: Show the effect of government borrowing by adding the extra spending to current consumption (the horizontal coordinate of *A*) and subtracting the future tax liability from future consumption (the vertical coordinate of *A*). Label the new point *B*.

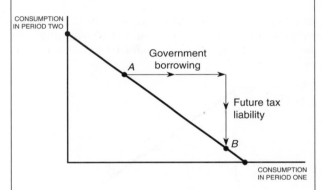

Step four: Determine if point *B* lies on or above the original budget constraint.

Step five: If *B* is on the original budget constraint, then Ricardian equivalence holds, and the household will save to return to point *A* because *A* indicates their preferred decision. If *B* is above the original budget constraint, Ricardian equivalence is not true, and the household may choose to consume more today.

---

4   (Worked problem: Barro-Ricardo) Doctor Campbell and her husband make £210,000 per year and expect that their real earnings will continue for at least ten years. Although they expect a 50 percent real interest rate over the ten-year period, they neither borrow nor save. The government passes an expenditure package which includes abolishing tuition fees and which will give the Campbells an extra £10,000 this year. It finances this program by issuing ten-year bonds that pay a 50 percent real rate of return over the period. The Campbells expect that they will pay their share of the tax liability when the bonds come due in ten years. Analyse how the program will affect the Campbells' savings decision and whether Ricardian equivalence would hold.

Step-by-step solution

Step one: Draw the two-period budget constraint. The present discounted value of their income equals £210,000 + [£210,000 × (1/1 + .50)] = £350,000, which is the horizontal intercept. The future equivalent is £210,000 × (1 + .50) + £210,000 = £525,000, which is the vertical intercept. The slope is 525,000/350,000 = 1.50, which is 1 plus the interest rate.

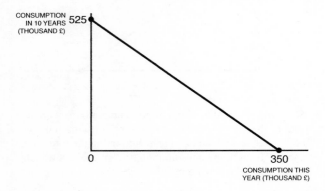

Step two: Choose a point that reflects the household's consumption and savings decisions. The Campbells neither save nor borrow, so they choose to consume £210,000 in each year.

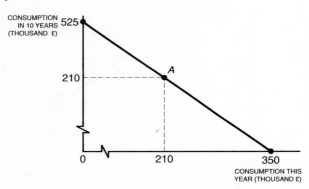

Step three: Show the effect of the program. It gives the Campbells £10,000 now, but it takes away £10,000 × (1 + .50) = £15,000 in ten years. This moves their chosen point from *A* to *B*.

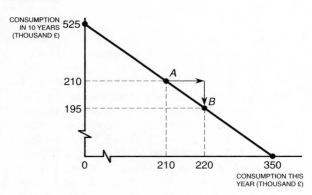

Step four: Determine if point *B* lies on or above the original budget constraint. Clearly, *B* is on the same budget constraint.

Step five: If *B* is on the original budget constraint, then Ricardian equivalence holds, and the household will save to return to point *A* because *A* indicates their preferred decision. The Campbells merely increase their savings to £10,000. The principal and interest will be just enough to pay the tax increase that they expect in ten years. The government borrowing is exactly offset by private savings.

5 (Practice problem: Barro-Ricardo) The typical person in Ricardania earns 20,000 ricks (the local currency) annually. The real interest rate is 5 percent per year, and the typical person borrows 2,000 ricks. The government decides to stimulate the economy by giving each person 5,000 ricks. To finance this grant, the government sells one-year bonds that also pay 5 percent. Taxes will be increased next year to pay off the bonds. Analyse how the grant will affect the typical person's borrowing and savings decisions and also whether Ricardian equivalence would hold in Ricardania.

6 (Worked problem: Barro-Ricardo) Return to the Campbells of problem 4. All information is the same except the real interest rate for borrowing, which is now 100 percent over the ten-year period. Analyse how the program will affect the Campbells' savings decision and whether Ricardian equivalence would hold.

Step-by-step solution

Step one: Draw the two-period budget constraint. The vertical intercept remains as in problem 4, but the horizontal intercept now equals the present value of income discounted at 100 percent = £210,000 + £210,000 × 1/(1 + 1.00) = £315,000.

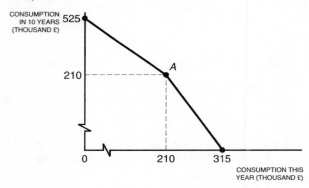

Step two: Choose a point that reflects the household's consumption and savings decisions. The Campbells continue to choose to consume £210,000 in each period.

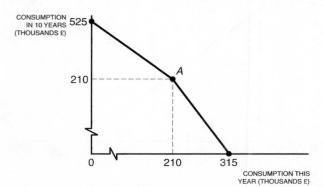

Step three: Show the effect of the government program. As in problem 4, it increases current consumption by £10,000 and reduces future consumption by £15,000, as shown by point *B.*

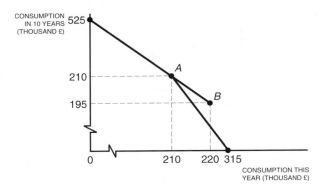

Step four: Determine if point *B* lies on or above the original budget constraint. It is now above.

Step five: If *B* is above the original constraint, Ricardian equivalence is not true, and the household may choose to consume more today. Deficit finance allows the Campbells to consume more today than it would if they had to borrow the money from a bank. They may choose any point on the line segment between *B* and *A,* and their choice will indicate more consumption. In this case, the government deficit increases consumption.

7   (Practice problem: Ricardian equivalence) Return to problem 5, and suppose that all information is the same except that the borrowing interest rate is 20 percent. Analyse how the grant will affect the typical person's borrowing and saving decisions and also whether Ricardian equivalence will hold in Ricardania.

8   (Practice problem: Ricardian equivalence) Although the Johnsons earn £50,000 per year after taxes and expect to continue to earn the same in real terms for the next five years, they have a bad credit history and cannot borrow. They could earn 25 percent on their savings, but they do not have any. Analyse the effect on the Johnsons' budget constraint of a current tax cut of £10,000 financed by a five-year bond paying 25 percent over the period. The bond will be repaid with tax increases, and the Johnsons expect that their share of the tax increase will pay off the bonds issued to finance their share of the current tax cut.

Answers to Problems

2   The increase in real interest rates reduces consumption (durable goods purchases fall) and investment, shifts aggregate expenditures down, and reduces output.

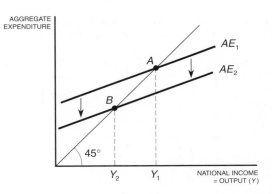

3   *a*   Investment falls, shifting the aggregate expenditure curve down and reducing output.

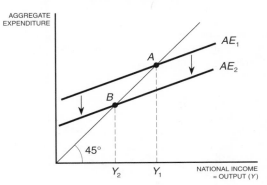

b   Investment falls, shifting the aggregate expenditure curve down and reducing output.

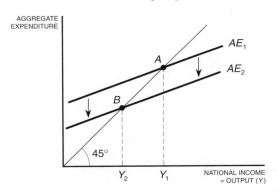

c   Consumption falls, shifting the aggregate expenditure curve down and reducing output.

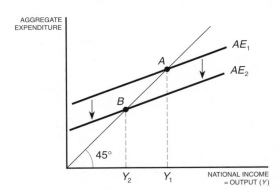

d   Investment increases, shifting the aggregate expenditure curve up and increasing output.

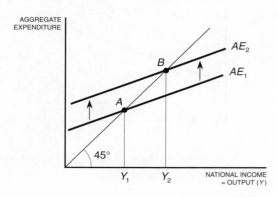

e   Investment and purchases of durable goods fall, shifting the aggregate expenditure curve down and reducing output.

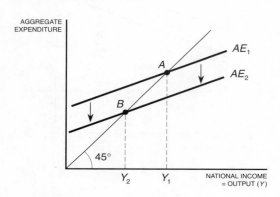

f   Investment and purchases of durable goods rise, shifting the aggregate expenditure curve up and increasing output.

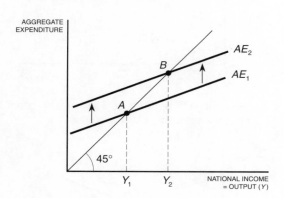

g   Investment falls, shifting the aggregate expenditure curve down and reducing output.

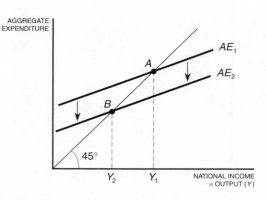

h   Investment increases, shifting the aggregate expenditure curve up and increasing output.

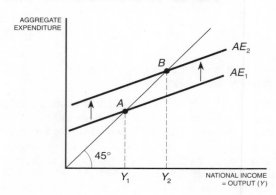

5

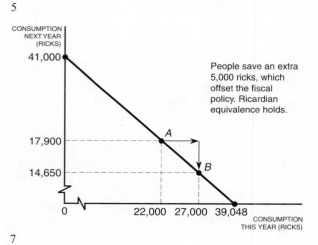

People save an extra 5,000 ricks, which offset the fiscal policy. Ricardian equivalence holds.

7

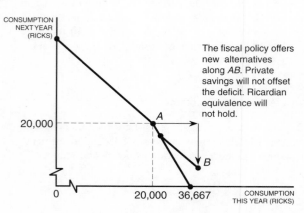

The fiscal policy offers new alternatives along *AB*. Private savings will not offset the deficit. Ricardian equivalence will not hold.

8

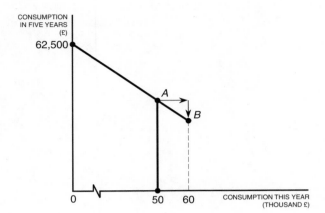

Chapter 28

MONEY, BANKING, AND CREDIT

Chapter Review

This chapter begins the study of money. What money is and the purposes it serves in the economy are the first two topics. The discussion then introduces the concept of the money supply and explains how the banking system creates money. The chapter also discusses the central bank, the institution of government responsible for regulating the money supply, ensuring the availability of credit, and promoting the stability of the banking system. In Britain, the central bank is the Bank of England; in Germany, the Bundersbank; in France, the Banque de France; in the United States, the Federal Reserve; and in Japan, the Bank of Japan. This material on money, banking, and credit is complemented by the next chapter's study of how money affects the real economy in the short run. This part concludes with Chapter 30, the analysis of monetary and fiscal policies.

ESSENTIAL CONCEPTS

1   Economists define **money** by what it does. Money serves three functions. It is a **medium of exchange,** facilitating trades between firms and households. It is a **store of value,** permitting individuals to buy and sell at different times. Finally, it is a **unit of account,** helping people measure the relative value of different goods.

2   Since there are many financial assets that perform money's three functions to some degree, the **money supply** is measured in several ways. The narrowest definition is **M0** which comprises notes and coin in circulation and bankers' operational deposits in the banking department of the Bank of England. A wider definition is **M2** which consists of notes and coin, and sterling retail deposits held at U.K. banks and building societies by U.K. residents. Bank retail deposits consist of all non-interest-bearing deposits plus "chequable" sight, or time, deposits, plus other deposits up to £100,000 with less than one month to maturity. Building society retail deposits are defined as transaction accounts and other deposits up to £100,000 with less than one month to maturity. A wider definition still is **M4,** this is the same as M2 but has no limit on the size of the accounts specified in M2; hence it includes the specified accounts over £100,000. A fourth measure is **M3H** which is a harmonised measure designed to be comparable with other European Union countries. M3H comprises M4 plus foreign country deposits by U.K. residents with banks and building societies in the United Kingdom, and sterling and foreign currency deposits held by public corporations at

U.K. banks and building societies. The Bank of England used to publish M1, **M3,** and **sterling M3** measures of the money supply, but these have become redundant as banking practices have changed. For example, M1 excluded interest-bearing current accounts from its definition, but this measure became increasingly irrelevant when banks introduced interest-bearing current accounts which became more and more popular. Likewise the use of M3, which excluded building society deposits, was compromised when the building societies began to offer cheque accounts similar to those of the banks.

3   The **financial system** includes all the institutions that help savers and borrowers transact. **Financial intermediaries,** such as banks and building societies, are the firms that stand between savers and borrowers. The central bank regulates banks to ensure their financial health and also controls the money supply and availability of credit to promote and stabilise overall economic activity.

4   While the central bank controls the money supply, money itself is created by the banking system. Banks operate on the **fractional reserve system,** which means that they keep only a fraction of deposits on hand as reserve assets. Thus, an initial deposit (or other increase in reserves) results in additional loans, which ultimately return to the banking system as more deposits. The process of deposit expansion continues until total deposits have grown by a multiple of the initial deposit. The **money multiplier** is the relationship between the initial deposit and the ultimate change in total deposits.

5   Central banks have three instruments for controlling the money supply. They can buy and sell government bonds. This activity is called **open market operations.** They can specify the level of **required reserves** or reserve assets that banks must keep on hand or on deposit at the central bank. Finally, they can change the **discount rate,** which is the interest rate which they set and which is charged to banks when they borrow from the central bank.

6   Ensuring the stability of the banking system and reducing the threat of bank runs are important responsibilities of the central bank and other government agencies. The central bank acts as a lender of last resort, providing liquidity to troubled banks, and it sets reserve requirements. Government-mandated capital requirements add to the incentives that bank owners have to manage risks carefully. In 1988 regulators from a number of countries agreed on an international minimum capital adequacy requirement. From 1992 this agreement imposed a minimum capital adequacy requirement of 8 percent of assets. In the United States, depositors are also afforded protection by the Federal Deposit Insurance Corporation which insures depositors against bank failure.

BEHIND THE ESSENTIAL CONCEPTS

1   How do the central bank's instruments affect the money supply? Each works by increasing or decreasing banks'

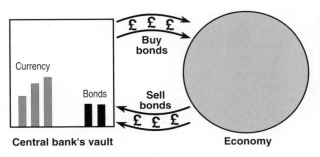

Figure 28.1

reserves, affecting the money available for loans, or by financing interest rates.

a   When the central bank engages in open market operations, it buys and sells bonds. If it buys a bond, for example, the money that it pays is deposited in a bank. The bank's reserves increase, and it in turn can grant new loans.

b   When the central bank decreases reserve requirements, banks can reduce their reserves and again make new loans.

c   When the central bank increases the discount rate, banks know that borrowing will be more expensive. They guard against having to borrow by keeping more reserves and making fewer loans.

Note that when the central bank buys or sells Treasury bills or government bonds their price changes, and so therefore does their interest rate. If the central bank buys, prices get bid up and interest rates fall. If the central bank sells, prices fall and interest rates rise. Hence, open market operations affect not only reserves but also interest rates.

2   Figure 28.1 will help you keep straight how open market operations affect the money supply. On the left is the central bank's vault, where it keeps stacks of bonds and currency. The currency in the vault is not money, because it is not in the economy. On the right is the economy. If the central bank buys bonds, currency flows from the vault into the economy and increases the money supply. If the central bank sells bonds, the money it receives leaves the economy and goes into the vault, where it is no longer money.

3   How are the central bank's three instruments used in Britain? First, **open market operations** include the sale and purchase of Treasury bills and short-term government bonds. Daily trading by the Bank of England (acting on behalf of the government) has a direct effect on the price of Treasury bills and government bonds, and thus on interest rates. Such control of short-term interest rates is the principal instrument of monetary policy used by the Bank of England. In 1997 the Bank of England began to widen the range of assets it dealt in by also using the repo market in its open market operations. Second, the Bank of England could change the level of **required reserves** that banks must deposit with it. In the United Kingdom, banks are required to hold cash reserves at the Bank of England equal to at least 0.5 percent of their deposits. Changes in required reserves were commonplace in Britain up to 1980 and are

still used in other countries, for example, the United States. Since 1980 changes in reserve requirements have not been used by the Bank of England as a means of controlling the money supply; the interest rate at which funds are available has been used instead. This is because the use of variable reserve requirements is like a tax on banks, and like all taxes, it can distort the allocation of resources and lead to inefficiencies. Finally, the Bank of England can set the **discount rate,** which is the interest rate it charges banks for borrowing. The discount rate used to be set by the Bank of England in accordance with government policy. Since 1997, the bank has been given a degree of independence from government and the newly established Monetary Policy Committee (a committee of experts drawn from industry, banking, and academia and chaired by the governor of the Bank of England) sets interest rates in accordance with the government's inflation target.

4   You should not confuse the money multiplier in this chapter with the fiscal multiplier introduced in Chapter 26. They are two different concepts. The fiscal multiplier shows that an increase in aggregate expenditure—for example, in investment—brings about a larger increase in output. The money multiplier shows that an increase in reserves leads to a larger increase in total deposits.

5   The *workings* of the fiscal and money multipliers, however, are similar. With the fiscal multiplier, an initial increase in spending creates additional income, which leads to a second round of spending when some of the income is consumed. The sequence is spending—income—additional spending—and so on. Each successive round of spending is smaller, and the process ultimately settles down.

     With the money multiplier, an initial increase in deposits leads to new loans, which ultimately are deposited back in the banking system. The sequence here is deposits—loans—deposits—additional loans—and so on. Each successive round of deposits is smaller, and again the process ultimately settles down.

6   The *formulas* for the multipliers are also similar. The fiscal multiplier equals 1 divided by the marginal propensity to save. You can think of savings as a leakage, which makes the next round of spending smaller than the last one. The formula for the money multiplier is 1 divided by the reserve ratio. Again, in that they are not loaned out, reserves are like a leakage, making the next round of deposits smaller than the previous round.

7   One of the fundamental trade-offs in economic life is risk and incentives. We have seen this notion many times, and it appears again in this chapter on the subject of deposit insurance. The U.S. Federal Deposit Insurance Corporation (FDIC) protects depositors against loss in case of bank failure. Because depositors know that their money is safe, they seek the highest rate of interest and have little incentive to worry about the financial health of the bank. Banks know this and are motivated to grant risky loans, seeking high average returns so that they can afford to pay high rates of interest. Thus, deposit insurance reduces the risk for depositors, but it creates incentives that lead to reckless lending. This problem led to the U.S. savings and loan crisis in the 1980s, and it is the motivation for regulations such as capital requirements that promote bank safety.

SELF-TEST

True or False

1   The term *money* refers only to currency and coins in circulation.

2   The store of value function of money refers to its use as a measure of the relative value of goods.

3   The money supply is an example of a flow variable.

4   M1 includes currency, traveler's checks, and demand deposits.

5   An asset is liquid if it is easily converted into money (M1).

6   Financial intermediaries are firms that provide a link between savers and borrowers.

7   The Bank of England is the central bank of the United Kingdom.

8   The U.S. Federal Reserve is an independent agency funded out of the profits of its operations.

9   A bank's net worth equals its liabilities minus its assets.

10   Banks operate on the fractional reserve or reserve assets system, which means that they hold only a fraction of the amount of deposits in reserve.

11   The money multiplier implies that total deposits increase by a multiple of an initial deposit.

12   Central banks control the money supply by mandating maximum interest rates that banks can charge their best customers.

13   The discount rate is the interest rate that the central bank charges on loans to banks.

14   Open market operations refer to the buying and selling of government bonds by the central bank.

15   In the United States, Federal deposit insurance lessens the risk faced by depositors but also reduces their incentives to monitor the performance of banks.

Multiple Choice

1   Trade without the use of money is called

     a   double coincidence of wants.

     b   medium of exchange.

     c   barter.

     d   unit of account.

     e   multiple deposit.

2   Double coincidence of wants refers to the

     a   fact that in order for two individuals to barter, each must have what the other wants and want what the other has.

b   fact that money must be both a store of value and a medium of exchange.

c   unlikely possibility that two individuals will have exactly the same tastes.

d   fact that dividends are taxed twice.

e   fact that the central bank engages in open market operations and sets the discount rate.

3   The use of money to facilitate exchange is its

   a   medium of exchange function.
   b   store of value function.
   c   unit of account function.
   d   double coincidence of wants function.
   e   fractional reserve function.

4   The use of money to measure the relative value of goods and services is its

   a   medium of exchange function.
   b   store of value function.
   c   unit of account function.
   d   double coincidence of wants function.
   e   fractional reserve function.

5   The use of money as a means of preserving purchasing power for a time period is its

   a   medium of exchange function.
   b   store of value function.
   c   unit of account function.
   d   double coincidence of wants function.
   e   fractional reserve function.

6   The economic definition of money is

   a   currency, traveler's checks, and demand deposits.
   b   M0.
   c   anything that acts as a medium of exchange, store of value, and unit of account.
   d   anything that avoids the double coincidence of wants problem.
   e   *a* and *b*.

7   In the United Kingdom, which of the following is *not* included in M0?

   a   Coins in circulation
   b   Notes in circulation
   c   Bankers' operational deposits at the Bank of England
   d   Retail deposits at U.K. banks and building societies
   e   None of the above

8   In the United Kingdom, which of the following is *not* included in M2?

   a   M0
   b   Sterling retail deposits held by U.K. residents at U.K. banks
   c   Sterling retail deposits held by U.K. residents at U.K. building societies
   d   Other sterling retail U.K. bank and building deposits up to £100,000 with less than one month to maturity
   e   All of the above

9   In the United Kingdom, which of the following is *not* included in M4?

   a   M0
   b   M2
   c   All sterling deposits at U.K. banks and building societies held by U.K. residents
   d   All sterling sight and time deposits held by U.K. residents at U.K. banks and building societies, regardless of size
   e   Deposits held at U.K. banks by non-U.K. residents

10   In the United Kingdom, M3H is

   a   a measure of the money supply that includes M4.
   b   a measure of the money supply that includes foreign currency deposits of U.K. residents held at U.K. banks and building societies.
   c   a measure of the money supply that includes sterling and foreign currency deposits of public corporations held at U.K. banks and building societies.
   d   a harmonised measure comparable to measures used in other European Union countries.
   e   all of the above.

11   Which of the following are *not* financial intermediaries?

   a   Banks
   b   Building societies
   c   Unit trusts
   d   Life insurance companies and pension funds
   e   None of the above

12   The objectives of government involvement in the financial system include

   a   protecting consumers.
   b   stabilising the level of economic activity.
   c   protecting banks from unfair competition.
   d   creating jobs in the financial sector.
   e   *a* and *b*.

13   The central bank of the United Kingdom is

   a   the Bank of Scotland.
   b   National Westminster Bank.
   c   the National Reserve.
   d   the Bank of England.
   e   the Royal Mint.

14   The Bank of England

   a   advises the government on how to finance its deficit and manage the national debt.
   b   is banker to the U.K. government.
   c   is involved in regulation of the banking system.
   d   is lender of last resort.
   e   all of the above.

15   The fractional reserve system in banking means that banks

   a   lend a fraction of their money to consumers and a fraction to businesses.
   b   hold a fraction of the amount on deposit in reserves.
   c   hold a fraction of the amount on loan in reserves.
   d   lend a fraction of their money to foreign businesses and a fraction to domestic businesses.
   e   may or may not belong to the federal reserve system.

16   The discount rate is the

  a   interest rate charged by the central bank on loans to banks.
  b   interest rate paid by the central bank on deposits.
  c   difference between the interest rate charged by the central bank and that charged in the market.
  d   maximum allowable difference between interest charged on loans to consumers and loans to banks.
  e   interest rate ceiling on credit card balances.

17   Which of the following is *not* a way in which a central bank can increase the money supply?

  a   Lowering the discount rate
  b   Reducing the reserve requirement
  c   Buying Treasury bills
  d   Selling Treasury bills
  e   None of the above

18   The money multiplier shows that

  a   the rich get richer.
  b   an increase in aggregate expenditures brings about a larger increase in national income.
  c   an increase in reserves leads to a larger increase in total deposits.
  d   a multiple of deposits must be held as reserves.
  e   deregulation leads to instability in the banking system.

19   Open market operations, the most important means by which the central bank controls the money supply, involve

  a   changing the discount rate.
  b   setting interest rates.
  c   changing the reserve requirement.
  d   buying and selling government bonds.
  e   placing varying restrictions on foreign borrowing and lending.

20   The U.S. Federal Deposit Insurance Corporation

  a   acts as the central bank of United States.
  b   ensures that banks will not fail.
  c   insures deposits (of up to $100,000) in case of bank collapse.
  d   protects banks against unfair foreign competition.
  e   sets the reserve requirement for bank deposits.

Completion

1   For a trade to take place in a barter economy, each individual must have what the other wants and want what the other has; that is, there must be a _____.

2   Money facilitates exchange; it is performing its _____ function.

3   Money holds on to its purchasing power; it is performing its _____ function.

4   People use money as a measuring rod, taking advantage of the _____ function of money operational deposits in the Banking Department of the Bank of England.

5   Currency in circulation and bankers' operational de-

posits in the banking department of the Bank of England are included in the _____ measure of money.

6   Firms that act as go-betweens for savers and borrowers are called _____.

7   The central bank in United Kingdom is called the _____.

8   When the central bank buys and sells bonds, it is engaging in _____.

9   In the United Kingdom, the minimum level of cash reserves that banks must keep at the Bank of England is _____ of their deposits.

10   The interest rate charged to banks by the central bank is called the _____.

Answers to Self-Test

True or False

1	F	6	T	11	T
2	F	7	T	12	F
3	F	8	T	13	T
4	T	9	F	14	T
5	T	10	T	15	T

Multiple Choice

1	c	6	c	11	e	16	a
2	a	7	d	12	e	17	d
3	a	8	e	13	d	18	c
4	c	9	e	14	e	19	d
5	b	10	e	15	b	20	c

Completion

1   double coincidence of wants
2   medium of exchange
3   store of value
4   unit of account
5   M0
6   financial intermediaries
7   Bank of England
8   open market operations
9   0.5 percent
10   discount rate

Tools and Practice Problems

In this section, we learn about the balance sheet of banks, where assets, liabilities, and net worth are recorded, and use this tool to see how open market operations lead to changes in deposits, to trace through the deposit expansion process, and to compute the money multiplier.

THE BALANCE SHEET

Before we can understand how banks create money, we must master the balance sheet. This keeps track of assets and liabilities as they change when money is deposited and loaned. Tool Kit 28.1 shows how to construct the bank's balance sheet and to compute its net worth.

Tool Kit 28.1 Constructing the Balance Sheet

The balance sheet is a "T account," with assets listed on the left and liabilities and net worth on the right. When anything changes, net worth must adjust to keep the right and left sides in balance. To create a balance sheet, follow this procedure.

Step one: Make a T account. Label the left column "Assets" and the right column "Liabilities and net worth."

Assets	Liabilities and net worth

Step two: Enter each of the assets (outstanding loans, holdings of government bonds, liquid assets, and cash reserves at the Bank of England) in the left-hand column, and add the assets.

Assets	Liabilities and net worth
Loans Government bonds Liquid assets Cash reserves at the Bank of England	
Total assets	

Step three: Enter each of the liabilities (deposits) in the right-hand column, and add the liabilities. Check that cash reserves at the Bank of England are at least 0.5 percent of deposits. Calculate the ratio of liquid assets to deposits and comment on whether the ratio is prudent.

Ratio of liquid assets to deposits

$$= \frac{\text{liquid assets plus cash reserves at the Bank of England}}{\text{deposits}}.$$

Prudential regulation by the Bank of England does not specify a minimum ratio of liquid assets to deposits; banks must keep a prudent amount depending upon the type of deposits they hold as liabilities.

Assets	Liabilities and net worth
Loans Government bonds Liquid assets Cash reserves at the Bank of England	Deposits
Total assets	

Step four: Compute net worth by subtracting liabilities from assets:

Net worth = assets − liabilities.

Enter net worth in the right-hand column and check that it is at least 8 percent of total assets to comply with international agreements regarding capital adequacy requirements.

Assets	Liabilities and net worth
Loans Government bonds Liquid assets Cash reserves at the Bank of England	Deposits
Total assets	

Step five: Add the right- and left-hand columns, and check that the balance sheet is in balance.

Assets	Liabilities and net worth
Loans Government bonds Liquid assets Cash reserves at the Bank of England	Deposits

Total assets = total liabilities + net worth.

1   (Worked problem: balance sheet) Green Bank has £18 million in outstanding loans, £3 million in government bonds, liquid assets of £4 million, cash reserves at the Bank of England of £1 million, and deposits equal to $20 million. Construct the balance sheet, compute its net worth, and check that it meets regulations regarding capital adequacy and cash reserves at the Bank of England.

Step-by-step solution

Step one: Make a T account.

Green Bank's Balance Sheet

Assets	Liabilities and net worth

Step two: Enter each of the assets (outstanding loans, holdings of government bonds, liquid assets, and cash reserves at the Bank of England) in the left-hand column, and add the assets.

Green Bank's Balance Sheet

Assets	Liabilities and net worth
Loans = £18 million Government bonds = £3 million Liquid assets = £4 million Cash reserves at Bank of England = £1 million	
Total assets	

Step three: Enter each of the liabilities (deposits) in the right-hand column, and add the liabilities. Check that cash reserves at the Bank of England are at least 0.5 percent of deposits.

Green Bank's Balance Sheet

Assets	Liabilities and net worth
Loans = £18 million Government bonds = £3 million Liquid assets = £4 million Cash reserves at Bank of England = £0.1 million	Deposits = £20 million
Total assets	

Cash reserve ratio = 0.1/20 = 0.5 percent of deposits

Calculate the ratio of liquid assets to deposits and comment on whether the ratio is prudent.

Ratio of liquid assets to deposits
= (4 + 0.1)/20 = 20.5 percent

Prudential regulation by the Bank of England does not specify a minimum ratio. Banks must keep a prudent amount depending on the type of deposits they hold as liabilities; the ratio of 20.5 percent appears to be more than adequate.

Step four: Compute net worth by subtracting liabilities from assets:

$$\text{Net worth} = 18 + 3 + 4 + 0.1 - 20 = \text{£5.1 million.}$$

Enter net worth in the right-hand column and check that it is at least 8 percent of total assets to comply with international agreements regarding capital adequacy requirements.

$$\text{Ratio of net worth to deposits} = 5.1/20 = 25.5 \text{ percent.}$$

Capital adequacy requirements are met with room to spare.

Green Bank's Balance Sheet

Assets	Liabilities and net worth
Loans = £18 million	Deposits = £20 million
Government bonds = £3 million	Net worth = £5.1 million
Liquid assets = £4 million	
Cash reserves at Bank of England = £0.1 million	
Total assets = £25.1 million	

Step five: Add the right- and left-hand columns, and check that the balance sheet is in balance.

Green Bank's Balance Sheet

Assets	Liabilities and net worth
Loans outstanding = £18 million	Deposits = £20 million
Government bonds = £3 million	Net worth = £5.1 million
Liquid assets = £4 million	
Cash reserves at Bank of England = £0.1 million	
Total assets = £25.1 million	Total liabilities plus net worth = £25.1 million

2   (Practice problem: balance sheet) First West Bank has £220 million in outstanding loans, £20 million in government bonds, liquid assets of £4 million, cash reserves at the Bank of England of £1 million, and deposits equal to £240 million. Construct its balance sheet, compute its net worth, and check that it meets regulations regarding capital adequacy and cash reserves at the Bank of England. Calculate the ratio of liquid assets to deposits and comment on whether it is prudent.

3   (Practice problem: balance sheet) Second North Bank has £400 million in outstanding loans, £25 million in government bonds, liquid assets of £50 million, cash reserves at the Bank of England of £2 million, and deposits equal to £400 million. Construct its balance sheet, compute its net worth, and check that it meets regulations regarding capital adequacy and cash reserves at the Bank of England. Calculate the ratio of liquid assets to deposits and comment on whether it is prudent.

MONEY CREATION

Using the fractional reserve system, banks create money. When banks receive a new deposit, they keep only a fraction on hand in reserve and loan out the remainder. But the loans find their way back into the banking system, increasing deposits further and setting off a new round of loans. When the process settles down, total deposits in the banking system have increased by a multiple of the initial deposit.

Tool Kit 28.2 Understanding Deposit Expansion and the Money Multiplier

Banks create money. Through the fractional reserve system deposits result in additional loans and further deposits. Follow these steps to see how the money creation process works through the banking system. In this example, we ignore liquid assets and all reserves are cash reserves held in the bank's vaults or at the central bank.

Step one: Construct a combined balance sheet for the banking system.

Step two: Identify the initial deposit, and add it to the banking system's deposits.

Step three: Identify the reserve ratio. Calculate the required increase in reserves made necessary by the initial deposit, and add it to the banking system's reserves:

New required reserves = reserve ratio × initial deposit.

Step four: Calculate the new loans that the deposit allows, and add the amount to the banking system's loans:

New loans = initial deposit – new required reserves.

This completes round one of the deposit expansion process. (Remember to recompute the total assets and liabilities and net worth.)

Step five: Trace through a few more rounds by repeating steps two through four. The initial deposit for round two is the amount of new loans from round one.

Step six: Compute the final expansion in deposits. This will be the increase in the money supply:

Final deposit expansion = initial deposit/reserve ratio.

Because there are no other leakages in this example, the money multiplier equals 1 divided by the reserve ratio.

---

4   (Worked problem: deposit expansion and money multiplier) The banking system in Costa Guano has £4 billion in outstanding loans, £1 billion in government bonds, £1 billion in reserves, and deposits of £5 billion. Its reserve ratio is 0.20. (Monetary magnitudes are converted to U.K. pound sterling equivalents.)

a   Construct the combined balance sheet.
b   A new deposit of £1 billion arrives from abroad. Trace through three rounds of the deposit expansion process, and compute the final deposit expansion.

Step-by-step solution

Step one (a): Construct a combined balance sheet for the banking system.

Costa Guano's Combined Balance Sheet

Assets	Liabilities and net worth
Loans outstanding = £4 billion Government bonds = £1 billion Reserves = £1 billion	Deposits = £5 billion Net worth = £1 billion
Total assets = £6 billion	Total liabilities plus net worth = £6 billion

Step two (b): Identify the initial deposit, and add it to the banking system's deposits. The deposit is £1 billion.

Step three: Identify the reserve ratio. Calculate the required increase in reserves made necessary by the initial deposit, and add it to the banking system's reserves:

$$\text{New required reserves} = 0.20 \times 1 = \text{£}0.2 \text{ billion.}$$

Step four: Calculate the new loans that the deposit allows, and add the amount to the banking system's loans:

$$\text{New loans} = 1 - 0.2 = \text{£}0.8 \text{ billion.}$$

Costa Guano's Combined Balance Sheet (round one)

Assets	Liabilities and net worth
Loans outstanding = £4.8 billion Government bonds = £1 billion Reserves = £1.2 billion	Deposits = £6 billion Net worth = £1 billion
Total assets = £7 billion	Total liabilities plus net worth = £7 billion

This completes round one of the deposit expansion process. (Note the new totals.)

Step five: Trace through a few more rounds by repeating steps two through four. The initial deposit for round two is the amount of new loans from round one.

Costa Guano's Combined Balance Sheet (round two)

Assets	Liabilities and net worth
Loans outstanding = £5.44 billion Government bonds = £1 billion Reserves = £1.36 billion	Deposits = £6.8 billion Net worth = £1 billion
Total assets = £7.8 billion	Total liabilities plus net worth = £7.8 billion

Costa Guano's Combined Balance Sheet (round three)

Assets	Liabilities and net worth
Loans outstanding = £5.95 billion Government bonds = £1 billion Reserves = £1.49 billion	Deposits = £7.44 billion Net worth = £1 billion
Total assets = £8.44 billion	Total liabilities plus net worth = £8.44 billion

Step six: Compute the final expansion in deposits. This will be the increase in the money supply:

$$\text{Final deposit expansion} = 1/0.2 = \text{£}5 \text{ billion.}$$

5 (Practice problem: deposit expansion and money multiplier) In El Dorado, the banking system has outstanding loans of £200 million, government bonds of £10 billion, reserves of £30 million, and deposits of £210 billion. Its reserve ratio is 1/7. (Monetary magnitudes are converted to U.K. pound sterling equivalents.)

a Construct the combined balance sheet.
b A new deposit of £49 million arrives from abroad. Trace through two rounds of the deposit expansion process, and compute the final deposit expansion.

6 (Practice problem: deposit expansion and money multiplier) The Erehwemos banking system has outstanding loans of £45 billion, government bonds of £2 billion, reserves of £5 billion, and deposits of £50 billion. Its reserve ratio is 0.10. (Monetary magnitudes are converted to U.S. dollar equivalents.)

a Construct the combined balance sheet.
b A new deposit of £5 billion arrives from abroad. Trace through three rounds of the deposit expansion process, and compute the final deposit expansion.

Answers to Problems

2

First West Bank's Balance Sheet

Assets	Liabilities and net worth
Loans = £220 million Government bonds = £20 million Liquid assets = £4 million Cash reserves at Bank of England = £1 million	Deposits = £240 million Net worth = £5 million
Total assets = £245 million	

Cash reserve ratio = 0.1/240 = 0.42 percent of deposits and does not meet the minimum requirement of the Bank of England of 0.5 percent.

$$\text{Capital adequacy} = \text{ratio of net worth to deposits}$$
$$= 5/240 = 2.1 \text{ percent.}$$

Capital adequacy does not meet the international requirement of 8 percent.

Ratio of liquid assets to deposits = (4 + 1)/240 = 2.1 percent.

Prudential regulation by the Bank of England does not specify a minimum ratio. Banks must keep a prudent amount depending on the type of deposits they hold as liabilities; the ratio of 2.1 percent is low and may be deemed imprudent.

3

Second North Bank's Balance Sheet

Assets	Liabilities and net worth
Loans = £400 million Government bonds = £25 million Liquid assets = £50 million Cash reserves at Bank of England = £2 million	Deposits = £400 million Net worth = £77 million
Total assets = £477 million	

Cash reserve ratio = 2/400 = 0.5 percent of deposits and meets the minimum requirement of the Bank of England of 0.5 percent.

Capital adequacy = ratio of net worth to deposits
= 77/400 = 19.3 percent.

Capital adequacy meets the international requirements with room to spare.

Ratio of liquid assets to deposits = (50 + 2)/400 = 13 percent.

Prudential regulation by the Bank of England does not specify a minimum ratio. Banks must keep a prudent amount depending on the type of deposits they hold as liabilities; the ratio of 13 percent appears to be prudent.

5 *a*

El Dorado's Combined Balance Sheet

Assets	Liabilities and net worth
Loans outstanding = £200 million	Deposits = £210 million
Government bonds = £10 million	
Reserves = £30 million	Net worth = £30 million
Total assets = £240 million	Total liabilities plus net worth = £240 million

b

El Dorado's Combined Balance Sheet (round one)

Assets	Liabilities and net worth
Loans outstanding = £242 million	Deposits = £259 million
Government bonds = £10 million	
Reserves = £37 million	Net worth = £30 million
Total assets = £289 million	Total liabilities plus net worth = £289 million

El Dorado's Combined Balance Sheet (round two)

Assets	Liabilities and net worth
Loans outstanding = £278 million	Deposits = £301 million
Government bonds = £10 million	
Reserves = £43 million	Net worth = £30 million
Total assets = £331 million	Total liabilities plus net worth = £331 million

Final deposit expansion = 49/(1/7) = £343 million.

6 *a*

Erehwemos's Combined Balance Sheet (round one)

Assets	Liabilities and net worth
Loans outstanding = £45 billion	Deposits = £50 billion
Government bonds = £2 billion	
Reserves = £5 billion	Net worth = £2 billion
Total assets = £52 billion	Total liabilities plus net worth = £52 billion

b

Erehwemos's Combined Balance Sheet (round two)

Assets	Liabilities and net worth
Loans outstanding = £49.5 billion	Deposits = £55 billion
Government bonds = £2 billion	
Reserves = £5.5 billion	Net worth = £2 billion
Total assets = £57 billion	Total liabilities plus net worth = £57 billion

Erehwemos's Combined Balance Sheet (round three)

Assets	Liabilities and net worth
Loans outstanding = £53.55 billion	Deposits = £59.5 billion
Government bonds = £2 billion	
Reserves = £5.95 billion	Net worth = £2 billion
Total assets = £61.5 billion	Total liabilities plus net worth = £61.5 billion

Final deposit expansion = 5/0.1 = £50 billion.

Chapter 29

MONETARY THEORY

Chapter Review

Chapter 28 showed how central banks can use policy instruments to bring about changes in the money supply and the availability of credit. This chapter discusses how these changes affect the economy. The most important issues involve changes in the money supply that affect output, prices, or both, and the channels through which these changes operate. There is some disagreement among economists concerning the latter issue, and the chapter outlines the sources of contention and the consequences for monetary policy. The concluding section explains how monetary policy works in the international monetary system of the world's interdependent economies.

ESSENTIAL CONCEPTS

1   With fixed prices, if the money supply is increased, people may either hold onto the money or spend it. If they hold it, aggregate demand will remain unchanged. If they spend it, aggregate demand will shift to the right, and output will increase. This can be seen from the definition of **velocity:**

$$V = pQ/M,$$

where p is the fixed price index, Q is output, and M is the money supply. An increase in M results in a decrease in V or an increase in Q. The big question in this chapter is how a change in M can affect output.

2   **Traditional monetary theory** starts with the demand for money to facilitate transactions. The opportunity cost of holding money is the **nominal interest rate,** which is determined by the intersection of supply and demand for money. An increase in the money supply lowers interest rates, stimulates investment, and shifts aggregate demand. The resulting increases in output and income shift the demand for money to the right, mitigating the fall in the interest rate.

3   The effectiveness of monetary policy depends upon three factors. First, there is the elasticity of money demand, which indicates how much the interest rate will fall for a given increase in money supply. Second is how much additional investment will result from the fall in the interest rate—sensitivity of investment to the interest rate. Finally there is the size of the multiplier, which measures how much output will increase for a given change in investment. In deep recessions each of these factors is likely to be small, and most economists agree that at these times monetary policy is unlikely to provide much stimulus.

4   Another view, held by monetarists, rearranges the definition of velocity as $M = pQ/V$ and interprets this equation as the demand for money. They assume that velocity is constant and that output is at its full employment level; therefore, an increase in money supply must increase Q by shifting aggregate demand to the right. The assumption about velocity implies that money demand does not depend upon the interest rate.

5   Criticism of traditional monetary theory centers around two relationships. First, there is the relationship between money and income. Even if the supply of money affects the volume of transactions, most transactions involve exchanges of financial assets, which have no direct bearing on output. Also, the rise of credit card and switch card use make traditional forms of money unnecessary. Second, the assumed relationship between interest rates and the demand for money may be undermined by interest-bearing checking accounts. If the checking account pays market interest rates, then the opportunity cost of holding money is zero. At any rate, the fact that real interest rates vary little casts doubt on the traditional view.

6   Monetary policy does work, however. Some recent theories stress alternative mechanisms. A likely channel through which money can affect output is credit availability. Tight monetary policy may reduce the supply of loans. In addition, there may be portfolio effects whereby, for example, changes in nominal interest rates alter the value of bonds and stocks, affecting the incentives to raise new capital. In Britain, changes in interest rates, house prices, and consumption have been closely correlated in recent years.

7   In an open economy monetary policy also works through exchange rates. For example, lower interest rates reduce the demand for pounds and lower the exchange rate. This depreciation makes exports attractive to foreign buyers and the resulting increase in net exports shifts aggregate demand. The open economy does limit the ability of the Bank of England to restrict credit, however, because U.K. borrowers can go elsewhere for funds.

BEHIND THE ESSENTIAL CONCEPTS

1   There are areas of disagreement about monetary theory and policy, but there is also a good deal of common ground. Concerning monetary theory, most economists recognise that the central bank can control the money supply through the use of its three instruments: open market operations, reserve requirements, and the discount rate. Most economists also agree that the demand for money depends upon income. In the area of monetary policy, economists believe that in deep recessions increases in the money supply will likely be ineffective, in mild recessions increases will shift aggregate demand and help the economy recover, and when the economy is operating at capacity, they will result only in higher prices. Severely restricting the money supply and credit availability, on the other hand, will cause a recession.

2   There is no consensus about how credit availability and the money supply work their way through the economy, but there are four possibilities.

   a   A larger money supply lowers interest rates and increases investment.

   b   A larger money supply directly shifts aggregate demand because velocity is constant.

   c   A larger money supply brings about higher stock and bond prices, which lead to more consumption and investment.

   d   Looser credit motivates more lending.

3   The logic of credit rationing is as follows. Banks ration credit because they fear that raising the interest rate would attract low-quality (risky) borrowers, many of whom would default. Because the interest rate remains below the market clearing rate, there is excess demand for loans.

SELF-TEST

True or False

1   The velocity of money is the ratio of nominal GDP to the price level.

2   The demand for money arising from its use as a unit of account is called the transactions demand for money.

3   The transactions demand for money increases as nominal income increases.

4   The opportunity cost of holding money is the nominal interest rate.

5   According to traditional monetary theory, the nominal interest rate is determined by the intersection of the supply and demand for money.

6   According to traditional monetary theory, an increase in the money supply will lower interest rates and increase investment except during deep recessions.

7   Monetary policy is more effective when the multiplier is large.

8   The theory that the velocity of money is constant and thus increases in the money supply bring about equal proportional increases in income is called the quantity theory of money.

9   Monetarists believe that money is important and that the government should use active monetary policy to influence the fluctuations in the economy.

10 Until recently, the velocity of money has increased steadily, although the upward trend slowed during recessions.

11 Central bank policies may affect the ability of banks to make loans, but they cannot force banks to lend.

12 Because of credit rationing, interest rates may not rise even though there is an excess demand for money.

13 If the interest rate falls and banks are willing to lend, investment will increase unless firms have an elastic demand for loans.

14 In an open economy an increase in the money supply appreciates the currency and increases net exports.

15 In an open economy, the central bank's attempt to restrict the availability of credit may be undermined if borrowers look abroad for funds.

Multiple Choice

1 When the central bank increases the supply of money,

    a individuals may hold the additional money, decreasing the velocity of money.
    b individuals may spend the money, leading to more output.
    c individuals may spend the money, shifting aggregate demand to the left.
    d all of the above.
    e *a* and *b*.

2 Which definition of money is used in this chapter?

    a M0
    b M2
    c M4
    d Eurodollars, money market mutual funds, and deposits in excess of £100,000
    e All of the above

3 The velocity of money is defined as the ratio of

    a GDP to the price level.
    b the price level to GDP.
    c GDP to the money supply.
    d the money supply to GDP.
    e M2 to M0.

4 According to traditional monetary theory, changes in the money supply affect the economy through

    a the interest rates.
    b the velocity of money.
    c the foreign exchange market.
    d the quantity theory of money.
    e credit availability.

5 The transactions demand for money refers to money held as a

    a medium of exchange.
    b store of value.
    c unit of account.
    d precaution against unexpected need such as illness or job loss.
    e hedge against deflation.

6 An increase in which of the following will cause an increase in the demand for money?

    a Real income
    b Nominal income
    c Velocity of money
    d The nominal interest rate
    e The real interest rate

7 The opportunity cost of holding money is

    a the exchange rate.
    b the velocity of money.
    c the real interest rate.
    d the nominal interest rate.
    e none of the above.

8 Which of the following is *not* a principle of traditional monetary theory?

    a The nominal interest rate is the opportunity cost of holding money.
    b The demand for money decreases as the interest rate rises.
    c The interest rate is determined by the intersection of money demand and money supply.
    d The velocity of money is stable.
    e None of the above.

9 Which of the following is a tenet of the traditional theory of monetary policy?

    a Monetary policy is ineffective because it cannot affect the interest rate.
    b Monetary policy is especially effective in deep recessions when money is scarce.
    c Monetary policy is ineffective in deep recessions.
    d Monetary policy is ineffective because investment is not affected by changes in interest rates.
    e Monetary policy is effective but is too dangerous to use.

10 Monetary policy is more effective when

    a the elasticity of money demand is low.
    b investment is sensitive to changes in the interest rate.
    c the multiplier is low.
    d prices are flexible.
    e the economy is in deep recession.

11 According to traditional monetary theory, monetary policy affects output by

    a altering the availability of credit.
    b changing the exchange rate and thus net exports.
    c affecting stock prices and thus firms' incentives to raise funds for investment on the stock market.
    d changing interest rates and investment.
    e changing the size of the government deficit.

12 One criticism of traditional monetary theory is

    a real interest rates are too variable to explain the variation in investment.
    b most transactions involve the exchange of assets, not the purchase of goods.
    c most cheque accounts pay no interest.
    d the velocity of money is not a constant.
    e there are many definitions of money.

13 Monetarists believe that

    a the velocity of money is stable over time.
    b the velocity of money is unpredictable.
    c the quantity theory of money is no longer a sensible way to look at the economy.
    d money serves no function as a store of value.

e the velocity of money increases as the money supply grows.

14 According to credit availability theories, an increase in the money supply will stimulate the economy when

a interest rates fall.
b stock prices rise.
c bond prices rise.
d interest rates rise.
e banks make more loans on easier terms.

15 According to credit availability theories, central bank policies

a affect the ability of banks to lend but cannot force them to lend.
b affect the willingness of banks to lend but cannot affect the ability of banks to lend.
c affect the ability and willingness of banks to lend by lowering interest rates.
d may not stimulate the economy if banks buy fewer Treasury bills.
e c and d.

16 Banks may be reluctant to lend even though the return on Treasury bills is lower if

a default rates are high.
b their net worth is low.
c other banks have gone bankrupt.
d all of the above.
e none of the above; banks will not be reluctant to lend.

17 Even though there is an excess demand for credit, banks may not increase the interest rate if

a Treasury bill interest rates are high.
b increased interest rates have an adverse selection effect by attracting riskier borrowers.
c Treasury bill interest rates are low.
d credit rationing is illegal.
e borrowers cannot afford higher interest rates.

18 Portfolio theories of how monetary policy affects the economy focus on the role of money as a

a medium of exchange.
b store of value.
c unit of account.
d precaution against unexpected need such as illness or job loss.
e hedge against deflation.

19 According to portfolio theories, the central bank can increase the money supply, lower interest rates, and shift aggregate demand because

a when interest rates fall, stock prices rise and firms invest more.
b when interest rates fall, stock prices rise and people increase consumption because they are wealthier.
c open market operations increase banks' reserves, and their response leads to higher stock prices.
d all of the above.
e none of the above.

20 In an open economy, an increase in the money supply

a depreciates the exchange rate.
b increases exports.
c reduces imports.
d increases net exports.
e all of the above.

Completion

1 Gross domestic product divided by the money supply equals the _____.

2 Money held for use as a medium of exchange forms the _____.

3 The opportunity cost of holding money is the _____.

4 The view that money affects the economy through changes in interest rates and investment is the _____ monetary theory.

5 According to _____, the velocity of money is constant and increases in the money supply bring about proportionate increases in national income.

6 _____ believe that there is a stable and predictable relationship between the money supply and national income.

7 _____ occurs when there is an excess demand for credit but banks do not raise interest rates for fear of attracting less credit-worthy borrowers.

8 According to _____ theories, changes in the money supply may lead to different levels of investment without changing interest rates.

9 A decrease in the supply of money leads to an _____ of the exchange rate.

10 An open economy _____ the ability of the central bank to limit credit.

Answers to Self-Test

True or False

1	F	6	T	11	T
2	F	7	T	12	T
3	T	8	T	13	F
4	T	9	F	14	F
5	T	10	T	15	T

Multiple Choice

1	e	6	b	11	d	16	d
2	c	7	d	12	b	17	b
3	c	8	d	13	a	18	b
4	a	9	c	14	e	19	d
5	a	10	b	15	a	20	e

Completion

1 velocity
2 money supply
3 nominal interest rate
4 traditional
5 monetarism
6 Monetarists
7 Credit rationing
8 portfolio

9   appreciation
10 reduces

Tools and Practice Problems

The traditional theory of how changes in the money supply affect the economy argues that money supply determines interest rates in the money market. Although there are problems associated with this theory, it represents the best starting point for the study of monetary policy. In this section, we work problems that trace the channels through which money moves to shift aggregate demand and alter the equilibrium output of the economy. Tool Kit 29.1 explores traditional monetary theory.

Tool Kit 29.1 Using Traditional Monetary Theory

   According to this view of money and the economy, the nominal interest rate, which is the opportunity cost of holding money, is determined by the intersection of the supply and demand curves for money. An increase in the supply of money shifts the supply curve to the right and lowers the interest rate. Finally, lower interest rates induce more investment and shift aggregate demand to the right.

Step one: Identify the demand curve for money, the supply curve for money, and the investment function.

Step two: Start with an equilibrium in which the supply and demand curves for money intersect at the nominal interest rate. The level of investment is read off the investment function at this interest rate.

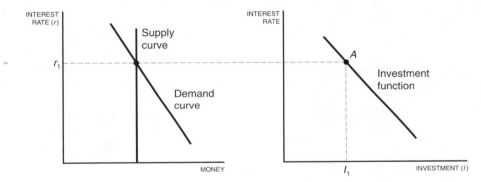

Step three: Shift the money supply curve to reflect the change in the money supply.

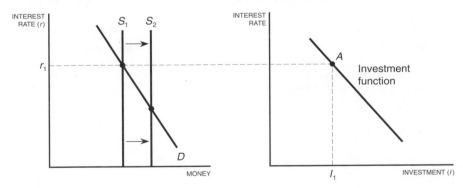

Step four: Find the new equilibrium interest rate.

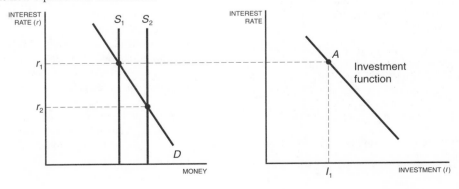

Step five: Determine the change in investment by reading the new level of investment off the investment function.

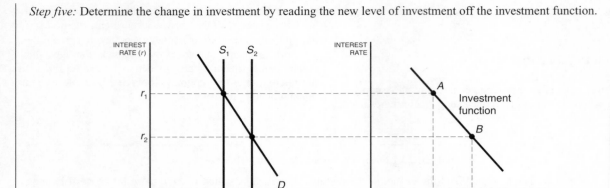

---

1   (Worked problem: traditional monetary theory) The money demand and investment function are given in Table 29.1. The initial money supply is £1.8 billion.

Table 29.1

Money demand		Investment function	
Nominal interest rate	Money demand (billion £)	Real interest rate	Investment (100 million £)
10%	1.0	10%	2
9%	1.2	9%	3
8%	1.4	8%	4
7%	1.6	7%	5
6%	1.8	6%	6
5%	2.0	5%	7
4%	2.2	4%	8

a   Find the equilibrium interest rate and level of investment.
b   Suppose the central bank lowers required reserves, and the money supply increases to £2 billion. Determine the new interest rate and level of investment.
c   How does aggregate demand shift?

Step-by-step solution

Step one (a): Identify the demand curve for money, the money supply, and the investment function. See Table 29.1 for the money demand and the investment function. The money supply is £1.8 billion.

Step two: Start with an equilibrium in which the supply and demand curves for money intersect at the nominal interest rate. The level of investment is read off the investment function at this interest rate. The initial equilibrium interest rate is 6 percent, which induces firms to invest £600 million.

Step three (b): Shift the money supply curve to reflect the change in the money supply.

Step four: Find the new equilibrium interest rate. It is 5 percent.

Step five: Determine the change in investment by reading the new level of investment off the investment function. Firms increase their investment levels to £700 million, which represents an increase of £100 million.

Step six (c): Aggregate demand shifts to the right.

2   (Practice problem: traditional monetary theory) The money demand and investment function are given in Table 29.2. The initial money supply is £4.2 billion.

Table 29.2

Money demand		Investment function	
Nominal interest rate	Money demand (billion £)	Real interest rate	Investment (100 million £)
10%	2.5	10%	2.0
9%	3.0	9%	4.0
8%	3.3	8%	5.0
7%	3.6	7%	6.0
6%	3.9	6%	7.0
5%	4.2	5%	7.5
4%	4.5	4%	8.0

a   Find the equilibrium interest rate and level of investment.
b   Suppose the central bank sells bonds, causing the money supply to decrease to £3.6 billion. Determine the new interest rate and level of investment.
c   How does aggregate demand shift?

3   (Practice problem: traditional monetary theory) The money demand and investment function are given in Table 29.3. The initial money supply is £5.5 billion.

Table 29.3

Money demand		Investment function	
Nominal interest rate	Money demand (billion £)	Real interest rate	Investment (100 million £)
10%	4.5	10%	12.0
9%	5.0	9%	14.0
8%	5.5	8%	15.0
7%	6.0	7%	16.0
6%	6.5	6%	17.0
5%	7.0	5%	17.5
4%	7.5	4%	18.0

a   Find the equilibrium interest rate and level of investment.

b   Suppose the central bank buys bonds, causing the money supply to increase to £7 billion. Determine the new interest rate and level of investment.

c   How does aggregate demand shift?

Answers to Problems

2   a   Interest rate = 5 percent; investment = £750 million.
    b   Interest rate = 7 percent; investment = £600 million.
    c   Aggregate demand shifts to the left.

3   a   Interest rate = 8 percent;
        investment = £1,500 million.
    b   Interest rate = 5 percent;
        investment = £1,750 million.
    c   Aggregate demand shifts to the right.

FISCAL AND MONETARY POLICY

Chapter Review

The basic model of unemployment macroeconomics is completed in this chapter, which pulls together the material on the real economy from Chapters 26 and 27 with that on the monetary system in Chapters 28 and 29. The chapter compares the effects of fiscal and monetary policies and analyses some issues concerning their use in the current economy. The next chapter begins the section on dynamics.

ESSENTIAL CONCEPTS

1 **Fiscal policy** is the use of government tax and expenditure policies to improve the performance of the economy. When there is excess capacity, an increase in government expenditure or a tax cut shifts aggregate demand to the right, moving the economy towards full employment. Whether the gain in current output is worth the increased indebtedness depends upon how much private investment is crowded out, whether government spending is for consumption or investment, and how much of the deficit is financed by borrowing from abroad.

2 The government can still use fiscal policy even if it is constrained to keep a balanced budget. Although the required tax increase offsets somewhat the effect of higher government expenditures, some stimulus remains. The **balanced budget multiplier** equals 1; this means that aggregate demand shifts to the right by exactly the amount of the extra government spending.

3 Monetary policy can also be used. A larger money supply lowers interest rates and makes credit available, increasing private investment. Also, the exchange rate falls, stimulating a rise in net exports. Both combine to shift aggregate demand to the right. Monetary policy is also important as it interacts with fiscal policy. In response to a fiscal stimulus the central bank may pursue an **accommodative monetary policy.** This stance keeps interest rates from rising, which would limit the fiscal stimulus.

4 Monetary and fiscal policies differ in how they affect the composition of output. Monetary policy's lower interest rates bring about more investment. The impact of fiscal policy depends upon the mix of additional expenditure and tax cuts and also upon how government expenditure is divided between consumption and investment.

5   Monetary policy is certainly ineffective in deep recessions. Fiscal policy's power may be limited if consumers anticipate future tax increases to pay off the deficit, if government borrowing increases interest rates (crowding out investment), or if changes in the exchange rate reduce net exports. None of these is likely in deep recessions, however.

6   Monetary policy's impact is delayed by the time it takes lower interest rates to stimulate investment. Government spending in principle can work immediately. It does take time for government to pass laws and administer the spending. Certain programs, such as unemployment benefits and progressive income taxes, act as **automatic stabilizers,** quickly causing greater spending and reduced taxes during recessions.

7   In the United States, the **balanced budget amendment** requiring the government to avoid deficit would probably destabilise the economy because it would prevent the automatic stabilisers from doing their job. In this case all of the responsibility for stabilization would rest with monetary policy. One compromise would keep the **full-employment deficit** at zero. This is what the deficit would be if the economy were operating at full employment, and it is a measure of fiscal responsibility.

BEHIND THE ESSENTIAL CONCEPTS

1   Government can use fiscal policy in two ways. First, it can stimulate the economy during recessions. Here government takes an active role, making up for the shortfall in private spending. Another approach works automatically. Taxes, such as income and corporation tax, which decrease as income decreases, and social security programs such as income support and the unemployment benefit act as automatic stabilisers. These programs provide additional spending during downturns without explicit government action.

2   The instruments of government policy include fiscal policy measures such as tax rates and levels of expenditure, and monetary instruments such as open market operations, reserve requirements, and the discount rate. In different circumstances some form of each policy may be appropriate. They differ in their effectiveness, how they change the mix of output, and their speed of implementation.

3   The actual budget deficit computes the difference between government expenditure and tax revenue. When the economy falls into recession, however, tax collections diminish. Households earn less income and pay less income tax. Business profits fall and so do corporation tax collections. Spending increases on unemployment benefit and other welfare programs. All of these combine to bring about a deficit without any change in policy. The full-employment deficit measures what the deficit would be at full employment. Tax and expenditure policies that result in no full-employment deficit will nevertheless lead to actual budget deficits when the economy is operating below capacity.

SELF-TEST

True or False

1   Fiscal policy aims to improve macroeconomic performance by promoting fiscal responsibility among banks and other financial intermediaries.

2   When the government increases expenditures or cuts taxes to provide a fiscal stimulus, there is an increase in the national debt.

3   Government borrowing to finance the deficit may crowd out private investment.

4   If government spending and taxes increase by the same amount, then aggregate demand will not change.

5   The balanced budget multiplier equals 1.

6   In a closed economy, monetary policy works by changing interest rates and investment.

7   In an open economy, monetary policy works by changing exchange rates and net exports.

8   If the central bank pursues an accommodative monetary policy, it will cut the money supply when government spending increases.

9   While monetary policy stimulates investment, fiscal policy may crowd it out.

10   Most economists agree that fiscal policy is ineffective in deep recessions.

11   One problem with fiscal policy is the time it takes for government to take action.

12   The impact of monetary policy is delayed while firms take time to respond to lower interest rates with new investment.

13   Unemployment benefits help stabilise the economy by increasing government expenditure during recessions.

14   Amending the law to require a balanced budget would place all of the responsibility for stabilising the economy on monetary policy.

15   The full-employment deficit is what the actual budget deficit would be if the economy were operating at full employment.

Multiple Choice

1   Fiscal policy includes
   a   maintaining a stable money supply.
   b   using consumer product safety regulation to promote consumer confidence.
   c   regulating the banking and securities industries to encourage sound investment.
   d   using government expenditure and taxation to improve macroeconomic performance.
   e   funding audit agencies, such as the National Audit Office, to ensure that government carries out its fiduciary responsibilities.

2   Providing fiscal stimulus with a current budget deficit affects future generations by

a   accumulating a national debt for which they are responsible.
b   reducing current private investment by driving up current interest rates.
c   incurring foreign indebtedness by financing the deficit with bonds sold abroad.
d   all of the above.
e   *a* and *b*.

3   An increase in government spending holding the level of taxes constant will

a   shift the aggregate expenditures schedule up.
b   leave the aggregate expenditures schedule unchanged.
c   shift the aggregate expenditures schedule down.
d   rotate the aggregate expenditures schedule to the left.
e   rotate the aggregate expenditures schedule to the right.

4   An increase in taxes holding the level of government spending constant will

a   shift the aggregate expenditures schedule up.
b   leave the aggregate expenditures schedule unchanged.
c   shift the aggregate expenditures schedule down.
d   rotate the aggregate expenditures schedule to the left.
e   rotate the aggregate expenditures schedule to the right.

5   An increase in both government spending and taxes, keeping the overall budget balanced, will

a   shift the aggregate expenditures schedule up.
b   leave the aggregate expenditures schedule unchanged.
c   shift the aggregate expenditures schedule down.
d   rotate the aggregate expenditures schedule to the left.
e   rotate the aggregate expenditures schedule to the right.

6   Deficit spending is financed by

a   taxes.
b   spending cuts.
c   borrowing through the sale of Treasury bills and bonds to investors.
d   printing money.
e   the multiplier.

7   Increased government expenditure

a   reduces total investment.
b   reduces private investment but may increase total investment if the additional government expenditure includes public investment, such as roads or research and development.
c   increases private investment.
d   reduces foreign indebtedness.
e   may reduce total investment if the central bank pursues an accommodative monetary policy.

8   The balanced budget multiplier equals

a   1.
b   zero, because the stimulus provided by increased government spending is offset by the fiscal drag of the tax increase.
c   1 divided by the marginal propensity to consume.
d   one divided by the reserve ratio.
e   2.

9   When there is excess capacity, an increase in the money supply leads to

a   lower interest rates.
b   increased investment.
c   greater credit availability.
d   exchange rate depreciation.
e   all of the above.

10 Accommodative monetary policy refers to

a   keeping a strong currency to accommodate importers.
b   driving down the exchange rate to promote exports.
c   complementing the objectives of fiscal policy by adjusting the money supply to keep interest rates from rising.
d   maintaining a stable money supply.
e   letting the money supply grow at a rate equal to the growth in output.

11 Crowding out refers to the

a   possibility that taxes reduce private investment.
b   effect of inflation on the real value of the accumulated government debt.
c   possibility that government borrowing may reduce private investment.
d   effect of protectionism on the trade balance.
e   effect of imports on the market share of domestic firms.

12 Which of the following illustrates problems with the effectiveness of a policy instrument?

a   Even though the central bank undertakes policies that increase bank reserves, it may not be able to motivate banks to make new loans.
b   Looser monetary policy, even though it was designed to increase investment, might instead cause the pound to depreciate and increase net exports.
c   Monetary policy often concentrates its effects on particular sectors, such as export-competing industries or consumer durables.
d   There are lags in the government's ability to recognise and implement fiscal programs.
e   Individuals may treat tax cuts as temporary and increase consumption.

13 Which of the following illustrates a concern with the effect of a policy instrument on the composition of output?

a   Even though the central bank undertakes policies that increase bank reserves, it may not be able to motivate banks to make new loans.
b   Looser monetary policy, even though it was de-

signed to increase investment, might instead cause the pound to depreciate and increase net exports.

c   Monetary policy often concentrates its effects on particular sectors, such as export-competing industries or consumer durables.

d   There are lags in the government's ability to recognise and implement fiscal programs.

e   Individuals may treat tax cuts as temporary and increase consumption.

14   Mechanisms that increase the government deficit during recessions and decrease it during economic booms are called

a   balanced budget multipliers.
b   full-employment deficits.
c   automatic stabilisers.
d   political business cycles.
e   none of the above.

15   Automatic stabilisers are

a   programs, such as the unemployment benefit or progressive taxation, that increase spending during recessions and reduce it during economic booms.

b   policy rules that restrain the use of discretionary fiscal and monetary policies.

c   the adjustments that individuals with rational expectations make to offset fiscal and monetary policies.

d   market responses, such as increased interest rates, that limit the ability of government to stimulate the economy.

e   *a* and *c*.

16   Which of the following is *not* an automatic stabiliser?

a   Income taxes
b   The unemployment benefit
c   The child benefit
d   social security benefit
e   None of the above

17   Which of the following relates to the issue of lags in monetary and fiscal policies?

a   Monetary policy's effectiveness is delayed while businesses wait to undertake new investments.

b   Governments take time to make decisions about tax and expenditure changes.

c   Exchange rates adjust slowly.
d   All of the above.
e   *a* and *b*.

18   Central and local government spending tends to

a   increase in booms and decrease in recessions, thus reducing the volatility of the economy.

b   increase in booms and decrease in recessions, thus increasing the volatility of the economy.

c   decrease in booms and increase in recessions, thus reducing the volatility of the economy.

d   decrease in booms and increase in recessions, thus increasing the volatility of the economy.

e   be stable over the business cycle and neither increase nor reduce the volatility of the economy.

19   A balanced budget amendment in the United States or elsewhere would

a   eliminate the ability of the government to provide fiscal stimulus.

b   place most of the burden of stabilization on monetary policy.

c   probably destabilise the economy by limiting the impact of automatic stabilisers.

d   all of the above.
e   *b* and *c*.

20   The deficit that would occur if the economy were at full employment under current spending and tax policies is called the

a   balanced budget multiplier.
b   full-employment deficit.
c   trade deficit.
d   total accumulated government debt.
e   real budget deficit.

Completion

1   _____ involves the use of taxation and government spending to improve macroeconomic performance.

2   The balanced budget multiplier equals _____.

3   If the government spends more than it raises in taxes, the deficit is financed by _____.

4   _____ includes infrastructure and spending for education and research.

5   _____ monetary policy furthers the goals of fiscal policy by adjusting the money supply to keep interest rates from rising and crowding out private investment.

6   _____ refers to the possibility that government borrowing may reduce private investment.

7   Mechanisms that reduce government spending or raise taxes in recessions are called _____.

8   Central and local government expenditures vary _____ than GDP.

9   In the United States, the _____ would preclude the use of deficit financed fiscal policy.

10   The _____ equals the deficit that would have occurred if government revenues and spending were at their full-employment levels.

Answers to Self-Test

True or False

1	F	6	T	11	T
2	T	7	T	12	T
3	T	8	F	13	T
4	F	9	T	14	T
5	T	10	F	15	T

Multiple Choice

1	*d*	6	*c*	11	*c*	16	*c*
2	*d*	7	*b*	12	*a*	17	*e*
3	*a*	8	*a*	13	*b*	18	*b*
4	*c*	9	*e*	14	*c*	19	*d*
5	*a*	10	*c*	15	*a*	20	*b*

Completion

1 Fiscal policy
2 one
3 borrowing
4 Government investment
5 An accommodative
6 Crowding out
7 automatic stabilizers
8 more
9 balanced budget amendment
10 full-employment deficit

Tools and Practice Problems

Fiscal policy involves the use of government expenditure and taxation to influence the macroeconomic performance of the economy. It works by shifting aggregate demand, up in the cases of tax cuts or expenditure increases, down when taxes are raised or expenditures decreased. The multiplier plays a crucial role, determining the magnitude of the change in aggregate demand that results from an initial fiscal policy measure. In this section we use income-expenditure analysis to study balanced budget changes in fiscal policy. Tool Kit 30.1 shows how to analyse the impact of changes in government spending accompanied by tax changes of equal size.

Tool Kit 30.1 Analysing Government Spending with Tax Changes

When there are equal changes in government spending and taxes, output will change by an equivalent amount. Economists say that the balanced budget multiplier is 1. Follow these steps.

Step one: Identify the marginal propensity to consume, the initial tax rate, investment, and the level of government spending.

Step two: Compute the consumption function.

Step three: Compute the aggregate expenditures schedule and find the equilibrium level of output.

Step four: Identify the new tax rate and use this information to calculate the new aggregate consumption function.

Step five: Identify the new level of government spending and compute the new aggregate expenditures schedule.

Step six: Find the new equilibrium level of output.

Step seven: Verify that the change in tax revenue equals the change in government spending:

Change in tax revenues
= new tax rate × new output − original tax rate × original output.

Step eight: Verify that the balanced budget multiplier equals 1:

$$\text{Multiplier} = \frac{\text{change in output}}{\text{change in government spending}}.$$

---

1 (Worked problem: balanced budget fiscal policy) In Isle de Guano (a neighbor of Costa Guano) the marginal propensity to consume is 0.75 and the tax rate is a rather high 50 percent. Autonomous consumption is 10 million guanos, investment is zero, and government spending is 40 million guanos.

  a Compute the aggregate consumption function.
  b Compute the aggregate expenditures schedule.
  c Find the equilibrium level of output.
  d Is the budget balanced?

Suppose that government spending is increased to 60 million guanos and the tax rate is increased to 60 percent.

  d Compute the new aggregate consumption function.
  e Compute the new aggregate expenditure schedule.
  f Find the new equilibrium level of output.
  g Compute the change in tax revenue. Is this a balanced budget change in fiscal policy?
  h Verify that the change in output equals the change in government spending, that is, that the multiplier equals 1.

Step-by-step solution

Step one: Identify the marginal propensity to consume, the initial tax rate, autonomous consumption, investment, and the level of government spending. The marginal propensity to consume is 0.75 and the tax rate is 50 percent. Autonomous consumption is 10 million guanos, investment is zero, and government spending is 40 million guanos.

Step two: Compute the consumption function. When national income is zero, consumption is 10 million guanos. When national income is 20 million guanos, consumption equals $0.75(1 − 0.5) × 20 + 10 = 17.5$. Continuing, we derive the consumption function.

National income (millions of guanos)	Consumption (millions of guanos)
0	10
20	17.5
40	25
60	32.5
80	40
100	47.5
120	55

Step three: Compute the aggregate expenditures schedule and find the equilibrium level of output. Since investment equals zero and there is no trade, aggregate expenditure equals consumption plus government expenditures.

National income	Consumption	Government expenditure	Aggregate expenditure
(millions of guanos)			
0	10	40	50
20	17.5	40	57.5
40	25	40	65
60	32.5	40	72.5
80	40	40	80
100	47.5	40	87.5
120	55	40	95

Equilibrium output is 80. The budget is balanced; taxes = $0.5 \times 80 = 40$ = government expenditure.

Step four: Identify the new tax rate and use this information to calculate the new aggregate consumption function. The new tax rate is 60 percent. When national income is 20 million guanos, consumption equals $0.75 \times (1 - 0.6) \times 20 + 10 = 16$. Continuing, we derive the consumption function.

National income (millions of guanos)	Consumption (millions of guanos)
0	10
20	16
40	22
60	28
80	34
100	40
120	46

Step five: Identify the new level of government spending and compute the new aggregate expenditure schedule. Government now spends 60 million guanos. The new aggregate expenditure schedule is as follows.

National income	Consumption	Government expenditure	Aggregate expenditure
(millions of guanos)			
0	10	60	70
20	16	60	76
40	22	60	82
60	28	60	88
80	34	60	94
100	40	60	100
120	46	60	106

Step six: Find the new equilibrium level of output. It equals 100.

Step seven: Verify that the change in tax revenue equals the change in government spending.

Change in tax revenues
= new tax rate × new output – original tax rate
× original output
= $0.60 \times 100 - 0.50 \times 80 = 20$ million guanos.

Step eight: Verify that the balanced budget multiplier equals 1.

$$\text{Multiplier} = \frac{\text{change in output}}{\text{change in government spending}}$$
$$= (100 - 80)/(60 - 40) = 1.$$

2 (Practice problem: balanced budget fiscal policy) In Silverado (a neighbor of El Dorado) the marginal propensity to consume is 0.8 and the tax rate is one-third. Both autonomous consumption and investment are 100 billion guanos, and government spending is 500 billion dorals.

a Compute the aggregate consumption function.
b Compute the aggregate expenditures schedule.
c Find the equilibrium level of output.
d Is the budget balanced?

Suppose that government spending is decreased to 200 billion dorals and the tax rate is decreased to one-sixth.

e Compute the new aggregate consumption function.
f Compute the new aggregate expenditures schedule.
g Find the new equilibrium level of output.
h Compute the change in tax revenue. Is this a balanced budget change in fiscal policy?
i Verify that the change in output equals the change in government spending, that is, that the multiplier equals 1.

3 (Practice problem: balanced budget fiscal policy) In Wohon (a neighbor of Erehwemos) the marginal propensity to consume is 0.9 and the tax rate is one-sixth. Autonomous consumption equals 5 billion hons and investment is 15 billion hons, and government spending is 40 billion hons.

a Compute the aggregate consumption function.
b Compute the aggregate expenditures schedule.
c Find the equilibrium level of output.
d Is its budget balanced?

Suppose that government spending is increased to 120 million hons and the tax rate is increased to three-eighths (0.375).

e Compute the new aggregate consumption function.
f Compute the new aggregate expenditures schedule.
g Find the new equilibrium level of output.
h Compute the change in tax revenue. Is this a balanced budget change in fiscal policy?
i Verify that the change in output equals the change in government spending, that is, that the multiplier equals 1.

Answers to Problems

2   *a* and *b*

National income	Consumption	Investment	Government expenditure	Aggregate expenditure
(billions of dorals)				
0	100	100	500	700
300	260	100	500	860
600	420	100	500	1,020
900	580	100	500	1,180
1,200	740	100	500	1,340
1,500	900	100	500	1,500
1,800	1060	100	500	1,660

c Equilibrium output is 1,500 billion dorals.
d Tax revenue = 1/3 × 1,500 = 500 billion dorals = government expenditure.

e and f

National income	Consumption	Invest- ment	Government expenditure	Aggregate expenditure
(billions of dorals)				
0	100	100	200	400
300	300	100	200	600
600	500	100	200	800
900	700	100	200	1,000
1,200	900	100	200	1,200
1,500	1,200	100	200	1,400
1,800	1,500	100	200	1,600

g Equilibrium output is 1,200 billion dorals.
h Tax revenue = 1/6 × 1,200 = 200 billion dorals = government revenue. The budget is still balanced.
i Multiplier = (1,500 − 1,200)/(500 − 200) = 1.

3   a and b

National income	Consumption	Invest- ment	Government expenditure	Aggregate expenditure
(billions of dorals)				
0	5	15	40	60
40	35	15	40	90
80	65	15	40	120
120	95	15	40	150
160	125	15	40	180
200	155	15	40	210
240	185	15	40	240
280	215	15	40	270
320	245	15	40	300

c Equilibrium output is 240 billion hons.
d Tax revenue = 1/6 × 240 = 40 billion hons = government expenditure.

e and f

National income	Consumption	Invest- ment	Government expenditure	Aggregate expenditure
(billions of dorals)				
0	5	15	120	140
40	27.5	15	120	162.5
80	50	15	120	185
120	72.5	15	120	207.5
160	95	15	120	230
200	117.5	15	120	252.5
240	140	15	120	275
280	162.5	15	120	297.5
320	185	15	120	320

g Equilibrium output is 320 billion hons.
h Tax revenue = 0.375 × 320 = 120 billion hons = government revenue. The budget is still balanced.
i Multiplier = (320 − 240)/(120 − 40) = 1.

Part Seven

DYNAMICS AND MACRO POLICY

Chapter 31

INFLATION: WAGE AND PRICE DYNAMICS

Chapter Review

This chapter begins the study of dynamics, that is, how things change. The focus is on inflation, its costs, and, in particular, its relationship with unemployment. The Phillips curve summarises this relationship, and the chapter explains how the Phillips curve relates to the aggregate demand and supply framework. The role of monetary policy receives attention both in its closed and open economy varieties. A more microeconomic discussion of price rigidities closes the chapter.

ESSENTIAL CONCEPTS

1   **Inflation** is a general rise in the price level over time. If anticipated, it causes little disruption because households and firms can plan for and offset any troublesome effects. Inflation hurts lenders because they are repaid with cheaper pounds. It hurts investors because they are taxed on returns from their investments that barely compensate for the higher price level. Holders of currency see inflation erode its purchasing power. Inflation causes further trouble because it distorts relative prices and, when variable, contributes to the riskiness of borrowing and lending. The costs of inflation

can be softened somewhat by **indexing,** which means linking future payments to some measure of inflation.

2   When at the current price level aggregate demand exceeds aggregate supply, there is full employment but upward pressure on prices. The opposite is the case when aggregate demand is less than aggregate supply and unemployment is high. The **Phillips curve,** shown in Figure 31.1, illustrates the trade-off between unemployment and inflation. Decreases in inflation increase un-

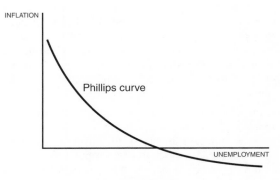

Figure 31.1

employment (at least in the short run) until unemployment reaches its so-called **natural rate,** when the price level is constant.

3   When workers and firms expect inflation, the Phillips curve shifts up. This higher curve is called the **expectations-augmented Phillips curve.** When inflation equals the expected rate, the economy is at its natural rate. If government tries to keep unemployment below this level, inflation will continue to rise, even accelerate. Thus, the natural rate equals the **NAIRU** (non-accelerating inflation rate of unemployment), and it is the unemployment rate consistent with constant inflation. The NAIRU itself varies over time with factors such as the entry of women in the labour force. Recent estimates put the NAIRU in the range of 5.5 to 7 percent of the labour force in Britain.

4   In the long run firms and workers use all available current and past information and adjust their expectations of inflation. Economists say that they have **rational expectations.** The unemployment rate returns to the NAIRU, which implies that the **long-run Phillips curve** is vertical. This fact means that a country experiencing high inflation may be able to put in place a credible program that convinces firms and workers of its resolve to lower inflation. As they expect lower inflation, the Phillips curve shifts down rapidly, allowing inflation to fall without a rise in unemployment. In other circumstances, a long recession may be required.

5   In the long run, when prices and wages have time to adjust, the long-run aggregate supply curve is vertical. The **short-run aggregate supply curve** shows the levels of output at different price levels, holding wages fixed. It is horizontal at low levels of output, then upward sloping, and nearly vertical at high price levels. Because machines and workers temporarily can be worked overtime, the vertical portion of the short-run aggregate supply curve lies to the right of the long-run aggregate supply. Finally, equilibrium in the short run depends upon the price level. If the price level is above the intersection of short-run aggregate supply and demand, then output is determined by aggregate demand, the short side of the market. A price level below the intersection implies that output equals short-run aggregate supply.

6   Increases in aggregate demand do not increase the price level when there is excess capacity; otherwise, they put upward pressure on prices. Similarly, when short-run aggregate supply shifts to the left, inflationary pressures form. The former is called **demand-pull inflation;** the latter, **cost-push inflation.** Once underway, **inflation inertia** sets in as expectations of price increases lead workers to demand wage increases.

7   In the long-run full-employment economy, more money simply means higher prices. In the short run, when prices are fixed, the money supply affects only output. Monetary policy can set off demand-pull inflation by shifting aggregate demand to the right when the economy is at full employment. Regardless of the reason for the start of inflation, monetary policy has a role in its continuation. Restrictive monetary policy dampens inflation, but accommodative monetary policy may accelerate it if the money supply is allowed to grow faster than the sum of the real growth rate and the existing inflation rate.

8   Relatively high inflation depreciates a country's currency because investors realise that if they hold assets in that currency, inflation will erode its value. Thus, monetary policy affects exchange rates. Investors, of course, form expectations about future monetary policy and inflation rates, and these expectations get built into exchange rates in much the same way that expectations of inflation affect the price level. Investors' expectations can reinforce or counteract the intentions of the monetary authorities.

9   Firms may be reluctant to change prices for three reasons. First, changing prices is expensive. Economists refer to this reason as **menu costs,** analogous to the expenses restaurants incur when printing new menus. Second, the uncertainties associated with changing prices may be greater than those associated with changing output. Customers may revise their expectations about prices and postpone purchases if they see prices falling. Finally, in oligopolies, firms may face *kinked demand curves*. Firms can facilitate cooperation by offering to match price cuts. This strategy puts a kink in each firm's demand curve at the current price. Cutting prices gains few extra customers, and firms may prefer to postpone price decreases.

BEHIND THE ESSENTIAL CONCEPTS

1   When inflation is anticipated, its effects are limited. To understand this better, imagine that you are borrowing £10,000 from your uncle for this year's tuition and living costs. To be compensated for living without his money for a year, he wants a 3 percent real rate of return. If there is no inflation, you simply agree to pay him 3 percent interest. If inflation is expected to be 7 percent, you pay him 10 percent interest, which gives him 7 percent to make up for the increase in prices and leaves a 3 percent real return. All contracts can be indexed in this way; therefore a mild, steady rate of inflation does not impose serious costs on the economy.

2   An unpredictable rate of inflation is very costly. Suppose that inflation is uncertain, that it might be 14 percent or 0 percent with equal probability. The average inflation rate is still 7 percent, but now when you borrow from your uncle, there is risk. If you pay the same 10 percent and inflation is zero, your uncle earns a 10 percent real return—a bonanza! On the other hand, if inflation turns out to be 14 percent, he nets negative 4 percent, and receives back less in real terms than he lent. You can see how a variable and unpredictable rate of inflation imposes risks on capital markets.

3   When the price is stuck at somewhere other than its market-clearing level, the quantity of output is determined by the short side of the market. If the price is too high to clear the market, then demand is the short side. Although suppliers would like to produce more, there is not enough demand, and thus the output equals the quantity demanded. On the other hand, when the price is too low to clear the market, supply is the short side. Demanders would like to purchase more goods, but only what suppliers can profitably produce is made available. In this case, the output equals the quantity supplied.

4   Inflation in the long run is a simple issue: money growth determines inflation. In the time before relative prices have adjusted to their market-clearing levels, however, inflation is a complex issue, involving shocks to aggregate demand and supply, accommodating or restrictive monetary policy, the credibility of the monetary authorities, and expectations. Inflation can arise for nonmonetary reasons, and if it is expected to continue, it can persist for a period. Eventually, it will adjust to a rate determined by the growth in the money supply, but the time of adjustment depends upon what investors think the monetary authorities will do. Expectation formation is not an exact science.

SELF-TEST

True or False

1   The U.K. tax system is fully indexed for inflation.

2   Inflation makes it expensive to hold money, because as the price level rises, money becomes less valuable.

3   The Phillips curve shows the relationship between unemployment and inflation.

4   The natural rate of unemployment is the rate that would occur if inflation were zero.

5   When workers and firms expect inflation to increase, the expectations-augmented Phillips curve shifts up.

6   If the government tries to keep the unemployment rate below the NAIRU, the result will be increased inflation.

7   The long-run Phillips curve is downward sloping.

8   The short-run aggregate supply curve can never lie to the right of the long-run aggregate supply curve.

9   When the price is stuck above the level at which aggregate demand and aggregate supply intersect, output equals aggregate supply.

10   When the price is stuck below the level at which aggregate demand and aggregate supply intersect, output equals aggregate supply.

11   Because inflation is always a monetary phenomenon, demand-pull inflation must start with an increase in the money supply.

12   If international investors expect a restrictive monetary policy, the currency will appreciate.

13   Menu costs refer to the expense of changing prices.

14   Firms perceive greater risk during economic downturns and may choose the safer path of reducing output rather than reducing price.

15   Firms facing a kinked demand curve are unlikely to change price when their costs decrease.

Multiple Choice

1   Linking wages and returns to the rate of inflation is a type of

   a   wage and price control.
   b   indexation.
   c   monetary target.
   d   discretionary monetary policy.
   e   inflation tax.

2   If not anticipated, an increase in inflation will

   a   hurt both borrowers and lenders.
   b   help both borrowers and lenders.
   c   hurt borrowers but help lenders.
   d   hurt lenders but help borrowers.
   e   have no effect on either borrowers or lenders.

3   Inflation

   a   does not affect taxpayers, because the tax system is fully indexed.
   b   does not affect taxpayers, because only real income is taxed.
   c   does not affect taxpayers, because only nominal income is taxed.
   d   frequently injures investors, who are taxed on high nominal incomes, even though inflation makes their real income small or even negative.
   e   hurts wage earners but not investors.

4   The inflation tax refers to the

   a   fact that inflation makes it expensive to hold money.
   b   fact that the earnings of investors are not adjusted for inflation.
   c   fact that wages are not adjusted for inflation.
   d   injury suffered by borrowers in inflationary times.
   e   injury suffered by lenders in inflationary times.

5   Inflation often distorts

   a   nominal prices.
   b   relative prices.
   c   absolute prices.
   d   average prices.
   e   none of the above.

6   The trade-off between inflation and unemployment is illustrated by the

   a   aggregate demand curve.
   b   aggregate supply curve.
   c   Phillips curve.

d aggregate expenditure schedule.
e money demand curve.

7 The natural rate of unemployment is the rate that prevails

a when there is no inflation.
b during hyperinflation.
c when inflation equals its natural rate.
d when there are no wage and price controls.
e in inflationary spirals.

8 If people expect inflation to be higher, then the Phillips curve

a is vertical in the short run.
b shifts to the right.
c shifts to the left.
d does not shift, because it assumes that expectations are always rational.
e is horizontal in the long run.

9 If the government tries to keep unemployment below the NAIRU,

a inflation will decrease.
b there will be no effect on inflation.
c inflation will increase.
d there will be stagflation.
e the Phillips curve will shift to the left.

10 In the long run the Phillips curve is

a downward sloping.
b upward sloping.
c horizontal.
d vertical.
e increasing at a decreasing rate.

11 When people form expectations on the basis of the structure of the economy, their expectations are said to be

a irrational.
b rational.
c adaptive.
d unrealistic.
e myopic.

12 If the price level is stuck above the level at which aggregate demand and aggregate supply intersect, then output is

a less than firms are willing to supply.
b more than firms are willing to supply.
c less than the economy is willing to purchase.
d more than the economy is willing to purchase.
e *a* and *d*.

13 When the price level is stuck above the intersection of aggregate demand and long-run aggregate supply, output

a equals the level at which aggregate demand and long-run aggregate supply intersect.
b equals aggregate demand at the current price level.
c equals short-run aggregate supply at the current price level.

d s greater than it is at the intersection of aggregate demand and aggregate supply.
e *c* and *d*.

14 When the price level is stuck below the intersection of aggregate demand and short-run aggregate supply, output

a equals the level at which aggregate demand and aggregate supply intersect.
b equals short-run aggregate supply at the current price level.
c equals aggregate demand at the current price level.
d is less than it is at the intersection of aggregate demand and short-run aggregate supply.
e *b* and *d*.

15 Which of the following can cause inflation to begin?

a Demand shocks
b Supply shocks
c Monetary shocks
d Wage and price controls
e *a, b,* and *c*

16 If investors expect restrictive monetary policy,

a the exchange rate will appreciate.
b the exchange rate will depreciate.
c there will be no change in the exchange rate.
d the exchange rate may move up or down depending upon whether these expectations are rational.
e the exchange rate will rise if there is excess capacity but fall if the economy is operating at full employment.

17 The costs of changing prices are called

a variable costs.
b sunk costs.
c fixed costs.
d pricing costs.
e menu costs.

18 During recessions, firms perceive that

a cutting prices is riskier than cutting production.
b increasing prices is riskier than increasing production.
c cutting production is riskier than cutting prices.
d increasing prices is riskier than increasing production.
e none of the above.

19 Which of the following is *not* true of the beliefs of firms facing a kinked demand curve?

a Their customers will quickly learn of price increases, and they will lose business.
b Other firms' customers will be slow to learn of any price cuts, so the firm will gain little new business.
c Rivals may match price cuts.
d Rivals will not match price increases.
e None of the above.

20 For a firm facing a kinked demand curve for a product or a service, when its marginal cost increases slightly, its

a   price will rise.
b   price will stay the same.
c   price will fall.
d   output will increase.
e   output will decrease.

Completion

1   Formally linking any payment, such as wages or taxes, to inflation is called _____.

2   The trade-off between unemployment and inflation is represented by the _____.

3   The rate of unemployment that would result if there were no inflation is the _____.

4   If the government tries to maintain the unemployment rate below the _____, inflation will increase.

5   Inflation perpetuated by increases in government or investment spending is _____ inflation.

6   Inflation perpetuated by wage increases is an example of _____ inflation.

7   When both the unemployment rate and inflation rate are high, there is _____.

8   If investors expect increased inflation, the exchange rate will _____.

9   The costs of changing prices are called _____.

10   Firms that believe that rivals will match price cuts but not price increases face a _____ demand curve.

Answers to Self-Test

True or False

1	F	6	T	11	F
2	T	7	F	12	T
3	T	8	F	13	T
4	T	9	F	14	T
5	T	10	T	15	T

Multiple Choice

1	*b*	6	*c*	11	*b*	16	*a*
2	*d*	7	*a*	12	*e*	17	*e*
3	*d*	8	*b*	13	*c*	18	*a*
4	*a*	9	*c*	14	*e*	19	*e*
5	*b*	10	*d*	15	*e*	20	*b*

Completion

1   indexing
2   Phillips curve
3   natural rate
4   NAIRU
5   demand-pull
6   cost-push
7   stagflation
8   depreciate
9   menu costs
10   kinked

Tools and Practice Problems

In Chapter 24, we learned how to measure inflation and construct the price index. In this chapter, we use those tools to study indexation provisions in contracts and to make comparisons between prices at different times. The goals are to understand how the economy deals with steady and predictable inflation and to develop a feel for the difference between real and nominal values.

Tool Kit 31.1 Indexing Wages, Prices and Pensions for Inflation

Wage agreements between employers and employees, contracts between firms and their suppliers, pensions, and benefits can all be index linked to protect them from inflation. Index linking adjusts wages, prices, or other important economic variables for inflation. The problems in this section show how to do this using the retail price index, the producer price index, and pensioner indices. Table 31.1 shows the producer price index, the retail price index, and pensioner indices for various years between 1948 and 1998. (You can look up these figures and a wealth of other economic data in *Economic Trends* produced by the Office for National Statistics.)

Step one: Identify the pound amount to be adjusted, that year's price index, and the current price index.

Step two: Convert the amount to current pounds:

$$\text{Current pound equivalent} = \text{amount} \times \frac{\text{current price index}}{\text{past price index}}.$$

---

1   (Worked problem: wage indexation) Alpha Steel Company offered a wage of £10 per hour in 1985. A wage indexation clause in the contrast guaranteed that the nominal wage would be increased to compensate for inflation. Use the general index of retail prices (all items) in Table 31.1 to calculate the wage in each year since 1985.

Step-by-step solution

Step one: The wage in 1985 was £10. To find the inflation-adjusted wage in 1986, we need the price index in 1985, which is 100, and in 1986, which is 103.4.

Step two: Convert the wage to 1986 pounds:

Wage in 1986 = £10(103.4/100) = £10.34.

The wage in 1987 is £10(107.7/100) = £10.77. Proceeding similarly, we derive the information in Table 31.2.

Table 31.1

Two-person	Producer price index (1995 = 100)		General index of retail prices[1] (1985 = 100)				Pensioner indices[2] (1985 = 100)	
	Materials and fuel purchased by manu- facturing industry	Output: all manufactured products: home sales	All items	Total food	All items except food	All items except seasonal food	One-person households	households
	PLKW	PLLU	FRAG	FRAH	FRAI	FRAK	FRAL	FRAM
1948	..	..	8.4	7.1	9.3	..	..	..
1949	..	..	8.6	7.5	9.4	..	..	..
1950	..	..	8.8	8.1	9.5	..	..	..
1951	..	..	9.6	9.0	10.2	..	..	..
1952	..	..	10.6	10.4	10.8	..	..	..
1953	..	..	10.9	11.0	10.9	..	..	..
1954	..	..	11.1	11.3	11.0	..	..	..
1955	..	..	11.6	12.1	11.3	..	..	..
1956	..	..	12.1	12.7	11.9	12.2	..	..
1957	..	..	12.6	13.0	12.4	12.7	..	..
1958	..	..	13.0	13.3	12.9	13.0	..	..
1959	..	..	13.0	13.4	12.9	13.1	..	..
1960	..	..	13.2	13.3	13.2	13.3	..	..
1961	..	..	13.6	13.5	13.7	13.7	..	..
1962	..	..	14.2	14.0	14.4	14.3	13.9	14.0
1963	..	..	14.5	14.4	14.6	14.6	14.2	14.3
1964	..	..	15.0	14.8	15.1	15.1	14.7	14.8
1965	..	..	15.7	15.3	15.9	15.8	15.3	15.4
1966	..	..	16.3	15.9	16.6	16.4	15.9	16.1
1967	..	..	16.7	16.3	17.0	16.8	16.3	16.4
1968	..	..	17.5	16.9	17.8	17.6	17.1	17.2
1969	..	..	18.4	18.0	18.8	18.5	18.0	18.1
1970	..	..	19.6	19.2	19.9	19.7	19.2	19.3
1971	..	..	21.4	21.4	21.7	21.6	21.2	21.3
1972	..	..	23.0	23.3	23.1	23.1	22.8	22.8
1973	..	..	25.1	26.8	24.8	25.0	25.0	25.2
1974	32.0	19.8	29.1	31.6	28.5	29.0	29.0	29.2
1975	35.3	24.3	36.1	39.6	35.3	36.0	39.5	36.6
1976	44.3	28.4	42.1	47.6	40.8	41.7	43.5	43.5
1977	50.5	33.8	48.8	56.6	46.9	48.4	50.7	50.8
1978	50.5	36.8	52.8	60.6	50.9	52.7	54.9	54.8
1979	59.0	41.1	59.9	67.9	58.0	59.7	61.3	61.4
1980	69.3	47.6	70.7	76.1	69.4	70.7	71.4	71.3
1981	78.5	52.8	79.1	82.5	78.3	79.1	79.5	79.5
1982	83.4	57.3	85.9	89.0	85.1	85.8	86.9	86.7
1983	88.1	61.0	89.8	91.8	89.4	89.8	90.8	90.7
1984	96.6	64.6	94.3	97.0	93.7	94.1	95.4	95.3
1985	96.6	68.6	100.0	100.0	100.0	100.0	100.0	100.0
1986	81.0	69.5	103.4	103.3	103.5	103.3	103.2	103.2
1987	82.6	71.9	107.7	106.4	108.0	107.6	105.6	105.8
1988	84.5	74.6	113.0	110.1	113.6	113.0	109.5	109.8
1989	89.1	78.2	121.8	116.4	122.9	121.9	115.4	115.8
1990	88.5	83.0	133.3	125.7	134.9	133.5	124.2	124.5
1991	86.6	87.4	141.1	132.2	143.0	141.3	133.0	133.5
1992	86.3	90.2	146.4	135.0	148.7	146.9	137.6	138.7
1993	90.2	93.8	148.7	137.5	150.9	149.3	140.5	142.4
1994	91.9	96.1	152.4	138.9	155.1	152.9	143.0	145.4
1995	100.0	100.0	157.6	144.2	160.2	158.0	146.9	149.5
1996	98.8	102.6	161.4	148.9	163.9	162.0	150.2	153.3
1997	90.6	103.6	166.5	149.0	169.9	167.4	151.8	155.8
1998	82.5	104.2	172.2	150.9	176.3	173.0	153.9	158.5

1 The index numbers given here are for comparative purposes only and should not be regarded as accurate to the last digit shown.
2 All items except housing.
Source: Office for National Statistics, Enquiries Columns 1-2 01633 812106; Columns 3-9 020 7533 5874.

Table 31.2

Year	Wage
1985	£10.00
1986	£10.34
1987	£10.77
1988	£11.30
1989	£12.18
1990	£13.33
1991	£14.11
1992	£14.64
1993	£14.87
1994	£15.24
1995	£15.76
1996	£16.14
1997	£16.65
1998	£17.22

2   (Practice problem: producer prices) The Alpha Steel Company has forward contracts for the annual purchase of materials and fuels. In 1990 the nominal value of the annual contract was £2,000,000, and Alpha's suppliers decided to protect themselves against inflation by specifying that the price of future annual deliveries of materials and fuels must be adjusted for inflation using the producer price index for materials and fuels purchased by manufacturing industry. Calculate the cost of the materials and fuels contract in all years between 1990 and 1995.

3   (Practice problem: indexing pensions) Pensioners successfully campaign to have their pensions index linked. In 1990 the value of a pension for a married couple was £80 per week. Use the pensioner index for two-person households to show how the nominal value of the pension must increase each year between 1990 and 1998 in order to stay constant in real terms.

Answers to Problems

2   The cost of the materials in 1990 = £2,000,000; the cost in 1991 = £2,000,000(86.6/88.5) = £1,957,062; the cost in 1992 = £2,000,000(86.3/88.5) = £1,993, 072; the cost in 1993 = £2,000,000(90.2/88.5) = 2,090,382; the cost in 1994 = £2,000,000(91.9/88.5) = £2,037,694; and the cost in 1995 = £2,000,000(100/88.5) = £2,176,279. Note that in 1990 and 1992 the suppliers lose out from indexation because the price of manufacturing materials and fuels fell in the early 1990s recession; from 1993 onwards the suppliers gain.

4   The value of the pension in 1990 is £80;
the values in 1991 = £80(133.5/124.5) = £85.78;
the values in 1992 = £80(138.7/124.5) = £89.12;
the values in 1993 = £80(142.4/124.5) = £91.50;
the values in 1994 = £80(145.4/124.5) = £93.43;
the values in 1995 = £80(149.5/124.5) = £96.06;
the values in 1996 = £80(153.3/124.5) = £98.51;
the values in 1997 = £80(155.8/124.5) = £100.11; and
the values in 1998 = £80(158.5/124.5) = £101.85.

Chapter 32

UNEMPLOYMENT: UNDERSTANDING WAGE RIGIDITIES

Chapter Review

The last chapter focused on inflation. This chapter focuses on the labour market to examine the causes of unemployment more closely. The key issue is why wages fail to adjust to clear the market and bring about full employment. In recent years economists have put forward several new ideas about this problem, and these ideas are discussed and evaluated here. The next chapter completes Part Seven on dynamics with some analysis of the policy issues involved in the unemployment-inflation trade-off.

ESSENTIAL CONCEPTS

1 While unemployment fluctuates substantially in the United Kingdom, there is little variation in real wages. Why not? We know that changes in product demand cause the labour demand to shift. Unless supply shifts to match the shifts in demand or supply is perfectly elastic (two propositions that are surely wrong), the explanation must lie in a microeconomic analysis of sticky real wages.

2 Wages may not adjust to bring about full employment for several reasons.

a **Union contracts** may specify wages above the market-clearing level. If the demand for labour falls, the union may not agree to accept lower wages.

b Firms may have informal agreements, or **implicit contracts,** with their risk-averse workers to provide fixed wages as a kind of insurance against economic downturns.

c **Insider-outsider theory** observes that because existing workers must train new employees, the current workforce may not be willing to provide training to newly hired workers unless they are paid the same wage.

d **Minimum wage laws** mandate a price floor in the labour market.

e **Efficiency wage theory** shows how firms may make higher profits by paying wages that are above the market-clearing level, because workers have incentives to work harder and be more productive.

3 There are three reasons why firms can increase the productivity of their workers by paying the higher efficiency wage rather than the market wage.

a When a firm cuts its wage, some workers leave. These workers are likely to be the firm's most productive workers who will have good alternatives elsewhere. The pool of the firm's new employees will be of lower quality when the wage offer is less. Thus, the overall quality of the workforce is poorer at lower wages. This phenomenon is called adverse selection.

b   Workers may put forth greater effort on a job that pays more than alternative jobs. In effect, the higher wage makes the job more valuable to the worker and motivates her to work harder for fear of losing the high-paying job.

c   By paying higher wages, firms can reduce the rate at which workers quit—the labour turnover rate. Because it is costly to hire and train new workers, a firm's profits may be higher than they would if it paid lower wages.

4   **Okun's law** says that a 2 percent increase in output is needed to bring about a 1 percent decrease in unemployment. One explanation for this is **labour hoarding,** where firms retain workers during downturns in order to have them available when demand returns. This is a form of disguised unemployment.

5   One policy option is to attempt to increase wage flexibility through profit sharing or substituting bonuses for some percentage of the wage bill. Another recommends reducing the costs of unemployment with a more generous unemployment insurance and benefits system. Both proposals run into the risk-incentive trade-off, which shows that when workers are protected from risk, they lose incentives to put forth effort.

a   If workers receive more of their wages in the form of profit sharing, their earnings become more flexible, rising in booms and falling in recessions. Such a policy reduces the risk of unemployment, yet increases the risk of income loss during economic downturns.

b   Unemployment insurance and benefits protects workers against income loss if they are laid off, but reduce their incentives to find and accept new jobs.

BEHIND THE ESSENTIAL CONCEPTS

1   While each of the reasons for wage rigidity listed above has some validity, the efficiency wage theory is the most satisfactory explanation. Economists favour efficiency wage theory because it explains three important facts about the labour market: the failure of wages to adjust to market-clearing levels, the fact that firms lay off excess workers during downturns rather than share the available work equally among the firm's total labour demand, and the fact that wages adjust slowly when economic conditions change.

2   The efficiency wage theory explains rigid wages in the following way. Suppose you are an employer. You need quality workers who put forth a lot of effort and remain loyal to your firm. Your problem is how to keep and motivate your good workers. If you pay the market-clearing wage, jobs with your firm will be worth no more than those of other firms. Your workers will know that they can quickly find work elsewhere at the going wage. The efficiency wage solves the problem in a very clever way. It is part carrot and part stick. You offer the carrot of higher wages and gain influence over your workers with the stick, which is the threat to take away the job. Your workers have good incentives to stay, because the job is now worth more than their alternatives.

3   Once you understand why one firm gains by paying its workers wages above market-clearing levels, you can then see that other firms will do the same. It might seem to you that if all firms pay higher wages, then no firm offers anything special. But because all wages are higher than the market-clearing level, there remains a surplus of unemployed workers and not enough jobs to go around. Losing a valuable job represents a substantial cost to your workers, not because other jobs pay less, but because workers without jobs face a considerable time of unemployment.

4   Unemployment is a surplus of labour, or workers. You might ask, "Why don't the unemployed offer to work for less?" After all, the usual explanation for why the price of anything adjusts down to the market-clearing level is that the suppliers who cannot find buyers offer to sell at lower prices. In the efficiency wage world, however, if the unemployed offer to work at lower wages, the manager of the firm will conclude that they are either low-quality workers who will not make the required effort or that they will soon look for other employment. Remember that the efficiency wage is just high enough to attract, motivate, and keep quality workers. Any offer to do quality work for less is simply not credible.

5   When the demand for labour falls during economic downturns, firms use layoffs and redundancies to reduce the size of the workforce rather than share the available work among their workers. Why? According to efficiency wage view, sharing work lowers average earnings in the same way that cutting wages does. If you let your employees share the work, you will lose your high-quality workers and have difficulty motivating those who stay. It is better to use layoffs.

6   A final implication of efficiency wage theory is that wages adjust slowly. Put yourself again in the shoes of an employer. If business falls off, you may want to cut wages, but first you must see whether your competitors will reduce *their* wages. If you move too soon, you may lose your best workers. Efficiency wage theory counsels waiting, perhaps spending a few pounds more in labour costs.

SELF-TEST

True or False

1   The real wage is the nominal wage adjusted for inflation.

2   If supply is perfectly elastic, then when demand shifts, real wages will not change.

3   Unions reduce the responsiveness of wage rates to changes in labour market conditions.

4   Employment levels fluctuate quite dramatically; nevertheless, real wages are rather stable.

5   Most union contracts contain provisions for adjusting wages downwards when the firm's demand for labour shifts.

6   Indexation of wages allow real wages to remain stable even though inflation increases.

7   An implicit contract is an informal arrangement between workers and firms, often involving the firm's paying constant wages even as the wages its workers could receive elsewhere change.

8   Implicit contract theory also explains why real wages of job seekers do not decline significantly during recessions.

9   According to insider-outsider theory, a firm's current workers refuse to train new employees unless the new workers receive similar wages.

10   The minimum wage is a price ceiling in the market for unskilled labour.

11   According to efficiency wage theory, the firm can make more profits by paying higher wages.

12   One reason firms may not wish to pay lower wages is the adverse selection effect, whereby the average quality of the pool of workers willing to accept a job with a firm depends upon the wage offered.

13   As a general rule, the efficiency wage is less than the market-clearing wage.

14   Efficiency wage theory implies that wages will adjust slowly because firms are reluctant to change wages before their competitors do.

15   Unemployment affects most demographic groups equally.

Multiple Choice

1   The demand curve for labour studied in this chapter

   a   shows the total amount of labour demanded by all firms in the economy at each wage.
   b   is drawn assuming that product prices are fixed.
   c   may shift to the right but never shifts to the left.
   d   is upward sloping, according to efficiency wage theory.
   e   a and b.

2   The real wage equals the

   a   efficiency wage.
   b   nominal wage when expectations have adjusted to the actual rate of inflation.
   c   nominal wage adjusted for errors in forming expectations.
   d   nominal wage adjusted for inflation.
   e   wage negotiated in the union contract and modified by indexation.

3   Which of the following is *not* a possible explanation for wage rigidity?

   a   The supply curve of labour is horizontal (perfectly elastic).
   b   The labour supply curve shifts along with the demand curve for labour.
   c   The demand curve for labour is perfectly inelastic.
   d   Union contracts restrict wage adjustment.
   e   Some firms have implicit contracts with their risk-averse workers to provide insurance by paying the same wage even as the market wage varies.

4   Unemployment results if

   a   the demand for labour shifts to the left and wages fail to adjust.
   b   the supply of labour shifts to the left and wages fail to adjust.
   c   the demand for labour shifts to the right and wages fail to adjust.
   d   the supply of labour shifts to the right and wages fail to adjust.
   e   a and d.

5   If the supply of labour is upward sloping and demand shifts to the right, then if wages

   a   adjust to the market-clearing level, anyone willing to work at the going wage can eventually find a job.
   b   adjust to the market-clearing level, any unemployment will be involuntary.
   c   adjust to the market-clearing level, employment will decrease.
   d   do not adjust to the market-clearing level, any unemployment will be involuntary.
   e   do not adjust to the market-clearing level, the supply of labour will shift to the right.

6   In modern economies, when the demand for labour falls, the real wage

   a   always falls to clear the market.
   b   does not change but workers share the available jobs by each working fewer hours.
   c   does not change but workers share the available jobs by rotating between full time and unemployment.
   d   does not change and some workers are made redundant while others retain employment.
   e   b and c.

7   Which of the following is an explanation of the failure of real wages to adjust to changes in the demand and supply of labour?

   a   Union contracts
   b   Implicit contracts
   c   Insider-outsider theory
   d   Efficiency wage theory
   e   All of the above

8   The minimum wage is a price

   a   floor in the labour market, causing the quantity of workers demanded to exceed the quantity supplied.
   b   floor in the labour market, causing the quantity of

workers demanded to be less than the quantity supplied.

c ceiling in the labour market, causing the quantity of workers demanded to exceed the quantity supplied.

d ceiling in the labour market, causing the quantity of workers demanded to be less than the quantity supplied.

e *a* and *d*.

9 The theory that argues that firms have an informal agreement to protect risk-averse workers from variations in their incomes by paying the same wage even though their alternative wage changes is

a efficiency wage theory.
b implicit contract theory.
c insider-outsider theory.
d minimum wage theory.
e none of the above.

10 The theory that points out that it is not in the interests of the firm's workers to train newcomers if the new employees receive lower wages is

a efficiency wage theory.
b implicit contract theory.
c insider-outsider theory.
d minimum wage theory.
e none of the above.

11 The theory that says that wages above market-clearing wages motivate workers to put forth effort and remain with the high-paying firm is

a efficiency wage theory.
b implicit contract theory.
c insider-outsider theory.
d minimum wage theory.
e none of the above.

12 Typically, when the firm's demand for labour falls, it

a immediately cuts wages for all workers.
b shares the available work among all its workers.
c reduces the size of its labour force through layoffs.
d idles some of its capital stock in order to keep its workers busy.
e retains its entire workforce at current wages, hoping that business will return.

13 Efficiency wage theory emphasises that higher wages are important to

a motivate workers.
b retain high-quality workers.
c attract high-quality job applicants.
d reduce turnover.
e all of the above.

14 Unemployment typically affects

a different groups in the economy equally.
b high-skilled, high-wage workers more because employers can save more in labour costs by laying them off.
c lower-skilled and part-time workers more.
d only those paid on a piece-work basis.
e none of the above.

15 The system under which workers are paid on the basis of what they produce is called

a efficiency wages.
b implicit contracts.
c the insider-outsider system.
d minimum wages.
e piece work.

16 If wages and prices fall in the same proportion, then real wages

a increase.
b decrease.
c stay the same.
d may increase or decrease depending upon the absolute level of the real wage.
e may increase or decrease depending upon the absolute level of the nominal wage.

17 Firms that keep their best workers on the payroll hoping that business will pick up are engaging in

a piece work.
b labor hoarding.
c profit sharing.
d layoffs.
e union busting.

18 Okun's law asserts that for every 1 percent decrease in

a output, unemployment increases by 1 percent.
b unemployment, output increases by 2 percent.
c unemployment, output increases by less than 1 percent.
d output, unemployment increases 2 percent.
e output, unemployment increases by less than 1 percent.

19 If workers received some of their compensation in the form of bonuses tied to the profit level, then

a wages would be more flexible.
b unemployment would fall.
c workers would be exposed to a greater risk of income fluctuations.
d all of the above.
e none of the above.

20 Unemployment compensation

a increases the risk of income fluctuations for workers.
b reduces unemployment.
c gives unemployed workers more incentive to look for and accept job offers.
d increases both risk and incentives to look for work.
e decreases both risk and incentives to look for work.

Completion

1 Wage _____ refers to the failure of wages to adjust sufficiently to changes in the demand or supply for labour.

2 An understanding between a firm and its workers that requires the payment of constant wages is called an _____.

3   According to _____ theory, the current employ-
    ees of a firm refuse to train new workers unless their
    wages are comparable.

4   The minimum wage is a government-mandated price
    _____ in the labour market.

5   Paying higher wages can increase _____ by at-
    tracting more qualified workers, increasing effort, and
    reducing turnover.

6   The wage that minimises total labour costs is called
    the _____ wage.

7   Because it is expensive to hire and fire workers, firms
    may _____ employees during recessions.

8   _____ says that if output increases by 2 percent,
    unemployment falls by 1 percent.

9   Making wages more flexible by substituting some
    form of profit sharing may be unattractive to workers
    who are relatively _____ .

10 Unemployment insurance and benefits reduces the
    risk associated with unemployment but also reduce
    the _____ of the unemployed to search for
    work.

Answers to Self-Test

True or False

1	T	6	T	11	T
2	T	7	T	12	T
3	T	8	F	13	F
4	T	9	T	14	T
5	F	10	F	15	F

Multiple Choice

1	e	6	d	11	a	16	c
2	d	7	e	12	c	17	b
3	c	8	b	13	e	18	b
4	e	9	b	14	c	19	d
5	a	10	c	15	e	20	e

Completion

1   rigidity
2   implicit contract
3   insider-outsider
4   floor
5   productivity
6   efficiency
7   hoard
8   Okun's law
9   risk averse
10 incentives

Tools and Practice Problems

Involuntary unemployment results when the wage does not
adjust to clear the market. Efficiency wage theory explains
the failure of wages to bring about full employment. It also
implies that firms will use redundancies and layoffs (rather
than job sharing) to reduce the workforce when the demand

Tool Kit 32.1 Determining the Efficiency Wage

Firms perceive that the productivity of their workers
depends upon the wage. Higher wages motivate workers
to put forth effort, attract a high-quality pool of applicants, and reduce labour turnover. When productivity depends upon the wage, the profit-maximising strategy for
the firm is to set the wage at the level that attains the
highest output per pound. This level is achieved when
the ratio of productivity (output per hour) to the wage
rate is maximised.

Step one: Identify and graph the productivity-wage relationship.

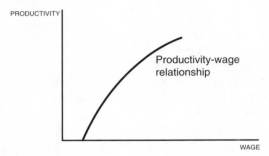

Step two: Calculate the ratio of productivity to the wage
for each wage level. This ratio gives output per pound
spent on labor:

Output per pound = productivity/wage.

Step three: Choose the wage for which the corresponding
productivity-wage ratio is the highest. Label this point *A*
on the graph of the productivity-wage relationship.

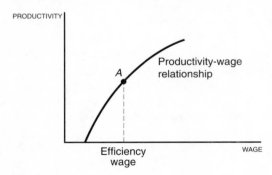

Step four: Draw a line from the origin to *A*. The slope of
this line is the productivity-wage ratio. The line should
be tangent, and so indicate that output per pound is maximised.

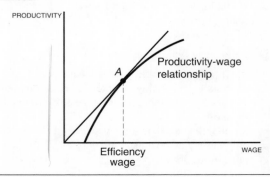

for labour is low, and wages will adjust slowly as conditions change. In this section, we learn how to determine the efficiency wage.

1   (Worked problem: efficiency wage) Murray's Auto Parts has had trouble with labor turnover. Once its workers are trained, they leave. A consultant points out that productivity would be higher if the firm could keep its workers and that one way to discourage them from quitting is to pay higher wages. The consultant estimates that the relationship between productivity and wages is as shown in Table 32.1.

Table 32.1

Wage (£ per hour)	Productivity (£ sales per hour)
4	8.00
5	12.50
6	18.00
7	24.50
8	26.00
9	27.00

Determine the efficiency wage for Murray's.

Step-by-step solution

Step one: Identify and graph the productivity-wage relationship.

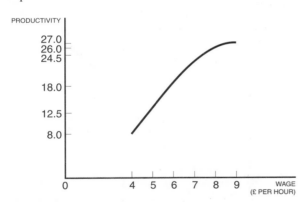

Step two: Calculate the ratio of productivity to the wage for each wage level. This ratio is shown in Table 32.2.

Table 32.2

Wage (£ per hour)	Productivity (£ sales per hour)	Productivity Wage
4	8.00	2.00
5	12.50	2.50
6	18.00	3.00
7	24.50	3.50
8	26.00	3.25
9	27.00	3.00

Step three: Choose the wage for which the corresponding productivity-wage ratio is the highest. The efficiency wage is £7 per hour and is shown as point *A*.

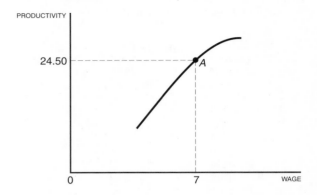

Step four: Draw a line from the origin to *A*. The slope of this line is the productivity-wage ratio, which is 3.5. The line is tangent, indicating that output per dollar is maximised.

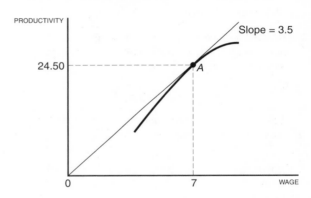

2   (Practice problem: efficiency wage) Moe's Lawn Care has plenty of customers, but Moe is having difficulty getting his mowers to work hard. He cannot monitor each worker all the time and suspects that there is considerable shirking on the job. His brother-in-law, always ready with helpful advice, suggests that if wages were higher, his workers would put forth more effort for fear of losing a well-paid job. Moe considers this and estimates that the relationship between wages and productivity is as appears in Table 32.3.

Table 32.3

Wage (per month)	Productivity (acres mowed per month)
£ 900	800
£1,000	1,000
£1,100	1,320
£1,200	1,680
£1,300	1,950
£1,400	1,960

Determine the efficiency wage for Moe's business.

3   (Practice problem: efficiency wage) Luke's Warm and
     Now food delivery business needs good drivers. He
     thinks that he may get a better pool of applicants if he
     offers higher wages. Table 32.4 shows the relationship
     between the wage and productivity.

Table 32.4

Wage (per week)	Productivity (deliveries per week)
£200	110
£220	114
£240	130
£260	146
£280	160
£300	168

Determine the efficiency wage.

Answers to Problems

2   Table 32.5 shows the productivity-wage ratio. The effi-
     ciency wage is £1,300 per month, as shown in the dia-
     gram.

Table 32.5

Wage (per month)	Productivity (acres moved per month)	Productivity / Wage
£ 900	800	0.89
£1,000	1,000	1.00
£1,000	1,320	1.20
£1,200	1,680	1.40
£1,300	1,950	1.50
£1,400	1,960	1.40

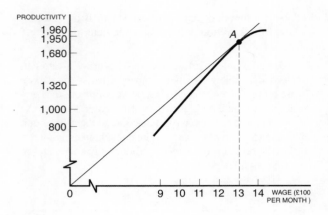

3   Table 32.6 shows the productivity-wage ratio.

Table 32.6

Wage (per week)	Productivity (deliveries per week)	Productivity / Wage
£200	100	0.50
£220	114	0.52
£240	130	0.54
£260	146	0.56
£280	160	0.57
£300	168	0.56

The efficiency wage is £280 per week, as shown in the
diagram.

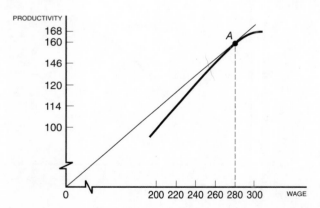

Chapter 33

INFLATION VERSUS UNEMPLOYMENT: APPROACHES TO POLICY

CHAPTER REVIEW

In closing the discussion of dynamics this chapter brings together the insights of Chapter 31, on the trade-off between inflation and unemployment, and Chapter 32, on the reasons for the slow adjustment of real wages. Here the emphasis is on policy alternatives: what can be done to stabilise the economy, control inflation, and reduce the rate of unemployment. The book returns to the other major macroeconomic goal—growth—in the next chapter.

ESSENTIAL CONCEPTS

1   Attempting to push the unemployment rate below the NAIRU only results in increased inflation. There is always some uncertainty about the exact level of the NAIRU, however, and thus there is some room for disagreement. The main policy question is how aggressive should the government be in lowering unemployment or fighting inflation. The answer depends upon how one values the relative costs of inflation and unemployment.

2   Facing the problem of the business cycle with its varying levels of output and occasional episodes of high un-employment, economists split into two camps. **Interventionists** believe that government has an important role to play in fostering a more stable economy. **Non-interventionists** see little prospect that government can succeed and much risk that government actions will exacerbate the economy's fluctuations.

3   Among the alternative schools of thought, there are the following.

a   **Real business cycle theory** places the blame for fluctuations on exogenous shocks, such as the oil price increases of the 1970s. It recommends that government follow a hands off approach, letting the money supply increase at the rate of growth of real GDP.

b   **New classical macroeconomics** stresses the concept of rational expectations, whereby households and firms recognize and offset the effects of government actions. For example, current deficits motivate households to rationally anticipate future tax increases. They save more, and that counteracts the fiscal stimulus of the deficit.

c   **Monetarism** stresses the inability of government to effectively carry out an interventionist program. Monetarists emphasise the lags in determining the need for and completing the interventionist policies and also the perverse incentives that the political environment gives to governments.

4   Noninterventionists recommend tying the hands of government with **fixed rules,** such as balanced budgets and stable monetary growth. They stress that this policy would remove one source of instability, namely uncertainty surrounding future government policy. Fixing government policy mitigates the problem of **dynamic consistency** by giving households and firms confidence that government will not reverse direction when conditions change.

5   Interventionists counter with arguments that downturns can persist for a long time and that government can reduce their duration both with automatic and discretionary policies. The leading school, new Keynesianism, emphasises the endogenous forces in the economy that amplify shocks and cause their effects to persist. These include the **multiplier-accelerator,** which shows that as firms try to keep a constant inventory to sales ratio, output varies much more than sales. These variations are further amplified by the multiplier process. The economy expands rapidly, only to bump against capacity constraints at full employment and then slump into recession.

6   Interventionists call for policies, such as automatic stabilisers, that alter the structure of the economy and strengthen its ability to dampen shocks. They also support the use of discretionary fiscal and monetary policies. In recessions, government should increase the budget deficit to stimulate the economy. Also, the central bank should use active monetary policy to counteract economic fluctuations. Finally, interventionists advocate labour market policies that lower the NAIRU, including promoting labour mobility, reducing some types of business regulation, and opening the economy to free trade.

7   The macroeconomic history of the United Kingdom illustrates the ideas of this chapter. In the 1950s and 1960s the U.K. government used discretionary fiscal and monetary policies to fine-tune the economy. This period was characterised by a consensus that Keynesian demand management was the most appropriate model for policy. In the 1970s the effectiveness of Keynesian demand management policies was questioned. In this decade economic uncertainty and instability increased as the Bretton Woods system of fixed exchange rates broke down and the economy was hit by a number of exogenous shocks, including the oil price crisis. By the end of the 1970s controlling inflation had become the primary objective of policymakers. The Thatcher government adopted a monetarist stance based on controlling the money supply. Inflation continued to be the primary concern of macroeconomic policy for much of the 1980s and 1990s, although issues relating to Economic and Monetary Union in Europe also shaped policy. Britain's short membership in the Exchange Rate Mechanism between 1990 and 1992 ended in a speculative attack on the pound, a rapid rise in interest rates, and recession. Since this period, U.K. macroeconomic policy has been based on using interest rates to meet announced targets to limit inflation.

8   The political business cycle is the result of governments' using macroeconomic policy to manipulate the business cycle to maximise their chance of reelection. The political business cycle appears to have been stronger in Britain than other countries because U.K. governments have more freedom to determine the timing of elections. A good example of this occurred in 1987 when the government continued to cut taxes despite signs that the economy was overheating. The so-called Lawson boom was followed by rapid inflation and a reversal of policy with tax rises and high interest rates, ending in a prolonged recession in the early 1990s.

BEHIND THE ESSENTIAL CONCEPTS

1   Economists use the term *business cycle* to refer to the ups and downs of the economy. Although there are certain regularities (in recessions output falls, unemployment rises, the working week shortens, and inflation slows), the length of the cycle is quite unpredictable. The length and amplitude of the economic cycle in Britain increased in the 1980s and 1990s in comparison to the 1960s and 1970s. All of this makes predicting the path of the economy a hazardous and uncertain endeavour.

2   When the economy is hit with a shock, such as an increase in oil prices, households and firms take actions. Some of these actions offset the impact of the shock and dampen its effects. For example, while you would reduce your demand for petrol, you and others might buy cars with higher kilometres per gallon ratings. Similarly, firms invest in energy-saving equipment, leading to increased production and employment in that sector. All of these responses to changes in relative prices keep aggregate demand, output, and employment high. On the other hand, there are mechanisms in the economy that amplify the shock. High-energy-use industries contract, firms go out of business, and workers are laid off. Income and consumption fall and the multiplier process worsens the decline. Sometimes the dampening activities dominate; for example, when the stock market crashed in 1987, the economy continued its expansion. On other occasions, the shock is amplified and the economy is thrown into recession.

3   If inflation is undesirable, why not simply outlaw it with **wage and price controls?** Although they have been used by various governments at various times, wage and price controls do not have much support among economists. Suppose that the government mandated that no price rise by more than 1 percent per year. In some markets where relative prices were stable or falling, this regulation would make no difference. But in others where relative prices were rising, market prices would hit the ceiling and shortages would appear. An alternative policy with a lighter touch is **moral suasion,** where the government tries to persuade firms to keep prices in check. However, there is little evidence that such policies have had much effect.

4   The discussion in this chapter draws clear distinctions among policies to emphasise the differences among

economists and explore the logic of their arguments. For example, noninterventionists forswear discretionary policy and argue for fixed rules, such as a steady growth rate for the money supply. Interventionists point out that some discretion must be used in the choice of **monetary aggregate** and in the timing of open market operations. Once room for some discretion is admitted, they recommend a more active use of monetary policy.

SELF-TEST

True or False

1   If the government attempts to keep the inflation rate below the NAIRU, unemployment will accelerate.

2   Investors in financial assets, such as non-index-linked bonds, generally advocate an aggressive anti-inflationary policy stance.

3   Interventionists favour fixed policy rules such as balanced budgets and steady money growth.

4   There is little variation in the length of expansions in the United Kingdom since the Second World War.

5   The amplitude and length of economic cycles in U.K. output and employment were greater in the 1980s and 1990s than they were in the 1960s and 1970s.

6   The political business cycle arises because governments engineer a boom before an election.

7   Economic downturns in the United Kingdom have tended to be proceeded by reductions in interest rates.

8   Real business cycle theory attributes the variability of output to exogenous shocks.

9   The dynamic consistency problem refers to the difficulty of maintaining full employment when wages and prices change.

10   New classical economists such as Robert Lucas have emphasised the importance of rational expectations.

11   New Keynesians differ from older Keynesian economists in their emphasis on microeconomics.

12   The effectiveness of fiscal policy may be undermined by the lags in the time it takes government to make decisions.

13   If the economy slips slightly below the NAIRU, rapid inflation results.

14   The multiplier accelerator is an example of an endogenous cause of economic downturns.

15   In the United Kingdom, the NAIRU is probably around 10 percent.

Multiple Choice

1   The political business cycle is a situation where

 a   government policy is set by politicians.
 b   the business cycle is determined by economic factors.
 c   government policy is used to engineer a boom before an election.
 d   the business cycle is determined by factors outside the control of policymakers.
 e   the business cycle is predictable.

2   In Britain, the recession of the early 1990s was

 a   mitigated by the fall in the price of houses.
 b   exacerbated by the fall in the price of houses.
 c   unaffected by changes in the housing market.
 d   ended by a rise in interest rates that made house prices fall.
 e   none of the above.

3   Which of the following best describe(s) the shift in British macroeconomic policy between the 1950s and 1960s, on the one hand, and the 1980s and 1990s, on the other?

 a   In the 1980s and 1990s governments became less concerned about inflation and more concerned about unemployment.
 b   In the 1980s and 1990s governments became more concerned about inflation and less concerned about unemployment.
 c   In the 1950s and 1960s macroeconomic policy was more Keynesian.
 d   In the 1950s and 1960s macroeconomic policy was more monetarist.
 e   *b* and *c*.

4   The idea that variations in output are due to exogenous shocks to which the market reacts quickly to restore full employment is a tenet of

 a   real business cycle theory.
 b   new classical macroeconomics.
 c   monetarism.
 d   new Keynesianism.
 e   supply-side economics.

5   The idea that actions of rational individuals offset the impact of government actions is associated with

 a   real business cycle theory.
 b   new classical macroeconomics.
 c   monetarism.
 d   new Keynesianism.
 e   supply-side economics.

6   Doubts about the government's ability to carry out discretionary fiscal and monetary policy are stressed by believers in

 a   real business cycle theory.
 b   new classical macroeconomics.
 c   monetarism.
 d   new Keynesianism.
 e   supply-side economics.

7   The belief that government can be effective with discretionary fiscal and monetary policies is part of

 a   real business cycle theory.
 b   new classical macroeconomics.
 b   monetarism.
 d   new Keynesianism.
 e   supply-side economics.

8   Noninterventionist economists view government as a source of instability and advocate

    a   binding fiscal and monetary policies with fixed policy rules.

    b   using fiscal and monetary policies with discretion.

    c   returning oversight of the money supply to the private sector.

    d   dynamic inconsistency.

    e   repealing the accelerator.

9   Which of the following is *not* an example of a policy rule advocated by noninterventionists?

    a   The money supply should increase at a fixed rate each year.

    b   The money supply should be adjusted to stimulate aggregate demand in recessions and constrain aggregate demand in inflation.

    c   The budget deficit should be zero.

    d   Government expenditure should be a fixed percentage of GDP.

    e   The money supply should increase with the rate of output.

10   Dynamic consistency refers to the

    a   fact that most business cycles follow the same pattern.

    b   recommendation that government policy follow certain fixed rules.

    c   issue of whether the government will carry out its promises.

    d   political business cycle explanation for economic fluctuations.

    e   need to harmonise fiscal and monetary policies.

11   The new Keynesian view is that economic fluctuations are due

    a   to endogenous forces and predictable.

    b   to random, exogenous shocks and unpredictable.

    c   chiefly to misguided monetary and fiscal policies.

    d   to exogenous shocks but are amplified and made persistent by the economic system.

    e   none of the above.

12   The accelerator model of the economy assumes that firms want to keep the

    a   ratio of output to labour constant.

    b   ratio of investment to sales constant.

    c   level of unemployment constant.

    d   rate of growth in the money supply constant.

    e   level of full-employment GDP constant.

13   New Keynesians advocate

    a   policies to lower the NAIRU, such as reducing business regulation.

    b   discretionary monetary policy.

    c   discretionary fiscal policy.

    d   automatic stabilisers.

    e   all of the above.

14   Most economists agree that in the long run the Phillips curve is

    a   vertical.

    b   horizontal.

    c   upward sloping.

    d   downward sloping.

    e   inelastic.

15   The idea that the economy expands rapidly until it hits capacity constraints and then plunges into recessions argues that the causes of fluctuations are

    a   exogenous shocks.

    b   endogenous.

    c   uncertainty over government policy.

    d   rational expectations.

    e   dynamic consistency.

16   Which of the following represents a mechanism that amplifies shock to the economy?

    a   The multiplier

    b   Changes in relative prices that lead households and firms to change their consumption and production patterns

    c   Changes in interest rates that affect the demand for investment

    d   The anticipation the effects of shocks by households and firms with rational expectations

    e   Government use of discretionary monetary and fiscal policies

17   Which of the following might reduce the NAIRU by shifting aggregate supply to the right?

    a   Moral suasion

    b   Wage and price controls

    c   A fixed rule mandating steady money growth

    d   Unemployment insurance

    e   Policies that promote labour mobility

18   Which policy is likely to promote labour mobility?

    a   Training programs for displaced workers

    b   Moral suasion

    c   Regulations requiring notification in anticipation of layoffs

    d   Increasing the availability of rental housing

    e   *a* and *d*

19   During Britain's membership in the Exchange Rate Mechanism (ERM) between 1990 and 1992, the exchange rate for the pound was

    a   fixed against other ERM currencies.

    b   fixed against the deutsche mark (DM).

    c   allowed to vary within a band of DM2.95 plus or minus 6 percent.

    d   allowed to vary within a band of DM2.95 plus or minus 2 percent.

    e   allowed to vary against the DM and other ERM currencies.

20   In Britain, the Monetary Policy Committee established in 1997

    a   offers the Bank of England greater independence.

    b   was intended to depoliticise monetary policy.

    c   sets interest rates to meet an intermediate policy target.

    d   *a* and *b*.

    e   *a* and *c*.

Completion

1 _____ shocks such as wars or monetary restrictions start outside the economy.

2 _____ argues that prices and wages are quite flexible and recommends that the government not try to smooth economic fluctuations.

3 Households and firms that understand the structure of the economy are said to have _____.

4 The _____ refers to the inability of government to credibly promise not to change policy.

5 _____ advocate discretionary fiscal and monetary policies, automatic stabilisers, and policies to reduce the NAIRU.

6 New Keynesians stress that although externally generated shocks may hit the economy, the system can _____ them and cause the effects to _____.

7 Regulations that prohibit rapid increases in wages and prices are called _____.

8 When the government attempts to persuade firms to keep prices and wages low, it uses _____.

9 Targets, such as M0 and M4, are called _____.

10 Unemployment benefits and income taxes are examples of _____.

Answers to Self-Test

True or False

1	T	6	T	11	T
2	T	7	F	12	T
3	F	8	T	13	F
4	F	9	F	14	T
5	F	10	T	15	F

Multiple Choice

1	c	6	c	11	c	16	a
2	b	7	d	12	b	17	e
3	e	8	c	13	e	18	a
4	a	9	b	14	a	19	c
5	b	10	d	15	b	20	d

Completion

1 Exogenous
2 Real business cycle theory
3 rational expectations
4 dynamic consistency problem
5 New Keynesian economists
6 amplify, persist
7 wage and price controls
8 moral suasion
9 monetary aggregates
10 automatic stabilisers

Tools and Practice Problems

The economy is continually buffeted by shocks. Consumer tastes change, new technologies are discovered, bad weather appears, or import prices surge. There are mechanisms within the economy that dampen the impact of shocks. These include flexible prices, rational expectations, labour mobility, and government policies, such as automatic stabilisers. On the other hand, there are factors such as the multiplier and accelerator that amplify shocks. Tool Kit 33.1 illustrates how these mechanisms can exacerbate instability.

Tool Kit 33.1: The Multiplier-Accelerator Process

The accelerator is the capital-output ratio. Firms in many industries try to keep this constant. The multiplier determines how much aggregate demand shifts when there is a change in spending, such as an increase in investment. These mechanisms can combine to amplify shocks. Follow these steps.

Step one: Identify the accelerator, the multiplier, and the change in spending.

Step two: Multiply the change in spending by the accelerator. This gives the extra investment needed to keep the capital-output ratio constant.

Required investment = change in spending × accelerator.

Step three: Multiply the product in step two by the multiplier. This gives the change in output resulting from the extra investment.

Change in output = new investment × multiplier.

Step four: Multiply the product in step three by the accelerator. This gives the second round of additional investment needed to keep the capital-output ratio constant.

Required investment = change in output × accelerator.

---

1 (Worked problem: multiplier-accelerator) Output is £5 billion and the capital stock equals £15 billion. The multiplier is 2. Suppose that a new investment project of £10 million is undertaken.

   a Trace through the impact of this using the multiplier-accelerator.

   b Do you think the process can continue unabated? Why or why not?

Step-by-step solution

Step one: Identify the accelerator, the multiplier, and the change in spending. The accelerator is 15/5 = 3 and the multiplier is 2. The initial change in spending is £10 million.

Step two: Multiply the change in spending by the accelerator. This gives the extra investment needed to keep the capital-output ratio constant.

Required investment = change in spending × accelerator
= £10 million × 3 = £30 million.

Step three: Multiply the product in step two by the multiplier. This gives the change in output resulting from the extra investment.

Change in output = new investment × multiplier
= £30 million × 2 = £60 million.

Step four: Multiply the product in step three by the accelerator. This gives the second round of additional investment needed to keep the capital-output ratio constant.

Required investment = change in output × accelerator
= £60 million × 3 = £180 million.

Of course, the process cannot continue too long, because the economy has capacity constraints.

2   (Practice problem: multiplier-accelerator) Output is £2 billion and the capital stock equals £4 billion. The multiplier is 2.5. Suppose that a new investment project of £30 million is undertaken.

   a   Trace through the impact of this using the multiplier-accelerator.
   b   Do you think the process can continue unabated? Why or why not?

3   (Practice problem: multiplier-accelerator) Output is £7 billion and the capital stock equals £14 billion. The multiplier is 1.5. Suppose that a new investment project of £15 million is undertaken.

   a   Trace through the impact of this using the multiplier-accelerator.
   b   Do you think the process can continue unabated? Why or why not?

Answers to Problems

2   *a*   Required investment = £30 million × 4/2 = £60 million; change in output = £60 million × 2.5 = £150 million; additional investment = £150 million × 2 = £300 million.
   b   No. The economy will eventually run into capacity constraints.

3   *a*   Required investment = £15 million × 14/7 = £30 million; change in output = £30 million × 1.5 = £45 million; additional investment = £45 million × 2 = £90 million.
   b   No. The economy will eventually run into capacity constraints.

Part Eight

ISSUES IN MACROECONOMIC POLICY

Chapter 34

GROWTH AND PRODUCTIVITY

Chapter Review

This chapter of the text begins Part Five, which builds on the lessons of the previous four parts and takes a detailed look at some major macroeconomic problems. The chapter focuses on the causes of growth and the potential for continued expansion. The key concept is productivity, defined as output per worker. A small increase in productivity growth over a sustained period is capable of generating a very large increase in living standards. Our main aim is to understand what determines economic growth and why growth rates differ over time and between countries.

ESSENTIAL CONCEPTS

1   The period 1950 to 1973 is often referred to as the Golden Age of economic growth. During this time continental Europe, and to a lesser extent the United Kingdom and the United States, enjoyed high and stable economic growth. Despite the fact that U.K. growth was high by historic standards, Britain experienced relative economic decline as some continental European countries had faster output and productivity growth and overtook Britain in terms of living standards. Since 1973, growth in the United States, the United Kingdom,

and continental Europe has slowed, although for a period in the 1980s Britain's growth rate improved and outstripped that of many other European countries.

2   The four causes of growth in productivity are the accumulation of capital goods, an improvement in the quality of the labour force, an increase in the efficiency of resource allocation, and technological advance. Concerns about productivity slowdown have led economists to propose policies designed to restore rapid growth.

3   Figure 34.1 represents the production function, which shows the relationship between inputs and outputs. It illustrates that the accumulation of capital goods per worker brings about an increase in output per worker; however, the increase is subject to the **law of diminishing returns.** Economists call the increase in capital per worker **capital deepening**.

4   Although today's world capital market allows international borrowing, **capital accumulation** clearly requires more domestic savings and investment. Savings rates in Britain are low by international standards and have fallen significantly since their peak in 1973. Low and falling savings rates have been attributed to periods of negative real interest rates, the development of the social security and benefits system, financial market deregulation, increases in wealth associated with

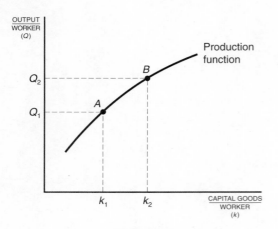

Figure 34.1

rising house prices, and demographic factors. British governments have introduced policies designed to increase the supply of savings, such as tax breaks for Personal Equity Plans (PEPs), Tax Exempt Special Savings Accounts (TESSAs), and Individual Savings Accounts (ISAs). These policies may have had the effect of diverting savings, from taxable to nontaxable accounts, rather than significantly increasing the overall amount. Investment in Britain has tended to be low in comparison to other countries, and investment as a share of GDP in Britain has been falling since its peak in 1974. Reasons for Britain's lacklustre investment performance include high real interest rates, short-termism in financial markets, a history of large cyclical fluctuations in output, and distortions caused by policies designed to encourage investment in housing.

5   Investment in skills and education improves the quality of the labour force. Economists call this **human capital.** Although the U.K. educational system has considerable strengths, especially in higher education, there is concern about the level of funding, the standards in education, the quality and recruitment of teachers, the participation rate in higher education, and other problems.

6   The economy expanded during this century as resources moved from traditional agriculture to higher productivity employment in manufacturing. Presently, the movement is towards the service sector, where some economists think the potential for productivity gains is more limited.

7   **Technological change** shifts the production function up and can outstrip diminishing returns. Although not everyone benefits from every innovation, technological change increases productivity, employment, and living standards overall. **Learning by doing** and **research and development** are important sources of technological progress. Sound macroeconomic policies that encourage full employment, R & D funding and tax subsidies, more science and technology education, and better government regulation all promote technological advance.

8   Total factor productivity analysis helps quantify the role of different factors in increasing productivity. After ac-

counting for the increase due to more physical and human capital, economists attribute the residual increase to improvements in technology. This analysis shows that most productivity increases are due to technological change.

9   Economic growth both creates and destroys jobs. As new techniques of producing drive old ways from the market, displaced workers see declining standards of living. The difficulty involved in transition to new lines of employment may call for government programmes to finance retraining and ease the transition.

BEHIND THE ESSENTIAL CONCEPTS

1   You should be clear about the distinction between factors that lead to movements along the production function and those that cause shifts. Capital accumulation moves the economy along its production function, as shown in Figure 34.1. An improvement in technology, on the other hand, shifts the production function. In Figure 34.2, the technological advance increases output without increasing the capital stock.

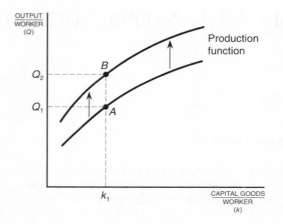

Figure 34.2

2   Productivity equals output per worker. As population grows, capital goods must be accumulated for the new workers to use. Because output per worker depends upon how much capital each has to work with, this extra capital only keeps productivity constant. Additional capital goods must be accumulated to increase the amount of capital per worker, so that productivity can grow.

3   One theory that explains variations in savings rates is the **life-cycle theory of savings.** According to this view, people save in order to consume more in the future. Thus, the trade-off is current versus future consumption. Most of us will probably save during our working years to build up funds for retirement. The life-cycle theory of savings shows that people save less when they are young, most when they are in established jobs (aged

approximately 25 to 60), and less, or even dissave, in retirement. This means that a fall in the fraction of the working population in the middle years (25 to 60) will lead to a fall in the share of savings. Other factors that may have affected savings in the United Kingdom include better health care and social security, and increases in real wealth associated with house price inflation. All of these factors mean that people have to save less for their retirement. Many of these developments are good, but an unfortunate side effect is the accompanying disincentive to save.

4 Giving workers more capital to work with—capital deepening—accounts for only one-eighth of the growth in productivity. How do economists know this? One reason is that until recently productivity grew at a steady rate, a fact that cannot be explained by capital accumulation. If it were capital deepening, then the movement along the production function would run into diminishing returns. Therefore it must be a shift in the production function, probably brought about by human capital accumulation or technological advance.

5 Some have argued that the available natural resources set up limits to growth. Certain natural resources, such as petroleum and agricultural land, are privately owned and traded in well-organized markets. These markets provide good incentives for conservation and preservation. If oil becomes scarce, for example, its price will rise, and world oil stocks will be conserved. This type of natural resource will probably not limit the world's growth. The ozone, the oceans, and the genetic diversity in threatened natural habitats, on the other hand, are natural resources that are commonly owned and not traded in markets. The world's economy provides no incentive to conserve or preserve these resources. Their destruction is an external cost, not captured by prices. These global environmental problems may pose threats to increased living standards. Their solution requires cooperation among the world's governments.

SELF-TEST

True or False

1 Productivity measures output per unit of capital goods.

2 Productivity growth in the United Kingdom slowed in the late 1980s.

3 Over the postwar period, U.K. productivity growth has tended to be high by historical standards but low by international standards.

4 The law of diminishing returns says that technological advance must bring about slower growth in the future.

5 Capital deepening refers to increases in the number of workers per unit of capital.

6 During the 1980s taxes on savings rose in the United Kingdom.

7 A fall in the fraction of the population between the ages of 25 and 60 is likely to decrease the savings rate.

8 A country's infrastructure includes its roads, bridges, sewer systems, and airports.

9 Investment in infrastructure has increased substantially during recent years.

10 Human capital refers to the plant and equipment that workers use on the job.

11 Participation in higher education in the United Kingdom is low compared to that in the United States, Canada, France, and Japan.

12 The shift of resources out of manufacturing into services has dragged overall productivity growth down, but recent advances in electronics and information technology are likely to mitigate against this effect.

13 Everyone benefits from each technological advance through higher productivity and growth.

14 Total factor productivity analysis is used to distinguish between growth due to increases in labour and capital from that due to technological advance.

15 Market incentives ensure that such natural resources as rain forests and the global environment will be preserved.

Multiple Choice

1 Productivity is

   a the extra output from the marginal worker.
   b hours worked divided by output.
   c output per hour worked.
   d the number of workers required to produce the next unit of output.
   e output divided by the total number of inputs.

2 The U.K. rate of growth of per capita real GDP between 1965 and 1990 has been

   a faster than that of any G7 country.
   b equal to the average rate for the G7 countries.
   c slower than that of any G7 country except the United States.
   d faster than that of any G7 country except the United States.
   e slower than that of any G7 country except Italy.

3 Over the business cycle, productivity

   a grows at approximately the same rate.
   b falls as the economy enters a downturn but rises faster than output as the economy commences recovery.
   c rises as the economy enters a downturn but falls as the economy recovers.
   d grows faster during recessions because output falls less than employment.
   e may grow at a faster or slower rate, depending upon monetary and fiscal policies.

4 The causes of growth include

   a the accumulation of capital goods.
   b improvement in the quality of the labour force.
   c more efficient allocation of resources.
   d technological advance.
   e all of the above.

5   Capital deepening refers to

   a   increased numbers of workers per unit of capital.
   b   increases in capital per worker.
   c   decreases in capital per worker.
   d   reallocation of capital from less productive to more productive sectors.
   e   government investment in infrastructure.

6   According to the law of diminishing returns, as the economy accumulates more capital, output increases

   a   at the same rate as capital grows.
   b   at a slower rate than capital grows.
   c   at a faster rate than capital grows.
   d   only if new workers enter the labour force.
   e   only if the new capital equipment takes advantage of new and better technologies.

7   Savings accumulated for retirement are called

   a   life-cycle savings.
   b   target savings.
   c   precautionary savings.
   d   bequest savings.
   e   permanent income savings.

8   Savings accumulated for use in emergencies are called

   a   life-cycle savings.
   b   target savings.
   c   precautionary savings.
   d   bequest savings.
   e   permanent income savings.

9   According to life-cycle theory, savings in the United Kingdom were low in the 1980s because

   a   the fraction of the population that is retired decreased.
   b   the fraction of the population in the prime savings years (25 to 60) increased.
   c   the fraction of the population in the prime savings years (25 to 60) decreased.
   d   the population as a whole increased.
   e   the fraction of the population in the prime savings years (21 to 44) decreased.

10 In the United Kingdom during the 1980s, the introduction of PEPs and TESSAs was designed to

   a   encourage savings by increasing the real after-tax rate of return to savings.
   b   encourage savings by decreasing the real after-tax rate of return to savings.
   c   discourage savings by increasing the real after-tax rate of return to savings.
   d   discourage savings by decreasing the real after-tax rate of return to savings.
   e   leave savings unaffected.

11 Which of the following policies is likely to stimulate investment by firms?

   a   An increase in the rate of mortgage tax relief
   b   A decrease in the real after-tax rate of return
   c   Greater availability of long-term finance at the going rate of interest
   d   *a* and *c*
   e   *b* and *c*

12 The production function shows the relationship between

   a   the levels of inputs and the level of output.
   b   technology and growth.
   c   productivity and real wages.
   d   learning and experience.
   e   productivity and output.

13 In the United Kingdom, the share of domestic investment as a percentage of GDP

   a   rose by 5 percentage points between 1974 and 1994.
   b   stayed roughly constant between 1974 and 1994.
   c   fell by about 5 percentage points between 1974 and 1994.
   d   fell by 2 percentage points between 1974 and 1994.
   e   rose by 7 percentage points between 1974 and 1994.

14 Human capital refers to

   a   the capital goods that individuals own.
   b   education and skills that increase the productivity of individuals.
   c   fertility.
   d   output per hour worked.
   e   the capital goods that workers use on the job.

15 Investment in human capital

   a   increases the skills of the workforce.
   b   increases productivity.
   c   increases unit wage costs.
   d   *a* and *b*.
   e   *b* and *c*.

16 The expansion of the telecommunications sector in the United Kingdom will

   a   raise overall productivity because productivity is higher than average in these sectors.
   b   raise overall productivity because productivity is lower than average in these sectors.
   c   reduce overall productivity because productivity is higher than average in these sectors.
   d   reduce overall productivity because productivity is lower than average in these sectors.
   e   leave overall productivity unchanged.

17 Technological change

   a   shifts the production function so that the same number of inputs produce more output.
   b   shifts the production function so that more output is produced but only if additional capital goods are used.
   c   shifts the production function so that more output is produced but only if additional workers are hired.
   d   increases productivity for capital but not for workers.
   e   increases productivity but does not shift the production function.

18 The method that attributes that part of the growth in productivity that cannot be explained by increases in labour and capital to technological advance is called

a   total factor productivity analysis.
b   partial productivity analysis.
c   capital deepening.
d   capital widening.
e   sustainable development.

19   The economy's growth in output is equal to

a   its growth in productivity.
b   the sum of its growth in the labour force and its capital accumulation.
c   the sum of its growth in hours worked and its growth in productivity.
d   the marginal product of labour times the number of hours worked plus the marginal product of capital times the capital stock.
e   the sum of private savings, government savings, and net inflows of capital from abroad.

20   Sustainable development refers to growth without excessive

a   technological advance.
b   population increase.
c   capital investment.
d   natural resource exploitation.
e   all of the above.

Completion

1   _____ is defined as output per hour worked.

2   The _____ relates the levels of inputs to the level of output.

3   A country's roads, airports, bridges, sewer lines, and railroads make up its _____.

4   Economists refer to education and skills as _____.

5   Increases in capital per worker are called _____.

6   Savings for a specific purpose, such as university tuition fees, are called _____.

7   According to the _____, successive increments in capital lead to smaller increases in output per worker.

8   The savings that a household sets aside in case of emergency or illness are called _____.

9   Economists use _____ to discover the magnitude of technological advance.

10   Advocates of _____ seek policies to preserve the environment and natural resources while increasing living standards.

Answers to Self-Test

True or False

1	F	6	F	11	T
2	F	7	T	12	T
3	T	8	T	13	F
4	F	9	F	14	T
5	F	10	F	15	F

Multiple Choice

1	c	6	b	11	c	16	a
2	c	7	a	12	a	17	a
3	b	8	c	13	c	18	a
4	e	9	c	14	b	19	c
5	b	10	a	15	d	20	d

Completion

1   Productivity
2   production function
3   infrastructure
4   human capital
5   capital deepening
6   target savings
7   law of diminishing returns
8   precautionary savings
9   total factor productivity analysis
10   sustainable growth

Tools and Practice Problems

Two important factors that explain Britain's low productivity growth are low savings and low investment. In this section, we study some reasons for low savings rates: demographic changes, improved opportunities for consumer borrowing, and more generous social security benefits. Also, we see how favourable tax treatment of certain types of investment can reduce investment in other sectors of the economy.

REASONS FOR LOW SAVINGS RATES: THE LIFE-CYCLE MODEL AND DEMOGRAPHIC CHANGES

As the life-cycle model predicts, individuals save at different rates during their lifetimes. Generally, people will save little in their early years, a great deal in middle age, and less when retired. When generations are of different sizes, then the national savings rate will fluctuate as the relatively large generation moves through the high-savings years.

1   (Worked problem: low savings rates) There was zero population growth in the country of Steady for centuries until now. People in Steady behave exactly as the life-cycle model predicts, saving at different rates during the successive periods of their lives. The savings supply schedules for three age classes of equal size are given in Table 34.1.

Table 34.1

Interest rate	Savings		
	Young	*Middle*	*Old*
4%	£1,000	£20,000	£5,000
6%	£1,100	£25,000	£5,000
8%	£1,200	£30,000	£5,000
10%	£1,200	£35,000	£5,000

a   Suppose the generation that is now young is twice as large as the other generations, which are of equal size. Calculate the supply of savings for the economy.

b   Twenty years from now, the large generation will be middle aged. The currently old will die and be replaced by the cohort that is now middle aged. Calculate the supply of savings for the economy in 20 years.

c   Forty years from now, the large generation will be old. The young and middle generations will be half the size of the large generation. Calculate the supply of savings in 40 years.

d   Plot the three savings supplies, and notice the fluctuations in savings supply caused by the demographic transition.

Step-by-step solution

Step one (a): We find the market supply of savings by summing the total amount of savings at each interest rate. If the interest rate is 4 percent, then total savings will be

$$(2 \times £1,000) + (1 \times £20,000) + (1 \times £5,000) = £27,000.$$

We multiply the £1,000, which is the savings of the young, by 2 because there are twice as many young people.

Step two: At a 6 percent interest rate, the supply of savings is

$$(2 \times £1,100) + £25,000 + £5,000 = £32,200.$$

Continuing the process derives the entire supply of savings, which is as follows.

Interest rate	Savings
4%	£27,000
6%	£32,200
8%	£37,400
10%	£42,400

Step three (b): To find the total supply of savings 20 years from now when the large generation will be middle-aged, multiply the supply of savings in the middle-aged generation by 2 and add it to the others. For example, at a 4 percent interest rate, total savings are

$$£1,000 + (2 \times £20,000) + £5,000 = £46,000.$$

Continuing gives the supply of savings in 20 years.

Interest rate	Savings
4%	£46,000
6%	£56,100
8%	£66,200
10%	£76,200

Step four (c): Total savings 40 years from now are found by multiplying the savings of the old by 2 and adding them to the savings of the others. The supply curve is given by

Interest rate	Savings
4%	£31,000
6%	£36,100
8%	£41,200
10%	£46,200

Step five (d): Plot the curves. Clearly, the supply curve shifts to the right as the large generation moves into the high-savings years and shifts to the left when they retire.

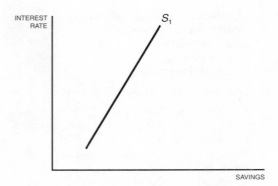

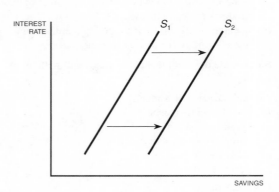

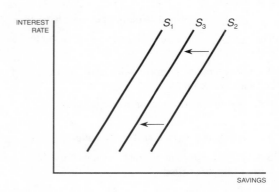

2   (Practice problem: low savings rates) Using the same data as in problem 1, suppose that a baby boom generation follows 40 years behind the large generation. In other words, every other generation will be twice as large as the generations were in Steady for centuries. Derive the supply of savings for the economy for 20-year intervals. Begin with a small young generation.

REASONS FOR LOW SAVINGS RATES: LOWER INTEREST RATES FOR BORROWING

One of the great strengths of the U.K. economy is its efficient capital market. Recently a combination of factors, for example credit cards, home equity loans, and bank deregulation, have increased access for borrowers. Lower interest rates for borrowers rotate part of the budget constraint out, giving the household more opportunities to consume more today.

3   (Worked problem: low savings rates) Harold and Myla take home £60,000 each year. They can earn 4 percent on any savings, but they must borrow at 14 percent.

a   Plot their two-period budget constraint.
b   A preapproved application for a new credit card arrives. The interest rate on the unpaid balance will be 8 percent. Plot their new two-period budget constraint, and compare it with the answer to part a.

Step-by-step solution

Step one (a): Plot the budget constraint with the 4 percent interest rate. The slope is 1.04, and it passes through the point £60,000 now and £60,000 next year.

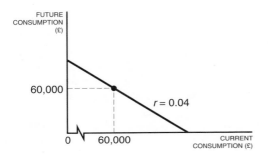

Step two: Plot the budget constraint with the 14 percent interest rate. The slope is 1.14, and it passes through the point £60,000 now and £60,000 next year.

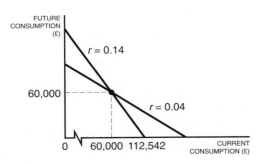

Step three: Darken the portion of each budget constraint that lies under the other constraint. This is the answer to part a.

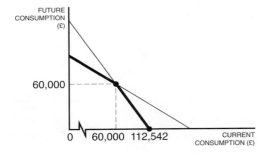

Step four (b): Again, plot the budget constraint with the 4 percent interest rate as in step one.

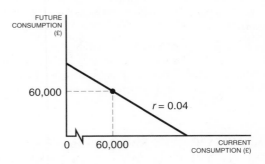

Step five: Plot the budget constraint with the 8 percent interest rate. The slope is 1.08, and it passes through the point £60,000 now and £60,000 next year.

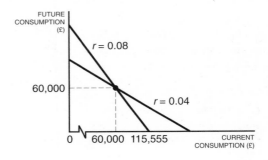

Step six: Darken the portion of each budget constraint that lies under the other constraint. This is the answer to part b.

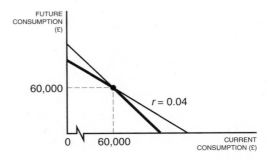

Step seven: Compare the two budget constraints. The lower interest rate gives Harold and Myla more opportunities, but the extra opportunities all involve borrowing.

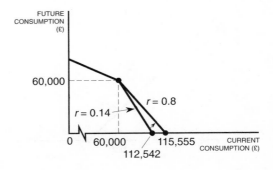

4   (Practice problem: low savings rates) Bill takes home £10,000 this year, but he anticipates taking home £30,000 next year. He can earn 8 percent on savings, but he has a poor credit rating and must pay 19 percent to borrow.

   a   Plot his two-period budget constraint.
   b   Through his credit union at his new job, Bill can obtain loans for 10 percent. Plot his new two-period budget constraint, and compare.

REASONS FOR LOW SAVINGS RATES: INCREASED SOCIAL SECURITY BENEFITS

Social security can reduce people's incentives to save for retirement, and because it is financed on a pay-as-you-go basis, it reduces national savings. The next two problems use the two-period budget constraint to illustrate this idea.

5   (Worked problem: low savings rates) Juwan has 10 years until retirement. He earns £40,000 after taxes and expects to receive a pension of £20,000 when he retires. He expects that over the 10-year interval until retirement he can earn a 100 percent rate of return, and he currently saves £5,000 per year.

   a   Calculate the present discounted value of his pension benefits.
   b   Draw his two-period budget constraint, and plot his chosen point.
   c   Suppose that his pension is increased to £30,000. His National Insurance contributions are also increased by £5,000: this reduces his current net income to £35,000. Draw his two-period budget constraint.
   d   How much does Juwan now save?

Step-by-step solution

Step one (a): The present discounted value of his pension payment is £20,000/(1 + *r*) = £20,000/(1 + 1) = £10,000.

Step two (b): Draw his two-period budget constraint. Label the axes "Current consumption" and "Retirement consumption." The slope is 1 + *r*, and the interest rate for the 10-year period is 100 percent. The horizontal intercept is the present discounted value of all income, which is £40,000 + £10,000 = £50,000.

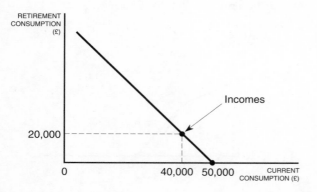

Step three: Plot his chosen point. Juwan chooses to save £5,000; thus, he consumes £40,000 − £5,000 = £35,000 now. The £5,000 grows to £10,000 in 10 years, which enables consumption of £20,000 + £10,000 = £30,000.

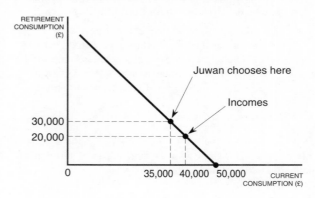

Step four (c): Plot his new budget constraint. The present discounted value of his pension is now £30,000/2 = £15,000. The horizontal intercept is £15,000 + £35,000 = £50,000, which is unchanged. Because neither the present discounted value of his two-period income nor the interest rate changes, the budget constraint remains the same.

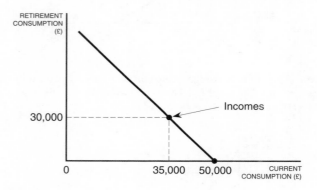

Step five (d): Because he has the same budget constraint, he chooses the same point. But he achieves this combination of current and retirement consumption by reducing his savings to zero. The increase in his pension has reduced Juwan's savings by exactly £5,000.

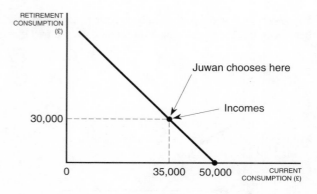

6   (Practice problem: low savings rates) Jane is only 10 years from retirement. She can expect to receive £2 in interest for every £1 saved for retirement. She takes home £60,000 annually, saves £10,000 each year, and expects a pension of £30,000 when she retires.

   a   Plot her two-period budget constraint.

   b   Suppose the pressure group Pensioner Power wins a 50 percent increase in pensions. Taxes also rise, so the budget constraint does not change. How will Jane's consumption now and during retirement change? How will her savings change?

Subsidies and the Allocation of Investment

Preferential tax treatment of certain types of investment can reallocate an economy's capital stock. A subsidy to a particular type of investment will raise its return, and since investors always seek the highest rate of return, they will reallocate their portfolio to take advantage of the subsidy. Tool Kit 34.1 shows the link between subsidies and reallocation.

Tool Kit 34.1 Showing How Subsidies Can Reallocate Investment

   Subsidies shift up the demand for investment in the subsidised sector. This reallocates investment. These steps outline the procedure for analysing the impact of a subsidy in one sector.

Step one: Add up the demands of each sector for capital.

Step two: Find the market-clearing rate of interest.

Step three: Substitute the market-clearing rate of interest into each demand to determine the allocation of investment that occurs without subsidy.

Step four: Add the subsidy to the demand for capital in the subsidised sector.

Step five: Repeat steps one through three.

Step six: Compare the allocation found in step five with that found in step three.

---

7   (Worked problem: allocation of investment) Suppose the government scrapped mortgage tax relief. To see the effect that this tax subsidy had, consider Table 34.2, which gives the demands for investment in the housing and manufacturing sectors. The supply of financial capital for the two sectors is £3,900 million.

Table 34.2

Interest rate	Demand for housing investment (millions)	Demand for investment manufacturing (millions)
10%	£1,000	£2,000
9%	£1,100	£2,200
8%	£1,200	£2,400
7%	£1,300	£2,600
6%	£1,400	£2,800
5%	£1,500	£3,000
4%	£1,600	£3,200

   a   Find the market allocation.

   b   Suppose the tax subsidy amounts to an extra 3 percent annual return for investment in housing. Find the allocation.

   c   How does the tax subsidy alter the equilibrium allocation of capital?

Step-by-step solution

Step one (a): Add the demands of each sector for capital. We choose an interest rate, and sum the quantity demanded in each sector. When the interest rate is 10 percent, the total quantity demanded is £1,000 + £2,000 = £3,000 million. Continuing, we derive Table 34.3.

Table 34.3

Interest rate	Housing	Manufacturing	Total
		(millions)	
10%	£1,000	£2,000	£3,000
9%	£1,100	£2,200	£3,300
8%	£1,200	£2,400	£3,600
7%	£1,300	£2,600	£3,900
6%	£1,400	£2,800	£4,200
5%	£1,500	£3,000	£4,500
4%	£1,600	£3,200	£4,800

Step two: Find the market-clearing rate of interest. Quantity supplied, which is £3,900 million, equals quantity demanded when the interest rate is 7 percent.

Step three: Substitute the market-clearing rate of interest into each demand to determine the allocation of investment. The 7 percent rate of interest brings about an allocation of £1,300 million in housing and £2,600 million in manufacturing.

Step four (b): Add the subsidy to the demand for capital in the subsidised sector. Simply add 3 percent to the interest rate column for the housing sector. Table 34.4 gives the result.

Table 34.4

Interest rate	Housing (millions)
13%	£1,000
12%	£1,100
11%	£1,200
10%	£1,300
9%	£1,400
8%	£1,500
7%	£1,600

Step five: Repeat steps one through three. Table 34.5 gives the new total demand.

Table 34.5

Interest rate	Housing	Manufacturing	Total
13%	£1,000	£2,000	£3,000
12%	£1,100	£2,000	£3,100
11%	£1,200	£2,000	£3,200
10%	£1,300	£2,000	£3,300
9%	£1,400	£2,200	£3,600
8%	£1,500	£2,400	£3,900
7%	£1,600	£2,600	£4,200
6%	£1,600	£2,800	£4,400
5%	£1,700	£3,000	£4,700
4%	£1,800	£3,200	£5,000

The market clears at an 8 percent interest rate with an allocation of £1,500 billion to housing and £2,400 million to manufacturing.

Step six (c): Compare the allocation found in step five with that found in step three. The tax subsidy increases investment in the housing sector's allocation from £1,300 to £1,500 million, reducing the manufacturing sector's allocation from £2,600 million to £2,400. In effect, £200 million is reallocated from manufacturing to housing.

8   (Practice problem: allocation of investment) Table 34.6 gives the demands for financial capital in the United States in the sector that produces goods for export and the sector that produces goods that compete with imports. The available supply of capital is $200 million.

Table 34.6

Interest rate	Demand in the import-competing sector (billions)	Demand in the export sector (billions)
12%	$ 30	$ 40
11%	$ 50	$ 50
10%	$ 60	$ 60
9%	$ 70	$ 80
8%	$ 80	$ 90
7%	$100	$100
6%	$120	$110
5%	$140	$120

a   Find the market allocation.
b   Worried about lost market share to imports, a protectionist U.S. Congress passes a series of tax subsidies and trade barriers. Suppose that the tax subsidies and import controls amount to an extra 5 percent of annual earnings for import-competing investment. Find the new allocation.
c   How does the tax policy alter the equilibrium allocation of capital?

9   (Practice problem: allocation of investment) Preferential tax treatment can reallocate investment capital across regions. The European Union structural funds alter financial incentives to firms that locate in specified areas in the United Kingdom with high unemployment. To see

how this policy might work, consider Table 34.7, which gives demands for capital in enterprise zones and elsewhere. Assume that the investment incentives are worth 6 percent and the total quantity supplied equals £10 million.

Table 34.7

Interest rate	Demand in regions eligible for structural funds (millions)	Demand elsewhere (millions)
9%	£0.6	£ 8.2
8%	£0.8	£ 8.6
7%	£1.0	£ 9.0
6%	£1.2	£ 9.8
5%	£1.4	£10.8
4%	£1.6	£12.0
3%	£1.8	£15.0
2%	£2.0	£20.0

a   Find the market allocation without the investment incentives and the corresponding interest rate.
b   Find the demand curves with the investment incentives.
c   Find the new allocation brought about by the investment incentives. How does the tax policy alter the equilibrium allocation of capital?

Answers to Problems

2   With a small young generation, a large middle-aged generation, and a small old generation, the supply of savings is as follows.

Interest rate	Savings
4%	£46,000
6%	£56,100
8%	£66,200
10%	£76,200

When the young generation is large, the middle-aged generation small, and the old generation large, the supply of savings is as follows.

Interest rate	Savings
4%	£46,000
6%	£56,100
8%	£66,200
10%	£76,200

4   a

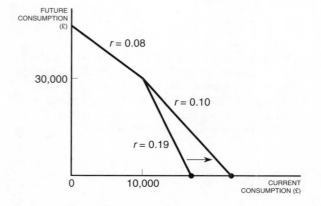

b With the lower interest rate for borrowing, Bill's budget constraint rotates out, giving him new opportunities, all of which involve borrowing more.

6 *a*

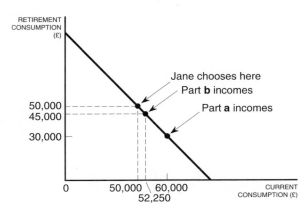

b The budget constraint does not change, so neither do her current and retirement consumptions. The increase in her pension reduces her savings by £7,500.

8 *a* The equilibrium interest rate is 7 percent, and the allocation is $100 billion to each sector.
   b Table 34.8 gives the demands with the tax subsidy and trade protection policies.

Table 34.8

Interest rate	Demand in the competing import sector	Demand in the export sector	Total
	(billions)		
17%	$ 30	$40	$ 70
16%	$ 50	$40	$ 90
15%	$ 60	$40	$100
14%	$ 70	$40	$110
13%	$ 80	$40	$120
12%	$100	$40	$140
11%	$120	$50	$170
10%	$140	$60	$200
9%	$140	$80	$220
8%	$140	$90	$220

c The market clears at an interest rate of 10 percent with an allocation of $140 billion to the import-competing sector and $60 billion to the export sector. The policies shift $40 billion from the export to the import-competing sector.

9 *a* The market allocation without the investment incentive is £1 million in the zones and £9 billion elsewhere and the interest rate is 7 percent.
   b Table 34.9 gives the demands with the investment incentive.

Table 34.9

Interest rate	Demand in the regions eligible for structural funds	Demand elsewhere	Total
	(billions)		
15%	£0.6	£ 8.2	£ 8.8
14%	£0.8	£ 8.2	£ 9.0
13%	£1.0	£ 8.2	£ 9.2
12%	£1.2	£ 8.2	£ 9.4
11%	£1.4	£ 8.2	£ 9.6
10%	£1.6	£ 8.2	£ 9.8
9%	£1.8	£ 8.2	£10.0
8%	£2.0	£ 8.6	£10.6
7%	£2.0	£ 9.0	£11.0
6%	£2.0	£ 9.8	£11.8
5%	£2.0	£10.8	£12.8

c The new equilibrium allocation is £1.8 million to the eligible regions and £8.2 billion elsewhere at an equilibrium interest rate of 9 percent. The investment incentives shift £0.8 million to the eligible regions from elsewhere in the economy.

Chapter 35

ECONOMIC INTEGRATION: THE EUROPEAN UNION

Chapter Review

This chapter extends our analysis of the open economy and trade by considering economic integration in the European Union (EU). While there are several examples of blocs of countries coming together to agree to mutually beneficial trading arrangements (for example, NAFTA, ASEAN, and APEC), the EU represents the most extensive and developed model of economic integration in the world. The chapter explores a number of economic aspects of European integration including **customs unions** and the single market, the Common Agricultural Policy (CAP), the social chapter, the European Monetary System (EMS), Economic and Monetary Union (EMU), and the **single currency**.

ESSENTIAL CONCEPTS

1   Economic integration in Europe is an ongoing process that started with the formation of the European Coal and Steel Community by France, West Germany, Italy, and the Benelux countries in 1951 and evolved into the European Community (EC), and then the EU. During the 1970s and 1980s the number of countries joining the EC grew. In the 1980s two main treaties shaped the fu-

ture of European integration: the Single European Act, in 1986, and the Treaty on European Union (the Maastricht Treaty) which led to the formation of the European Union in 1993 and monetary union in 1999. The EU now comprises 15 member states and the process of enlargement and integration is continuing.

2   The European Economic Community was set up as a **customs union:** a bloc of countries with no tariffs, taxes, or quotas on trade between members of the customs union. Goods entering the customs union from non-member states are liable to a **common external tariff** imposed by all members of the union. Customs unions have the effect of both creating and diverting trade. The effects on welfare depend upon the balance of trade creation and trade diversion, the extent of increasing returns to scale, the effects on X-efficiency, and the possible effects on the rate of economic growth. Tariff barriers between member states of the EC were removed by 1968, but restrictions on trade in the form of nontariff barriers remained.

3   The Single European Act was designed to remove all nontariff barriers within the EC by the end of 1992 to create the Single European Market. The idea—which goes a long way beyond a customs union—was to promote free trade and free mobility of capital and labour

by removing nontariff barriers, such as national standards, regulations, and public procurement policies that favour home producers. The removal of all such barriers requires radical policies to impose common standards, for example, common electricity and wiring standards, across member countries. The aim is to increase competition in the EU even further and improve economic welfare and living standards. The downside is that there are costs involved in establishing common standards and regulations. Not surprisingly, it has proven difficult to remove all nontariff barriers.

4   The Common Agricultural Policy was established at the outset of the EC with the aim of stabilising agricultural production and farm incomes. While the CAP is a key feature of European integration, it is not a necessary or intrinsic part of the process of economic integration. The CAP works by setting prices for agricultural produce and imposing variable import levies for agricultural produce imported from the rest of the world. Thus, consumers often pay higher prices for agricultural produce. If EC production exceeds EC consumption, surplus produce is purchased under the CAP at the intervention price. This has the effect of protecting farm incomes but encouraging overproduction and the creation of EC wine lakes, butter mountains, and frozen beef mountains. The CAP has absorbed a large part of the total EC budget.

5   The European Monetary System was designed to stabilise exchange rates in the EC. Under the EMS Exchange Rate Mechanism (ERM) currencies can vary within a target zone or band (initially plus or minus 2.25 percent of their central parity values). Once a currency hit the edges of its band, the monetary authorities intervened to defend weak currencies. Capital controls were also used to limit speculation and support the EMS but were removed under the single European market programme at the end of 1992. Persistent differences in inflation rates between countries were accommodated by occasional realignments of parities. Britain joined the ERM in 1990 but was forced out in 1992 following a speculative attack on the pound. Speculation in the ERM increased in the 1990s as capital controls were removed. As a result, the acceptable bands of fluctuation for ERM currencies were increased from ±2.25 to 15 percent.

6   European Monetary Union was enshrined in the Maastricht Treaty signed in 1993. It set out a three-step programme for monetary union and a single currency in Europe. Stage three was completed in January 1999 when 11 EU countries joined the single currency, called the Euro. Their exchange rates are now fixed. The advantages of a single currency are lower transactions costs and greater exchange efficiency. The disadvantages include loss of the exchange rate as a policy instrument a loss of control over monetary policy. The creation of a single currency in Europe required the formation of a European Central Bank (ECB) which manages the money supply and monetary policy in Europe. The ECB has been given considerable independence from political influence and is responsible for maintaining price stability.

7   The experience of economic integration in the European Union illustrates the inextricable links between economic and political processes. Economic integration requires cooperation between countries, coordination of monetary policy, and agreement on common standards and laws regarding, for example, aspects of product and labour market regulation. The social chapter of the Maastricht Treaty sets out measures affecting employment and industrial relations to ensure a level playing field and avoid social dumping. A central debate in Europe concerns the extent to which increased integration should be brought about by cooperation between nation-states (sometimes referred to as the Gaullist view) or by the creation of supranational European institutions (federalism).

BEHIND THE ESSENTIAL CONCEPTS

1   A **customs union** has two main effects. First, the removal of tariff barriers, quotas, and taxes on trade between members of the custom union creates trade and shifts production to low-cost producers within the union. This effect is termed **trade creation.** It represents a movement towards free trade and is likely to raise economic efficiency and welfare (although as with all gains from trade, there may well be winners and losers). Second, the imposition of a common tariff barrier causes some trade to be diverted away from countries outside the union to countries within the union. **Trade diversion** occurs when the tariff barrier makes imports from outside the union more expensive than imports from countries within the union, despite the fact that nonunion countries may be able to produce at lower cost. Trade diversion represents a movement away from free trade and is likely to reduce economic welfare. Since customs unions result in both **trade creation** and **trade diversion** the overall effect on economic welfare is ambiguous.

2   The preceding analysis of customs unions is based on the assumption that industries are perfectly competitive. If economic integration takes place between countries with imperfectly competitive industries, there may be more scope for gains from trade. Imperfect competition arises when there are significant economies of scale in production that make large firms more cost efficient. When there are increasing returns to scale, the size of the market affects costs of production. As the market grows, costs of production fall. A customs union generates a larger market and leads to more competition between firms within the union. Unit costs of production fall, and there is more competitive pressure on firms to pass on cost savings in the form of lower prices.

3   Three further effects of removing tariff barriers within customs unions with imperfectly competitive markets are greater consumer choice, X-efficiency, and higher investment and growth. Competition in imperfectly competitive industries often takes place via product

differentiation. Removing barriers to trade within a customs union may mean that consumers also benefit in terms of access to a wider variety of goods and services. A further possibility is that increased competition between firms within the customs union increases X-efficiency, or output efficiency, by causing firms to innovate, lower costs of production, and raise productivity. Finally, it has been argued that lower prices and higher real incomes generated by the removal of tariffs within a customs union will encourage higher savings and investment, and therefore higher growth. In practice, it is difficult to measure the significance of each of these potential gains.

4   The CAP works by setting minimum import prices (MIP) for agricultural products. Imports into the EC were subject to a variable import levy that brought their price up to the intervention price (IP). If EC production was less than EC consumption, prices in the EC were not able to fall below the minimum import price. If, on the other hand, EC production exceeded EC consumption, prices could fall to the intervention price—the price at which surplus produce would be bought under the CAP. How the system works in practice depends upon the levels at which the MIP and IP are set in relation to the market price. In general, the MIP and IP were set at a levels that meant EC production exceeded EC consumption; this encouraged EC production which had to be bought up under the CAP. As a result, the CAP has proved to be extremely costly.

5   The EMS and the ERM were designed to stabilise exchange rates. Restricting exchange rate movements also has the advantage of preventing individual countries that are members of a customs union from using strategic depreciation of their currency as a means of gaining unfair competitive advantage. Maintaining exchange rate parities in narrow bands is difficult when countries have different underlying rates of inflation that affect the real exchange rate. For example, if prices in Italy are increasing by 10 percent per annum, while prices in Germany are constant, demand for Italian goods in Germany will fall, causing a fall in the demand for Italian lira. Under floating exchange rates, equilibrium could be restored by a depreciation of the lira. Under the ERM, currencies were periodically realigned to cope with different underlying rates of inflation.

6   The creation of a single currency brings benefits in terms of reduced transactions costs, but costs in terms of the loss of the exchange rate as a policy instrument. If Italian goods become less competitive relative to German goods, the Italians may want the lira to depreciate to avoid a large trade deficit or unemployment. Under a single currency this adjustment is not possible. Instead, adjustment would have to take place by Italy's reducing its inflation rate, say through a cut in fiscal policy, or Germany's increasing its inflation rate. The former option involves costs in terms of unemployment, the latter costs in terms of inflation. The extent of these costs depends upon the degree of wage and price flexibility. The lower the flexibility of wages and prices, the higher the costs.

SELF-TEST

True or False

1   The European Union was established in 1993.

2   A country that is a member of a customs union is unprotected by tariff barriers.

3   Subsidiarity means that decisions should be taken at the lowest possible level.

4   The European commissioners are elected in their member states.

5   The welfare gains from a customs union are greater when there is imperfect competition.

6   The European Monetary System has been a system of target zones for exchange rates.

7   The European Central Bank has responsibility for price stability in "Euroland."

8   A benefit of the single currency is that participating countries have greater control over monetary policy.

9   Removal of capital controls made the Exchange Rate Mechanism susceptible to speculative attack.

10   The Common Agricultural Policy stabilised farm incomes and encouraged overproduction.

Multiple Choice

1   Economic integration in Europe involves

   a   lowering tariff barriers.
   b   lowering nontariff barriers.
   c   monetary union.
   d   developing common policies in areas, such as industrial relations.
   e   all of the above.

2   The concept of subsidiarity is best described as the practice where decisions are taken

   a   in the best interests of the greatest number of countries.
   b   at the most centralised level possible.
   c   at the most decentralised level possible.
   d   at a variety of levels.
   e   at the local level.

3   The treaty on European Union (the Maastricht Treaty) was signed in

   a   1958.
   b   1965.
   c   1973.
   d   1986.
   e   1992.

4   In a customs union

   a   there are no taxes, tariffs, or quotas on trade between member countries.
   b   there are no nontariff barriers on trade between member countries.
   c   there is a common external tariff imposed by all members of the union.
   d   a and c.
   e   a and b.

5   Improvements in economic welfare associated with a customs unions are likely to be greatest when

  a   there is perfect competition.
  b   there is imperfect competition.
  c   there are decreasing returns to scale.
  d   trade diversion exceeds trade creation.
  e   none of the above.

6   The single European market is best described as

  a   a union of European countries with free trade in goods and services.
  b   a union of European countries with free trade in goods and services and free mobility of capital and labour.
  c   a market within which nontariff barriers to trade are being removed.
  d   a market protected by a common external tariff.
  e   all of the above.

7   The Common Agricultural Policy was designed to

  a   raise the prices of food in the European Community.
  b   create wine lakes and butter mountains.
  c   limit the production of agricultural produce.
  d   stabilise the incomes of farmers in the European Community.
  e   all of the above.

8   The Common Agricultural Policy works by setting

  a   prices for agricultural produce (minimum import prices) in the EC.
  b   a variable import levy on agricultural imports.
  c   an intervention price at which agricultural produce would be purchased by the CAP.
  d   *a* and *c*.
  e   all of the above.

9   Selling goods abroad at a lower price than they sell for in the country where they are produced is called

  a   social dumping.
  b   dumping.
  c   pricing at cost.
  d   perfect competition.
  e   imperfect competition.

10   If the CAP intervention price is set above the price that would equate EC supply and demand,

  a   demand will equal supply.
  b   there will be a shortage of agricultural produce.
  c   a surplus will be produced.
  d   the cost of financing the CAP will increase.
  e   *c* and *d*.

11   The General Agreement on Trade and Tariffs (GATT)

  a   governs trading conditions within the EU.
  b   governs trading conditions between the EU and other countries and trading blocs.
  c   outlaws the use of tariffs.
  d   outlaws the use of nontariff barriers to trade.
  e   is negotiated by each individual member state of the EU.

12   When exchange rates are not fixed,

  a   a country may gain a competitive advantage by devaluing its exchange rate.
  b   a country may gain a competitive advantage by letting its exchange rate depreciate.
  c   countries with weak currencies will slump.
  d   countries with strong currencies will boom.
  e   none of the above.

13   The Exchange Rate Mechanism (ERM) of the European Monetary System (EMS) is best described at a system

  a   of fixed exchange rates.
  b   of freely floating exchange rates within the EU.
  c   of exchange rate target zones.
  d   of pegged exchange rates.
  e   fixing the rate of exchange between the U.S. dollar and European currencies.

14   Under the ERM, if the Italian lira became weak against the deutschemark,

  a   the German monetary authorities would be required to buy deutschemarks.
  b   the Italian monetary authorities would be required to buy lira.
  c   the German monetary authorities would be required to sell deutschemarks.
  d   *a* and *b*.
  e   *b* and *c*.

15   The removal of capital controls

  a   made the ERM more vulnerable to speculation.
  b   made it easier to fight off speculative attacks.
  c   reduced the need for frequent realignments.
  d   allowed the width of the target bands to be narrowed.
  e   all of the above.

16   The Maastricht criteria for entry into the EMS specified a maximum

  a   ratio of national debt to GDP of 60 percent.
  b   ratio of government debt to GDP of 50 percent.
  c   government deficit of 3 percent of GDP.
  d   *a* and *c*.
  e   *b* and *c*.

17   The main economic benefit of a single currency is it

  a   is cheaper to mint just one currency because there are economies of scale in the production of notes and coin.
  b   gives member countries greater say over how their economies are run.
  c   makes it easier to resolve problems of divergent inflation rates between member countries.
  d   lowers transactions costs and reduces risk.
  e   none of the above.

18   Under a single currency if the French economy became uncompetitive relative to the German economy, then to restore competitiveness,

  a   Germany should have lower inflation than France.
  b   France should increase its aggregate demand.

c France should have lower inflation than Germany.

d Germany should lower its aggregate demand.

e inflation in both countries should fall by the same amount.

19 Under a single currency

a member countries cannot pursue independent monetary policies.

b member countries cannot pursue independent fiscal policies.

c the economic costs of divergence are higher when prices are sticky.

d *a* and *b*.

e *a* and *c*.

20 The European Central Bank

a takes decisions according to majority voting by EMS member states.

b is responsible for maintaining price stability.

c is under the political control of the European Parliament.

d takes account of employment when setting policy.

e is responsible for fiscal policy in member states.

Completion

1 Decision making in Europe on some issues may mean states transfer their _____ to European institutions; on other issues they may retain it.

2 The single market was to be created by the removal of all _____.

3 A customs union causes both _____ and _____.

4 The _____ sets import tax levels for all goods entering the EU.

5 Trade diversion is likely to _____ economic welfare.

6 Under increasing returns to scale, increasing the size of the internal market is likely to _____ economic welfare.

7 The CAP sets _____ and _____ prices.

8 The CAP was designed to _____.

9 The removal of _____ made the exchange rate mechanism more vulnerable to speculative attacks.

10 The _____ means that member countries lose control over the exchange rate as a policy instrument.

Answers to Self-Test

True or False

1	T	3	T	5	T	7	T	9	T
2	F	4	F	6	T	8	F	10	T

Multiple Choice

1	*e*	6	*e*	11	*b*	16	*d*
2	*c*	7	*d*	12	*b*	17	*d*
3	*e*	8	*e*	13	*c*	18	*c*
4	*d*	9	*b*	14	*e*	19	*e*
5	*b*	10	*e*	15	*a*	20	*b*

Completion

1 sovereignty
2 nontariff barriers
3 trade creation, trade diversion
4 common external tariff
5 reduce
6 increase
7 minimum import, intervention
8 stabilise farm incomes
9 capital controls
10 single currency

Tools and Practice Problems

Customs unions do away with tariff barriers between member countries and impose a common external tariff. The removal of internal tariff barriers and the imposition of a common external tariff lead to trade diversion and trade creation. Tool Kit 35.1 illustrates how these effects work in the case of a single industry.

Tool Kit 35.1

To see how customs unions create and divert trade, this tool kit uses a simple three-country example (Britain, Italy, and Japan) of the computer industry to determine the extent of trade creation and trade diversion when two of the three countries form a customs union.

Step one: Identify the demand and domestic supply of computers in Britain.

Step two: Identify the pre-customs union tariffs, and posttariff import prices for Italian and Japanese goods.

Step three: Identify the level of imports from Italy and Japan.

Step four: Form a customs union between Italy and Britain that removes tariff barriers on imports from Italy. Recalculate the supply of imports from Italy and Japan with the new tariff structure.

Step five: Calculate the extent of trade diversion, in this case, the amount of imports into Britain that are switched from outside to inside the customs union.

Step six: Calculate the amount of trade creation, which is equal to the increase in the amount of imports into Britain.

---

1 (Worked problem: customs unions) Suppose that the demand and supply of computers in Britain is given by Table 35.1. Japan can supply the British market at a pretariff price of £1,600. Italy can supply the British market at a pretariff price of £1,700. Before the formation of the customs union, the tariff barrier for both Italy and Japan is set at 20 percent. After the formation of the customs union between Italy and Britain, the

tariff barrier on Italian imports is removed. The common external tariff barrier on imports from Japan is set at 20 percent. Calculate the extent of trade creation and trade diversion.

Table 35.1

Price of computers in Britain	Demand for computers in Britain (thousands)	Supply of computers produced in Britain (thousands)	Demand for imports into Britain (thousands)
£1,000	7,900	4,000	3,900
£1,200	7,800	4,200	3,600
£1,320	7,700	4,400	3,300
£1,600	7,600	4,600	3,000
£1,700	7,500	4,800	2,700
£1,800	7,400	5,000	2,400
£1,920	7,300	5,200	2,100
£2,160	7,200	5,400	1,800
£2,300	7,100	5,600	1,500
£2,500	7,000	5,800	1,200

Step-by-step solution

Step one: Identify the demand for, and domestic supply of, computers in Britain from Table 35.1.

Step two: Calculate the posttariff prices before the formation of a customs union between Italy and Britain. The tariff is set at 20 percent for both countries. Japan can supply any quantity of computers at a posttariff price of £1,920 = £1,600 + 0.2(£1600). Italy can supply any quantity of computers at a posttariff price of £2,040 = £1,700 + 0.2(£1,700).

Step three: Given that Japan can supply any quantity at a lower price, it will supply all imports into Britain. Japanese imports are equal to the difference between British supply and demand at the price of £1,920. Japan will supply 2,100,000 computers into Britain. Italy will supply zero. Domestic producers will supply 5,200,000.

Step four: Recalculate the posttariff prices from Italy and Japan after the formation of the customs union. Italy now has no tariff on its imports; therefore its supply price is £1,700. Japan's posttariff supply price is the same, £1,920, because the new common external tariff is still equal to 20 percent. Under the customs union, Italy has a lower posttariff price and will supply 2,700,000 imports into Britain. Domestic producers will supply £4,800,000 computers.

Step five: Trade diversion is equal to the amount of imports that are diverted from outside the customs union to within the customs union. This is equal to 2,100,000 units.

Step six: Trade creation is equal to the increase in imports into Britain which is 2,700,000 − 2,100,000 = 6,000,000 units.

2   (Practice problem: customs unions) Suppose that the demand and supply of washing machines in Britain is given by Table 35.2. Japan can supply the British market at a pretariff price of £250. Germany can supply the British market at a pretariff price of £270. Before the formation of the customs union, the tariff barrier for imports into Britain from both Germany and Japan is set at 10 percent. After the formation of the customs union between Germany and Britain the tariff barrier on German imports is removed. The common external tariff barrier on imports from Japan is set at 10 percent. Calculate the extent of trade creation and trade diversion.

Table 35.2

Price of washing machines in Britain	Demand for washing machines in Britain (thousands)	Supply of washing machines produced in Britain (thousands)	Demand for imports into Britain (thousands)
£200	6,900	3,500	3,400
£220	6,800	3,700	3,100
£230	6,700	3,900	2,800
£250	6,600	4,100	2,500
£270	6,500	4,300	2,200
£275	6,400	4,500	1,900
£297	6,300	4,700	1,600
£300	6,200	4,900	1,300
£350	6,100	5,100	1,000
£368	6,000	5,300	700

3   (Practice problem: customs unions) Suppose that the demand and supply of refrigerators in Britain is given by Table 35.3. Iceland can supply the British market at a pretariff price of £1,600. France can supply the British market at a pretariff price of £1,700. Before the formation of the customs union, the tariff barrier for imports into Britain from both Iceland and France is set at 33.3 percent. After the formation of the customs union between Germany and France, the tariff barrier on Italian imports is removed. The common external tariff barrier on imports from Japan is set at 33.3 percent. Calculate the extent of trade creation and trade diversion.

Table 35.3

Price of refrigerators in Britain	Demand for refrigerators in Britain (thousands)	Supply of refrigerators produced in Britain (thousands)	Demand for imports into Britain (thousands)
£100	8,900	4,500	4,400
£120	8,800	4,700	4,100
£130	8,700	4,900	3,800
£150	8,600	5,100	3,500
£165	8,500	5,300	3,200
£180	8,400	5,500	2,900
£190	8,300	5,700	2,600
£200	8,200	5,900	2,300
£220	8,100	6,100	2,000
£240	8,000	6,300	1,700

Answers to Problems

2   Before the formation of the customs union the posttariff prices are:

Japanese posttariff price = £250 + 0.2(£250) = £300.

German posttariff price = £270 + 0.2(£270) = £324.

Japan supplies 1,300,000 units into Britain. After the formation of the customs union the posttariff prices are:

Japanese posttariff price = £250 + 0.2(£250) = £300.

Germany is now exempt form tariffs and its price is £270.

Germany supplies 2,200,000 units into Britain. Trade diversion is equal to 1,300,000 units. Trade creation is equal to 900,000 units.

3   Before the formation of the customs union, the posttariff prices are:

Iceland's posttariff price = £200 + 0.333(£150) = £300.

France posttariff price = £180 + 0.333(£180) = £240.

Iceland supplies 2,300,000 units into Britain. After the formation of the customs union the posttariff prices are:

Iceland's posttariff price = £180 + 0.333(£180) = £240.

France is now exempt form tariffs and its price is £150.

France supplies 3,500,000 units into Britain. Trade diversion is equal to 2,300,000 units. Trade creation is equal to 1,200,000 units.

Chapter 36

TRADE POLICY

Chapter Review

Governments affect the flows of traded goods through tariffs, quotas, other nontariff barriers, and a series of fair trade laws. This chapter discusses how these measures affect markets, who wins, who loses, and their political rationale. There is also discussion of the major international institutions governing trade. Many countries have formed **trading blocs**. One of the most important of these is the **European Union** (EU) as discussed in Chapter 35.

ESSENTIAL CONCEPTS

1   Countries practicing protection use commercial policies to restrict imports. These trade barriers include tariffs, quotas, other nontariff barriers, and fair trade laws. Tariffs, which are taxes on imported goods, raise domestic prices, injuring consumers while providing some benefit to producers. Overall the economy suffers, losing consumer surplus and wasting resources producing goods that could be imported more cheaply.

2   Quotas are limits on the quantity of imports. By restricting supply, they force up prices and lead to the same types of deadweight burdens as tariffs do. Rather than collecting tariff revenues, the government confers on certain firms extra profits from importing, called quota rents. Other nontariff barriers, such as voluntary export restraints (VERs), have similar effects. In the case of VERs the quota rent accrues to foreign exporters.

3   While ostensibly designed to promote competition, fair trade laws are protectionist. These include antidumping laws, which prohibit the sale of imports below the cost of production, and subsidies to domestic producers, usually justified to offset the impact of foreign subsidies.

4   The political rationale for trade protection lies in the fact that certain groups lose from trade. Competition from imports may lead firms to close plants or even cease operation. Their displaced workers suffer large losses. Also, foreign competition may drive down wages in certain sectors or erode market power. Lost profits and laid-off unionised workers create a demand for protectionist relief.

5   Other arguments for protection may have some limited validity. The **infant industry argument** claims that import barriers may allow a young industry time to acquire the experience necessary to be competitive on the world market. Usually, however, direct assistance is a better policy. There is also the strategic trade argument,

whereby protected domestic firms exploit economies of scale to undercut their foreign competitors.

6   After the Second World War the **General Agreement on Tariffs and Trade (GATT)** was founded to reduce trade barriers. Its three basic principles were reciprocity, nondiscrimination, and transparency, and it succeeded in greatly reducing tariffs. In 1995 it was replaced by the **World Trade Organization (WTO)** as attention turned to nontariff barriers and intellectual property. The WTO has procedures for adjudicating trade disputes.

7   Regional trading blocs, such as the **European Union** and the **North American Free Trade Agreement (NAFTA),** remove trading barriers for member countries, and this brings about the benefits of trade creation, expanded trade within the bloc. On the other hand, the discrimination against those outside the bloc causes trade diversion. Goods that may be less costly from outsiders are produced within the bloc.

BEHIND THE ESSENTIAL CONCEPTS

1   A tariff is just a tax on imports, and we analyse its effects in the same way that we analyse a tax on a domestic good. As you recall from Chapter 3, if the suppliers must pay the tax, it shifts the supply curve up by the amount of the tax and the price rises to the intersection of the demand and the new supply curve. In the case of a tariff, the price is set on the world market. This price simply shifts up by the amount of the tariff, and the new equilibrium is read off the demand and supply curves. There is more on how to do this in Tool Kit 36.1.

2   Tariffs, quotas, and voluntary export restraints are equivalent in one sense. Each raises prices to consumers, reduces the quantity demanded, reduces imports, and increases domestic supply. In another way, however, they are quite different. Tariff revenue is collected by the government. In the case of quotas, there is an equivalent amount of money collected by importers. They can earn excess profits because the quota protects them from competition. In the case of voluntary export restraints, the two governments force the foreign suppliers to restrict output. But we know from monopoly theory that this results in higher prices and monopoly profits. In each case there is extra revenue collected: tariff revenue to the government, quota rents to the licensed importer, and VER excess profits to foreign firms.

3   When a country enters a regional trading bloc, it eliminates trade barriers with the other members, while keeping barriers up against nonmembers. This discrimination favours production within the bloc. Trade that otherwise would have occurred with nonmember countries is diverted to member countries. Since this likely goes against the principle of comparative advantage, there is a waste. Balanced against this inefficiency are the benefits of expanded trade among member countries. When trade agreements are global, however, there is no downside. It is all trade creation.

4   Why do we care about dumping? After all, if foreign producers want to sell us goods below cost, then should we not just accept their generosity? One fear is that after driving domestic producers from the market, the foreign firms will take advantage of their monopoly position and raise prices. This practice is called predatory pricing and it is illegal in the European Union and the United States. In theory, antidumping laws make the practice illegal for foreign firms. In practice, however, these laws are used to protect domestic firms from low-cost foreign competition.

5   The infant industry argument claims that temporary protection may allow firms to grow more efficient and ultimately to prosper. The policy is like an investment, sacrificing the current gains from importing cheaper goods for long-run profitability. Of course, it should only be applied if the present value of the future profits exceeds the current costs. But in that case firms in the industry should be able to raise capital to stay in business while they are gaining experience. Governments are in no better position to evaluate the prospects of infant industries than the capital market.

SELF-TEST

True or False

1   Policies that restrict the import of foreign goods are examples of protection.

2   Tariffs are taxes on exports.

3   Tariffs reduce the quantity supplied domestically.

4   Although they also result in higher prices, quotas differ from tariffs in that firms licenced to import earn quota rents.

5   Voluntary export restraints allow foreign firms to collude and raise prices.

6   Antidumping laws make it illegal to sell goods abroad below the cost of production.

7   Predatory pricing refers to selling below cost in order to drive rivals from the markets.

8   Strategic trade theory points out the possibility of protecting domestic firms so that they can exploit economies of scale to undercut their foreign rivals.

9   When there is free trade between two countries, the net benefits are positive in each country.

10   When there is free trade between two countries, all individuals gain.

11   Most of the recent slowdown in wage growth in the United Kingdom is due to international trade.

12   Regional trading blocs such as the EU, divert trade from nonmember to member countries.

13   Regional trading blocs, such as the EU, expand trade both among member and nonmember countries.

14   The GATT successfully reduced tariffs among most of the world's countries.

15 The WTO adjudicates trade disputes among the United States, Canada, and Mexico.

Multiple Choice

1 Which of the following are trade barriers?

   a Tariffs
   b Quotas
   c Voluntary export restraints
   d Fair trade laws
   e All of the above

2 Policies that affect imports or exports are called

   a commercial policies.
   b protection.
   c free trade.
   d nontariff barriers.
   e fair trade laws.

3 Tariffs are

   a taxes on exports.
   b subsidies on exports.
   c taxes on imports.
   d subsidies on imports.
   e voluntary export restraints.

4 When a small country imposes a tariff, the domestic price

   a rises by more than the amount of the tariff.
   b rises by an amount equal to the tariff.
   c rises by less than the amount of the tariff.
   d stays the same because only imported goods pay the tariff.
   e falls.

5 Tariffs, quotas, and voluntary exports restraints are similar in that each

   a raises domestic prices.
   b reduces domestic prices.
   c reduces domestic consumption.
   d increases domestic output.
   e a, c, and d.

6 When a tariff is imposed, the net loss to the European Union includes

   a tariff revenues.
   b lost consumer surplus due to less consumption of the good.
   c higher costs of producing the good domestically.
   d all of the above.
   e b and c.

7 When a quota is imposed, the net loss to the European Union includes

   a quota rents.
   b lost consumer surplus due to less consumption of the good.
   c higher costs of producing the good domestically.
   d all of the above.
   e b and c.

8 When a voluntary export restraint is imposed, the net loss to the European Union includes

   a excess profits.
   b lost consumer surplus due to less consumption of the good.
   c higher costs of producing the good domestically.
   d b and c.
   e all of the above.

9 Dumping refers to selling

   a goods abroad for less than the going price.
   b goods abroad without paying tariffs.
   c goods abroad below the cost of production.
   d goods abroad above the cost of production.
   e excess inventories abroad.

10 Predatory pricing refers to

   a pricing above cost to reap excess profits.
   b pricing below cost to drive rivals from the market.
   c bribing politicians to receive licenses to import.
   d not reducing price when the firm is subsidised.
   e using intellectual property without paying for it.

11 Which of the following groups generally favors free trade?

   a Exporters
   b Unions
   c Firms earning monopoly profits
   d Workers in import industries
   e Low-wage workers

12 When labour markets are inflexible, shifts in comparative advantage and growth of trade can lead to

   a structural unemployment.
   b frictional unemployment.
   c long-term unemployment.
   d all of the above.
   e a and b.

13 Beggar-thy-neighbour policies attempt to

   a increase national consumption by reducing exports.
   b increase national savings by reducing foreign aid.
   c increase national output by reducing imports.
   d decrease national savings by reducing imports.
   e decrease the budget deficit by exporting taxes.

14 During the Great Depression, the Hawley-Smoot tariffs in the United States

   a raised tariffs on imported goods.
   b drastically reduced imports.
   c led to foreign retaliation.
   d contributed to the economic downturn.
   e all of the above.

15 During the first years of the Great Depression,

   a U.S. imports fell.
   b U.S. exports fell.
   c U.S. GDP fell.
   d all of the above.
   e none of the above.

16 Which of the following is not a result of international trade in the United Kingdom?

   a Lower wages for skilled workers

b   Lower wages for unskilled workers

c   Lower profits in industries where competition is limited

d   Lower wages in industries where competition is limited

e   None of the above

17   The infant industry argument advocates

a   temporary protection while firms gain experience needed to compete with foreign rivals.

b   lowering prices to drive foreign rivals out of business.

c   protection so that domestic firms can take advantage of economies of scale.

d   subsidising firms that face competition from foreign firms subsidised by their governments.

e   quotas rather than tariffs.

18   Strategic trade theory can be used to argue for

a   temporary protection while firms gain experience needed to compete with foreign rivals.

b   lowering prices to drive foreign rivals out of business.

c   protection so that domestic firms can take advantage of economies of scale.

d   subsidising firms that face competition from foreign firms subsidised by their governments.

e   quotas rather than tariffs.

19   The organization established after the Second World War for the purpose of reducing trade barriers is called

a   WTO.

b   GATT.

c   NAFTA.

d   European Union.

e   OECD.

20   Regional trading blocs, such as the EU, can lead to

a   the diversion of trade from member to nonmember countries.

b   the diversion of trade from nonmember to member countries.

c   the creation of trade among member countries.

d   the creation of trade between member and nonmember countries.

e   *b* and *c*.

Completion

1   _____ involves restricting the import of foreign goods.

2   Policies that affect imports or exports are called _____.

3   Taxes on imports are called _____.

4   When the government imposes quotas, firms licenced to import may earn extra profits, called _____.

5   An agreement whereby foreign firms limit sales of their good in domestic markets is called a _____.

6   Selling products abroad at prices below the cost of production is called _____.

7   The _____ proposes temporary protection while firms gain experience to become competitive.

8   Formed after the Second World War, the _____ promoted free trade among most of the world's countries.

9   The global trading organization that directed attention towards nontariff barriers, agricultural subsidies, and intellectual property is called the _____.

10   Regional trading blocs, such as NAFTA or the EU, expand trade within the bloc, but the net benefits may not be positive if there is too much _____.

Answers to Self-Test

True or False

1	T	6	T	11	F
2	F	7	T	12	T
3	F	8	T	13	F
4	T	9	T	14	T
5	T	10	F	15	F

Multiple Choice

1	*e*	6	*e*	11	*a*	16	*a*
2	*a*	7	*e*	12	*d*	17	*a*
3	*c*	8	*d*	13	*c*	18	*c*
4	*b*	9	*c*	14	*e*	19	*b*
5	*e*	10	*b*	15	*d*	20	*e*

Completion

1   Protection
2   commercial policies
3   tariffs
4   quota rents
5   voluntary export restraint
6   dumping
7   infant industry argument
8   General Agreement on Tariffs and Trade
9   World Trade Organization
10   trade diversion

Tools and Practice Problems

We use the small open economy model introduced in Chapter 24 to study the effects of three commercial policies: tariffs, quotas, and voluntary export restraints. This model starts with the idea that price is determined on world markets and that relative to that world market, the country's output is too small to affect price. The country, in other words, is a price taker. For each of the policies we will determine the effects upon the market equilibrium and also the deadweight burdens. Tool Kit 36.1 shows how to get started.

Tool Kit 36.1 Finding the Free Trade Equilibrium in a Small Open Economy

In a small open economy the quantity demanded is what consumers demand at the fixed world price, and the quantity supplied is what producers offer for sale at that price. These quantities need not be equal. The difference is the level of imports or exports. Follow these steps.

Step one: Identify the world price, the demand curve, and the supply curve.

Step two: Find the quantity demanded. This is read off the demand curve at the world price.

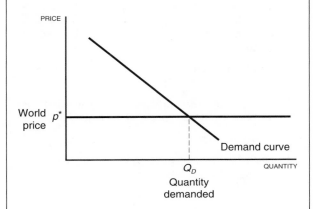

Step three: Find the quantity supplied. This is read off the supply curve at the world price.

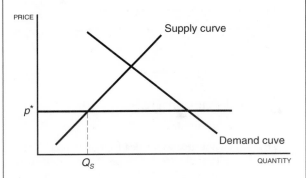

Step four: Find the level of imports or exports. If the quantity demanded exceeds the quantity supplied, then the country imports the goods. Otherwise the good is exported.

Imports =
    quantity demanded – quantity supplied (if positive).

Exports =
    quantity supplied – quantity demanded (if positive).

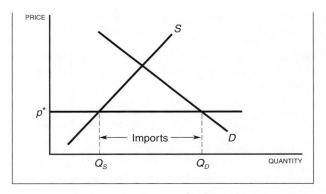

1   (Worked problem: small open economy) The world price of high-grade aluminium is 1,200 Euros per metric ton. The European Union demands and supplies are given below in Table 36.1.

  a   Find the quantity demanded and the quantity supplied.
  b   Is high-grade aluminium exported or imported? What is the amount?

Table 36.1

Demand		Supply	
Price (Euros)	Quantity (metric tonnes)	Price (Euros)	Quantity (metric tonnes)
2,000	100,000	2,000	400,000
1,800	150,000	1,800	300,000
1,600	200,000	1,600	200,000
1,400	250,000	1,400	100,000
1,200	300,000	1,200	50,000
1,000	350,000	1,000	25,000

Step-by-step solution

Step one: Identify the world price, the demand curve, and the supply curve. The world price is 1,400 Euros and the demand and supply curves are given in Table 36.1.

Step two: Find the quantity demanded. When the price is 1,200 Euros, the quantity demanded is 300,000 metric tonnes.

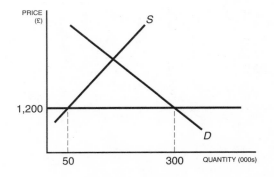

Step three: Find the quantity supplied. When the price is 1,400 Euros, the quantity supplied is 50,000 metric tonnes.

Step four: Find the level of imports or exports. The quantity demanded exceeds the quantity supplied, so the country imports the good.

Imports = quantity demanded – quantity supplied
= 300,000 – 50,000 = 250,000 metric tonnes.

2   (Practice problem: small open economy) The world price of coffee is 4 cents per pound. The U.S. demands and supplies are given in Table 36.2.

   a   Find the quantity demanded and the quantity supplied.
   b   Is coffee exported or imported by the United States? What is the amount?

Table 36.2

Demand		Supply	
Price (cents per pound)	*Quantity (million pounds)*	*Price (cents per pound*	*Quantity (million pounds)*
8	14,000	8	20,000
7	16,000	7	18,000
6	18,000	6	16,000
5	20,000	5	14,000
4	22,000	4	12,000
3	24,000	3	10,000
2	26,000	2	8,000
1	28,000	1	6,000

3   (Practice problem: small open economy) The world price of sugar is 1 pence per pound. The U.K. demand and supply curves are given in Table 36.3.

   a   Find the quantity demanded and the quantity supplied.
   b   Is sugar exported or imported? What is the amount?

Table 36.3

Demand		Supply	
Price (pence per pound)	*Quantity (million pounds)*	*Price (pence per pound)*	*Quantity (million pounds)*
4.0	1,000	4.0	900
3.5	1,100	3.5	850
3.0	1,200	3.0	800
2.5	1,300	2.5	750
2.0	1,400	2.0	700
1.5	1,500	1.5	650
1.0	1,600	1.0	600

Tariffs

Tariffs are taxes on imported goods. Economists analyse their impact by looking at how markets adjust. Like other taxes, they change market outcomes and bring about deadweight burdens. Fewer goods are sold and consumers lose surplus. Also, the economy wastes resources by producing goods that are more cheaply obtained abroad. We follow the usual procedure of starting with an equilibrium, shifting curves, finding the new equilibrium, and comparing. Tool Kit 36.2 shows how to find the deadweight burden of tariffs.

Tool Kit 36.2 Determining the Effects of Tariffs

Tariffs raise domestic prices above world price. This increase reduces consumption, increases production, and creates deadweight burdens. These steps show how to analyse tariffs.

Step one: Identify the world price, the demand curve, the supply curve, and the tariff.

Step two: Find the new world price. The new world price increases by exactly the amount of the tariff.

New world price = old world price + tariff.

Step three: Find the new equilibrium quantity demanded, quantity supplied, and level of imports. Follow the steps of Tool Kit 36.1.

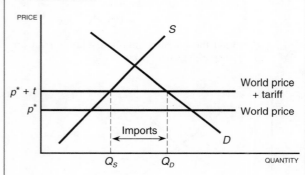

Step four: Calculate tariff revenue.

Tariff revenue = tariff × imports.

Step five: Show the area of the deadweight burden. There are two parts. Triangle *DEF* represents the loss in consumer surplus due to reduced consumption. Triangle *ABC* represents the waste of resources brought about by producing domestically when it is less expensive to import.

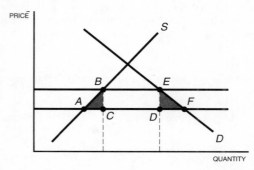

4   (Worked problem: tariffs) This problem continues with the market for high-grade aluminium. The demand and supply data are given in Table 36.1. The world price is 1,400 Euros and the tariff rate is 200 Euros per metric ton.

a   Find the new equilibrium.
b   Calculate tariff revenue.
c   Show the deadweight burden.

Step-by-step solution

Step one: Identify the world price, the demand curve, the supply curve, and the tariff. The world price is 1,200 Euros, the demand and supply curves are in Table 36.1, and the tariff rate is 200 Euros per metric tonne.

Step two: Find the new world price. The new world price increases by exactly the amount of the tariff.

New world price = old world price + tariff
= 1,200 + 200 = 1,400 Euros.

Step three (a): Find the new equilibrium quantity demanded, quantity supplied, and level of imports. When the price is 1,400 Euros, the quantity demanded is 250,000, the quantity supplied is 100,000, and the level of imports is 250,000 − 100,000 = 150,000.

Step four (b): Calculate tariff revenue.

Tariff revenue = tariff × imports
= 200 × 150,000
= 30,000,000 Euros.

Step five (c): Show the area of the deadweight burden. There are two parts. Triangle *DEF* represents the loss in consumer surplus due to reduced consumption. Triangle *ABC* represents the waste of resources brought about by producing domestically when it is less expensive to import.

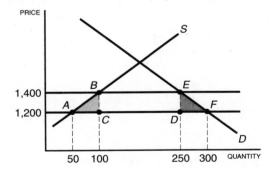

5   (Practice problem: tariffs) This problem continues with the market for coffee. The demand and supply curves are given in Table 36.2. The world price is 6 cents per pound and the tariff rate is 2 cents per pound.

a   Find the new equilibrium.
b   Calculate tariff revenue.
c   Show the deadweight burden.

6   (Practice problem: tariffs) This problem continues with the market for sugar. The demand and supply curves are given in Table 36.3. The world price is 1

pence per pound and the EU tariff rate is amounts to 1/2 pence per pound.

a   Find the new equilibrium.
b   Calculate tariff revenue.
c   Show the deadweight burden.

Quotas and Voluntary Export Restraints

Both quotas and VERs reduce imports. Quotas are imposed by the importing country, and VERs are "voluntarily" agreed to by the exporting country. Both raise prices, reduce consumption, and increase domestic production. Accordingly, both lead to deadweight burdens of exactly the same type as tariffs do. Follow along with Tool Kit 36.3.

Tool Kit 36.3 Quotas

Quotas, whether imposed or voluntary, raise prices, reduce consumption, increase production, and cause deadweight burdens. Follow these steps.

Step one: Identify the world price, the demand curve, the supply curve, and the quota.

Step two: Find the total supply curve. This is just the domestic supply curve added to the quota.

Total supply = domestic supply + quota.

Step three: Find the equilibrium price. Simply equate the total supply with the demand.

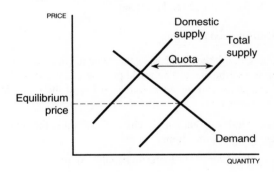

Step four: Find the domestic quantity supplied. This is read off the domestic supply curve.

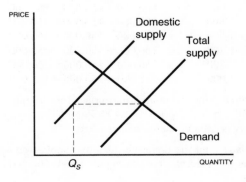

Step five: Calculate the quota rents. This is the extra money earned by licensed importers.

Quota rents = (new price – world price) × imports.

Step six: Show the area of the deadweight burden. There are two parts. Triangle *DEF* represents the loss in consumer surplus due to reduced consumption. Triangle *ABC* represents the waste of resources brought about by producing domestically when it is less expensive to import.

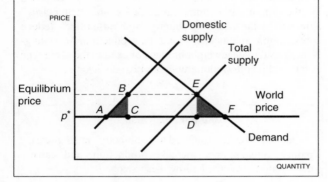

7   (Worked problem: tariffs) This problem continues with the market for high-grade aluminium. The demand and supply curves are given in Table 36.1. The world price is 1,200 Euros and the import quota is 150,000 metric tonnes.

   a   Find the new equilibrium.
   b   Calculate quota rents.
   c   Show the deadweight burden.

Step-by-step solution

Step one: Identify the world price, the demand curve, the supply curve, and the quota. The world price is 1,200 Euros, demand and supply are given in Table 36.1, and the quota is 150,000 metric tonnes.

Step two: Find the total supply curve. This is just the quota added to the domestic supply curve.

Total supply = domestic supply + quota.

Supply

Price (Euros)	Quantity (metric tonnes)
2,000	400,000 + 150,000 = 550,000
1,800	300,000 + 150,000 = 450,000
1,600	200,000 + 150,000 = 350,000
1,400	100,000 + 150,000 = 250,000
1,200	50,000 + 150,000 = 200,000
1,000	25,000 + 150,000 = 175,000

Step three: Find the equilibrium price. Total supply equals demand when the price is 1,400 Euros. The equilibrium quantity is 250,000 metric tonnes.

Step four: Find the domestic quantity supplied. When the price is 1,400 Euros, domestic supply equals 100,000 metric tonnes.

Step five: Calculate the quota rents. This is the extra money earned by licenced importers.

Quota rents = (new price – world price) × imports
          = (1,400 Euros – 1,200 Euros) × 150,000.

Step six: Show the area of the deadweight burden. There are two parts. Triangle *DEF* represents the loss in consumer surplus due to reduced consumption. Triangle *ABC* represents the waste of resources brought about by producing domestically when it is less expensive to import.

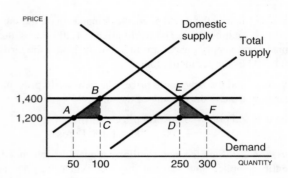

8   (Practice problem: quotas) This problem continues with the market for coffee. The demand and supply curves are given in Table 36.2. The world price is 6 cents and the U.S. import quota is 10,000 million pounds.

   a   Find the new equilibrium.
   b   Calculate quota rents.
   c   Show the deadweight burden.

9   (Practice problem: quotas) This problem continues with the market for sugar. The demand and supply curves are given in Table 36.3. The world price is 1 pence and the EU import quota for the U.K. is 1,000 million pounds.

   a   Find the new equilibrium.
   b   Calculate quota rents.
   c   Show the deadweight burden.

Answers to Problems

2   *a*   Quantity demanded = 22,000; quantity supplied = 12,000.
   b   Imports = 22,000 – 12,000 = 10,000.

3   *a*   Quantity demanded = 1,600; quantity supplied = 600.
   b   Imports = 1,600 – 600 = 1,000.

5   *a*   Quantity demanded = 18,000; quantity supplied = 16,000; imports = 18,000 – 16,000 = 2,000.
   b   Tariff revenue = 2 × 2,000 = 4,000 million cents = $40,000,000.

c

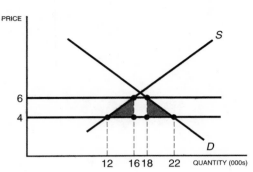

c

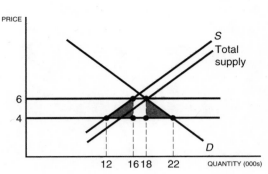

6   *a*   Quantity demanded = 1,500 million pounds; quantity supplied = 650 million pounds; imports = 1,500 – 650 = 850 million pounds.

     b   Tariff revenue = 0.5 × 850 = 425 million pence = £4,250,000.

     c

9   *a*   New price = 1.5 pence per pound; quantity demanded = 1,500 million pounds; quantity supplied = 650 million pounds; imports = 1,500 – 650 = 850 million pounds.

     b   Quota rents = 0.5 × 850 = 425 million pence = £4,250,000.

     c

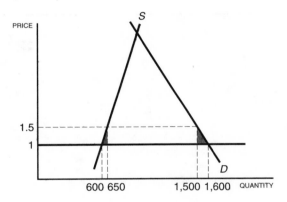

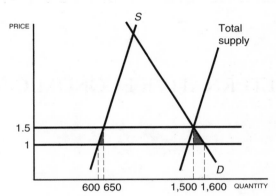

8   *a*   New price = 6 cents per pound; quantity demanded = 18,000 million pounds; quantity supplied = 16,000 million pounds; imports = 18,000 – 16,000 = 2,000 million pounds.

     b   Quota rents = 2 × 2,000 = 4,000 million cents = $40,000,000.

Chapter 37

ALTERNATIVE ECONOMIC SYSTEMS

Chapter Review

This chapter compares the nature and performance of the system we have studied throughout this book, the mixed economy, with some alternatives, namely the economic systems that evolved in the former Soviet Union and Eastern Europe in this century. The chapter includes some discussion of the worker-managed firms found in what used to be Yugoslavia as well as the incorporation of markets into the socialist economies of Hungary and Communist China. The book concludes in the next chapter with the topic of developing economies.

ESSENTIAL CONCEPTS

1 In **socialist** economies, the government owns the means of production; in **communist** countries, it owns all property. Both systems have a high degree of government control of economic decisions, or **central planning,** which stands in contrast to that in the market system prevalent in the **market economies** (also called capitalist because of the prominent role played by private capital). The economies of Western Europe, Japan, and the United States rely on private property and markets for most economic decisions.

2 Appalled by the extreme economic inequality that accompanied the industrial revolution, Karl Marx predicted the downfall of capitalism and its replacement by a communist state. His ideas were implemented to some extent by Vladmir Lenin and Joseph Stalin in the Soviet Union from 1917 until recently.

3 **Soviet-style socialism** coordinated economic activity through a series of centrally administered plans that answered the basic economic questions of what is to be produced, how it is to be produced, and for whom. A system of political controls and rewards backed up by force replaced market incentives. In the labour market, this system assigned workers to jobs and limited labour mobility. The capital market was replaced by central directions that pursued a low-consumption, high-investment strategy emphasising heavy industry. Goods were produced according to the plan and sold at prices controlled below market-clearing levels, leading to shortages and long lines at stores. Despite the ideology of "to each according to his needs," much inequality remained.

4 Soviet-style socialism failed for at least two reasons. It provided no *incentives* to managers; they could not keep

any profits, nor were they responsible for losses. Furthermore, the planning mechanism was unable to gather the needed *information* to allocate resources efficiently or to monitor workers and firms in order to ensure that the plan was carried through effectively. Prices, which were set arbitrarily, did not convey information about relative scarcity and value, as do market prices.

5 Under **market socialism** the central planners set prices and order managers to maximise profits. This revision of the system performs only a little better than Soviet-style socialism; prices are set without good information, and managers, still without property rights, have no incentives to pursue profits. Some success was achieved with the "responsibility system" in China, where farmers were allowed to sell their produce and keep some of the proceeds. Yugoslavia instituted worker-managed firms as a partial step towards markets.

6 The transition from Soviet-style socialism to market economies is difficult and fraught with problems. It begins with a period of disruption, falling living standards, and high unemployment as old, inefficient factories are closed and resources are reallocated. Inflation rises as price controls are relaxed. Limiting budget deficits, controlling credit, and privatization of government-owned assets, including land, are difficult in countries making the transition. Finally, it will take a long time for all of the various institutions that support market economies to evolve. Nearly all of the former communist countries are moving towards the market economy, although the pace of transition varies widely.

BEHIND THE ESSENTIAL CONCEPTS

1 The main disadvantages of central government control are gathering the information needed to determine the optimal decisions and giving incentives to managers and workers. Every organization, whether it operates within a market or a socialist economy, faces these problems. The difficulty with the socialist system is that the economy is simply too large an organization to control from the center.

2 The experiment with worker-managed firms in Yugoslavia showed interesting results. Since workers shared the profits, their goal was not to maximise total profits but rather to maximise profits per worker. This reduced the incentive to hire additional workers, because any new worker would cause the profit pie to be sliced more thinly. Further, the incentives to invest and increase the value of the enterprise were limited because it could not be sold.

3 The Soviet-style socialist economies bottled up inflation by controlling prices below the market-clearing levels and by providing fewer goods than people wanted to buy. Because there were so few goods to spend money on, savings rates were especially high, a phenomenon known as monetary overhang. As prices are freed from

government control, they rise to market-clearing levels, but inflation grows even more as people spend their monetary overhang.

4 Despite claims of eliminating unemployment, the Soviet-style socialist economies did have disguised unemployment. Workers were assigned to firms, and layoffs were banned. Plants with excess workers simply kept them on the payroll. Because they were subject to the **soft budget constraint,** any losses resulting from the excess payroll were covered by the central government.

SELF-TEST

True or False

1 Under socialism, the state owns the means of production.

2 In mixed economies, there is a reliance on markets for most decisions, but government also plays a substantial role.

3 Karl Marx led the Russian revolution of 1917, establishing a Marxist state.

4 Under central planning, important decisions are made at the plant level.

5 In Soviet-style economies, incentives were provided by force.

6 In Soviet-style economies, there was little job mobility and some disguised unemployment.

7 The Soviet Union pursued a high-investment, low-consumption economic plan.

8 Soviet-style socialist economies nearly eliminated economic inequality.

9 Although socialist economies lost the competition for efficient production, they were able to protect their environments.

10 Most economists believe that the experiment in Soviet-style socialism was a failure.

11 Bureaucrats lacked the information to make efficient decisions under Soviet-style socialism.

12 Under market socialism, prices replace planning in determining investment decisions.

13 Worker-managed firms have little incentive to hire more workers.

14 The movement from socialism to a more market oriented economy has caused prices to increase.

15 Privatization refers to the process of eliminating price controls and returning the function of setting prices to private firms.

Multiple Choice

1 Socialism is the system under which

  a the state owns all property, including the means of production and all land.

b   the state owns the means of production.

c   there is a heavy reliance on firms and households interacting in markets.

d   there is a heavy reliance on markets and a considerable role for government.

e   workers own and manage the firms.

2   Under communism,

a   the state owns all property, including the means of production and all land.

b   the state owns the means of production.

c   there is a heavy reliance on firms' and households' interacting in markets.

d   there is a heavy reliance on markets and a considerable role for government.

e   workers own and manage the firms.

3   In a mixed economy,

a   the state owns all property, including the means of production and all land.

b   the state owns the means of production.

c   there is a heavy reliance on firms' and households' interacting in markets.

d   there is a heavy reliance on markets and a considerable role for government.

e   workers own and manage the firms.

4   The Russian revolution of 1917, which installed communism, was led by

a   Marx.

b   Lange.

c   Lenin.

d   Stalin.

e   Mises.

5   The forced collectivization of agriculture was ordered by

a   Marx.

b   Lange.

c   Lenin.

d   Stalin.

e   Mises.

6   Under Stalin, the Soviet Union increased investment by

a   maintaining high rates of return for savings.

b   keeping wages low.

c   limiting the supply of consumer goods.

d   attracting foreign investment.

e   *b* and *c*.

7   Under central planning,

a   the government makes all significant economic decisions.

b   government-owned property is sold or given to individuals.

c   workers own and manage their firms.

d   prices are set by the interplay of supply and demand.

e   land is redistributed to those who have worked it.

8   Under socialism, in the labour market,

a   wages adjust to clear the market.

b   firms pay above market-clearing efficiency wages to keep and motivate their best workers.

c   workers are assigned jobs, and there is very little labour mobility.

d   unions set wages through collective bargaining.

e   workers own and manage their own firms.

9   In Soviet-style socialist economies, the allocation of investment capital is determined by

a   workers who own and manage their own firms.

b   the capital market.

c   the government.

d   majority vote.

e   none of the above.

10   In Soviet-style socialist economies, prices were

a   outlawed.

b   set equal to market-clearing levels.

c   set above market-clearing levels.

d   set below market-clearing levels.

e   determined by the forces of supply and demand.

11   The Soviet Union pursued a policy of

a   high investment and low consumption.

b   high consumption and low investment.

c   high investment and high consumption.

d   low investment and low consumption.

e   none of the above.

12   Socialist enterprises often face soft budget constraints; this means that

a   workers share the profits equally.

b   firms that continue to make losses are absorbed by larger firms.

c   the government makes up any losses.

d   workers do not have to work unless the firm makes a profit.

e   workers are assigned jobs and thus are never unemployed.

13   Among the problems of central planning are

a   the lack of incentives that managers have to operate firms efficiently.

b   the lack of information needed to make efficient decisions.

c   the fact that prices, not determined by markets, could not provide informative signals.

d   the difficulty in monitoring the performance of managers and workers.

e   all of the above.

14   Under market socialism,

a   government makes the investment decisions.

b   firms maximise profits at the prices they face.

c   workers own and manage their own firms.

d   all of the above.

e   *a* and *b*.

15   In China, farmers were allowed to sell most of what they produced and keep the profits under

a   collectivized agriculture.

b   farmer cooperatives.

c   the responsibility system.

d land reform.

e privatization.

16 Worker-managed farms were instituted in

a China.

b the Soviet Union.

c Poland.

d Hungary.

e Yugoslavia.

17 Which of the following was *not* a problem with worker-owned cooperatives?

a Workers had little incentive to undertake investments that paid off after they left the firm.

b Keeping a share of the profits motivated workers to work hard in smaller firms.

c Cooperatives had little incentive to hire new workers.

d The aging workforce diminished investment incentives.

e The reluctance to hire workers contributed to the unemployment problem.

18 Environment policy in the Soviet Union was characterized by

a low energy prices.

b lack of antipollution measures.

c intensive farming with high pesticide use and much soil erosion.

d lack of nuclear safety equipment.

e all of the above.

19 Privatization refers to

a the transfer to individuals of property formerly owned by the state.

b the fact that managers under Soviet-style socialism kept information private.

c the consolidation of agriculture into large firms.

d the policy that allowed private farmers in China to sell much of what they produced.

e the attempt to combine the best features of socialism and private enterprise.

20 Which of the following are problems involved in the transition from socialism to market economies?

a Inflation

b Unemployment

c The lack of a safety net

d Falling living standards

e All of the above

Completion

1 The government owns and operates the means of production under _____.

2 Under _____, the government owns all property.

3 The system of _____ gives the government and its ministries control over economic decisions.

4 Economies with a heavy reliance on markets but also a considerable role for government are referred to as _____.

5 _____ believed that the capitalist system would eventually collapse and evolve into communism.

6 _____ forced the collectivization of farms, causing a famine in which millions died.

7 According to _____, economies can combine the advantages of market mechanisms with public ownership of the means of production.

8 Worker-owned _____, in which workers hired managers and received the profits, were countenanced in Yugoslavia.

9 Transferring businesses and property from public ownership to individuals is called _____.

10 Among the formerly Communist countries _____ proceeded most quickly in the macroeconomic aspects of the transition to a market economy.

Answers to Self-Test

True or False

1	T	6	T	11	T
2	T	7	T	12	F
3	F	8	F	13	T
4	F	9	F	14	T
5	T	10	T	15	F

Multiple Choice

1	*b*	6	*e*	11	*a*	16	*e*
2	*a*	7	*a*	12	*c*	17	*b*
3	*d*	8	*c*	13	*e*	18	*e*
4	*c*	9	*c*	14	*e*	19	*a*
5	*d*	10	*d*	15	*c*	20	*e*

Completion

1 socialism

2 communism

3 central planning

4 mixed economies

5 Karl Marx

6 Stalin

7 market socialism

8 cooperatives

9 privatization

10 Poland

Tools and Practice Problems

In a planned economy, such as Soviet-style socialism, the state owns and must allocate the means of production. To gain some understanding of the allocation problem the state must solve, we first look at some relatively simple problems involving how to allocate a resource between different plants or regions that produce the same good. The next topic involves a Yugoslavian experiment with firms owned and managed by the workers. We explore the problem of how many workers to hire.

Efficient Resource Allocation

Compared to market economies, socialism allocated resources poorly. This means that resources were not assigned to tasks efficiently and that the economy produced inside its production possibilities curve. While markets use prices to guide allocations, socialist managers must gather a great deal of information about productivity in alternative uses, form a coherent plan, direct the allocation, and monitor performance to see that the plan is carried out. The combined information and incentive problems overwhelmed the capacity of planners. Tool Kit 37.1 shows how to solve allocation problems when the information is available.

Tool Kit 37.1 Finding the Efficient Allocation of a Resource

When new productive resources become available, state bureaucrats must decide how to use them. The solution to this problem requires information about production functions. Tool Kit 37.1 looks at how to allocate resources efficiently. Follow the steps.

Step one: Identify the production functions for each possible use.

Step two: Compute the marginal product for each quantity of the resource:

Marginal product = change in output/change in input.

Step three: Allocate the first unit of the resource to the activity with the highest marginal product.

Step four: Allocate the second unit of the resource to the activity with the next highest marginal product.

Step five: Continue until the available supply of the resource is exhausted.

---

1 (Worked problem: planning and efficient allocation) The commissar of fishing has received eight new trawlers for cod. She must decide how to allocate the new vessels between the Black Sea and the Caspian Sea fleets. The production function for each fleet is given in Table 37.1.

Table 37.1

Number of trawlers	Harvest of Black Sea cod (tonnes per week)	Harvest of Caspian Sea cod (tonnes per week)
1	9	20
2	17	36
3	24	50
4	30	62
5	35	72
6	39	80
7	42	86
8	44	90

a Find the efficient allocation of trawlers.
b Suppose the commissar does not know the production functions and simply allocates the trawlers equally between the fleets. How many fewer tonnes of cod will be harvested?

Step-by-step solution

Step one (a): Identify the production function for each possible use. They are given in Table 37.1.

Step two: Compute the marginal product for each quantity of the resource. The first trawler in the Black Sea harvests 10 tonnes. The second one increases the harvest to 19, which is a marginal product of $19 - 10 = 9$. Continuing, we derive Table 37.2.

Table 37.2

Number of trawlers	Harvest of Black Sea cod (tonnes per week)	Marginal product	Harvest of Caspian Sea cod (tonnes per week)	Marginal product
1	9	9	20	20
2	17	8	36	16
3	24	7	50	14
4	30	6	62	12
5	35	5	72	10
6	39	4	80	8
7	42	3	86	6
8	44	2	90	4

Step three: Allocate the first unit of the resource to the activity with the highest marginal product. The highest marginal product is 20 in the Caspian Sea.

Step four: Allocate the second unit of the resource to the activity with the next highest marginal product. The next highest marginal product is 16, again in the Caspian Sea.

Step five: Continue until the available supply of the resource is exhausted. If 6 trawlers are allocated to the Caspian Sea, where the output is 80 tonnes per week, and 2 to the Black Sea, where the output is 17 tonnes per week, then the output of cod is 97. The allocation is efficient, and this is the answer to part *a*.

Step six (b): If 4 trawlers are sent to each region, total output is $30 + 62 = 92$ tonnes per week, which is 5 less than if the allocation were efficient.

2 (Practice problem: planning and efficient allocation) Nine new tractors roll off the assembly line at the huge state-owned tractor works in Braslov. Many cooperative farms have requested new tractors, and the minister in charge must allocate them. The production functions for three farms are given in Table 37.3. Output is measured as thousands of bushels of wheat.

a Find the efficient allocation of tractors;
b Compute the waste if the tractors are divided equally among the three farms.

Table 37.3

Tractors	Output at farm 1	Output at farm 2	Output at farm 3
0	30	100	50
1	40	150	90
2	49	180	120
3	57	200	140
4	64	210	150
5	70	215	155
6	75	218	160
7	79	220	164
8	82	220	166
9	82	220	167

3 (Practice problem: planning and efficient allocation) Six new locomotives are made available for either the north-south route or the east-west route. The production functions for each route is given in Table 37.4. Output is measured as numbers of standard containers per week.

Table 37.4

Locomotives	East-west route output	North-south route output
1	1,000	1,000
2	1,800	1,600
3	2,500	2,000
4	3,000	2,200
5	3,300	2,300
6	3,500	2,400

a   Find the efficient allocation of locomotives.
b   How much output is wasted if all are allocated to the east-west route?

Worker-Managed Firms

One experiment in market socialism occurred in the former Yugoslavia when the government sanctioned the creation of firms owned and managed by workers. The profits from each firm were shared equally among the workers. Worker-managed firms do seek profits, but they do not maximise total profits; rather, their goal is to make profits per worker as large as possible. Generally, this practice results in fewer workers hired than under a full-fledged market system. Tool Kit 37.2 demonstrates this.

Tool Kit 37.2 Finding the Level of Employment in a Worker-Managed Firm

Because it is run by workers who share in the profits, a worker-managed firm will seek to maximise profits per worker. This differs from the goal of firms in market economies, which maximise profits. Follow these steps to find the level of employment in worker-managed firms.

Step one: Identify the production function and the product price.

Step two: Compute the total revenue at each level of employment by multiplying the output by the product price:

$$\text{Revenue} = \text{output} \times \text{product price}.$$

Step three: Compute profits by subtracting costs from revenue:

$$\text{Profits} = \text{revenue} - \text{costs}.$$

Step four: Compute profits per worker by dividing profits by the corresponding number of workers. This is the share of profits going to each worker.

$$\text{Profits per worker} = \text{profits/number of workers}.$$

Step five: Find the level of employment for which profits per worker is highest. This is the equilibrium level of employment in the worker-managed firm.

4 (Worked problem: worker-managed firms) The new branch of the Hair Cuttery is ready to open. It will be owned and managed by the stylists. The price of haircuts is £10, and the production function is given in Table 37.5. Fixed costs equal £50 per day. Find the equilibrium number of stylists.

Table 37.5

Stylists	Haircuts per day
1	6
2	16
3	30
4	42
5	50
6	56
7	60

Step-by-step solution

Step one: Identify the production function and the product price. The production function is given in Table 37.5, and the price is £10.

Step two: Compute the total revenue at each level of employment by multiplying the output by the product price. When the number of stylists is 1, output is 6 and revenues equals 6 × £10 = £60. Continuing, we complete the column as shown in Table 37.6.

Step three: Compute profits by subtracting costs from revenue. We subtract £50 from the revenue column. The completed information is given in Table 37.6.

Table 37.6

Stylists	Haircuts per day	Revenue	Profits
1	6	£ 60	£ 10
2	16	£160	£110
3	30	£300	£250
4	42	£420	£370
5	50	£500	£450
6	56	£560	£510
7	60	£600	£550

Step four: Compute profits per worker by dividing profits by the corresponding number of workers. This is the share of profits going to each worker. For example, profits per worker when there is one stylist equal £10/1 = £10. Continuing, we derive Table 37.7.

Table 37.7

Stylists	Haircuts per day	Revenues	Profits	Profits per stylist
1	6	£ 60	£ 10	£10.00
2	16	£160	£110	£55.00
3	30	£300	£250	£83.33
4	42	£420	£370	£92.50
5	50	£500	£450	£90.00
6	56	£560	£510	£85.00
7	60	£600	£550	£76.57

Step five: Find the level of employment for which profits per worker is highest. The equilibrium level of employment is 4, where profits per worker equal £92.50.

5 (Practice problem: worker-managed firms) Moe's Lite-Brite Charcoal Company soaks charcoal in lighter fluid for £1 per bag. Its production function is given in Table 37.8. Moe is selling his business and all of the equipment to the employees. Their fixed costs including the payment on the loan to finance the sale will be £500 per day. Find the equilibrium level of employment when Moe's becomes worker managed.

Table 37.8

Workers	Output per day
1	100
2	500
3	1,500
4	2,500
5	2,900
6	3,300

6 (Practice problem: worker-managed firms) The Thelonius Thimble Company is to become worker owned and managed next month when the likable Thelonius retires. He is giving the business to the workers, and they will have no fixed costs. Thimbles sell for 10 pence each. The production function is given in Table 37.9. Find the equilibrium number of employees of the worker-managed thimble company.

Table 37.9

Workers	Thimbles
1	2,000
2	5,000
3	10,000
4	13,000
5	15,000
6	17,000

Answers to Problems

2 Table 37.10 gives the marginal product of tractors at each of the farms.

Table 37.10

	Farm 1		Farm 2		Farm 3	
Tractors	Output	Marginal product	Output	Marginal product	Output	Marginal product
0	30	30	100	100	50	50
1	40	10	150	50	90	40
2	49	9	180	30	120	30
3	57	8	200	20	140	20
4	64	7	210	10	150	10
5	70	6	215	5	155	5
6	75	5	218	3	160	5
7	79	4	220	2	164	4
8	82	3	220	0	166	2
9	82	0	220	0	167	1

a The efficient allocation is 1 tractor to farm 1, 4 tractors to farm 2, and 4 tractors to farm 3.

b The output of the tractors divided equally is 57 + 200 + 140 = 397. The output at the efficient allocation is 40 + 210 + 150 = 400. The waste is 400 – 397 = 3, and since output is measured in thousands of bushels, this represents 3,000 bushels.

3 Table 37.11 gives the marginal product along each route.

Table 37.11

	East-west route		North-south route	
Locomotives	Output	Marginal product	Output	Marginal product
1	1,000	1,000	1,000	1,000
2	1,800	800	1,600	600
3	2,500	700	2,000	400
4	3,000	500	2,200	200
5	3,300	300	2,300	100
6	3,500	200	2,400	100

a The efficient allocation is 4 to the east-west route and 2 to the north-south route.

b Output is 3,500 if all are allocated to the east-west route. Output is 3,000 + 1,600 = 4,600 at the efficient allocation. The waste is 4,600 – 3,500 = 1,100.

5   Table 37.12 gives profits per worker, which are maximised when the firm has 4 workers.

Table 37.12

Workers	Output per day	Revenue	Profits	Profits per worker
1	100	£ 100	−£ 400	−£400
2	500	£ 500	£ 0	£ 0
3	1,500	£1,500	£1,000	£333
4	2,500	£2,500	£2,000	£500
5	2,900	£2,900	£2,400	£480
6	3,300	£3,300	£2,800	£466

6   Table 37.13 gives profits per worker, which are maximised when the number of workers is 3.

Table 37.13

Workers	Output per day	Revenue	Profits	Profits per worker
1	2,000	£ 200	£ 200	£200
2	5,000	£ 500	£ 500	£250
3	10,000	£1,000	£1,000	£333
4	13,000	£1,300	£1,300	£325
5	15,000	£1,500	£1,500	£300
6	17,000	£1,700	£1,700	£283

Chapter 38

DEVELOPMENT

Chapter Review

This chapter takes up developing countries. It examines living standards in these countries as well as the causes of underdevelopment and the prospects for bringing the living standards up to those of the developed countries. The chapter closes with a look at the policies some countries have pursued, namely the relative advantages of the export-led and import-competing strategies.

ESSENTIAL CONCEPTS

1 In **developing countries** GNP per capita was less than US $785 in 1992. The per capita income gap among developed countries has narrowed over the past century, while it has widened between the developed and developing world. Although a few countries have successfully raised their living standards, most of the developing countries remain in grinding poverty. Agricultural gains from the **green revolution,** improvements in health and life expectancy, and the emergence of the **newly industrialized countries** of East Asia are some examples of successful economic development.

2 Although there is considerable variation among developing countries, agriculture dominates the economy in most. In the rural sector, farming takes place on small, labour-intensive farms with poorer techniques and less fertilizer than in the developed world. **Sharecropping** remains a widespread arrangement. Redistribution of land ownership through **land reform** has at times been successful, but dramatic inequality remains. In the urban sector, wages are far higher, and many individuals have migrated to the cities. Such migration has caused massive unemployment and squalor. The term **dual economy** describes the vast difference between the rural and urban sectors.

3 The institutions and structure of the economy in developing countries do not facilitate growth. Although savings rates are high, there is a shortage of capital. The absence of efficient capital markets keeps the limited capital from its most productive use. An inadequate supply of skilled workers accompanies burgeoning population growth, which reduces the ratio of capital to workers and lowers productivity. Also, the lack of developed capital markets and ill-advised government interventions have kept the limited capital from its most productive use. All of this plus extreme inequality characterize developing countries.

4   The failure of markets in their countries has led most developing countries to adopt *central planning*. Because planners do not have sufficient information to make correct decisions, central planning has not been successful. An overreliance on heavy industry, corruption, and widespread interference in trade and foreign exchange are common problems of actual developing country development efforts. A common policy, import substitution, emphasises the development of domestic markets by substituting domestic production for imports. The pervasive role of government also motivates wasteful rent seeking. Another clear failure has been in providing needed **infrastructure**, especially a sound legal system.

5   The success of the East Asian economies points to several policy successes. These countries practiced the sound macroeconomic policies of low budget deficits and low inflation. Other policies encouraged high savings rates, literacy, college education, and the explicit promotion of certain export-oriented industries. This export-led strategy protects and encourages certain industries judged to be potentially successful against world competition. Dynamic comparative advantage, based on acquired education and skills, has guided the most successful of these policies, but there have been some failures. One final benefit is the high level of economic equality, suggesting that there is not necessarily a trade-off between growth and equality.

BEHIND THE ESSENTIAL CONCEPTS

1   The case for central planning in developing countries has always rested on the pervasive *market failures*. Clearly, markets do a poor job allocating resources in these countries. Yet the failure of planning provides a salient example of *government failure*. Although the potential for beneficial government intervention exists, governments have made matters worse.

2   Real-world markets are complicated, and the institutions that help them work have taken time to evolve. Reputations, repeated business arrangements, implicit contracts, and other institutions help ease the information problems that trouble imperfectly competitive markets. In the developing countries, these institutions are not present, and in their absence, resource allocation is worse.

3   Observing varying levels of success and failure around the world, we can compile a list of good development policies. First, there must be sound macroeconomics, that is, fiscal responsibility and a stable monetary system. Second, the economies must direct themselves towards the rest of the world by reducing trade barriers, encouraging foreign investment, and promoting exports. This approach helps to transfer more-advanced technology from abroad and provides a natural test for success. Government can allocate more of its budget to investment and less to consumption, such as food subsidies. Finally, policies such as land reform and universal education (including women) not only contribute to development but also promote equality.

4   The term *vicious circle* is often used with respect to developing countries. Poor households cannot afford education and must scratch out a living in labor-intensive activities, such as subsistence farming. They not only lack the education to practice birth control, but also have incentives to raise more children, who are economically useful. The population growth reduces capital per worker, keeping the economy in underdevelopment.

5   The education of women plays an especially important role in development. You can see this in terms of the costs and benefits of children. More educated women understand and practice birth control. Also, as education allows their earnings to increase, they realize that the opportunity cost of having children is high and limit family size. Lower population growth means more capital per worker and higher output.

SELF-TEST

True or False

1   Over the past century, the income gap between the industrialised and developing economies has narrowed.

2   One success story in the developing world has been the emergence of the newly industrialised countries, such as Singapore and Taiwan.

3   Increases in life expectancy and improvements in infant mortality have allowed rapid population growth in many developing countries.

4   In poor countries, agriculture plays a more prominent role, often accounting for 80 percent of GNP.

5   The developing countries have much less capital per person than the United States because their savings rates are very low.

6   The absence of capital markets in developing countries prevents the limited supply of capital from finding its most efficient use.

7   Land reform transfers agricultural land to those who work it.

8   Inequality can inhibit development by leading to political instability and a poor climate for foreign investment.

9   Sharecropping gives good incentives for the tenant farmer to work hard and maintain the productivity of the land.

10   Central planning enables developing countries to coordinate all the related activities in a single coherent development strategy.

11   An important element of a country's infrastructure is its legal system.

12   A difficulty with the export-led strategy is that it protects inefficient domestic producers from the competition of foreign firms.

13   One problem with import substitution is that it is difficult to remove trade barriers once they are imposed.

14 The successful East Asian economies have achieved high growth rates, but this has occurred at the cost of extreme inequality.

15 Educating women leads to lower birth rates because as their education brings higher wages, the opportunity cost of devoting time to raise children rises.

Multiple Choice

1 What fraction of the world's population lives in developing countries?

    a One-fourth
    b One-half
    c Three-fourths
    d One-third
    e One-sixth

2 Over the past century, the income gap has

    a widened among high-income countries.
    b narrowed among high-income countries.
    c grown wider between high- and low-income countries.
    d narrowed between high- and low-income countries.
    e b and c.

3 The green revolution refers to

    a the spread of concern for the environment in the developing countries.
    b the World Bank's largely successful efforts to aid development by lending money for infrastructure investment.
    c the development and spread to developing countries of new agricultural technologies, which brought about huge increases in output.
    d improvements in life expectancy and infant mortality statistics in the developing countries.
    e none of the above.

4 Agriculture in the developed countries

    a uses larger farms than in the developing countries.
    b uses fewer workers per acre than in developing countries.
    c uses more fertilizer per acre than in developing countries.
    d is more mechanised than in developing countries.
    e all of the above.

5 Sharecropping refers to the

    a fact that much of the agricultural output in the developing countries is taken in taxes.
    b World Bank's policy of matching agricultural gains in developing countries with food shipments.
    c sharing of technological know-how between agricultural research centers in the developed world and the developing countries.
    d system in which the landlord takes a share of the output of a farm.
    e system in which farmers set aside a fraction of their output to support religious institutions.

6 The term *dual economies* refers to the disparity between

    a the developed and developing economies.
    b men's and women's earnings in the developing countries.
    c upper and lower incomes in the developing countries.
    d rural and urban life in the developing countries.
    e the efficiency of the market sector and the inefficiency of governments in developing countries.

7 In developing countries, it is generally true that

    a savings rates are low.
    b because it is in short supply, capital is used very intensively.
    c because the capital stock is so low, the marginal return to capital is much higher than in developed countries.
    d the lack of effective capital markets keeps capital from its most productive uses.
    e the stable political environments attract foreign investment.

8 The debt crises experienced by several developing countries in the 1980s were caused by

    a high interest rates.
    b the world recession in the early 1980s.
    c lack of prudence in lending by banks.
    d U.S. government deposit insurance.
    e all of the above.

9 In developing countries, the population is

    a large and well educated.
    b falling because of the poor medical care and meagre diets.
    c growing too rapidly, causing an excess supply of trained workers.
    d growing too rapidly but includes too few vocationally trained, skilled workers.
    e none of the above.

10 The low returns to capital in the developing countries are the result of

    a shortages of capital.
    b low supplies of capital.
    c lack of markets to allocate capital efficiently.
    d all of the above.
    e b and c.

11 In developing countries,

    a both labour and capital markets work well.
    b while labour markets work well, capital markets fail to allocate the scarce capital efficiently.
    c while capital markets work well, ethnic divisions and language barriers hinder the labour market.
    d neither capital nor labour markets work efficiently.
    e there are no labour or capital markets.

12 Sir Arthur Lewis argued that the surplus of labour contributes to economic growth by

    a supporting strong governments that can provide the stability needed to attract foreign investment.
    b keeping wages low, which leads to high profits and investment.

c   discouraging population growth through high unemployment.

d   emigrating and sending earnings home.

e   attracting foreign investment with low wages.

13   Export-led growth strategies have promoted

a   agriculture where developing countries have had comparative advantage.

b   the substitution of domestic production for imported goods.

c   land reform.

d   export industries aligned with the principle of dynamic comparative advantage, which is based on acquired skills, education, and technology.

e   government control of production in order to maximise exports.

14   What best describes the relationship between inequality and economic growth?

a   The countries that have developed most rapidly have lower levels of inequality.

b   The countries that have developed most rapidly have higher levels of inequality.

c   There is no consistent relationship between inequality and the pace of development.

d   Planned economies have developed rapidly with low inequality, but unplanned ones have only developed when inequality is high.

e   Planned economies have developed rapidly with high inequality, but unplanned ones have only developed when inequality is low.

15   Inequality may inhibit development by

a   leading to political instability and a poor investment climate.

b   fostering the development of sharecropping.

c   leading governments to impose high tax rates.

d   forcing governments to spend on food subsidies rather than investment.

e   all of the above.

16   Most economists

a   favor central planning by developing countries because planners can better coordinate all the aspects of major projects.

b   favor central planning by developing countries because planners have better information about whether projects will be successful.

c   are skeptical about central planning because planners lack the needed information.

d   see no need for planning of any kind.

e   view planning as neither beneficial nor harmful because of the policy ineffectiveness proposition.

17   Rent seeking refers to

a   the payments made by sharecroppers.

b   activities by individuals to get special benefits from governments.

c   campaigns to attract foreign investment.

d   the failure of sharecroppers to maintain the land.

e   none of the above.

18   Which of the following is *not* part of a country's infrastructure?

a   Roads

b   Bridges

c   Ports

d   Legal system

e   None of the above

19   Encouraging the production and export of goods in which the country has a comparative advantage is the strategy called

a   export-led growth.

b   central planning.

c   dynamic comparative advantage.

d   import substitution.

e   laissez-faire.

20   Encouraging the development of a domestic market by substituting domestically produced goods for imports is called

a   export-led growth.

b   central planning.

c   dynamic comparative advantage.

d   import substitution.

e   laissez-faire.

Completion

1   Economists refer to the poorest countries of the world as _____.

2   Countries that have recently moved from being quite poor to being middle-income countries, including South Korea and Hong Kong, are called _____.

3   The development of new seeds, fertilisers, and agricultural practices that brought about increases in agricultural output in the developing countries during the 1960s and 1970s was called the _____.

4   In many developing countries, there is a _____, which includes a poor rural sector alongside a relatively more advanced urban sector.

5   A country's roads, ports, bridges, and legal system compose its _____.

6   _____ is a strategy according to which governments encourage exports to stimulate growth.

7   _____ is a strategy whereby the focus is on substituting domestic goods for imports to develop self-sufficiency.

8   Countries that have large numbers of unemployed or underemployed workers are said to have _____.

9   _____ refers to activities designed to secure government favors, such as import licences or access to foreign exchange.

10   The _____ is the most important of the international agencies that lend funds to developing countries to aid in development.

Answers to Self-Test

True or False

1	F	6	T	11	T
2	T	7	T	12	F
3	T	8	T	13	T
4	T	9	F	14	F
5	F	10	F	15	T

Multiple Choice

1	c	6	d	11	d	16	c
2	e	7	d	12	b	17	b
3	c	8	e	13	d	18	e
4	e	9	d	14	a	19	a
5	d	10	d	15	e	20	d

Completion

1   developing countries
2   newly industrialised countries
3   green revolution
4   dual economy
5   infrastructure
6   Export-led growth
7   Import substitution
8   labour surplus
9   Rent seeking
10 World Bank

Tools and Practice Problems

Two important problems that impede growth in developing countries are the absence of markets to allocate resources efficiently and the prevalence of institutions, such as share-cropping, that provide weak incentives. We study both of these problems in this section. Developing economies not only have limited supplies of capital and skilled labour, they also lack good markets to allocate what supplies they have. In this section, we consider the efficient allocation of resources, how markets achieve this allocation, and the losses that result from misallocation.

1   (Worked problem: absence of markets) The World Bank has made £10 million available for development projects in Costa Guano. Two possible uses for the money are building roads and building irrigation systems. The present discounted value of investments in each sector is given in Table 38.1.

Table 38.1

Investment	Irrigation projects	Roads
	(millions)	
£ 1	£10	£ 25
£ 2	£18	£ 45
£ 3	£25	£ 60
£ 4	£31	£ 72
£ 5	£36	£ 83
£ 6	£40	£ 93
£ 7	£43	£102
£ 8	£45	£110
£ 9	£46	£116
£10	£46	£120

a   Find the efficient allocation of the £10 million.
b   How would competitive markets allocate the money?
c   The party in power in Costa Guano draws much of its support from agriculture. If it used all of the money for irrigation, how much less would the benefits be?

Step-by-step solution

Step one (a): To find the efficient allocation, we adapt the procedure outlined in Tool Kit 38.1. Identify the production functions for each possible use. Here we are given the relationship between investment and the benefits of investment in Table 38.1.

Step two: Compute the marginal benefit for each quantity of the resource. We compute marginal benefit in the usual way. For example, the marginal benefit of the first £1 million in investment in irrigation is £10 million. Continuing, we derive Table 38.2.

Table 38.2

Investment	Irrigation projects	Marginal benefit	Roads	Marginal benefit
		(millions)		
£ 1	£10	£10	£ 25	£25
£ 2	£18	£ 8	£ 45	£20
£ 3	£25	£ 7	£ 60	£15
£ 4	£31	£ 6	£ 72	£12
£ 5	£36	£ 5	£ 83	£11
£ 6	£40	£ 4	£ 93	£10
£ 7	£43	£ 3	£102	£ 9
£ 8	£45	£ 2	£110	£ 8
£ 9	£46	£ 1	£116	£ 6
£10	£46	£ 0	£120	£ 4

Step three: Allocate the first unit of the resource to the activity with the highest marginal benefit. The first £1 million is allocated to road building, where it has a marginal benefit of £25 million.

Step four: Allocate the second unit of the resource to the activity with the next highest marginal benefit. The second £1 million is allocated to road building, where it has a marginal benefit of £20 million.

Step five: Continue until the available supply of the resource is exhausted. We allocate £8 million to roads and £2 million to irrigation.

Step one (b): To find the competitive market allocation, simply interpret the marginal benefits as the demand for the investment money, and follow the procedure in the first three steps of Tool Kit 34.1. Add each sector's demand for capital. When the price is £25 million, the total quantity demanded is £1 million by the road-building industry. When the price falls to £20 million, the quantity demanded is £2 million. Continuing, we derive the demand in Table 38.3.

Table 38.3

Price (million/million)	Quantity (millions of investment)
£25	£ 1
£20	£ 2
£15	£ 3
£12	£ 4
£11	£ 5
£10	£ 7 (£1 each for roads and irrigation)
£ 9	£ 8
£ 8	£10
£ 7	£11
⋮	⋮

Step two: Find the market-clearing price. The market clears at a price of £8 million.

Step three: Substitute the market-clearing price into each demand to determine the allocation of investment. At a price of £8 million, road builders will purchase £8 million, and irrigation firms will purchase £2 million. This is exactly the efficient allocation.

Step four (c): If all the investment money is used in irrigation projects, then the total benefit will be £46 million. The efficient allocation gives benefits equal to £18 million (irrigation) + £110 million (roads) = £128 million. Thus the waste that is due to misallocation is £128 − £46 = £82 million.

2 (Practice problem: absence of markets) Eight engineers return to their home country of Zandip after studying abroad. They can work for the government building bridges or in the mining sector. The (pound sterling equivalent) value of output produced in each sector is given in Table 38.4.

Table 38.4

Engineers	Roads	Mining
1	£200,000	£100,000
2	£280,000	£190,000
3	£350,000	£270,000
4	£410,000	£330,000
5	£450,000	£360,000
6	£480,000	£380,000
7	£500,000	£400,000
8	£500,000	£400,000

a Find the efficient allocation of the 8 engineers.
b How would competitive markets allocate the engineers?
c The president of Zandip likes roads. How much is wasted if all 8 engineers are sent to build roads?

3 (Practice problem: absence of markets) The Zambizi River can provide up to 100 million litres annually for irrigation. Both the cotton and millet crops would benefit from irrigation, and the benefits are given in Table 38.5.

Table 38.5

Water (millions of litres)	Cotton (millions)	Millet (millions)
1	£ 50	£ 25
2	£ 95	£ 50
3	£135	£ 75
4	£170	£100
5	£200	£125
6	£225	£150
7	£245	£175
8	£260	£190
9	£270	£200
10	£275	£200

a Find the efficient allocation of the water.
b How would competitive markets allocate the water?
c The president of Zandip allocates 80 million to millet and the rest to cotton. How much value is wasted?

Sharecropping

In developing economies, much farming takes place under conditions of sharecropping, where the landlord receives a fixed percentage of the output of the farm. The landlord's share of output is an externality from the point of view of the tenant, and as in all similar situations, there are incentive problems. Tool Kit 38.1 shows how to analyze sharecropping.

Tool Kit 38.1 Analysing Sharecropping

Under sharecropping the farmer pays a fraction of the output to the landlord. This creates poor incentives to work hard and maintain the land and equipment. Follow these steps.

Step one: Find the full marginal benefits and costs of the tenant's effort.

Step two: Find the efficient level of effort, which is the level at which marginal benefits equal marginal cost.

Step three: Calculate the tenant's marginal private benefits, multiplying the full marginal benefits by the tenant's share.

Step four: Find the equilibrium level of effort, which is the level at which marginal private benefits equal marginal cost.

Step five: Compare the equilibrium and efficient levels of the activity.

---

4 (Worked problem: analysing sharecropping) Mahragh grows corn on 20 acres in Zandip. He gives one-half of his output in rent to the landlord. The current price is £1 per bushel, and Table 38.6 gives the production function. Finally, Mahragh could devote time each day to his wife's bicycle manufacture business, where he could earn £30 for each daily hour.

Table 38.6

Effort (hours per day)	Corn (bushels)
1	120
2	210
3	270
4	300
5	315
6	321
7	324

a   Find the efficient level of effort.
b   Find the equilibrium level of effort.

Step-by-step solution

Step one (a): Find the full marginal benefits and costs of the tenant's effort. We first compute the marginal product in bushels of corn and then multiply by the price of corn to find the pound value. The first 2 hours of daily effort increase output to 120 bushels, which sell for £120. Continuing, we derive Table 38.7.

Table 38.7

Effort (hours per day)	Corn (bushels)	Marginal product (bushels per daily hour)	Marginal benefits (per daily hour)
1	120	120	£120
2	210	90	£ 90
3	270	60	£ 60
4	300	30	£ 30
5	315	15	£ 15
6	321	6	£ 6
7	324	3	£ 3

Step two: Find the efficient level of effort, which is the level at which marginal benefits equal marginal cost. The marginal cost, which is £30, equals marginal benefits at 4 hours per day.

Step three (b): Calculate the marginal private benefits by multiplying the full marginal benefits by the tenant's share. Mahragh's share is one-half; so if he works 1 hour each day, his marginal private benefits equal £120 × 1/2 = £60. Continuing, we derive Table 38.8.

Table 38.8

Effort	Marginal private benefits (per daily hour)
1	£60.00
2	£45.00
3	£30.00
4	£15.00
5	£ 7.50
6	£ 3.00
7	£ 1.50

Step four: Find the equilibrium level of effort, which is the level at which marginal private benefits equal marginal cost. The marginal private benefits equal marginal cost at 3 hours per day.

Step five: Compare the equilibrium and efficient levels of the activity. Mahragh works 3 hours each day, which is 1 less than the efficient number of hours.

5   (Practice problem: analysing sharecropping) Mr. Droulig is a sharecropper on a farm owned by the bank. He gives one-third of his revenues from farming 20 acres in rural Mali to the bank. Table 38.9 gives the relationship between his effort and the revenue from the farm.

Table 38.9

Time (hours)	Total revenue
1	£18
2	£33
3	£45
4	£54
5	£60
6	£63

Mr. Droulig, when not sharecropping, can work in town and make £6 per hour.

a   If he owned the farm himself and did not share revenue with the bank, how much would he work on the farm?
b   How much does Mr. Droulig choose to work on the farm?

6   (Practice problem: analysing sharecropping) Protecting farms against soil erosion is vital in the Sahel region of sub-Saharan Africa. The benefits of effort (in pound sterling equivalent) for a typical farm are given in Table 38.10. Assume that the marginal cost of effort is £100 and that sharecroppers pay one-half their yield in rent.

a   Find the level of effort for owners.
b   Find the level of effort for sharecroppers.

Table 38.10

Effort (days)	Benefits
1	£ 500
2	£ 900
3	£1,200
4	£1,400
5	£1,500
6	£1,500

Answers to Problems

2   The marginal benefits of the engineers in each sector are given in Table 38.11.

Table 38.11

Engineers	Roads	Marginal benefits	Mining	Marginal benefits
1	£200,000	£200,000	£100,000	£100,000
2	£280,000	£ 90,000	£190,000	£ 90,000
3	£350,000	£ 80,000	£270,000	£ 80,000
4	£410,000	£ 60,000	£330,000	£ 60,000
5	£450,000	£ 40,000	£360,000	£ 30,000
6	£480,000	£ 30,000	£380,000	£ 20,000
7	£500,000	£ 20,000	£400,000	£ 20,000
8	£500,000	£ 0	£400,000	£ 0

a   The efficient allocation is 4 engineers to each sector.

b   The market would allocate 4 to each sector with a wage of £60,000.

c   The total benefits if all are allocated to roads equal £500,000. At the efficient allocation, the total benefits equal £410,000 + £330,000 = £740,000. The waste is £740,000 − £500,000 = £240,000.

3   Table 38.12 gives the marginal benefits of irrigation water for each crop.

Table 38.12

Water	Cotton	Marginal benefits	Millet	Marginal benefits
1	£ 50	£50	£ 25	£25
2	£ 95	£45	£ 50	£25
3	£135	£40	£ 75	£25
4	£170	£35	£100	£25
5	£200	£30	£125	£25
6	£225	£25	£150	£25
7	£245	£20	£175	£25
8	£260	£15	£190	£15
9	£270	£10	£200	£10
10	£275	£ 5	£200	£ 0

a   The efficient allocation is 6 million litres to cotton and 4 million to millet.

b   The market would allocate 6 million to cotton and 4 million to millet with a price equal to £25.

c   Using 8 million for cotton and 2 million for millet gives benefits equal to £260 + £50 = £310. The efficient allocation gives benefits equal to £225 + £100 = £325 million. The waste is £325 − £310 = £15 million.

5   Table 38.13 gives the full marginal benefits and the private marginal benefits of time.

Table 38.13

Time	Total revenue	Full marginal benefits	Private marginal benefits
1	£18	£18	£12
2	£33	£15	£10
3	£45	£12	£ 8
4	£54	£ 9	£ 6
5	£60	£ 6	£ 4
6	£63	£ 3	£ 2

a   The efficient amount of time is 5 hours.

b   Mr. Droulig works 4 hours each day.

6   Table 38.14 gives the owner's and sharecropper's marginal benefits of efforts to reduce soil erosion.

Table 38.14

Effort	Benefits	Owner's marginal benefits	Sharecropper's marginal benefits
1	£ 500	£500	£250
2	£ 900	£400	£200
3	£1,200	£300	£150
4	£1,400	£200	£100
5	£1,500	£100	£ 50
6	£1,500	£ 0	£ 0

a   The owner would devote 5 days.

b   The sharecropper would devote 4 days.